COURTING JUSTICE

GAY MEN AND LESBIANS
V. THE SUPREME COURT

Joyce Murdoch
and Deb Price

BASIC
BOOKS

A Member of the Perseus Books Group

Also by Joyce Murdoch and Deb Price

And Say Hi to Joyce:
America's First Gay Column Comes Out

Cataloging-in-Publication data is available from the Library of Congress.
ISBN 0-465-01513-1

Set in 11-point Fairfield

01 02 03 04 / 10 9 8 7 6 5 4 3 2 1

*Dedicated to all the gay people
who believe in American justice
enough to fight for it*

CONTENTS

ACKNOWLEDGMENTS

OUR HEARTFELT THANKS go to the hundreds of people who jogged their memories and recounted their experiences to help us bring a slice of U.S. Supreme Court history to life. We owe special debts of gratitude to Sally Smith, for a priceless window into the court; to Billy Glover, for helping us track down copies of *ONE*; Cheryl Phillips, for locating several lost souls; and Supreme Court librarian Brian Stiglmeir, for superb special assistance. Ramsey Clark generously agreed to study his father's homosexual rulings for us. Laurence Tribe provided invaluable, in-depth, written replies to what must have seemed like an endless stream of *Hardwick* questions. Cathy Rudder, Cynthia Harrison and E. Joshua Rosenkranz kindly assisted in our failed bid to gain access to Justice Brennan's papers. Stu Ross graciously helped us figure out the chronology of Justice Clark's undated *Boutilier v. INS* draft opinions. Alison Howard provided important feedback on an early draft of Chapter 1. Matt Coles, Chai Feldblum, Art Leonard and Evan Wolfson have tirelessly shared their legal insights with us over the years. Also, the works of Arthur Leonard and Jonathan Ned Katz gave us an essential grounding in the historical period we studied. Norman MacAfee, our keen-eyed copy editor, provided many helpful suggestions. This project would not have been possible without the matchmaking skills of our agent, Charlotte

Sheedy, and the extraordinary patience of our editor, Jo Ann Miller. Finally, our secret thanks go to those former clerks and court insiders who agreed to interviews only after saying, "Promise that you won't mention my name even in the acknowledgments!"

Joyce Murdoch
Deb Price

INTRODUCTION

"PAY NO ATTENTION
TO THAT MAN
BEHIND THE CURTAIN"

Justice is not to be taken by storm.
She is to be wooed by slow advances.

—*Justice Ruth Bader Ginsburg,*
quoting former justice Benjamin Nathan Cardozo

FOR NEARLY HALF A CENTURY, gay Americans have been courting justice. This is the story of that courtship.

Courting Justice is the first in-depth account of how the U.S. Supreme Court has dealt with gay and lesbian cases over the past five decades. From the 1958 triumph of a tiny homosexual magazine to the 2000 defeat of gay assistant scoutmaster James Dale, this chronicle offers a behind-the-scenes look at the influences shaping the court's decisions. This is also the saga of the often-inspiring gay men and lesbians who reached out to the nation's top court during terrifying junctures in their lives—when threatened with deportation, for example, or when barred from seeing a desperately injured partner. Together, the two histories provide a unique window from which to view how the gay civil rights movement in America has unfolded.

Like an old-fashioned melodrama, this account is bursting with heroes—the Rosa Parkses, Martin Luther King Jr.'s and Susan B. Anthonys of the push for gay legal equality. Other than ignorance, villains are harder to identify; individual justices must be judged by the times in which they lived. Without a doubt, though, the brightest star is the U.S. Constitution. The Constitution's majestic promises of freedom and fairness haven't changed in recent times. It's the world that has changed dramatically, both inside and outside the court's marble palace. And, consequently, the court's justices have slowly begun reading protections for gay Americans into the Constitution.

Written by a privileged set of men using quill pens and whale oil lamps more than 200 years ago, the Constitution's unsurpassed ability to transcend time and help far different generations of Americans settle disputes is nothing short of miraculous. Certainly, our forefathers could not have imagined the Constitution being used to decide whether a boys' club should be forced to accept a gay man as a role model. After all, when the Constitution was drafted in 1787, only Pennsylvania had abolished the death penalty for sodomy—one year earlier. Yet the drafters could no more easily have imagined that the *Boy Scouts* case, or any case for that matter, would be decided by a court whose members included two women, two Jews and a black man. But our forefathers didn't need to imagine gay Scout leaders or female, black or Jewish justices to know that the document they created needed flexibility. Rather than write a rigid rule book, they created promises supple enough to grow with their new nation.

Most simply stated, it's the Supreme Court's role to use the Constitution as a scale on which to weigh competing legal claims. Obsessively, excessively cloaked in secrecy, the Supreme Court encourages the impression that it is a monolithic institution whose rulings are the disembodied voice of timeless wisdom. The nine justices, the most private of public officials, sit in their public courtroom to listen to one single hour of argument over even the most complicated case, then disappear back behind their heavy, burgundy velvet curtains to deliberate and decide in secrecy. Months later, the court hands down its written ruling, explaining itself as much or as little as it pleases, sometimes in less than a sentence. Doing their utmost to draw attention away from themselves as individuals—refusing, for example, to put nameplates in front of their courtroom seats—the justices are like the Wizard of Oz, who commanded Dorothy: "Pay no attention to that man behind the curtain!" But like Dorothy's little dog Toto, this book, written by "friends of Dorothy," pulls the curtain back to reveal the life-sized, fallible human beings behind.

Twice in the early years of this history, the very human justices of a staid, tradition-bound court handed surprising victories to homosexual publications, even as other federal officials waged war on homosexuals. Then, for long decades, a majority of justices rebuffed virtually every gay overture. In recent years, most justices have learned to say "gay" and "lesbian" and to treat gay pleas with respect. In 1996, striking down Colorado's attempt to brand gay citizens second-class, six justices eloquently extended the Constitution's guarantee of equal protection to gay Americans. Yet five years later, the promise implicit in that 1996 ruling—that other laws rooted in animosity toward gay people will be struck down—still has not been kept.

The gay men, lesbians and bisexuals who fought all the way to the Supreme Court shared an unshakeable faith that the U.S. Constitution protected their rights. Most often, their cases were turned away unheard. Whether victorious or not, the tenacious gay people who reached the nation's top court showed—as the John Wayne movie would have put it—true grit. Many, many other people walked—or ran—away when targeted by the government for arrest, harassment or dismissal simply because of their sexual orientation. Especially in the hyper-closeted days of the 1950s and '60s, walking away was the "reasonable" response.

A few who proved their grit became mini-celebrities within gay civil rights folklore: Dr. Thomas Waddell, the Olympic athlete who started the Gay Games; Miriam Ben-Shalom, a decorated Army Reserve drill sergeant; Michael Hardwick, a fun-loving Atlanta bartender who became an unlikely gay-rights poster boy; Sharon Kowalski, whose partner Karen Thompson waged a one-woman crusade to bring her home; and James Dale, the ousted scoutmaster with Kennedyesque clean-cut good looks. But whether famous or virtually unknown, the gay people who went to court to fight back describe their legal bids with words that are both proud and bitter, words that express undying faith in American ideals as well as disillusionment.

"I just couldn't walk away," recalled Frank Kameny, a brilliant Harvard-educated astronomer who became nearly destitute after being fired from his government job in 1957. The phrase echoed through many interviews with gay people who fought against dreadful odds after losing a job, being embarrassed by a "sex crime" arrest or suffering some similar humiliation. "For the rest of my life, I wouldn't have been able to live with myself," Kameny added. "I would be dead of stomach ulcers by now. There's simply a burning sense of injustice."

That burning sense of injustice turned a few gay fighters into outlaws. Australian Tony Sullivan lives illegally in the United States because the court refused to help him remain with the American man he has loved for a quarter century. "There's only so much you can allow governments to restrict your life," Sullivan says of his decision to defy U.S. immigration rules. "There's a point at which you become outlaws. There's a point at which you say, 'Wait a second. No one has a right to do this to me. And if the law is in my way, then I will break the law.'"

Regardless of whether they won or lost, gay people who battled all the way to the Supreme Court tend to recall the fight as life-altering:

"It changed me from being an American to being a gay man," former Navy aviator Jim Woodward explained of his unsuccessful 15-year effort to persuade the Supreme Court that the military shouldn't have been allowed to kick him out. "I no longer felt a loyalty to the United States of America that caused me to join the Navy at a period when probably the majority of my peers would have gone to Canada instead."

The gay people whose pleas reached the nation's highest tribunal included gifted teachers, an undercover Central Intelligence Agency technician, a quiet hotel clerk from Switzerland, a 290-pound albino philosopher-turned-pornographer and an in-your-face activist who routinely showed up for work at the Equal Employment Opportunity Commission decked out in a dress, long hair and nail polish because he wanted to better understand sexism. Their crusades frequently consumed large portions of their lives and often left them deeply in debt.

Accountant Daniel Miller, for example, who was shocked when he was held to an anti-gay contract, borrowed money from everyone he knew, including his grandmother, to pay $148,000 in legal fees and court-ordered restitution to his ex-boss. "You lose some faith in America," Miller said. "People knew it wasn't right, yet allowed it to happen."

Nearly all the gay people who shared their stories said they wished they could have spoken to the justices. "I am in this position because I refused to lie," former soldier Miriam Ben-Shalom wanted to tell them. "There just comes a point in your life where you just can't lie, when you realize there's something more than just words that are in the balance. I believe I would have lost my soul if I had lied." Her unsuccessful legal battle cost Ben-Shalom her home and custody of her daughter.

No Supreme Court justice ever laid eyes on Miriam Ben-Shalom, Frank Kameny, Tony Sullivan or Daniel Miller. Unlike trial court judges, justices don't get to meet—and size up—the people whose lives they hold in the balance. Justice William J. Brennan Jr. reacted with glee when he saw a TV interview with one of the real human beings behind a loyalty-oath case that the court had decided decades earlier. "It was fascinating," Brennan said. ". . . I had no idea how much they had to lose personally if the case had gone the other way. They would have lost everything they had ever done as teachers."

Similarly, Supreme Court justices keep themselves in the shadows, making them the ultimate un-celebrities. Even after presiding over President Clinton's post-impeachment Senate trial, Chief Justice William Rehnquist probably wouldn't be recognized by most Americans if he were behind them in line at a grocery store. Justice John Paul Stevens—best known for his bow ties—once had tourists wave him out of the way as they prepared to photograph the court's handsome façade. In a 1995 national poll, three times as many adults (59 percent) could name all Three Stooges—Larry, Moe and Curly—as could name any three justices (17 percent).

The chapters ahead gradually pull in from the shadows the three chief justices and 23 associate justices who've served since the late 1950s—when the Supreme Court first ruled on a homosexual case—and defined the legal status of gay Americans. Appointed by 10 different presidents, none of them brought a gay-friendly record to the Supreme Court. Since the 1950s, quite a few far-sighted federal judges have stood up forcefully for basic gay civil rights in the absence of Supreme Court leadership and in the face of government-sponsored discrimination. Yet not one of them has been nominated to the nation's highest court.

Though sometimes described as "nine scorpions in a bottle," the Supreme Court justices serving at any given time might be more aptly called "nine scorpions in nine bottles." Their isolation, even from each other, is astonishing. Each works primarily with his or her own tiny personal staff—three or four young law clerks serving a one-year apprenticeship plus two or three permanent clerical workers. The entire court's personal staff is smaller than that of just one U.S. senator. The justices communicate with one another primarily in writing or when announcing their votes in private conference. Most aren't known for dropping by their colleagues' offices to chat. Justices are paid to think for a living, yet their isolation restricts even their intellectual stimulation. Arthur Goldberg, who had been a Cabinet secretary before being tapped for the court in 1962, lamented that his phone stopped ringing once he joined the court. Justices can easily avoid close contact with the public during working hours: They drive into a private underground garage, take a private elevator up to their private chambers and dine in a private section of the court's cafeteria.

Even in Washington, D.C., where social sightings of the president, lawmakers and Cabinet officials are a dime a dozen, personal anecdotes about Supreme Court justices are rare. It was big news, for example, in 1985 when professional football player John Riggins drunkenly disrupted a formal banquet by crying out to table-mate Justice Sandra Day O'Connor, "Come on, Sandy baby, loosen up!" Tales of this justice offending his Georgetown neighbors by standing in his front window in his underwear each morning or that justice double-dipping at an hors d'oeuvre table are relished as clues to their mysterious personalities. Justice Ruth Bader Ginsburg shocked and amused one of this book's authors—a "juror" during the incident in question—in 1999 by rigging the verdict in a mock trial over whether William Shakespeare was guilty of anti-Semitism for writing A Merchant of Venice. Ginsburg, an opera and theater buff, had earlier made headlines by appearing in full costume on stage in Henry the VI to deliver Shakespeare's line, "First thing we do, let's kill all the lawyers."

Cut off from the world far more than if they taught at Harvard Law School, headed a major law firm or served on a lower court, the justices can be quite insulated from changes that blow through American society with hurricane force. But change does reach them eventually. Since the early 1950s, American homosexuals have gone from being an invisible, defensive minority hounded out of the closet by a hostile and ill-informed government to being a proud gay community, whose members assertively demand full legal and social equality. While the justices of yesteryear could go through life oblivious to the homosexuals around them or pity them as lesser beings, the justices of today—no matter how cocooned—can't avoid bumping into openly gay people who are respected pillars of society.

Close Encounters of a Gay Kind

On April 22, 1993, hundreds of thousands of gay men and lesbians began flooding into Washington, D.C., for the record-breaking gay-rights march three days later. Among them were two dozen gay men and lesbians who met in the U.S. Capitol as part of the first organizational meetings of a national association of openly gay judges.

Afterward, most of the judges, judiciously dressed in staid business attire, streamed across the street to the Supreme Court's imposing, white marble building. As they walked up the enormous front staircase, whose length slows all but the youngest tourists to a properly contemplative pace, the gay judges could see the guarantee carved high above the court's entranceway: EQUAL JUSTICE UNDER LAW. The powerful phrase wasn't the inspired creation of a founding father. It was the handiwork of the building's architect, who needed words that fit the space he wanted to fill. The words also fit the American dream of equality, the magnetic force that pulls wave after wave of gay Americans to the Supreme Court.

The judges hoped to drop in on a justice or two. They soon discovered that even the crimson-carpeted corridors outside the justices' offices are closed to the public. Turning to leave, the judges spotted Justice David Souter, whose gently stern demeanor brings to mind a beloved schoolmaster. In a flash, a quick-thinking judge politely ensnared Justice Souter in a handshake. "Hello, my name is Rand Hoch. I'm a workers' compensation judge visiting from Florida. And I'm here with a group called the International Association of Lesbian and Gay Judges. We were wondering if you'd have some time this afternoon to meet with us?" Hoch kept a firm grip on Souter's hand until he was sure the justice had heard the words "lesbian and gay judges."

Without missing a beat, Justice Souter respectfully replied, "Nice to meet you, Judge Hoch. Unfortunately my calendar is rather full for this afternoon. Had you given notice, I'm sure we could have arranged something."

A handshake, a smile, a shared profession. Even within their marble fortress, justices are touched by gay lives. Our chronicle examines gay influences on them: the lesbian dude ranchers who lived next to one justice, for example, and the troubled gay nephew of another. A liberal justice wrote a play with gay elements. A conservative justice presided over a make-believe Supreme Court as it heard a same-sex marriage case. Several gay clerks have come out to their justices, and some have taken their partners to court reunions. One of the court's highest-ranking professional employees is a gay man who received handwritten letters of condolence from two conservative justices when his partner died of leukemia. Another justice sent a lesbian couple a gift for their holy union ceremony.

How did knowing gay people affect the justices and their legal judgments? There are no easy answers. Unlike other public officials, justices almost never grant substantive interviews. All nine sitting justices—as well as the four retired justices alive when this project began—declined our interview requests. However, seizing our invitation to correct the record, Justice Stevens wrote back to confirm our suspicion that he'd been misquoted as saying, "I hate homos," during a private conference with other justices in 1986.

Our job was gumshoe detective work, tracking down what justices said about homosexuality, how they secretly voted in gay-related cases and how gay influences have sometimes colored their outlook. As Justice Stevens pointed out in his powerful dissent from the court's ruling against gay Scout James Dale, justices' attitudes toward homosexuality do evolve and justices are very aware of the remarkable advances in society's acceptance of gay Americans.

While justices haven't spoken publicly about how knowing gay people has affected their understanding of gay issues, several have described how firsthand experiences sensitized them to the plight of others. Justices O'Connor and Ginsburg have talked about the sex discrimination they experienced after law school. Thurgood Marshall, the first black justice, continually tried to educate his colleagues by describing the racism he'd fought all of his life. Justice William O. Douglas, a die-hard defender of individual rights, never forgot the vulnerability he felt hopping freight trains and dodging cops because he was too poor to buy a ticket. Justice Brennan credited his almost superhuman capacity for empathy for all sorts of people to the suffering he'd witnessed growing up in a poor neighborhood. Justice Lewis Powell Jr. was a reliable abortion-rights vote partly because, as a Virginia attorney, he'd seen his 19-year-old office boy nearly go to prison after the young man's girlfriend died from an illegal abortion. Justice Anthony Kennedy says he came to understand Hispanics better while performing free legal work for them. Justice Stephen Breyer says having daughters makes him more sensitive to sex discrimination.

Perhaps the best example of how justices' experiences influence their decisions is the court's crowning achievement, its unanimous 1954 *Brown v. Board of Education* school desegregation ruling. Chief Justice Earl Warren's opinion declared racial segregation unconstitutional largely because of the psychological damage it did to black schoolchildren when it "puts the mark of inferiority . . . upon their little hearts and minds." Warren drew on conversations he'd had with his black chauffeur, Edgar Patterson, while governor of California. According to Patterson, Warren had said, "'Tell me about how you felt when you were a little kid, going to school.' . . . [*Brown v. Board*] almost quoted the ideas that he and I used to talk about on feelings."

The court did not reach its famous *Brown* decision quickly or easily. Resting on the foot of lampposts outside the Supreme Court building are bronze tortoises, a symbolic reminder that justice moves slowly and cannot be rushed. In dealing with basic gay civil rights, most justices have taken the turtle mimicry to extremes—pulling in their heads to ignore serious inequities and counting on the hard shell of lifetime tenure to shield them from confrontation with topics they wished to avoid. As a result, the court has often seemed to more closely resemble a lamppost tortoise than a live one that actually moves.

Yet, as is often the case with the mysterious Supreme Court, appearances can be deceiving. The most powerful court in the world's oldest democracy has moved from branding all homosexuals as psychos "afflicted with homosexuality" to having the four *Boy Scouts* dissenters warn, in a forceful echo of the *Brown* decision, that creating a gay exception to the Constitution places on gay people a "symbol of inferiority."

Understandably, many readers will feel outraged by much of the way the high court has dealt with gay issues. But there's good reason for optimism because, down through the centuries, it has treated other minority groups far worse—and later recanted. The court's approach to any civil rights issue tends to reflect the attitudes and prejudices of its members as well as the tenor of the times at least as much as it does the Constitution's wording. The justices have repeatedly failed to "do unto others" as they would have others do undo them—doling out a more meager portion of legal rights to people whose race, sex or sexual orientation is different from their own.

Five slave-owning justices were the driving force behind the all-white court's infamous 1857 *Dred Scott* decision, which called blacks "beings of an inferior order . . . [with] no rights which the white man was bound to respect." Abolitionist Horace Greeley said he "would rather trust a dog with my dinner" than trust a slave-holding Supreme Court with questions of slavery.

When, in its 1873 *Bradwell v. Illinois* decision, an all-male Supreme Court upheld a state statute barring women from practicing law, one justice explained, "The paramount destiny and mission of woman are to fulfill the noble and benign offices of wife and mother." Two years later, the court refused to read voting rights for women into the Constitution. As late as 1961, forty-one years after the 19th Amendment explicitly granted women voting rights, all nine male justices upheld a Florida law excluding women from jury duty unless they went to considerable effort to volunteer. Ruling against a woman convicted by a male jury of murdering her philandering husband, the nation's highest court of married men declared that treating women differently wasn't really discrimination like excluding blacks. "Woman is still regarded as the center of home and family life," the justices ruled. In other words: Who'll wash our socks if our wives are out serving on juries? It wasn't until 1971 that the all-male court struck down a law as unconstitutional sex discrimination.

In another stain on its record, a Supreme Court of Caucasian justices of European descent upheld forcing Japanese Americans into detention camps during World War II, while U.S. citizens of German and Italian extraction were assumed to be loyal unless proven to be traitors.

Obviously, serving on the Supreme Court doesn't magically rid any-one of judgment-clouding prejudices. Consider the anti-Semitism of Justice James McReynolds, who refused to speak to Jewish colleagues, and the racism of Justice Stanley Reed. The Supreme Court did not pose for its annual group photo in 1924 because McReynolds refused to stand beside Jewish Justice Louis Brandeis. In 1947, the court canceled its Christmas party after Justice Reed declared that he would not attend if the court's black employees were invited.

An Imprecise Art

To fully appreciate the importance of individual justices' prejudices and predilections, it is necessary to know a bit about how the court works and the almost total discretion its members have in choosing which cases to hear and how to rule on them. The Supreme Court neither commands armies nor controls purse strings. Yet it can overrule the elected officials who do. The court's awesome power flows from its two main duties—deciding what the U.S. Constitution means and deciding what federal laws and regulations mean. (Each state's top court inter-prets the laws of its state. The U.S. Supreme Court then can rule on whether a particular state law—as interpreted by the state's court—vio-lates the U.S. Constitution.) When lower-level federal judges wrestle with the meaning of a law or a constitutional provision, they're bound by any prior Supreme Court rulings that seem relevant. Supreme Court justices themselves, however, pay as little or as much attention to their court's precedents as they wish.

The unelected Supreme Court is intended to check and balance the power of the federal government's elected executive and legislative branches. The justices are supposed to safeguard the constitutional rights of the minority so that majority rule doesn't cross the invisible line into tyranny. Theoretically, the more downtrodden, misunderstood, ma-ligned and oppressed a minority group is, the more zealous the Supreme Court is supposed to be about protecting its members' basic civil rights. As Justice Hugo Black proudly proclaimed in a 1940 decision overturn-ing the convictions of several black men coerced into false confessions, "Under our constitutional system, courts stand against any winds that blow as havens of refuge for those who might otherwise suffer because they are helpless, weak, outnumbered, or because they are nonconforming victims of prejudice and public excitement." Yet for all its fine phrases, the Supreme Court has very rarely provided a safe haven for those "nonconforming victims of prejudice and public excitement" who happen to be homosexual.

If interpreting federal laws and the Constitution were an exact science instead of an imprecise art, there would be no 5-to-4 Supreme Court decisions: Nine learned people would automatically agree on, say, whether the Constitution protects two adults engaging in oral sex in the privacy of their home. In reality, however, interpreting the grand, intentionally vague promises that the Constitution makes to all Americans is much like interpreting the Bible or a Rorschach inkblot test—what someone reads into it often tells more about that person than about what's on the printed page. Consider the Fifth Amendment guarantee that no citizen shall be deprived of "liberty . . . without due process of law." What is "liberty"? What is "due process"? Since the 1960s, most justices have read "privacy" into "liberty," though the Constitution never uses the word "privacy." And the invisible "privacy" guarantee has further been interpreted as protecting access to birth control devices and as establishing a right to abortion. A string of "privacy" decisions essentially put the Constitution's seal of approval on heterosexual recreational sex—first for married couples, then unmarried adults and even minors. But the vague "liberty" and unwritten "privacy" guarantees cannot be read as protecting gay sex, or so the majority in a bitterly split court declared in 1986. The Constitution is silent about sex of any sort, sexual orientation and homosexuality—the justices are on their own when they venture into that territory.

The Constitution's ambiguity can be quite unnerving to those of us raised to revere it as the surefire protector of the American ideals of individual freedom and equal rights. Realizing just how much power that ambiguity places in the hands of nine very human interpreters is even more rattling. Soon after being appointed by President Franklin D. Roosevelt, Justice Douglas lost his illusions about constitutional verities. As Douglas told the story, Chief Justice Charles Evan Hughes "made a statement to me which at the time was shattering but which over the years turned out to be true: 'Justice Douglas, you must remember one thing. At the constitutional level where we work, 90 percent of any decision is emotional. The rational part of us supplies the reasons for supporting our predilections.' I knew that their moods as well as their minds were ingredients in their decisions. But I had never been willing to admit to myself that the 'gut' reaction of a judge at the level of constitutional adjudications, dealing with the vagaries of due process, freedom of speech and the like, was the main ingredient of his decision."

Justice Brennan, who ardently believed that Supreme Court justices were supposed to breathe life into the Constitution's grand promises by making society more just and humane, delighted in giving his law clerks a memorable lesson in constitutional math. Brennan would wait until the inevitable moment when the clerks—top graduates of the finest law schools—were wailing about some Supreme Court decision they considered a gross miscarriage of justice. Blue eyes twinkling, Brennan would hold up one hand, wiggle his fingers and explain, "Five votes can do anything."

Handicapping how the Supreme Court will respond to even the most blatant violation of legal rights that other Americans can take for granted remains impossible because of what gay-rights attorneys gnash their teeth about and call the "gay exception." That's the thumb that prejudice slips onto the scales of justice. That's the asterisk that heterosexism puts beside the 14th Amendment's guarantee that government won't deny "any person . . . the equal protection of the laws." That's the double standard that results in gay people being punished by the government for saying and doing things that never cost similarly situated heterosexuals their freedom, their livelihood or custody of their children. The "gay exception" means that, a great deal of the time, standards of judging suddenly change because a case involves homosexuality. A midnight kiss on New Year's Eve suddenly becomes illegal "lewd" behavior if it involves two people of the same sex. And suddenly no law is too vague if, like those condemning the unnamed "crime against nature," it's routinely used to harm homosexuals. Laws that overtly discriminate against homosexuals—such as the military's "Don't ask, don't tell" statute—are rare. What's far more common is for police officers, prosecutors, judges and even Supreme Court justices to twist neutral laws to the detriment of homosexuals.

In 1996, the Supreme Court finally confronted the double standard and found it unconstitutional—at least in the case of Colorado's anti-gay Amendment 2. What the full Supreme Court has never publicly confronted is the question lurking just beneath the surface of every gay case: Who are homosexuals? The answer is the keyhole through which every justice must look to determine the Constitution's relationship to gay Americans. Are homosexuals weak-willed, anti-social sex perverts engaged in destructive behavior that threatens to undermine national security, the family and all civilization? Are homosexuals pathetic creatures who nevertheless deserve the court's protection? Are homosexuals much like heterosexuals, except for having had to cope with a particularly insidious brand of ostracism? Is homosexuality immoral or morally neutral, like having perfect pitch?

Ironically, the Constitution says very little about the federal court that has so much to say about its meaning. The Constitution created "one Supreme Court," whose members serve "during good behavior"—a requirement taken to mean that justices serve for life unless ousted for misconduct. (No justice has ever been removed from office.) The size of the court's membership is set by Congress and has varied from six to 10. The number of justices has been fixed at nine since 1869. A chief justice, whose formal title is "chief justice of the United States," presides over eight "associate justices" during the court's public sessions and private conferences. The chief justice also chooses which justice will write the court's opinion in a given case—provided the chief voted with the majority. When a Supreme Court justice dies or chooses to retire, the president may nominate anyone as a successor. There are absolutely no requirements for the job. FDR was shocked to learn that a justice needn't even be a lawyer. In practice, though, presidents pick prominent lawyers—most often federal appeals court judges, at least in recent decades. Every full-term president in history, except Jimmy Carter, has gotten to make at least one Supreme Court appointment. Before taking a seat on the nation's top court, a nominee must be confirmed by the Senate—that is, win the votes of a majority of senators. Until 1967, when President Lyndon Johnson appointed Thurgood Marshall, the Supreme Court was the exclusive bastion of white men. At the time of the *Boy Scouts* decision, the court had six white men, two white women and a black man. Seven current justices are married, one is widowed and one is a lifelong bachelor. All are presumably heterosexual.

Each year, more than 7,000 cases raising questions of federal or constitutional law reach the U.S. Supreme Court. In recent times, fewer than 100 a year win the court's full attention. Though a few cases are a special sort that the justices technically must take, the Supreme Court easily finds excuses for brushing aside any case it doesn't want. Most cases land on the Supreme Court's doorstep in the form of 25-page legal documents pleading with the justices to grant a *writ of certiorari*. Derived from *certiorari volumus*—Latin for "we wish to be informed"— a petition for *certiorari* is simply a request by the losing side of the legal battle for the Supreme Court to review the lower court's record in the case. A *cert* petition, as it is commonly called, is essentially an argument that a particular case raises significant enough issues to be worthy of the justices' attention. If any justice thinks a case merits discussion, it is listed on the court's secret "discuss" list. When the court announces "*certiorari* denied," meaning the case is being turned away, it gives no clue about whether the justices ever discussed the case with one another. Usually, they didn't.

Although "five votes can do anything," as Brennan was fond of pointing out, only four are needed to accept a case. In taking a case, the justices can simultaneously issue a decision called a "summary judgment." If the court instead wants to know more before ruling, it schedules the case to be argued in open court by the attorneys on either side. Before "oral argument," as it is called, the attorneys file 30-page written summaries of the facts of the case, the legal issues involved and what they would like the court to rule. When the justices meet a few days after oral argument to vote, no one else—not even a stenographer—is allowed inside their small conference room. (In one of the court's many quirky traditions, the most junior justice goes to the door if anyone knocks.) The justices' handwritten notes are the only records of their secret sessions. Justices are free to switch their votes right up until the time the court publicly releases its closely guarded ruling. Observers are frequently left wondering what, exactly, a ruling means.

For decades, the Supreme Court seems to have been intent on saying as little as possible about homosexuality, a subject widely considered unmentionable in polite company when the first homosexual-rights case reached the court in 1957. Determined not be an engine driving social change in the area of gay rights, the Supreme Court has instead been a drag on the nation, holding back the pace of progress toward the full acceptance of gay people.

Despite most justices' clear aversion to dealing with homosexuality, the court has turned its full attention to homosexual cases more than a dozen times—getting fully briefed and hearing oral arguments before rendering a decision—and summarily decided another six. Those decided cases, plus more than four dozen that the Supreme Court refused to hear, form the backbone of this book. (We don't scrutinize AIDS cases, which might eventually make a book of their own, or deal with transgendered issues, although we did find one male-to-female transsexual ex-clerk.) A substantial number of pages are devoted to gay cases in which the court denied cert—that is, turned the case away unheard. From a technical legal standpoint, denial of cert is usually dismissed as meaningless. It constitutes a non-decision, setting no precedent and offering no guidance to lower courts. However, especially in an area of law as controversial and unsettled as gay rights, the denial of cert can have significant impact. Lower court judges often cite the high court's refusal to hear a gay plea in justifying their own anti-gay decisions. Also, gay cases that the court avoided provide important windows into what the justices were being told about homosexuality and society's attitudes toward it, how they reacted to what they were being told and what they were hearing from lower court judges.

Court watchers who claim that a denial of cert tells us nothing about the Supreme Court's attitudes often point to the sheer volume of petitions that reach the court and the fact that only a tiny portion are accepted for review. Yet, in reality, the court isn't so burdened that gay cases just get lost in the shuffle. Instead, there's clear evidence of justices recognizing the importance of gay cases—individually and collectively—and intentionally avoiding them decade after decade.

In *Deciding to Decide: Agenda Setting in the United States Supreme Court*, H. W. Perry persuasively debunks the myth that denial of cert is meaningless. Perry shows how justices use the cert process strategically to further their legal goals. In his study of the 1976–80 court terms, Perry found insiders saying without prompting that homosexuality was the one topic the court consistently ducked. One clerk recalled justices' reaction to a case involving a sodomy conviction: "The feeling was that, 'Oh, God, we really don't need this.'" Another told Perry that "some of the more liberal justices were afraid to take [a gay case] because they thought they would lose on the merits. In other words, they were defensively denying *[cert]*. Other justices did not even see it as an issue, having no doubt that states could prohibit such behavior. There were also some justices who felt, why get involved in such a messy, controversial issue, perhaps doing reputational damage to the court, when no one was really being prosecuted?"

The behind-the-scenes tug-of-war over the court's intentional ducking of gay cases broke into public view in 1978. Dissenting from the court's refusal to take the case of a university fighting a lower court order that it recognize a gay student group, conservative William Rehnquist, then an associate justice, scolded his brethren: "[T]he existence of discretion [in case selection] does not imply that it should be used as a sort of judicial storm cellar to which we may flee to escape from controversial or sensitive cases." Rehnquist was clearly upset that rulings supporting gay rights were becoming more common as liberal lower court judges exercised the leeway that the high court's inaction gave them.

Seven years later, Justice Brennan, Rehnquist's ideological opposite, took his turn in prodding justices who found gay cases too upsetting, distasteful or hot to touch. Dissenting from the court's refusal to take the case of a fired bisexual guidance counselor, Brennan declared, "Whether constitutional rights are infringed in sexual preference cases, and whether some compelling state interest can be advanced to permit their infringement, are important questions that this court has never addressed, and which have left the lower courts in some disarray." Translation: We're being derelict in our duty. In the absence of a Supreme Court directive saying that gay cases merit serious scrutiny, lower courts generally operate on the assumption that governments' anti-gay actions are rational and permissible.

Gay-supportive clerks have often lobbied against the Supreme Court taking gay cases because it is so conservative. According to Michael Conley, a gay clerk during 1990–91, "To the extent that you are looking at pool memos from clerks indicating that a [gay] case shouldn't be taken, very often that's a defensive posture. You realize that it is much better for a case not to be taken. . . . There is room for judgment on whether it is now the right time."

The Supreme Court is structured to be a fairly passive institution. It must wait for controversies to boil up to its level. Yet the history of gay

Americans' interactions with the Supreme Court is largely the history of the court repeatedly passing up chances to help a beleaguered minority group. A historical account that focused only on the gay cases in which the Supreme Court issued formal rulings would overlook crucial elements in the court's slow, unsteady evolution.

A Gay Justice?

A joke sometimes heard in gay legal circles goes like this: Why are there nine Supreme Court justices? Because one in 10 people is gay. Joking aside, the Supreme Court quite possibly has had a gay justice—Frank Murphy, who served from 1940 until his death in 1949 at age 59. As is maddeningly true of other mysterious figures, such as poet Emily Dickinson, who have been "read" as gay by contemporary biographers, there is no steamy, confessional statement that proves Murphy was homosexual. However, with modern-day gay eyes, it's easy to read Murphy as a closeted homosexual making a great display of going through the motions of a heterosexual social life while deflecting attention from his lifelong bond with another man.

Welcomed in 1939 as U.S. attorney general to "a socially-conscious capital, where presentable, unattached males are more precious than rubies," Murphy was hailed by a society columnist as "the answer to ladies' prayers." Heterosexual women were charmed by him, perhaps for the same reasons many now enjoy the company of polished gay men. He was impeccably dressed, enjoyed the social whirl, kept himself fit, exuded such righteousness that he was dubbed saintly, was "sentimental and tender-hearted" and could be counted on to be a perfect gentleman—one who never made sexual demands. The debonair demeanor of "Fragile Frank," as he was dubbed, was quite strange. A tall, thin Irish Catholic with receding red hair and gigantic, bushy eyebrows, Murphy had a quiet manner and "birdlike" gestures. He carried his family Bible and neither smoked nor drank in an era when Washington ran on scotch and cigars. His speech was wispy, "a deliberate, soft purr." One newspaperman growled, "What in heck is this bird, a whispering baritone?" Another called him "Holy Joe, the Airedale Angora."

Rumors of homosexuality dogged Murphy all his adult life but were considered unprintable in his day. Gossip columnists contented themselves with reporting which starlet or socialite Murphy had most recently squired around town and whom he was engaged to at the moment. The diaries of Murphy's contemporaries tell a different story. Investigative columnist Drew Pearson confided to his diary that a woman who "should know" insisted that Murphy "died a male virgin" and that when Washington insider Harry Hopkins heard a woman claim to have spent the night with Murphy, Hopkins wryly observed, "Well, there's no place where you could be safer." A man who served with Murphy in FDR's Cabinet wrote in his diary that the president's son-in-law considered Murphy a "pansy."

Historian Sidney Fine pursued the homosexual rumors when writing his exhaustive three-volume biography of Murphy. "I was never able to find anything that could pin it down," he told us. "I could not stick my neck out and say he was gay. All I can say is that there were rumors to that effect but not corroborated." Fine's theory about Murphy's perpetual bachelor status is that he was a momma's boy who never met a woman measuring up to her idealized image. The biographer's search of Murphy's personal papers turned up one letter that, Fine wrote, "if the words mean what they say, refers to a homosexual encounter some years earlier between Murphy and the writer." That January 10, 1940, letter—a congratulatory note on Murphy's nomination to the Supreme Court—cannot be quoted, according to the terms of the agreement under which it was obtained for this book from the University of Michigan. On stationery belonging to a Nina Garfinkel, Abe Garfinkel—apparently a soldier stationed in the Philippines while Murphy was governor-general—implied that he and Murphy had become lovers in Hong Kong on June 13, 1933. Garfinkel wrote that he felt that Murphy had belonged to him ever since. Stressing that he had no intention of asking Murphy for favors, Garfinkel expressed admiration for Murphy and regret about a breakup apparently caused by a jealous Murphy.

Fine saw no other hints of homosexuality in Murphy's life story. But a gay reading of Fine's work suggests that Murphy's homosexuality was hiding in plain sight. For more than 40 years, Edward G. Kemp was Frank Murphy's devoted, trusted companion. Like Murphy, Kemp was a lifelong bachelor. From college until Murphy's death, the pair found creative ways to work and live together. They met as University of Michigan undergraduates, then attended law school there before continuing their studies in England. After returning, they shared an apartment with a friend, starting a pattern of sharing living quarters in ways unlikely to raise eyebrows. After World War I broke out, Murphy and Kemp served together, then became law partners.

When Murphy appeared to have the better future in politics, Kemp stepped into a supportive, secondary role, much as Hillary Clinton would later do for Bill Clinton. "In a curious reversal of roles, Ed Kemp . . . became the silent and self-effacing partner of the Murphy-Kemp team," Fine notes. Kemp helped Murphy get elected mayor of Detroit in 1930 and became Mayor Murphy's closest adviser. The mayor, Kemp and the mayor's brother shared a small apartment. Murphy's support of Roosevelt's successful 1932 presidential bid soon paid off. In 1933, Murphy became governor-general of the Philippines; his "closest friend and confidant" became his legal adviser. In 1936, Murphy returned to Michigan—at FDR's urging—to run successfully for governor. Governor Murphy's tiny staff was headed, naturally, by the ubiquitous Kemp. When Murphy lost the governorship two years later, FDR made room in his Cabinet. At 49, Murphy—who sometimes vainly lied about his age—was attorney general and Kemp was his special assistant. "Whatever his title, Kemp functioned as Murphy's chief of staff. . . . [He was] indispensable to Murphy, who could not imagine himself getting along without Kemp at his side," according to Fine.

Murphy settled into a furnished suite at the Washington Hotel, a block from the White House. Kemp, Murphy's personal secretary and two department secretaries also moved into the hotel. Remarking on his living arrangements, Murphy said, "We have a gay society." (FBI Director J. Edgar Hoover kept a file on his boss, Attorney General Murphy. But declassified FBI documents are conspicuously silent about Murphy's rumored homosexuality.) After a year as attorney general, Murphy was elevated by FDR to the Supreme Court. Kemp officially became general counsel of the U.S. Bureau of the Budget. Unofficially, Kemp was Justice Murphy's closest adviser, speechwriter and—in a total breach of court tradition—sometime opinion drafter.

It's not difficult to imagine Kemp spending his evenings poring over court documents while the less-scholarly Murphy was at society parties. In their era, homosexuals usually thought of their orientation as a personal failing and knew that exposure would mean ruin. Whether Murphy's nods toward heterosexuality were merely out of deference to society's expectations or reflected ambivalence, even shame, about something his religion branded sinful is impossible to know. Yet they have the earmarks of contrived efforts. His heart, quite literally, wasn't in them. Prodded by FDR, Murphy became engaged, then delayed the marriage by insisting that his fiancée convert to Catholicism. When she agreed, Murphy was hospitalized with chest pains. The wedding was postponed so many times that the woman—like others before her—gave up. Murphy became engaged to a different woman. He had told her—in what sounds like a Freudian slip—that "To say that I love you is a misunderstandment." The wedding, planned for August 1949, was to be attended only by his personal secretary and, of course, Kemp. Murphy instructed the secretary to find a Washington house where she, Murphy, Murphy's bride and Kemp could live together after the wedding. "We would have great fun," Murphy told his secretary. A month before the wedding date, Murphy's heart gave out. He died in his sleep. He left all his worldly goods to Kemp and the secretary. The press stamped Murphy's dubious heterosexual credentials even after his death. His obituary in *The Washington Post* declared, "He was romantically linked with names of a number of pretty girls, and one kissed him in public." Kemp retired and left Washington immediately after the death of his longtime companion. Kemp died in 1962 at age 75.

A results-oriented liberal, Justice Murphy tailored his votes to fit the dictates of his compassionate conscience. He is best remembered for standing up for the civil rights of minorities, including Japanese Americans, Jehovah's Witnesses, picketing workers, defendants, Native Americans and blacks. Critics smirked about "justice tempered with Murphy." Yet many Murphy dissents—including his 1948 view that "separate but equal" racially segregated schools were unconstitutional—became Supreme Court majority positions after his lifetime. Three of the 26 justices who later dealt with homosexual cases had served with Murphy. His successor, Truman appointee Tom Clark, took a hard line against homosexuals.

An Archeological Dig

Your authors are Washington journalists who have long been fascinated by the Supreme Court but frustrated by how difficult it is to learn about its gay history. Supreme Court histories and biographies, with a couple of recent exceptions, have tended to ignore even the most significant gay cases. For example, the 1979 bestseller *The Brethren: Inside the Supreme Court* devoted just three paragraphs to the sodomy decision that fell within its time frame. (Twenty years later, co-author Bob Woodward said he'd be happy to share his files with us on that case, except that he couldn't remember ever having any.)

The court's secretive and undemocratic traditions make ferreting key bits of information out of its past always difficult and sometimes impossible. That makes discoveries all the more rewarding. Justices' personal records reveal, for example, that rather than being a unanimous decision, as it has been celebrated, the breakthrough 1958 *ONE* magazine ruling that has allowed the gay press to flourish was the result of a 5-to-4 vote. The shift of a single justice would have dealt a stunning defeat to the budding homophile community.

The story that unfolds in the chapters ahead was pieced together from tens of thousands of pages of official Supreme Court documents; National Archives originals of petitions the court discarded long ago; justices' private memos, notes and drafts; the homophile and beefcake magazines missing from the court's records; scratchy audiotapes of oral arguments; FBI files; newspaper articles; books; and hundreds of interviews, including with family members and friends of justices and 103 former Supreme Court law clerks. Interviews with attorneys spanned the entire history of the court's homosexual evolution—from Eric Julber, who fought for *ONE* when most lawyers wouldn't touch anything homosexual; to renowned constitutional law scholar Laurence Tribe, who lost a gay heartbreaker; to Jean Dubofsky, who got Colorado's Amendment 2 knocked down; and to Evan Wolfson, the rising gay legal star who argued James Dale's *Boy Scouts* case. Sometimes the search for long-buried facts and missing explanations felt like an archeological dig as dusty shards of information were unearthed and reassembled.

Interviews with clerks proved especially helpful. Most justices nurture close relationships with their clerks, providing the clerk's insights into their justice's attitudes as well as into his or her legal reasoning. To widely varying degrees, justices rely on clerks' advice on how to respond to a particular case. Often, clerks—a generation or two younger than the justices—have served as a liberalizing influence in gay cases. However, at least twice, clerks successfully pressured justices to take significant anti-gay stands. Within the last decades, gay clerks have started coming out to justices to put a human face on homosexuality. Some justices have such a deep affection for their clerks that learning that one is gay is much like having a gay child or grandchild. Others don't connect on a human level with their clerks. Justice Breyer, for example, once failed to notice a goldfish in his office water cooler and pays just as little attention to his assistants.

We found 22 gay former Supreme Court clerks—18 gay men and four lesbians. Four of those men died of AIDS. (Another gay man and a lesbian clerked for appeals court judges who later became justices.) The earliest of the discovered gay clerks assisted Justice Harlan in the mid-1950s. Of those still alive, the first was Jim Graham, now a Washington, D.C., city council member and founder of one of the nation's largest gay health clinics. Graham was closeted in 1973–74 when clerking for Chief Justice Warren. The impact of gay Supreme Court clerks has been very muted until very recent years because clerks tended to come out only after the justice for whom they'd worked had left the court. Or, the clerks simply chose not to tell their justice. Justice Powell had an unconscious affinity for hiring gay men and lesbians. For six consecutive terms in the 1980s, one or more of Powell's four clerks was gay. Yet at the end of that streak, Powell dismayed his colleagues by announcing that in all his 78 years he'd never known a homosexual. Powell proceeded to cast the decisive vote to uphold Georgia's sodomy law. Doubts still gnaw at Powell's ex-clerks about whether they could or should have done more to educate him.

Searches by telephone, mail and the Internet resulted in interviews with dozens of gay men, lesbians and bisexuals whose cases reached the court. (At least four have since died.) A surprising number had to be persuaded to share their stories because they'd felt unappreciated for too long. Especially in the early decades, gay-rights pioneers tended to be so far ahead of most gay Americans in their thinking that their battles were very lonely indeed. They were publicly fighting for job rights when most homosexuals were still doing their best to remain invisible. They started fighting to remain in uniform when military service was derided in liberal circles. They pursued marriage when most gay couples still considered it an impossible dream or a patriarchal prison. Yet, most of the early gay court battles were born of desperation because government-sponsored discrimination had disrupted quiet, often quite closeted, lives.

Because the court shrouds itself in far too much secrecy, this story is maddeningly incomplete in places. Virtually nothing is known, for example, about why the court summarily upheld Virginia's sodomy law in 1976. Documents that ought to have become public after a decent interval remain hidden from view. In any other arm of government, the thinking behind a quarter-century-old decision would be more accessible.

But Supreme Court justices persist in behaving as if they are the high priests in ancient Greece who supposedly deciphered the unintelligible utterances of the Delphic oracle in order to know the will of the gods. The justices act like the court can maintain its power only as long as the public believes in magic and doesn't understand its inner workings. As a result, the tapes and transcripts of oral arguments give no clue about which justice is speaking. The court forbids the press to tape or televise its public proceedings. Although the justices' papers were created by government officials at taxpayer expense, they are treated as justices' personal property. Some justices burn or shred most of their priceless documents. Others place absurd, posthumous restrictions on them. The papers of Chief Justice Warren Burger, for example, are closed to everyone except his chosen biographer until 50 years after Burger's death.

One goal of this project is to give the court a slice of its history that was in danger of being lost. The court's institutional memory is often more like institutional amnesia. Cases in which *cert* was denied—especially those filed by petitioners too poor to pay filing fees—can vanish with barely a trace. The court's library has no record, for example, of the 1971 sodomy case in which a gay man was sentenced to 15 years in prison. After turning that case away, most justices continued cavalierly acting as if sodomy laws were unenforced anachronisms.

Like an archeological exhibit that prominently displays its best reconstructions, this chronology turns its biggest spotlights on pivotal cases and the ones that can be described from both inside and out. The complicated saga of the 1986 *Bowers v. Hardwick* decision, which found homosexual sodomy laws constitutional, is showcased. The most devastating gay legal setback of the 20th century, the *Hardwick* decision provides the clearest view of a very human justice struggling to understand how the Constitution requires the court to treat homosexuals. In general, early cases offer the least-obstructed peek behind the velvet curtain. We encourage anyone who can help fill in remaining gaps to contact us at murdoch@erols.com or debprice@erols.com.

Part of this project naturally involved pursuing persistent but unsubstantiated rumors that Justice Souter is gay. Such rumors about the lifelong bachelor made it into print as soon as he was nominated to the court and have continued to swirl in gay circles. We interviewed longtime friends, old girlfriends, gay clerks, journalists who printed the rumor and quite a number of people who continue to repeat it. We found not one shred of evidence to confirm the rumor, nor the kind of details that set off "gaydar" as much of Justice Murphy's life story does. Unsubstantiated gay rumors about public officials and their families abound in Washington. We consider it a testament to Justice Souter's integrity that, despite being aware of these rumors, he has emerged as one of gay Americans' most dependable allies.

We began this project a bit squeamish about the cases involving sleazy public sex arrests of gay men caught with their pants down. Our queasiness quickly turned to outrage as our research exposed the naked underbelly of American law enforcement. The patterns of abuse by police officers, prosecutors and judges ought to sicken every fair-minded American. The aggressive police targeting of homosexuals often associated with the 1950s has never stopped. We are appalled by how gay men have been arrested, decade after decade, for sexual remarks in gay bars or public places that would never land a heterosexual (other than a suspected prostitute) in a jailhouse. As recently as 1996, the Supreme Court turned away the case of a gay Oklahoma City man whose "crime" was being tricked into telling an undercover cop that he enjoys oral sex. No heterosexual has to fear that the good-looking stranger they've just met in a singles bar or lovers' lane is a police officer waiting to hear the magic words that will produce handcuffs. When no place feels safe, when entrapment is always a worry and when even propositions for legal sex can land a gay man behind bars, furtive sexual encounters in public restrooms are easier to understand. In case after case, prosecutors and judges made no attempt to disguise the fact that homosexuals had been singled out for punishment under laws that, at least on their face, apply to everyone. To fight back—rather than plea bargain or pay off a cop—arrested homosexuals had to risk insanely long sentences, sometimes up to life in prison or in a mental hospital. The Supreme Court has largely fluctuated between being willfully blind to the systematic injustices against gay Americans and actively encouraging disparate treatment.

We wholeheartedly believe the Constitution grants every citizen, regardless of sexual orientation, full legal equality and the right to be free from unwarranted government harassment. And we confidently predict the U.S. Supreme Court will one day agree. However, we're going to pull ourselves back out of view in order to tell the story of gay Americans' slow advances toward justice as objectively as possible.

1

ONE Standard
of Justice

AMERICAN HOMOSEXUALS' FIGHT for equal constitutional rights began not on New York City's Christopher Street or San Francisco's Castro Street but at "232 South Hill Street, Los Angeles 12, California." From that seedy, garment district address, an almost penniless publication demanded the attention of the U.S. Supreme Court. Against all odds, it won not only the court's attention but also an unprecedented legal victory that allowed the gay press to blossom.

By the fall of 1954, nearly 15 years before the Stonewall Rebellion that is marked as the start of the modern-day gay-rights movement, those few homosexuals bold enough to subscribe to the nation's first homosexual publication knew 232 South Hill as a return address. Most of the monthly magazine's 1,650 subscribers prudently paid extra—one dollar a year—for the supposed protection of receiving it in a sealed, first-class envelope bearing that nameless return address as its only identifying mark. The Los Angeles postal officials policing the mails for obscenity were equally familiar with that seemingly unremarkable return address.

232 South Hill was a run-down three-story office building with a Goodwill Store at street level. Upstairs, most of the offices housed a perpetually changing cast of fly-by-night sweatshops, the type that churned out women's clothes until the workers tried to get paid and the boss vanished. In the dingy third-floor hallway, the dull whir of sewing machines was jarringly punctuated by a soprano singing teacher, whose voice wan-

dered around on every note. In that undistinguished location straight out of a film noir set, a white-on-black hand-lettered sign on a frosted glass door read simply **ONE**, the name of the daring publication that frankly billed itself as "The Homosexual Magazine."

From its first issue, *ONE* attributed its name to a lofty quotation from 19th-century British writer Thomas Carlyle: ". . . a mystic bond of brotherhood makes all men one." But the name's roots also were in the insider code—"He's one"—and in "the ubiquitous World War II joke" that it produced, *ONE* news columnist Jim Kepner later wrote. In that joke, "an Army sergeant [was] teaching a group of rookies to count off, coming to one who didn't speak up and barking, 'Hey! You! Ain't you one?' 'Yes!' lisped the recruit, 'Are you one, too?'"

ONE's two-room office—half of it windowless—was just as shabby as the rest of the building. The mishmash of used bookshelves, furniture and office equipment looked like the donated castoffs that it was. But the small volunteer staff, which had launched *ONE* as a serious-minded voice for long-silent homosexuals in January 1953, was proud to no longer be working out of an editor's basement, proud to have exchanged P.O. Box 5716 for a real address. The editorial team tended to procrastinate, but as its end-of-the-month deadline approached "everybody would turn out and we'd smoke and have hamburgers and finish the damn magazine," a founder, Dale Jennings, recalled nearly a half century later. During those marathon sessions, "the rooms were filled with smoke and sparking conversation," said Don Slater, another founder.

The magazine was the obsession, indeed the primary occupation, of its devoted staff. Slater, for example, was largely supported by his long-time lover, Tony Reyes, the lead flamenco dancer at a Los Angeles nightclub. To disguise the size of *ONE*'s very small stable of writers, each regular contributor adopted several pen names. The most fearless wrote under their own names as well. The threat of government censorship always hung over the heads of *ONE*'s staff, but they did not have the luxury of being continually fearful of it.

"On a day-to-day basis, the danger from the censors seemed no worse than the others to us," Slater recalled. "For instance, we had to deliver the magazine to the newsstands ourselves. Circulation was crucial. At first no distributors would touch *ONE*. And I was more than once physically chased away from a newsstand with the proprietor behind shouting, 'You fucking cocksucker! You want me to carry that dirty rag? You bastard! Don't let me catch you around here again!'"

Continually dogged by shortages of money, help and publishable articles, ONE skipped its August and September issues in 1954. But managing editor Irma "Corky" Wolf, who used the pseudonym Ann Carll Reid, got the next issue into the mail right on time—October 1, 1954.

Soon readers who bought ONE at newsstands and pushed its circulation up to 5,000 were calling to ask, "Where's the issue?" A letter from Los Angeles postmaster Otto K. Olesen provided the answer. As ONE attorney Eric Julber explained at a November 12 staff meeting, Olesen said "he had been instructed by the U.S. Postal Dept. in Washington to detain the second-class mailing of ONE's October issue, pending final determination of [the] U.S. solicitor general as to its mailability." Six hundred copies had been seized.

Initially, ONE editors weren't particularly alarmed because the August 1953 issue had been held up three weeks before being cleared by postal officials. That issue's cover had asked "Homosexual Marriage?"—then an almost unimaginable question that the author, an unabashed advocate of promiscuity, answered by warning that acceptance of homosexuality would necessarily lead to homosexual marriage and mandatory monogamy. When the marriage issue was deemed fit to be mailed, the earnest little magazine's staff brashly declared on its October 1953 cover that "ONE is not grateful." And it prematurely declared victory: ". . . We have been pronounced respectable. The Post Office found that ONE is obscene in no way. . . . Never before has a government agency of this size admitted that homosexuals not only have legal rights but might have respectable motives as well."

Despite the bravado, ONE's first brush with federal authorities made a staff already vigilant about trying to avoid obscenity charges take the added precaution of having attorney Julber read every word in each issue at least twice before the copy was typeset. Yet when government censors in Washington finished inspecting ONE's October 1954 issue, they banned it under a law that forbade the mailing of any "obscene, lewd, lascivious or filthy" publication.

Julber was just a few years out of law school when he agreed to become ONE's unpaid attorney and try to protect its civil liberties. So far as he knew, he'd never before been acquainted with homosexuals. "I thought, 'This will help my reputation in the future,'" Julber recalled at age 74. "Actually, it didn't because everyone thought, 'Julber must be gay.' I didn't care. [ONE's editors] were so clearly in the right that I thought they deserved legal representation."

The ONE staff, "a tiny ever-shifting band of radicals" that had never numbered more than about a dozen, wanted to fight. The notion of publishing a magazine for and by homosexuals had originated at a 1952 discussion group of the Mattachine Society, an organization founded in 1951 on the then-radical premise that homosexuals might eventually improve their place in society by meeting to explore common concerns. ONE's founders and eventual staff saw a need to move from talk to activism by producing an unprecedented publication. None was a professional journalist, but that was one of their few common traits. Some were civil libertarians. Others considered themselves conservative Republicans. Several of ONE's early driving forces were ex-Communists. "I was a card-carrying Communist for almost a week. And then there was a knock on the door, and here came a gal that was in my cell, I guess you'd call it. And she said, 'We're going to have to ask for you to resign.' And I said, 'Why?' Yes, you guessed it, 'You're homosexual,'" recalled ONE founder Dale Jennings, whose sister owned a print shop and gave ONE the generous price-break on paper and printing that enabled it to get started.

The ONE staff, which included several women, didn't even have a unified position on whether "homosexual" described people or only particular sex acts. "The only thing that bound us together was a determination to escape the social inequality we faced. It was not so much a matter of the law, but its harsh and unequal enforcement," said founder Don Slater.

ONE itself was not Communist, a conclusion the Federal Bureau of Investigation reached before calling off its first secret investigation of the magazine in December 1953. In fact, a consistent, unspoken theme running through the issues leading up to the October 1954 ONE was a belief in democracy and education—that is, if homosexuals and the public at large could learn enough about the true nature of homosexuality, the government would stop discriminating against homosexuals.

Gay pride was an unknown concept. (Several editors almost resigned over a cover article entitled "I'm Glad I'm Homosexual." Kepner recalls,

"They said, 'How can you possibly be glad? Who would choose to be this way?'") Yet *ONE*'s staff had a healthy sense of indignation at being targeted by the government. With the seizure of their October 1954 issue, *ONE* editors were eager "to take the Post Office on" not only because they thought their fledgling magazine was the victim of a double standard but also because "we were all tired of the uncertainty facing each issue," Slater recalled.

ONE couldn't afford to fight, though. At the end of October, accounts receivable totaled $1,428.89; accounts payable, $1,433.70. Julber volunteered to handle a lawsuit free of charge. The young attorney turned to the American Civil Liberties Union (ACLU) for "heavyweight support. But, believe it or not, when I said it involved a homosexual magazine, they said they wouldn't get involved. I was astounded," Julber recalls.

After an 11-month delay that Julber attributed to the magazine's financial woes, *ONE* filed suit in federal court against Los Angeles postmaster Olesen, challenging the decision that the October 1954 issue was unmailable. Ironically, the cover of the disputed issue declared, "You Can't Print It!" In the anonymous cover article "by *ONE*'s legal counsel," Julber explained the censorship guidelines he'd cautiously instituted in trying to ensure that *ONE* did not run afoul of the federal law against mailing obscene material.

Julber's censorship explanation was needed, according to Jim Kepner, because "readers had complained bitterly that the magazine was so damn tame." Some thought they weren't getting their 25 cents' worth; if they had wanted a totally staid magazine, they could get *Time* for 20 cents. Kepner, then about 31, was a *ONE* news columnist who supported himself by working the midnight shift in a milk carton factory. Kepner, who died as this book was being written, never knew his exact age because he was a foundling, discovered as a toddler under an oleander bush. Reporting that discovery, *The Galveston* [Texas] *Daily News* hailed him as "our little visitor from Mars," he said.

Trying to readjust readers' expectations, Julber began by pointing out that anyone who knowingly broke the obscenity law could be fined $5,000 and/or imprisoned for five years. Noting that there was no way to be certain precisely what federal courts might see as "obscene, lewd, lascivious or filthy," he warned that "there is one extreme school of legal thought that would say that *ONE*, merely by its existence, is illegal. That reasoning would run as follows: Homosexual acts are made crimes in every state of the union. *ONE* is published specifically for homosexuals. Therefore, *ONE* is a magazine for criminals . . . [and, thus,] illegal. This, however, is too extreme a view for 1954." *ONE* tried to avoid being tarred as criminal by repeatedly stating that it did not advocate illegal behavior. Julber wrote that *ONE* probably was on safe legal ground as long as it discussed the "social, economic, personal and legal problems of homosexuals" and avoided stimulating "sexual desires." For that reason, he had deleted portions of the Walt Whitman poetry in an article exploring evidence that the poet was homosexual.

Julber told readers, "*ONE* cannot print the following: lonely hearts ads, cheesecake art or photos; descriptions of sexual acts or the preliminaries thereto. . . . Permissible: 'John was my friend for a year.' Not permissible: 'That night we made mad love'; descriptions of homosexuality as a practice which the author encourages. . . . Characters cannot rub knees, feel thighs, hold hands, soap backs or undress before one another. . . ." Julber's rules were "relaxed somewhat" for lesbian articles.

As Kepner later explained, "Our lawyer figured that, generally speaking, the law was a little easier on descriptions of lesbians because an awful lot of men were turned on by that." Kepner added, "We knew that the interpretation of the laws was unfair, that what was permissible for heterosexuals on a scale of one to 10 was 10—and less than one for us."

Julber had, in fact, relaxed his rules in the very issue that he spelled them out: ". . . Pavia pressed her knee conspiratorially against Jill's." In "Sappho Remembered," a four-page romance that playwright James Barr Hugate wrote as "Jane Dahr" to counteract a shortage of manuscripts from women, a 30ish singer and her 20-year-old secretary, Jill, touched four times. The singer, Pavia, gradually admitted to herself that she was in love with Jill. The younger woman, meanwhile, was torn between the singer and the "nice young man" who wanted to marry her. But unlike most lesbian pulp fiction of the day, there was no tragic lesbian death scene to keep government censors at bay. The lesbian relationship simply triumphed.

When federal officials had to justify branding *ONE*'s October 1954 issue "obscene," that short story was always the first evidence cited. In response to *ONE*'s lawsuit, the U.S. attorney's office in Los Angeles told federal District Court Judge Thurmond Clarke that the story was "obscene because [it is] lustfully stimulating to the average homosexual reader."

The postmaster's legal team also targeted as obscene the "filthy words" in "Lord Samuel and Lord Montagu." A bawdy 15-verse poem by a Canadian professor who used the pen name "Brother Grundy," it made light of the British uproar over the arrests of several prominent men, including the actor Sir John Gielgud, on homosexual "morals" charges. One member of Parliament was convicted of "importuning" other men at urinals. The most vulgar verse declared "Lord Samuel says that Sodom's sins / Disgrace our young Queen's reign, / An age that in this plight begins / May well end up in flame. . . . Would he idly waste his breath / In sniffing round the drains / Had he known 'King Elizabeth' / Or roistering 'Queen James'?" *ONE*'s Don Slater later admitted, "We knew we took a chance with Grundy, but we simply couldn't resist. Have you read the poem? Too delicious!"

Federal attorneys also contended that a small ad for a trilingual Swiss monthly, *Der Kreis*, or *The Circle*, rendered *ONE* unmailable "because it gives information for obtaining obscene material," meaning, the Swiss magazine itself.

The legal arguments against *ONE* initially proved persuasive. The magazine suffered back-to-back court defeats. First, on March 2, 1956, Judge Clarke handed down a decision declaring the October 1954 issue obscene for precisely the reasons offered by Postmaster Olesen's legal team. Clarke added, "The suggestion that homosexuals should be recognized as a segment of our people and be accorded special privilege as a class is rejected."

Then, on February 27, 1957, a three-judge panel of the Ninth Circuit Court of Appeals branded the October 1954 issue "morally depraving and debasing," in other words, obscene and unmailable. "The magazine . . . has a primary purpose of exciting lust, lewd and lascivious thoughts and sensual desires in the minds of persons reading it," the court found. Quoting a prior ruling that obscenity laws are not designed to fit the moral standards of "society's dregs," the appellate judges declared, "Social standards are fixed by and for the great majority and not by or for a hardened or weakened minority."

The judges were appalled by "Sappho Remembered." "The climax," they wrote, "is reached when the young girl gives up her chance for a al life to live with the lesbian. This article is nothing more than cheap pornography calculated to promote lesbianism. It falls far short of [ONE's stated goal of] dealing with homosexuality from the scientific, historical and critical point of view." As for the poem, the judges said it "pertains to sexual matter of such a vulgar and indecent nature that it tends to arouse a feeling of disgust and revulsion." The Swiss ad "appears harmless" but is not, the judges said, because it tells readers "where to get more of the material contained in ONE."

"Perverts Called Government Peril"

Missing from the seemingly endless accusations that federal judges and executive branch officials hurled at ONE was the underlying reason that the weight of the federal government was bearing down on an impoverished little periodical. ONE was under assault for the same reason that both it and the Mattachine Society had been founded: The federal government had adopted an aggressive new posture in 1950 that treated homosexuals as a national menace.

Until 1950, cautious, closeted American homosexuals—except those in the military—had little reason to fear that their sexual orientation would cost them their jobs. Society's consistent message was, "Just stay out of sight. We want to pretend you don't exist." (The military had found it expedient during World War II to ignore most homosexuals in its ranks. After the war, involuntary discharges for homosexuality tripled, according to historian Allan Berube.)

The rapid spread of Communism early in the Cold War heightened America's fear of being undermined from within—by infiltrators, traitors or persons with so-called weak moral fiber. With the nation gripped by the notion that the enemies of democracy could be lurking anywhere, homosexuals—long practiced at hiding in plain sight—became targets. In 1950, the federal government began unprecedented attempts to expose and expel the homosexuals in its civilian workforce.

The notion that homosexuals posed a threat to national security was planted in the minds of many members of Congress early in 1950 by Deputy Under Secretary of State John E. Peurifoy, who was in charge of ridding his department of security risks. He informed a Senate panel in February that 91 employees "in the shady category" had resigned since the start of 1947. "Most of these were homosexuals," he revealed. Already obsessed with charging that under Democratic President Harry Truman the State Department was soft on Communism, Republican leaders seized the idea that the State Department was riddled with homosexuals. Senator Joseph McCarthy soon took time out from his red baiting to accuse the State Department of poisoning the Central Intelligence Agency, which he claimed had unwittingly hired a homosexual whom the State Department had allowed to resign quietly. Next, the Republican Party's national chairman fired off a warning to 7,000 party members that, "Perhaps as dangerous as the actual Communists are the secret perverts who have infiltrated our government in recent years." *The New York Times* reported that GOP warning under the headline that epitomized societal attitudes toward homosexuals: "PERVERTS CALLED GOVERNMENT PERIL."

One Republican senator rhetorically demanded to know, "Who put the 91 homosexuals in our State Department?" Historian David K. Johnson notes, "The question implied that 'an unseen master hand' had placed them there in order to weaken America's foreign policy apparatus. . . . Homosexuals might not be intrinsically disloyal, but they could be used by those who were, so the thinking went. They were, in the words of one contemporary tabloid magazine, 'Stalin's Atom Bomb.'"

Senate Minority Leader Kenneth Wherry, a Nebraska Republican, took the lead in demanding an investigation of the extent to which homosexuals had "infiltrated" the federal Civil Service. Those demands were heightened by an out-of-thin-air estimate offered by the chief of the District of Columbia's vice squad, Lieutenant Roy Blick. His "quick guess," as he put it, was that the executive branch harbored 3,500 homosexuals—with 300 to 400 lurking inside Truman's State Department.

Besides being driven by Republicans' desire to gain a partisan advantage, the rapid escalation in the national fear of homosexuals was propelled by two other phenomena: The first was the fear of Communism that gripped the postwar American public, which was perpetually fed propaganda claiming that Communist agents—ordinary looking and undetected—lurked behind every corner. The second was researcher Alfred Kinsey's 1948 bestseller, *Sexual Behavior in the Human Male*, which shocked a nation that had considered homosexuality rare. Kinsey's findings indicated that 37 percent of white male adults had had at least one adult homosexual encounter to the point of orgasm. Oddly, the news that homosexual behavior was not so aberrant after all didn't make homosexuals seem less strange and frightening to the general population. Instead, it served "to magnify suddenly the proportions of the danger they allegedly posed," according to historian John D'Emilio.

Suddenly, the homosexual wasn't easily picked out of the crowd on the basis of a few telling mannerisms. Suddenly, the homosexual, like the Communist spy, could be anyone—the person sitting at the next desk or asking you for a light. Even though Kinsey's findings depicted homosexual desire as a natural human variation, as a deviation only from a statistical norm, they inadvertently buttressed the belief that homosexuality is a vice that everyone is vulnerable to being enticed into. Paradoxically, homosexuality was feared both as an individual weakness and as a menacing force—perhaps powered by some sort of conspiracy—capable of undermining national security. Homosexuals holding positions of public trust became the sum of all fears because they were both powerful and invisible. Writing "The Washington Sex Story" for *The New York Post* on July 10, 1950, columnist Max Lerner pointed out, "This is a story in which only the accusers and the hunters—Senate probers, security officers, police officials—get their names in the papers. The hunted remain anonymous—unspecified, uncounted, nameless men."

The Senate officially launched its investigation in June 1950. A special seven-member subcommittee reported back December 15 on *Employment of Homosexuals and Other Sex Perverts in Government*. As the panel noted, much had already changed since the revelation about the number of homosexuals forced to resign from the State Department: The FBI had begun coordinating a national effort to identify and oust homosexuals holding federal jobs. "The FBI . . . began furnishing to the Civil Service Commission the criminal records of persons currently arrested by the police throughout the country on charges of sex perversion who were known to be government employees," the subcommittee reported.

Although noting that "reliable, factual information on . . . homosexuality and sexual perversion is somewhat limited," the Senate subcommittee concluded that homosexual federal employees were security risks. They are easy prey for blackmailers, the panel said, pointing to a single example in Austria in 1912. And their "lack of emotional stability" and "the weakness of their moral fiber" makes them vulnerable to foreign agents, the panel added. "These perverts will frequently attempt to entice normal individuals to engage in perverted practices. . . . One homosexual can pollute a government office," the subcommittee asserted.

With the exception of the military, the federal government had been far too lax in dealing with homosexuals, the report claimed: "There is no place in the United States government for persons who violate the laws or the accepted standards of morality, or who otherwise bring disrepute to the federal service by infamous or scandalous personal conduct. . . . [T]hose who engage in acts of homosexuality are unsuitable for employment in the federal government," the subcommittee declared. "To pussyfoot or take half measures will allow some known perverts to remain in government," it warned.

The FBI, under the direction of J. Edgar Hoover (quite possibly a closeted homosexual), led a national crackdown on homosexuals. "Once the government assumed the position that homosexuals and lesbians threatened the welfare of the country, it had to devise methods to cope with the problem that gay people could conceal their identity. Since hidden homosexuals allegedly posed the most serious danger, national security seemed to depend on the ability to break their cover," historian D'Emilio observes. Beginning in 1950, "The FBI sought out friendly vice squad officers who supplied arrest records on morals charges, regardless of whether convictions had ensued. Regional FBI offices gathered data on gay bars, compiled lists of other places frequented by homosexuals. . . ."

The Immigration and Naturalization Service pounced on the vice squad arrest records collected by the FBI to target homosexual immigrants for deportation. Meanwhile, the Post Office deviously used its power to try to identify homosexuals by snooping in their mail, tracking who received homosexual publications and having postal inspectors join pen pal clubs. When homosexuals were found, postal officials "placed tracers on victims' mail in order to locate other homosexuals," D'Emilio reports. Some homosexuals lost jobs after their employers were alerted that they'd received homosexual publications.

Within the federal government, dismissals of homosexuals jumped from just five a month before the "government peril" alarm sounded in

April 1950, to more than 60 a month. Soon after President Dwight Eisenhower's inauguration in 1953, he issued an executive order listing "sexual perversion" as disqualifying anyone from a federal job. Being barred from the federal government, the nation's largest employer, was just the beginning of the new hardships inflicted upon homosexual workers. State and local governments as well as government contractors mimicked the federal government in imposing security rules intended to keep out homosexuals. D'Emilio estimates that more than 20 percent of the American workforce was subjected to "loyalty-security investigations." Even quite a few private industries without government contracts conducted witch hunts to expose and drive out homosexuals.

With public and private employers aggressively attempting to ferret out homosexuals, police forces acted as if they'd been given a "no-holds-barred" signal to harass, abuse and arrest homosexuals. Vice squads peeped into restrooms, set traps for homosexual men cruising public parks or bars and routinely raided homosexual bars, sometimes beating up the patrons but more commonly arresting them for innocuous touching or for dancing with someone of the same sex. Especially for homosexual men, vice squads turned the world upside down: Anyone in what was supposedly safe homosexual territory—whether a bar or a cruising spot—might actually be a cop. So a touch or a proposition could result in being arrested and fired.

The role of defending the federal government's new anti-homosexual policies in court automatically fell to the Justice Department, which continues to play that role today.

In the 1950s, very few voices countered the idea that homosexuals were a national menace that must be dealt with decisively and harshly. Psychiatry claimed to take a more enlightened approach to homosexuality than clerics and lawmakers by calling it a mental illness rather than a sin or a crime. Yet the illness label, which the American Psychiatric Association made official in 1952, created an effective new weapon that could be used in court against homosexuals. In 1957, psychologist Evelyn Hooker began publishing research revealing that homosexual men were as mentally healthy as their heterosexual counterparts. Hooker's homosexuals were Los Angeles men associated with *ONE* and/or Mattachine. Her work had little initial impact, though. Meanwhile, a draft of the American Law Institute's model penal code first proposed decriminalizing sodomy in 1955. Six years later, Illinois became the first state to follow that advice.

In 1957, the ACLU's board of directors defended the constitutionality of laws that made homosexual behavior criminal. Homosexuals simply were not viewed as a mistreated minority group. Thinking of homosexuals in that way would have seemed as inappropriate to most Americans as considering purse snatchers or Communists an oppressed group.

Yet because of the intense new government campaigns against them, a few homosexuals did start to see themselves as members of a persecuted minority group. For the great mass of homosexuals, hiding no longer provided any real guarantee of safety. And for a few, fighting back was no longer prohibitively dangerous because they had little left to lose: They'd already lost a career or the right to stay in the United States. The Mattachine Society's formation in 1951 marked the first attempt of homosexuals to band together to explain themselves, at least to one another. *ONE*'s creation in 1953 gave homosexuals a publication that gave voice to their new and growing sense of being wrongly oppressed.

Reaching the High Court

Given the intense societal hostility to homosexuals and government officials' fear of being accused of pandering to them, it was perhaps inevitable that the U.S. Post Office would try to ban the first homosexual magazine to hit the newsstands. Yet FBI, Supreme Court and *ONE* records yield no definitive clues about why the crackdown came with the October 1954 issue. Kepner's theory—spread in several accounts of the early days of the gay-rights movement—that the seizure was triggered by FBI fury over *ONE*'s passing reference to homosexuality within the bureau turns out to be mistaken. The reference and the fury came later.

The actual trigger might have been Senate Foreign Relations Committee Chairman Alexander Wiley's "vigorous protest against the use of the United States mails to transmit a so-called 'magazine' devoted to the advancement of sexual perversion." Having stumbled upon the March 1954 issue ("The Importance of Being Different," read the cover), the Wisconsin senator angrily wrote to U.S. Postmaster General Arthur Summerfield. Allowing a homosexual magazine to use the U.S. mail,

Wiley charged, "(a) runs utterly contrary to every moral principle, (b) runs utterly contrary to our intentions to safeguard our nation's youngsters, (c) likewise, it is the very opposite of the entire purpose of our governmental security program. . . ."

Perhaps most likely, postal officials continually kept tabs on ONE but waited to act until the comparatively racy October 1954 issue gave them confidence that an obscenity charge would stick.

Less than a decade after the federal government aggressively turned up the heat on homosexuals in 1950, homosexual cases began bubbling up to the Supreme Court. The first, of course, was ONE's. Despite the tenor of the times and the ferocity of the appellate court's slaps at ONE, attorney Julber remained confident that at the Supreme Court "a rational view of the matter would prevail and 20th-century standards of free discussion of human problems would be upheld."

Yet even though the U.S. Constitution's First Amendment guarantees freedom of the press, ONE had little reason to expect a Supreme Court victory. From 1953 to 1969, Chief Justice Earl Warren presided over what is often recalled as "the liberal Warren court" because of its groundbreaking decisions against school segregation and in favor of the rights of the accused. But by the time ONE's appeal landed on its doorstep, the Supreme Court had not extended the constitutional ideal of "equal protection" much beyond racial minorities.

Cases tinged with sexuality seemed to bring out a conservative desire among most justices not to rock the status quo of the gender-stereo-typed, conformist '50s. For example, the court had yet to strike down as unconstitutional any law based on stereotypical notions about women's roles in society. And the justices were actively dodging the most sexual of all race discrimination questions: Are state laws against interracial marriage unconstitutional? The court had yet to hand down any of the sexual freedom decisions that established a "right to privacy." The first of those—knocking down laws against the sale of contraceptives to married couples—was still nearly a decade away. Meanwhile, sodomy was still illegal in all 48 states. Although those "crime against nature" laws generally applied to anyone—even married couples—who engaged in specific behavior, they were commonly thought of as outlawing homosexuality. The subject of homosexuality was engulfed in silence, rarely mentioned in "polite society." The court had never pondered the constitutional rights of homosexuals.

As soon as *ONE* attorney Julber filed his petition, dated June 13, 1957, the question implicitly before the U.S. Supreme Court was: Is there one standard of justice for all Americans—heterosexual and homosexual alike? The question explicitly before the court was whether the Post Office had the legal right to bar *ONE*'s October 1954 issue from the mail.

Julber's nine-page, mildly worded *cert* petition asked the Supreme Court to decide whether *ONE* was being "discriminated against" and deprived of "equal protection" by being held to a "stricter standard" of mailability. It definitely was not a passionate homosexual-rights treatise. Julber merely pointed to federal court decisions allowing the advocacy of polygamy and nudism. Those cases and his own, he argued, involved written works "attempting to explain to the layman problems of human life that have plagued the human race through the centuries." He concluded by defensively telling the justices, ". . . There is nowhere . . . in any issue of *ONE* magazine any *advocacy* of homosexuality as a way of life, but only a discussion of the problems, social, economic, and personal, which confront those persons possessed of that particular neurosis, or complexion." Julber was challenging the judicial determination that *ONE*'s October 1954 issue was obscene, not the widely held assumption that homosexuality was a mental illness.

Postmaster Olesen was represented by the U.S. solicitor general, who speaks to the Supreme Court on behalf of the federal government's executive branch. Solicitor General J. Lee Rankin tersely responded to Julber's petition by noting that two courts had ruled *ONE* obscene. "There is no need for this court to review these findings," Rankin concluded. Then, in a footnote, he added, "The courts below did not find the magazine non-mailable simply because it deals with the subject of homosexuality." While *ONE* claims to take a "scientific, historical and critical" approach, "the magazine appears primarily to deal with sex . . . 'in a manner appealing to [the] prurient interest' of those the magazine tries to reach," Rankin said, quoting the new Supreme Court ruling upholding the constitutionality of the federal law against mailing obscene material. That decision, *Roth v. United States,* had been announced just days after Julber filed *ONE*'s petition. In *Roth,* a five-member majority of the court offered this definition: "Obscene material is material which deals with sex in a manner appealing to prurient interest." The ruling helpfully explained that "prurient" means "having a tendency to excite lustful thoughts."

Most justices' first impressions of *ONE Inc. v. Olesen, postmaster of Los Angeles*—as the case was known—were gleaned largely from memos written by their clerks. (The party listed first in the case title is always the "petitioner," that is, the one seeking a Supreme Court hearing after having lost in the court below.) Only Justice William J. Brennan Jr., who in 1957 was beginning the second of what would be an awesome 33 terms on the court, personally reviewed the documents filed in almost every case. In Brennan's chambers, whenever a cart overflowing with new petitions arrived, it was wheeled directly to him. In every other justice's chambers, the daunting cart was tackled not by seasoned jurists confirmed by the U.S. Senate but by bright young men, usually no more than a year out of law school.

On battered manual typewriters, the clerks banged out rapid-fire summaries of the legal arguments in every case that reached the high court, sometimes spending as little as five minutes digesting and spitting out a case's highlights. In every "paid" case—those in which normal filing fees were tendered—each of Brennan's eight colleagues read the "*cert* memo" prepared in his own chambers and never laid eyes on the memos written by clerks in the seven other chambers. (Summaries of cases involving impoverished petitioners asking that all fees be waived—usually prisoners seeking a new day in court—were quickly written by one of the chief justice's clerks and then circulated to every justice.)

In *ONE*'s era, clerks routinely let their personal attitudes seep into their restatement of the facts of a case, the legal arguments raised and their assessment of how the court should respond. With homosexual cases, clerks—who at 27 or 28 were 35 years younger than the average justice in 1957—have tended to be a liberalizing influence on the court. In *ONE v. Olesen cert* memos written in late August 1957, several clerks—including one repulsed by *ONE*—declared *ONE* was being held to a tougher standard because it was a homosexual magazine, thought that was unfair and pushed their justices to take the magazine's case.

The personal records of the late Justice Harold H. Burton contain the four-page *cert* memo that he received about *ONE v. Olesen*. In the fall of 1957, the 69-year-old Burton was starting his 13th and last term on the court. A former mayor of Cleveland, he'd represented Ohio in the Senate until his old colleague Harry Truman tapped him for the high court in 1945, making him the first Republican associate justice appointed by a Democratic president. Burton once compared his job change to going from "a circus to a monastery." An avid bird watcher who tried to keep the peace when other justices quarreled, Burton had the air of a "supremely cultured English butler one might see in a movie," according to William Rehnquist, who observed Burton while clerking for another justice. Because Parkinson's disease drove Burton from the bench in 1958, *ONE* was his only homosexual case.

One of Burton's two law clerks wrote, "I read the issue of *ONE* with some mild interest. I must say that I found it relatively inoffensive, far less offensive than the average 'men's' magazine. I think the decision below is an example of the tyranny of the majority. . . . The [appeals] court seems to feel that homosexuality is disgusting and therefore allusions to homosexual practices are disgusting and obscene. . . . I think *ONE* is no more descriptive of sexual practices than dozens of magazines. The fact that the practices differ from those of the 'normal' person should not make the magazine obscene.

"If the story in *ONE* is 'calculated to promote lesbianism' certain stories in *Woman's* [sic] *Home Journal* are probably calculated to promote adultery," Burton's clerk concluded, recommending that the justices send the case back to the appeals court to be reconsidered in light of the new obscenity standard established by *Roth*.

Likewise, a four-page memo to Chief Justice Warren recommended that the court "grant" *cert* (that is, take the case), reverse the lower courts and send it back for reconsideration under the *Roth* standard. Warren's clerk suggested that the *ONE* material targeted by the lower courts might be "just bad taste," not obscene. "Were the contributions dealing with heterosexual matters, it is doubtful the community would find them prurient. Possibly because the topic is homosexuality, where the community has expressed an aversion, a stricter standard is available even under *Roth*, . . ." Warren's clerk concluded.

Civil libertarian William O. Douglas, a Roosevelt appointee who in 1957 had already served 18 terms though he was only 59, had been one of three dissenters from *Roth*. Douglas believed it was none of the government's business whether a piece of literature excited lustful thoughts. "The arousing of sexual thoughts and desires happens every day in normal life in dozens of ways. . . . The test of obscenity that the court endorses today [in *Roth*] gives the censor free range over a vast domain," Douglas wrote in dissent.

For the 1957–58 term, Douglas had just one law clerk, not the two that most associate justices had. (Chief Justice Warren had three.) Douglas's lone clerk devoted just half a page to his *ONE* memo:

> There is no doubt in my mind that the [court of appeals] applied a different standard to this magazine than it would have to a magazine portraying sexual relations between males and females. The real question is whether this standard is valid or whether these people are entitled to express their thoughts and customs under the same standard that publishers of girly magazines operate. The fact that any incitement to do a physical act in this magazine is inciting the commission of a crime in every state while the same cannot be said of girly magazines is difficult to ignore in arguing the standards should be the same.

Actually, state laws against fornication—unmarried heterosexual intercourse—were widespread, sodomy laws generally applied to anal and oral sex regardless of whether the participants were the same sex and plenty of homosexually stimulating physical activities fell outside the reach of most laws. Douglas's clerk was far from alone, however, in equating homosexual activity with illegality. He concluded by confessing, "I am torn between the desire to cut down on this sort of administrative censorship and the revulsion the magazine gives me. I suppose in the long run it is better to let the American people make the choice than a postmaster."

The justices' easiest response to *ONE v. Olesen* would have been to turn it away unheard. That's the course the court takes in all but a tiny fraction of cases. The court's jurisdictional rules at the time certainly did not require that it take the case. The court normally prefers to wait to take up a given legal question until conflicting appellate court decisions need to be sorted out. But there was no appeals court ruling in conflict— even indirectly—with the Ninth Circuit's condemnation of *ONE*. In fact, other than *ONE*'s petition, nothing external pushed the court to pay attention to an impoverished homosexual magazine's plea. The justices could have safely assumed that if they just let the Post Office's victory over ONE stand, the mainstream press would ignore the case. The media routinely treated denial of *certiorari* as a non-decision and, thus, a non-story. By turning ONE away, the justices could avoid whatever embarrassment might come from having their court publicly linked with a mention of homosexuality.

Yet, remarkably, the Supreme Court quickly decided to at least think about accepting the case. The court had taken it upon itself to be the national arbiter of exactly what constituted obscenity and, apparently, did not want to cede that power either to the Post Office or lower courts. Soon after the Supreme Court's 1957–58 term began by tradition on the first Monday in October, the justices secretly voted 8 to 1 on October 9, 1957, to withhold judgment on whether to take ONE *v. Olesen.* They wanted to wait until an obscenity case involving two nudism magazines reached the court, according to Chief Justice Warren's conference notes. The lone dissenter was Texan Tom C. Clark, who had been a career Justice Department attorney until President Truman elevated him first to attorney general, then to the nation's top court.

By privately agreeing to consider accepting their first homosexual-rights case, the justices put themselves in the position of needing to begin thinking about homosexuality: Does "homosexual" describe only (mis)behavior? Should homosexuals be thought of as a national menace, as criminals, as sick or as just another minority group? Does homosexual content automatically render a publication obscene?

After voting to defer its decision on whether to take ONE's case, the court put the matter aside for three months. Then on Friday, January 3, 1958, the justices considered both ONE *v. Olesen* and the obscenity appeal brought on behalf of the two nudist magazines, *Sunshine and Health* and *SUN,* formally known as *Solaire Universelle Nudisme.* Normally, the justices vote once on whether to accept a case; if at least four justices want to grant *cert,* the case is taken. The vast majority of cases fail to make the cut. On January 3, five justices—Roosevelt appointees Felix Frankfurter, Douglas and Hugo Black as well as Eisenhower appointees Charles E. Whittaker and John Marshall Harlan—voted to take the case, according to Douglas's tally sheet. Frankfurter, Douglas, Harlan and Whittaker—one short of the necessary majority—wanted to reverse the lower court judgment and immediately rule in favor of ONE.

Usually, such an outcome (enough votes to take the case but too few to hand down a final ruling) would mean that the court would actually hear the case: Attorneys for both sides would file written briefs—far more extensive than the original *cert* petition and its response—laying out their best legal arguments, then the attorneys would argue the case in open court. But in *ONE*'s case and that of the nudist magazines, the court simply voted a second time a week later.

By tradition, the most junior associate justice votes last. In January 1958, Charles E. Whittaker was not only the newest justice, having been confirmed less than a year earlier, he was the second youngest at 56. A former Kansas farm boy who'd been admitted to night law school even though he was a high school dropout, Whittaker felt he didn't measure up to his learned Supreme Court brethren. He worked himself to the point of complete exhaustion trying to master a job that the brilliant Douglas didn't even consider a full-time occupation. Yet, ironically, in the 1957–58 term Whittaker often found himself casting the swing vote on a bench split 4-to-4 between those labeled "liberal"—Warren, Douglas, Black and Brennan—and the "conservatives"—Frankfurter, Burton, Harlan and Clark. The court's first homosexual case, *ONE* didn't split the justices along predictable ideological lines, but Whittaker's vote proved decisive just the same.

On January 10, as the justices voted aloud, enacting a tradition-bound drama never witnessed in recent decades by a non-justice, first Frankfurter, then Douglas reiterated support for reversing the appeals court's decision against *ONE*. Then in a switch, Clark, who'd cast the lone vote against taking the case and who'd voted January 3 to deny *cert*, announced he favored reversal. Harlan again backed reversal. Whittaker gave *ONE* its fifth vote—and victory. The reasons Whittaker sided with *ONE* are lost to history; he is one of 24 former justices with no surviving papers.

On January 13, 1958, three days after the justices' closed-door vote, the Supreme Court decreed in a one-sentence unsigned ruling in *ONE v. Olesen*, "The petition for writ of *certiorari* is granted and the judgment of the United State Court of Appeals for the Ninth Circuit is reversed. *Roth v. United States*." *ONE* had won. The *Roth* reference meant the court was applying that case's obscenity standard. The court gave no hint of the narrowness of *ONE*'s historic victory. That story can be told now only because Douglas, who died in 1980, made arrangements for his court papers to become public after his death. The court's *ONE* ruling meant that, despite the rest of the federal government's aggressive hostility toward homosexuality, homosexual content in a publication did not automatically equal obscenity. A homosexual magazine could legally be sent through the U.S. mail.

"We Made It"

When *ONE*'s telephone began ringing the next day with word of the magazine's amazing Supreme Court victory, Jim Kepner raced to a newsstand for confirmation. He searched the Los Angeles and San Francisco newspapers in vain before spotting a squib in *The New York Times*. *ONE*'s staff and attorney had not even known their case had been accepted.

Founder Dale Jennings got the stunning news of victory when a friend called him at home. "I said, 'Look, don't joke. The year 2000, yes. But not today.' I rather resented his joking about such a serious thing. And he said, 'No, honestly.' We had realized that no one had ever won a case on this subject before. So it dawned on us rather slowly that we made it. We just said, 'My God, this is too soon! I'm supposed to be an old man before this happens!'" an elderly Jennings recalled decades later.

The Supreme Court's refusal to join the federal war against homosexuals was not front-page news in the nation's premier newspaper, *The New York Times*. The top story on January 14, 1958, was President Eisenhower's record-high peacetime budget, including a proposal to raise the postage on out-of-town letters to five cents. The paper was filled with oh-so-modern airline ads bragging that particular planes were "radar-equipped." Two Supreme Court rulings did make front page. One dealt with rail fares for Chicago commuters, the other with union organizing. Way inside, on page 35, a one-column headline read, "NUDIST MAGAZINES WIN MAIL RIGHTS." *The Times* thoroughly described the legal battle of the nudist magazines, whose victory also had been announced in a one-sentence, unsigned ruling. Buried inside the account of the court's decision not to ban frontal nudity from the mail were two brief paragraphs about *ONE*, whose name was confusingly written as "one."

The realization that the tiny magazine had won a giant legal victory didn't make 232 South Hill Street rock with the joyous shouts of hundreds of homosexuals. "We were jubilant, but we had no party," founder Slater recalled shortly before his death. "We may have boozed it up a little more than usual. . . . Because we were so sure of ourselves, in a way the decision was sort of anticlimactic. We were relieved, of course, and became freer in our writing and editing. . . . It wasn't long after that outright advocacy of homosexuality burst into being."

Slater had the privilege of announcing ONE's victory in the periodical's next issue. ". . . This decision was rendered UNANIMOUSLY," ONE bragged. (The tiny publication's staff had no way of knowing that, although no justice dissented publicly, they had come within a single vote of losing.) Without exaggeration, Slater's celebratory article declared, "By winning this decision ONE magazine has made not only history but law as well and has changed the future for all U.S. homosexuals. Never before have homosexuals claimed their rights as citizens. . . . ONE magazine no longer asks for the right to be heard; it now exercises that right."

Homosexual G-Men—"It's True!"

Unbeknownst to the Supreme Court or ONE's staff, the high court's 1958 decision handed the homosexual magazine a victory not just over the Post Office but also over the FBI. Director Hoover and his top assistant, Clyde Tolson, wanted to crush ONE and gave up only after the court ruled.

In January 1956—more than a year after the start of ONE's protracted battle with the Post Office—someone in New York City anonymously sent Hoover ONE's November 1955 issue. The lead article, "How Much Do We Know About the Homosexual Male?" by circulation manager "David L. Freeman," blithely divided the gay male world into revolutionaries, conservative Tories and liberals. "The Tories are the elegant ones who have decided to express their social hostility by being more correct than the foremost representatives of the dominant (and dominating) culture," Freeman wrote. ". . . They are in the diplomatic service; they occupy key positions with oil companies or the FBI (it's true!)." That passing reference started a commotion within the FBI that generated a multitude of official memos and sparked a bumbling investigation, FBI records show.

First, a top Hoover aide advised, "In view of the nature of this publication, it is believed *ONE* should not be dignified by a reply to the completely baseless and unfounded writings. . . ." But Hoover and Tolson, obsessive about squelching anything that could be construed as hinting that they were lovers, manned their battle stations. For decades the two G-men had been together at lunch, together at dinner, together when socializing, together on vacation. Now they were together in wanting to silence *ONE* permanently for a single provocative comment. (Anthony Summer's 1993 bestseller, *The Secret Life of J. Edgar Hoover,* provides evidence strongly suggesting that Hoover and Tolson were a couple for four decades.) Reacting to the memo recommending no action, Tolson wrote: "I think we should take this crowd on and make them 'put up or shut up.'" Beside Tolson's response, Hoover scrawled, "I concur. H."

Hoover commanded the FBI's Los Angeles office to tell Freeman "the bureau will not countenance such baseless charges." The L.A. supervisor dispatched agents to *ONE*'s office in a futile attempt to intimidate someone there into revealing Freeman's real identity. FBI officials were furious that the lone *ONE* staffer on duty sassily refused to give even his own name.

Frustrated, Hoover repeatedly attempted to get the Post Office and Justice Department to crack down on *ONE*. Both agencies responded that they had no interest in taking more action until litigation over *ONE*'s October 1954 issue was settled. Hoover's top aides began investigating whether federal criminal charges could be leveled against *ONE*—presumably against its editors—for "interstate transportation of obscene matter."

If Hoover was indeed a self-hating homosexual who abused his awesome police powers to protect the secret that surely would have cost his career, he must have been fascinated and terrified by a publication openly written by fairly self-respecting homosexuals. His taxpayer-financed vendetta against *ONE* ran out of steam only when the Supreme Court ruled in the magazine's favor.

On March 31, 1958, Hoover told his L.A. office that, because of the court's ruling and the Justice Department's refusal to prosecute, there was no need to keep sending him *ONE*. If the Supreme Court had not protected *ONE*, Hoover and Tolson very likely would have found a way to put it out of business.

The Path Out of Isolation

The significance of *ONE*'s three-year, largely forgotten legal battle is almost impossible to overstate. The written word has been the first path that countless gay men and lesbians have found out of isolation. The 1958 *ONE* ruling flung open the door for gay publications, which began to proliferate. Gay magazines and newspapers became a cornerstone for building gay communities by encouraging people to come out, to connect with one another and to share a sense of identity and injustice. Millions of American gay men and lesbians have learned to hold their heads up high in part because an obscure little magazine successfully stood up for itself long before many of them were born.

Had the justices instead ruled that *ONE*'s homosexual viewpoint made it inherently obscene, launching a gay-rights movement worthy of the name would have been infinitely more difficult. Imagine if gay-themed magazines, newspapers and books could not be distributed through the mail. It would not have been a major leap from that level of censorship to an outright ban on homosexual publications.

Had the government war on homosexuals never started, the Supreme Court might not have handed down any homosexual decision until 1972, when a male couple went to the court seeking recognition of their right to marry. Instead, *ONE v. Olesen* was just the first of many involving homosexual litigants under siege because of government action against them. Employment, deportation and sodomy cases all soon reached the nation's highest court as a direct result of the government assault on homosexuals. Just three years after its surprising *ONE* decision, the court inadvertently created a homosexual-rights giant by slamming its door in the face of a young astronomer.

2

"A Burning Sense of Injustice"

Shortly before the dawn of the Space Age, astronomer Franklin E. Kameny accidentally launched his undeniably brilliant career—in a San Francisco men's room.

Dr. Kameny was in California in August 1956—just two months after receiving his Ph.D. from Harvard University—to deliver a paper at the annual conference of the American Astronomical Society. On August 29, the young scientist took a bus from Berkeley into San Francisco, got off the bus and walked into the depot rest room to relieve himself. The stranger standing at the next urinal made an unsolicited advance, attempting to grope Kameny's penis. "Where I made the mistake is that I responded," Kameny said later. Kameny had responded in kind, by touching the stranger. Two plainclothes officers with the San Francisco police force's "Sex Detail" burst out of a closet where they'd been peeping through ventilation grillwork. Mortified, Kameny was arrested along with the stranger.

Hoping to put the incident behind him quickly, Kameny, then 31, pled guilty the next morning. He was fined $50 and placed on six months' probation. Under California law, it was a simple and routine matter to get such convictions erased. Kameny completed probation, then changed his plea to "not guilty" in order to get his conviction set aside. The original charge was dismissed in March 1957.

Unaware of the federal government's intense efforts to rid itself of homosexuals, Kameny, then a university professor, soon applied for a Civil Service job with the Army Map Service (now known as the Defense Mapping Agency). The job application asked whether he had an arrest record. He answered yes: "August 1956; Disorderly conduct; San Francisco; not guilty; charge dismissed." "Disorderly conduct" was one of the vague catchall phrases commonly used in charging homosexuals with taboo physical contact.

In July 1957, Kameny was hired as a GS-9 astronomer, a mid-level government rank then paying $5,440 a year. A mere three months later, on October 4, astronomers' job prospects quite literally skyrocketed as the Soviet Union shot the world's first satellite, Sputnik 1, into orbit. The Space Age brought with it the terrifying prospect of intercontinental nuclear missiles and intensified U.S. fears about real and imagined threats to national security. Kameny soon found himself treated as just such as threat. He had been a federal worker for only four months when government investigators delivered shattering news: "Information has come to the attention of the U.S. Civil Service Commission that you are a homosexual. What comment, if any, do you care to make?" Though providing no clues about the source or content of their "information," Kameny's interrogators pressed him for details about his sex life. Kameny refused to answer. His personal life, he insisted, was not the government's business and had no bearing on his job performance.

Within days, the commander of the Army Map Service notified Kameny that he was being dismissed for allegedly falsifying the nature of his San Francisco arrest. Kameny's court documents had obscurely listed the charge only as "215 MPC" without any explanation of what that meant. And despite his awesome memory, Kameny didn't recall ever having heard the exact charge. Yet the Map Service accused him of lying about the fact that he'd actually been arrested for "lewd and indecent acts," another catchall phrase used in booking homosexuals.

Declaration of War

With a tenacity that would come to characterize the rest of his life, Kameny, who'd previously been "very, very, very shy and retiring," badgered his higher-ups, demanding to know why he was being targeted. In the eyes of the government, he learned, his real crime was homosexuality. On December 20, 1957, he was fired. Then on January 15, 1958 (two days after the Supreme Court handed down its decision in favor of ONE magazine), the Civil Service Commission blackballed Kameny from holding or seeking federal employment for three years. The grounds: "immoral conduct."

"I took that as a declaration of war by my government upon me," Kameny recalls. "And I don't grant my government the right to declare war on me!"

Instantly radicalized, Kameny knew he had to fight back. He couldn't let himself walk—or run—away as so many others had. "For the rest of my life I wouldn't have been able to live with myself. I would be dead of stomach ulcers by now," Kameny passionately explains. "There's simply a burning sense of injustice. You've got to fight."

The United States jumped into the space race with its first successful satellite launch two weeks after Kameny's dismissal. Scrambling feverishly to catch up to the Soviet Union, President Eisenhower and Congress created the National Aeronautics and Space Administration that same year. The space agency was a magnet for young, ambitious scientists, including the astronomers who'd been Kameny's immediate supervisors. Kameny, too, felt powerfully pulled to get in on the launching pad of the U.S. space program. But an astronomer barred on moral grounds from government work wasn't just kept out of NASA. Private government contractors and universities would not want him either.

Desperate to clear his name and regain his eligibility for federal employment, Kameny carried his fight to all three branches of government. His formal appeal to the chairman of the Civil Service Commission proved fruitless. He failed to get the Eisenhower White House interested in helping him. Likewise, the chairmen of the congressional committees overseeing federal employment practices gave him what he recalls as "brusque brush-offs." By mid–1959, Kameny was still out of work, struggling to survive on 20 cents' worth of food a day. "Every once in a while I got an extra nickel and ended up with a pat of margarine on my potatoes and frankfurters," he recalls.

Finally, Kameny took his fight to court in June 1959. A federal judge summarily dismissed his complaint on December 28, 1959. A three-judge panel of the U.S. Court of Appeals for the District of Columbia seconded that decision, saying it was "satisfied" that valid regulations had been properly followed when the Army Map Service fired Kameny. Since the firing had proceeded by the book, the appeals court added, there was no need to examine whether the Civil Service blackball was inappropriate.

Total defeat at the hands of the appeals court on June 23, 1960, meant Kameny's war was lost as far as his attorney, Byron N. Scott, was concerned. Kameny was in no mood to surrender, though. So Scott gave him a copy of the Supreme Court's rules and turned the case over to him. Kameny read the U.S. Constitution and prepared to petition the Supreme Court. He'd already learned useful legal zingers like "arbitrary and capricious" from Scott. And whenever Kameny had a question about how to structure a *cert* petition, he called the court's administrative office for help. But a professionally worded petition wasn't enough. Kameny wanted one that was intellectually sound.

Was the Civil Service wrong in branding him—and by extension homosexuality—immoral? Kameny had accepted his homosexuality on his 29th birthday after getting involved with a more experienced younger man while working at a Tucson observatory. Six years had passed since then, but he'd never really pondered whether homosexuality was immoral. Before writing his Supreme Court petition, he forced himself to wrestle with the question of morality. In the process of answering it to his own satisfaction, he formulated an equal-rights position that would provide much of the intellectual underpinnings for what would come to be known as the gay-rights movement.

When Frank Kameny sat down to write his *cert* petition, he was no activist. Years before, he'd once dropped into *ONE*'s seedy headquarters while traveling on business, but he belonged to no homophile groups, as they were then called. A man with a 148 I.Q., he was quite used to thinking for himself. Born in 1925 to a Jewish family in Queens, Kameny was the son of "good, decent people." His father was an electrical engineer for an auto parts company. His mother was a legal secretary turned homemaker. By the time he graduated from high school at 16, Kameny was an atheist. He had total faith only in the "products of my own intellectual processes."

"Therefore, I have always taken the position that if society and I differ on something, I will give them a second chance to show that they're right and I am wrong. And if they don't, then I am right and they are wrong. And that is that, as long as they don't get in my way. If they get in my way, then there is going to be a fight—and I tend not to lose my wars," Kameny said, sitting at his battered desk in his home in northwest Washington, D.C., just a mile from his old office at the Army Map Service.

Coming from someone else, such self-satisfied confidence might sound arrogant. But Kameny's David-and-Goliath achievements over the last four decades render his assessment of his success a simple statement of fact: "Over the years, on those battles I have chosen to fight, I have chosen not to adjust myself to society. With considerable success I have chosen to adjust society to me. And society is considerably better off for the adjustment."

"The Passion of the Aggrieved"

Faced with the Civil Service's conclusion that homosexual behavior made him "immoral," Kameny weighed that assessment, found it wrong and demanded that the federal government be the one to change. Armed with a passionate belief that his rights as a U.S. citizen were being violated, Kameny filed an indignant 60-page petition with the Supreme Court on January 21, 1961.

"Our government exists to protect and assist *all* of its citizens, not, as in the case of homosexuals, to harm, to victimize, and to destroy them," Kameny argued in *Franklin Edward Kameny v. Wilber M. Brucker, secretary of the Army, et al.* Though "suspected of being a homosexual," as his petition phrased it, Kameny staked his claim to the right "to compete for government employment on the same basis as other citizens of the United States."

Aware that the justices accept very few petitions, Kameny tried to educate them about the tremendous national significance of his employment case. "This case, involving matters never before examined by the courts, is one of extreme importance to a very large number of American citizens," he began. Then, extrapolating from Kinsey's findings about the incidence of homosexual behavior, Kameny offered his own estimate that 10 percent of the U.S. adult population was homosexual.

Kinsey had described a continuum of human sexual behavior ranging from exclusively heterosexual throughout life to exclusively homosexual throughout life. Concluding that sexuality cannot be tidily divided into two types, Kinsey intentionally steered clear of labeling people "heterosexual" or "homosexual." Kameny, however, needed an estimate of the number of American homosexuals to underscore the significance of his case. Kameny's 10 percent figure came from the proportion of adults that Kinsey had found were "more or less exclusively homosexual."

Kameny's view that 10 percent of Americans can be labeled homosexual—widely attributed to Kinsey—gradually became accepted almost as an article of faith among gay Americans. Kameny estimated that the U.S. homosexual population was "comparable in size" to both the nation's "Negro minority" and "Catholic minority" as well as to the worldwide Jewish population.

The homosexual minority, Kameny forcefully argued, "is a group which, in this country, has borne and is bearing the brunt of a persecution and discrimination of a harshness and ferocity at least as severe as that directed against these other minorities, but which persecution instead of being mitigated and ameliorated by the government's attitudes and practices, has instead been intensified by them; a persecution and discrimination not one whit more warranted or justified than those against Negroes, Jews, Catholics or other minority groups."

Kameny contended that it was "abundantly clear" that the executive branch was not going to deal realistically with homosexuals "unless it is forced to do so." Therefore, he wrote, "it is necessary that . . . the court be instructed in regard to certain factual, sociological and other realities which the government ignores, and of which the court, certainly in a formal sense, through an almost total lack of previous cases, arguments, decisions, and precedents, is uninformed." The long sentences of Kameny's petition echoed his speaking style, with clause piled upon clause in an orderly, if complicated, way.

The ousted astronomer wanted the Supreme Court to understand not just how many homosexuals were being targeted—so many the government "would dissolve into chaos" if it succeeded in tossing them all out—but also that homosexuals had only their homosexuality and their oppression in common. "Despite this common popular stereotype of a homosexual which would have him discernible at once, by appearance, mannerisms and other characteristics, these people run the gamut of physical type, of intellectual ability and inclination, and of emotional make-up, with no distinguishing marks or characteristics of any sort whatsoever except their homosexuality itself, . . . " declared Kameny, whose rumpled appearance fits the stereotype of a scientist but not that of a homosexual man.

"The average homosexual is as well-adjusted in personality as the average heterosexual," Kameny further instructed the court. Kameny found a "thread of madness" in what he saw as the government's irrational policies on homosexuality.

He stopped just short of openly declaring his homosexuality to the court. He feared that an outright declaration of homosexuality would prevent him from getting a government security clearance even if the Supreme Court ruled his firing unfair, he recalls.

Kameny was not the least bit reticent, however, in his general defense of homosexuals. Homosexuality, he declared, is not immoral, is not sick and is not in need of fixing in any way. Indeed, he argued, what is immoral is the government's persecution of homosexuals.

In what ranks as the first gay-pride statement to reach the court (even though the term "gay pride" had not yet been coined), Kameny told the justices: "Petitioner asserts, flatly, unequivocally, and absolutely uncompromisingly, that homosexuality, whether by mere inclination or by overt act, is not only not immoral, but that for those choosing voluntarily to engage in homosexual acts, such acts are moral in a real and positive sense, and are good, right and desirable, socially and personally."

Kameny nevertheless asked the court to believe that he had "immediately repelled" the sexual advance of the stranger who had groped him in San Francisco.

He argued that the Constitution did not grant the government the right to decide what is immoral (as opposed to illegal). What's more, he argued that the regulation allowing federal workers to be fired for "immoral conduct" was "so broad and vague as to be meaningless." He pointed out that some people consider dancing, liquor and even drinking coffee or tea immoral.

"Will they, next year, term as immoral left-handedness, red-headedness, a liking for horsemeat steaks, or membership in either political party or none at all?" asked Kameny. He noted that his taste for horsemeat did not disqualify him for federal employment, despite the "repugnance and revulsion" his fancy inspired in many others. "Yet on the grounds that [petitioner] is a homosexual—a taste shared by a far higher number of citizens than one for horsemeat . . . the [Civil Service] Commission considers him disqualified to work as an astronomer."

Kameny also claimed that his Fifth Amendment rights were trampled by discrimination "so unjustifiable as to be violative of due process," phrasing he'd picking up from a Supreme Court ruling. ("Due process" basically means government must follow proper legal procedures.)

The unemployed scientist denounced the government's anti-homosexual policies as "nothing more than a reflection of ancient primitive, archaic, obsolete taboos and prejudices, [and] . . . an incongruous, anachronistic relic of the Stone Age carried over into the Space Age—and a harmful relic!" He was especially outraged that the very government that was "admirably" attempting to reduce racial and religious prejudice was inflaming anti-homosexual sentiments.

In his petition's final pages, the castoff astronomer gave full vent to what historian John D'Emilio calls "the passion of the aggrieved." That passion was then propelling the movement for racial equality but was conspicuously absent from public discussion of homosexuality. Nearly a decade before the outraged howl of gay liberation began reaching the nation as a whole, Frank Kameny told the Supreme Court, "The government's regulations [against homosexual employees] . . . are a stench in the nostrils of decent people, an offense against morality, an abandonment of reason, an affront to human dignity, an improper restraint upon proper freedom and liberty, a disgrace to any civilized society, and a violation of all that this nation stands for."

He pleaded with the court to take his case so that he could "fight for . . . his chance to contribute to society to the fullest extent of his ability, and [for] his good name, against infamous, tyrannical, immoral and odious actions of his government. . . ."

Kameny filed his petition a few days after the inauguration of President John F. Kennedy. Much of the nation saw the start of the Kennedy administration as heralding a more sophisticated era. Yet the progressiveness of the young president's team didn't extend to overturning government policies making homosexuals pariahs.

When Kennedy's solicitor general, Archibald Cox, responded to Kameny's petition, he urged the justices to turn the case away unheard. Cox didn't delve into whether the government's anti-homosexual policies were moral, rational or constitutional. Instead, he echoed lower courts in insisting that government dismissal procedures had been properly followed. How a federal worker was dismissed, not why, should be the judiciary's only concern, Cox said. Then in a gratuitous slap at a non-lawyer's legal draftsmanship, Cox charged that Kameny's long-winded petition should be denied for violating the court's "requirement of brevity."

Kameny's history-making plea for equal treatment of homosexuals was both short and passionless by the time it reached most justices. In a half-page memo to Justice John Marshall Harlan in March 1961, clerk Philip Heymann wrote, "[Petitioner] would have us strike down the whole idea that homosexuals can be discriminated against, but I doubt if that presents a substantial issue." More than 35 years later, Heymann, by then a Harvard law professor, commented that "it probably didn't present a substantial issue back then. I hope it does now."

Like Heymann, Douglas clerk Bernard Jacob recommended that Kameny's petition be denied. Jacob thought there was "sufficient evidence to show [Kameny] in fact did intend to deceive" in misstating the criminal charge he'd faced.

Kameny found a somewhat more sympathetic audience in Chief Justice Warren's clerk Markham Ball, who was appalled that Kameny had been expected "to answer the incredible question, 'What and when was the last [sexual] activity in which you participated?'" Ball thought Kameny's "candor" about his arrest indicated he had not meant to deceive.

However, Ball added, "It may be argued . . . that homosexuality is a reasonable ground for disqualification from government service. It seems, at least, to be widely believed that homosexuals are likely subjects of blackmail and likely to cause dissension and unpleasantness at work. I doubt the court would be willing to find this belief unwarranted. . . . I doubt the Fifth Amendment would permit the refusal to hire Negroes on the basis of color. The question must be faced whether there is a reasonable basis for a refusal to hire homosexuals. I recommend denial only because I do not think the court is ready to declare the prevailing view unreasonable."

Ball was right; the court wasn't ready. Chief Justice Warren and Justices Black, Frankfurter, Douglas, Clark, Harlan, Brennan, Whittaker and Stewart voted unanimously to deny Kameny's petition. Douglas's files, often the only window into the court's private conferences, contain no clues about the justices' thinking on *Kameny v. Brucker*. The court's reasoning remains a mystery. The outcome of the justices' secret vote on Friday, March 17, 1961, was tersely announced the next Monday as *"Certiorari* denied." With thousands of cases turned away every year, *The New York Times* considered Kameny's case too insignificant to mention.

More than 35 years later, as he gazes out from beneath bushy eyebrows, Frank Kameny gets a far-away look when he pauses to reflect on how his life might have turned out differently. He likes to imagine that if the Supreme Court had helped him get rehired by the government, he would have followed his former bosses to NASA—perhaps becoming an astronaut and certainly retiring with a comfortable pension. Who knows, maybe a 1961 Supreme Court ruling in favor of a "suspected homosexual" really could have cleared the way for an openly gay astronaut.

What's not in doubt is that whatever slim chance remained of Kameny's having a stellar career in astronomy vanished like a shooting star the instant the court turned his case away. Two weeks later, the Soviets rocketed the first human being into space. America again was struggling to catch up, just as it did after the launch of Sputnik 1. This time, though, it was clear that the U.S. space program would forever have to chart its course without Frank Kameny.

The Undefeated

The greatest unintentional favor the Supreme Court has ever done gay Americans was infuriating Kameny by turning his case away unheard. The court's refusal to restore a 35-year-old astronomer to an obscure government post arguably did more to advance homosexual rights than any ruling it has ever handed down in favor of homosexual litigants.

Losing his battle to regain his job made Kameny all the more determined to win his war for equal treatment. The court's denial of *cert* kept alive the full fury of a man who believed that his constitutional rights had been blatantly and idiotically denied. Being turned away from the nation's top court without so much as a hearing transformed the once shy Kameny into an astoundingly effective political dynamo.

Just months after being rebuffed by the justices, Kameny became the driving force behind a more militant brand of homosexual activism—unapologetic, unwilling to accept anything less than full equality, determined to persuade the nation that homosexuals are the only true experts on homosexuality.

Kameny deserves enormous credit for an awesome portion of the social and political strides made by gay Americans since 1961. He certainly ranks among the most accomplished civil rights leaders in U.S. history. When the gay-rights struggle is finally won, public schools may bear his name and postage stamps may show him standing in front of the Supreme Court's locked doors.

As a mortar-shell loader in World War II, 18-year-old U.S. Army private Frank Kameny had learned the value of battlefield tenacity. "I dug my way across Germany, slit trench by slit trench," he recalls. It was a never-give-an-inch warfare style that served him well nearly 20 years later when he found himself heroically warring with his own government. Propelled by righteous indignation at having been treated as a second-class citizen, Kameny helped found the Washington, D.C., chapter of the Mattachine Society just eight months after being turned away by the nine jurists he now derides as "the supreme injustices." As the chapter's first president, he forcefully shaped it into a dynamic civil rights organization.

"The gay movement had started in '51. It was . . . very defensive, apologetic and unassertive and unaggressive. Which is why I changed things. Because that didn't suit my personality at all," Kameny recalls.

He dug in for his protracted war against the government, certain in his own mind that society as a whole would not change its attitudes toward homosexuals until the federal government stopped discriminating. Under Kameny's command, the Washington Mattachine Society politely carried out the first organized attacks on the federal government's attempts to rid the Civil Service and the military of homosexuals and to deny all homosexuals security clearances. Those attacks first took the form of letter-writing campaigns, then homosexual-rights picket lines outside the White House and Philadelphia's Independence Hall. At Kameny's insistence, picketers wore conservative business attire, including skirts and heels for the lesbians.

Meanwhile, in November 1961, the same month the Washington Mattachine group formed, Kameny also help found the Washington chapter of the American Civil Liberties Union. After he persuaded that ACLU chapter to champion homosexual rights, the chapter convinced the national ACLU to do a 180-degree turn and recognize homosexuals as an oppressed minority group. In 1964, the national ACLU renounced its 1957 stand that had called constitutional both sodomy laws and government prohibitions against hiring homosexuals. By the end of the 1960s, ACLU attorneys were helping to lead the fight for homosexuals' civil liberties. The ACLU was instrumental, for example, in forcing the Post Office to stop routinely targeting homosexuals.

Continuing to give himself a do-it-yourself education in the law, Kameny evolved into the leading authority on government regulations involving homosexual employees. He began eking out a living by advising fellow homosexuals, eventually handling hundreds of gay Civil Service, military and security clearance cases.

Government officials rarely pointed to the possibility of blackmail in justifying efforts to target homosexual employees, Kameny quickly discovered. Instead, they relied on psychiatry's assessment that homosexuals were sick. "In our culture," Kameny observes, "to be considered mentally ill destroys you. And, therefore, that had to be looked at. And, again, I had no idea what I was going to come out with. I looked at whatever [research] there was, as a scientist by training and background. And what I found was absolutely appalling. Slovenly, slipshod, sleazy reasoning and scientific work, moralistic and theological value judgments cloaked and camouflaged in the language of science but with none of the substance of science."

Kameny had stumbled upon a promising new battlefront. According to Ronald Bayer's 1981 book, *Homosexuality and American Psychiatry*, "no one was of greater importance" than Kameny in relentlessly pressuring the American Psychiatric Association to change its inaccurate and powerfully stigmatizing assessment of homosexuals. "They surrendered about noon time on December 15, 1973," Kameny recalls. That's when the association's trustees voted that homosexuality was not, in fact, an illness. "In one fell swoop, 15 million gay people were cured!"

Eventually, the American Psychiatric Association, joined by other national mental health associations, enlisted in Kameny's war against the government. Those professional groups now routinely urge the Supreme Court to side with gay Americans fighting discrimination.

Like a five-star general rallying his troops, Kameny demanded that homosexuals stop thinking of themselves as damaged goods and, instead, get angry and fight for nothing less than full equality. His message helped radicalize the entire tenor of the tiny homophile movement in a way that's generally overlooked when the Stonewall rebellion of 1969 is marked as the start of the gay rights movement. Because of Kameny's encouragement, a Minnesota couple in 1971 filed the only same-sex marriage suit that has ever reached the high court. And when Virginia's sodomy law was challenged in federal court in 1974, Kameny was the sole "expert witness" on homosexuality.

For more than 35 years, Kameny has kept up the fight. Surrounded by towering piles of books and papers in the crowded home office that has long served as his command headquarters, Kameny readily ticks off his astounding victories in the war that became his life's work. In the sweetest success of all, the Civil Service Commission "surrendered to me on July 3, 1975." Eighteen years after barring Kameny from federal employment, "they called me up to say they were changing their policies to suit me," he proudly recalls. Homosexuality would no longer be grounds for dismissal. Then, in 1995, President Bill Clinton issued an executive order saying that a security clearance could not be denied simply because someone was homosexual. In 1998, Clinton issued another presidential order protecting the federal civil workforce from discrimination based on sexual orientation. Five years earlier, Kameny had won a 30-year struggle to get Congress to allow Washington, D.C., to repeal its sodomy law.

Both Kameny and his house are battle-scarred. During a January 1998 interview at his home, Kameny, then 72, was wearing clothes so old they were literally coming apart at the seams. The right sleeve of his faded orange shirt had come open nearly to his armpit. The ancient orange drapes hanging near his computer terminal dated from 1967, when his mother made them. The no-longer-hip purple carpet likewise dated from 1967.

Kameny's surroundings betray not absent-minded neglect but financial hardship. The gay-rights awards covering two walls had not helped pay the mortgage. Financially, Kameny has never progressed far from the era when an extra nickel meant more to eat. But as he gleefully recounts his wartime tactics, ambushes and territorial gains, he leaves no doubt that he considers himself very successful. Five prestigious libraries are vying for his papers.

"I can look back and say with a considerable amount of confidence that I feel that the world in general and a great many people individually are better off for my having been around. And this is a very good feeling to have," Kameny says. "If somehow it were possible in some sort of great, cosmic, absolutely just and fair way to do a measuring and a balancing, I would come out being owed more than owing. I feel very comfortable about that."

Kameny's petition is arguably the most important homosexual plea that the Supreme Court ever turned away—because that action gave the gay-rights movement its most successful field marshal. In many ways, though, Kameny's case was far from unique. It contained two elements running through many homosexual cases in the 1960s and '70s: First, an American citizen had lost a government job because of being homosexual. (The Constitution protects against government-sponsored discrimination but not private discrimination. Thus, in the absence of laws against anti-homosexual job discrimination, homosexuals fired by private employers have no grounds on which to sue.) Second, homosexual behavior had been punished as criminal.

In 1957, Kameny was a twin victim of the government war on homosexuals. He was caught by one of the vice squads that had stepped up the surveillance of homosexual cruising spots. And, probably with the aid of the FBI, he was caught by the Civil Service Commission, which had been ordered by Eisenhower and Congress to rid the government of "perverts." The ruination of Frank Kameny's astronomy career four decades ago hasn't destroyed his love of the night sky. In 1997, he rose every morning before dawn to observe the wondrous Comet Hale-Bopp as it passed by. Franklin Kameny doesn't live with regrets, though. The Supreme Court's refusal to grant him a hearing redirected his life to what he's come to see as a far higher calling than astronomy.

3

BEEFCAKE ON THE MENU

HERMAN LYNN WOMACK, who traded in a career as a George Washington University philosophy professor to become a peddler of male erotica, was a massive 290-pound Caucasian albino whose appearance was far more striking than any of the lean young men who filled the beefcake photo spreads of his magazines.

A homosexual known as "Lynn" to his friends, Dr. Womack stumbled into the publishing business and out of academia after investing in a holding company. The company went sour, leaving Womack in control of a Washington, D.C., printing plant in 1952. He soon started testing a straitlaced society's limits.

Womack's run-ins with authorities over freedom of expression dated from his youth, when he'd almost been expelled from his Bible Belt high school for taking evolutionary ideas—a copy of Darwin's *The Origin of Species*—to class. But Womack's troubles didn't end with his boyhood in Hazelhurst, Mississippi, where he'd been teased about his looks. After plunging into male erotica, he first tangled with postal authorities in 1960 when he mailed unsolicited ads for nude photos.

Four boys—ages 13, 15, 18 and 19—testified before a federal jury in Washington that they had received Womack's unsolicited ads, which included photos of men and women wearing only a genital drape. A postal inspector testified that Womack admitted the photos were aimed at homosexuals. The prosecution introduced a letter in which Womack told a photographer that "physique fans want their truck driver types cleaned up, showered and ready for bed."

On March 21, 1960, Womack was convicted of knowingly mailing obscene material and of advertising where obscene material could be obtained. When his appeal—*Womack v. U.S.*—eventually reached the Supreme Court, the justices voted 8-to-1 to turn it down.

Taking the March 1960 conviction of the 37-year-old Womack as permission to crack down on his enterprises, the Post Office seized copies of three beefcake publications four days later. Postal censors held up 255 copies of the April 1960 issue of *MANual,* 75 copies of the May issue of *Trim* and 75 copies of *Grecian Guild Pictorial* that had been mailed in Alexandria, Virginia.

Lightly camouflaged with a few bodybuilding tips, the 50-cent magazines were filled with photos of gorgeous, muscular young men in come-hither poses. Most of the "bodybuilders" wore so-called posing straps, essentially pouches that gave viewers a clear outline of bulging crotches, although some were shot naked from behind as they coquettishly showed off their perfectly sculpted buns. "California athlete ROBERT KIMBALL, 18 years old, 5' 10" and weighing 180 pounds, shows in these photos by BRUCE what his program of spear fishing, mountain climbing and surfing has done for his physique," gushed one typical caption of a voluptuous guy shown wielding a long bamboo pole.

Postal authorities, in an action reminiscent of the 1954 seizure of *ONE,* promptly declared the magazines unmailable because, allegedly, they contained obscene material and told where to obtain more. Womack's attorney, Stanley Dietz, responded by demanding an administrative hearing on behalf of Womack's magazine companies, Manual Enterprises Inc., Trim Enterprises Inc. and Grecian Guild.

The result was a strange and explicit hearing in which Post Office attorneys set out to persuade Post Office Judicial Officer Raymond J. Kelly that although Womack's magazines might look fairly tame to the untrained, heterosexual eye, they ought not be tolerated as just another flavor of cheesecake. For three days in late April 1960, Officer Kelly listened to testimony inside the Post Office Department's towering Washington, D.C., headquarters.

Post Office attorneys asked questions like, "What other type of sexual activity will the male homosexual resort to other than the annual [sic] intercourse?" The government relied heavily on the views of two psychiatrists and a psychologist in contending that Womack's magazines were dangerously obscene. Government attorneys argued for a separate, tougher obscenity standard for material intended for homosexuals, claiming that such readers were more vulnerable to being enticed into criminal behavior.

The government's key witness was Dr. Frank S. Caprio, a psychiatrist who termed himself an expert on homosexual arousal. Going photo by photo, he offered reasons they would not interest "a normal well-adjusted man" but would excite homosexual men. Caprio homed in on what *MANual* labeled a "dramatic shot of TED BORT"—a well-built young man with a '60s crewcut reclining in the shadows against a fence railing and wearing only a bulging G-string and cowboy boots. "Many male homosexuals have reported to psychiatrists that the picture of a nude male wearing shoes gives them added excitement," Caprio testified.

The recurrence of swords among the studio props in the Greek-themed *Grecian Guild Pictorial* gave Caprio a chance to expound on the hazards of allowing such magazines: "Many homosexuals are very weak. They suffer from a terrific sense of inferiority, sexual inferiority. In fact, this is one of the causes of homosexuality. They are afraid that they cannot satisfy a woman. . . . [C]ompensating for their inferiority they have to have fantasies with men of power, men with a whip, men with a sword, gladiators. . . . [T]hey don't have a Chinaman's chance of becoming cured as long as they are constantly stimulated by this type of picture."

Warning that the photos could turn boys into homosexuals, Caprio said, "out of curiosity they look through magazines of this kind and before they know it start masturbating. . . . You can't masturbate thinking of a man's penis . . . and hope to make a normal sexual adjustment."

Defending Womack's magazines, Dietz got Caprio to say that countless things, including photos in nudist magazines, *ONE* and *Time*, could conceivably arouse homosexual men. Then Dietz summoned his own mental health team.

Child psychiatrist Dr. Michael Miller said photographs don't have the power to create homosexuals. "What creates the homosexual," according to Miller, "is an abnormal relationship of the child to the parent . . . [an] emotional imbalance which has nothing to do with pictures."

Dietz psychologist Dr. S. Gordon Link wryly remarked that a photo of women's shoes in a popular women's magazine "might have a very bad effect on some segments of the population. . . . I should not for a moment think of suggesting that *McCall's* be investigated because they have catered, unknowingly I am sure, to the foot fetishists."

Judicial Officer Kelly ruled April 28, 1960, that the "average reader" of *MANual, Trim* and *Grecian Guild Pictorial* was a male homosexual, that the magazines appealed to their average reader's "prurient interest" and that boys attracted to the publications were in danger of being lured "into the abnormal paths of the homosexual." He therefore found the magazines obscene and unmailable.

The magazines lost again on August 17, 1960, when U.S. District Judge George L. Hart Jr. summarily ruled—that is, without having a full-scale hearing—that the Post Office's decision to seize Womack's magazines was "supported by substantial evidence."

A three-judge panel of the U.S. Court of Appeals for the District of Columbia then ruled against the magazines on March 23, 1961. In order to hold them obscene, two judges—the third endorsed the ruling's result—found it necessary to adjust the *Roth* obscenity standard. Under *Roth,* obscenity depended on "whether to the average person, applying contemporary community standards the dominant theme of the material taken as a whole appeals to prurient interest." However, the appeals court said, "The proper test in this case, we think, is the reaction of the average member of the class for which the magazines were intended, homosexuals." Evidence showed, the court added, that their prurient interest would be aroused.

Undeterred by Womack's earlier petition having been turned away, attorney Dietz asked the justices to take *Manual Enterprise Inc. et al. v. J. Edward Day, postmaster general of the United States.* Womack has been posthumously hailed by Cornell University historian Jackie Hatton as "an unsung anti-hero of the gay liberation movement," but in 1961 he certainly didn't have a gay-rights tune sung on his behalf when Dietz petitioned the high court. Characterizing *MANual, Trim* and *Grecian Guild Pictorial* as "physique magazines," Dietz contended that there was no way for anyone to determine the nature of their readership since they were sold at newsstands and bookstores rather than by subscription. "If these magazines would not appeal to the prurient interest of an average, normal, adult they are not obscene and are constitutionally protected. . . . A salacious reader who might purchase one of petitioners' magazines from a bookstore is more likely to feel cheated than excited," Dietz argued.

Then, as if to cover himself just in case the justices recognized the magazines' obvious target audience, Dietz closed by saying, "However, even if these magazines were intended for homosexuals, which petitioners do not admit, they would still be constitutionally protected as such." As evidence, he pointed to the court's groundbreaking decision in favor of *ONE*, "which states on its cover that it is beamed at homosexuals" and "surely . . . would appeal to the prurient interests of its average viewer." Dietz also argued that for the Post Office to decide on its own—without a court order—to impound the magazines amounted to unconstitutional prior restraint.

Urging the justices to reject the petition, the government's rebuttal noted that even "a cursory glance" reveals the seized magazines have "nothing to do with bodybuilding." Hoping to distinguish Womack's magazines from the victorious *ONE*, the government's revisionist attorneys said, "The magazine *ONE* dealt with the general problems of the homosexual and only contained two isolated items which could conceivably have been regarded as lewd."

The *Manual* case put the Supreme Court squarely in the middle of the question swirling through the nation's legal community: Who should control—the emphasis was on control—homosexuals? Should it be cops and courts or psychiatrists? For the first time the court was confronted with the testimony of mental health professionals presenting themselves as the experts on homosexual desire.

A fresh crop of Supreme Court clerks tackled *Manual v. Day* in August 1961, while their bosses were still on the court's traditional three-month summer break. The fact that Womack was a convicted pornographer was virtually the only thing that the clerks learned about him in poring over the first round of documents filed in *Manual v. Day*. As a clerk to Justice William O. Douglas pointed out, Womack's conviction meant he "was in the same business as his [magazines'] advertisers" and, thus, seemed to undermine the claim that Womack did not know he was running ads for obscene material. "The magazines, tho purporting to be bodybuilding publications, were found to be nothing but pictures of nearly nude male models displayed in such manner as to stimulate the erotic fantasies of homo's [*sic*]," the Douglas clerk wrote in urging that Womack's petition be denied. Civil libertarian Douglas responded, "Grant."

A clerk advised Justice Tom Clark that there was no need to take the case because ads for obscenity rendered the magazines unmailable. Clark wrote "Deny" atop the memo.

Clerk Gordon Gooch, meanwhile, urged Warren to grant, saying, "Perhaps the most important issue presented is whether a special test of obscenity can be used in judging photography aimed at a group classified as abnormal." Warren tentatively agreed to grant for a different reason. "This is a case of prior restraint," he wrote.

But the argument for why *Manual v. Day* was worthy of Supreme Court consideration was perhaps best articulated by University of Virginia law school graduate John B. Rhinelander, a clerk to John Marshall Harlan:

> When publications are intended for a particularly susceptible group are they to be judged on whether they appeal to the prurient interests of that group or by the appeal to the average person applying contemporary community standards[?] . . . Unless the post office department is to be the censor of our morals and the judge of what matter should be mailed to deviates, this case raises questions that only this court can answer. Finally, if the test is to be the appeal to special groups, such as homosexuals, will the judiciary have to step aside and rely on the opinions of experts as to whether a particular object, image or fetish appeals to the prurient interests of deviates? . . . This is a difficult case and although perhaps unsavory I think the court should hear it.

Justice Harlan initially disagreed, writing, "I'm inclined to leave this one alone—especially in the absence of a conflict as to the scope of the 'class' relevant to judging obscenity." Yet Harlan's overriding instinct was to see the magazines for himself and not rely on the judgment of mental health professionals or postal censors. "Tentatively, deny, subject to an inspection of the material in question," he wrote. Under that note, Harlan added, "On further consideration, the 'intended reader' point seems important enough to take."

The justices privately voted 5 or 6 to 3 to grant Womack's petition—a decision announced October 9, 1961. Since the *ONE* decision, Justice Burton had retired and another Ohio Republican, Potter Stewart, had been appointed by Eisenhower to replace him. In voting to take the case, Warren was joined by Hugo Black, Douglas, Harlan, Brennan and perhaps Stewart—justices' notes differ on whether Stewart participated. (Black, Womack's lone supporter the previous term in *Womack v. U.S.*, often remarked that after what he'd seen growing up in rural Alabama, nothing shocked him.) Frankfurter, Clark and Whittaker voted to deny *cert*.

Aroused Angels and the Empire State Building

In his formal written argument on behalf of Womack's risqué magazines, Dietz expounded on his contention that the Post Office erred in labeling their readers "homosexual." The term describes "activities and psychic reactions, rather than persons," he contended, citing Kinsey's data on the prevalence of homosexual acts. Dietz's point, though sketchily made, was that if the only thing postal censors knew about the readers of male pin-up magazines was that they had bought those magazines, then censors could not say whether any or all of those readers also engaged in the homosexual behavior then classified as criminal.

"Is the word 'homosexual' synonymous with the term 'sexual psychopath'?" Dietz asked, foreshadowing a question that would occupy the court as it wrestled with the deportation of homosexual immigrants. "There is no basis for the assumption that all homosexuals are psycho-biologically predisposed to commit prohibited sexual acts with other males or that they thus necessarily are sex perverts," Dietz added.

Then, lapsing into calling Womack's readers "homosexuals," Dietz rose to their defense. ". . . Persons with homosexual inclinations are not [by their very nature] criminals or detrimental to civilization, nor are they necessarily afflicted by disease . . . nor is homosexuality as such intrinsically evil. Our Constitution does not state that only heterosexuals may receive and read the literature of their choice, . . . " he told the court. The Post Office's interpretation of obscenity laws is based on "blind prejudice, superstition, hatred and condemnation of non-conformity," Dietz charged. "The Post Office Department would suppress . . . Michelangelo, Leonardo da Vinci, all overt homosexuals," he added.

Despite the rampant inconsistencies in his brief, Dietz was pushing the court to begin thinking about whether homosexuality is just a matter of behavior or something more: Should homosexuality be treated as a vice that anyone could fall prey to? Or, are homosexuals a class of people with their own particular appetites and a constitutional right to express them?

In reply to Dietz, Solicitor General Cox argued that "homosexuals are more easily stimulated to overt sexual activities than are normal persons" and that porn is more likely to result in criminal activity when it is aimed at homosexuals because "the average person . . . in most instances has a lawful outlet for his sexual drive." The solicitor general equated controlling Womack's magazines with controlling homosexuals. ". . . It seems scarcely open to question that society has a legitimate interest . . . in preventing overt homosexual activities while refusing to condemn comparable activities when indulged in on a heterosexual basis," he said. Nevertheless, in an effort to keep ONE's victory from undermining his side, Cox added, "The vice of petitioners' magazines is not, of course, that they are directed to homosexuals. Their vice, we emphasize, is that they are designed as sexual stimulants." He warned against adopting an obscenity standard that shielded "those who gain their livelihood by pandering to the warped interests of perverts."

But neither the government's argument nor Dietz's made as much of an impression on clerks as the racy material seized from Womack's advertisers. Thirty-five years later, two clerks vividly recalled—without prompting—Christmas cards that could be purchased through one ad. A Clark clerk recalled being amused by one card: "You'd open it up and an erect penis would jump out at you." Another pictured little boy angels kneeling, penises erect, before an altar, former Warren clerk Gordon Gooch said, adding, "I hadn't seen that in my local Hallmark store."

Before the Supreme Court actually hears a case argued, most justices have their clerks prepare what the court calls a "bench memo"
summarizing both sides' arguments and making a recommendation. Because Gooch had happened to handle the *Manual v. Day cert* petition
for Warren, he wrote the bench memo on it as well.

Gooch, a rare University of Texas law school grad among the
Supreme Court's endless waves of Ivy League clerks, admired Chief
Justice Warren. But, "Politically and philosophically, we were the opposite ends of the poles. Those were the days of the 'Impeach Earl Warren' billboards. I used to say to him, 'If you'll just fire me, I can go back
to Texas and run unopposed for governor on both tickets!'" Gooch, a
gregarious Washington, D.C., attorney, recalls with a hearty laugh.
Gooch's 25-page memo on *Manual* urged Warren to reverse the lower
court's ruling against Womack's magazines. Saying that heterosexuals
and homosexuals "should be on parity," Gooch proposed "banning
pornography for [homosexuals] on the same terms as that of other people." Gooch probably was more knowledgeable about homosexuality
than most court insiders. "In college I was a roommate once to a guy
who was clearly a homosexual. I was purely heterosexual myself, but we
were friends and got along fine and all," he says.

A passage in Gooch's account of the government's argument against
Womack caught Warren's attention. Warren underscored and marked
the margin alongside these statements: "The publisher admitted that he
was beaming his material to homosexuals, he wrote a letter suggesting
this, and he introduced no evidence to rebut the gov'ts [*sic*] showing of
the effect on the average homosexual. No evidence that these were
'physique magazines' was offered.'" Warren later showed that he'd really
seized on the image of Womack "beaming" his wares to homosexuals.

In the Supreme Court's ornate courtroom, where carvings of lotus
and tobacco leaves decorate the high ceiling, oral arguments in *Manual
v. Day* began on February 26, 1962, and continued to the next day. Each
side had a full hour to make its case and field justices' questions. (Today each side routinely gets half an hour.) With *Manual*, the American
people—at least those in attendance—got their first chance to see
Supreme Court justices react to discussion of homosexuality and even
talk about the subject themselves.

The rudimentary audiotape system in place during the *Manual* arguments relied on each justice to turn on his own microphone. Since the justices tended to forget that requirement, most of their *Manual* remarks are indecipherably garbled. Yet audible comments provide clues about their thinking. Warren, for example, described the magazines as "beamed toward a certain class of deviates," while an unidentifiable justice called homosexuals "an unfortunate class of people."

Because Dietz represented the side that had successfully petitioned for the hearing, he went first. More rough-edged than most attorneys who argue before the Supreme Court, Dietz sounded as if he were struggling to rise to the grandeur of the occasion: "The first argument which I would set forth to this court I would divide into three parts." Dietz was repeatedly interrupted by Chief Justice Warren, whose microphone was off. A Warren question, missed by the tape, triggered the court's first open-session discussion of the nature of homosexuality. Dietz answered Warren, ". . . there is no community that has no homosexuals. Every community has them. Possibly they are not . . . discovered. See, because we keep these people suppressed. So maybe they haven't been ferreted out and brought to the light."

Dietz implored the justices to actually look at Womack's magazines: "In all these photographs, the genitalia is draped or covered. Now these photographs are no worse than what we so-called normal people call pin-up photographs. . . . You see photographs of such female beauties as Marilyn Monroe nude on calendars on walls all over the country." Signaling that he was heterosexual and presuming that the justices were, Dietz argued, "Their pin-up is no worse than our pin-up."

Oh, but appearances are deceiving, countered Justice Department attorney J. William Doolittle, assistant to the solicitor general. Pushing the justices to consider the magazines "hard-core porn," he warned that they were dealing with "a peculiarly insidious form of obscenity in that while it appears to the average man to be far less objectionable than usual forms of pornography, in fact, it has a far more serious effect upon its audience than ordinary pornography has on the average audience." Precisely because the magazines look harmless, the justices need to rely on psychiatric expertise, Doolittle insisted.

He told the justices that homosexuals are more easily stimulated than "normal adults," have less self-control, are less likely to have legal sexual outlets and, thus, are "those most in need of protection against pornography." Allowing homosexuals access to Womack's magazines would "make it more difficult to treat and to cure them," the government attorney added.

"Average people cannot be expected to appreciate the great effect this kind of material can have on human beings," Doolittle insisted. "But where do you stop?" asked Potter Stewart, the newest justice. "I suppose there are some people who might be adversely affected by a picture of the Empire State Building." Though Stewart served 22 years on the court before retiring in 1981, that remark represented one of the few times he is known to have played an active role in a homosexual case. (Stewart's dubiousness in *Manual* about relying on anything other than his own judgment foreshadowed his most quoted statement. In 1964, Stewart declared that he might not be able to define hard-core porn, "but I know it when I see it.")

Justice Felix Frankfurter assisted Doolittle by comparing using psychiatrists to interpret a photo's effect on a homosexual to getting the help of a translator in determining whether an article written in Sanskrit is obscene.

Yet the court needed no assistance in figuring out—despite government attorneys' protests to the contrary—that Womack's magazines were seized because of their intended audience, not their content. "I take it, Mr. Doolittle," if all the magazines had been mailed to women's colleges, "you wouldn't be here," one justice asserted. "I don't suppose that I would," Doolittle admitted.

"No Worse Than Striptease Calendars"

Less than a week later, on March 2, 1962, the justices gathered in their private conference room to vote on *Manual v. Day*. Conference votes and remarks are never publicly announced. However, we can now reconstruct the *Manual v. Day* conference from Douglas's notes.

By tradition, the chief justice summarizes each case, then stakes out his position. Associate justices then speak in order of seniority. The orderly explanations rarely spark a true debate. The outcome of many cases is set before the most junior justices get their turns.

Chief Justice Warren voted to affirm the appeals court finding that Womack's muscle magazines were unfit to be mailed. "Congress has the right to regulate the mails + keep them for decent purposes," he argued. ". . . They are beaming to homosexuals."

Gooch never heard Warren discuss homosexuality. "I didn't detect Warren having any different standard for obscenity whether it was heterosexual or homosexual. He was a very fair man. . . . He was a very moral man, and he wanted to protect people that he thought would be exploited," Gooch says. Warren may well have viewed Womack as preying upon the vulnerable.

Unlike his brethren, Warren might not have examined Womack's beefcake magazines. According to Warren biographer Bernard Schwartz, the chief justice was so offended by sexually explicit material that he couldn't bring himself to review obscenity exhibits until 1966. When his clerks urged him to be more broadminded about pornography, Warren responded, "You boys don't have any daughters yet." And he once told a colleague, "If anyone showed that book to my daughters, I'd have strangled him with my own hands."

After the chief justice kicked off discussion of *Manual* in conference, Hugo Black spoke next, since with 24 years of service he ranked as the most senior associate justice. Black, who had just celebrated his 76th birthday, was an Alabama Democrat who in 1937 had gone from being the Senate's most zealous booster of President Franklin D. Roosevelt's New Deal to being FDR's first Supreme Court appointee. Once on the court, Black's liberalism was expressed most passionately in his relentless advocacy of taking First Amendment guarantees literally. In public appearances he stressed that when the Constitution states that "Congress shall make no law . . . abridging the freedom of speech, or of the press," it means precisely that. "No law means no law," Black declared, emphasizing the point by pulling a 10-cent copy of the Constitution out of his suit pocket and tapping on it. Black's embrace of the First Amendment was no secret to his colleagues, who could easily predict how he'd vote on *Manual v. Day* regardless of the nature of the censored material or its target audience. Douglas's conference notes said simply that Black "reverses." Reversal would mean victory for Womack, since he'd lost in the lower courts.

Justice Frankfurter, who had equated psychiatric testimony about homoerotic material with foreign language translation, voted to affirm and said he agreed with the chief.

Justice Douglas then voted to reverse, making no other comment that he chose to record. Douglas believed the court had wandered into dangerous territory when it deputized itself to police sexual literature.

Justice Clark provided the third vote for reversal. Justice Harlan, who from the first had wanted to judge the seized magazines for himself, also wanted to reverse. "We cannot, without [a] broad view of obscenity, render [obscene] something on [its] face not obscene by supplying the missing ingredient with the testimony of a psychiatrist," he declared in conference.

Justice William J. Brennan Jr. seized on a different facet of the case, saying the Post Office's seizure constituted "prior restraint." Brennan, who had written the *Roth* obscenity standard, said, "The 'hard core' stuff is not in this case—it was seized [at advertisers' studios]." He cast the crucial fifth vote to reverse, giving Womack a majority.

Justice Charles L. Whittaker, who four years earlier had cast the decisive vote in favor of *ONE*, voted to affirm. (Four days later, Whittaker, depressed and exhausted from struggling in vain to master duties that most better-educated colleagues took in stride, was hospitalized for a nervous breakdown. He resigned before the end of the month.)

Voting last, Stewart supported reversal, saying, "this literature for homosexuals is no worse than striptease calendars are to others."

Douglas's 6-to-3 conference vote tally is confirmed by the records of Warren and Clark. Had the chief justice voted in the majority, he would have had the privilege of choosing the author of the court's majority opinion. With the chief in the minority, the power of assigning that opinion fell to Black, as the most senior associate in the majority. Black tapped his close friend Harlan. Though the two justices' judicial philosophies clashed, they respected one another's integrity. "Black often remarked that he would not worry about giving power to judges if they were all like Harlan," according to Black's biographer, Roger K. Newman.

In *ONE v. Olesen,* the court had sided with a homosexual magazine against the Post Office but had given no reason, except for citing *Roth.* Having voted in *Manual* to side again with what quite clearly—despite Dietz's protests—were homosexual magazines, the court chose to start explaining itself.

The job of speaking for the court for the first time on homosexuality went to Harlan, a 62-year-old Eisenhower appointee who was a "quint-essential patrician," a man so unfailingly polite that after his eyesight began to fail he once greeted a lamppost "Good morning!" John Marshall Harlan was the grandson of a Supreme Court justice who bore an identical name and who is best remembered for his eloquent dissent from the court's 1896 "separate but equal" *Plessy v. Ferguson* decision. The younger Harlan had had a prosperous Chicago upbringing followed by education at Princeton and Oxford and a high-powered legal career in New York City. On the Supreme Court, he swam against the tidal wave of liberal judicial activism during Chief Justice Warren's era. Harlan's mild manner led critics to dismiss him as a "colorless conservative," "a Frankfurter without the mustard." He believed the nation's top court should exercise restraint, usually deferring to the states and the other branches of the federal government. Yet Harlan's was not a stodgy or moralistic conservatism. And he had an excellent sense of humor.

By 1964, Harlan, the justice most insistent on seeing Womack's magazines for himself, was nearly blind with cataracts. Whenever the court was asked to rule on whether particular photos were obscene, Harlan found himself holding graphic pictures two inches from his face—a fact that continually amused him. When the allegedly obscene material was a film, the justices gathered in a darkened room to view it, giving Harlan a prime opportunity to needle prudish colleagues. With the truthful excuse that he couldn't see the action, Harlan would sit beside some justice he knew was disturbed to have to watch porn movies. Harlan would insist on hearing a blow-by-blow description and then exclaim, "Oh, extraordinary!" recalls Harvard law professor Robert Mnookin, who clerked for Harlan.

Mnookin is one of the few ex-clerks who confirms having discussed homosexuality with any justice. He clearly remembers Harlan saying he wouldn't mind having a homosexual clerk. (A Harlan clerk from the

1950s later lived a double life as a gay married man before his death in the 1980s.) Despite being viewed as a traditional conservative, Harlan was "less personally prejudiced with respect to homosexuals than some much more liberal judges I had known," says Mnookin. "What I remember is feeling that particularly for his age and that era—this was 1969—Justice Harlan was really quite open-minded. I attributed that to the fact that he'd been a Rhodes Scholar in England and my sense that there may have been some openly gay people at Oxford when he was there and that it didn't trouble him at all," Mnookin added.

Philip Heymann, who clerked for Harlan the year before Womack's magazines were under the justice's nose, says, "He struck me as an almost completely unbigoted person and quite sort of sexually relaxed. He was sort of patrician, and he was sort of starched. He just wasn't nervous about sexual matters. He wouldn't have been frightened by talk about homosexuality."

In his landmark *Manual v. Day* decision, Harlan refused to permit a separate, tougher obscenity standard for material beamed at homosexuals. He favored one obscenity standard and, though he didn't cast his decision in such terms, one standard of justice. Harlan's opinion assumed Womack's pecs-and-ass picture spreads stimulated "sexual deviates" and held no interest for "sexually normal individuals." Yet Harlan considered the question of who bought Womack's magazines irrelevant. The real question to Harlan was, "Are these magazines offensive on their face?" Harlan flatly rejected the notion that homosexuals are so freakish that courts cannot judge whether material targeted to them is obscene without having psychiatrists decode it. Having examined them closely, Harlan concluded that "the magazines in question, taken as a whole, cannot, under any permissible constitutional standard be deemed to be beyond the pale of contemporary notions of rudimentary decency."

Being sexually stimulating is not sufficient to render material obscene, Harlan wrote. It must also be "inherently sexually indecent." Stewart suggested that another Harlan phrase—"obnoxiously debasing portrayals of sex"—might be closer to the mark. Harlan ultimately settled on "patent offensiveness" as the obscene quality that Womack's magazines lacked.

Although ruling there was no legal justification for barring Womack's magazines from the mail, Harlan branded them "dismally unpleasant, uncouth, and tawdry." Harlan steadfastly tried to keep his feelings from coloring his judicial decisions, clerks say. Yet pity for homosexual readers and disgust at Womack comes through even as Harlan judged the magazines by the same yardstick as heterosexual publications. "Divorced from their 'prurient interest' appeal to the unfortunate persons whose patronage they were aimed at capturing, . . . these portrayals of the male nude cannot fairly be regarded as more objectionable than many portrayals of the female nude that society tolerates," his final opinion stated. The phrasing in Harlan's first longhand draft had been "divorced from their repulsive purpose."

As if his attitude weren't already clear, Harlan concluded, ". . . nothing in this opinion of course remotely implies approval of the type of magazines published by these petitioners, still less of the sordid motives which prompted their publication."

Harlan had attempted to write for what had begun as a six-member majority. Yet only Stewart joined Harlan's opinion.

Intentionally or not, Harlan, who had dissented from Brennan's *Roth* decision because he thought policing sexual morality generally should be left to the states, had stepped on Brennan's toes. Brennan was unhappy with what he took as "an effort to refine the *Roth* test," as Brennan told Harlan in a letter. Brennan wrote a separate *Manual* opinion, agreeing with reversal because in his view the Post Office had overstepped its authority. He made no mention of homosexuality. Douglas signed onto Brennan's opinion.

Black simply concurred with the reversal without joining the written explanation.

In a switch from his conference vote, Clark voted against the magazines. Warren then switched in the opposite direction, joining Brennan, perhaps because additional Gooch memos nudged him in that direction or because of his well-known dislike of five-vote majorities, which clerks say he thought undermined the court's authority by making it look indecisive. Though the court ended up with six justices agreeing the magazines were not obscene, "those in the majority like ancient Gaul are split into three parts," Clark chided in dissent.

Clark, a University of Texas graduate who had risen through the ranks at the Justice Department all the way to attorney general before being appointed to the high court by President Truman, thought students at lesser-known law schools ought to have a shot at clerking for the Supreme Court. Drake University law graduate James Knox, son of Iowa farmers, was a grateful beneficiary of Clark's outreach. After reading Harlan's first circulated draft in *Manual*, Knox encouraged Clark to switch his original vote. Clark agreed and wrote a very strong dissent, accusing the court's majority of requiring "the United States Post Office to be the world's largest disseminator of smut and Grand Informer of the names and places where obscene material may be obtained."

Clark's fierce rhetoric caused Harlan to privately gasp "Wow!" in a margin note.

Clark's dissent would have affirmed the lower court's decision against Womack's magazines solely on the grounds that they advertised obscene material. Clark said he was taking no position on whether the magazines—minus their advertising—were obscene. According to Knox, Clark approached cases by asking, "'Has the law been correctly applied?' Whether he agreed or disagreed with the law was not a primary concern."

Clark never discussed homosexuality while considering the case, Knox added. "He was generally a very tolerant human being," Knox remarked, adding that Clark gave no indication that his approach to *Manual* was influenced by the magazines' subject matter. Likewise, former U.S. attorney general Ramsey Clark examined his father's dissent and concluded, "I don't think the analysis he made would have been any different if homosexuality wasn't involved."

Overall, Clark's language in discussing the magazines was milder than Harlan's. "The magazines have no social, educational, or entertainment qualities," Clark wrote, "but are designed solely as sex stimulants for homosexuals. . . . The publishers freely admit that the magazines are published to appeal to the male homosexual group. . . .

"Turning to Womack . . . it is even clearer that we are not dealing here with a 'Jack and Jill' operation," Clark solemnly declared. Harlan's witty retort, penned in the margin of his copy of Clark's draft dissent, was, "Certainly not. If anything, it was a 'Jack and Jack' operation.'"

After an April stroke, the 79-year-old Frankfurter was too ill to cast a final vote in *Manual v. Day*. He went on to retire that year. Whittaker, of course, had left the court by the time it handed down its splintered 6-to-1 decision in Womack's favor on June 25, 1962.

A Second Green Light

The lead story in the next morning's *New York Times* was the court's decision banning official prayers in New York State public schools. Rulings strengthening the hands of government trust-busters also got front-page play. Elsewhere on the front, Soviet Premier Nikita Khrushchev pushed his demand that Allied forces vacate West Berlin. Two atomic tests were set for Nevada. *Manual* was buried inside in a 14-paragraph article headlined, "COURT LIFTS BAN ON 3 MAGAZINES; Overrules the Post Office on Homosexual Periodicals."

"Womack was proud of [his Supreme Court] victory, fully aware of its political import and keenly interested in the ongoing challenges of both gay and sexual liberation," according to historian Jackie Hatton. His magazines rapidly became much more sexually explicit and more overtly homosexual. Womack continued to run afoul of federal censors until at least 1970, when the FBI arrested him on child-pornography charges. Days after that arrest, Womack, surrounded by illustrations from Japanese "pillow books" and overflowing piles of nude photos, told a reporter, "If I do anything to advance the freedom of the press, I'll consider myself lucky. I'm not a martyr. But if homosexuals want a literature they have a right to it. They pay taxes and die. A hell of a lot of them have died in Vietnam."

A search for Womack led to his longtime attorney. Asked where Womack might be found, Dietz, sounding like a film noir detective, ghoulishly replied, "Got a spade?" Womack died in 1985 at age 63 after moving to Florida. Under "usual occupation," his death certificate lists "college professor."

Together, the *ONE* and *Manual* decisions represented huge victories for the fledgling homosexual-rights movement. Together, they gave a green light to the gay publishing industry. With *Manual*, it became a settled area of law that homosexuality does not automatically equal obscenity and that homosexuals may receive sexually explicit materials that, in the Supreme Court's view, are no worse than those commonly available to heterosexuals. In *Manual,* the Supreme Court decided that, regardless of how much psychiatrists did or didn't know about homosexual desire, it would not cede its role as final arbiter of what is obscene.

For an era when hostility and ignorance reigned over most discussions of homosexuality, the *ONE* and *Manual* rulings are amazingly progressive. Thus, in 1958 and 1962, the Supreme Court appeared well ahead of the general public and the rest of the federal government in moving toward an equal standard of justice that included homosexuals. Yet, as soon as the court broadened its focus beyond freedom of the press, homosexuals ran into serious, lasting trouble.

Twisting a Shield into a Weapon

With *Manual v. Day,* John Marshall Harlan became the first justice to hand down a signed opinion in a homosexual-rights case. However, he wasn't writing about homosexuality for the first time. What he wrote a year earlier, when he repeatedly broached the subject of homosexuality while dissenting in a birth control case, is cited far more often. Harlan's words in that 1961 contraception case have been used ever since by jurists and government attorneys trying to justify second-class treatment of homosexuals. Yet there's no evidence that Harlan intended his *Poe v. Ullman* dissent to erect a new barrier to the advancement of homosexuals.

Poe v. Ullman involved a Connecticut statute making it a crime for anyone, even married couples, to use contraceptives for birth control. Nowadays, when condoms are easier to buy than cigarettes, it's difficult to grasp how controversial "family planning" was in the early 1960s. The Catholic Church contended reproduction was the sole purpose of sexual intercourse and that sex for pleasure was sinful. In defense of its law, Connecticut denounced contraception as immoral. When *Poe v. Ullman* reached the Supreme Court, a five-man majority found a procedural excuse—no one had been prosecuted—for not ruling in a case they found too hot to handle.

Harlan, then a 62-year-old married man with one child, dissented and laid the foundation for recognition of a constitutional right to privacy. All of the sexual privacy rights that generations of heterosexual Americans have taken for granted—including the right to abortion—have built on Harlan's now-classic dissent.

Ironically, the dissent that was used to expand most Americans' sexual freedom has been used to hold back homosexuals' progress. The clash between those uses was most obvious—and, in terms of gay rights, most costly—in the court's 1986 *Bowers v. Hardwick* decision: When the court ruled 5-to-4 that the right to privacy does not extend to private consensual homosexual sodomy, both the majority and minority views could be traced back to Harlan's *Poe* dissent.

How did homosexuality get mixed up in a quintessentially heterosexual conflict—whether a husband and wife can legally be barred from using contraceptives? Understanding that requires a bit of background on the status of constitutional law when Connecticut's ban was being challenged by two anonymous married couples.

In 1960, when Columbia law graduate Howard Lesnich wrote the first *Poe v. Ullman* memo to Harlan, the court had few recognized tools for knocking down laws restricting individual rights. The 14th Amendment declares, "No State shall . . . deny to any person within its jurisdiction the equal protection of the laws." Yet the Constitution's "equal protection" guarantee was not yet viewed as extending beyond race discrimination. Harlan was on record as essentially saying that almost any rationale would make a law reasonable and, therefore, constitutional.

In trying to differentiate a birth control ban from other laws expressing moral attitudes, Lesnich injected homosexuality into the debate. ". . . Laws against consensual homosexuality between adults can be justified on some theory that such practices 'weaken the nation's moral fiber.' Farfetched as this may be, it is probably not so ridiculous as to make the statute unconstitutional," he wrote.

Where did Lesnich get the idea that such justifications were "farfetched"? He says, "I haven't got the foggiest idea. It seems obvious to me [that they were], but I don't think I ever met a gay person up until then. The word was never used. 'Gay' was associated with 'divorcee.'"

When *Poe* carried over to the next term, it was inherited in Harlan's chambers by 25-year-old Charles Fried, a Czechoslovakian-born naturalized citizen with an English wife. After the court voted to dismiss *Poe*, Harlan asked Fried to craft a dissent. Harlan's Fried-drafted dissent draws a distinct line between marital and nonmarital sex. "The right of privacy most manifestly is not an absolute. Thus, I would not suggest that adultery, homosexuality, fornication or incest are immune from criminal enquiry, however privately practiced. . . . Adultery, homosexuality and the like are sexual intimacies which the state forbids altogether, but the intimacy of husband and wife is necessarily an essential and accepted feature of the institution of marriage, . . . " Harlan declared. He argued that allowing government to intrude "into the very heart of marital privacy . . . is surely a very different thing indeed from punishing those who establish intimacies which the law has always forbidden and which can have no claim to social protection."

Though the Constitution does not mention marriage, Harlan read into it the right of married couples to engage in non-procreative sex—that is, sex purely for pleasure. His dissent didn't treat homosexuality differently from any other form of extramarital sex in placing it outside the protective line he was attempting to draw to create a very narrow protected zone for sexual intimacy within marriage. Plus, he did not pass judgment on homosexuality. A little-quoted portion of his dissent states, "Certainly, Connecticut's judgment [that contraception is immoral] is no more demonstrably correct or incorrect than are the varieties of judgment, expressed in law, on marriage and divorce, on adult consensual homosexuality, abortion, and sterilization, or euthanasia and suicide."

Having clerked for Harlan the year of his *Poe* dissent, Philip Heymann says, Harlan's sole focus was "contraceptives in the bedroom," adding, "I can't imagine him being morally outraged by homosexuality."

Harlan's *Poe* dissent soon began being quoted in ways that made it appear that Harlan had put homosexuality farther from the protected zone of privacy than some other forms of unmarried sex. The process began with Justice Arthur Goldberg's 1965 concurrence in *Griswold v. Connecticut*. That case involved a Planned Parenthood clinic's doctor and director, who'd been fined $100 each for advising married couples about contraceptives.

Justice Douglas's opinion knocking down the Connecticut statute put the court on record as recognizing a right to privacy. Goldberg's concurrence brought homosexuality back into the discussion. Goldberg flatly declared that the constitutionality of laws against adultery and fornication "is beyond doubt." He added that "the court's holding today . . . in no way interferes with a state's proper regulation of sexual promiscuity or misconduct. As my Brother Harlan so well stated in his dissenting opinion in *Poe v. Ullman* . . . 'Adultery, homosexuality and the like are sexual intimacies which the state forbids. . . .'" Harlan's dissent had lumped all unmarried sex together. By citing the Harlan language that did not include "fornication" (unmarried heterosexual intercourse), Goldberg planted the idea that he and Harlan considered homosexuality farther from the protected zone of privacy than fornication was.

Yet Goldberg's son, Robert, a retired Virginia attorney, contends his father was "absolutely not" trying to make any point about homosexuality in *Griswold*.

Federal court decisions directly relying on Harlan's dissent to rule against gay Americans soon followed *Griswold*, though.

Lesnich, who introduced homosexuality into the Supreme Court's privacy debates, wishes Harlan's dissent in a contraception case would stop being used as an excuse for anti-gay rulings. "The whole thing is so absurd—parsing the language of older cases to try to make an argument about what [justices] meant about a case that wasn't before them. . . . You grab a phrase or a comma from an old opinion and say, 'See, this shows they agree with me.' It's silly."

Ironically, the Supreme Court string of heterosexual privacy rulings has in some ways weakened the legal position of homosexuals. In 1961, when Harlan issued his *Poe* dissent, no one's sexual privacy was protected, so the court's failure to protect homosexuals' privacy was no particular reflection on homosexuals. Then Harlan's dissent and *Griswold* drew a line that put married couples into a protected zone of privacy. Homosexuals were outside that protected zone, just like everyone else who engaged in nonmarital or extramarital sex.

The court purposely erased its first privacy line—the one based on marriage—in 1972 to overturn the Massachusetts ban on distributing contraceptives to couples who in Harlan's day were called fornicators. Each time the court redrew the privacy line to bring in a new group— unmarried straight couples, heterosexual minors, interracial couples, pregnant women—homosexuals became more marginalized.

Gradually, homosexuality's unprotected status left gay couples in a class not with the great mass of sexually active adults but with rapists, bigamists, prostitutes, pederasts and incestuous pairs. By the 1986 *Hardwick* decision upholding sodomy laws, the fact that homosexuals had not yet been brought inside the Harlan-created protected zone was being used as an indictment against them—as if an absence of protection equaled being unworthy of it. Also, because homosexuality was classed only with the most disreputable forms of sex, opponents of gay civil rights could play on the fear that bringing gay couples into the zone of privacy would lead to legalization of every imaginable type of sex, including bestiality.

Reinforcing Stereotypes

In Harlan's *Poe* dissent, homosexuality was an abstraction, just as it had been in *ONE* and *Manual*. In all three, homosexuals were name- less, faceless shadow figures—occupants of the netherworld outside the protected zone of privacy or anonymous readers of magazines that government attorneys branded filth. Then, in late 1962, homosexuality took on more human proportions for the court as it began accepting cases involving individuals—as opposed to publications—ensnared by the government's aggressive campaign against homosexuals. The court was confronted with homosexuals as fairly ordinary people with names, hometowns, careers. Yet the first homosexuals whose lives the court chose to scrutinize were hardly positioned to make the strongest argument for recognition of American homosexuals' constitutional rights: Those homosexuals weren't even U.S. citizens. They were legal immigrants facing deportation because of their sexual orientation.

In retrospect, the fact that foreigners were the first people to have homosexual-rights cases argued before our nation's top court isn't really surprising. Unlike, say, homosexuals purged from the State Department, they had nothing to gain from quietly acquiescing in the government's judgment against them.

The first large wave of homosexual-rights challenges to reach the Supreme Court generally involved men—whether aliens or citizens—whose cases had grown out of sleazy public sex arrests. At least superficially, these early challenges look quite unlike the squeaky-clean ones later filed by gay poster boys (and the occasional poster girl) fighting to preserve an exemplary military or teaching career. Thus, when the Supreme Court began to get acquainted through court documents with specific homosexuals, a great many stereotypes were quickly reinforced: The homosexuals were male, convicted criminals who, at least in the government's view, had been engaged in promiscuous public sex. What the justices weren't seeing in the 1960s was the homosexual equivalent of the heterosexual couples who won the right to marital privacy.

Swiss-born George Ernst Marcel Fleuti, the first individual to have a homosexual-rights case accepted by the Supreme Court, was a double victim of the U.S. war on homosexuals. After the Senate told the FBI to get tough on homosexuals, the FBI passed the word to police departments. When vice squads cracked down, Fleuti was among the many men repeatedly arrested. The mild-mannered immigrant soon found the full weight of the federal government bearing down upon him.

4

"More Than a Homosexual"

GEORGE FLEUTI WAS A POLISHED, mild-mannered man with a slight build and a light complexion. He had the demeanor of a front desk clerk at a fairly posh hotel. And that's exactly what he was by the time he ran into trouble with U.S. authorities.

Before immigrating to this country at age 40, Fleuti had worked in hotels all over Switzerland. Since his mid-20s, he'd been having sex with other men "whenever the opportunity would present itself, and one of my friends felt the same way at the same time," he once recalled. When he was admitted to the United States as a permanent resident on October 9, 1952, there was nothing in U.S. immigration law that could have been construed as making him ineligible to enter simply for being homosexual.

In early 1954, Fleuti settled into a permanent job as a valued and trusted employee at the Ojai Valley Inn and Country Club, a resort in Ojai (pronounced "Oh-hi"), California. Sixty miles northwest of downtown Los Angeles, Ojai was a lush and peaceful valley overflowing with avocado and lemon trees. Hollywood's idea of utopia, the Ojai valley starred as the mythical "Shangri-La" in the 1937 film *Lost Horizon*. The idyllic valley then became Fleuti's American Shangri-La. Within four years of his arrival he'd been promoted to the inn's front office manager, supervising eight workers and personally handling at least $500,000 in cash a year.

The Supreme Court's voluminous record on Fleuti fails to pinpoint the moment the INS set its sights on deporting him. But it seems likely

89

that the FBI alerted immigration officials in 1958 that he was probably
a homosexual. Fleuti had been arrested in November 1958 in nearby
Oxnard, California, "on suspicion"—as he later put it—of a crime involving homosexuality. The charges—unspecified in his records—were
dismissed after his fingerprints were forwarded to the FBI. Four months
after the Oxnard arrest, the INS interrogated Fleuti. Without the benefit of legal advice, he volunteered that he'd been arrested three times on
homosexual vice charges and convicted twice. His sworn statement of
March 25, 1959, revealed that he'd been a sexually active homosexual
for at least 16 years and that he'd left this country once since his arrival
in 1952. Fleuti recalled crossing the U.S. border sometime in August
1956 for a day trip to Ensenada, a Mexican tourist town near San Diego
known for bullfights and jai alai handball games.

The INS promptly demanded that he "show cause" why he shouldn't
be deported. Fleuti, 46, stood accused of having entered the United
States unlawfully because, the INS charged, he had previously been
convicted of a crime involving "moral turpitude." As proof, the INS
cited Fleuti's statement that he had been convicted in March 1956 of
having had oral sex with another man in a Los Angeles park. That conviction, the INS pointed out, was before his August 1956 "entry" back
into the United States after a couple of hours in Mexico.

Despite his dire legal situation, Fleuti showed up for his deportation
hearing on April 14, 1959, without an attorney. ". . . I didn't want anybody to know about my case, if possible," he explained at the hearing.
Six days later, an INS official ordered Fleuti deported. That order was
soon invalidated, however, because Fleuti's punishment for the 1956
oral sex arrest—a $200 fine—was too minor for him to be deported for
"moral turpitude."

Undeterred, the INS soon accused Fleuti of having been excludable—and thus deportable—when he returned from Mexico because he
was "afflicted with psychopathic personality." To the INS, immigration
law required that homosexuals be classified as psychopaths. Congress
had rewritten the law after Fleuti settled in the United States.

When Congress started panicking over the supposed threat posed by
homosexuals, a Senate Judiciary subcommittee recommended in 1950
that U.S. borders be closed to homosexual immigrants: "[T]he purpose
of the [existing] provision against 'persons with constitutional psycho-

pathic inferiority' will be more adequately served by changing that term to 'persons afflicted with psychopathic personality,' and that the classes of mentally defectives should be enlarged to include homosexuals and other sex perverts." However, the legislation that passed did not actually mention homosexuals. The U.S. Public Health Service had advised Congress that language requiring "the exclusion of aliens afflicted with psychopathic personality or a mental defect . . . is sufficiently broad to provide for the exclusion of homosexuals and sex perverts," a Senate committee report noted. The revised immigration law barred "aliens afflicted with psychopathic personality, epilepsy, or a mental defect." It took effect in December 1952, two months after Fleuti's original arrival but more than three years before his brief visit to Mexico.

Fleuti's second round of deportation hearings featured dueling psychiatric evaluations, then a mainstay of legal wrangling over homosexuals' rights. Citing Fleuti's arrest record, Dr. Arthur R. Dahlgren, a Public Health Service surgeon with no psychiatric training, testified that he had classified Fleuti as a psychopath because "this gentleman is a sexual deviate."

However, Dr. David R. M. Harvey, the psychiatrist retained by Fleuti's attorney, insisted that Fleuti's "deviation is not sufficient to justify the diagnosis of psychopathic personality."

Fleuti attorney Hiram Kwan recalls, "There were not very many psychiatrists that wanted to take the case. I had to shop around. And [Harvey] had a lot better vision than I had. He says, 'You know, if I treat him too much, then they'll say there's something wrong with him. I'll just see him three or four times and then pronounce him okay.'"

In support of Fleuti, Harvey reported,

> He does not frequent homosexual hangouts, has no evident interest in youths, manifests no irresponsible trends, and has his main social contacts with respected members of the community. . . . He is a lonely man and the main focus of his life is his work. . . . [H]is arrests have had a good effect on his homosexual trend and . . . my repeated examinations have also heightened his sense of sexual control and lessened his interest. . . . I do not find that Mr. Fleuti is a danger to any other person. In many ways he seems to have traits of a better than average citizen, in the sense of hard work, general morality and honesty.

Nevertheless, on September 22, 1959, the INS ordered Fleuti deported as a psychopath. After the Board of Immigration Appeals upheld that order, Kwan took Fleuti's case to federal court. As applied by the INS, the immigration law was unconstitutionally vague, he argued. The Supreme Court had repeatedly ruled that statutes must be clear enough for people of average intelligence to know what is forbidden. However, on January 4, 1961, U.S. District Judge James M. Carter ruled against Fleuti, saying, "from the legislative history, it is clear that Congress intended that sexual deviates would be classified by the enforcing agencies as psychopathic personalities."

Kwan, an immigration attorney in private practice in Los Angeles's Chinatown, had taken over Fleuti's defense because the hotel clerk needed an expert. Kwan recalls getting "a lot of flak" from fellow attorneys and INS investigators for "helping a faggot," as they put it. But Kwan, who says "I don't duck any case," soon won an impressive victory at an appeals court.

The Ninth Circuit Court of Appeals ruled unanimously on April 17, 1962, that the immigration law was unconstitutionally vague. Deciding that Fleuti's homosexual behavior in this country "was not compulsive, but was a matter of choice," the three-judge panel said he might have acted differently had he known he risked deportation. "The conclusion is inescapable that the statutory term 'psychopathic personality,' when measured by common understanding and practices, does not convey sufficiently definite warning that homosexuality and sex perversion are embraced therein," the panel declared. In other words, if Congress wanted to keep out homosexuals, it would have to actually say so. (The Supreme Court views the Constitution as granting Congress nearly absolute control over immigration. The court sees its own job not as ensuring that immigration rules are fair but that they are constitutionally interpreted and enforced.)

On behalf of INS District Director George Rosenberg, Solicitor General Archibald Cox petitioned the Supreme Court to reverse the Ninth Circuit. Mimicking the immigration law's language, Cox said Fleuti had been "afflicted" with the desire to have sex with men for 22 years and had "indulged" once a month. Cox argued that "Congress intended to include all sexual deviates, including homosexuals, in this [psychopathic] category." He added, "the statutory ground for expulsion is not the alien's conduct after entry, but his condition at the time of entry." Thus, in his view, the question of adequate warning was irrelevant. Cox also argued that the Ninth Circuit's decision conflicted with a Fifth Circuit ruling upholding a lesbian's deportation.

Kwan countered that there was no reason for the justices to intervene: The Ninth Circuit was correct, and there was no conflict with another appellate decision because the Fifth Circuit case had not addressed the vagueness question at the heart of Fleuti's case.

"He Performs Publicly"

Shortly after their 1962–63 term began, the justices gathered behind closed doors to decide whether to accept *Rosenberg v. Fleuti*. Chief Justice Warren, as usual, summarized the case at hand, then cast the first vote on October 12, 1962. He voted to deny, meaning he wanted to let Fleuti's victory stand. On the front of his clerk's *cert* memo, Warren had penciled a long note to himself, saying that "it was conceded by the gov't doctors that all homosexuals are not medically psychopaths." (Actually, the Public Health surgeon who labeled Fleuti deportable had danced around that issue.) Black and Douglas also voted to deny. Clark, who had so strongly dissented from the court's decision allowing homosexual beefcake magazines, favored granting *cert*. Clark was seconded by Harlan, who saw a conflict between circuits. Brennan voted for denial. Then Stewart voted to take the case. Byron White, whom President Kennedy had appointed to succeed Whittaker in the spring, cast the decisive fourth vote to grant *cert*. With his first vote in a homosexual-rights case, White started a pattern of voting against the homosexual litigant—one that culminated in his writing a 1986 decision upholding sodomy laws.

Arthur Goldberg also voted to take *Rosenberg v. Fleuti,* making the decision 5 to 4 in favor of the INS district director's request. Goldberg, whom Kennedy had chosen to replace Frankfurter, had taken his oath of office just 11 days earlier. As it turned out, Fleuti's fate rested in Goldberg's hands.

Once the court accepted *Rosenberg v. Fleuti,* attorneys filed competing briefs. The government's brief declared that the Ninth Circuit had erred in thinking it matters that psychiatrists don't agree on what "psychopathic" means. The brief approvingly quoted the Fifth Circuit: "Whatever the phrase 'psychopathic personality' means to the psychiatrist, to the Congress it was intended to include homosexuals and sex perverts. It is that intent that controls here."

Since homosexuality was still classified as a mental illness by the American Psychiatric Association, Fleuti's attorney, Kwan, made no attempt to argue that homosexuals are as likely as heterosexuals to be mentally healthy. Instead, he pushed his void-for-vagueness argument by quoting psychiatric texts saying that "psychopathic personality" is an almost meaningless label.

Before Kwan and Justice Department attorney Philip R. Monahan reiterated all their main points during their oral arguments March 26, 1963, Warren clerk Peter R. Taft made a somewhat different one in a bench memo. Taft, a Yale law school graduate, urged that the justices send the case back down for a ruling on whether "psychopathic"—as used by psychiatrists—actually applied to Fleuti. "The only alternative to this disposition . . . is to conclude that Congress intended to exclude every individual who ever took part in a homosexual act. I do not find such a statement in the legislative history. Moreover . . . I do not see how the term psychopathic personality could be stretched to cover it as it would be outside any known meaning of the term, common or uncommon."

Taft says he was not aware at the time of having any homosexual co-clerks. (John D. Niles, who clerked for Warren the same year as Taft, came out as a gay man before dying of AIDS in 1990.) Taft never talked about homosexuals with Warren but says, "My feeling is he'd just be a product of his time and not have any particular sympathy for them. . . . I seriously doubt that he would have had a huge objection to enforcing [sodomy laws] as a prosecutor."

Neither clerk's bench memos nor the oral arguments in *Rosenberg v. Fleuti* swayed the justices. At their private conference March 29, 1963, the justices again split 5 to 4 against Fleuti, lining up exactly as before. The chief justice voted to affirm the Ninth Circuit's ruling in Fleuti's favor. "But not too sure—psychopathic personality means little, according to many doctors," Douglas's notes quote Warren as saying. Arguing that "due process and equal protection protect aliens as well as citizens," Hugo Black pronounced the law "too vague" and voted to affirm. Douglas also affirmed "on vagueness." Tom Clark, rapidly becoming the bane of homosexual-rights litigants, voted to reverse. The concept of vagueness only applies to criminal cases, not civil immigration proceedings, he argued. Harlan agreed with Clark, adding that the "legislative history is clear that this phrase includes homosexuals." Brennan voted to affirm. Stewart supported reversal, saying that warnings of what is forbidden have "no relevance in deportation cases." White voted to reverse. Casting the decisive vote against Fleuti, Goldberg told his colleagues, "He is more than a homosexual. He has such a dominant sex drive that he performs publicly. He was a psychopath in the conventional sense."

As the senior justice in the majority, Clark had the prerogative of choosing who would write the court opinion holding it constitutional to use the term "psychopathic personality" as a blanket excuse for deporting homosexual immigrants. Clark may well have been intent on seeing that the newest justice—the one with the unique approach—didn't stray and destroy the slim, five-vote majority. Clark tapped Goldberg on April 3.

Two months later, Goldberg jolted his brethren with a memo announcing that he had changed his mind. "I am herewith circulating a draft opinion which incorporates my new thoughts about the case," Goldberg wrote. He had decided to duck the only real issue argued in the case—whether "psychopathic personality" was unconstitutionally vague when used by the INS as a synonym for "homosexual." His opinion instead turned on a new issue—whether Fleuti's return to the United States after a quick trip across the Mexican border constituted an "entry" as defined by immigration law. To Goldberg, it did not. Nothing in U.S. law had barred Fleuti in 1950 when he made what Goldberg viewed as his only "entry," so Fleuti was not deportable, Goldberg concluded.

U.S. immigration law flatly stated that coming into the United States was "entry" unless the departure "was not intended." Clearly intent on squeezing Fleuti into that very narrow exception, Goldberg insisted that if Fleuti's trip abroad was "innocent, casual, and brief" and not meant to jeopardize his legal residency, then departure—in a legal sense—was not intended. In a real stretch, Goldberg compared Fleuti's border crossing to that of a rescued seaman who'd been taken to Cuba after his merchant ship was torpedoed. The Supreme Court had ruled in 1947 that the sailor's post-shipwreck return was not an entry. In a note to

Douglas, Goldberg confided that he'd gotten the idea for his inventive approach from Douglas's 1947 shipwreck ruling.

The justices who'd been in the minority—Black, Douglas, Brennan and Warren—leapt at the chance to turn Goldberg's change of heart into a victory for Fleuti. The day after Goldberg circulated his unusual draft, he got the votes of all four—a notable occurrence on a court where it can take months for a majority to coalesce around an opinion. "Dear Arthur," Black wrote in longhand, "I agree although I would prefer (1) to hold the statute void for vagueness . . . or (2) that under the facts as shown deportation was not justified under this statute. Hugo."

Only Brennan suggested a modification. In an almost offhand way, Goldberg's draft declared, "Congress unquestionably has the power to exclude homosexuals and other undesirables from this country." Goldberg's court papers reveal that Brennan, who over the course of decades was to evolve into a gay-rights champion, kept that powerfully anti-homosexual statement from becoming part of a Supreme Court majority opinion. On June 6, 1963, when it was virtually unheard of for public officials to rise to the defense of homosexuals, Brennan wrote: "Dear Arthur: I think this is a splendid job. . . . May I suggest, however, that you delete the words 'homosexuals and others' in line 12 of page 12. I agree that Congress unquestionably has the power to exclude undesirable aliens, but I think it may be, at least medically, a matter of doubt whether homosexuals necessarily fall into the category of undesirable aliens. In any event, I'd rather not put us on record as deciding that." Goldberg revised the sentence to read, "Congress unquestionably has the power to exclude all classes of undesirable aliens from this country."

Even before that change was made, Douglas told Goldberg, "I think you have written a fine opinion. . . . It gives a slightly new meaning to the conception of 'entry'. . . . But I think this is in the direction of a just, liberal construction and I hope you get a court for it." (The justices call securing a majority "getting a court.")

Goldberg, like Douglas, would have considered "liberal" a compliment. Generally recalled as an advocate of individual rights, Goldberg was a Kennedy Democrat. The son of poor Ukrainian Jewish immigrants, he knew what it felt like to be on the receiving end of prejudice. As a schoolboy he was pummeled with anti-Semitic epithets, and sometimes even stones. Although he graduated with honors from Northwestern University law school in 1929, many doors were closed to him. "As a Jew, Goldberg was automatically barred from Chicago's oldest and largest [law] firms," according to his biographer. A labor lawyer, Goldberg became general counsel of the United Steelworkers of America, then special counsel of the newly merged AFL-CIO. He used his influence to get organized labor on board for John F. Kennedy's presidential campaign. President Kennedy repaid the favor by appointing Goldberg secretary of labor, then elevated him 15 months later to the Supreme Court. Goldberg was no advocate of judicial restraint. Rather, he believed the nation's highest court should ferociously fight injustice.

"He wasn't a gentle humanitarian. He was very fierce. He didn't believe [that as a justice] you were in charge of a mausoleum. You weren't maintaining a museum. The Constitution was a living part of government," his daughter-in-law, Barbara Goldberg, recalls.

When Goldberg circulated his activist formula in 1963 for keeping the INS from deporting Fleuti, his less liberal colleagues had no intention of going along. "Arthur—If you've ever been to Ensenada, you would not be so ready to assume that its purpose was innocent!!" teased Harlan. Goldberg at least got points for creativity. As a Harlan clerk put it, "the statute does not bear this interpretation very comfortably, but it surely is ingenious!" Having failed to get Goldberg to write an opinion that would maintain the original majority, Clark swiftly announced that he'd be writing a dissent.

On June 17, 1963, the court announced its 5-to-4 ruling in Fleuti's favor. Although Goldberg's majority decision vacated the Ninth Circuit finding of unconstitutional vagueness and sent the case back down, the court made clear that Fleuti was not to be deported unless new evidence showed there had been some nefarious purpose for his afternoon jaunt to Mexico. In dissent, Clark, joined by Harlan, Stewart and White, lectured their newest colleague that the court's job is to "construe" statutes, not "construct" them. Rather than create a loophole to fit Fleuti, the court ought to have decided whether "psychopathic personality" was unconstitutionally vague, they argued.

The next day's *New York Times* led with the court's ruling banning required Bible reading from public schools. Also on the front page was news that Senate Minority Leader Everett Dirksen, an Illinois Republican, would not support the Kennedy administration's expected effort to outlaw racial segregation by restaurants, motels and movie theaters. The *Fleuti* ruling, handed down on the final day of the court's 1962–63 term, was reported in a five-paragraph Associated Press story on page 29. Headlined "COURT SEEKS RULING IN ALIEN'S BRIEF TRIP," the article did not mention homosexuality.

"The Yellow Person of Today"

After Fleuti's Supreme Court victory, an immigration judge ruled that there was no reason to deport him. "They gave him back his Green Card. He was very happy," says Kwan. In about 1975, Fleuti, then in his early 60s, became a naturalized U.S. citizen. The INS couldn't prevent that final triumph, Kwan recalls, because Fleuti had "more than five years of 'good moral character.' No more arrests. He was very cautious. It was like walking a tightrope."

Fleuti was able to stay in his adopted homeland largely because of Justice Goldberg's change of heart. However, the court's Goldberg-authored *Fleuti* decision also meant that other homosexual immigrants remained vulnerable to being deported as psychopaths, regardless of their mental health. Ironically, the only homosexual that Goldberg ended up protecting was the one whom he originally singled out as properly labeled deportable. Goldberg had stepped, untrained, into the role of a psychiatrist. Once there, Goldberg judged Fleuti a "psychopath" because of his history of public sex. The tenor of Goldberg's remarks suggests that in the absence of evidence of public sex, he would have provided the decisive fifth vote for finding the immigration law unconstitutionally vague as applied to homosexuals.

Fleuti, who earned $400 a month when his INS troubles began, ended up paying legal bills totaling $3,000 to $4,000. "That's all I thought he could afford," explains Kwan. Fleuti remained in the hotel business at least until he won his U.S. citizenship, according to Kwan, who then lost track of him. Social Security records indicate Fleuti lived in southern California until his death, at age 70, in 1983.

Originally, Kwan didn't see Fleuti's struggle as a civil rights battle. "And now I see it from the bigger picture," Kwan says. "He was discriminated against as much as the blacks and the yellows and the Indians and the Jews." Intimately familiar with the long history of U.S. discrimination against Asian immigrants, Kwan believes the place of gay people in America hasn't improved much. "I would say the homosexual is the yellow person of today," he observed.

After the Supreme Court's *Fleuti* decision, the INS remained an active combatant in the U.S. war on homosexuals. Unlike their *ONE* and *Manual* rulings, the justices chose not to signal that a federal agency's attack on homosexuality was out of bounds. The court essentially called a technical foul on the INS, saying one man's border crossing had been misclassified but leaving intact the agency's blanket exclusion of homosexuals.

The court's handling of *Fleuti* is indicative of justices' general unwillingness over the past four decades to consider the impact of police harassment on everyday homosexuals. Unlike the ease with which heterosexuals met and mingled with potential partners, homosexuals of Fleuti's day were locked in what Harry Hay, a grandfather of gay rights, called "the solitary confinement of social persecution and civil insecurity." A society in which homosexuals knew that asking for someone's phone number might lead to a charge of "lewd" conduct wasn't one in which they found it easy to form lasting relationships. A great many men searched for intimacy in the furtive, anonymous, public sexual encounters that Goldberg considered pathological.

In passing judgment on Fleuti's behavior, Goldberg—and by extension the court—overlooked how vice squads targeted homosexual cruising spots while heterosexuals mated undisturbed along lovers' lanes. Goldberg's psychological assessment of Fleuti also failed to consider how loneliness and self-loathing could lead many homosexual men to act in desperate, risky ways that socially accepted heterosexuals had the luxury of finding despicable.

Goldberg seemed oblivious to the ways that Fleuti's arrest record was a product of oppressive times. In pondering Fleuti's case, Goldberg didn't talk more broadly about homosexuals, according to ex-clerk Peter Edelman. But measuring Goldberg's liberalism by today's standards would only compound the misunderstandings. His attitudes toward homosexuals cannot be neatly labeled. Unlike some justices, Goldberg was neither unaware of having known homosexuals nor unempathetic.

"Dad was a man without prejudice entirely. He had no prejudice toward homosexuals or anyone. . . . He was very saddened by the discrimination that the non-predatory homosexuals faced," Robert Goldberg recalls. He says that his father, a U.S. military intelligence chief in Europe during World War II, had known homosexuals during the war and been "troubled by what they went through. . . . Freedom to live without discrimination—that was Dad."

Pressured by President Lyndon Johnson, Arthur Goldberg resigned from the court he loved in 1965—after just three terms—to become ambassador to the United Nations because he wanted to try to help end the Vietnam war. Goldberg's understanding of homosexuality grew after leaving the court. His daughter-in-law, Barbara Goldberg, says she helped educate him: "As [homosexuality] became something that people were much more able to talk about, he was curious. . . . He married very, very young; he was only 21 or 22 . . . and in that regard he was very unworldly. . . . So in terms of other people's private lives he really didn't know much."

In 1970, when Goldberg was the Democratic nominee for governor of New York, the Gay Activists Alliance pressured him to update his liberalism. GAA members swooped down on his limousine to demand that he discuss gay rights. Waging a losing challenge to Republican Governor Nelson Rockefeller, Goldberg shot back, "I have more important things to talk about." With GAA "zaps" disrupting his campaign, he endorsed basic gay rights just before the election.

Barbara Goldberg recalls a dinner-table conversation later in the 1970s that focused on lesbianism. Her father-in-law revealed that he couldn't fathom why anyone discriminated against gay people on the basis of something "over which they had no control." He saw being gay like having "blue eyes or size 8 shoes. And he felt that this was just another area that society needed to address. He was a true liberal," his daughter-in-law adds. The former justice knowingly hired a lesbian couple in Virginia's horse country to teach his grandchildren to ride. The women's orientation, she says, "would have been a non-issue. That's what he would say, 'Non-issue!'"

She thinks that her father-in-law might well have evolved into a gay-rights leader on the court had he not resigned so early. "I'm not a lawyer, but I know where he stood on issues of that kind—where people are suffering. He would get very ferocious," she explains. If he had not stepped down at 56, he might have served another quarter century because he remained mentally sharp until the day he died in 1990. Johnson considered nominating him to be chief justice in October 1968. Goldberg clung to his dream of returning to the court until Richard Nixon won the White House that November. Justice Brennan, two years older than Goldberg, did stay on the court until 1990 and gradually emerged as gay Americans' foremost ally on the court.

Goldberg was quite moved by watching an AIDS-awareness march in the early 1980s. "What really struck him was the youthfulness of the marchers and the predicament they were in. And the fact that nobody was really taking it seriously because many of them were homosexual," Barbara Goldberg says. Lapsing into phrasing from her Scottish girlhood, she adds, "And it really bothered, that. He said, 'They're talking about discrimination. That's what this is about.'"

The insights Arthur Goldberg gained after leaving the court were useless, of course, to gay Americans. Had the liberal, increasingly open-minded Goldberg not viewed Fleuti as sick, the court almost certainly would have declared that a government policy unconstitutionally violated homosexuals' rights. In *ONE* and *Manual,* the court had not addressed questions of constitutionality. In those cases, the court was merely interpreting a federal statute. Thus, a ruling of unconstitutional vagueness in *Fleuti* would have been a tremendous breakthrough. As it turned out, the court would wait another three decades before saying that the Constitution's guarantee of equal protection applies to gay Americans.

Fleuti left unanswered whether the INS could constitutionally deport homosexuals by automatically diagnosing them as "psychopathic." Soon after that decision, Fleuti's attorney, Kwan, bumped into Justice Clark at a Washington, D.C., party. Clark informed Kwan that he'd wanted to kick Fleuti out of the country. The justice, Kwan recalls, strongly hinted that if the court ever received the question again, he would vote "with gusto" to deport.

5

"AFFLICTED WITH HOMOSEXUALITY"

JUST THREE YEARS AFTER FAILING to get Fleuti deported, Justice Clark got another crack at a homosexual alien. When Canadian Clive Michael Boutilier appealed to the Supreme Court for help in 1966, he unwittingly provided exactly the kind of case for which Clark had been waiting.

By the time the INS began trying to deport him, Boutilier was even more deeply rooted in American soil than George Fleuti had been during his own immigration troubles. Whereas Fleuti lived alone and had no close relatives in this country, Boutilier was involved in a seven-year relationship with an American man. They lived together in the same Brooklyn apartment building as Boutilier's mother, a naturalized U.S. citizen, and his stepfather. Boutilier also had three brothers and a sister in the United States. Only his eldest sister was back in Canada.

Born in Sheet Harbor, Nova Scotia, in 1933, Clive Michael Boutilier had grown up on his large Catholic family's small farm. The oldest son, he dropped out of school at 13 to help the family make ends meet. At 21, Boutilier immigrated to New York City, where he found steady work. He served as an attendant to a mentally ill person, then became a building maintenance man.

In September 1963, the month he turned 30, Boutilier applied for U.S. citizenship. He volunteered that he'd been arrested in 1959 on a sodomy charge that was reduced to assault, then dismissed because the alleged victim refused to press charges. That admission, of course, set off INS alarms. The agency interrogated Boutilier, getting him to acknowledge three or four homosexual encounters a year since age 16.

Four days after the interrogation, Dr. Paul G. Smith, chief of psychiatry for the Public Health Service, and Dr. Maria Sarrigiannis, the health service's medical director, diagnosed Boutilier. He had been "afflicted with a Class A condition, namely, psychopathic personality, sexual deviate, at the time of his admission to the United States for permanent residence on June 22nd, 1955," they said. In doing medical gymnastics to assess what Boutilier's mental health had been eight years earlier, the government doctors relied solely on the sworn statement of "the above named alien." They did not examine Boutilier. Apparently, they did not even meet him.

Facing a threat of deportation, Boutilier got legal help and began fighting back. In March 1964, he was examined by a Brooklyn psychiatrist, Dr. Edward F. Falsey, who concluded, "He is not psychotic. From his own account, he has a psychosexual problem but is beginning treatment for this disorder. Diagnostically, I would consider him as having a character neurosis, believe that the prognosis in therapy is reasonably good and do not think he represents any risk of [decline] into a dependent psychotic reaction nor any potential for frank criminal activity."

Boutilier's struggle with U.S. authorities was taking an emotional toll, according to the second psychiatrist to privately evaluate him at his attorneys' request. Noting Boutilier was periodically teary-eyed during the exam, Dr. Montague Ullman wrote,

> His initial spontaneous outburst was to the effect that the proceedings against him over the past six years [since his arrest] were forcing him to make bank loans and for the first time in his life he was unable to financially cope. . . . He has abandoned all sexual practices within the past several months because of his annoyance and disgust with the problems these activities have brought about. . . . He has moved back to living with his mother and his stepfather. . . . His evenings are spent mostly at home. He occasionally goes bowling. He attends Mass. . . . He feels as if he has made his life in this country and is deeply disturbed at the prospect of being cut off from the life he has created for himself.

Finding Boutilier dependent and immature but not a psychopath, Ullman added, "[H]is own need to fit in and be accepted is so great that it far surpasses his need for sex in any form."

INS Special Inquiry Officer Ira Fieldsteel brushed aside findings about Boutilier's actual mental state. ". . . We are not here concerned with the niceties of meaning indulged in by psychiatrists, but rather with words of legal art," Fieldsteel said. To him, Congress meant to close U.S. borders to homosexuals. On August 5, 1965, he ordered Boutilier deported. Five months later, the Board of Immigration Appeals dismissed Boutilier's appeal, saying that "'psychopathic personality' is a term of art . . . [that] includes an alien upon mere proof that he is a homosexual."

The appeal jumped to the Second Circuit Court of Appeals, which ruled 2 to 1 against Boutilier in July 1966. Judge Irving R. Kaufman, joined by Judge J. Joseph Smith, began with a slap at the nation's budding counterculture: "Although a relatively young segment of contemporary society prides itself on its readiness to cast off conventional and tested disciplines and to experiment with nonconformance and the unorthodox merely to act out its contempt for traditional values, certain areas of conduct continue to be as controversial in modern and *beau monde* circles as they were in bygone and more staid eras. Homosexual behavior . . . remains such a fervently debated issue that too often emotions on both sides obscure reason."

As if to demonstrate his fairness by giving a nod to one of the other side's best arguments, Kaufman quoted Sigmund Freud: "Homosexuality is no advantage, but it is nothing to be ashamed of, no vice, no degradation, it cannot be classified as an illness. . . ." The court's function is not to judge homosexuality but "simply to interpret a statute," Kaufman said. Though conceding that "'psychopathic personality' is not a model of clarity," he ruled that it was a "legal term of art" adequately expressing Congress's intention to keep out homosexual immigrants.

Kaufman cast his decision as a triumph of reason over emotion. Yet he had read anti-homosexual language into a statute that made no mention of homosexuals.

Circuit Judge Leonard P. Moore dissented forcefully. Moore emphasized the human toll of the INS's blanket rule against homosexuals, sympathetically describing Boutilier as a respected worker with extensive blood ties to U.S. residents. (The judge did not mention Boutilier's longtime American lover.) To Moore, Boutilier, who'd had sex with a woman three or four times in his youth, was not so thoroughly homosexual that the law required his deportation: "I cannot impute to Congress an intention that the term 'psychopathic personality' . . . be construed to cover anyone who ever had a homosexual experience. . . . To label a group so large 'excludable aliens' would be tantamount to saying that Sappho, Leonardo da Vinci, Michelangelo, André Gide, and perhaps even Shakespeare, were they to come to life again, would be deemed unfit to visit our shores."

Moore's argument, advanced for its day, was that "at most" Congress sought to exclude "sexual deviates." Though admitting "sexual deviate" was itself vague, Moore said it "suggests someone with a longstanding and perhaps compulsive orientation towards homosexual or otherwise 'abnormal' behavior." Moore didn't think "sexual deviate" or "psychopath" fit Boutilier. To Moore, people with psychopathic personalities were "individuals who show a lifelong . . . tendency not to conform to group customs, and who habitually misbehave so flagrantly that they are continually in trouble with the authorities."

Moore concluded that Boutilier entered this country with "a psychological condition which he probably would have been able to correct had he had any reasonable warning" that it could result in deportation. The law, Moore said, was too vague because it gave no warning.

Boutilier's appeal reached the Supreme Court in August 1966. In asking the justices to take the case, attorneys Blanch Freedman and Robert Brown of New York City argued that a "proper interpretation of the statute limits it to sexual deviates who are suffering from a mental disease or disorder." Echoing Kwan's argument on behalf of Fleuti, they said the immigration law—as applied by the INS—was unconstitutionally vague.

Solicitor General Thurgood Marshall also wanted the justices to settle the "void for vagueness" question that Goldberg had ducked in *Fleuti*. The Second Circuit's Boutilier decision conflicted with a Ninth Circuit decision. Marshall urged the justices to clear up the confusion.

The Ninth Circuit had blocked the deportation of Gerard Joseph Lavoie, a 42-year-old Canadian who managed a cosmetology school. In June 1961, seventeen months after becoming a permanent U.S. resident, Lavoie was arrested in a San Francisco Woolworth's on charges of "lewd and indecent" conduct. When the INS investigated, Lavoie said he was homosexual.

The Boutilier-Lavoie conflict caught the justices' attention. On the Boutilier memo written by one of his clerks, Harlan wrote, "Hold for 513

[*Lavoie*] + Grant Both." Likewise, Warren saw a "clear conflict."

After noting the conflicting decisions, Clark clerk Stuart Ross concluded, "The legislature was certainly capable of spelling out in more precise terms exclusionary language for sexual misfits." On Ross's memo, Clark summarized the case: "Finding is Boutilier was afflicted [with] a Class A condition namely psychopathic personality—sexual deviate—admitted he was homo—got draft classification 4F as such. Legislative history shows that homosexuals + sex perverts were explicitly included by name—on testimony of Public Health Service—draftsmen then changed language to psychopathic personality. . . ."

The justices voted October 21, 1966, to hold Boutilier's petition until *Lavoie* reached the court. Once the justices saw *Lavoie*, they decided on November 4 to focus solely on *Clive Michael Boutilier v. Immigration and Naturalization Service.*

In accepting Boutilier's petition, the Supreme Court put itself in the unusual position of agreeing to hear a repeat of a challenge it had heard, then sidestepped, three years earlier. Boutilier was challenging the same INS interpretation as Fleuti. Goldberg might have been more sympathetic to Boutilier, since he had no history of public sex arrests. But by the time Boutilier reached the high court, Goldberg had retired and much else had changed as well.

"Daddy, What Did You Do Today?"

On October 14, 1964, President Lyndon Johnson's closest aide, Walter Jenkins, had been arrested for having sexual contact with another man in a YMCA restroom not far from the White House. Word of the arrest leaked to the Washington *Evening Star,* which then uncovered a nearly identical arrest five years earlier. Jenkins, a married man with six children, hit the panic button, summoning Johnson's trusted outside legal adviser, Abe Fortas. A skillful Washington operator, Fortas hustled Jenkins into a hospital and talked *Star* editors out of reporting the arrests. News of them broke anyway. With the election just days away, Johnson unceremoniously flushed the man who'd been his confidant for a quarter century out of his administration. Technically, Jenkins resigned. Rather than appear in court, he forfeited the bond he'd posted.

Washington, D.C., in those days was still very much a company town, with top-level officials in all three branches of government mingling socially to an extent that's now rare. The pain of Jenkins's downfall was felt inside the Supreme Court. Fellow Texan Tom Clark and his wife, Mary, were close to Jenkins and his family. The Clarks' son, Ramsey, recalls that his parents "both remained enormously sympathetic with Walter Jenkins and were both a little upset with the president for not standing by him." Mimi Clark Gronlund says her father "felt that Walter Jenkins was probably just an exhausted individual who kind of broke down."

The Johnson White House, in fact, attributed Jenkins's behavior to exhaustion. Ramsey Clark recalls that Jenkins vanished from the capital after being released from the isolation ward where he'd been put to keep the press at bay: "It was heartbreaking. I never saw him in Washington again. It was as if he didn't exist, you know? I saw him later . . . always in Austin."

The Jenkins incident deeply affected Justice Douglas, "who mentioned it many times," according to his widow, Cathy Douglas Stone. "He kept saying to me, 'Can you imagine somebody on the police force actually hanging out in public toilets?' And he said, 'What do they say to their children when they say, "Daddy, what did you do today?" It was so ludicrous to him. It was pathetic and sad to him the way people were treated."

The Jenkins scandal brought homosexuality home to the Supreme Court far more personally than the cases the justices decided without ever meeting the people involved. For justices who were not as worldly as Douglas, Jenkins's downfall might well have reinforced the popular view that homosexuality was a personal weakness, something shameful that could ruin a career in a careless instant and something that the court would not wish to seem to be condoning.

Meanwhile, the Civil Rights Act of 1964 outlawed discrimination on the basic of race, religion, national origin or sex. The court's *Griswold v. Connecticut* birth control decision the next year protected the privacy of married couples. Thus, the gradual recognition and protection of other groups' civil rights was well underway before homosexuals had even begun to take to the streets to fight for theirs. As a result, homosexuals were even more marginalized because their rights were not yet even the subject of debate in society at large.

In 1965, Congress had again amended the immigration law, adding "sexual deviation" to a list of prohibitions that included "psychopathic personality." Congress said it was acting to "resolve any doubt" about whom it intended to bar. Since the amendment was not retroactive, it technically didn't apply to Boutilier. Yet by revising the immigration law to explicitly target "sexual deviation"—a term then commonly equated with homosexuality—Congress signaled that it wanted "psychopathic personality" to be read as a euphemism for "homosexual."

Also in 1965, Abe Fortas joined the Supreme Court, filling the vacancy that President Johnson had created by persuading Goldberg to leave. Fortas tends to be remembered as a Johnson crony—the fat-cat corporate attorney nominated for the court without his consent by a manipulative president and as a justice who kept too-close ties to a sitting president. Yet Fortas was a man of more backbone and intellectual depth than might be imagined in someone commonly recalled as residing in a president's back pocket.

Like Goldberg, Fortas was the son of impoverished Jewish immigrants. As a Memphis youth, he developed into a talented violinist and debater. The violin became a lifelong joy; even as a justice he played in a string quartet. Debate led him to Yale law school. There he became a protégé of a professor who also had escaped the downward pull of poverty, William O. Douglas. After graduating second in his class, Fortas spent a decade in New Deal government posts, including a stint working for Douglas at the new Securities and Exchange Commission.

After entering private practice in 1946, Fortas amassed a small fortune. That enabled him to flaunt the lavish trappings of wealth, such as having an office desk made from a Victorian grand piano and—as the story goes—playing his violin in the backseat of his Rolls Royce.

Early in his legal career, Fortas, a "fine-boned, polite, soft-spoken . . . refined" man made an unlikely friend—the earthy, pushy, domineering Congressman Lyndon Johnson. Fortas won Johnson's abiding thanks by deftly rescuing him from a ballot-box–stuffing scandal.

While cashing in by representing big business, Fortas fought free of charge for the little guy. He was the ultimate "limousine liberal" before that became a pejorative phrase. As McCarthyite madness gripped the capital, Fortas defended government officials smeared with trumped-up accusations of disloyalty. And Fortas—as gifted in writing clear, concise legal briefs as he was in arguing—was the attorney who secured the famous "Gideon's Trumpet" Supreme Court decision establishing the right of indigent accused criminals to have court-appointed attorneys. In 1954, he successfully challenged rules governing the insanity defense. "Using his knowledge of psychiatry gained from serving as a trustee of the William Alanson White Psychiatric Foundation and as a frequent contributor to psychiatric journals, Fortas persuaded [federal courts] to use new scientific evidence in creating a broader competency test," notes biographer Bruce Allen Murphy. Thus, when Fortas became a justice at 55, he brought with him a firm grasp of psychiatry and a belief that law should keep up with science.

Once on the court, Fortas continued using all the tools at his disposal to defend individual rights. "He was not afraid to interpret loosely . . . the Constitution in order to safeguard the rights of others, . . ." Murphy says. "For Abe Fortas, the very job of a jurist was to expand the rights of the Constitution in order to protect minorities, the downtrodden, and the oppressed."

"A Homo Might or Might Not Be Psychotic"

In *Boutilier v. INS*, Fortas and the eight more senior justices had to wrestle with a psychiatric term and the question of how far the INS and/or Congress could legitimately stretch it. Clive Boutilier was no psychopath, according to the psychiatrists hired by his legal team. But what was psychiatry's view of homosexuality at that time? In 1952, the year that Congress passed the immigration law in question, the American Psychiatric Association (APA) adopted its first formal list of mental illnesses. Homosexuality was counted among them. It was classed among "sociopathic personality disturbances," disorders "characterized by the absence of subjectively experienced distress or anxiety despite the presence of profound pathology," Ronald Bayer writes in *Homosexuality and American Psychiatry*. In the hyper-conformist 1950s, homosexuals were automatically diagnosed as mentally ill because they didn't fit in. As the psychiatrists' diagnostic manual explained, people with sociopathic personality disturbances were "ill primarily in terms of society and of conformity with the prevailing cultural milieu."

(After a long debate, the Mattachine Society of Washington voted in 1965 that "homosexuality is not a sickness." The APA eventually agreed in 1973—six years after the justices finished tussling with the INS diagnosis of Clive Boutilier.)

Once the justices accepted *Boutilier v. INS*, Boutilier's attorneys filed their written brief, arguing that the case grew out of the government's misunderstanding of homosexuality: "The source of the evil lies in the apparent belief that there is some kind of recognizable human being that is a 'homosexual'—like one might recognize a 'redhead'. . . . By and large homosexuality is a kind of behavior, evidently very widespread, and not the manifestation of a particular kind of person. . . . [N]ot everyone who engages in a homosexual act is suffering from a psychopathic disorder."

Boutilier's attorneys argued for the right to engage in homosexual behavior, saying, "In the light of modern scientific investigation, making private, consensual homosexual practices between adults the subject of oppressive legislation and ostracism is reminiscent of history's other witch hunts. To the extent that the statute involved here applies sanctions to persons labeled 'homosexuals' . . . it is factually wrong, socially wasteful and morally inexcusable."

Solicitor General Marshall's brief countered that Congress intended to exclude "homosexuals and other sexual deviates." While conceding that it might sometimes be difficult to know whether the "homosexual" label fit, Marshall nevertheless saw "no ambiguity" about Boutilier.

In a memo preparing the chief justice for oral arguments, clerk Douglas Kranwinkle, who was aware of having had several gay friends in college and law school, recommended taking Boutilier's side. Since the deportation order was largely based on Boutilier's behavior in this country, the law should have provided a clearer warning, he told Warren.

Manhattan lawyer Blanch Freedman went first when the court heard oral arguments on March 14, 1967. In a confident-sounding voice, she briskly summarized the case of her 33-year-old client. She assured the justices that Boutilier "could have, and in all probability would have, refrained" from homosexual conduct if he'd been properly warned. In fact, she said, he had refrained from it in the years since learning it could result in deportation. "He does not suffer from any condition," she insisted. Justice Stewart took some wind out of her warning argument by noting that the existence of criminal laws against certain homosexual acts had not prevented Boutilier from having sex.

Justice Department attorney Nathan Lewin followed with a half-hour presentation stressing the government's view that "Congress did consider [homosexuality] a condition. And that Congress did intend to encompass that condition within the words used in the statute."

Perhaps because he knew more about psychiatry than most of the court, Fortas was Lewin's most persistent and aggressive questioner. Fortas interrupted Lewin to point out that the Public Health Service had advised Congress that not all homosexuals were psychopaths. In response to one Fortas question, Lewin said the INS was targeting homosexuals, not everyone who might have engaged in an isolated homosexual act.

Fortas asked, "[What if] Congress had said, instead of 'psychopathic personality,' 'afflicted with dandruff' and the legislative history showed they meant to include homosexuals?" Lewin responded that the hypothetical situation wasn't comparable to the actual INS policy. Fortas pressed Lewin on whether homosexuals were, in fact, the only people deported as "psychopathic." The government attorney did not know.

Firing pointed questions during oral argument was Fortas's best chance to influence his colleagues. Tradition dictated that when the court met in private three days later, Fortas, as the most junior justice, would get to speak only after the others had voted.

On March 17, 1967, in their small private conference room, Chief Justice Warren started the *Boutilier* discussion. Three years earlier, Warren had sided in conference with Fleuti. Black, Douglas and Brennan had joined him in wanting to declare the INS policy unconstitutionally vague. If, as seemed likely, Fortas also saw that policy as fatally flawed, Boutilier and similarly situated homosexuals would escape deportation—provided the original four votes held tight.

Warren's vote against the INS had been shaky in *Fleuti*, but he reiterated it in *Boutilier*, according to the conference notes of Douglas and Fortas. Saying his decision did not "rest on vagueness," Warren said, "Congress spoke meaningfully but in a medical sense a homo might or might not be psychotic." Warren added that "very little" of Boutilier's homosexual behavior occurred before he became a U.S. resident.

Then Justice Hugo Black voted, and Boutilier lost his fight to stay in the country that had been his adopted home for 11 years. When voting in *Fleuti,* Black had flatly pronounced the deportation law as interpreted by the INS "too vague." But the invisible thumb Congress had slipped onto the scales of justice when rewriting the law in 1965 apparently made Black shift his position. "Stat[ute] can be construed either way—psychopathic personality means sexual deviate," Black said in voting to affirm the lower court's ruling against Boutilier. Although Black was casting what would be the decisive vote in one of the Supreme Court's most anti-homosexual decisions, he didn't have strong feelings about his position. In fact, he said he would be willing to go along with the opposite decision. "If majority thinks homos are not included, [Black will] not dissent," Douglas recorded in his conference notes.

Soon after being appointed to the court in 1937 by Franklin D. Roosevelt, Black began turning the institution toward protection of the downtrodden. Ironically, shortly after his confirmation, the Alabamian was caught up in a furor over his having joined the Ku Klux Klan in 1923. It died down only after he made a national radio address saying that he'd resigned from the KKK in 1925 and that his Senate record proved he wasn't a bigot.

Although he believed in interpreting the Constitution's language strictly, Black saw the Constitution and the court as the protectors of human rights. He authored a 1940 decision that eloquently overturned the death sentences of four black men coerced into falsely confessing to murder. Black had declared that it was the court's duty to be a refuge for "nonconforming victims of prejudice" being punished for "manufactured crime." Yet a quarter-century later, Black didn't see homosexuals as nonconforming victims of prejudice being punished for manufactured crime and manufactured mental illness. In 1967, Black apparently could dismiss homosexuals as "deviants" without seeing that he was voting to deport Boutilier for nonconformity.

As the justices' voting continued, Douglas joined Warren in siding with Boutilier. Douglas noted that the law's 1965 amendment "adds 'sexual deviates,'" which he took as a congressional admission that the original language wasn't sufficient to bar all homosexual aliens.

Predictably, Clark voted against Boutilier, saying that "sex perversion was included in psychopathic personality." Harlan also voted against Boutilier. Brennan voted to reverse it, saying that he agreed with the chief justice. Stewart, voting against Boutilier, then said the question of "notice is not important here. Congress intends to ban homos." Byron White cast the fifth vote to affirm the lower court's ruling against Boutilier.

Fortas closed out the discussion by voting to reverse the lower court. His reading of the Public Health Service's stance was that "ordinarily a homo is a psycho but many are not," according to Douglas's notes.

As senior justice in the majority, Black had the power to decide who would write for the court, just as he had in *Manual*. Ten days after the 5-to-4 conference vote, he tapped Clark. After a three-year wait, Clark would finally get the chance to put the court's stamp of approval on the INS policy labeling homosexual aliens sick and deportable. The fact that Chief Justice Warren didn't assign any of the three opinions written in homosexual cases during his tenure is an indication of how little a role he played in shaping the court's posture toward homosexuality.

The 67-year-old Clark had announced his retirement by the time he was assigned to write for the majority in *Boutilier*. Fellow Texan Lyndon Johnson was elevating Clark's son, Ramsey, to attorney general. Saying he was "filled with both pride and joy over Ramsey's nomination," the elder Clark had decided to step down to avoid conflict-of-interest questions that might arise from having to decide cases involving a Justice Department led by his son.

Clark often worked up his own first drafts. But with the court's pace picking up as it headed toward the close of his 18th and final term, Clark enlisted the help of clerk Stuart Ross. The two never discussed the justice's attitudes toward homosexuality. Ross, now a Washington, D.C., trial lawyer, says, "There was never any talk of, 'God, let's keep the homos out!'. . . For him, this was a case where the government was right: The Congress was clear."

Ross's task was to craft language reflecting Clark's outlook. Clark generally had what his son characterizes as a "pro-government, pro-prosecution" bent. Before being appointed to the high court in 1949 by Truman, Clark had worked his way up through the Justice Department to attorney general. Earlier, he'd been an assistant district attorney in Dallas, then gone into private practice. Over the course of his career, he developed a very mixed human-rights record. After the bombing of Pearl Harbor, he was in charge of corralling Japanese Americans into detention camps. He later called that "the biggest mistake in my life." As attorney general, Clark aggressively prosecuted accused Communists and published lists of allegedly subversive groups.

Once on the Supreme Court, Clark first sided with the government against civil liberties, especially in national security cases. Gradually, he moderated his views, writing, for example, the 1961 decision barring courtroom use of illegal evidence. On race, Chief Justice Warren could count on Clark as a reliable vote against segregation.

Warren also counted on Clark's good relations with the fellow southerners who controlled key congressional committees. Year after year, the chief dispatched Clark to sweet-talk Congress into looking favorably upon the court's budget request. Clark had worked closely with the INS while at Justice and maintained fond friendships with INS officials while on the court, according to his son. *Boutilier* gave Clark the opportunity to endorse what he saw as the INS's proper interpretation of Congress's intent.

"I remember he was pretty convinced that the Congress, in its infinite wisdom, had meant to exclude people who at the time of entry had engaged in homosexual activity," Ross says.

Soon after getting his *Boutilier* assignment, Ross knocked out a 14-page, double-spaced draft. Clark drew on Ross's work in writing a longhand draft that underwent only minor changes before becoming the court's official decision. Clark's chief conclusion was, "Congress used the phrase 'psychopathic personality' not in the clinical sense, but to effectuate its purpose to exclude from entry all homosexuals and other sex perverts."

Like Justice Harlan's decision for the court in *Manual*, Clark brushed psychiatrists aside—though with Harlan that had worked in homosexuals' favor. Clark wrote that "the test here is what the Congress intended, not what differing psychiatrists think."

With a double dose of *Alice in Wonderland* reasoning, Clark concluded that a word meant whatever the Supreme Court thought that the Congress wanted it to mean. In Clark's defense, Ross says, "Well, the thing about this case was: What the hell is a 'psychopathic personality'? I expect you could get enough 'experts' to give you a listing of 800 things that would constitute a 'psychopathic personality'."

Clark's decision summarized Boutilier's sexual history, calling him a "passive participant" in his first homosexual encounter but an "active participant" the next time. "[W]hen petitioner first presented himself at our border for entrance, he was already afflicted with homosexuality.

The pattern was cut, and under it he was not admissible." That language remained unchanged from Clark's handwritten draft to the court's published opinion.

Three decades after Clark coined the phrase "afflicted with homosexuality," that language is jarring, offensive to many ears. Stuart Ross says he has always been bothered by it. "I had trouble in the case with the use of the word 'afflicted.' I had trouble with that personally. Back then, the word 'afflicted' sounded inappropriate," he says, recalling that he'd had gay friends at George Washington University law school. To Ross, homosexuality "was never a threatening thing. They were just gay people."

A majority of the Supreme Court in 1967 had no problem with characterizing homosexuality as an affliction. Clark circulated his opinion April 20. Justices Black and White signed onto it the next day. Harlan soon joined them.

Harlan clerk Burt Rein, who worked on *Boutilier*, said Harlan was concerned solely with determining whether the INS was following Congress's wishes. As for Harlan's attitudes toward homosexuality, Rein said, "He would be appalled if anyone said he decided a case on that basis."

On May 16, Stewart's vote gave Clark "a court," a majority. No justice asked Clark for substantive changes.

Once it was clear the court would stick with its conference decision to uphold the constitutionality of closing U.S. borders to homosexuals by automatically diagnosing them as psychopaths, Chief Justice Warren added his name to Clark's opinion. Clark, more gracious than some of his egotistical brethren, congratulated Ross when the chief justice joined. Ross was delighted because the chief was his hero. Ross didn't learn until three decades later that Warren's May 19 vote was a switch away from his shaky conference vote in Boutilier's favor.

"The chief led a lot of revolutions, but I'm not so sure the chief necessarily had focused in on the rights of lesbian and gay people back then. It might not have been a major concern for him. And he was of a different era," Ross noted. "Those guys [the justices of that era] probably thought a homosexual was somebody who tried to pick you up when you were hitchhiking. It could well be that's why the chief decided to switch."

Warren clerk Douglas Kranwinkle says, "I remember the case, but I can't remember at all what caused the chief to flop around. The chief hated 5-4 decisions. He just felt the court ought to be not as badly split as that. And he would sometimes, if he didn't feel strongly on an issue, move off the minority to the majority just to make it 6-3 rather than 5-4. That could have been what happened here."

To Chief Justice Warren, one of the greatest civil rights advocates in American history, the court risked damaging its greatest intangible asset—its authority—if it appeared indecisive. Protecting that authority was vital to Warren; protecting homosexuals clearly was not.

A Beloved Homosexual Nephew

The court's 6-3 *Boutilier* decision is one of the last to bear Tom Clark's name. Like Clark's dissents in both the *Fleuti* deportation case and the *Manual* beefcake case, his *Boutilier* ruling is bereft of empathy for homosexuals. While there is not the overt animosity some justices would show later, there is also no recognition of the havoc the decision would wreak in the lives of Boutilier and many others. Clark's opinion was as impersonal as if the court were ruling on whether a law barring importation of "carrots" could be used to block all foreign turnips.

Clark's decision certainly didn't sound as if it had been written by a man who knew his nephew was homosexual and who treated him like a beloved son. But that, in fact, was the case.

Tom Clark was like a father to his younger brother's son, Bobby Clark, according to both of the justice's children. Tom Clark's brother, Bob, had married a wealthy woman whose family pampered the couple's only child. Bobby Clark, who wore little camel's hair coats as a preschooler, was just too spoiled, in the eyes of the Clark side of the family. Bobby and his father "had a terribly strained relationship from the earliest childhood," recalls Ramsey Clark, who was always "very fond" of his younger cousin. Bob Clark had such a poor relationship with his son that when he gave Bobby an Oldsmobile convertible as a high school graduation present Ramsey Clark was asked to deliver it.

Tom Clark stepped into the void created in Bobby Clark's life by the absence of his real father. And Bobby Clark was closer to his Aunt Mary, Tom Clark's wife, than he was to his own mother. By the 1960s, the Clarks knew Bobby was homosexual. "I know his father had a hard time with it, a very hard time with it. . . . I'm not sure I heard Dad ever talk about it, although I know he certainly knew," Ramsey Clark says.

His sister, Mimi Clark Gronlund, agrees. Yet, she says, "it's not a subject that he would have opened up a discussion about. I mean, he would talk about Bobby but not in those terms or that aspect of his life." Gronlund thinks her father "disapproved of" homosexuality. "On the other hand," she says, "he was extremely compassionate. And on an individual basis I don't think he would let that really bother him that much. He would never, ever, sever a relationship or even let a relationship with a family member cool because he learned something like that."

Looking back, Ramsey Clark says,

> There was nothing about my father's attitudes toward homosexuality that overcame his humanity toward his nephew. That's very clear to me. I have to say I don't think he looked at Bobby as the all-American boy, which he wasn't. He wasn't a Tom Sawyer or even a Boy Scout. . . .
>
> Dad would have fought for Bobby. I have no question about it—and not as an injured member of the family or a different member of the family but as a member of the family. He was just intensely loyal. You could feel he had no sense of common interest with Bobby. But he was able to do something that Bobby's own father couldn't do. And that is to overcome that [lack of common interest]. Whenever Bobby was around [my parents] would take him out to dinner. If it was Christmas or Thanksgiving or something like that, he would always be there when he was in Washington.

Bobby Clark was a opera aficionado and was instrumental in bringing world-famous soprano Maria Callas to sing in Dallas in the 1950s, Ramsey Clark recalls. "He had a ear you can't believe. If anybody made the slightest off-key sound, he would sneer. He wasn't impolite. He wasn't like the Italians. He didn't throw vegetables or anything, but he was a perfectionist. He was close to Joan Sutherland. But Callas he absolutely adored. It was quite beautiful, really. And she was fond of him." Bobby Clark eventually moved to Paris and lived near Callas.

Bobby Clark was very open about his homosexuality with his cousin Ramsey, who visited him several times at a predominantly gay section of Fire Island in the early 1960s. Over the years, Bobby Clark had a "very rough time" with alcoholism, at times drinking several bottles of champagne a day and periodically having to be institutionalized. It may well be, according to Ramsey Clark, that Justice Clark thought Bobby's homosexuality "was what caused the alcoholism, or vice versa."

In 1965 or 1966, shortly before Justice Clark wrote the court's *Boutilier* decision, Bobby Clark was severely beaten by a man he'd picked up in Vienna. Ramsey Clark says his cousin told him the truth but told others that he'd fainted, fallen and hurt himself. "He was hospitalized, and he was in really bad shape," Ramsey Clark says. "I remember thinking at that time that my father was really quite heroic about trying to help Bobby because he got on the phone and called the embassy over there personally."

Justice Clark didn't live to see his nephew turn his life around after getting involved with "a really wonderful Frenchman," as Ramsey Clark puts it. "Dad died in '77. That was very close to the time that Bobby was getting together with Bernard, the man he spent 20 years with. I don't think Dad ever knew about or met Bernard. On the other hand, Mother had them [stay] in her home whenever they came to Washington. . . . She knew, of course, that there was a homosexual relationship there. It didn't cause her to say, 'You're not welcome.' Quite the contrary."

Ramsey Clark's sister adds that she's talked with their mother "about how lucky Bobby was to find someone like the young man he lived with for a number of years. . . . My cousin was not an easy person. He was a very difficult person—and it had nothing to do with sex. . . . I think Mother—and I think my father would have felt the same way—felt that this relationship was a very positive thing and that Bobby was lucky to have it."

Bobby Clark spent the last 20 years of his life in France and died there in 1996. He was "a wonderful person who had a sad life. Very, very bright. Very cultured," Ramsey Clark recalls.

Under the INS policy that Justice Clark upheld as constitutional, the foreigner credited with being a wonderful partner to Bobby Clark could not have immigrated to the United States. Unbeknownst to Justice Clark, his *Boutilier* decision forced his beloved nephew to choose between living in his own country and living with the man who gave him his best chance at happiness.

Justice Clark's children describe him as a compassionate but prudish man, as an Eagle Scout who grew up before World War I. "I don't remember ever discussing homosexuality with him. I don't remember ever discussing sex with him or Mother. They would have been very embarrassed and shocked just to discuss sex generally," Ramsey Clark says. He doesn't recall his father making derogatory remarks about homosexuals or saying someone must be homosexual. "It's hard to believe, probably, in this generation but then it was a very serious thing to say that about somebody. In those days, it was worse than being a Communist," Ramsey Clark says.

Yet, Ramsey Clark adds, "I never had any sense of any deep prejudice [in my father] about homosexuality. . . . Ordinarily, if there's strong prejudice, you get the message. It's very difficult to conceal a strong prejudice from children. And I could name a number of prejudices I believe my father had."

Before Ramsey Clark became attorney general, he and his father had a strict unspoken policy of never discussing law with each other since they never knew which of Ramsey's cases might end up before the Supreme Court. "I have never tried to make an analysis of my father's opinions," Ramsey Clark remarked after agreeing to review his father's homosexual cases.

The hallmark of Ramsey Clark's career since leaving government service has been standing up for the legal rights of pariahs, such as the accused mastermind of the World Trade Center bombing. As one who believes in taking a very humanistic and civil libertarian approach to the law, Ramsey Clark was bothered by reading his father's *Boutilier* decision. "The use of the word 'afflicted' is very offensive to me and not true. If words have meaning, this is not an 'affliction.' But I have great trouble with the phrase 'psychopathic personality.' I don't think that tells you a damn thing, except maybe we don't like these people. That's extremely vicious stuff," he said. Yet, he concluded, "As bad as *Boutilier* is, I don't think you can make the case that it shows strong emotional feelings or animus toward homosexuals."

Ramsey Clark's overall conclusion about his father's approach to homosexual cases is, "The votes were generally bad, but the votes were based upon an approach that was neutral as far as homosexuality is concerned." Justice Clark's handling of those cases shows, according to his son, that "he is one of the judges that believes you can identify objective legal standards by legal reasoning and you have an absolute duty to keep your personal emotions out. . . . I'm not sure you can keep your emotions out, so you're misleading yourself or others. But beyond that, I'm not sure that you want to keep compassion out. . . . What judges are supposed to do is protect fundamental rights even against the will of the overwhelming majority."

A librarian, not a lawyer, Justice Clark's daughter sees an element of compassion peeking through the *Boutilier* opinion. "An 'affliction'— there's an aspect of being a victim. You know, he doesn't sound like he would necessarily be judgmental. He saw this person as 'afflicted' with something that maybe to some extent was beyond his or her control," she remarked. "My father, I've never really known a more compassion- ate person, but he was also a product of his time. And that was certainly an unfavorable era for homosexuals."

As for the seeming contradiction between her father's willingness— perhaps eagerness—to deport homosexuals and his lovingly paternal re- lationship with his homosexual nephew, she observes, "It's one thing to rule on something that is impersonal and then can be totally different when it happens to be someone you know and is a member of your own family, particularly."

A Dissenting Diagnosis

Justice Clark's *Boutilier* opinion attracted its sixth vote—the chief jus- tice's—the day after Justice William O. Douglas circulated a dissent attacking the McCarthyite labeling of people as outcasts. Undeniably brilliant, Douglas was also arrogant, cantankerous and a loner. He put a far higher premium on speaking his own mind than on writing opin- ions that would attract the support of a majority of his brethren. In fact, Douglas, an avid outdoorsman, often seemed to prefer to blaze his own trail. Appointed in 1939 by poker buddy Franklin Roosevelt, he developed into an ardent civil libertarian and judicial activist. He cared far less about the intent of Congress or prior rulings than about protecting the downtrodden. More worldly than most justices, Doug- las traveled the globe, absorbing as much as he could from other cul- tures.

Even Douglas's personal life and habits set him apart. A man ahead of his time in many ways, Douglas had tousled hair and rumpled clothes that today would get him mistaken for a stylish college professor. But in the regimented gray flannel suit era, his appearance probably struck many observers as almost subversively sloppy. And on a court dominated by men who seem to have mated for life, Douglas was a 68-year-old newlywed in 1967. He'd married his fourth wife, Cathy, the year before, when she was 23. Their age difference made them the object of public comment ranging from good-natured ribbing to outright ridicule.

Douglas derided his court work as less than a full-time job. He proved the point by cranking out travel journals, autobiographies and speeches. He leaned on clerks less than many justices—far less than most recent justices—but sometimes overestimated his ability to juggle. Fortas, who counted Douglas as a personal hero and a genius, remarked that "unfortunately Bill just got bored, and so, in his later years, he got sloppy in writing his opinions."

Douglas's *Boutilier* dissent, written 28 years into his 36-year stint on the court, is a slapdash muddle with glaringly contradictory attitudes toward homosexuality. In fairness to Douglas, one source of the problem, no doubt, was the confused state of psychiatric opinion. Douglas's dissent attempted to be the very things that Clark's opinion wasn't—passionate, compassionate, scientific, sexually sophisticated and undeferential to either lawmakers or bureaucrats. What fails to come across in Douglas's dissent is that he was, according to his widow, Cathy Douglas Stone, "completely comfortable with homosexuality."

Douglas's dissent began boldly by declaring that the term "psychopathic personality" was unconstitutionally vague, period—not just when used to target homosexual immigrants. "The term 'psychopathic personality' is a treacherous one like 'communist' or in an earlier ear 'Bolshevik.' A label of this kind when freely used may mean only an unpopular person. It is much too vague by constitutional standards for the imposition of penalties or punishment." Citing psychiatric texts showing the term was so amorphous as to be essentially meaningless, Douglas argued the immigration law's use of the term handed bureaucrats a net in which "anyone can be caught who is unpopular, who is off-beat, who is nonconformist."

The dissent quickly became mired in an intellectual morass. Douglas clearly wanted to make a statement about the nature of homosexuality, but what he wanted to say is anything but clear. His was a unique undertaking. Neither before nor since has an official Supreme Court opinion attempted to delve deeply into the subject.

Douglas portrayed homosexuals as victims of arrested development, people to be pitied rather than persecuted. His original draft, not circulated to the rest of the court, was considerably more empathetic than his final version, a close examination of his papers shows. In between the first and final versions, an uncharacteristically hostile footnote was added, then dropped. The impression created by reading Douglas's various rewrites isn't that his attitudes toward homosexuality were shifting but that he kept finding quotes that he wanted to slap into his work.

The great pity, from the perspective of anyone favoring equal rights for homosexuals, is that Douglas wanted to be scientifically up-to-date yet shows no sign of being aware of groundbreaking psychological research that was already a decade old: By 1957, Dr. Evelyn Hooker was publishing her evidence that homosexual men were as mentally healthy as their heterosexual counterparts.

After reading Douglas's first draft, Lewis Merrifield, Douglas's only clerk during the 1966–67 term, recommended tightening the prose, dropping most of the discussion of homosexuality. Unlike justices who treated their unseasoned assistants as trusted junior partners or beloved sons, Douglas brusquely dealt with his as, well, clerks. He ignored Merrifield's advice.

Douglas dove into his examination of homosexuality by quoting from books on criminal psychiatry dating from the 1940s. He wrote, "Those 'who fail to reach sexual maturity (hetero-sexuality), and who remain at a narcissistic or homosexual stage' are the products 'of heredity, of glandular dysfunction, [or] of environmental circumstances.'"

In his original draft, Douglas moved from there immediately into a sympathetic quote, apparently from the same source. That paragraph, missing from his published dissent, read: "We should not condemn them; we have no right to do so, they are as much the victims of their constitutions as we are of ours, and we can only step in when their conduct becomes subversive of society, or when they request help so as to enable them to reach a more mature level. Because of this anomaly only in their sexual development we are not entitled to describe them as psychopaths; in all other respects they may be perfectly decent, law-abiding citizens."

The biggest shift in tone between the dissent's first and final versions came next, when Douglas made his own declaration about homosexuality before moving into a quote from *Crime and the Human Mind*, a 1944 text. Douglas originally stated, "The homosexual is one, who but for the grace of God, might be almost anyone: 'One may within certain limits say that the homosexual is an individual who really belongs to the opposite sex. All people have originally bisexual tendencies which are more or less developed.'" Douglas's published dissent instead began, "The homosexual is one, who by some freak, is the product of an arrested development."

Although the freak-of-nature attitude is now officially recorded as Douglas's perspective, that's not how he sounded at home, according to Cathy Douglas Stone. "That was never the attitude," she insists. "That earlier ['but for the grace of God'] phrase is much more characteristic of Bill. And one which he used in many contexts." He often used it, she says, in talking about the necessity of standing up for the defenseless, for people who were especially vulnerable to government harassment simply because they lacked power or money. Douglas had grown up poor in rural Yakima, Washington. Later, as a man of power and privilege, he never forgot having had to dodge policemen as he hopped freight trains as a law student too poor to buy a ticket.

In writing about homosexuality, Douglas tried with only partial success to look beyond the fact that it was forbidden. His dissent cited Freud, Second Circuit Judge Leonard Moore's list of great homosexuals and Kinsey's belief that, "It is not possible to insist that any departure from the sexual mores, or any participation in socially taboo activities, always or even usually, involves a neurosis or psychosis. . . .'" On his own, Douglas added, "It is common knowledge that in this century homosexuals have risen high in our own public service—both in Congress and in the Executive Branch—and have served with distinction."

Douglas's first draft concluded that it has not been determined whether Boutilier "is 'afflicted' in the statutory sense." But by his final draft, Douglas had followed Judge Moore's lead in saying that Boutilier wasn't enough of a homosexual to be deportable. Suddenly, Douglas had shifted from protecting homosexuals from McCarthyite labeling to protecting one man as someone who should be forgiven a few slips off the prescribed heterosexual path. Did Douglas forget that he'd dismissed "psychopathic personality" as a meaningless "epithet" and turned his nose up at the notion that breaking sexual taboos is necessarily sick?

"'Afflicted' means possessed or dominated by," Douglas wrote in his published dissent. "Occasional acts would not seem sufficient. 'Afflicted' means a way of life, an accustomed pattern of conduct. Whatever disagreement there is as to the meaning of 'psychopathic personality,' it has generally been understood to refer to a consistent, lifelong pattern of behavior conflicting with social norms without accompanying guilt. . . . Nothing of that character was shown to exist at time of [Boutilier's] entry. The fact that he presently has a problem, as one psychiatrist said, does not mean that he is or was necessarily 'afflicted' with homosexuality."

In the end, Douglas, too, was casting his vote in favor of the notion that homosexuality was an affliction.

The original draft not only had ended on what at least sounded like a more supportive note for all homosexuals but also had included a quite sympathetic "Appendix," as Douglas labeled a Murray Schumach news analysis piece recently clipped from *The New York Times*. The original header was "Morals," but Douglas kept only the subhead, "On the Third Sex." Schumach described how Columbia University's recognition of a campus homosexual-rights group "brought a few rays of sunshine to the twilight world that alternates between the furtive and the flagrant." The climate for New York City homosexuals "has improved decidedly," he wrote, citing the fact that prospective city employees no longer had to say whether they were "parolees, unwed mothers or homosexuals." An "important police official" said, "A guy can mince down the street with marcelled blond hair and if he doesn't bother anyone it is not illegal." The article concluded with a "self-styled homosexual" saying, "Things are better, in New York anyhow, but none of us is ever going to see the day when we are treated as humans."

If Douglas wanted his Appendix to tweak the consciences of his colleagues, he undercut himself. Before circulating his dissent, he tacked an aggressively anti-homosexual footnote onto the heart-rending quote at the end of his Appendix. Excerpted from psychiatrist Edmund Bergler's 1956 diatribe, *Homosexuality: Disease or Way of Life?*, it claimed: "Homosexuals are essentially disagreeable people, regardless of their pleasant or unpleasant outward manner. . . . Like all psychic masochists, they are subservient when confronted with a stronger person, merciless when in power, unscruplous [*sic*] about trampling on a weaker person. The only language their unconscious understands is brute force. . . ."

After Douglas circulated his dissent, Fortas—at the urging of clerk John Griffiths—asked him to "consider knocking out the Appendix." Douglas was probably more open to listening to Fortas than anyone else in a case involving psychiatry. Not only did Fortas have considerable knowledge, he also had encouraged Douglas's interest. In 1954, for example, Fortas had successfully lobbied Douglas to become a trustee of the William Alanson White Psychiatric Foundation, telling him that "a formal connection is enough to cause me to keep in touch with this fascinating, infant art."

Fortas and Douglas had always been close. Douglas had been Fortas's best man. In sexual matters, Douglas saw most of his colleagues as prudes of limited experience. He knew Fortas, however, had a ribald sense of humor, one that had shown itself when the court heard arguments in a 1967 interracial marriage case, *Loving v. Virginia*. Fortas penned doggerel verses that day. He seems to have passed them like a naughty schoolboy while he and Douglas were supposed to be listening to attorneys argue. One poem makes a racy allusion to oral sex, an activity that Fortas and Douglas apparently did not consider an unspeakable "crime against nature":

To WOD—a poem—No. 395
[*Loving's* case number] 4/10, 1967

A number of spouses
Is not like grouses—
Many spouses add up to spice
Many grouse mean lots of grice.
A grouse in hand is worth a lot
A spouse in hand may be or not
But grice in the bush are wasted
While spice in the bush may be tasted.

—A.F.

A month later, when Fortas sent his more serious memo on Boutilier, Douglas responded by deleting both his sympathetic Appendix and the ferociously anti-homosexual footnote grafted onto it. Douglas's dissent attracted only Fortas's support.

Justice William J. Brennan Jr. dissented separately, "for the reasons stated by Judge Moore of the Court of Appeals," but making no other comment. In taking a lower court judge's dissent as his own, Brennan was paying Moore a very high compliment. Moore focused on the human cost of the INS's automatic classification of homosexual aliens as deportable; Brennan, a man of enormous empathy, wanted to do the same.

The court's 6-to-3 decision against Boutilier was not preordained by its makeup in 1967. It's not difficult to imagine there having instead been a six-man majority—Douglas, Fortas, Brennan, Warren, Black and Harlan—in Boutilier's favor. Warren, after all, had sided with Boutilier in conference. Douglas might have held the prudish chief justice by drafting a dissent that was less outrageously sexual. But Douglas "thought it was his role to shake people up, including his brethren, and to point out to them their Sunday School flaws," his widow recalls.

Douglas's published *Boutilier* dissent reads in places as if he were trying to shock colleagues such as Warren. Douglas quotes Kinsey as concluding, "The impression that such 'sexual irregularities' as 'excessive' masturbation, pre-marital intercourse, responsibility for a pre-marital pregnancy, extra-marital intercourse, mouth-genital contacts, homosexual activity, or animal intercourse, always produce psychoses and abnormal personalities is based upon the fact that the persons who do go to professional sources for advice are upset by these things." Douglas could not have expected Warren to sign on to an opinion that appeared to condone bestiality.

A more sharply focused Douglas dissent that undermined the undeniably weak argument that the INS was merely following the original intent of Congress might well have drawn both Black and Harlan. Such an opinion could have emphasized that all pending legislation dies at the end of each two-year Congress. It is doubtful that the legislative history of a law can accurately be said to start before the Congress in which it passed. Thus, a Senate subcommittee report in the 81st Congress on the meaning of "psychopathic personality" might not accurately reflect what the 82nd Congress meant by using that ambiguous phrase in the 1952 immigration law. In *Fleuti*, Black had pushed for a finding of unconstitutional vagueness. Although Black's position had changed by *Boutilier*, he signaled his opinion was not set in stone. Meanwhile, Harlan, Mr. Judicial Restraint, might well have supported

Boutilier if he could have been persuaded that doing so would not have violated Congress's intent. Harlan had proven with his 1962 *Manual* beefcake magazine opinion that he had no objection to siding with a homosexual litigant.

Brennan was a master at crafting compromises that could overcome or sidestep the objections of enough justices to win a majority. Although the glad-handing Irishman with twinkling blue eyes bristled at being described as a politician, he clearly focused on results and on trying to steer the court in the humanitarian direction he believed it ought to go. He apparently made no attempt to control the outcome of *Boutilier v. INS*, however.

Despite what—at least from the gay-rights perspective of today—appears to be its shortcomings, Douglas's dissent stood up more explicitly for the basic civil rights of homosexuals than anything else written by a justice before 1985. Douglas protested the government's slapping pejorative labels on homosexuals and singling them out for punishment because their sex lives deviated from the popular conception of normalcy. Cathy Douglas Stone is certain her husband considered sodomy laws unconstitutional, explaining that "the whole panoply of restrictions on consensual adult behavior was such an anathema to him."

The Lesbian Couple Next Door

In his 1974 autobiography, *Go East, Young Man*, Douglas wrote about meeting "the first homosexual I ever knew" while working his way through college.

> I liked him for his humor, friendship, and helpfulness. I had only normal feelings toward him, and I suppose that if in those days I had been asked to name the 10 men I most admired, he would have been on the list. One day when we were working alone he grabbed me and expressed his sexual interest in an unmistakable way. I pushed him away and left, and I avoided him thereafter. I was not angry, I was only sad.
>
> Years later I discovered from legal cases and from books the nature of the "disease." I knew one United States senator who was reputed to be homosexual and one undersecretary of State. I learned that Lafayette Park, opposite the White House, . . . became at dusk the

meeting place for homosexuals. Friends of mine, innocently relaxing there, had been accosted. I later learned that the District of Columbia hires 12 men whose sole job is to patrol parks and men's rooms trying to induce homosexuals to solicit them. . . .

I saw these miserable people hounded and solicited by the police; many were driven from the lower echelons of government. I learned that the condition is not explicable in terms of the Puritan ethic. I also learned that some who denounce homosexuality the loudest and proclaim against it the most vociferously may be the ones closest to being its victims.

Douglas's sensitivity to homosexuals arose out of his overall championing of individual rights, which he considered one of the twin pillars of his government service. The other was protection of the great outdoors. "I believe that he believed that there is a biological basis for homosexuality. It simply was his view that society was quite wrong, backward," Stone says.

"He also was very sympathetic to personal loneliness. And finding happiness later in life gave him enormous sympathy for people struggling to find an emotional base in a partner. In his era, people did the most unusual things to not be outed and to find personal happiness," says Stone, who first met Douglas while waiting tables to put herself through college. "His curiosity made him open to everyone, including me," she adds.

In a series of interviews, Stone, then a high-ranking Boston city official, described Douglas as a man who viewed homosexuality as part of the "tapestry of life" and "had many friends over the years who were homosexual." Some of Douglas's male homosexual friends were married, but even those of his generation who were single generally felt the need to present a heterosexual façade by, say, bringing a female date to dinner parties. His much younger wife's law school classmates were much more open about being gay.

But Douglas's biggest taste of how homosexuality could be dealt with matter-of-factly came through his decades-long friendship with an openly lesbian couple, Kay Kershaw and Isabelle Lynn. The women were his next-door neighbors in Goose Prairie, Washington, his beloved summer retreat, population 8. Kershaw was the original proprietor of the Double K Mountain Ranch, a dude ranch drawing a sophisticated clientele. "Kay built it. Isabelle came out [from Pennsylvania] as a guest and then ultimately came out permanently and was Kay's partner—a business partner and a personal partner—for all those years. And they died only recently. It's a wonderful story," Stone says.

Kay Kershaw taught Douglas's young bride to ride a horse. Isabelle Lynn taught her to cook. "They were our closest friends there. We spent endless hours in each others' homes and with many of their friends, some of whom were lesbian couples from other parts of the country. But the dude ranch catered to anyone who was smart enough to love *The New Yorker* and who could take Isabelle's tart tongue," Stone fondly recalls, adding that the Double K attracted "people who didn't want to be like everybody else."

In *Go East, Young Man,* Douglas wrote warmly about the women next door—but in terms that would not have tipped off the average reader to the fact that they were a lesbian couple: "Some 30 years ago Kay Kershaw, who was born and grew up in Yakima, bought some land in the Prairie, erected a ranch house, and opened one of very few dude ranches in the state. It is a ranch for people who really love the wilderness, not for those who litter the trails or who look at trees to estimate the board feet in them. . . . Kay acquired a partner, Isabelle Lynn, born in the East but a real wilderness zealot now and the best cook west as well as east of the Cascades."

Letters in Douglas's files capture the closeness of that friendship. As the court's 1971–72 term headed to a close, for example, Kay Kershaw wrote that Douglas's car would be waiting at the airport June 26 and "we'll be looking forward to you joining us for Happy Hour and dinner." And in February 1978, two years after a stroke forced Douglas's retirement, Isabelle Lynn wrote to update him on efforts to keep developers at bay and to gripe about Boy Scouts on snowmobiles. "Thank you," she closed, "for the lovely Valentine, Bill; we hope you got ours, too."

Douglas clearly viewed his attitudes toward homosexuality as enlightened. In 1970, adopting the name of a different fir tree, William "Frazier" wrote "The Couch." In that unpublished play, Douglas puts his *Boutilier* views into the mouth of the lead character—a surrogate for himself—psychiatrist Sigmund Brock. The time is the early 1980s. A married president rumored to be homosexual has appointed Brock secretary of mental health. Brock, like Douglas himself, is threatened with impeachment by conservatives. Brock comes under heavy fire as anti-American, possibly even Communist, for his remarks during a press conference:

AP [Associated Press]: Then you think that the handbag snatchers, bank robbers, arsonists, rapists, homosexuals who run wild in the nation's capital should be pampered?

BROCK: Pampered is your word, not mine. I am interested in causes of maladjustment. . . . I would treat these culprits, not punish them. . . .

UPI: Do homosexuals have a place in government?

BROCK: There have been many distinguished men in the federal government over the last 50 years who have been homosexuals.

UPI: Can you name them?

BROCK: You could, if you had done your homework. Actually the war records show that homosexuals have an extraordinary degree of valor. As a class they are highly perceptive and very creative. They have, you see, a prominent feminine component.

UPI: They are like women?

BROCK: Roughly so.

Even though Douglas counted an openly lesbian couple as dear friends, whenever he wrote about homosexuals he assumed them to be male. Perhaps Kay Kershaw and Isabelle Lynn were so well-adjusted that when Douglas thought about homosexuality in terms of mental problems they slipped his mind.

In *Boutilier,* Douglas's most vigorous attempt to get the court to take what he saw as a rational approach to homosexuality flatly failed. And the facts that two of Douglas's best friends were a lesbian couple, that Clark was as close as a father to his homosexual nephew and that Fortas was something of an expert in psychiatry ultimately were of no help to 33-year-old Clive Boutilier. After a dozen years as a legal U.S. resident, he lost his right to remain in this country.

The court's decision of May 22, 1967, that homosexual immigrants could be deported as persons "afflicted with psychopathic personality" rated one sentence in a court news roundup on page 33 of *The New York Times*. The paper led with Egypt barring Israel from using the Gulf of

Aqaba. Also on the front page was President Johnson's call for a national day of prayer for peace in Vietnam, a State Department warning not to visit Israel or its Arab neighbors, the nomination of a new secretary of commerce and the court's narrowing of its "one-man, one-vote" rule.

In 1999, Clive Boutilier, 65, was living in a rest home in Willand, Ontario, just 20 minutes from the U.S. border at Niagara Falls. Speaking haltingly, he confirmed that he moved back to Canada immediately after losing his legal fight. His seven-year relationship with Eugene O'Rouke, the American he lived with before the INS turned his life upside down, was his only long-term relationship. O'Rouke has "passed away," Boutilier said. Twenty-one years after being deported, Boutilier contended that he'd made a mistake in telling the U.S. military that he was homosexual—though the records indicate his INS troubles were triggered by his citizenship application. How did he feel when he heard the court's decision? "No comment!"

A "True Homosexual"?

In taking *Boutilier,* the court had chosen to hold a nearly identical case, *INS v. Lavoie.* Three weeks after ruling against Boutilier, the court reversed Lavoie's lower court victory and sent his case back down "for further proceedings in conformity with the opinion of this court," meaning that the Ninth Circuit was supposed to read *Boutilier* as requiring Lavoie's deportation. The conference vote was 7 to 2; only Douglas and Fortas backed Lavoie. Although Brennan had supported Boutilier's failed bid to remain in this country, he voted against Lavoie, perhaps for the sake of consistency in the court's rulings. Douglas publicly dissented, saying he would have denied the government's *cert* petition—a move that would have prevented Lavoie's deportation.

Lavoie attorney Norman Leonard of San Francisco immediately petitioned for a rehearing, a rarely successful plea after losing at the Supreme Court. Leonard argued that Lavoie's case was fundamentally different from Boutilier's because Lavoie wasn't homosexual.

Lavoie had told the INS that he'd considered himself homosexual since his first sexual experience with another man in 1946. Yet Public Health Service psychiatrist Daniel Beittel concluded: "[H]e is more accurately characterized as a sexual deviate manifested by auto-eroticism and homo-eroticism. Patient's major mode of sexual gratification since puberty . . . has been masturbation. . . . [H]is admission of homosexuality is largely promoted by guilt. . . . [T]here is evidence of a pathological relationship between the patient and his mother and the fact that he returned to Canada in 1960 to nurse her during the last two months of her life even though he had brothers and sisters living in the area, is but a manifestation of this."

Lavoie had had sex with men about 12 times over the next 16 years, according to his psychiatrist, Bernard Diamond. That doctor's conclusion was that Lavoie was simply neurotic. "I do not even regard him as a homosexual in any sense of the word," Dr. Diamond said.

In asking the justices for a rehearing, Lavoie's legal team made one of the most anti-homosexual arguments ever presented to that court. The justices were told that Dr. Diamond "pointed out the absence of factors which characterize the 'true homosexual': no molesting of children, no interest in adolescents, no sustained relationships 'with some abnormal individual in any perverted way,' no feminine characteristics, no love affairs with men."

On October 16, 1967, the justices announced that they had reconsidered. The court signaled that it now wanted the Ninth Circuit to figure out whether Lavoie was homosexual and, thus, deportable. Thurgood Marshall, who as solicitor general had handled the government case against Lavoie before being appointed to succeed Clark, didn't participate in consideration of the case.

The Ninth Circuit found Lavoie was indeed homosexual. The cosmetologist's case returned to the Supreme Court in 1970. By then President Nixon had appointed law-and-order advocate Warren Burger to succeed Earl Warren as chief justice. Nixon had appointed Harry Blackmun to succeed Abe Fortas. On October 12, 1970, nine years after Lavoie's Woolworth's arrest, the court turned down Lavoie's petition. By a secret 7-to-1 vote, the court ended Gerard Lavoie's chances of legally remaining in his adopted homeland. Marshall, again, didn't vote. And, again, "Mr. Justice Douglas is of the opinion that *certiorari* should be granted," the court officially noted.

After *Boutilier* and *Lavoie,* the Supreme Court never again accepted a homosexual immigration case. The question of whether immigrants could be deported for being homosexual was ultimately taken out of its hands.

In August 1979, U.S. Surgeon General Julius Richmond decided that because homosexuality was not a "mental disease or defect" the INS should stop sending homosexuals to the Public Health Service for declarations of deportability. However, in December 1979, the Justice Department decreed the surgeon general had overstepped his authority. The exclusionary policy was reinstated. All homosexual immigrants remained in jeopardy until 1990, when gay Congressman Barney Frank (D-Massachusetts) persuaded Congress to delete the language barring "sex deviates" so that the INS would stop targeting homosexuals.

With its 1967 *Boutilier* decision, a court that had been ahead of the nation in advocating one standard of justice for heterosexuals and homosexuals alike abandoned that egalitarian approach. In allowing homosexuals to be targeted even when the law in question did not mention them, the nation's highest court signaled lower courts that it was open season on homosexuals: Feel free to rule against homosexuals because the Supreme Court will not rise to their defense.

Although there's no evidence that any of the justices was consciously motivated in *Boutilier* by animosity toward homosexuals, prejudice undoubtedly came into play. It's difficult to imagine that the justices serving in 1967 would have passively allowed the INS to target all left-handed immigrants under a federal law that barred, say, "misfits." If the justices had seen no legitimate link between the targeted group and the language of the law, they surely would not have let the INS policy stand, regardless of how they interpreted the law's legislative history. Most justices must have seen a connection between being homosexual and being psycho.

After *Boutilier*, the Supreme Court quite literally stopped listening to homosexual-rights arguments. Just as most of the nation was about to begin hearing gay-liberation arguments for the first time, the court tuned out debates over homosexuality. The court didn't hear oral arguments in another homosexual case until 1984. Instead, by letting hostile lower court rulings stand or by ruling itself without benefit of briefs and oral arguments, the justices signaled homosexuals that the courthouse was a dangerous place to be honest.

For a decade, 1967 to 1977, the justices sent no other message to American homosexuals. The justices never acknowledged—perhaps didn't know—the broader implications of *Boutilier*: With that ruling, the U.S. Supreme Court joined the government war against homosexuals.

6

NOWHERE TO HIDE

THE FRONT PAGE OF THE *Mansfield* (Ohio) *News-Journal* screamed:

HIDDEN MOVIE CAMERA USED BY POLICE
TO TRAP SEXUAL DEVIATES AT PARK HANGOUT

"Spurred by a sex deviate's confession that he wantonly murdered two little girls who cried out for help when he attempted to molest them, Mansfield Police are completing one of the most spectacular investigations of homosexual depravity ever undertaken," the August 22, 1962, article breathlessly began.

"Sex deviate" was such a broad and horrifying concept for many law enforcement officers in the 1950s and '60s that a ghastly crime could trigger a crackdown on male homosexuals even when the crime was heterosexual and the victims weren't male.

In targeting homosexuals for harassment, police in many states were armed with more than the power to arrest them on charges of "lewd and indecent" conduct for touching or far more serious "sodomy" charges for actual sexual relations. Cold War–era "sexual psychopath" laws had been enacted in 21 states by 1955. These laws, propelled by the fear that anyone who deviated from perceived sexual norms was a menace to society, often allowed so-called sexual psychopaths to be locked away indefinitely in mental institutions.

According to historian Allan Berube,

During the nationwide campaigns against sexual psychopaths, the terms "child molester," "homosexual," "sex offender," "sex psychopath," "sex degenerate," "sex deviate," and sometimes even "Communist" became interchangeable in the minds of the public, legislators, and local police. . . . The press added to the national hysteria by portraying gay men as molesters of children, corrupters of youths, and even perpetrators of violent sexual crimes; lesbians were sometimes portrayed as malevolent seducers of women and girls.

After the 1955 murder of a Sioux City, Iowa, boy, a prosecutor used a sexual psychopath law to commit 29 homosexual men to an insane asylum without even allowing them to stand trial.

In Mansfield, Ohio, the police response to a heinous heterosexual attack on two little girls was to arrest men for homosexual activity. In 1962, Mansfield, population 47,000, was known for manufacturing electrical appliances. For two months, plainclothes policemen used a hidden camera to make color movies of sexual activity inside the men's restroom at a local park. Police Chief Clare W. Kyler said the undercover operation was in response to two girls, ages 7 and 9, having been kicked to death in another park by an 18-year-old boy.

The *News-Journal* named 13 men facing sodomy charges and one accused of exposing himself to a boy. "The things which some of these men did cannot be printed. They did break the laws of Ohio, of decency and of humanity," reporter Donn Gaynor wrote. And Chief Kyler warned, "Any sex deviate may be a potential killer."

Police Lieutenant Bill Spognardi found secretly filming the Central Park men's room "very degrading, very sickening." His revulsion intensified when, he says, he saw James Chamberlain having sex with another man. "It shocked the hell out of me! He was a friend of mine in grade school," recalls Spognardi, who testified against Chamberlain.

Two days after the undercover operation hit the news, Spognardi summoned Chamberlain to police headquarters and arrested him for sodomy. Chamberlain, the married father of three, was accompanied only by his boss. "Greatly distraught and anxious to avoid adverse publicity for his family," according to court documents, Chamberlain, 32, pled guilty.

Ohio law defined sodomy as "carnal copulation with a beast, or in any opening of the body, except sexual parts, with another human being." A sodomy conviction automatically meant a prison sentence of one to 20 years. Sodomy was one of eight crimes that then carried no possibility of probation in Ohio. The others were murder, arson, house burglary, incest, rape, attempted rape and poisoning. A mental exam was mandatory after an Ohio sodomy conviction.

After consulting an attorney, Chamberlain formally pled guilty. Before being sentenced, he attempted to withdraw that plea. A judge refused to let him. Chamberlain lost his state court appeal. He was then sent to the Lima State Hospital for a 60-day mental exam, which he passed. If Chamberlain had been found "psychopathic," "mentally ill" or "mentally deficient," he could have spent the rest of his life in an insane asylum. On March 10, 1965, he was sentenced to serve one to 20 years behind bars. The Supreme Court was his last hope of avoiding prison.

Chamberlain's attorneys told the justices that Chamberlain ought to have been allowed to withdraw his plea because he had not understood it meant an automatic prison sentence and perhaps life in a mental institution. They also contended that "surreptitious, exploratory motion picture taking of the users of a public toilet constituted an unreasonable search and seizure." The state of Ohio replied that Chamberlain had been warned that there was no probation for sodomy.

Douglas clerk Lewis Merrifield was sympathetic to Chamberlain: "I just don't see how a guilty plea can be held to waive a right when the plea is induced by evidence illegally obtained."

On October 10, 1966, the court denied *cert.* Douglas had wanted to take the case. Three months later, Chamberlain, 37, entered the Ohio Penitentiary. He served one year in prison and 13 months on parole.

Still living in Mansfield at 68, Chamberlain declined to discuss his case at length, saying, "It's too long ago—36 years—too long ago. And it's over with and it's done. . . . I spent lots and lots of money with lawyers and court costs, Supreme Court costs. . . . And I don't want nothing to do with it anymore."

More than 20 men were ensnared in the police department's attempt to rid Mansfield of "deviates," says Larry Inscore, Chamberlain's lead attorney. Some of the men thought of themselves as homosexuals; others didn't. Most served a year in prison, Inscore added, explaining that the judge refused to let sodomy charges be reduced to a probation-level offense.

The fact that probation was not an option prodded those arrested to challenge the evidence against them, says Inscore, who spent years defending them because he knew "instinctively" that "homosexuality is not supposed to be a crime." He also thought the punishment in the restroom arrests was totally out of proportion. "It was supposed to be a 'disturbance of the peace' at most—doing something like that in a public place," he says.

Inscore's *Chamberlain* petition did not challenge the constitutionality of Ohio's sodomy law or its cruel, if not unusual, "sexual psychopath" law. However, it brought to the Supreme Court's attention not only that sodomy laws were being enforced but also how fierce that enforcement could be. In refusing to hear *Chamberlain,* the court took its first tentative step toward its 1986 *Bowers v. Hardwick* ruling upholding the constitutionality of sodomy laws.

"I Know I Look Like I'm a Queer"

The first wave of Supreme Court cases that grew out of arrests for homosexual physical contact might create the misimpression that police departments were merely attempting to drive homosexual behavior out of public places where it might offend a heterosexual passerby. After all, Frank Kameny, like James Chamberlain, had been arrested in a restroom. George Fleuti was nabbed in a park. But, in reality, the police wanted to entrap, intimidate and harass homosexuals wherever they could find them. And gay bars, the very place that homosexuals congregated to escape the oppressive heterosexual world, were prime police targets in the 1950s and '60s.

Generally, an establishment could lose its liquor license for being a gay bar or, as a 1955 California law put it, a "resort for sexual perverts." Even when such laws began changing in the late 1960s, bars still could lose their licenses if illegal physical contact took place or was proposed. In other words, if a customer accidentally made a pass at an undercover cop, the bar could be closed down.

Gay bars are sometimes mythologized as having been a haven for deeply closeted homosexuals in the era before the Stonewall rebellion of 1969. The sad reality was quite different: Nowhere was completely safe for homosexuals. Bars, both those catering to lesbians as well as those mainly for homosexual men, were particularly dangerous because they were magnets for undercover vice cops passing themselves off as homosexuals. The most innocuous behavior—a suggestive remark, a hug between friends of the same sex—could lead to arrest.

Los Angeles attorney Herb Selwyn, who defended several homosexual men accused of "lewd" conduct, recalls that handsome young officers were assigned to lure men into compromising situations. Once, Selwyn was supposed to meet a homosexual client at the courthouse. Selwyn thought he spotted the man: "I said, 'Are you Mr. So-and-so?' He laughed. He says, 'No. I'm the cop that arrested him.' He says, 'I know I look like I'm a queer. That's why they chose me for this.'"

A classic case of police entrapment reached the Supreme Court just before its 1966–67 term. At 1:50 A.M. on May 23, 1965, New York City Patrolman Anthony De Greise had walked into a crowded homosexual bar in Greenwich Village. De Greise was wearing white slacks, light sneakers and a polo shirt in order to "be in" with the men there, he later testified. According to De Greise, he ordered a beer, sat down and was approached by Francis Robillard, who asked for a light. In De Greise's version of events, Robillard introduced him to two friends, Leroy Snowden and John Wrenn, then asked if he frequented "this type of bar." De Greise confirmed that he did. Five minutes into the conversation, the banter turned sexual with Robillard allegedly telling De Greise, "I think your joint is big enough to fuck me in the ass," and rubbing the officer's thigh. Wrenn and Snowden allegedly chimed in with similarly ribald remarks. Moments before the group headed out to De Greise's car, Robillard allegedly said, "Let's go and I will watch you girls suck and fuck; man I'll beat your ass with a strap." Once outside the patrolman arrested his new acquaintances. In previous weeks, he had made nine similar arrests.

Robillard, Wrenn and Snowden were charged with "disorderly conduct" under a state law targeting "any person who with intent to provoke a breach of the peace, or whereby a breach of the peace may be occasioned, . . . frequents or loiters about any public place soliciting men for the purpose of committing a crime against nature or other lewdness." The three defendants pleaded not guilty but were convicted and sentenced to 30 days in a "workhouse." None of them actually served any time even though a New York appeals court upheld their convictions.

In petitioning the Supreme Court to take the case, New York Civil Liberties Union attorney Morton P. Cohen argued that New York had doubly violated the three bar patrons' constitutional right to due process. The convictions were baseless, since the peace was not disturbed, he said. Second, he contended that the arrests were the result of "abhorrent," unconstitutional entrapment. Cohen asked the justices to decide whether "police officers may dress and behave as homosexuals in order to entice others to solicit said police officers for a lewd purpose." The justices were not asked to find the New York law unconstitutionally sexist. (It was illegal to solicit men—but not women—for so-called crimes against nature.)

The *Robillard et al. v. New York* petition explained the dynamics of same-sex pickups: The last thing most homosexuals wanted was to create a public disturbance by making a pass at someone who wasn't interested. Quoting a 1966 law review article, Cohen argued, "The majority of homosexual solicitations are made only if the other individual appears responsive and are ordinarily accomplished by quiet conversations and the use of gestures and signals having significance only to other homosexuals." Cohen listed ways that Officer De Greise had led the men he met in the bar to think that he was homosexual. The patrolman, for example, had not objected when Robillard rubbed his thigh. Thus, the case offered the justices a rare opportunity to weigh the constitutionality of tricking homosexuals into making an illegal pass.

The district attorney of New York County, Frank S. Hogan, vigorously urged the justices to deny *cert*. Hogan told the court exactly what the patrolman accused Robillard, Snowden and Wrenn of having said. Hogan very likely assumed the justices would not be eager to take a case where coarse language might well be quoted in open court.

Hogan argued that the "disorderly conduct" statute had been violated because a homosexual pass could be expected to upset a "reasonable man" so much that the peace would be disturbed. "Public solicitation, degrading the addressee and implying, as it does, that the addressee is a pervert, constitutes no less than 'fighting words,'" Hogan said. There's no entrapment, he argued, if the person ensnared had a "predisposition" to commit the crime.

Warren clerk Douglas Kranwinkle echoed the district attorney's no-entrapment conclusion. However, Douglas clerk Lewis Merrifield, again bothered by the police tactics, observed, "Perhaps the average person would be tempted to hit a person who made homosexual advances. But I doubt that this can be said of a person who has gone to a homosexual bar dressed as a homosexual."

Fortas clerk Daniel Levitt saw it differently: "Because the patrolman entered a queer bar dressed like a homosexual, petitioners propositioned him in the crudest imaginable way (let those who regard our homosexuals as 'blithe spirits' more refined than the mainstream human being cast an eye on the conversations set out on page 7 of the state's response) and began to paw him. If that's entrapment, then banks 'entrap' bank robbers by virtue of their very existence."

Without bothering to vote, the justices passed up the chance to object to the kind of police tactics used in *Robillard*. They turned away *Robillard* on November 7, 1966.

By the time the court announced its non-decision, New York City's police commissioner had forbidden such entrapment. Nine months before, in February 1966, newly elected Mayor John Lindsay, known as a liberal Republican, had announced a crackdown on "honkytonks, promenading perverts . . . homosexuals and prostitutes." The Mattachine Society and the New York Civil Liberties Union orchestrated a surprising uproar, and the city relented. The police commissioner "instructed officers not to lure homosexuals into breaking the law. . . . [A]nd entrapment, for years a scourge of gay men in New York came to an end," historian John D'Emilio points out.

Nightstick Nightmares

But New York was only one city, and entrapment was only one common police method of making life more difficult for homosexuals. Actual bar raids were another. By the time the first bar raid case reached the Supreme Court, Tom Clark had retired. His departure was no loss for Americans who were, as he put it in *Boutilier*, "afflicted with homosexuality."

President Johnson was not known for patiently waiting to get what he wanted: He made things happen even in political territory that other presidents considered off-limits. In 1965, Johnson had talked Justice Goldberg into hanging up his robe to become a UN ambassador, making room for Johnson confidant Fortas. The vigorous 67-year-old Clark—younger than Warren, Black, Douglas and Harlan—no doubt would have remained on the court if Johnson had not chosen Clark's son to be attorney general. Regardless of whether the wily Johnson intentionally maneuvered Clark into retiring, the opening on the court gave the president a chance to achieve a civil rights milestone. On June 13, 1967, he nominated 58-year-old Solicitor General Thurgood Marshall, the nation's most famous black attorney, to integrate what had been a white-male institution from its founding.

As director of the NAACP Legal Defense and Education Fund, Marshall had won 29 Supreme Court victories in pursuit of racial equality. He successfully attacked segregation in interstate transportation, all-white election primaries and racist restrictions on home sales. His most historic breakthrough, the 1954 *Brown v. Board of Education of Topeka* ruling declaring "separate but equal" schools innately unequal, drove a stake into the evil heart of legalized racial segregation.

President Kennedy had appointed Marshall, grandson of a freed slave, to a federal appeals court in 1961. Four years later, Johnson chose him to be solicitor general, a position so influential that it is sometimes called the "tenth justice." The solicitor general not only represents the U.S. government in cases before the Supreme Court but also plays a key role as a gatekeeper—choosing among the cases that federal agencies want to pursue.

As solicitor general, Marshall had successfully pushed the court to side with the INS in deporting homosexuals. As a justice, however, he gradually showed that his concept of civil rights was broad enough to include homosexuals. Ramsey Clark, who worked with Marshall at the Justice Department, notes that a solicitor general's job is to defend federal laws and agencies, regardless of his own views. "I think Thurgood equated [gay rights] with civil rights. . . . He also knew the persecution of African-American gays could be very vicious," Clark says.

The first homosexual case to reach the court during Marshall's tenure as a justice grew out of a Los Angeles bar raid. Police harassment frequently crossed the line into police brutality during such raids. In one Greenwich Village bar raid, policemen put their hands down lesbians' pants and said things like, "Oh, you think you're a man. Well, let's see what you've got here," historian Lillian Faderman reports. In another lesbian bar raid, patrons were strip-searched.

One extraordinarily brutal raid in Los Angeles turned a New Year's Eve celebration into a nightstick nightmare and sparked an equal-protection plea that reached the Supreme Court. The Black Cat Beer Bar on Sunset Boulevard was one of about 10 homosexual bars in a six-block area. A small sign out front showed a black cat with an arched back, its face turned toward incoming customers. Inside, the rather ordinary tavern was one long room with a handful of tables, a jukebox and a pool table. Bar stools stood in a semi-circle around the Black Cat's mirror-backed bar.

On the last night of 1966, the Black Cat was decked out with party balloons and packed with 60 to 75 revelers—15 of them in drag because the nearby New Faces bar was having a drag contest. At the stroke of midnight, the Black Cat crowd sang "Auld Lang Syne," then started kissing to celebrate the arrival of 1967. At least six undercover vice cops immediately pounced.

"One queen . . . ran out and was followed to New Faces, where the police beat the tall woman owner, thinking that she was a drag queen. And her two bartenders jumped to her defense and were left unconscious in the gutter, one with ribs and spleen busted and a couple fractures in his skull," recalled *ONE* columnist Jim Kepner.

Community activist Buddy Ball rushed to console the victims. "Quite a number were taken to jail. The belief was that the police were terribly homophobic and felt that the [November 1966] election of Ronald Reagan [as governor] was a green light for more brutality," Ball says.

In response to the brutal Black Cat raid, Ball and Kepner helped organize a protest—an unheard-of reaction by homosexuals. Some 30 to 40 people picketed along Sunset Boulevard; 200 attended a rally. A block away, police nervously set up "machine gun nests," Kepner recalled.

Six Black Cat patrons had been arrested for kissing. All six were tried and convicted of disorderly conduct for "lewd or dissolute conduct" in a public place. Under California law, their convictions meant that they had to register as "sex offenders."

Two convicted kissers, Charles W. Talley and Benny Norman Baker, pursued their appeal to the Supreme Court. According to one police officer, Talley and another man had "kissed on the mouth for three to five seconds." Two other officers testified that Baker, who had worn a white dress on New Year's Eve, had kissed three men for two to five seconds.

Los Angeles attorney Herbert E. Selwyn had not handled the Black Cat patrons' trial but petitioned the Supreme Court on behalf of Baker and Talley. "I represented a lot of gay men because there weren't any gay lawyers in those days who would admit it," the heterosexual Selwyn recalls. "There are a lot of intellectuals in the gay movement, but usually they don't get arrested in bars. These people at the Black Cat were simple working-class types," he added.

Selwyn had gotten involved with the Los Angeles homosexual community at the request of a lesbian patient of his physician father's. Selwyn lectured the Mattachine Society on homosexuality and the law, incorporated the Mattachine Society and helped *ONE*. When psychologist Evelyn Hooker began researching the mental health of homosexual men, Selwyn helped her find homosexual volunteers. "I was her guinea pig for her heterosexual control group," he says.

Less than a year after the Black Cat raid, Selwyn filed a forceful homosexual-rights *cert* petition with the Supreme Court. He didn't claim his clients weren't really homosexual; he didn't claim entrapment. Rather, he declared that homosexuals deserve equal rights.

Selwyn's 12-page petition first argued that the California "disorderly conduct" law was unconstitutionally vague because "lewd" and "dissolute" have no fixed meaning. The trial judge had defined those terms as meaning "lustful, libidinous, lascivious, unchaste, sexual impurity, wanton, debauched, and loose in morals and conduct." But, as Selwyn pointed out, all those definitions are just as nebulous. Selwyn found that trying to pin down the meaning of any of the words was like a dog chasing its own tail. When he looked up "lustful," "wanton" and "debauched" in dictionaries, he found "lewd" given as a definition of each. Thus, lacking clear guidelines as to what behavior was illegal, the jury was "left free to convict" on whatever grounds it chose, Selwyn argued.

Selwyn hit his stride in arguing that convicting homosexual men of kissing violated the Constitution's guarantee of equal protection. "The Fourteenth Amendment . . . demands that persons be treated equally regardless of sex or creed and that the same standard of conduct exists between homosexuals and heterosexuals; that behavior not illegal between a man and woman would not be illegal between two men," Selwyn told the justices.

The "lewd or dissolute" statute, theoretically, could be used against any couple who kissed lewdly in public. The reality, of course, was that the law was being enforced selectively to harass homosexuals. "The simple fact of the matter is that on that festive occasion [New Year's Eve], no men in all Los Angeles County were arrested for kissing women in a lewd manner at any public place. Any public official in Los Angeles County who even condoned such an enforcement policy would be laughed out of the state," Selwyn argued.

"Unenforced and unenforceable against conduct between men and women," the statute "denies equal protection" if it is used against men who lewdly kiss men, Selwyn contended.

> A conviction which results from discriminatory enforcement of a valid statute is just as constitutionally void as would be a conviction under a statute which was discriminatory on its face. . . . The constitutional command is clear: the law must be enforced equally to, for and against all with no exemption—none as to Chinese, none as to Negroes and none as to homosexuals. . . . If two persons, both male, wish to pursue happiness (without injury to others) by engaging in affectionate behavior in a bar at midnight on New Year's Eve, that is their natural and inherent right . . . and that conduct which may merely be offensive to others cannot be and must not be prohibited by the state. It may seem to some of us offensive to watch others chewing gum, chewing or smoking tobacco, drinking alcohol beverages . . . yet we certainly would not and should not attempt to proscribe these activities except by influence or example.

In reply, Los Angeles City Attorney Roger Arnebergh contended, "all [lewd public kissing] will be prosecuted." He told the justices, "The mere act of two males kissing is not a crime. . . . The president of France kissing a decorated hero, the premier of the Soviet Union kissing a returning cosmonaut, men from the 'old country' kissing a male relative or a father kissing a son—these acts engaged in a public place are not done in a lewd and dissolute manner."

But as Selwyn had noted, "The statute nowhere sets up any standards relating to how long a kiss may be prolonged with safety. . . . Had the legislature wanted to proscribe kissing between non-related males in public for more than two seconds, provided neither party was the president of France nor the premier of the Soviet Union, it could have done so."

According to City Attorney Arnebergh, the California law was not too vague. What took the Black Cat smooching "out of the realm of a normal kiss" and into illegality, he explained, was "the manner of the . . . kiss," "the gender of the parties," "the mode of dress" and "the place." Despite his focus on gender, he insisted that Talley and Baker "were not convicted for the 'status' of being homosexuals."

To Selwyn, however, the case was a clear-cut example of selective, discriminatory prosecution. "It took almost a century to grant the constitutional rights of our ethnic minorities in this country. Let us hope that the homophile minority will achieve its equal rights with more dispatch," his petition concluded. Selwyn was the first attorney to make a totally undefensive homosexual-rights argument in a *cert* petition. He later said, "There are two kinds of lawyers—those who argue what the law is and those who argue what the law should be. And I like to be the latter."

Talley v. California offered the justices yet another window onto harassment of homosexuals. However, the court wasn't told how violently the police executed the Black Cat raid. After reading the limited account of the bar raid contained in court documents, Clark clerk Larry Nichols jumped to the conclusion that Talley and Baker were transvestites. "The petition is frivolous," he concluded dismissively. Meanwhile, a Douglas clerk recommended that the court grant *cert* "on vagueness only," not equal protection.

A Fortas clerk—probably Peter Zimroth, based on the handwriting— expressed outrage at the police tactics and suggested the court take *Talley* to send a message that the police could spend their time more productively if they got out of homosexual bars.

In the court's April 19, 1968, conference, only Douglas voted to accept the kissing case.

The year before, in allowing the INS to brand all homosexual immigrants as deportable psychopaths, the Supreme Court had clearly signaled that it was not interested in interfering with government attempts to crack down on homosexuality. With the Black Cat kissing case, the court suggested through inaction that there was no limit to the double standard that it would allow police to use in punishing same-sex behavior. Homosexual publications had rights in the eyes of a majority of the court; homosexual people apparently did not.

Nixon's "Law and Order" Chief Justice

At the end of the court's 1967–68 term, Chief Justice Warren, 77, announced his intention to retire. Though a Republican, Warren wanted his successor to be chosen by Democrat Lyndon Johnson, a president whose support for the active pursuit of racial equality matched his own. Warren knew that, if he waited longer, he risked the possibility that a man he loathed, Republican Richard Nixon, would get a chance to pick a right-winger as chief justice. Battered by growing opposition to the war in Vietnam, Johnson had already announced that he would not seek reelection. Nixon was the leading candidate to replace him.

As chief justice, Earl Warren breathed new life into the Constitution's elusive promise of equal protection—for some Americans. No legal scholar, Warren used his judicial power to try to make the country fairer, especially for blacks. "His greatest concern was expressed in the question so often asked when the cases were argued before the court: 'But was it fair?' . . . When the chief justice concluded that an individual had been treated in an unfair manner, he would not let legal rules stand in the way in his effort to remedy the situation," according to the Supreme Court Historical Society. Warren's greatest triumph—the court's unanimous *Brown v. Board* decision—was a direct result of his having pushed fellow justices to see the case in human terms. In conference, Warren warned that "separate but equal" schools could continue to be upheld only if the court believed in the "inherent inferiority of the colored race." He added, "I don't see how in this day and age we can set any group apart from the rest and say that they are not entitled to exactly the same treatment as all the others." Justices who'd previously defended segregation were unwilling to cast themselves as overt racists; Warren won them over. His *Brown v. Board* ruling relied heavily on psychological evidence that segregation harmed black schoolchildren.

Yet Warren did not push the court to see homosexual cases in human terms, did not urge that homosexuals be treated just like heterosexuals, did not ask "But was it fair?" when confronted with carnage from the government's war on homosexuals. Far from seeing homosexuals as a minority group in dire need of the court's protection, Warren repeatedly endorsed policies that legalized their oppression. He did not care that the psychiatric profession did not share the INS view that "psycho-pathic" described all homosexuals.

However, Warren doesn't seem to have expressed overt hostility to-ward homosexuals. And he did not aggressively attempt to steer the court toward anti-homosexual rulings. His own record, in fact, was mixed—the legacy of a man who deeply believed in equality but to whom the phrase "homosexual rights" would have seemed an incom-prehensible contradiction in terms.

With Warren's retirement, the nation might have gotten its first chief justice sympathetic to homosexuals. In mid-1968, Johnson nominated Justice Fortas to lead the nation's highest court. In *Boutilier*, Fortas had demonstrated his willingness to aggressively challenge the government's blanket classification of all homosexuals as psychopaths. As chief justice, Fortas almost certainly would have tried to keep the court abreast of the growing scientific understanding of homosexuality. Fortas's health was good enough that he might well have led the court until his death in 1982 at 71. But it was not to be. Johnson's adversaries in the Senate, seeing the lame duck president as weakened and vulnerable, forced the withdrawal of Fortas's nomination in October 1968. Nixon won the White House the next month. Then, amid allegations of financial improprieties, Fortas re-signed on May 14, 1969. Nixon would get to pick not only a chief justice to replace Warren but also an associate justice to replace Fortas.

If Chief Justice Warren exhibited ambivalence about the pleas of ho-mosexuals, his 61-year-old successor, Warren Burger, did not. Before being appointed to the nation's top court, Burger showed his lack of sympathy for homosexual rights. While on the U.S. Court of Appeals for the District of Columbia, Burger dissented from a 1965 decision over-turning the Civil Service's refusal to rehire a 17-year veteran of the La-bor Department because he'd been arrested for loitering in Lafayette Park, then a male homosexual cruising spot. The court ruled that the Civil Service couldn't base a disqualification for "immoral conduct" on "such vague labels as 'homosexual' or 'homosexual conduct.'" Dissent-ing from that first federal employment victory for homosexuals, Burger wrote, "Whether it is sound legislative policy to attempt to deal with sex deviates under the criminal law is not open to judges, but one can hardly doubt that such conduct is regarded as immoral under contemporaneous standards of our society. This court is in no position, then, to overturn, or even to question an executive determination authorized by Congress that homosexual conduct warrants a disqualification from federal employment."

During his 17 years on the Supreme Court, Burger was consistently hostile to homosexual litigants. His deep animosity burst into full public view in the final days of his tenure, when he approvingly quoted an eighteenth-century description of sodomy as being "an affliction of 'deeper malignity' than rape." Extending privacy protections to include homosexual sodomy "would be to cast aside millennia of moral teaching," Burger added.

A "law and order" court judge elevated to the Supreme Court by a president intent on seeing that criminals were not coddled, Burger treated homosexuals as unconvicted felons and saw them as sinners. He scheduled conference discussions only in those few homosexual cases that government attorneys wanted the court to take in order to overturn a homosexual victory. Under Burger, when a homosexual petitioned the court, the case was turned away undebated unless another justice added it to the "Discuss" list.

The Burger era, which began after Chief Justice Warren formally retired on June 23, 1969, was bleak indeed for homosexual Americans who sought Supreme Court protection. But beyond the court's marble walls, the homosexual-rights movement was undergoing a radical transformation. The tiny, cautious homophile movement was swept aside by the explosive arrival of the gay liberation movement. Suddenly, men and women from all walks of life were pouring out of the closet and into the streets to demand equal rights. The birth of gay pride as a widely shared emotion represented such a profound break with the past that a great many gay Americans today don't realize that a homosexual-rights movement existed before June 1969, when gay Americans began to fight back not just in the courts but in the streets.

The bar raids had long been fairly routine affairs in which police rounded up bar patrons on flimsy excuses, loaded them into paddy wagons and hauled them down to the stationhouse for booking and/or more harassment. Homosexuals tried to flee or passively did what they were told. When San Francisco police arrested 89 men and 14 women in a

1961 homosexual bar raid, a reporter described the roundup as "vaguely reminiscent of leading sheep from a packed corral."

The raids often increased during mayoral campaigns as police pitched in to show the incumbent was tough on crime. In the summer of 1969, New York Mayor Lindsay was running for reelection, and a new police precinct commander was busily raiding bars. The crackdown on the Stonewall Inn, a sleazy unlicensed Greenwich Village bar with no running water, began in typical fashion. As the only homosexual nightspot that allowed dancing, the Stonewall Inn drew a mixed crowd, heavy on young Puerto Rican drag queens and street hustlers.

Just before midnight on June 27, 1969, the police made their move. A 45-year-old man was arrested for being unable to prove that he was at least 18, the legal drinking age. Drag queens were rounded up for violating the city dress code, which required everyone to wear at least three articles of clothing "appropriate" to their gender. The bartender, bouncer and several patrons went peacefully to the waiting police van. Then, according to a *Village Voice* account, a lesbian angrily "put up a struggle. . . . [T]he scene became explosive. Limp wrists were forgotten. . . . Almost by signal the crowd erupted in cobblestone and bottle heaving."

Spontaneous rioting continued the next night, with "Gay Power!" echoing through Greenwich Village as some 400 nightstick-wielding police officers battled to control a homosexual uprising 2,000 strong. Years of pent-up rage were unleashed.

News of the rebellion drew little mainstream attention. Buried on page 33 of *The New York Times* was a six-paragraph story, "4 Policemen Hurt in 'Village' Raid." But among homosexuals, word of the "Stonewall rebellion" spread quickly, changing the way vast numbers of homosexuals here and abroad conceived of themselves and their rightful place in the world. Almost overnight, gay liberation groups sprang to life in cities across the nation.

After its violent birth, the gay-rights movement immediately turned peaceful but kept its determination to fight back. The ideas weren't new; the breakthrough was one of sheer numbers.

Trouble in Sexual Paradise

Shortly after the Stonewall rebellion, a gay legal challenge by a fired high-

level civil servant reached the Supreme Court. Richard Schlegel had
been fired from the Department of the Army in July 1961, just months after the court turned away Frank Kameny. Eight years later, Schlegel's petition for *cert* distilled the issues raised by Kameny down to their essence:
Is it constitutional to dismiss a federal worker for homosexuality?
Schlegel was homosexual; both sides agreed that was why he was fired.

Schlegel, a lanky, genial man whose demeanor in recent years brings
to mind an aging Clark Kent, laughingly traces his homosexuality back
to his first crush—at age five. He traces his ancestry back to German
"Pennsylvania Dutch" immigrants who settled in Philadelphia in 1734.
He was raised in tiny Milroy, Pennsylvania, by thrifty parents. His father
operated a steam shovel at a Bethlehem Steel limestone quarry. Midway
through college, Schlegel, then 18, was drafted into the Air Force,
where he passed up a chance to become an officer because "I thought I
was too sissified." After his 18-month stint in uniform, he completed his
undergraduate work, then got an entry-level GS 6 federal job while
working on a graduate degree in public administration.

Putting his early training in pinching pennies to good use, Schlegel
whizzed up through the ranks as a federal budget officer, landing a
GS 13 job before age 30. As budget director of the Federal Civil Defense Administration, Schlegel routinely handled some of the nation's
most sensitive, top-secret documents while U.S. elected officials franti-
cally scrambled to prepare for the possibility of a Soviet missile attack
in the wake of the 1957 Sputnik launch. The very government that was
trying to rid itself of homosexuals for fear that they posed a threat to national security was unknowingly trusting a homosexual to supervise its
civil defense spending.

In 1958, Schlegel moved to Honolulu to oversee Army transportation
for the entire Pacific theater. "I always like to joke that I had in my budget more aircraft in that theater than the Air Force and I had more ships
than the Navy," Schlegel says.

Hawaii was a sexual paradise for Schlegel, who at 31 delighted in
casting himself as a sugar daddy for handsome playmates. "The tempta-
tion was like a never-ending smorgasbord, so far as military men," he recalls with a naughty smile. "They always enjoyed someone who would
entertain them, who would buy them drinks, who would take them
around the island. . . . Army boys were not so readily available. But

sailors or Marines, you name it, you got it." Schlegel rented a cliff-side apartment overlooking Diamond Head, downtown Honolulu and the sea. In his spare time, he was president of the failing Tahiti U Drive, which had 16 rental cars but few customers. He allowed his financially strapped military buddies to borrow cars or the key to his apartment. In exchange, he got sex play that, he says, stopped short of oral or anal sex because of his concern about Hawaii's sodomy law. "That certainly was satisfactory to me. If they were indulging in oral sex elsewhere, they didn't with me . . . because I drew that line," Schlegel says.

Schlegel's tropical antics quickly came under fire. In mid-1959, the Army notified him that he was being dismissed for "infamous, immoral and notorious misconduct off duty." An infantryman had sworn to the military police that he regularly had sex with Schlegel and had attended a party at his apartment in which men "danced together in their *lava-lavas,*" South Sea islands–style skirts. Schlegel hired an attorney: "I lied to him through my teeth. I said, 'This never happened. I'm incensed!'" With roommates backing up his denial, Schlegel kept his job.

Less than two years later, the Army told him he was being fired for "immoral and indecent conduct." He was accused of fondling three Marines, bringing two to orgasm, in private, one-on-one encounters.

Lying had won him "a hollow victory," Schlegel realized. "What had I gained other than just a little time and a lot of mental anguish?" Also, he was unlikely to be able to discredit affidavits from three Marines. So instead of trying to duck the new accusations, Schlegel composed a 36-page treatise claiming a right to a homosexual private life. "I contend . . . that any legal or regulatory interference in the sexual activities of two mature persons, carried on by agreement, in privacy, is invasion of the basic rights of the individual," Schlegel wrote in July 19, 1961, quoting almost verbatim from the stance taken that May by the American Law Institute. "I accept the moral responsibility to account to my God for my own conduct. I accept the moral responsibility to account to my fellow men for any conduct which causes 'demonstrable harm.' I ask only that a spirit of tolerance prevail in the exchange," he concluded.

Schlegel recalls, "I was furious. The individual should have some right to be let alone in his own home. That's what sticks in my craw today. If this had been a public restroom, if this had been Kahala Avenue on Waikiki Beach or if I had importuned someone and caused him great distress and the police had been called. But in my own four walls! . . . I had to account to a bunch of Army officers and Civil Service Commission officials for the right to enjoy my own privacy."

His protest, remarkable for its time, failed. After 11 years as a federal employee, Schlegel lost his Army job on July 31, 1961. As a military veteran, he couldn't be fired, except to "promote the efficiency of the [Civil] Service." He appealed on the grounds that government efficiency wasn't advanced by firing someone with sterling evaluations and that the charge of "immoral and indecent conduct" was unconstitutionally vague. The Civil Service regional director ruled against Schlegel, saying that "acts of sexual perversion . . . constitute indecent and immoral conduct, disqualifying an employee from further service." A board of appeals, though "not professing to be a guardian of the public morals," also upheld Schlegel's dismissal.

Seeking reinstatement and back pay, Schlegel sued in 1963 in the U.S. Court of Claims, which handles claims against the United States, because he wanted his case heard by several judges instead of just one federal district judge. Six years later, he discovered how hostile a seven-judge panel could be. It unanimously lectured him: "Any schoolboy knows that a homosexual act is immoral, indecent, lewd and obscene. . . . If activities of this kind are allowed to be practiced in a government department, it is inevitable that the efficiency of the service will in time be adversely affected."

By then, the frugal Schlegel was broke. He'd run through the $4,700 in his federal pension plan. And he'd lost another government job. Pennsylvania had hired him in 1963 to oversee spending for its $10 billion interstate highway system. He was forced to resign after postal inspectors informed his supervisor that he had received a homosexual magazine, he says.

Schlegel continued battling to regain his federal post. On February 28, 1970, New York City attorney Norman Dorsen and American Civil Liberties Union attorney Melvin Wulf petitioned the Supreme Court, casting *Schlegel v. United States* as a homosexual-rights case of enormous importance. "This case presents the court with an opportunity to rectify, in the context of a specific instance of discrimination by the federal government, an aspect of the historic, severe and unjustified prejudice against a despised minority—individuals whose sexual preference is for members of their own sex," they told the justices.

The petition, which said Schlegel's right to due process had been violated, argued that anti-homosexual prejudice is fed by "fear and ignorance" and "supported by a popular conception of the causes and characteristics of homosexuality that is no more deserving of our deference than the Emperor Justinian's belief that homosexuality causes earthquakes."

Yet, Schlegel's attorneys continued, "the public attitude toward the homosexual community is altering." They cited an October 1969 report by the National Institute of Mental Health, which said, "Discreet homosexuality . . . is being recognized more and more as the private business of the individual rather than a subject for public regulation through statute. Many homosexuals are good citizens, holding regular jobs and leading productive lives." Though much of Schlegel's petition had a post-Stonewall tenor, it assumed that homosexual civil servants would remain closeted and, thus, would not be "readily identifiable" by co-workers.

Labeling government discrimination against homosexuals evil, Schlegel's petition noted that in 1952 the Supreme Court had ruled that no group can be barred from government employment based on "an 'arbitrary or discriminatory' classification." Then, foreshadowing a break-through 1996 gay-rights ruling, it argued, "irrational fears and prejudices abound, but it is clear that the government may not add its approval or sanction to these prejudices." The petition added, "Otherwise, Negroes, communists, and bastards [children born out of wedlock] would not have been entitled to the constitutional protection that the court has consistently provided. . . . Presumably, there are many employees who would find it distasteful to work alongside Negroes, Jews, and persons of illegitimate birth. Does this mean the government could bar these groups from the Civil Service?"

In response, Nixon administration Solicitor General Erwin Griswold argued that "there are many who find homosexual conduct so distasteful that they could not work efficiently with a known homosexual." Griswold conceded that Schlegel had been considered a "superior employee" whose colleagues had been unaware of his homosexuality before government investigators tipped them off. Griswold's concession inadvertently begged the justices to see the investigators, not Schlegel, as the disruptive influence.

Griswold also conceded that attitudes were changing. Schlegel's petition suggests, Griswold said, "that it would be wiser for the government not to act on the basis of its views of sexual propriety among its citizens. Many hold such views, and they may ultimately prevail. Until corresponding legislation is adopted, however, we believe neither changes in public attitudes nor information pointing to the desirability of a corresponding official change itself warrants review by this court." Griswold added that "so long as homosexual behavior is permissibly deemed criminal, the government offends no constitutional strictures against arbitrariness by making it, when known, cause for dismissal." Yet, sodomy laws no more outlawed all homosexual activity than they outlawed all heterosexual behavior.

The Supreme Court rarely jumps into a controversy unless lower court opinions conflict. The Court of Claims's decision against Schlegel seemed to be at odds with a ruling handed down by the U.S. Court of Appeals for the District of Columbia. In *Norton v. Macy,* the appeals court had overturned the dismissal of a federal worker who allegedly had "felt the leg" of another man while off duty. That court ruled in July 1969 that Uncle Sam's "embarrassment" over a civil servant's presumed homosexuality was not a legitimate reason for firing the worker. (The government did not appeal its *Norton* defeat, so that case never reached the Supreme Court.)

Solicitor General Griswold argued that, despite appearances, *Norton* and *Schlegel* did not conflict because Schlegel's "alleged conduct was neither minor nor wholly consensual." Virtually accusing Schlegel— never arrested on any charge—of attempted rape, Griswold said Schlegel had ripped the underwear of a "resistant victim." The "victim," by the government's own account, was a Marine whom Schlegel brought to orgasm before the underwear got torn. The two had had sex at least once before, the government acknowledged.

According to Schlegel, the Marines he fondled "were no shrinking violets. If I had ever tried to force them to do anything they didn't feel like doing at the time, believe me I certainly would have gotten my comeuppance." He adds, "The underwear were ripped. I have to say that. . . . We were both lying in this great big oversized bed out in the living room and were getting undressed. And it just so happened that his underwear got caught under him."

Schlegel's Army supervisor learned of Schlegel's homosexuality after recommending him for a security-clearance upgrade to "top secret," the level he had enjoyed while overseeing civil defense spending. In reviewing *Schlegel v. United States,* Harlan clerk Robert Mnookin focused on the tangential issue of security clearances: "If it were not for the security aspect of this case, I would think it should be clearly granted. . . . [I]t must be true that the government has greater leeway when national security is involved."

Douglas clerk Thomas Armitage did not see a strong enough link between off-duty homosexual behavior and government efficiency to justify Schlegel's firing. Armitage was pleased that anti-gay attitudes were changing and assumed that meant Supreme Court involvement wasn't needed. He wrote, "it seems that some progress is being made by the courts in this area, and this court would probably do best to leave it alone."

On April 20, 1970, an eight-man Supreme Court—Burger, Black, Douglas, Harlan, Brennan, Stewart, White and Marshall—denied *cert.* The justices unanimously turned Schlegel away without even discussing his case. (Fortas had resigned but had not yet been replaced.)

If Schlegel had won, he would have returned to the Civil Service: "I didn't visualize myself as any crusader. I did visualize myself as an honest employee and a hard worker."

Schlegel instead spent most of his career as a self-employed consultant, working briefly for Lynn Womack's beefcake magazines. In retirement, Schlegel gets just $429 a month in Social Security and $150 from the Veterans Administration, far from the $50,000-a-year federal pension he'd been on track to receive. Living in a modest frame house in Lewisburg, Pennsylvania, Schlegel, 69 when interviewed in 1996, had maintained his frugal habits—taking delight in buying still-fresh pies after they've been marked down. But he is hardly poor. After the U.S. and Pennsylvania governments threw away their chances to benefit from his budgetary skill, he put it to his own use. His investments made him a millionaire. In 1999, he set up a trust to benefit gay students at nearby Bucknell University.

"A Reckless, Irresponsible or Wanton Nature"

Schlegel attorneys Dorsen and Wulf filed a *cert* petition in what they called "a companion case" on the same day in 1970 that they submitted Schlegel's petition. The second case tackled security clearances head-on, challenging the constitutionality of denying a security clearance to a worker in private industry because of private, consensual homosexual behavior.

Electronics technician Robert Larry Adams had secured a "secret" clearance in 1957 while working for a defense contractor, Melpar Inc. After transferring to National Scientific Laboratories Inc., he applied in 1962, at his employer's request, to get his clearance upgraded. Government investigators eventually summoned him to discuss his application. Under questioning, he described homosexual encounters dating back to his fourteenth birthday. After that disclosure, he continued to work with classified material. Then, in 1965, the Defense Department turned down his "top secret" application and revoked his security clearance, rendering him virtually unemployable within the defense industry.

Since Adams wasn't a federal employee, the government could not claim that targeting him was an attempt to avoid embarrassment or to promote its own efficiency. Instead, it raised the specter of blackmail and carelessness of the "loose lips sink ships" variety.

Quoting almost verbatim from guidelines on denying clearances, a review board told Adams his sexual history "reflects acts of a reckless, irresponsible or wanton nature which indicate such poor judgment and instability as to suggest you might disclose classified information" and "furnishes reason to believe that you may be subjected to coercion, influence, or pressure which may be likely to cause you to act contrary to the national interest."

A federal judge then ruled against Adams. He also lost a 2-to-1 decision by the U.S. Court of Appeals for the District of Columbia. That court said homosexuals have difficulty getting clearances because the guidelines target "emotional instability and possible subjection to sinister pressures and influences which have traditionally been the lot of homosexuals living in what is, for better or worse, a society still strongly oriented towards heterosexuality."

Judge J. Skelly Wright strongly dissented, saying the review board ought to have to figure out whether there really was any link between Adams's "unfortunate affliction"—meaning, his homosexuality—and his ability to keep classified information secret. "Generalized assumptions that all homosexuals are security risks cannot outweigh almost eight years of faithful service," Wright declared.

Pushing the justices to take Adams's case, Dorsen and Wulf argued that it is "cruel and arbitrary . . . to tag [all homosexuals] with the virtually indelible tar of 'security risk.'" They noted that there was no evidence that homosexuals were particularly susceptible to blackmail and that Adams's homosexuality is now "public knowledge," surefire protection against blackmail. "The discrimination [against homosexuals seeking security clearances] should not continue unreviewed by this court," they argued.

But 20 years into the federal war on homosexuals, Solicitor General Griswold didn't want the court to declare an armistice. He contended that "homosexuals are still looked on with much disfavor, and their sexual conduct is frequently made criminal. As long as this continues to be the case, homosexuals will be susceptible to coercion and pressure to reveal secrets as the price for silence. The willingness of a person to engage in behavior which flouts social and legal norms equally justifies a reluctance to trust him with national secrets."

As in *Schlegel*, an eight-man court denied *cert* without discussing *Adams v. Melvin R. Laird, secretary of defense.* The denial was announced April 20, 1970, the day Richard Schlegel was turned away. Thus, the court not only refused to intervene in the federal government's ongoing efforts to rid its ranks of homosexuals but also turned its head as the government essentially labeled millions of private jobs off-limits to homosexuals.

"An Outlaw of Society"

As *Adams* and *Schlegel* underscore, the existence of sodomy laws was—and is today—used to justify viewing homosexuals as unindicted criminals or, at least, as shady characters unworthy of equal rights. Right from the start, sodomy laws had lurked just under the surface in every homosexual-rights case that reached the Supreme Court. And justices who were ex-prosecutors were far more likely than their brethren to treat homosexuals as just another variety of criminal. Yet until mid-1970 the justices were not asked to rule on the constitutionality of sodomy laws, then still on the books in every state except Illinois. In June 1970, a pair of clashing appeals reached the high court—both of them stemming from a three-judge federal panel's decision striking down Texas's sodomy law.

Dallas police aggressively enforced their state sodomy law, making an average of 69 arrests a year from 1963 to mid-1969. In February 1969, Alvin Leon Buchanan was arrested for having oral sex in a men's room in a park. Two months later, Buchanan, a stocky man with dark piercing eyes, was arrested for having oral sex in a Sears department store restroom. Buchanan, "a confessed homosexual," as his lawyer put it, responded by challenging the state sodomy law in federal court. (Texas's expansive definition of sodomy covered all oral and anal sex, bestiality and being genitally stimulated by a minor.) While his challenge was pending, Buchanan was tried, convicted and sentenced to two concurrent five-year sentences.

A special three-judge federal panel heard Buchanan's case because he was challenging the constitutionality of a state law and seeking to block its enforcement. Judges Sarah T. Hughes, Irving L. Goldberg and W. M. Taylor Jr. let Michael and Janet Gibson join as plaintiffs because Buchanan couldn't adequately represent the interests of married couples fearing prosecution for private acts of sodomy. Similarly, Dallas gay-rights activist Travis Lee Strickland was added as a plaintiff to represent "homosexuals who do not commit acts of sodomy in public places" but nevertheless fear prosecution.

In a unanimous decision January 21, 1970, the judges ruled that Texas may not outlaw sodomy—within marriage. Because it encroached on the "private, consensual acts of married couples," Texas's law was unconstitutionally broad, they declared. Never before had a federal court knocked down a sodomy law. The judges brushed aside the homosexual challenges with the obvious observation that they "do not involve private acts of the marriage relation."

Federal rules allowed Henry Wade, criminal district attorney of Dallas County, to jump directly to the Supreme Court in asking that the panel's decision be overturned. Buchanan and Strickland asked the justices to expand the lower court ruling to protect them.

On behalf of Wade, Texas Attorney General Crawford C. Martin argued that the right of privacy spelled out in *Griswold,* giving married

couples the green light to use contraceptives, is limited to vaginal intercourse. "Unlike the marital union of intercourse from which offsprings
[sic] are born . . . sodomy in marriage often leads to distaste, revulsion
and divorce," he said. ". . . The crime of sodomy, like the crimes of murder, incest, and narcotic abuse, must not be protected merely because it
is performed behind the marital door."

Homosexuality remained in the background in the appeal filed for
Buchanan and Strickland. Attorney Henry J. McCluskey Jr., who also
represented the Gibsons, argued that the lower court erred "in drawing
a distinction between the private sexual conduct of married and unmarried couples. Nowhere in the Constitution does such a distinction
exist." (Less than two years later, in a decision striking down a Massachusetts law making it a felony to sell contraceptives to unmarried people, the Supreme Court essentially agreed with McCluskey.)

McCluskey contended that Texas had no legitimate reason and, thus,
no constitutional right to regulate the private sex lives of consenting
adults. He also argued that the state sodomy law violated the First
Amendment's guarantee of freedom of religion by imposing "an essentially religious view . . . that sex which is not directed at procreation is
sinful." The attorney added that Buchanan's privacy had been unconstitutionally invaded by the cops who spied upon him in public restrooms. While accepting the state's right to criminalize public sodomy,
McCluskey stressed the extreme disparity between the 15-year prison
sentence that could result from a public sodomy arrest and the maximum punishment for public heterosexual intercourse: a $100 fine.

As interested bystanders, the North American Conference of Homophile Organizations filed a brief arguing that sodomy laws exist "primarily to punish, harass and otherwise denigrate the male homosexual,
to make him feel inferior, unworthy, and an outlaw of society." NACHO
inadvertently illustrated that true gay pride remained scarce in the first
years after Stonewall. Homosexuals, it said, usually don't realize their
orientation "until it is too late to change."

The justices postponed a decision on the Texas cases until after determining who had standing to sue in federal court. They then ruled in 1971
that anyone who had not been arrested, indicted or threatened with prosecution could not challenge a state law's constitutionality in federal
court. In addition, anyone who was being prosecuted could not file a fed-

eral challenge until state appeals had been exhausted. The justices then voted 8 to 1 to vacate the Texas sodomy ruling because of the new restrictions. (Douglas had wanted to hear the two homosexuals' plea.)

Back in Texas, a state court threw out one of Buchanan's convictions, saying that peeking at him inside a closed toilet stall violated his right against unreasonable search and seizure. Buchanan was "not the ideal plaintiff," as gay legal scholar Arthur Leonard has noted. But Buchanan was the only plaintiff left standing after the Supreme Court cut the floor out from under the Gibsons and Strickland.

Buchanan's remaining conviction was challenged in a November 1971 *cert* petition. A Douglas clerk noted, "The only serious question is whether there is a right to privacy in a three-sided john in a public restroom." The court unanimously turned the case away February 22, 1972.

By then Harlan and Black had been succeeded by Nixon appointees William H. Rehnquist and Lewis F. Powell Jr. Black, 85, had stepped down in September 1971 after a stroke. Harlan, 72, resigned a week later after being diagnosed with spinal cancer. Both died that year. Harlan and Black left a mixed legacy. They had helped protect the gay press yet had almost always refused to help gay people, despite their own lack of squeamishness. Their replacements joined the court in January 1972 and immediately began developing records hostile to gay rights.

The final page of Buchanan's original challenge was written by the Texas legislature in 1974: Because of that case, sodomy was reduced to a misdemeanor carrying a $200 fine, and the crime was narrowed to cover only homosexual oral and anal sex. (Buchanan had served prison time for sodomy. According to Social Security records, he died in 1999 at age 61, and Strickland died in 1993 at age 57.)

By the early 1970s, the nation's top court had shown no interest in the plight of homosexual U.S. citizens who'd been imprisoned, entrapped, fired or denied security clearances. In addition, the tighter "standing" requirements that the court applied to the Texas sodomy law challenge appeared to outfit the young gay-rights movement in lead running shoes. The restrictive guidelines seemed to mean that gay people whom the justices might view as nice and respectable had no chance of challenging sodomy laws and their stigmatizing impact. How would the court react when actually faced with a wholesome gay couple demanding equal rights?

7

NOTHING TO HIDE

MIKE McCONNELL MET JACK BAKER on a blind date at a Halloween party in an Oklahoma barn in 1966 when they were 24-year-old graduate students. Distinctly unimpressed, McConnell scolded the matchmaker: "Don't ever fix me up again! I really don't like him." The matchmaker confidently responded, "You don't know what you're talking about. You two were destined for one another." McConnell admits, "He was right. It was true. I fell in love." On Baker's twenty-fifth birthday, the two young men became "betrothed," as they put it, in a private ceremony.

If Frank Kameny is the visionary Martin Luther King Jr. of the gay-rights movement, James Michael "Mike" McConnell and Richard John "Jack" Baker together are its Rosa Parks. Refusing to let their relationship be relegated to the back of the bus, they eventually seized a privilege that the dominant majority assumed was restricted, in the natural order of things, to itself: legal matrimony. As rapidly growing numbers of gay people gained self-respect and moved out from the shadows, the nature of the homosexual cases reaching the Supreme Court gradually changed. McConnell and Baker brought the court the first gay cases that fundamentally were about love, not sex.

The couple's first introduction to gay liberation was through Frank Kameny and fellow gay-rights pioneer Barbara Gittings. "That's what lit our fires of pride," McConnell says, recalling that he and Baker met the activists while living in Kansas City, Missouri, in the late 1960s. "These fine people were willing to say, 'Look, I'm as good as anybody else.' That's all I needed to hear."

163

Just two years after the Stonewall rebellion, McConnell petitioned for the justices' attention in what in many ways was the first true gay-rights case to reach the court. McConnell's case stemmed neither from allegations of illegal sexual activity nor from his sexual orientation having been uncovered by government investigators. Rather, McConnell's legal challenge was a direct result of his determination to pursue what he calls "absolute and full equality—no exceptions." McConnell lived his life openly as a gay man and wanted the court to make good on the Constitution's guarantees of equal protection and freedom of speech. He believed he ought not have to hide his identity, his views or his love in order to enjoy first-class citizenship.

McConnell's legal saga began in April 1970 when he accepted a $11,000 job as head of cataloging at a campus library at the University of Minnesota, where Baker was a first-year law student. Three weeks later, on May 18, the couple applied for a marriage license in Minneapolis. "PROSPECTIVE NEWLYWEDS REALLY IN A GAY MOOD," announced the *St. Paul Pioneer Press*. A *Minneapolis Tribune* photo showed two serious-looking young men in coats and ties. The university's student daily paper reported that the couple "caused only a minor stir" in the county licensing bureau, where "office workers stood in small clusters and tittered." Baker was quoted as saying, "If there's any legal hassle, we're prepared to take it all the way to the Supreme Court." He added, "This is not a gimmick. We really want to do it. A homosexual ought to have equal rights, privileges and responsibilities."

The university's regents were apoplectic, even though news accounts did not mention that McConnell had just been offered a university job. In an emergency resolution, Elmer Anderson and the rest of the regents refused to approve McConnell's appointment, charging that "his personal conduct . . . is not consistent with the best interests of the university." McConnell, 28, had moved to Minneapolis to accept the University of Minnesota's offer. Unemployed and with only $200 to his name, he sued to force the university to hire him.

The resulting trial demonstrated how sodomy laws taint gay legal proceedings. McConnell testified that he'd never broken Minnesota's sodomy law, which applies to both straight and gay couples. Yet, the regents' unanimous view, as federal Judge Philip Neville summarized it, was that McConnell's "professed homosexuality connotes to the public generally that he practices acts of sodomy . . . [and] that by applying for a license to marry another man plaintiff intended . . . [to] engage in such sodomous criminal activities . . . and thus plaintiff has rendered himself unfit to be employed." To the regents, homosexuality equaled criminality.

Judge Neville viewed applying to marry another man as "rather bizarre," yet ruled August 10, 1970, in McConnell's favor. "Plaintiff's [job] will not expose him to children of tender years who conceivably could be influenced or persuaded to his penchant. What he does in his private life . . . should not be his employer's concern unless it can be shown to affect in some degree his efficiency in the performance of his duties. . . . An [sic] homosexual is after all a human being and a citizen. . . . He is as much entitled to the protection and benefits of the laws . . . as are others," wrote Neville, forbidding regents to block McConnell's hiring because of his homosexuality.

While the regents appealed, McConnell and Baker continued pursuing a marriage license. Minnesota's marriage application did not ask the sex of the applicants. Yet state Judge Tom Bergin ordered the Hennepin County clerk not to issue them a license. The couple appealed.

Their marriage fight made them "the first national media celebrities of the gay rights movement," as a gay history book phrased it. They were featured in *Look* on January 26, 1971, when that photo-filled magazine still shaped the way America saw itself. "Not all homosexual life is a series of one-night stands in bathhouses, public toilets or gay bars (those queer, mirror images of the swinging singles straight scene). Some homosexuals—a minority—live together in stable, often long-lasting relationships like Baker's and McConnell's," *Look* told readers.

In August 1971, McConnell legally adopted Baker. (Partner adoption was once fairly common among couples seeking legal protection otherwise unavailable for gay relationships.) The adoption enabled Baker, student body president of the University of Minnesota, to legally use the androgynous name Pat Lynn McConnell. Mike McConnell then went to Blue Earth County, Minnesota, and obtained a license to marry Pat Lynn McConnell. Blue Earth's county attorney soon declared the license void.

Nevertheless, the couple wed in a private ceremony in South Minneapolis on September 3, 1971. "We were legally married by two Methodist ministers. Both signed the documents, and they were properly filed," recalls McConnell, whose partner still goes by the name Jack Baker.

In October 1971, the trailblazing couple's luck with the heterosexist legal system ran out. The Minnesota Supreme Court ruled that Minnesota law prohibits same-sex marriage, even though it is not listed as forbidden. In that court's view, a "sensible reading" of a marriage law is that it applies only to male-female couples. Going out on an historically shaky limb, the court declared, "The institution of marriage as a union of a man and woman, uniquely involving the procreation and rearing of children within a family, is as old as the book of *Genesis*."

The court's biblical scholarship was skewered in a 1994 law journal article by William M. Hohengarten, later a clerk to Supreme Court Justice David Souter. "At best," Hohengarten noted, "*Genesis* appears to be authority for the institution of marriage as a union of one man and several women. See *Genesis* 29:1–30:24 (narrating story of Jacob's marriage to more than one woman at the same time); cf. 1 *Kings* 11:3 (stating that Solomon had 700 wives, in addition to 300 concubines)."

In 1967, the U.S. Supreme Court had knocked down state laws against interracial marriage. To the Minnesota court, that action was irrelevant to a gay marriage because there was no comparison "between a marital restriction based merely upon race and one based upon the fundamental difference in sex." Yet for centuries, many courts had viewed racial differences as a fundamental, insurmountable barrier to marriage. The Supreme Court's infamous 1857 *Dred Scott* ruling that blacks could not be citizens was partially based on the fact that states treated interracial marriage as criminal, unnatural and immoral.

Three days after the Minnesota Supreme Court ruled against Baker and McConnell in their marriage suit, the Eighth Circuit Court of Appeals overturned Judge Neville's favorable decision in McConnell's library-job lawsuit. A three-judge Eighth Circuit panel ruled that the regents' action had not been "arbitrary or capricious." That court saw McConnell's openness as a reason to rule against him. This was not a case involving "a desire clandestinely to pursue homosexual conduct," the judges stressed. Labeling McConnell's first attempt to marry an "antic," the appeals court charged that the librarian "demands . . . the right to pursue an activist role in implementing his unconventional ideas concerning the societal status to be accorded homosexuals and, thereby, to foist tacit approval of this socially repugnant concept upon his employer. . . ."

McConnell's *cert* petition reached the Supreme Court January 31, 1972. Minneapolis attorney Lynn S. Castner argued that the librarian's rights to due process, equal protection, free speech and privacy had been violated. The justices were told, "Attitudes are changing toward homosexuality. . . . The time is ripe for examination by this court of the constitutional issues presented in this case." McConnell was well within his rights in peacefully seeking legal benefits "presently enjoyed by heterosexuals," Castner argued.

Since the regents had won in lower court, they saw no reason for the justices to hear the case. Regents' attorney Richard A. Moore of St. Paul contended that Mike McConnell had lost his job offer because he "made a public spectacle of himself." Moore argued, "It is no deprivation of constitutional rights for an institution of higher learning to choose not to hire one whose deliberate intentional conduct is so bizarre as to be a probable source of embarrassment and ridicule. . . ." He cited the *Poe* dissent in which Justice Harlan stressed he wasn't proposing a right of privacy broad enough to protect "adultery, homosexuality, fornication and incest."

After reviewing McConnell's case for Justice Douglas, clerk Richard L. Jacobson concluded that it "flatly implicates First Amendment freedoms." Twenty-five years later, Jacobson said Douglas would have considered the homosexual aspects of the case "irrelevant," adding, "They basically took [McConnell's] appointment away because he advocated gay marriage. And Douglas would see that as a clear First Amendment violation." Yet the cantankerous Douglas wasn't one to try to drum up a majority for his vision of civil liberties. "Douglas really never cared that much about what other people thought. . . . Basically, he did what he thought was right, and if people came along, great," Jacobson recalls.

When the justices discussed *McConnell v. Anderson* in conference, only Douglas voted to take the case. Denial of *cert* was announced April 3, 1972. Douglas was listed as dissenting.

The Baker-McConnell marriage lawsuit had reached the U.S. Supreme Court in February 1972. (The case was an "appeal"—not a *cert* petition—since it was one sort of constitutional dispute that the justices were then required to settle.) Because Hennepin County Attorney George M. Scott was slow to respond, the marriage case was held over until the 1972–73 term.

The American Civil Liberties Union passed up its chance to join the fight for gay marriage. In an internal memo, attorney Mel Wulf confessed, "I don't know whether it's my objective judgment as a constitutional lawyer or my subjective reaction as an old-time Calvinist Puritan, but . . . to bring this case to the Supreme Court might well jeopardize what I would characterize as our more serious efforts on behalf of the homophile movement."

Throughout the 1970s and 1980s, marriage was not taken seriously as a goal by most gay-rights organizations. Some gay leaders were hostile to pushing for inclusion in a patriarchal institution that they viewed as irredeemably flawed. To them, the heart of the gay-rights movement was the pursuit of unfettered sexual and personal freedom, not the legal bondage marriage entailed. Marriage finally shoved its way to the forefront of the gay movement in the 1990s only because marriage-minded couples sued for equal treatment. In 1993, the Hawaii Supreme Court shocked the world by handing down a preliminary opinion in favor of same-sex marriage. Suddenly, countless couples saw marriage as a possible dream—the golden ring from which truly equal rights would ultimately flow. On July 1, 2000, in the biggest breakthrough in the history of the gay civil rights movement, Vermont began recognizing "civil unions," a new legal status providing gay couples all the state-level rights and responsibilities of marriage.

In 1972, however, gay marriage would have seemed like a contradiction in terms to most Americans. Undaunted by the prospect of trying to get the Supreme Court to take such an avant-garde topic seriously, R. Michael Wetherbee of the Minnesota Civil Liberties Union appealed on behalf of the Minnesota couple. Since the Minnesota Supreme Court had read a prohibition on same-sex unions into its state marriage law, the only question before the U.S. Supreme Court was whether that prohibition violated the U.S. Constitution. Wetherbee asked the justices: May two people, "solely because they are of the same sex," constitutionally be denied the opportunity to make their relationship a legal marriage? "At first, the question and the proposed relationship may well appear bizarre—especially to heterosexuals. . . . [T]hat first impulse provides us with some measure of the continuing impact on our society of prejudice against non-heterosexuals," he argued.

Wetherbee briefly touched on a few of the tangible and intangible benefits that McConnell and Baker were being denied because they were refused the right to marry: tax benefits, inheritance rights, veterans' benefits, the right to sue for wrongful death, property ownership rights, the right not to testify against one another and priceless emotional symbolism. The denial of a host of benefits routinely granted through marriage to "similarly situated" childless heterosexual couples meant equal protection rights were being violated, Wetherbee argued. Foreshadowing the Hawaii same-sex marriage fight, he contended that "the discrimination in this case is one of gender," noting that in 1971 the justices had finally struck down a law as unconstitutional sex discrimination.

Wetherbee assured the justices that public attitudes were changing. Prime evidence of that transformation was Wetherbee's own argument: He said his clients weren't the ones who were sick. ". . . Prejudice against homosexuals, which tends to be phobic, is unlikely to be cured until the public acknowledges that homosexuals, like all people, are entitled to the full protection and recognition of the law," he contended. "Only then will the public perceive that homosexuals are not freaks or unfortunate aberrations [*sic*], to be swept under the carpet or be reserved for anxious phantasies about one's identity or child rearing techniques."

Yet "unfortunate aberration" pretty well summarized the attitude that Douglas and Brennan—far more progressive than most justices—had expressed toward homosexuals in their 1967 *Boutilier* immigration dissents. There was no reason to think their attitudes had shifted.

If the justices wanted to dismiss the marriage appeal unheard, County Attorney Scott suggested justifications: "The appeal does not present a substantial federal question, and the power to regulate marriages within a state belongs exclusively to that state." (Five years earlier the U.S. Supreme Court had forcefully injected itself into regulation of marriage by declaring laws against interracial marriage unconstitutional.) Arguing on behalf of Gerald Nelson, the county court clerk being sued to issue a marriage license, Scott contended the interracial marriage case, *Loving v. Virginia,* had been an exception to the unwritten rule against federal involvement because it involved race discrimination. Scott also argued that if McConnell and Baker were already married, as they claimed, there was no longer any reason for the suit.

But the core of Scott's argument implied that the questions raised by the case were not only substantial but potentially earthshaking. ". . . [I]t is patently obvious that to permit same sex marriage would create absolute chaos in our system of jurisprudence, government and culture," he contended. The Baker-McConnell lawsuit "must be considered as an attack upon the very foundation itself of the institution of marriage," he said, arguing that the Constitution's framers would never have envisioned its protections being used to legalize a same-sex marriage. (He offered no opinion on what the framers, who allowed slavery, would have thought of using the Constitution to overturn 16 states' bans on interracial marriage.) Ignoring that the Constitution guarantees freedom of religion and doesn't mention marriage, Scott emotionally concluded, "Our country, and our Constitution, were founded upon basic religious principles . . . [including] that marriage is an institution ordained by God and that such institution is to be entered into by a man and a woman as husband and wife."

As a black man married to a woman of Hawaiian ancestry, Justice Marshall might have been expected to take more interest than his colleagues in the federal government's role in regulating marriage. In his chambers, review of the gay marriage case, *Baker v. Nelson*, fell to clerk Barbara Underwood. In an April 1972 memo, she said, "it is probably reasonable, within the limits imposed by equal protection, for a state to limit the institution known as marriage to heterosexual couples (though it is surprisingly hard to justify this except by reference to custom . . .)." The exclusion might be justified "on the ground that homosexual marriage would entail criminal conduct," she added, urging that the appeal be dismissed.

Douglas clerk Carol Bruch thought the county attorney had failed to "adequately distinguish" gay marriage from interracial marriage. She recommended that the appeal be heard.

Writing for a unanimous Supreme Court in *Loving*, Chief Justice Warren had declared, "The freedom to marry has long been recognized as one of the vital personal rights essential to the orderly pursuit of happiness by free men." But five years later, when free men wanted to marry one another, the court's vision of civil rights was not broad enough to protect them. At the start of the court's 1972–73 term, just months after Democrat George McGovern became the first presidential nominee of a major party to advocate gay rights, the justices met in private conference on *Baker v. Nelson*. They unanimously voted to "dismiss for want of a substantial federal question," the phrasing the court routinely used in turning an appeal away unheard.

Unlike turning away a *cert* petition, dismissing an appeal counts as a decision on the case's merits and, thus, is considered a precedent when similar cases arise. However, the precedent set by the October 10, 1972, dismissal of *Baker v. Nelson* is anyone's guess since the justices offered no clue about what they found wanting. Was the court saying that a ban on same-sex marriage raises no federal question of equal protection? Or, was the court saying that this particular case didn't properly raise a federal question? Certainly, from the justices' perspective, there were plenty of reasons to shove the case aside. There was no conflict among the lower courts to be settled; no court in the world had ruled in favor of gay marriage. Simply taking the case would have plunged the court into a controversy that the nation as a whole would have considered absurd, if not obscene, jeopardizing the court's authority and rendering it a laughingstock in the eyes of many. An integration-minded court had stalled for 13 years before toppling racist marriage laws that clearly violated equal protection. A court that had raised no objections to the targeting of homosexuals for arrest or deportation could hardly be expected to give its blessing to homosexual marriage. Plus, even though *Baker v. Nelson* presented the court with a squeaky-clean gay couple, the case was muddied by McConnell's adoption of Baker and by the couple's claim to have already gotten married.

The truth probably is that it was difficult, if not downright impossible, for the nine married men then serving on the Supreme Court to see *Baker v. Nelson* as anything but frivolous, perhaps even disrespectful. The justices' personal lives and court traditions were grounded in that era's assumptions of heterosexual marriage—a man took a wife; she took his name and became his satellite. (Inside the justices' courtroom, brass nameplates reserved chairs for "Mrs. Douglas" and each of the other court wives.) Although five justices had joined the court since *Loving*, that decision's language offers a telling glimpse of the liberal thinking of that era. "Marriage," the court hyperbolically declared, "is one of the 'basic civil rights of man,' fundamental to our very existence and survival." Marriage was equated with procreation, so much so that the court acted as if reproduction were impossible outside wedlock.

The lingering puzzle of *Baker v. Nelson* isn't that nine presumably heterosexual justices saw no reason to accept the case. It's impossible to imagine that a majority of those justices would have ever contemplated rocking the nation by overturning bans on gay marriage. Unlike on racial issues and women's rights, the court wasn't getting encouragement from Congress or the White House to reassess the second-class citizenship of homosexuals. What's puzzling is that the justices unanimously passed up their chance to second the Minnesota Supreme Court by voting to "affirm" its decision against gay marriage.

On March 10, 1997, Mike McConnell and Jack Baker, both 55, celebrated their thirtieth anniversary, dating their relationship from their betrothal. In 1997, McConnell, who'd briefly worked as a bartender after losing his university job offer, had been a librarian in Hennepin County's nationally respected library system for nearly 25 years. Baker continued to pursue his career as a lawyer, engineer and businessman. They'd kept battling for equality even after their Supreme Court defeats. Baker, an Air Force veteran, for example, unsuccessfully tried to get spousal veteran's benefits for McConnell. Baker's idealism was so uncompromising that in 1973 he testified against a proposed Minnesota gay-rights law because it used "homosexual," a word he found as offensive as "cocksucker" because it emphasized the sexual aspect of gay relationships. Baker's critics found his brand of purity an impediment to the young movement's progress. By 1980, Baker and McConnell shifted their focus away from gay liberation. They've stayed out of recent gay-marriage struggles. Baker is no longer willing to talk publicly about their marriage fight.

"When our 15 minutes on stage expired some time ago, we exited the limelight comforted by the knowledge that we accomplished our goal," McConnell says. "I think that we got the entire world talking about gay relationships and gay marriage."

Their gay marriage case, the only one to reach the Supreme Court thus far, marked a tremendous milestone: For the first time, gay Americans petitioning the nation's highest court didn't stand accused of anything and had not been punished in any way. Instead, they were suing for full recognition of the constitutional rights routinely granted to other citizens.

If the court had handed down a full opinion in the case, it surely would have been a profoundly negative one, providing language that could be cited to rationalize denying same-sex couples equal rights. The court's decision not to heave another major stumbling block onto the path makes the climb to legal gay marriage just a bit easier than it otherwise would have been.

"The Abominable and Detestable Crime Against Nature"

The court that had nothing to say about same-sex marriage regained its voice when the subject returned a year later to criminalization of sodomy. The idea that certain sexual acts were unspeakably horrid was reflected in the wording of Florida's sodomy law for more than 100 years. That 1868 statute declared, "Whoever commits the abominable and detestable crime against nature, either with mankind or with beast, shall be punished by imprisonment not exceeding 20 years." Florida courts long interpreted "crime against nature" as a euphemism for oral and anal sex. Then, in 1971, the Florida Supreme Court declared the law unconstitutionally vague. "The language of this statute could entrap unsuspecting citizens and subject them to 20-year sentences. . . . Such a sentence is equal to that for manslaughter and would no doubt be a shocking revelation to persons who do not have an understanding of the meaning of the statute," the court noted. The Florida court refused, however, to make its ruling retroactive.

Raymond R. Stone and Eugene F. Huffman were among the prisoners left serving sentences for breaking a law the state's top court had since struck down as unconstitutional. Stone had been sentenced in 1970 to two consecutive five-year sentences for "an act of copulation *per os* and *per anum*," as Florida's attorney general so delicately phrased it in Latin while arguing that the law and its judicial interpretations provided sufficient "clarity" to warn the average person what was forbidden. Huffman had been sentenced in 1968 to serve six months to 10 years for anal sex. Attorney General Shevin alleged Stone's sex acts were "forceful" and that Huffman's was committed "in a jail rape situation." Case records and interviews provided no details about either man's alleged crime. The Florida law made no distinction between consensual and nonconsensual sex.

In 1972, a federal judge ruled Florida's "crime against nature" law unconstitutionally vague and freed Huffman and Stone. On April 19, 1973, the Fifth Circuit Court of Appeals agreed. The Fifth Circuit's opinion, written by Judge Irving L. Goldberg, quoted a 1926 U.S. Supreme Court declaration that a law violates due process if it is "so vague that men of common intelligence must necessarily guess at its meaning."

Florida corrections chief Louie L. Wainwright and state prison superintendent James F. Tompkins asked the Fifth Circuit's overseer, Justice Lewis F. Powell Jr., to suspend the impact of the appeals court's decision until the Supreme Court could decide whether to hear their appeal. Powell refused, an action noteworthy because the prison chief's plea stressed that 85 people were then imprisoned in Florida for so-called crimes against nature. Thus, Powell was—or should have been—aware that, in Florida alone, a sizable number of people were serving sodomy sentences of up to 20 years. Yet 14 years later, when he cast the decisive vote in *Hardwick* upholding sodomy laws, Powell naively acted as if he would have voted differently if sodomy laws actually led to long prison sentences.

When the justices gathered early in their 1973–74 term to weigh Florida's appeal, 18 states had "crime against nature" laws like Florida's. A decision upholding the Fifth Circuit's finding of vagueness no doubt would have struck down all those laws. Only Douglas and Brennan wanted to affirm, however.

On November 5, 1973, the court, without public dissent, handed down a three-page unsigned opinion by Byron White in *Wainwright, Corrections Director, et al. v. Stone*. White had been the quintessential scholar-athlete, having delayed going to Oxford on a prestigious Rhodes Scholarship in order to play pro football for the Pittsburgh Pirates (a name later associated with Pittsburgh's baseball team) for a record-high $15,000 in 1938. While serving in the Navy during World War II, he wrote the official report on John F. Kennedy's heroism after the sinking of his patrol boat. As president, Kennedy appointed White deputy attorney general. Then, after passing over a black appeals court judge because it was "just too early" to appoint the first black justice, Kennedy tapped the keenly competitive, zealously private White for the Supreme Court in 1962.

According to White's "crime against nature" opinion, Florida's law was not unconstitutionally vague because when Stone and Huffman were convicted Florida's highest court still read "crime against nature" as a coded reference to oral and anal sex. Thus, White, who adopted the stilted *"per os* and *per anum"* terminology, ruled that the Florida men had been warned. As a result of the court's action, Stone and Huffman presumably were reincarcerated, although, when we inquired about them, Florida prison officials were unable to trace them.

The same day the justices refused to find Florida's crime-against-nature law too vague, they dismissed a pair of fellatio appeals "for want of a substantial federal question." In one, Kenneth Dale Canfield had been sentenced to 15 years in prison for oral sex.

Canfield, a thin young man with black hair, delicate hands and a twangy accent, had met another man in an Oklahoma City bar on April 17, 1971. The two left together, drove around, then pulled 100 yards off the road to have oral sex. A police officer peered into the car and arrested then for a "crime against nature." The maximum sentence was 10 years, but Canfield was sentenced to 20 (later reduced to 15) because of a prior felony. An Oklahoma court of appeals then upheld his conviction, ruling "crime against nature" is as "inherently understandable as . . . 'murder.'"

Though the justices weren't told, Canfield was already a free man when his appeal reached them. A few months after Canfield went to prison, his attorney, William P. Porter, was walking near the Oklahoma City courthouse when someone tapped his shoulder. Turning around, he was shocked to see Canfield. "Did you escape?" Porter asked incredulously. Laughing, Canfield replied, "They let me go," recalls Porter, who says homosexuality had somehow turned out to be a get-out-of-jail-free card for Canfield. Porter pursued the appeal anyway because he was excited to take a case to the nation's top court.

In the other dismissed fellatio case, John Martin Connor, 30, had been convicted under a law requiring a sentence of one to 21 years for "sodomy or buggery" after being arrested in a parked car. Arkansas's top court had ruled that the law covered oral sex, saying, "[I]t is an unnatural sex act which is condemned. It is the opposite of a natural sex act. . . ."

The justices dismissed *Connor v. Arkansas* and *Canfield v. Oklahoma* without discussing either in conference. Through action and inaction, the justices had created the impression by November 1973 that virtually no law was too vague if homosexuals were being punished by it. "Psychopathic" could be equated with homosexual. "Lewd and dissolute" could cover the most innocuous homosexual contact. "Crime against nature" could be a synonym for sodomy. "Sodomy" could mean anything "unnatural," which in turn could mean anything homosexual. When laws made no mention of homosexuality, the court allowed prohibitions to be read as anti-homosexual and benefits (such as marriage rights) to be read as excluding homosexuals. By consistently ignoring or ruling against homosexuals' pleas for fair treatment, the court was teetering on the brink of reading homosexuals out of the Constitution.

"A Duty of Privacy"

When the first gay teacher case reached the Supreme Court in June 1974—five years after the Stonewall rebellion—there was no evidence that the gay-rights movement had influenced any justice. Lower courts here and there, however, had begun showing queasiness about rubber-stamping overt discrimination against a group that was starting to arouse considerable sympathy within segments of the general population.

Yet in the high court's first gay teacher case, *Acanfora v. Board of Education of Montgomery County*, such queasiness translated not into favorable rulings but into far-fetched excuses for denying equal protection to a particular gay individual. Thus, in a textbook example of homophobia in action, lower court judges could feel broad-minded for acknowledging that homosexuals as a group have rights but refuse to allow a gay teacher to return to his classroom.

Joseph "Joe" Acanfora III, son of an Italian-American truck driver with a fourth-grade education, grew up two miles from the Jersey shore in Brick Town. Fascinated by weather as a boy, he measured the rain, took the ocean's temperature and gobbled chicken wings in hopes of flying up to the clouds. He taught his homemaker mother to stop being terrified of thunder.

"I was always the star in the family, you know the bright kid. I graduated valedictorian of my high school," recalls Acanfora, who in 1968 became the first member of his family to go to college. Planning to become a Navy pilot, he won a full Navy ROTC scholarship to Penn State and signed up as a meteorology major.

As he struggled to ignore internal tugs toward being gay, he dated women. "It was a complete farce. I felt like I was really hurting people, not being honest with them or myself," he says. At the end of his sophomore year, Joe Acanfora shifted direction. Realizing he disliked the military mindset and opposed the Vietnam war, he dropped out of ROTC. He switched his major to education. And he spotted a 3-by-5 card on a bulletin board announcing a free course on homosexuality. He signed up. Soon he found himself treasurer of Homophiles of Penn State (HOPS), a campus group that sprang out of the course. The student government recognized the gay civil rights group, but the administration balked. HOPS sued. In a 1972 newspaper interview about the fight, which HOPS won, Acanfora revealed that he was gay.

Penn State immediately yanked him out of his student teaching post at a nearby junior high. A court order quickly reinstated him. But when he tried to get certified to teach in Pennsylvania after graduation, the university reignited the controversy, requiring six deans to grill him to determine whether he had good character. The dean of education pressed Acanfora for intimate details: "What homosexual acts do you prefer. . . ?" He declined to answer. Deadlocked, the deans bucked the question of Acanfora's character up to the state secretary of education.

Meanwhile, Acanfora landed a job teaching eighth-grade earth science—a combination of geology, astronomy and his first love, meteorology—in Montgomery County, Maryland, a prosperous suburb of Washington, D.C. By all accounts, his performance during his first four weeks as a teacher in the fall of 1972 was excellent. His students and supervisors did not know he was gay.

Ironically, Acanfora's classroom career slammed to an abrupt, premature halt on Friday, September 22, 1972, when Pennsylvania's secretary of education called a news conference to declare he was certifying Acanfora to teach in his state. A brief item on the decision in Sunday's *New York Times* mentioned that Acanfora taught at Parkland Junior High School in Rockville, Maryland. On Monday morning, Parkland's principal ripped Joe Acanfora, known homosexual, out of his classroom and transferred him to a make-work assignment designed to keep him away from students. Acanfora sued to regain his teaching job.

Though the Supreme Court's evolution in dealing with homosexuality remained stalled, public outrage at Acanfora's ouster showed that attitudes indeed were changing. Not only did Washington-area gay activists—led by Frank Kameny—protest, 67 of Parkland's 83 faculty members petitioned the school board to return Acanfora to his classroom. Half the eighth grade begged the board to let Acanfora teach. A local newspaper demanded that Acanfora be judged on his teaching. The student paper at his alma mater declared that he had "taught us the meaning of courage, integrity and persistence." Meanwhile, the National Education Association bankrolled Acanfora's fight to teach. The news media clamored for interviews. *60 Minutes* introduced the nation to the handsome, sad-eyed, young idealist with fashionably long sideburns, modish haircut and drooping mustache.

At a trial before federal Judge Joseph H. Young in Baltimore, pediatricians and mental health professionals dueled over whether being taught earth science by Acanfora would turn eighth graders into homosexuals. Both sides assumed that preventing homosexuality would be desirable because homosexuals are stigmatized. To Acanfora's foes, the fact that he was a good teacher—or, as the superintendent of schools put it, "a good role model"—was all the more reason to keep him away from kids. Child psychiatrist Reginald Spencer Lourie of George Washington University Medical School compared keeping Acanfora out of the classroom to an "inoculation program" to keep schoolchildren from becoming gay. Acanfora's defenders pointed to evidence that "sexual orientation" is fixed by age five or six.

In ruling May 31, 1973, Judge Young objected to the school system's admitted unwillingness to hire known homosexuals. ". . . The time has come today for private, consenting adult homosexuality to enter the sphere of constitutionally protectable interests. Intolerance of the unconventional halts the growth of liberty. This case would be different if homosexuals were generically psychotic," Young declared.

But just as he was wrapping homosexuals in the Equal Protection Clause of the 14th Amendment, Young accused Acanfora of exceeding the First Amendment's free speech protections by speaking up for himself after losing his classroom. Seeing Montgomery County's reason for removing Acanfora as invalid, the judge came up with a new reason. Teachers, he declared, have "not only a right of privacy . . . but also a duty of privacy." Young compared Acanfora's tame interviews, such as appearing on PBS with his supportive parents, to shouting "Fire!" in a crowded theater. He refused to reinstate Acanfora.

Young's decision, Acanfora says, "told me judges are people—with all the same homophobia and bigotry as everyone else."

On February 7, 1974, the Fourth Circuit Court of Appeals flatly disagreed with Young about Acanfora's public statements: They were indeed protected by the First Amendment. The appeals court came up with yet another reason to rule against the young teacher: He had not listed Homophiles of Penn State on his job application when asked about "extracurricular activities" and membership in "professional, service and/or fraternal organizations." Acanfora could not challenge the constitutionality of an anti-gay employment policy because he had used "deception" to try to avoid it, ruled the three-judge panel, which included retired justice Clark. Driving home to visit his parents, Acanfora heard the verdict on his car radio and burst into tears.

In petitioning the Supreme Court, Acanfora's attorneys pointed out that the high court had already ruled that teachers cannot be required to list every membership; also, the Montgomery County form did not ask about political groups. The justices were urged to intervene to settle a conflict among the appeals courts. Five circuits had ruled that a public employee's firing must be overturned if any reason for it was unconstitutional.

At the heart of Acanfora's petition was the undeniable fact that he'd been removed from the classroom not for concealment but for honesty about being gay. Acanfora's petition told the court that "there appears to be general acknowledgement among the experts that concealment of one's homosexuality—living 'in the closet'—is psychologically harmful." In reply, the school board's attorney simply said the court should not allow anyone to lie to the government.

Without discussing *Acanfora v. Board of Education* in conference, the justices denied *cert* on October 15, 1974. For 24-year-old Joe Acanfora, being turned away by the Supreme Court felt like the ultimate verdict against his choice of careers. He never again tried to teach.

In a 1996 interview in the cozy Berkeley, California, home he shared with his partner of 15 years, Acanfora said that he'd wanted the justices to understand "that I am an American citizen, that I pay my taxes. I work hard. I was valedictorian. I did everything I was supposed to do. . . . I have an in-born, inalterable different sexual orientation. And it is injustice to punish people for that." Then a handsome 46-year-old with short graying hair and a clipped mustache, Acanfora was associate director of the University of California's office of technology transfer. He was convinced that had the Supreme Court returned him to his classroom he would still be teaching. "I enjoyed it, and I was good at it."

By then, Joe Acanfora's former students were old enough to have eighth graders of their own. And the Supreme Court still had not ruled on whether public school teachers can constitutionally be barred from the classroom simply for being gay.

Two months after the court unanimously turned away Acanfora in 1974, Justice Douglas, 76, suffered a stroke that dulled his mind. He resigned less than a year later. The rugged civil libertarian had been homosexual litigants' most consistent ally during his 36 years as a justice. Brennan took over the role of the court's liberal conscience on basic gay civil rights.

Douglas's successor, 55-year-old federal appeals court judge John Paul Stevens, had been nominated by President Gerald Ford in an attempt to restore the faith in government that had been severely damaged by the Watergate scandal and President Richard Nixon's resignation in disgrace. Confirmed in December 1975, Stevens, a moderate Republican with a penchant for bow ties, soon proved to be an independent thinker. Stevens almost immediately signaled gay Americans that he would not be among their knee-jerk opponents.

Rubber-stamping a Stigmatizing Law

Until the mid-1970s, the Supreme Court never directly confronted the question of sodomy laws' constitutionality. Yet every time a gay case had reached the court, the existence of sodomy laws weighed heavily on the scales of justice, often tipping the balance away from equal treatment of homosexuals. Sodomy laws were used elsewhere as a justification for denying gay parents custody and visitation, for opposing gay-rights statutes and for treating gay people as sex-crazed outlaws who deserve to be arrested for making a suggestive remark or fired for letting anyone discover their "secret." Sodomy equaled homosexuality equaled criminality. The fact that the vast majority of sodomy laws applied to anyone—even married couples—who engaged in oral or anal sex did almost nothing to change that equation.

In the second half of the 20th century, sodomy laws were used only secondarily to police sexual behavior. Their primary function was to stigmatize gay people. Did laws that served mainly to bolster prejudice violate the Constitution's promise of equal protection? Or, as the question was put to the justices in December 1975, did Virginia's sodomy law violate the rights of gay men?

In the years immediately after Stonewall, many gay-rights leaders began to think that the ultimate success of their movement depended on getting ordinary gay people to risk coming out so that they would no longer be nameless, faceless shadow figures to heterosexual lawmakers, judges and voters. The National Gay Task Force (NGTF), founded in 1973 by former Rockefeller University biology professor Bruce Voeller, was intent on demonstrating that gay people were not markedly different from heterosexuals and, thus, should enjoy the same rights.

Frustrated by his years in an anti-establishment ragtag gay liberation group dominated by unruly leftists, Dr. Bruce Voeller envisioned NGTF as a sort of gay ACLU that would calmly challenge discrimination. He wanted to attract middle-class gay professionals and to mainstream gay activism, moving it off the streets and into boardrooms, courthouses and Congress. Working to create a climate in which everyday gay men and lesbians would feel safe coming out, NGTF members began challenging sodomy laws. As a divorced father, Voeller was keenly aware of the stigmatizing effect of sodomy laws: He had had to fight for visitation rights after coming out.

Virginia's crime-against-nature law made oral sex, anal sex and bestiality a felony carrying a one-to-three-year sentence (later increased to five years). An NGTF-backed lawsuit, filed by "John Doe and Robert Roe" on behalf of all gay male Virginians, went directly to a three-judge federal panel.

"Expert Frank Kameny, Ph.D."—as court papers described him—testified by deposition against Virginia's law. Noting homosexuality was no longer officially listed as a mental illness, Kameny stated: Prosecution doesn't deter homosexual sodomy. Imprisonment doesn't change homosexuals into heterosexuals. Most child abuse is heterosexual. Homosexuals aren't a criminal class, except in terms of sodomy laws. And Virginia has no rational basis for criminalizing sodomy between consenting men in private.

Doe, meanwhile, told the court that he could satisfy himself sexually only by committing sodomy, that sodomy laws had a chilling effect on his enjoyment of sex and that he'd been harassed by police for being in a known gay gathering spot.

The state of Virginia offered no evidence of the law's constitutionality.

"We thought we had a wonderful chance of winning. There were very high hopes that this would end sodomy laws once and for all," Kameny recalls.

But by a 2-to-1 vote, the federal panel upheld the Virginia law in October 1975. Senior Circuit Judge Albert V. Bryan wrote that the Supreme Court's privacy rulings applied "exclusively" to "marriage," "the sanctity of the home" and "the nurture of family life," ignoring the fact that the right to privacy had been recognized as covering abortion and contraception for unmarried couples. "Homosexuality . . . is obviously no portion of marriage, home or family life," Bryan said. Citing Harlan's *Poe* dissent and Goldberg's *Griswold* concurrence as proof, Bryan ruled Virginia had the right to promote "morality and decency" by punishing homosexuality. He quoted Leviticus 20:13: "If a man also lie with mankind, as he lieth with a woman, both of them have committed an abomination: they shall surely be put to death. . . ."

In dissent, Judge Robert R. Merhige Jr. strongly argued that the majority's view of prior privacy rulings was too narrow: "I view those cases as standing for the principle that every individual has a right to be free from unwarranted governmental intrusion into one's decision on private matters of intimate concern. . . . Private consensual sex acts between adults are matters, absent evidence that they are harmful, in which the state has no legitimate interest."

Merhige was among the first federal judges unwilling to accept just any concocted justification for restricting homosexual behavior. "To suggest, as [Virginia does], that the prohibition of homosexual conduct will in some manner encourage new heterosexual marriages and prevent the dissolution of existing ones is unworthy of judicial response," he fumed.

Doe et al. v. Commonwealth's Attorney for the City of Richmond et al. advanced to the Supreme Court on appeal in December 1975. The case did nothing to put a human face on homosexuality. The justices were told only that "John Doe and Robert Roe are active homosexuals who regularly seek and enjoy sexual gratification in a private and consensual manner with other adults." The anonymous "Doe" was Bill Bland, Voeller's lover and a native of tiny West Point, Virginia. An NGTF photo of Bland standing in front of the Supreme Court shows a long-legged, dark-haired man wearing a heavy mustache, a suit jacket, necktie and bell-bottoms. "Robert Roe" did not exist, according to Kameny.

"Doe's" attorneys, Philip J. Hirschkop and John D. Grad, argued that Virginia's sodomy law violated gay men's right to privacy and trampled their First Amendment right to freedom of expression and association. (If saying that sexual behavior should be protected as freedom of expression seems a bit of a stretch, perhaps it is no more so than saying that about nude dancing. Yet, in 1991, eight justices ruled naked bar dancing enjoys some First Amendment protection.)

"Doe's" attorneys further claimed that it would violate the Constitution's equal protection guarantee to respect the privacy of unmarried heterosexual couples (as the court had done in a 1972 birth control case) but not provide homosexual unmarried couples similar cover.

Meanwhile, Virginia Attorney General Andrew P. Miller told the justices that the case was too insubstantial to merit their attention. He argued that because the sodomy statute applied to everyone it wasn't discriminatory—essentially the argument Virginia had long offered in defending its law against interracial marriage. Protecting "private consensual sodomitic acts," Miller warned, would undermine laws against fornication and adultery.

The window that Justice Douglas's records provided into the court's private machinations is keenly missed in trying to see how the court—

then required to rule on properly presented appeals—reached its decision in *Doe*. On Friday, March 26, 1976, the justices conferred privately about the case. The next Monday, a six-man majority "affirmed" the lower court's decision without explanation. (In choosing to affirm rather than simply dismiss *Doe*, the court seemed to be violating its 1971 guidelines, which decreed that individuals must have been arrested, indicted or directly threatened with prosecution to have standing to challenge a law's constitutionality.)

Justices Brennan, Marshall and Stevens were publicly listed by the court as having wanted to hear oral argument in *Doe*. Brennan had believed since at least 1971 that a "fundamental" aspect of the right to privacy was the "freedom to do with one's body as one likes." Marshall saw the Constitution's protections as expansive enough to cover everyone. Unlike many of his white brethren, he looked on the court's precedents not as building blocks but as acknowledgments of existing civil rights guaranteed all Americans. "The fact that he didn't exclude homosexuals is . . . noteworthy," a former Marshall clerk says. Stevens, on the court just three months when he voted against rubber-stamping the lower court's sodomy decision, was already emphasizing his belief in the importance of scrutinizing each case's facts and of not short-circuiting the process designed to reveal them.

According to *The Brethren*, Bob Woodward and Scott Armstrong's extraordinary peek behind the court's velvet curtain, Brennan and Marshall had tried without success to find the necessary fourth vote to secure a full hearing for *Doe*:

> Marshall was outraged. Privacy interests acknowledged explicitly in earlier opinions, particularly the 1973 abortion decision, should protect consenting adults in such matters. The Virginia law that had been upheld had also banned heterosexual oral sex. Marshall found it ridiculous that the state should exercise such police power. Worse, in Marshall's eyes, was the majority's unwillingness to face the issue squarely—to accept the case for argument and to write an opinion spelling out its reasoning. It was cowardly. The court's authority rested, in part, on its ability and willingness to offer its reasons for any decision. Where were the other votes—Blackmun, Stewart and Powell

[and Burger]—that had extended the concept of privacy as a basis for the right to have an abortion?

Nobody's Poster Boy

The day the Supreme Court affirmed the constitutionality of Virginia's sodomy law, it turned away Eugene Enslin, a gay man convicted of oral sex after being set up by a police detective intent—by his own admission—on running Enslin out of town. When arrested, Enslin was the 31-year-old manager of a massage parlor, a porn shop and a bar, side-by-side businesses in Jacksonville, North Carolina. He worked in the X-rated part of town, which was awash in the cold cash thrown around by hot-blooded young Marines from Camp LeJeune. The semi-cultured son of a Pennsylvania policeman, Enslin had hit quite a few bumps in the road before landing in the rough side of Jacksonville.

Born in 1942, Enslin knew by age nine—when he "wanted to hug and kiss Tarzan"—that he was attracted to men. As a young man, he was expelled first from a Quaker college for saying yes when a male student propositioned him, then from a Protestant missionary college for converting to Catholicism. After two years as a Navy hospital corpsman, he was dismissed because of a love letter from another man. "I am not a poster boy for a successful gay life. I am a poster boy for all . . . the varieties of homophobia that exist in society, the hypocrisy," Enslin says.

After working in Virginia adult bookstores, Enslin moved to North Carolina to open one in Jacksonville in 1972. He was repeatedly arrested as the police tried to shut down the bookstore, which carried straight and gay material, and the massage parlor. Police Detective Sam Hudson, who knew Enslin was gay, figured that the way to get rid of him was to recruit a young Marine to entice him into breaking North Carolina's "crime against nature" law. "This was a deliberate and planned effort on my part using this 17-year-old prosecuting witness, Herbert Morgan, to set Mr. Enslin up so that I could prosecute him for homosexual conduct," Hudson later testified.

With the policeman hiding in the bushes across the street with binoculars, the Marine entered the rundown building that housed Tri-Massage

Parlor, which Enslin had decorated incongruously with prints of paintings by Salvador Dalí and Rembrandt. The teenage Marine nervously told Enslin he was looking for "extra excitement." Enslin took him next door to the windowless back room behind the bookstore. The back room still had a double sink from its earlier incarnation as a greasy spoon's kitchen. There, on an old mattress, Enslin and the Marine had sex.

At Enslin's trial in September 1974, sociologist Albert D. Klassen Jr. of the Kinsey Institute for Sex Research testified that sodomy laws serve no useful purpose. He added that fellatio is common among heterosexuals and gay men, contact with homosexuals doesn't make anyone gay, that criminal laws only make homosexual activity more furtive. Suppression of homosexuality is bad for marriage because it pressures homosexuals into marrying people with whom they are sexually incompatible. Enslin, nevertheless, was convicted. North Carolina's top court then dismissed his claim that the sodomy law was unconstitutional.

Justice Brennan got the Supreme Court to discuss Enslin's petition before denying *cert*. Enslin argued that North Carolina had violated his rights to privacy and equal protection. North Carolina Attorney General Rufus Edmisten replied, "[T]his case concerns the criminal prosecution of an adult for the blatant and open pandering and solicitation of an act of fellatio with a 17 year old." Of course, the policeman who solicited the young Marine wasn't the one prosecuted. As Lambda Legal Defense and Education Fund noted in a friend-of-the-court brief, "The enforcement of the sodomy laws . . . habitually involves the police in the roles of procurer, panderer or seducer."

Gay-rights attorneys were reeling after the Supreme Court dealt their movement a major setback by upholding Virginia's sodomy law without even bothering to hear arguments. *Doe* "is quite disastrous, and no less so for the court's reasoning being unknown," Lambda general counsel E. Carrington Boggan lamented. Did the justices agree with an extremely narrow reading of their privacy precedents? Was the court affirming that the Bible was a justification for modern-day sodomy laws? Or, did the court just not want to discuss homosexuality?

Attorneys for "Doe" and Enslin filed a consolidated petition for rehearing. The National Gay Task Force pleaded for "specific guidance from the highest court of this land." In reply, the court offered two words: "Rehearing denied."

Eugene Enslin was still serving what turned out to be a six-month stint in a minimum-security prison when the justices turned away *Doe* and *Enslin v. North Carolina* for the second and last time in May 1976. He was assigned to clean highway ditches. "Prison wasn't that big a deal," he says, adding that what he most disliked was keeping his promise of celibacy. His attorneys feared that prison sex might damage his privacy claim, Enslin explains.

Despite the court's attempts to shield itself from public discussion of homosexuality, the subject did not vanish. A month after the court denied a "rehearing" to "Doe" and Enslin—who'd never gotten a hearing in the first place—G. Harrold Carswell was arrested in the men's room at a Tallahassee mall for allegedly making an "unnatural and lascivious" advance to an uncover cop. He was fined $100 after pleading no contest to a lesser charge.

Carswell, as news reports of his arrest dutifully pointed out, had very nearly been confirmed to the Supreme Court. Nixon had nominated him in 1970. After Carswell was revealed to be a mediocre judge and former advocate of "white supremacy," the Senate voted against him, 51 to 46. A switch of three Senate votes would have meant that Carswell, a married man, would have been confirmed and possibly would have still been on the Supreme Court in 1976. Carswell's 1976 restroom blunder may have reinforced many justices' impression that homosexual behavior was a source of humiliation, a vice that could sully even stained reputations. Despite the efforts of proud gay men like Mike McConnell, Jack Baker, Joe Acanfora and "John Doe," the court didn't seem to be modernizing its own attitudes toward homosexuality.

8

A MARBLE STORM CELLAR

THE WILD EXUBERANCE with which John Singer celebrated being gay was something quite new for the Supreme Court when his *cert* petition arrived in April 1976. Singer's insistence on being himself even at work had gotten him fired from the Equal Employment Opportunity Commission (EEOC), the federal agency designated to combat job discrimination. He was the radical son of ultraliberal New York City Jews; his mother had been briefly jailed for union organizing. And it never occurred to Singer not to fight back.

John Singer had graduated from high school in 1962, then drifted through the civil rights and antiwar movements, served in VISTA (Volunteers in Service to America) and completed a two-year hitch as an Army medic. Along the way, he accepted his homosexuality. By 1969, Singer had plunged headlong into the first wave of the gay liberation movement. Settling in Seattle, he applied in 1971 for a clerk-typist job with the local office of the EEOC. Cautioned that the work required empathy for minorities, Singer replied that wouldn't be difficult since he was a double minority—Jewish and gay. He got the job.

Ten months later, Singer was notified that an investigation had uncovered "adverse information" about his suitability for federal employment. What had the taxpayer-financed probe discovered? "You are homosexual. . . . [A]nd you have received widespread publicity in this respect in at least two states," Singer was gravely informed. "It was all so laughable," he recalls.

A holdover from the 1950s, the Civil Service's cloak-and-dagger technique of ferreting out homosexuals was a silly anachronism when directed at someone who proudly did his utmost to ensure that no one mistook him for a heterosexual. Singer drove a hippie Dodge van with bumper stickers proclaiming "Gay Power" and "Faggots Against Fascism." After EEOC hired him, he made a splash in the local press by applying for a license to marry Paul Barwick.

Singer and Barwick seriously wanted to marry, yet theirs was a political, not a romantic, union. They lived together in a rice-and-beans group house but were more friends than lovers. "I was married to the movement for many, many years. I would have little affairs with men," Singer says. He and Barwick agree that they would have married, if they'd won the right. "And God knows if we'd ever have gotten divorced," Barwick says with a chuckle.

By the time the Civil Service cracked down on Singer, he'd radically changed his name and his attire—though the Supreme Court was never told. He'd given up "John" in favor of "Faygele" (pronounced FAY-ga-la), which he says is Yiddish for "faggot." And he was cross-dressing at work to further his understanding of sexism. There he'd be, in long hair, heels, a dress and tights. "When I finished my typing, I could put on my nail polish at my desk just like any other secretary," he says.

The Civil Service Commission spelled out a long list of particulars for starting its quarrel with Singer: He had kissed a man in front of the elevator at the building where he'd worked in San Francisco. He'd told the *San Francisco Chronicle* that he was "openly gay." He had applied for a license to marry another man. He served on the board of the Seattle Gay Alliance. And he had identified himself as an "openly gay" EEOC employee when complaining to EEOC regional officials that a sensitivity training session on minorities' problems did not mention gay people.

Singer was notified on June 26, 1972, that he was being fired for "immoral and notoriously disgraceful conduct." He stood accused of having "flaunted" his homosexuality and of being "an advocate for a socially repugnant concept," presumably gay rights. According to a Civil Service examiner, Singer's continued employment would threaten federal efficiency because he might offend co-workers and embarrass the government. A Civil Service appeals board seconded Singer's dismissal, despite a letter from all his EEOC co-workers saying that working with him was "educational and positive" and calling him a respected employee.

Singer lost his job on January 6, 1973. The ACLU, which according to Singer had brushed off his marriage lawsuit as "too frivolous," agreed to fight for him. A federal judge dismissed Singer's lawsuit. Then the Ninth Circuit Court of Appeals ruled against him on January 12, 1976. (The unanimous three-judge panel included Anthony Kennedy, who would later be a Supreme Court justice.) Judge W. J. Jameson's appellate decision held that Singer had been fired for "flaunting his homosexual way of life." Jameson ruled that "notorious conduct" and the "careless display of unorthodox sexual conduct in public" could compromise government efficiency.

Petitioning the Supreme Court, ACLU attorney Melvin Wulf argued that Singer's privacy and free-speech rights had been violated. Arguing that it was wrong to punish Singer for being gay, Wulf said, "It would be extremely difficult and painful to reverse [Singer's] sexual preference," an assertion that made homosexuality sound flawed and fixable. "A favorable decision in this case would demonstrate a sensitivity to the problems of homosexuals," Wulf told the justices.

Then *Singer v. United States Civil Service Commission et al.* took a surprising and historic turn. For the first and—as yet—only time, a solicitor general essentially took the side of a gay-rights litigant. Rather than filing the expected "response in opposition" to *cert,* Solicitor General Robert H. Bork urged the justices to take the case, vacate the Ninth Circuit's ruling and send the case back to the Civil Service Commission. The commission had had a change of policy, Bork explained.

The Civil Service Commission had been forced to surrender in its long war against homosexuals. After Singer lost his job, a federal judge in a 1973 California case ordered the commission to "forthwith cease" branding homosexuals unfit simply because of fears they might embarrass the government. The commission instructed supervisors that no one was to be barred from the Civil Service for homosexuality. Then in 1975—the year before Singer's case reached the Supreme Court—the commission amended its regulations to end its ban on homosexuals.

(At 50, Frank Kameny had finally won his 18-year war with Civil Service. Federal personnel officials "surrendered to me on July 3rd, 1975," Kameny recalls. "They called me up to tell me they were changing their policies to suit me. And that was the end of it." In revising its grounds for dismissal, the Civil Service deleted the vague, damning word "immoral," which had galled Kameny ever since he'd been branded with it. Kameny felt that he had finally forced the most powerful government in the world to give him back his good name.)

As for Singer, Chief Justice Burger didn't want to schedule his case for discussion, despite the solicitor general's recommendation and the Civil Service's policy change. If a lower court had ruled against a homosexual, that apparently was the end of the matter as far as Burger was concerned. At Justice Brennan's insistence, *Singer* was debated in the last week of September 1976. Oddly, the case's outcome was not announced until January 10, 1977. A six-man majority—Brennan, Stewart, Marshall, Blackmun, Powell and Stevens—had followed Bork's advice in canceling the lower court ruling against Singer and sending his case back to the Civil Service Commission. Without explanation, Burger, White and Rehnquist dissented.

Singer's victory was the homosexual-rights movement's first Supreme Court triumph since 1962, when Lynn Womack's Manual Enterprises won the right to send beefcake magazines through the mail and to be judged by the same obscenity standards as heterosexual publications.

For 15 years, the Supreme Court had done nothing to help gay workers. But once the Civil Service Commission rescinded its homosexual ban, most justices had no objection to letting the commission apply its liberalized policy to an old case. The court's passive decision stopped far short of a declaration that gay people have the same First Amendment, privacy and employment rights as heterosexuals. Yet the outcome was a major breakthrough.

But as much as Singer's triumph was cause for celebration among gay-rights advocates, the court's 6-to-3 split was ominous. The Supreme Court clearly had a hard-core trio of justices deeply hostile to basic gay civil rights: White, Rehnquist and Burger were not ready to declare the government war on homosexuals over. They didn't want the Civil Service Commission laying down its weapons. Conservative justices of the previous era had been supremely deferential to the executive and legislative branches. Clark and Harlan, for example, almost certainly would have gone along with whatever the solicitor general and the Civil Service Commission wanted to do about Singer. There's no evidence the earlier conservatives had had any ax to grind against homosexuals. But times—and the court's makeup—had indeed changed.

Singer eventually won $50,000 in back pay from the Civil Service Commission. By then he didn't want his old job. He plowed part of his winnings into the gay movement and put a down payment on a North Carolina house. "It was a vindication. There weren't too many gay victories. This was a significant one," he remarked in 1997. Then 51 and HIV-positive, he was back in Seattle, active in the gay movement and still friends with the man he'd tried to marry. He was working to start a bagel shop, Faygele's Baygeles.

The day in January 1977 that the Supreme Court announced Singer's victory it received a *cert* petition from the tiny Mississippi Gay Alliance, which was trying to force Mississippi State University's student newspaper to run its paid advertisement. (The nation was on the verge of inaugurating Democrat Jimmy Carter, the first successful candidate to have promised to issue a presidential order advancing gay rights. He never kept that little-noticed pledge.) *Mississippi Gay Alliance v. Goudelock* is noteworthy mainly for underscoring yet again that, in the absence of Supreme Court guidance to the contrary, many judges equated homosexuality with criminality.

"An Off-Campus Cell of Homosexuals"

The Mississippi Gay Alliance was, in the view of the Fifth Circuit Court of Appeals, an "off-campus cell of homosexuals," language that was an echo from the vanishing era when homosexuals and communists were merged in many minds as threats to national security. Though court documents never spelled out the group's composition, the alliance was merely a trio of lesbians—25-year-old Anne DeBary, her lover Sally and a friend. Their group was an attempt to offer other gay people support and access to the small collection of gay books in DeBary's apartment, where a plaque over the fireplace read: "To say and believe gay is good." As DeBary recalls, "The only reason we [founded it] is because we felt that there was absolutely nothing in Mississippi for gays to feel that they could go to at all."

On August 16, 1973, DeBary tried to place a paid ad in *The Reflector*, the Mississippi State University's campus paper. It read,

> Gay Center—open 6:00 to 9:00 Monday, Wednesday and
> Friday nights. We offer—counseling, legal aid and a
> library of homosexual literature.
> Write to—The Mississippi Gay Alliance
> P.O. Box 1328
> Mississippi State University
> Mississippi 39762

When student editor Bill Goudelock turned down the ad, the alliance sued, drawing the local news media's attention. "Three people had everyone on campus saying, 'There's going to be a gay revolution here. It's those gay militants,'" DeBary proudly observed. A federal judge, who found the ad "innocuous," ruled that the student-run *Reflector*, though partially funded by mandatory student fees, was not a government publication and, thus, was protected by the First Amendment's freedom of the press rather than being bound by the Constitution's equal protection guarantees.

The Fifth Circuit agreed August 12, 1976. In a remarkably bald assertion of a gay exception to basic civil rights, Judge James P. Coleman declared on behalf of the 2-to-1 majority that the fact that the Mississippi Gay Alliance was a homosexual group was reason enough to rule against it. "There are special reasons for holding that there was no abuse of discretion by the editor of *The Reflector*. Mississippi Code of 1848 includes the following provision: 'Unnatural intercourse. . . ,'" Coleman began. He proceeded to recite the statute mandating a prison sentence of up to 10 years for committing a "crime against nature . . . with mankind or a beast."

Then, speaking only for himself, Coleman declared that a Mississippi newspaper could no more be required to "advertise solicitation for homosexual contacts" than it could be required to run prostitutes' ads. The gay ad's mention of "legal aid" might well be construed to mean "criminal activity is contemplated," he said.

Dissenting Judge Irving L. Goldberg stressed "this is not an 'unnatural intercourse' case," in a tone suggesting that he was profoundly annoyed by its being cast as one. Goldberg argued that state-supported newspapers must have nondiscriminatory ad policies. He would have sent the case back down to get details about *The Reflector*'s funding.

The Mississippi case interested Justice Brennan, who added it to the Supreme Court's "discuss" list for April 22, 1977. Three days later, the court announced: "*Certiorari* denied."

The alliance's "off-campus cell" never really grew. DeBary and her partner moved to Louisiana. In 1996, DeBary, 48, was managing a Ben & Jerry's ice cream parlor.

By the summer of 1977, the Supreme Court had been expanding the right to privacy for a dozen years. But the court had made no move to include gay people. Most justices were content to rubber-stamp or ignore any trampling of gay privacy rights. They perhaps didn't want to be bothered and/or embarrassed by having gay sexual privacy cases argued in open court.

Behind the scenes, justices on the far left and far right were locked in a tug-of-war over the constitutional rights of gay Americans. That struggle broke into public view June 9, 1977, in dueling footnotes in *Carey v. Population Services International*. The court's Brennan-written *Carey* decision struck down a New York law barring distribution of birth control devices to minors under age 16. Brennan, known for his chesslike gamesmanship in plotting moves that took the court toward his desired goals, used *Carey* to twice declare that "the court has not definitively answered the difficult question whether and to what extent the Constitution prohibits state statutes regulating [private consensual sexual] behavior among adults." Disguised as mere asides, Brennan's declarations clearly encouraged lower court judges to discount the Supreme Court's 1976 *Doe* ruling affirming (without explanation) the constitutionality of Virginia's sodomy law. A majority of Brennan's colleagues—Stewart, Marshall, Blackmun, Stevens and White—signed on to at least one of the two sections containing the intentionally manipulative footnotes. (White and Stewart had been part of *Doe*'s six-man anti-sodomy majority.)

Rehnquist could not, as he put it, let Brennan's power play "pass without comment." In a last-minute footnote to his *Carey* dissent, Rehnquist huffed, "While we have not ruled on every conceivable regulation affecting such [adult sexual] conduct the facial constitutional validity of criminal statutes prohibiting certain consensual acts has been 'definitively' established." He cited *Doe* and a 1975 ruling in which the court had said its summary decisions (reached without a full hearing) ought to be regarded as binding.

The Brennan-Rehnquist footnote duel foreshadowed far bigger court clashes over basic gay civil rights. The justice caught in the middle would be Lewis F. Powell Jr. Genteel to the point of prissiness, Powell was uncomfortable with any discussion of sexuality. In a note to himself and his clerks about *Carey*, Powell wrote, "This case is an extremely difficult one for me. I wish it were not here." As might be guessed about a man so ill at ease with talk of adolescent heterosexuality, Powell's discomfort level would skyrocket when the court did allow homosexual cases to be fully argued.

"I Had to Tell My Parents"

Since the court had ended its 1976–77 term sparring over just how hostile it had already been to gay privacy rights, some outsiders might have expected the court to treat important gay *cert* petitions more seriously when its new term began. It did not.

The case of a Washington State high school teacher offered the court a nearly ideal opportunity to squarely confront the question of the constitutionality of discrimination against public employees. James M. "Jim" Gaylord was fired for being gay. That fact was undisputed.

When the Supreme Court turned away Joe Acanfora three years earlier, a promising teaching career had died. If anything, the stakes were higher in Gaylord's case because it involved proven excellence. By all accounts, Gaylord had been an outstanding 12th-grade American history and world affairs teacher for 12 years.

Jim Gaylord, who'd discovered his sexual orientation by junior high, had graduated Phi Beta Kappa from the University of Washington in 1960 and immediately landed a teaching job at Wilson High School in Tacoma, Washington. For a decade he was terribly isolated. Always shy, he was 32 before he got up the nerve to join a Seattle gay group—a step that finally gave him gay friends and a social life.

One of Gaylord's newfound friends suggested that a Wilson High student struggling with his sexuality talk to Gaylord. The two had a "pretty innocuous" 10- or 15-minute conversation, recalls Gaylord, who did not reveal his homosexuality. However, the troubled student later told authorities—without meaning to harm Gaylord—that he thought Gaylord was gay. Vice Principal John Beer immediately confronted Gaylord, who admitted being gay.

Gaylord, 35, passed up a chance to resign quietly. "I'm sure others did slink away. But I really was a very strong believer in civil liberties and equal rights. . . . And I just could not see any way that I couldn't do what I had taught [students] we should all do—stand up for our rights," Gaylord says. On December 21, 1972, the school board fired him for "immorality."

John Singer's Supreme Court victory was no help to Gaylord because he wasn't a federal worker. The court had simply deferred to federal personnel officials, not declared homosexuality an improper basis for firing a public employee.

"Before I filed the lawsuit," Gaylord recalls, "I had to tell my parents I was gay. . . . Dad's first reaction was something like, 'Oh, I know what causes it, homosexuality, it's the parents.' So at that point I had to give a little lecture. Finally, Dad said, 'You know, I think if I was in your situation, I think I would do the same thing.'"

After a three-day trial, Judge James V. Ramsdell ruled against Gaylord. After a higher court found his original reasoning flawed, Ramsdell again ruled against Gaylord on December 30, 1975. The second verdict focused on two findings: First, homosexuality was immoral, a conclusion that the judge drew from the fact that "Gaylord didn't want his parents to know." Second, Gaylord's teaching would be impaired because "there would be those who would not take his class."

On January 20, 1977, the Supreme Court of Washington State upheld Gaylord's dismissal. The 6-to-2 ruling is a prime example of how anti-gay arguments shift so that a hostile conclusion can be reached even when earlier justifications for it vanish. The court used the fact that the American Psychiatric Association no longer classified homosexuality as a mental illness as a reason to judge Gaylord immoral: "One who has a disease . . . cannot be held morally responsible for his condition. Homosexuality is not a disease, however. . . . [Gaylord] has sought no psychiatric help because he feels comfortable with his homosexuality. He has made a voluntary choice for which he must be held morally responsible."

The Washington court stressed that homosexuality was "condemned as immoral in biblical times." Washington had repealed its sodomy law in 1976, after Gaylord was fired. Yet, in the court's view, "the fact that sodomy is not a crime no more relieves the conduct of its immoral status than would consent to the crime of incest."

Dissenting, James M. Dolliver stressed that "there is not a shred of evidence" that Gaylord had broken the sodomy law, which had applied to all couples. For all the court knew, he might be celibate, Dolliver added. "Presumably under [the majority's] reasoning, an unmarried male who declares himself to be heterosexual will be held to have engaged in 'illegal or immoral acts'. . . . There is no law against being a homosexual. All that is banned [by the sodomy law] are certain acts, none of which Mr. Gaylord was alleged to have committed and none of which can . . . be assumed . . . simply because of his status as a homosexual," Dolliver stated.

Jim Gaylord's *cert* petition reached the U.S. Supreme Court on July 14, 1977. At its heart was an undeniable fact: "If petitioner had been heterosexual, he would not have been fired." Gaylord's attorney Christopher Young of Seattle told the justices, "The rights to privacy and liberty are meaningless if they can be claimed only by those who think and act in accordance with the conventions and wishes of the majority." Gaylord's treatment, Young said, was a "lesson" in discrimination, a lesson that only the nation's highest court could correct. The school district countered that Gaylord had received due process.

Chief Justice Burger did not list Gaylord's case for discussion. Marshall got it listed. The court denied *cert* in *Gaylord v. Tacoma School District No. 10 et al.* on October 3, 1977. That day the court also turned away a New Jersey teacher who'd lost his classroom after refusing to take the psychiatric exam ordered because his decision to come out made his school board question his sanity. That teacher's case had been discussed at Brennan's request. Marshall and Brennan had wanted to accept both cases.

Jim Gaylord was 39 years old when the Supreme Court turned him away. Like Acanfora, he never returned to the classroom. Despite his master's degree in library science, Gaylord became a part-time library clerk, checking books in and out. Looking back, he says the great irony in his court case is "that I had to give up my privacy in order to defend it."

A Contagion Like Measles?

Until 1978, the Supreme Court's deep aversion to gay-rights cases consistently hurt gay Americans. Every time the court turned away a gay case, the gay litigant lost for one very simple reason: All those gay people had come to the high court seeking reversal of negative lower court decisions. But as lower court judges grew more receptive to gay-rights arguments, more gay victories reached the Supreme Court. In February 1978, for the first time, Supreme Court inaction sustained a gay-rights victory.

The case involved Gay Lib, a largely gay student group seeking formal recognition at the University of Missouri's Columbia campus. With gay-rights groups springing up all across the nation after Stonewall, Gay Lib applied for university recognition in early 1971. The group's goals were to help gay people shed "the unnecessary burden of shame," promote understanding between gay and straight people and create an atmosphere conducive to repealing Missouri's sodomy law.

The student Senate and a student-faculty committee endorsed recognition, which would allow the group to use university facilities and apply for funding. However, university officials—from the dean of students to President C. Brice Ratchford—vetoed recognition. Ratchford contended, "'Gay Lib' implies the liberation of homosexuality. [The group's] purposes are more than establishing an 'understanding and knowledge.' They are in fact an attempt to actively promote the practices of homosexuality by claiming that they are acceptable in our society. . . . Homosexuality is generally treated in the state of Missouri as a socially repugnant concept as is evidenced by the criminal statutes. . . ." Missouri state law mandated a prison sentence of at least two years for anyone convicted of "the detestable and abominable crime against nature, committed with mankind or with beast, with the sexual organs or with the mouth."

When Gay Lib's appeal reached the university's governing Board of Curators, it appointed Jefferson City attorney Cullen Coil to hold a hearing. Coil's August 1973 hearing delved into the history of the gay liberation movement as well as "whether orgies were standard homosexual practice, the alleged homosexual propensities of a mass murderer in Houston . . . and the detrimental effects on children of

'mothers who are overly protective or hostile or rejecting or clinging,'"
as a judge later summarized testimony. Coil's "findings of fact" warned:
Recognition of Gay Lib would "expand an abnormal way of life," turn
"latent homosexuals" into "overt" ones, increase violations of Missouri's
sodomy law and "be undesirable insofar as homosexuals will counsel
other homosexuals, i.e., the sick and abnormal counseling others who
are similarly ill and abnormal." In November 1973, a month before the
American Psychiatric Association decreed that homosexuality is not
sick, the university's curators accepted Coil's diagnosis that, as they put
it, "homosexuality is an illness and should and can be treated as such."

Gay Lib and four members of its board—students Sarah McNamara,
Doug Hudson and Darrell Napton and university employee Lawrence A.
Eggleston—sued for recognition, arguing that university officials had vi-
olated their rights to equal protection and freedom of association.

Federal Judge Elmo B. Hunter ruled in favor of the defendants—
President Ratchford and the Board of Curators—on June 29, 1976.
Hunter based his ruling against Gay Lib on two psychiatrists' prediction
that recognition of a gay campus group would increase sodomy law violations. Because Gay Lib's medical expert was not a psychiatrist,
Hunter gave his testimony no credence. Hunter said there was no equal
protection violation because Gay Lib wasn't comparable to groups that
did not present a "clear and present danger" of triggering sodomy law
violations. (Yet since any couple could violate the sodomy law, any
campus organization could theoretically boost the rate of sodomy law
violations simply by helping people get acquainted.)

Dr. Charles Socarides, a Columbia University psychiatrist, had told
the court, "I believe that whenever you have a convocation of homosexuals that you are going to have increased homosexual activities, which,
of course, includes sodomy." Deemed a "highly qualified expert" by
Judge Hunter, Socarides had already had his views renounced by his
profession when he led—and lost—the fight against deleting homosexuality from the APA's list of mental disorders. To Socarides, homosexuals were deeply disturbed, compulsive men who "hope to achieve a
'shot' of masculinity in the homosexual act. Like the addict, [the homo-
sexual] must have his 'fix.'"

The other psychiatrist relied on by Hunter, Dr. Harold Moser Voth,
was also one of the leading dissidents from the APA's 1973 public dec-

laration that there is no justification for considering homosexuality sick. The APA's declaration was virtually an admission of what Frank Kameny had long argued: Mental health professionals have no special claim to expertise about homosexuality since it is not a disorder. Judge Hunter signaled no awareness that Socarides and Voth were no longer in the mainstream of scientific thought.

Gay Lib appealed to the Eighth Circuit and won a 2-to-1 decision on June 8, 1977. Writing for the court, Judge Donald Lay dismissed Hunter's decision as based on two psychiatrists' unsubstantiated beliefs—what Judge William H. Webster's concurrence derided as "skimpy and speculative evidence." Lay declared that even if Socarides's and Voth's contentions were valid, that would not justify "prior restraint" of freedom of association at a public institution.

Lay pointed to a Supreme Court's 1972 ruling that required recognition of a university chapter of the radical antiwar group Students for a Democratic Society (SDS). The high court ruled that unless a student group was both inciting imminent lawless action and likely to provoke it, the group had to be granted recognition by a public university. In the wake of that SDS decision, the First and Fourth Circuit Courts of Appeal had sided with gay campus groups seeking recognition. Quoting that Fourth Circuit decision, Lay declared, "Individuals of whatever sexual persuasion have the fundamental right to meet, discuss current problems and to advocate changes in the status quo, so long as there is no 'incitement to imminent lawless action.'"

Lay saw equal protection problems since the University of Missouri presumably would have let a heterosexual group discuss sodomy law reform. He concluded, "To invoke censorship in an academic environment is hardly the recognition of a healthy democratic society."

The appeals court's dissenter saw homosexuality as an illness and contended university officials had a responsibility to protect "latent or potential" homosexuals.

The University of Missouri's legal team, led by Jackson A. Wright, petitioned the Supreme Court on September 20, 1977. The *cert* petition cast the Gay Lib case as largely a medical one "where formal recognition would likely bring about violation of the criminal law of the state of Missouri and likely cause students with latent homosexual tendencies to become overt homosexuals and deem homosexuality as normal behavior

rather than to seek medical treatment for the medical illness of homosexuality. . . ." Gay Lib's attorney, of course, disagreed, saying there was
no reason to think recognition of Gay Lib would lead to lawlessness.

By the time Gay Lib's case reached the Supreme Court, a new virulent strain of homophobia had infected the American body politic. The
menacing image of homosexuality as a national security threat had
largely faded from the national consciousness. Just eight years after
Stonewall, openly gay people seemed well on their way to integrating
themselves into the American mainstream, with gay-rights advocates
being invited to the White House. Then Dade County, Florida, officials
made Miami the first major southern city to protect gay rights, and
born-again Christian singer Anita Bryant launched a vicious backlash
whose reverberations are still being felt nationwide. Bryant, a former
beauty queen best known for TV commercials hawking Florida orange
juice, aggressively fanned fears that homosexuals prey on children. In a
full-page *Miami Herald* ad March 20, 1977, Bryant's new group, Save
Our Children, warned, "The recruitment of our children is absolutely
necessary for the survival and growth of homosexuality. Since homosexuals cannot reproduce, they must recruit, must freshen their ranks."

When Dade County voters overwhelmingly repealed their gay-rights
ordinance in June 1977, demonization of homosexuals was well on its
way to becoming a cash cow for newly emerging far-right fundamentalist Christian political groups. The backlash politicized countless young
gay men and lesbians who were shocked to find themselves so publicly
under attack. The nation now had a new vocabulary for articulating
anti-gay prejudice. There was a harsher, more aggressive edge to public
expressions of anti-gay feelings—an edge that was soon heard at the
Supreme Court when Justice William H. Rehnquist, joined by Justice
Harry Blackmun, compared homosexuality to a communicable disease
in the Gay Lib case.

Not surprisingly, since the anti-gay side was the one petitioning the
court, Chief Justice Burger scheduled *Ratchford, President, University
of Missouri et al. v. Gay Lib et al.* for discussion. The court voted December 9, 1977, to deny *cert*—sealing Gay Lib's victory by sidestepping
the controversy: The court's little-noticed "non-decision" tremendously
strengthened the hand of gay campus groups at public colleges and universities nationwide.

Appalled, Rehnquist pounded out a six-page dissent from denial of *cert* that he circulated to his brethren January 13, 1978. Rehnquist, who may well have written the dissent himself since none of his three clerks recalls the case, first lit into his colleagues for what he considered irresponsible inaction. "There is a natural tendency on the part of any conscientious court," he wrote, "to avoid embroiling itself in a controversial area of social policy unless absolutely required to do so. . . . The district court and the court of appeals were doubtless as chary as we are of being thrust into the middle of this controversy but were nonetheless obligated to decide the case. . . . [T]he existence of [the Supreme Court's] discretion does not imply that it should be used as a sort of judicial storm cellar to which we may flee to escape from controversial or sensitive cases." Labeling Missouri's sodomy law "admittedly" valid, Rehnquist equated homosexuality with criminality. "Writ large, the issue posed in this case is the extent to which a self-governing democracy, having made certain acts criminal, may prevent or discourage individuals from engaging in speech or conduct which encourages others to violate those laws," he said.

The clear implication of Rehnquist's dissent was that enacting a sodomy law gives a state carte blanche to discriminate against homosexuals, effectively trumping the Constitution's guarantees of freedom of speech and freedom of association. To Rehnquist, homosexuality apparently was not merely an illness but a contagion, a deeply hostile perspective he revealed in the analogy that he concocted to describe the University of Missouri's perspective. He noted that Gay Lib considered itself little different from other campus political clubs. "From the perspective of the university, however, the question is more akin to whether those suffering from measles have a constitutional right, in violation of quarantine regulations, to associate together and with others who do not presently have measles, in order to repeal a state law providing that measles sufferers be quarantined. The very act of assemblage under these circumstances undercuts a significant interest of the state, . . ." Rehnquist wrote, sounding very much like a "Save Our Children" recruitment warning.

Claiming that "expert psychological testimony below established" the danger of allowing homosexuals to meet together as part of an officially recognized group, Rehnquist argued that "this danger may be particularly acute in the university setting where many students are still coping with sexual problems which accompany late adolescence and early adulthood."

Rehnquist's opposition to protecting the basic civil rights of groups subjected to discrimination was nothing new. Rehnquist was a Supreme Court clerk in 1954 when the court handed down its landmark *Brown v. Board* desegregation ruling declaring unconstitutional the "separate but equal" standard established in 1896 in *Plessy v. Ferguson*. Rehnquist had advised upholding racial segregation, saying, "[I]n the long run it is the majority who will determine what the constitutional rights of the minority are. . . . I realize that it is an unpopular and unhumanitarian position, for which I have been excoriated by 'liberal' colleagues, but I think *Plessy v. Ferguson* was right and should be re-affirmed," Rehnquist wrote. His later claim that his memo was intended to reflect the views of his justice, Robert Jackson, has been widely discredited.

As a Phoenix attorney, Rehnquist, 39, mourned the enactment of an ordinance banning discrimination in public accommodations based on race, color or religion because it abolished what he called "the historic right of the owner of a drug store, lunch counter, or theater to choose his own customers." Later, Rehnquist urged the Nixon administration to oppose the Equal Rights Amendment, saying that banning sex discrimination would "turn 'holy wedlock' into 'holy deadlock.'" Once on the Supreme Court, Rehnquist, who ardently believed the Warren court had dragged the nation much too far to the left, consistently voted against women and racial minorities in civil rights cases. He insisted that the 14th Amendment, passed to protect black Americans after the abolition of slavery, did not safeguard the rights of all Americans.

Three days after Rehnquist circulated his *Ratchford v. Gay Lib* draft, Blackmun sent him a one-sentence memo: "Please join me in your dissent," court jargon meaning add Blackmun's name. Blackmun's clerks from that term do not recall the case. However, one intensely loyal clerk said Blackmun sometimes joined dissents from *cert* denials without much thought.

A former counsel for the Mayo clinic, Blackmun had a lifelong interest in medicine. Now best remembered for authoring the court's 1973 *Roe v. Wade* abortion-rights decision, Blackmun originally saw abortion as largely a question of doctors' rights. The supposed medical aspect of the Gay Lib case may have piqued Blackmun's interest. Or, he might have been interested in whether the Eighth Circuit had over-stepped its authority. (The day Rehnquist added Blackmun's name to his dissent he also added a sentence saying that which side was right about Gay Lib was less important than whether the lower court had vi-olated procedural rules.) Or, Blackmun may have shared Rehnquist's "measles" view of homosexuality. When denial of *cert* was announced February 21, 1978, Chief Justice Burger was listed simply as having wanted to take the case.

Needing to sway just one more justice to get its case accepted, the University of Missouri intensified its anti-gay rhetoric, calling Gay Lib "abhorrent" in a petition for rehearing. "If this court believes that by denying writs of *certiorari* in matters relating to homosexuals, the prob-lem will go away, then the court does not fully appreciate the tenacity of the Gay Lib movement. Homosexuals' burning desire is to have homo-sexual activities recognized as normal. This push has been in many forms such as constitutional attacks on sodomy laws, attempting legisla-tive repeal of sodomy statutes, forcing the medical profession to drop ho-mosexuality as an illness, obtaining minority status for housing, employment, etc. and to get recognition for homosexual organizations on college and university campuses across the country," the university argued. Gay Lib's real goal, the university warned, is "to obtain the badge of normalcy that comes from being a recognized student organization."

Gay Lib gay members were indeed seeking a badge of normalcy. And when, without comment, the Supreme Court denied the university's pe-tition for rehearing in April 1978, the court silently bestowed that badge on gay-rights organizations at public colleges and universities nation-wide. Regardless of whether most justices simply wanted to have noth-ing to do with homosexuality, Gay Lib had won.

"I Felt So Lonely, So Useless"

Three years later, the justices were again faced with the prospect that a gay-rights victory would stand if they rejected a case. New York's high-est state court—in seeming contradiction of the Supreme Court's 1976 *Doe* judgment upholding Virginia's sodomy law—had struck down its state sodomy law on the grounds that it violated the U.S. Constitution. New York's law had made "deviate sexual intercourse" a misdemeanor and defined it as unmarried oral or anal sex. New York's top court declared that the law violated constitutional guarantees of equal protection and privacy. A pair of challenges to that ruling reached the U.S. Supreme Court in March 1981.

The first involved Ronald Onofre of Syracuse, who admitted having oral and anal sex in his home in 1976 with a 17-year-old boy he'd met through his ministry at his tiny, non-denominational Universal Life Church. Onofre, then 34 and working as a punch press operator, was arrested on sexual assault charges: "It was on Ash Wednesday. I remember that day because it was very embarrassing because they came into work and accused me of raping him." Onofre was jailed for nine days. "Oh, God, it was horrible. I felt so lonely, so useless," he recalls.

The teenager, old enough under state law to legally consent, recanted his charges of forcible sex once confronted with photos establishing his consensual sexual relationship with Onofre. The older man was sentenced by Onondaga County Judge Ormand N. Gale to a year on probation; the youth wasn't charged. (Onofre says that, because of his arrest, he was fired and spent seven years on welfare.)

In upholding New York's sodomy law in 1978, Judge Gale noted that repeal efforts had repeatedly failed. "Today we live in a permissive society. If such a statute . . . should be wiped off the books . . . , now is the time for the legislature to do it," Gale declared.

On appeal, New York State Supreme Court—a mid-level tribunal, despite its name—refused to defer to lawmakers on a law it saw as unconstitutional. Citing U.S. Supreme Court decisions that had established and gradually expanded a protected zone of privacy, the panel found, "Personal sexual conduct is a fundamental right, protected by the right to privacy because of the transcendental importance of sex to the human condition, the intimacy of the conduct, and its relationship to a person's right to control his or her own body. The right is broad enough to include acts between non-married persons and intimate consensual homosexual conduct."

Demonstrating the unwillingness of a growing number of judges to accept anti-gay arguments at face value, that ruling added, "There are those who argue that homosexual conduct should be forbidden even when conducted in private by consenting adults because it is destructive of traditional principles of family and marriage. However, there is no empirical evidence to support that view."

Onondaga County District Attorney Richard A. Hennessy Jr. appealed to the state's top court. When it reached the New York State Court of Appeals, Onofre's case was combined with fellatio sex cases from Buffalo—one involving two men in a parked car; the other a supposed female prostitute. (In the homosexual case, the Buffalo man convicted of playing the oral role in oral sodomy was fined $200 while his partner was fined half as much—perhaps reflecting the notion that when it comes to oral sex it is better to receive than to give.)

New York's highest court ruled in 1980 that because the state's consensual sodomy law was broad enough to prohibit "noncommercial, cloistered" sex and because it exempted married couples, it trampled both the right to privacy and the Constitution's 14th Amendment guarantee of equal protection. As that court interpreted Supreme Court precedents, sexual privacy rights had already expanded well beyond the marital bed—including, for example, the right to read pornography at home. The court didn't feel bound by *Doe* because, it said, the U.S. Supreme Court might simply have thought the plaintiffs had no standing to challenge Virginia's sodomy law. The New York court instead relied on Justice Brennan's *Carey* footnotes saying the outer bounds of privacy rights had not yet been defined.

Judge Domenick Gabrielli, writing in dissent, warned that the majority's ruling was so permissive that "it is difficult to perceive how a state may lawfully interfere with such consensual practices as euthanasia, marijuana smoking, prostitution and homosexual marriage."

Urging the Supreme Court to reverse the New York court, Erie County (Buffalo) District Attorney Edward C. Cosgrove argued that married couples have sexual privacy rights no one else enjoys. "The statute recognizes that distinction; it does not . . . create it," he said. What's more, he argued, privacy rights certainly don't protect people having oral sex in a parked car. Onondaga County District Attorney Hennessy, meanwhile, called sodomy "a crime of ancient vintage" and quoted former Chief Justice Warren as saying government has a right to "maintain a decent society."

In reply, Onofre's attorney, Bonnie Strunk of Syracuse, called the New York court's ruling proper and said sodomy isn't "evil," pointing as proof to the fact that it was legal for married New York couples. Attorney William Gardner, representing the Buffalo litigants, argued that striking down a sodomy law was consistent with Supreme Court decisions that, "in effect, recognized the human right to enjoy private erotic pleasures."

Predictably, Chief Justice Burger listed *New York v. Onofre* and *New York v. Peoples et al.* for discussion. Yet on May 18, 1981, both cases were turned away. The state court decision deeming New York's sodomy law unconstitutional was allowed to stand. Not one justice objected, at least in public. The Supreme Court could have overturned that decision by simply saying, "Reversed. See *Doe v. Commonwealth's Attorney.*" In choosing not to do so, the court naturally made *Doe* seem even less definitive.

The court's inaction underscored just how little the justices as a group seemed to feel a responsibility to clear up confusion about significant gay legal questions. Were sodomy laws constitutional or not? Was the marriage exemption in New York's law a fatal flaw? How were lower court judges and ordinary citizens expected to know? Under rules that allow supreme unaccountability bordering on irresponsibility, the court offered no clue as to its thinking.

Onofre, who slowly accepted his orientation after being arrested, had his persistent loneliness punctured by celebrations of his Supreme Court success. His voice chokes with emotion as he describes his elation at parties honoring him and his attorney in Rochester and Albany, New York. "It was the most wonderful feeling that, 'Gee, maybe I did accomplish something after all,'" he recalls.

Stripped of Their Uniforms

Although the U.S. military had begun attempting to purge itself of homosexuals before World War II, individual gay-rights cases that reached the Supreme Court before 1981 involved civilians. The first gay service member to seek the high court's protection was Dennis R. Beller, whose *cert* petition arrived in February 1981 just as the nation was taking a hard right turn with the start of the Reagan administration.

Beller enlisted in the Navy the month before his twentieth birthday and served with distinction for 15 years. An "Aerographer's Mate First

Class" (a meteorologist) at a Navy weather station in Monterey, California, Beller said his career ran aground during a routine investigation launched because superiors wanted to upgrade his security clearance. Under questioning, Beller said he was president of the gay Monterey Dons Motorcycle Club, had sex with men, patronized gay bars and considered himself bisexual.

Under Navy regulations, sailors "involved in homosexuality" were intolerable "military liabilities" and "security risks," though the Navy's own Crittendon Report had thoroughly debunked the security risk stereotype in 1957. On December 19, 1975, the chief of naval personnel ordered Beller, 34, honorably discharged as unfit to serve.

Beller won a restraining order temporarily preventing his discharge. But then on April 14, 1976, Judge George B. Harris ruled in favor of the Navy, despite his disdain for its policy. Beller had not challenged the Navy's right to expel homosexuals. Rather, he had argued that the Navy's definition of "homosexual" was unconstitutionally vague because it could include anyone who'd "ever even patted affectionately a member of the same sex." Harris rejected the vagueness argument because Beller had known he was violating the Navy's gay ban.

Though ruling against Beller, Harris fired a broadside at the seeming mindlessness of the Navy's ban. Harris said "large numbers" of sailors probably had engaged in homosexual conduct, yet there was no evidence that they accounted for a disproportionate number of "disloyal or inefficient" sailors. If the Navy really wants to minimize security risks, it should let sailors admit homosexuality without fear of reprisal, he argued. "The emerging learning . . . is that there is no basis for homosexuality or homosexual conduct per se disqualifying one from positions of trust. . . . The Navy does itself and the public little good by removing an experienced and able serviceman such as [Beller] from its ranks," Harris concluded.

At the Ninth Circuit Court of Appeals, Beller's case was combined with those of Navy air traffic controller Mary Saal and Yeoman Second Class James Miller. Like Beller, they were being stripped of their uniforms for admitted homosexual acts despite fine service records. On October 23, 1980, future Supreme Court justice Anthony Kennedy, writing for a three-judge panel of the Ninth Circuit, ruled that Navy regulations requiring the discharge of homosexuals were constitutional:

"We recognize that to many persons the regulations may seem unwise, but if that be the case the political branches of the government, which most certainly are on notice of the controversy here or in similar cases, have the right and the prerogative to declare a different policy. Our role is more confined. We are limited to determining whether or not the Constitution prohibits the Navy from adopting the rule before us."

The Navy had submitted a long list of supposed justifications for excluding homosexuals: There would be hostility between known homosexuals and sailors who "despise/detest homosexuality." Homosexual emotional relationships would cause problems. Homosexual officers would have difficulty commanding respect. The presence of known homosexuals would damage recruitment. And "a homosexual might force his desires upon others."

Kennedy found, "Despite the evidence that attitudes toward homosexual conduct have changed among some groups in society, the Navy could conclude that a substantial number of naval personnel have feelings regarding homosexuality, based upon moral precepts recognized by many in our society as legitimate, which would create tensions and hostilities, and that these feelings might undermine the ability of a homosexual to command the respect necessary to perform supervisory duties." Emphasizing that naval service often involved long confinement in close quarters at sea, Kennedy concluded that "the constitutionality of the regulations stems from the needs of the military, the Navy in particular, and from the unique accommodation between military demands and what might be constitutionally protected activity in some contexts."

Kennedy's ruling was a major disappointment to gay-rights advocates. However, it also represented a breakthrough because, according to gay law scholar Arthur Leonard, for the first time a federal appeals court was suggesting that government discrimination against gay people (outside the military) might have to pass a test of "heightened scrutiny" to be constitutional. Most laws need only be "rational" to be constitutional. However, racist laws must be subjected to "strict scrutiny" and are unconstitutional unless justified by a "compelling state interest" and narrowly tailored to advance it. "The [gay military] case before us lies somewhere between those two standards" of strict scrutiny and mere rationality, Kennedy said. In between those extremes fall laws that discriminate on the basis of sex or against certain traditionally powerless groups; those mid-range laws must pass what the Supreme Court has called "heightened scrutiny"—in other words, the court must think there's a good reason for discriminating.

When a majority of Ninth Circuit judges voted against having the entire circuit hear the case, Judge William Norris blasted Kennedy's "knee-jerk acquiescence" to the Navy's contention that the anti-gay feelings of heterosexual sailors were a legitimate basis for declaring gay people unfit to serve. Norris said such deference would not be accorded the prejudices of racists or misogynists who did not want to work alongside blacks or women. "Intolerance is not a constitutional basis for an infringement of fundamental personal rights," Norris declared.

After Kennedy ruled in favor of the Navy's gay ban, only weatherman Dennis Beller appealed to the Supreme Court. Attorney Richard Fox of Los Angeles argued that Beller was entitled to know why his exemplary record didn't make him an exception to the ouster rule. Fox noted that lower courts' contradictory gay-rights decisions stemmed from their confusion over whether private consensual homosexual conduct is constitutionally protected in any way. "The time is ripe for this court to address this question," Fox declared. Then, in an ironic twist, Fox concluded by approvingly quoting Justice Rehnquist's angry dissent from denial of *cert* in *Ratchford v. Gay Lib*. The scolding words of the justice who had compared homosexuality to a contagious disease were put to a gay-friendly use as Fox urged the court not to let its power over its own schedule become a "judicial storm cellar" where it could hide from "sensitive cases."

In reply, the Navy said that, since it wanted to oust Beller, there was no need to explain why. Plus, the Navy argued, the court would be wasting its time in reviewing Beller's expulsion because the challenged Navy regulations had been revised when the Pentagon standardized the armed forces' rules for booting out homosexuals.

The Supreme Court did not discuss *Beller v. Lehman, secretary of the Navy, et al.* in conference. Dennis Beller lost his last chance of regaining his military career on June 1, 1981, when his case was unceremoniously turned away without comment. Just as Frank Kameny's Civil

Service victory was no help to public school teachers, it did nothing for gay men and lesbians in uniform. The Pentagon was nowhere near being ready to retreat from its war against gay Americans. Apparently unconcerned about the mounting casualties of that war, the U.S. Supreme Court passively watched from the safety of its marble storm cellar.

9

OMINOUS, "UNSETTLED" TIMES

THE SUPREME COURT STOPPED being a gentleman's club in 1981.
After 101 male justices, the nation's highest court finally got its first
woman. The court's 191-year history preceding that appointment was
steeped in male bias. It had long held, for example, that state laws forbidding women to vote did not violate the 14th Amendment's 1868
guarantee of equal protection. Male lawmakers had to amend the Constitution in 1920 for women to gain voting rights. Not until 1971 did
the court strike down any law for sex discrimination. A decade later, an-
ticipating that a woman would soon join their elite ranks, the men of
the court privately agreed to stop calling themselves "brethren." And
their title of address was neutered—"Mr. Justice So-and-So" became
simply "Justice So-and-So." One patriarchal flourish survived: "Mr.
Chief Justice."

Supreme Court appointments are often one of the most enduring
parts of a president's legacy. (A quarter century after President Nixon
resigned in disgrace, Nixon appointee Rehnquist was still on the court.)
President Carter had hoped that his legacy would include appointing
the first female justice. Instead, as progressives' bad luck would have it,
Carter became the first full-term president in history not to leave a
mark on the nation's highest court.

Just months after the Democratic Carter left office, Justice Stewart,
an Eisenhower appointee and former Republican elected official,
stepped down, giving the new Republican president, Ronald Reagan,
the opportunity to make the first of what would be three Supreme
Court appointments. Keeping a campaign pledge to put a woman on

the court, Reagan reached all the way down to the Arizona Court of Appeals to tap 51-year-old Sandra Day O'Connor.

After an Annie Oakley girlhood on a 198,000-acre Arizona ranch, she'd graduated third in her class at Stanford University's prestigious law school in 1952, then run smack into sexism. Unable to find a law firm that would hire a woman, O'Connor took a job as a lowly deputy county attorney in San Mateo, California. After returning to Arizona, she became active in Republican politics. In 1969, she was appointed to the state Senate, then twice won election as a moderate conservative and became the first female majority leader of a state Senate. Senator O'Connor, a married woman with three sons, demonstrated her sensitivity to women's rights, supporting ratification of the Equal Rights Amendment. Switching gears, she won election to a state judgeship and five years later was appointed to a state appeals court.

Would O'Connor, like Thurgood Marshall, the first justice without a white male perspective, extrapolate from her own experience enough to align herself with other victims of discrimination, including gay people? Or, would she be like Stewart, who—except in "obscenity" cases—almost invariably voted against homosexuals. O'Connor's past provided no clues.

During her U.S. Senate confirmation hearings, O'Connor gave no hint as to her view of the legitimacy of gay constitutional claims. Senator Jeremiah Denton, a far-right Alabama Republican, demanded to know whether she saw constitutional limits on laws restricting "the rights of homosexuals because of their sexual deviance." In a classic understatement, O'Connor replied that "the state of the law concerning homosexuality is, in one word, unsettled."

Signaling only that she'd done homework, O'Connor cited Brennan's 1977 *Carey* footnotes that said the court had not yet determined the limits of the constitutional protections for private sexual behavior. Then she cited the 1976 *Doe* decision upholding Virginia's sodomy law. "[T]hat is all we know I think at the moment on the Supreme Court holdings in the area," she said, showing no awareness of the landmark *ONE* and *Manual* freedom-of-the-press rulings. "The cases concerning the rights of people who are homosexuals in connection with being deprived of a position as an employee or having custody of children are really very confused on the lower court level. Some of those are working their way up to the Supreme Court and, I think, pose some very unsettled questions on which the court will indeed be asked to rule," she noted.

When O'Connor took her oath of office on September 26, 1981, the Supreme Court's lineup took a shape that would remain fixed for five terms. Chief Justice Burger and Justices Brennan, White, Marshall, Blackmun, Powell, Rehnquist, Stevens and O'Connor would be the nine who in 1986 would decide the Georgia sodomy case, *Bowers v. Hardwick,* that produced the century's most devastating defeat for gay Americans. In the years leading up to *Hardwick,* gay Americans received powerful warnings of the way the court, including its first woman, was headed.

Justice O'Connor's first gay-rights case was awaiting her when she arrived. The case of Army Lieutenant Joseph G. "Jay" Hatheway Jr. presented a classic example of discriminatory law enforcement. Was there a gay exception to the Constitution's guarantee of equal protection?

The Ninth Circuit seemed to think so, at least for gay men and lesbians in uniform. The military's sodomy ban prohibited "unnatural carnal copulation with another person of the same sex or opposite sex"—taken to mean oral and anal sex were crimes for everyone. Hatheway had been court-martialed for sodomy, convicted and sentenced to be discharged. His attorney argued, first in military courts, then in federal courts, that the case ought to be dismissed because Army prosecutors knew of heterosexual sodomy violations but ignored them.

A three-judge panel of the Ninth Circuit ruled April 20, 1981, that homosexuality was permissible grounds for "selective prosecution" of military sodomy. The court found homosexual sodomy was more likely than heterosexual sodomy "to undermine discipline and order."

Hatheway's *cert* petition, filed July 20, 1981, did little to help the justices see him as an individual, a young man whose faith in his country had been shaken by his treatment at the hands of the military. The justices weren't told, for example, that Jay Hatheway was a National Merit Scholar who'd been able to attend college only because he'd won a ROTC scholarship.

As an intelligence officer in the Green Berets, Hatheway, a short, muscular, blue-eyed blond, was stationed in West Germany. After homosexual rumors sparked an investigation, a frightened Hatheway secured a discharge. He spent a drunken evening saying goodbye to an enlisted man. They were caught naked together. Hatheway's bedmate was granted immunity and testified against him. Hatheway's first judge was a colonel who allegedly remarked, "I don't have anything against queers. I've always heard a blow job was as good from a man as from a woman." His second military judge filled a page with a giant doodle: "HOMO."

In petitioning the Supreme Court on Hatheway's behalf, attorney Christopher Coates argued that the selective prosecution of homosexual sodomy doubly violated the Constitution's equal protection guarantee: Hatheway was discriminated against because of his sexual orientation and his gender. Had Hatheway been female, the argument went, he could have performed the same sex acts with a man and not been prosecuted even though the military's rule, on its face, was not discriminatory. The Army did not bother to file a response.

Neither O'Connor nor any of her elders on the bench viewed the gay exception that the Ninth Circuit had tacked onto the Equal Protection Clause as something that the court ought to at least talk about in conference. Without discussion, the court denied *cert* in *Hatheway v. Marsh, secretary of the Army* on October 5, 1981.

Indirectly, the military's gay ban also triggered civilian Gary Van Ooteghem's Supreme Court case. Van Ooteghem had moved to Houston in January 1975 to take a job as assistant county treasurer. He'd been hired by Hartsell Gray, treasurer of Harris County, who suspected Ooteghem was gay. For six months, the county treasurer was delighted with Van Ooteghem, whom he considered a "brilliant accountant." Promoted to assistant treasurer, Van Ooteghem worked long hours and set his own schedule. He quickly developed a good working relationship with the county governing board, before which he testified twice a week.

Van Ooteghem was closeted at work, apolitical and, by his own assessment, materialistic. His only "activism" had been organizing a gay volleyball team in Chicago. In June 1975, Van Ooteghem read about Air Force Sergeant Leonard Matlovich, a Bronze Star winner who—at Frank Kameny's encouragement—had declared his homosexuality to challenge the constitutionality of the military's gay ban. Awed by the sergeant's courage, Van Ooteghem contacted him. Matlovich suggested that they meet in July in Washington, D.C., where he would be lobbying Congress with National Gay Task Force founder Bruce Voeller.

Van Ooteghem tagged along as Matlovich and Voeller (then challenging Virginia's sodomy law) buttonholed lawmakers. Because of his job, Van Ooteghem was able to secure a meeting with Senate Armed Services Committee Chairman John Tower of Texas.

Transformed by his day at the Capitol, Van Ooteghem returned to work eager to change the world. He came out to his boss—a revelation he followed up by saying he intended, as a private citizen, to ask the county board to protect gay people. Treasurer Gray feared that the board would slash his agency's budget in retaliation if Van Ooteghem pressed it on gay rights. Gray demanded that Van Ooteghem sign a statement requiring him to be on the job from 8 A.M. to noon and 1 to 5 P.M.—the only hours the board heard citizen grievances—and barring him from political activities during those hours. When Van Ooteghem, 33, refused, Gray fired him.

Van Ooteghem's friends begged him not to be "stupid," not to commit financial suicide. Undeterred, the day after being fired Gary Van Ooteghem addressed his county board. "After I gave the speech there were cameras. I'd never been in front of that many cameras. Press everywhere. One leg was shaking so bad I had all my weight on the other leg. As soon as I gave the speech . . . I was free. There was nothing anybody else could do to me because I said who I was. I was free. I was really free," Van Ooteghem recalled. With the ACLU's backing, he sued for reinstatement and back pay, charging that Treasurer Gray had violated his freedom of speech.

Federal Judge Ross N. Sterling agreed on March 29, 1978. He said "a state may discharge an employee for an immodest flaunting of his homosexuality," citing librarian Mike McConnell's unsuccessful attempt to regain a promised job and, oddly, John Singer's Civil Service triumph. "However," the judge continued, "where no improper conduct, such as applying for a marriage license with a person of the same sex, kissing a person of the same sex in public or participating in homosexual demonstrations, has occurred and where the individual has not purposely sought out notoriety, a discharge for a person's advocacy of homosexual rights is unconstitutional."

A three-judge panel of the Fifth Circuit Court of Appeals agreed in 1980 that Van Ooteghem's firing was unconstitutional. Judge Irving L. Goldberg's ruling declared, "the ability of a member of a disfavored class to express his views on civil rights publicly and without hesitation—no matter how personally offensive to his employer or majority of his co-employees—lies at the core of the free speech clause of the First Amendment."

When Harris County Attorney Mike Driscoll petitioned the Supreme Court to overturn the judgments in Van Ooteghem's favor, he argued it wasn't a "censorship" case. Instead, he said it involved the right to fire a worker for insubordination. Driscoll claimed the county treasurer would have acted no differently if Van Ooteghem had wanted to make a "Save the Whales" pitch to the county board. Van Ooteghem's legal team responded that the lower courts had established that Van Oogethem's rights had been violated and were mulling who should compensate him.

Since a gay victory would stand if the Supreme Court did not intervene, Chief Justice Burger predictably listed *Gray, treasurer of Harris County, Texas v. Van Ooteghem* for discussion. Without public comment, the court turned down the case on January 18, 1982.

In passively handing victory to Van Ooteghem, did the justices see themselves as saying that gay Americans enjoy equal First Amendment rights, as they had implied in *ONE* and *Manual?* Was the Fifth Circuit's decision so obviously correct that no justice—or, at least, no four justices—wanted to review it? Accountable to no one, the court explains its inaction to no one.

Van Ooteghem's case finally stopped bouncing around the lower courts in 1985, a decade after he had lost his job. Harris County was ordered to pay his attorneys' fees, give him back pay and to consider him for employment without prejudice. The court didn't order Van Ooteghem's reinstatement because treasurer Gray was no longer in office.

It had been a challenging decade for Van Ooteghem. In the early years, he was nearly destitute. Friends brought over food every Christmas Eve. "I lost my house. I lost my ability of getting a job," he recalled. He went into private practice but, ironically, whenever he won another legal round, his income plunged. "Every time it came out in the news, my clients left me—even my gay clients 'cause in those days people were afraid." That changed when his victory established "the right not to be afraid to say you are gay in Houston," said Van Ooteghem, who became president of the Log Cabin Republicans of Houston.

Although proud of what his lawsuit accomplished, Van Ooteghem, who died in July 2000, modestly recalled, "All I did was stand my ground. I didn't consider it a brave thing."

A Couple Without a Country

What would it take to get the Supreme Court actively involved in a gay case? In 1982, the court had not given full consideration—publicly hearing oral argument after attorneys on both sides had filed briefs—to any homosexual case in 15 years. The last time the court had focused its full attention on a homosexual case was in 1967, when it allowed Clive Boutilier to be deported under a policy equating "psychopathic" with homosexual.

A quite different immigration case reached the court in May 1982. It begged the question of how far the justices would allow lower courts to go in reading anti-gay restrictions into laws that, on their face, did not discriminate. When conservatives decry "judicial activism," they're usually upset that courts have read individual rights into laws or constitutions that do not explicitly spell out such rights. Gay Americans have long been the victims of a peculiar brand of judicial activism: Judges uphold an anti-gay status quo by discovering homophobic restrictions in laws that make no mention of gay people. Such judges seem to think, "If lawmakers had realized homosexuals would try to exercise equal rights, they surely would have written explicit prohibitions against them into this law. Thus, we can assume this law contains such restrictions."

In finding it legitimate to concoct anti-gay interpretations of laws, lower courts have relied heavily on the Supreme Court's *Boutilier* deportation decision. If the high court wanted to curtail anti-gay judicial activism, the deportation fight of Australian Anthony "Tony" Corbett Sullivan and his spouse, U.S. citizen Richard Frank Adams, presented a golden opportunity.

Stopping over in Los Angeles on a round-the-world trip in 1971, Tony Sullivan, then 29, met Richard Adams at a gay bar called The Closet. Adams, a 24-year-old Avis employee, found Sullivan, a former Quantas flight attendant then working as a model and surf shop manager, attractively "worldly." For their first real date, they romantically rendezvoused the next night at the Greta Garbo star in the sidewalk alongside Hollywood Boulevard. The two men quickly fell in love; Sullivan never finished his trip.

An Australian official soon informed them that Adams, a naturalized U.S. citizen born in Manila, could not immigrate to Australia because he was part Filipino. "That tipped us off that we were going to have problems," Sullivan recalls. He was legally extending his U.S. stay by crossing into Mexico, then getting a new six-month tourist stamp on his visa upon his return. He grew nervous that immigration authorities were going to stop him at the border.

Under U.S. immigration law, Sullivan could become a permanent resident if he were the "spouse" of a U.S. citizen. Two days before his visa was to expire in January 1974, Sullivan married Mary Egleston, a friend of a friend, who wanted to help him legally stay with Adams. The "green card" marriage was promptly annulled when Sullivan learned that the INS expected him to "copulate," as he puts it, with his wife. Sullivan's wealthy mother then warned she would disown him if he fought for his rights as a gay man. "She kept her promise," he says.

In consultation with the Reverend Troy Perry, founder of the predominantly gay Metropolitan Community Church (MCC), Sullivan and Adams planned a church wedding that, they hoped, would give them First Amendment freedom-of-religion grounds to claim to be legally wed. On March 20, 1975, the Reverend Perry united the couple in a holy union ceremony in Los Angeles.

Before the couple could pursue their religious-freedom challenge, they heard Johnny Carson joking on late-night television about a county clerk allowing gay couples to marry in Colorado. Seeing nothing in state law to prohibit same-sex marriages, Boulder County Clerk Clela Rorex felt she had a duty not to discriminate. Despite barbs hurled in her direction, Rorex kept her sense of humor. When an old codger tried to make a fool of her by gruffly demanding to marry his horse, Rorex charmed him by calmly informing him that the filly wasn't old enough.

Sullivan and Adams flew to Colorado with a pair of MCC ministers in tow. At 8:40 A.M. on April 21, 1975, Rorex issued the couple a marriage license. The marriage was performed immediately. By 11 A.M. it was registered with Boulder County. Three days later, Colorado's attorney general deemed Boulder's six same-sex marriages invalid. Rorex stopped licensing gay couples. However, Colorado never formally nullified the same-sex marriages.

After returning home to the Los Angeles suburb of Tujunga, the newly wed Adams and Sullivan learned the INS had begun deportation proceedings against Sullivan. Adams asked the INS to classify Sullivan as his "spouse." In reply, the INS district director wrote, "You have failed to establish that a bona fide marital relationship can exist between two faggots." That crude denial was quickly withdrawn as "legally insufficient" and replaced by a letter from Acting District Director Jo Dermet stating that the Adams-Sullivan relationship was not a true marriage because neither man "can perform the female functions in marriage." The Board of Immigration Appeals then ruled that the couple had failed to prove their wedding was valid under Colorado's marriage statute, which used "a man and woman" language at one point.

Beverly Hills attorney David M. Brown—who had already broken legal ground for nontraditional couples by winning the first successful "palimony" claim—sued in federal court on the couple's behalf. On December 18, 1979, Judge Irving Hill ruled against Adams and Sullivan. Though noting that nothing in Colorado law barred same-sex marriages, Hill construed the "man and a woman" reference to mean that the state recognized only male-female marriages.

Except for sham marriages entered into only to avoid deportation (which no one argued was the case for Adams and Sullivan), the INS normally accepts as valid any marriage that a state recognizes. However, Hill ruled that even if the men's marriage were valid in Colorado, the INS would not have to honor it because gay marriage "offends federal public policy."

Federal law was silent on same-sex marriage. Hill filled that void with his own conclusions. "Marriage exists as a protected legal institution primarily because of societal values associated with the propagation of the human race," he wrote, quoting the Washington State court blocking John Singer's bid to marry Paul Barwick. Unabashedly rooting his ruling in religion, Hill added, "The definition of marriage, the rights and responsibilities implicit in that relationship . . . are now governed by civil law. The English civil law took its attitudes and basic principles from canon [religious] law. . . . Canon law in both Judaism and Christianity could not possibly sanction any marriage between persons of the same

sex because of the vehement condemnation in the Scriptures of both religions of all homosexual relationships. Thus there has been for centuries a combination of scriptural and canonical teaching under which a
'marriage' between persons of the same sex was unthinkable and, by definition, impossible."

Hill concluded that "in light of this history," Congress did not intend
"spouse" to include a same-sex partner. The judge further ruled that
limiting federal recognition to male-female marriages did not violate the
Constitution's equal protection and due process guarantees. Of "paramount importance," he said, was the fact that the Supreme Court had
dismissed a gay marriage case, *Baker v. Nelson,* as not raising a "substantial federal question." Hill declared that the government interest in
procreation justified allowing male-female couples to marry while barring same-sex couples—even though many male-female couples are
sterile or childless by choice. Hill added that making male-female marriage licenses contingent on whether the couple intended to breed
would be unconstitutional.

Imagine the public uproar if Hill had ruled in 1979 that Congress's
use of "spouse" in 1965 legislation didn't include interracial partners
since mixed marriages were then illegal in much of the nation. Or, what
if he'd said "spouse" did not include interfaith marriages because many
religions refuse to recognize them. Or, what if he had ruled in favor of
an incestuous union and cited Old Testament patriarch Abraham's marriage to his half-sister, Sarah?

The Ninth Circuit Court of Appeals affirmed Hill's decision. A three-
judge panel's February 25, 1982, ruling focused on whether Congress
"intended that homosexual marriages confer spouse status." Congress
did not, the panel ruled. It based that conclusion on the fact that the
1965 immigration law, which added "sexual deviation" to prohibited
characteristics for aliens, "clearly expresses an intent to exclude homosexuals." As proof, the panel cited *Boutilier.*

To avoid exorbitant Supreme Court filing fees, Adams and Sullivan
filed paupers' affidavits. Adams swore that he had only $100 in savings
and that his only property was a 19-year-old Peugeot; Sullivan had $70
in the bank and an aged Ford. On May 28, 1982, attorney David Brown
petitioned the justices, arguing that Adams and Sullivan were legally
married, that "homosexual conduct" was legal in Colorado and their

home state of California and that Congress had not intended to block such lawful marriages.

Brown's plea was, of necessity, a marriage-rights argument even though his clients had been married for seven years at that point. "[A]n adult's sexual preference is either impervious or barely susceptible to change. As a result, state action forbidding persons of the same sex to marry is tantamount to forbidding homosexuals as a class from entering into any marriage save for a 'marriage of convenience'. . . . Government possesses few means of inflicting a stigma upon a class more effective than withholding the ability to marry. . . . Prohibition of homosexual marriage undercuts governmental interest in social stability for it discourages formal commitment to a lasting relationship by a substantial segment of society," Brown argued.

Reagan administration Solicitor General Rex E. Lee told the court that he saw no need to respond.

Tony Sullivan and Richard Adams presented the justices with the case of a gay family on the brink of being torn apart because of anti-gay interpretations of U.S. law. Unlike the Minnesota gay couple whose case the high court had dismissed in 1972, Adams and Sullivan had not had a state court declare their marriage void. Yet the justices saw no need to discuss the case. None of the eight associate justices objected when Chief Justice Burger failed to list it for discussion. *Cert* was denied in *Adams et al. v. Howerton, Acting District Director, Immigration and Naturalization Service* on June 28, 1982.

Adams and Sullivan kept struggling to remain together legally. Sullivan argued deportation would cause extreme hardship. The Board of Immigration Appeals ruled against him. Then in a 2-to-1 decision written by Judge Anthony Kennedy, the Ninth Circuit ruled on September 30, 1985, that the immigration board had not abused its discretion. (Kennedy was the future justice who in upholding the Navy's gay ban had indicated in 1980 that some anti-gay discrimination might be unconstitutional.) Kennedy had no problem with the fact that the board—saying Adams was not "a qualifying relative"—had refused to weigh the impact of Sullivan's deportation on Adams.

Dissenting Judge Harry Pregerson noted that Sullivan and Adams had been a couple for well over a decade. The board's "failure to recognize Sullivan's emotional hardship is particularly troublesome,"

Pregerson declared, "because he and Adams have lived together as a family. . . . [M]ost deported aliens can return to their native lands with their closest companions. But . . . Adams allegedly would not be permitted to emigrate to Australia."

The couple finally abandoned their futile U.S. legal battle. With Sullivan's deportation date closing in, the couple thought they had reached an agreement with Australia: The couple would go to Europe, stay out of the news, then enter Australia separately. Australia failed to keep its part of the bargain, the couple says. Adams received a temporary visa, not a permanent one.

A couple without a country, Adams and Sullivan fled to Ireland, where they existed for months on the equivalent of 69 cents a day and ate lamb shank stew night after night. Realizing that the United States was really home, they tried to return together, but Sullivan's request for a tourist visa was turned down. Having run out of legal options for staying together, Sullivan secretly slipped back into this country. Without the U.S. government's knowledge or blessing, he settled back down with his lawfully wedded spouse in 1986.

"There's only so much you can allow governments to restrict your life. There's a point at which you become outlaws. There's a point at which you say, 'Wait a second. No one has a right to do this to me. And if the law is in my way, then I will break the law,'" Sullivan said a decade later, celebrating 25 years of living with Adams. "I can be grabbed and deported at any time."

In 1996, Adams, 49, was a law firm's assistant office manager. At 54, Sullivan, who stressed that he pays U.S. taxes, had found ways to work without attracting INS attention. The couple remains angry that Sullivan's outlaw status forces them to struggle financially. Had the courts ruled differently, "We would probably own our own home. We both love to travel. We would have been able to travel. I would have been a professional of some kind," Sullivan says, who has a heart condition but no health insurance.

The couple still resents the pressure that gay-rights groups, fearful of more anti-gay court rulings, put on them to drop the case at a very early stage. "We were fighting for love rights at a time when the [gay] community was just fighting for sex rights. They weren't even fighting for employment rights," Sullivan says. "I'm a '60s idealist. I feel we made a major contribution."

Responding to lingering gay criticism of their losing legal battle, Adams and Sullivan declared on an Internet bulletin board,

> The bottom line was that we loved one another and wanted to remain together. The consequence of not fighting the oppression that existed and still exists because of the way legal marriage was set up and is still set up was that we would abandon our relationship and go our separate ways. Many do that. We could not. Love is important to us, more important than countries, governments, laws, regulations and even blood families. We still love one another and are still together and still paying the cost . . . of the society not recognizing gay and lesbian relationships.

Sullivan and Adams are willing to risk the consequences of this book's disclosing that they're living somewhere in the United States because, as Sullivan stresses, "It's important for people to realize that it was never resolved." Same-sex partners still are not considered spouses for immigration purposes. U.S. immigration policy purportedly values family reunification yet continues to offer committed gay couples three untenable choices: breaking up, living in separate countries or becoming outlaws. Australia, in response to criticism of its treatment of Sullivan and Adams, now offers permanent resident status to the gay partners of its citizens.

The Case of the "Soliciting Homo"

Shortly before its 1983–84 term began, the court finally agreed—for the first time since 1967—to give a gay case a full hearing. Ultimately, though, a five-member majority decided *cert* had been "improvidently granted"—the court's way of saying "Oops." *New York v. Uplinger et al.* was dismissed, letting a gay-rights victory stand.

Yet anyone who interpreted that dismissal as meaning the Supreme Court was warming to gay civil rights was very much mistaken. Inside the court, out of earshot of the American people, anti-gay warning signals were loudly sounding: The delicate sensibilities of Justice Lewis F.

Powell Jr., the middle-of-the-road conservative who often cast the decisive vote on social issues, were deeply offended by the mere mention of homosexuality.

Uplinger presented another case involving discriminatory enforcement of law that, on its face, made no distinction between homosexuals and heterosexuals. *Uplinger* grew out of the fact that the Buffalo vice squad was still targeting male homosexuals, even though New York's top court had ruled the state sodomy law unconstitutional. The U.S. Supreme Court had refused to review that sodomy decision, denying *cert* to *New York v. Onofre* in 1981. After the sodomy law's demise, police continued arresting gay men under a statute that outlawed loitering "for the purpose of engaging, or soliciting another person to engage, in deviate sexual intercourse or other sexual behavior of a deviate nature." New York defined "deviate intercourse" as unmarried oral or anal sex. What "other" behavior constituted illegal deviance was left undefined. The law prohibited all "deviate" solicitation, no matter how polite or welcome. (Other laws prohibited harassment and prostitution.) Anyone who propositioned someone in a public place, including a bar, was breaking the law if the spoken or unspoken goal was oral or anal sex.

When New York had a sodomy law, only gay men were arrested in Buffalo under that loitering law, according to the head of the city vice squad. Once the sodomy law vanished, the loitering law was also used against suspected prostitutes if the police didn't have enough evidence to sustain a prostitution charge. The loitering law's constitutionality was challenged by a gay man and by a woman who was, as one judge put it, "a known prostitute."

At 2:50 A.M. on August 7, 1981, Robert Uplinger, who was short and good-looking, was standing on the Lenox Hotel's front steps, a popular cruising spot for gay men in Buffalo. He struck up a conversation with a stranger, Steven Nicosia, and introduced him to friends. Uniformed police officers then told the tiny gathering to disperse. As they were walking away, Uplinger, who'd been chatting with Nicosia for 10 minutes, invited him to his apartment. Nicosia asked what Uplinger had in mind. "Well," Uplinger replied, "if you drive me over to my place . . . I'll blow you." The oral sex invitation was just what Nicosia, an undercover vice squad rookie, was waiting to hear. He immediately arrested Uplinger.

A city judge found Uplinger guilty of breaking the loitering law and fined him $100. ("What!" Justice Powell later gasped in a margin note, sounding shocked the fine wasn't higher.)

Convicted prostitute Susan Butler had been spotted waving at cars passing through a Buffalo intersection at 4 A.M. on April 1, 1981. A vice cop watched as a car pulled over. Butler talked briefly with the male driver, then got inside. The policeman followed and allegedly saw Butler performing fellatio on the driver. She was arrested under the loitering-for-deviate-sex law. A judge dismissed the charge, saying that in Butler's situation the law was too vague.

On appeal, Erie County Judge Joseph P. McCarthy ruled against both Uplinger and Butler. "Indiscriminate public solicitation for deviate sex constitutes a contemptuous disregard for community standards, facially defies moral and aesthetic sensibilities, and annoys individuals who do not wish to become involved in such activities," he declared.

Then New York's top court struck down the loitering law on February 23, 1983. In a short 6-to-1 decision that did not state the precise statutory or constitutional grounds for its conclusions, the court ruled: "The object of the loitering statute is to punish conduct anticipatory to the act of consensual sodomy. Inasmuch as the conduct ultimately contemplated by the loitering statute may not be deemed criminal, we perceive no basis upon which the state may continue to punish loitering for that purpose." In other words, if it's legal to, say, share a pizza in private, it can't be illegal to publicly invite someone home for pizza. The court added that the loitering statute was not an anti-harassment statute since it didn't require that conduct be annoying to be illegal.

In petitioning the Supreme Court to overturn that ruling, Erie County District Attorney Richard J. Arcara contended that the loitering law was indeed a harassment statute. Arcara made clear he was searching for a back-door route to reinstatement of New York's sodomy law. The loitering statute, he insisted, controlled invasions of the public's privacy.

In reply, Uplinger attorney William Gardner argued that the loitering statute was unconstitutionally vague and trampled the rights of free speech and freedom of association. What's more, it interfered with the right to privacy because it restricted public conversations about constitutionally protected (at least in the eyes of New York's top court) sexual activities. Gardner warned the justices to steer clear of the case unless they were prepared to address the underlying issue of whether private, consensual, non-commercial, adult sodomy is protected by the right to privacy.

On a clerk-written pool memo on *Uplinger*, Justice Powell emphatically wrote, "This is a subject (criminalizing homosexual solicitation in public) that we can <u>do without</u>." In that memo, Rehnquist clerk Gary B. Born flatly stated, "Whether or not it is constitutionally protected, deviate sexual conduct is highly offensive to most persons." ("Yes," Powell responded.) In recounting Uplinger's arrest, Born referred to the gay men gathered on the Lenox Hotel steps as "gentlemen." (Powell added quote marks around "gentlemen" and a question mark above the word.) Born said that neighborhood residents had expressed "humiliation at being propositioned" by homosexuals. (Powell underlined and put a check mark over that sentiment.)

Fourteen years later, Harvard law professor David Charny's clearest memory of *Uplinger* was Powell's "rabidly" hostile margin notes. Charny was one of the two young gentlemen who worked on *Uplinger* while clerking directly for Powell. Both were gay.

On September 26, 1983, Chief Justice Burger led off the court's private discussion of *Uplinger* by saying he favored immediately reversing the New York court decision that had struck down the loitering law. Brennan voted to deny *cert*. White wanted *cert* granted. Marshall voted to deny. Like a reluctant bridge player, Blackmun said he would "Join three," meaning he'd provide the crucial fourth vote for *cert* if it were needed. Powell, of course, wanted the court to have nothing to do with the case. Rehnquist, always pushing to go on record against homosexuality, cast the vote that assured the case would be taken. Stevens then voted for denial. O'Connor, the newest justice, lined up with the conservatives who wanted to hear the case.

District Attorney Arcara then filed a brief that called the loitering law a "clear and concise attempt to regulate offensive conduct." He was no longer trying to use the defunct sodomy law to justify the loitering law. Instead, raising a series of new arguments, he said the law protects children, targets speech that is "undeniably lewd" and extends not just to loitering to solicit oral and anal sex but also to solicit bestiality or necrophilia. Arcara did not explain how animals or the dead can be solicited.

Uplinger attorney William Gardner countered that the law was discriminatory, offering no protection to "women subjected to 'normal' sexual solicitation." He added, "What the present statute directly accomplishes is avoidance of injury to the male ego from the possibility of being solicited for a homosexual act." Susan Butler's attorneys added that "the real danger" of a law that makes no attempt to define the boundaries of prohibited sexual remarks is that it is used "only against those individuals who are deemed 'undesirable' by society, for example, against suspected prostitutes and suspected homosexuals. They . . . are easy prey to the vagaries of the statute and its arbitrary enforcement." The American Psychological Association was among the group urging the justices not to revive the loitering law.

To prepare for oral arguments, most justices had a clerk write a "bench memo" laying out both sides' arguments. On a seven-page *Uplinger* memo from one of his clerks, Justice Marshall put a large check mark beside advice that apparently expressed his views: "I would hold, at the outset, that consensual homosexual activity is constitutionally protected for the same reason that the use of contraceptives is constitutionally protected."

Meanwhile, Powell clerk David Charny, careful to frame his conclusions in terms Powell would not find objectionable, cautiously advised affirming—provided the New York decision was not interpreted as granting a constitutional right to solicit sex. Charny, a Powell favorite, consciously steered clear of anything smacking of a gay-rights plea.

Oral argument began at 2:14 P.M. on January 18, 1984. The court had not heard a public debate involving homosexuality since March 14, 1967; only Justices Brennan and White remained from that pre-Stonewall era. As the attorney seeking reversal, Erie County District Attorney Arcara went first. O'Connor and Rehnquist pressed him: Was the New York court's *Uplinger* ruling based on the U.S. Constitution or state law? What, exactly, had the lower court held? No one, including Arcara, seemed to know.

In response to another O'Connor question, Arcara said he was no longer challenging the state court *Onofre* decision striking down New York's sodomy law. Rehnquist swooped in, "Well," Rehnquist lectured, "certainly the assumption that *Onofre* was correctly decided is contrary to our summary affirmance of the *Doe* [sodomy] case in 1976. . . ." Arcara agreed.

When attorney Gardner's half-hour turn came, Rehnquist declared that the court could still rule on whether the *Onofre* sodomy decision was properly decided. Gardner cautioned the justices not to delve into sodomy's constitutionality without having a sodomy case fully argued.

Treating speech as conduct, O'Connor asked, "Why should the right to privacy—or to do things in private—extend on to do[ing] the same or some portion of those things in public?" In reply, Gardner pointed to freedom of speech.

Then in a long exchange with Gardner, who was gay though married to a woman, White seemed upset by the prospect of being propositioned by a man. White asked whether the state could make it illegal to solicit someone who turns the invitation down. Gardner said there would need to be harassment.

> WHITE: Well, an element of harassment—He says, "I am harassed, I don't like to be walking down the street and be accosted by a homosexual."
> GARDNER: The word "accosted" and the word—
> WHITE: Well, solicited by a homosexual.

Gardner then agreed, as Powell phrased it in his notes, that "a narrowly drawn statute lawfully may proscribe solicitation if the soliciting homo. [*sic*] has no reason to think his target is not also a homo."

According to Gardner, Robert Uplinger, who was a Buddhist, returned from oral argument "filled with fervor" to help the gay community and later founded a gay youth group.

Two days after oral argument, the court privately found itself deeply divided. Chief Justice Burger wanted to reverse the lower court because he saw the loitering law as a harassment law. "Statutes like this serve [a] compelling state interest," the law-and-order chief declared. Civil libertarian Brennan proposed that the muddy case either be "dismissed as improvidently granted" or affirmed. To Brennan, the loitering law violated free speech. White wanted to reverse and send the case back down to have the law, which he saw as a harassment statute, used against Uplinger and Butler. Marshall echoed Brennan: Dismiss or affirm. Declaring the New York ruling "incomprehensible," Blackmun voted to dismiss. Sharing Blackmun's uncertainty, Powell wanted to dismiss. Rehnquist, of course, favored reversal. "We affirmed [the] validity of sodomy statutes in *Doe*. Thus *Onofre* is erroneous," he insisted. Stevens gave dismissal a majority. O'Connor then voted to reverse, saying she agreed with Burger, White and Rehnquist.

As senior justice in the 5-to-4 majority, Brennan assigned himself to write the court's unsigned dismissal, which said "this case provides an inappropriate vehicle for resolving the important constitutional issues raised by the parties." Brennan originally also called those issues "sensitive" but dropped that adjective, apparently at the sensitive Powell's request.

Rehnquist, annoyed that the court had ducked a real decision, circulated a long dissent, written at Burger's request. Hiding his real view that *Onofre* was flat-out wrong, he said that decision was of "doubtful correctness." Rehnquist hailed the loitering statute as "designed to protect individual citizens and residential neighborhoods from lewd conduct that affronts peoples' sensibilities in the most intimate of matters." Brennan shot back in a footnote that the law definitely was not aimed at offensive conduct.

White then circulated a one-paragraph dissent saying the court ought to have issued a real decision. After talking with White, Rehnquist withdrew his dissent and joined White's. Brennan deleted his retort.

The dismissal, handed down May 30, 1984, left undisturbed the decisions eliminating New York's loitering and sodomy laws—but also left similar laws on the books elsewhere.

What court observers couldn't know at the time was that all four dissenters—Burger, White, Rehnquist and O'Connor—had cast forceful votes for upholding the loitering law that was undeniably being used to target gay men. If the minority could harness Powell's deep aversion to homosexuality, they would have a solid anti-gay majority.

"These Bastards Will Not Win!"

The same week *Uplinger* was dismissed, the Supreme Court disposed of a gay case that attempted to make it confront the ongoing damage of its

1967 ruling interpreting the congressional prohibition on "psycho-pathic" immigrants as a ban on homosexuals. *Longstaff v. Immigration and Naturalization Service* involved a 44-year-old gay Englishman who, after 18 years as a productive and upstanding U.S. resident, was fighting for U.S. citizenship.

Seeking "something different, adventure," Richard John Longstaff applied to immigrate to this country in 1965. The application form, he recalls, "was really quite offensive. . . . Mostly paranoia about Communism. 'Was your father a Communist? Were you? Was your mother a prostitute?'" He answered "No" to a long list of questions, including: "Are you now or have you ever been afflicted with psychopathic personality, epilepsy, mental defect, fits, fainting spells, convulsions or a nervous breakdown?" He paid no particular attention to the question. A self-respecting homosexual, he didn't consider himself mentally ill. He had no way of knowing that the INS treated "psychopathic personality" as a euphemism for homosexuality. Neither did he know that two years earlier the Supreme Court had ducked the issue of whether that phrase was unconstitutionally vague. And, of course, he couldn't predict that in 1967 the court would embrace "psychopathic" as a blanket prohibition on homosexual immigrants. Unaware of Longstaff's homosexuality, the INS admitted him as permanent U.S. resident in November 1965.

Longstaff eventually settled in Dallas, put down roots and opened Union Jack, a clothing store geared to a gay clientele. When political activism began percolating through his adopted hometown's gay community, Longstaff decided that he ought to become a U.S. citizen.

Processing his 1975 citizenship application, the INS summoned Longstaff to its Dallas office. An examiner repeatedly demanded to know, "Are you a homosexual?'" After initially saying, "No," Longstaff said, "Well, I have had some homosexual experiences, but that's my private life." Two months later, he was grilled again. After refusing to describe the frequency of his sexual encounters, Longstaff asked (according to an INS transcript), "How could it possible [*sic*] be relavent [*sic*] to my becoming an American citizen? . . . I don't feel anybody has the right to peak [*sic*] through my bedroom curtains."

An INS examiner urged that citizenship be denied. After a congressman got the INS to reconsider, examiner James Curry decided in 1978 that "while homosexual activity offends most of us," being homosexual isn't necessarily immoral. Curry recommended citizenship.

On March 9, 1979, Longstaff, then a U.S. resident for 13 years, went before Judge Joe Ewing Estes—"I thought to be sworn in as a citizen." Longstaff entered a huge, lofty courtroom in the federal courthouse in Dallas. Suddenly, he recalls, Judge Estes "was just screaming at me and really got me very frightened. . . . He was the most homophobic person I have ever seen in my life. I guess these people are still around, but I hate to think they are judges."

Judge Estes denied Longstaff's application on the grounds that same-sex sodomy was a crime—a misdemeanor carrying a maximum $200 fine—in Texas, that Longstaff had "exhibited a lack of candor" by refusing to answer some character (meaning sex) questions and that Longstaff had not proved he had good character. The Fifth Circuit Court of Appeals ruled that Longstaff had failed to prove "good moral character" but agreed to give him a chance to do so.

INS examiner Lee Reinfeld interviewed Longstaff. Until then, every U.S. official who had weighed in on Longstaff's case had referred to him as a "lawfully admitted" immigrant; nothing had indicated that Longstaff had been homosexual when he applied for admission in 1965. Fearing his application would be denied if he wasn't completely candid, Longstaff said he had been a homosexual "from birth." Reinfeld found Longstaff had finally proven his good character but had failed to prove he was a legal U.S. resident. Judge Estes then denied Longstaff's citizenship petition in March 1982, saying that he was "not lawfully admitted."

A Fifth Circuit panel then ruled 2-to-1 that Longstaff's entry into the United States was not legal because federal law, as interpreted by the INS and the Supreme Court, barred homosexuals. Judge Alvin Rubin, writing for the majority, was distressed by the decision he felt forced—by the Constitution, immigration law and the Supreme Court's *Boutilier* decision—to make. Rubin noted that the Constitution grants Congress virtually unlimited control over immigration, a power he said is unchecked by normal requirements of "rationality" and "non-discrimination."

Rubin wrote, "That homosexuality is no longer considered a psychopathic condition is established by the opinion of the government's highest medical officer, the surgeon general. We are bound, nonetheless, by *Boutilier's* ruling that the phrase 'psychopathic personality' is a term of art, not dependent on medical definition. . . . There is no evidence that, when [Longstaff] sought a visa 18 years ago, he was asked any question that would indicate to him or to any other intelligent layman that his sexual preferences might affect the issuance of a visa."

Longstaff's attorney had contended that, under federal law, no immigrant could be excluded for a medical reason unless a Public Health Service doctor certified the existence of that condition. Thus, since Congress had listed "psychopathic personality" in 1952 along with epilepsy, insanity and other medical bases for exclusion, homosexuals could not be barred unless they were certified homosexual by a doctor.

Dissenting Fifth Circuit Judge Albert Tate Jr. agreed. The problem, from the INS's perspective, was that government doctors were no longer branding homosexuals excludable. In 1979, Carter administration Surgeon General Julius Richmond had ordered Public Health Service physicians to stop accepting INS referrals whose only purpose was to certify homosexuals as sick. Richmond explained that "homosexuality is no longer properly characterized as a mental disorder" and homosexuality cannot be determined through any medical test.

After Longstaff's Fifth Circuit defeat, his attorneys pleaded with the Supreme Court for help in January 1984, stressing that U.S. immigration policy was in disarray because the circuit court decisions conflicted. The Ninth Circuit had decreed that medical certification of homosexuality was required before homosexuals could be deported.

Reagan administration Solicitor General Rex E. Lee's *Longstaff* response cast the INS's exclusionary policy as too "inconsequential" to merit the court's attention, as something that affected only foreign gay-rights advocates who arrived at U.S. borders vocally challenging it. He argued that "the only homosexuals who are excluded are those who insist on making an issue of their homosexuality." Lee ignored the fact that, as Longstaff's plight illustrated, homosexuals who immigrated after enactment of the 1952 law remained vulnerable to being denied citizenship or even deported for an admission that was anything but truly voluntary.

Once again the Supreme Court was faced with the question, Who is a homosexual? Did labeling one's self make the statement a legal reality or was a government doctor's assessment what mattered? Judicial attempts to define the exact parameters of homosexuality were reminiscent of the old "racial purity" laws under which states painstakingly spelled out precisely how much "Negro blood" rendered an American legally ineligible for privileges accorded whites. The goal was the same: Determine who could be "properly" discriminated against.

Courts had long wrestled with what behavior, exactly, rendered one homosexual for, say, deportation purposes. Was one drunken escapade enough? Did "flaunting" by refusing to pretend to be heterosexual make one more homosexual and, thus, less eligible for equal rights than homosexuals who cowered in the closet? The Pentagon, under President Reagan, had issued guidelines exempting from its gay ban heterosexuals caught in a one-time homosexual encounter. Just as rulings striking down racist laws gradually rendered "racial purity" laws obsolete, the Supreme Court could put an end to the need to legally define "homosexuality."

Longstaff v. INS offered the court the opportunity to say that sexual orientation is a matter of personal identity that cannot be accurately assessed by any outsider, including a doctor. The court could have then said that, since physicians are not equipped to diagnose homosexuality, there was no way to exclude homosexuals under the immigration law as then written.

However, despite the evidence that the court's 1967 decision equating homosexuals with psychopaths was still disrupting productive lives, most justices had no interest in Longstaff's case. *Cert* was denied on May 29, 1984. Justice Brennan publicly dissented. The only remaining *Boutilier* dissenter, Brennan had once left it to Justice Douglas to be the lone public wolf howling over the court's refusal to hear the homosexual pleas. The savvy, empathetic Brennan, a consummate strategist, had preferred to work behind the scenes in pursuing humane outcomes. Then Douglas retired. Times and Brennan changed. By the mid-1980s, Brennan did not object to being the lone justice publicly crying for the court to give homosexuals a fair hearing.

Richard Longstaff was shocked by his citizenship battle. "I thought, 'No, these bastards will not win!' But then they did," he recalls. If he'd had the chance to address the justices, "I'd just have tried to reassure them that I would make an excellent citizen. And I think I have been, except I don't have the right to vote. I have paid well over $1 million in taxes."

By 1996, his 25-year-old Union Jack was one of Dallas's oldest stores. "I'm probably boasting a bit, but it is the most successful gay retail store in the country right now. . . . I've got eight employees that are well-paid and happy. . . . So I have done very well," he said.

After Longstaff's Supreme Court disappointment, INS officials publicly hinted he might face deportation. They backed down because "there was so much publicity," he recalls.

In 1990, Congress stripped immigration laws of anything that could be construed as banning gay people. Later, President Clinton futilely wrote the INS on Longstaff's behalf. "I think I am a model citizen in many ways, except I am not a citizen, which I want to be," Longstaff said at 57. "I'll never give up. I think this is a fabulous country."

Longstaff's $30,000 battle also had high emotional costs. INS investigators outed him to neighbors and business associates. And publicity reaching Britain made it necessary for him to come out to his family. "I just had a mother back then, and she didn't take it well," he says. "But I don't think [the citizenship fight] was wasted time, and I would do it again. [My case] reminds people that things aren't quite right. We've still got lots of work to do."

Longstaff says his struggle "created an awareness in the [Dallas] gay community that things weren't too safe for them here. If I could be deported, what could happen to them?"

One of main things that could happen to gay American citizens, of course, was that they could be fired. Gay educators had good reason to be especially afraid. The persistent myth that gay adults were inappropriate role models meant gay educators often found themselves out of work soon after supervisors learned they were gay. Until 1982, no state outlawed discriminating against gay workers. Unlike people fired because of race, color, religion, national origin, sex or age, there was no federal civil rights law to protect gay workers.

Without a law to protect them, private employees had no recourse if they were fired for being gay. However, gay public employees could try to prove that a government had violated their constitutional rights. So, gay public school educators kept begging the Supreme Court to rescue their careers because—in the absence of a Supreme Court ruling protecting them—gay educators kept getting yanked out of school.

10

THE CHESS MASTER
MAKES HIS MOVE

WHEN 34-YEAR-OLD MARJORIE ROWLAND roared into work on the morning of November 26, 1974, she thought her life was finally falling into place. She felt accepted at school even though she wore jeans and rode a motorcycle. Teachers as well as students were signing up for counseling sessions with her. Privately, she was reveling in her new-found freedom to find herself sexually.

Reaching that point in her life had not been easy. Raised in Toledo, Marjorie was the youngest child and only daughter of austere funda-mentalist Christians. She describes her parents as sin-obsessed people who ranked dancing, card playing, makeup and jewelry as forbidden vices right along with drinking, smoking and unmarried sex. Oddly, they never seemed to mind that Marjorie was a tomboy who avoided dresses whenever possible.

From an early age, Marjorie tried without much success to break free of the restraints her parents had imposed. She was still sexually inexpe-rienced when she married at 23 after getting a college degree in Chris-tian education. Five years later, Rowland began a seven-year affair with another married woman, a substantially older friend from church. The stress of living what she calls "this double life" landed Rowland in a mental hospital briefly. For two years she saw a psychiatrist, who gradu-ally convinced her that there was nothing wrong with being bisexual.

Eventually, Rowland, then an English teacher and the mother of three daughters, got divorced, ended her affair and earned a master's degree in counseling. After graduation, she had a counseling job waiting for her at Stebbins High School in Mad River township just outside Dayton, Ohio. She started work there in August 1974.

Driving into the school parking lot three months later, on November 26, Rowland was in an especially good mood. She'd just fallen in love with a medical student, an energetic and unattached young woman who got along great with Rowland's kids. Curious about Rowland's elation, school secretary Elaine Monell asked what was up. Getting no real reply, Monell, who was chummy with Rowland, kept pressing. Her spirits up and guard down, Rowland blurted out, "Well, I met this person. . . ." She confided that she was bisexual and was in love with a woman. "I was beaming, and it got me in trouble. I could not tell a lie," Rowland recalls.

"Evidently," Rowland says, "as soon as we finished that conversation, she freaked out and went to talk to our supervisor." The next day Monell also told the principal that Rowland was bisexual. The principal soon asked Rowland to resign. She refused. Summoned to meet with the superintendent of schools, Rowland took along an ACLU attorney and a teachers' union representative. She sat quietly as she was accused of having revealed her bisexuality at school. But her attorney shot back, "How is that any different than if she told them she was a Democrat or a Rotarian?" Inside Rowland, "a part of me—the fighter—just came alive. And I wasn't going to give up because I knew it wasn't right," she recalls. "I stood up and I said, 'I won't resign.'" Instantly, she was suspended, not permitted even to return to her office to collect her belongings.

When a federal judge blocked the suspension, Rowland, like other gay teachers before her, was given a make-work job designed to ensure she had no contact with students. At the superintendent's recommendation, the school board refused to renew her one-year contract.

Rowland sued, claiming that school officials had violated her constitutional rights by ousting her for acknowledging her sexual orientation. In 1977, a federal district court dismissed the suit on the grounds that "sexual preference" is not a constitutionally protected trait like race or gender. The sixth Circuit Court of Appeals then ordered the case to be tried.

Meanwhile, even though the Ohio Education Association was paying her legal bills, Rowland was struggling. Unable to find a school willing to hire a counselor who was suing her previous employer, Rowland went on welfare and food stamps in order to feed and clothe her daughters. She went bankrupt before she could switch careers.

In 1981, after a trial in rural southwestern Ohio, Rowland briefly tasted victory. The jury unanimously found that she had lost her job solely because she was bisexual and had told secretary Elaine Monell. The jury also found that Rowland's revelation had caused no disruption and that school officials had treated Rowland differently because of her bisexuality. Based on those findings, U.S. Magistrate Robert A. Steinberg ruled that Rowland's rights to equal protection and free speech had been violated. Steinberg cited the 4th Circuit's *Acanfora* ruling in finding that a gay educator has free speech rights. The judge also found that while the Constitution doesn't create a right to "be bisexual," it does guarantee Rowland equal protection of the laws.

Noting that school officials had tried to justify their actions by branding Rowland a "free spirit," Steinberg declared that there's room in public education for people who march to "a different drummer." He said "such a person has a constitutional right to be different; to express her inner-most personal thoughts, her doubts, her fears, her insecurities, her likes, and her loves to fellow workers and to friends so long as she does not impede the performance of the public school function. The fact that these expressions may be repugnant to some and shocking to others is of no consequence in and of itself."

After Steinberg ruled, the jury awarded Rowland $55,973.14 in damages for mental anguish, humiliation and lost income. She was thrilled, even though every time her case was in the news she and her daughters received obscene phone calls.

The 6th Circuit overturned Rowland's victory in March 1984. In a 2-to-1 decision, Chief Judge Pierce Lively ruled that Rowland's speech was not constitutionally protected because it didn't involve "matters of public concern." The court also tossed out Rowland's equal protection claim, saying there was no evidence she had been treated differently from heterosexuals.

Judge George Clifton Edwards Jr. strongly disagreed, accusing the majority of silently treating Rowland as a "sick" person whose "homosexual status" justified dismissal. Edwards lectured his colleagues that homosexuality is not a mental illness and that perhaps 6 to 10 percent of women are bisexual or homosexual. Rowland's admissions of bisexuality propelled her into the national debate over homosexual rights, "a debate of far greater significance than the majority opinion recognizes," Edwards said. He compared Rowland's situation to a teacher who appears white being fired after revealing that she had a black parent. Edwards said there is "no logical . . . distinction" between firing a teacher for being black and firing a teacher for being bisexual: The 14th Amendment's equal protection guarantee should protect them both.

Petitioning the Supreme Court, Rowland attorney Alexander Spater of Columbus, Ohio, stressed that school officials never claimed to be upset that Rowland had disclosed "information about her love life." Their concern, he said, was that she had revealed she wasn't heterosexual. He noted that the case didn't involve sexual behavior. There was no allegation of sodomy, lewdness or a proposition that fell on the wrong ears. The case solely involved the question of whether a public employee may be dismissed for saying she is bisexual. "The court has the opportunity in this case to decide the protection to be afforded homosexuals," Spater said.

The school district's attorney, Michael Burdge of Dayton, countered that the Supreme Court had already "provided sufficient direction regarding homosexual rights and the Equal Protection Clause." To support his contention that the Constitution doesn't grant homosexuals equal rights, Burdge cited *Doe v. Commonwealth's Attorney* (the 1976 Virginia sodomy case), *Baker v. Nelson* (the 1972 Minnesota same-sex marriage case), Justice Powell's 1978 concurrence in *Zablocki v. Redtail* (a heterosexual marriage case) that noted the existence of state laws against incestuous, bigamous and homosexual marriages and, going way back to 1961, Judge Harlan's classic dissent in the *Poe v. Ullman* birth control case.

Rowland's trouble at Stebbins High had begun just weeks after the Supreme Court turned away a promising gay teacher, Joe Acanfora. That was at the start of the court's 1974–75 term. By the time Rowland's petition was filed a decade later, the court had discussed but denied similar pleas from two longtime teachers with outstanding records, Jim Gaylord and John Gish.

Wading into the Flood

By the time Rowland petitioned the Supreme Court to review the constitutionality of her dismissal, Justice William J. Brennan Jr. had finally lost patience with the court's passive acceptance of anti-gay job discrimination.

The pace of the Supreme Court's 1984–85 term was already getting hectic, at least for clerks, when Mad River school district responded to Rowland's plea for the court's attention. The school district's official reply was delivered to the court's administrative office on December 6, 1984—making the case "ripe" for the court's attention. Copies of the response and Rowland's *cert* petition were then bound together with rubber bands and plopped onto wheeled, wooden carts. Each justice had a messenger whose weekly duties included fetching a *cert* cart laden with hundreds of sets of petitions and replies. The messengers tended to be elderly black men, whose servant-like chores lent the almost blindingly white institution an air of an antebellum plantation.

In early December 1984, Justice Brennan's longtime messenger, Joe Thompson, slowly pushed the cart containing the documents in *Rowland v. Mad River Local School District, Montgomery County, Ohio* down a corridor of the court's main floor, then took the cart up an elevator and into Brennan's chambers. He parked the cart, as always, beside Brennan's desk. In deciding whether a particular case was one of the few that merited their court's full attention, most of Brennan's colleagues relied on a bland, clerk-written "pool" memo summarizing the arguments for and against granting *cert*. During the 1984–85 term, many clerks were unusually conservative, so much so that they hardly were the best people to weed through cases for a diehard progressive like Brennan. One clerk was so "reactionary," as a liberal clerk put it, that he flicked the lights to celebrate executions. A few justices, like Stevens, were too independent to dive into the *cert* pool. Yet they, too, relied on clerk memos; the only difference was that each holdout had his own clerks summarize every case.

Brennan was the only justice who personally waded through most of the flood of *cert* petitions and appeals that inundated the court. During the early part of each term, Brennan had his clerks sort through the petitions in order to "teach the boys about the law," as he put it, former clerk Charles Curtis recalls. But soon that training exercise was over. And every weekday morning, beginning at 7 o'clock, Brennan spent an hour reading pleas filed by solid citizens and ax murderers, millionaires and paupers, victims and victimizers.

Although Brennan and the late William O. Douglas had shared a liberal vision of individual rights, they were very different men. And those differences were reflected in their approach to their work.

Douglas was a brilliant loner, a curmudgeon with little patience for lesser mortals, an individualist who'd rather be the sole champion of a position he viewed as entirely correct than the author of a winning compromise. As Douglas continually told his brethren, much to Brennan's dismay, "I have no soul to worry about but my own."

Brennan, in contrast, was an Irish Catholic with a merry demeanor who felt duty-bound to worry about the soul of the entire nation. He ardently believed that as a justice his job was to work for the betterment of humankind. In a classic understatement, his widow remarked, "Justice Brennan wanted the court to go his way, which he thought was best for the country. I think Brennan could twist an arm." He saw the Constitution's purpose as "the protection of the dignity of the human being and the recognition that every individual has fundamental rights which government cannot deny him."

A charmer with twinkling blue eyes, Brennan devoted himself to trying to steer the court toward his egalitarian vision of a more just society. Although he bristled at being depicted as an arm-twisting pol, Brennan was a born glad-handing politician who used his clerks as an intelligence network that tried to scope out exactly how and where he'd need to compromise to reach the winning number five in any case.

Like a chess master searching for just the right opening move, Brennan was always on the alert for cases that might lead his court and country—10 or 20 years and a half dozen rulings later—to one of his goals: equal rights for women, for example, or abolition of the death penalty. "What I always thought was brilliant was Brennan's ability in the decision that was before him to start laying the groundwork for steps that were five steps removed from where he was. He was truly astounding. He would plant the seeds of decisions in cases that he would then reap a generation later," says E. Joshua Rosenkranz, director of the

Brennan Center for Justice at New York University's School of Law and a former Brennan clerk.

The vote-counting master craftsman behind many of the civil rights breakthroughs of the Warren and Burger courts, Brennan was always supremely aware of the power any five justices of the court could wield. By the mid-1980s, Brennan was deeply disturbed that the court had swung far to the right. His outright victories had become rare; more and more often he attacked discrimination through dissents in which only Marshall joined.

On those rare mornings in the fall of 1984 when he arrived before early-bird clerk Charles Curtis, Brennan made the office's coffee before tackling the *cert* cart. Having leafed through tens of thousands of petitions, the 78-year-old Brennan, then in his twenty-ninth term on the court, rarely needed long to see if a case was a standout. Did it raise a significant constitutional or statutory question? Were the lower courts in disarray and in need of guidance? Was it "pure," meaning were issues raised clearly enough?

Marjorie Rowland's plea caught Brennan's eye. Here was a young woman who'd lost her job as a high school guidance counselor solely because she had said she was bisexual. Because it raised both free speech and equal protection issues, *Rowland v. Mad River* was especially appealing to Brennan. His ability to spot an important case like *Rowland* buried in the *cert* pile was "exactly why he did his own *cert* work," Curtis says.

Chief Justice Burger, of course, left *Rowland* off the court's "Discuss" list. Brennan added it. As far back as 1963, Brennan had tried to temper the court's hostility toward homosexuals—persuading Goldberg not to gratuitously declare that Congress had the power to exclude all homosexual immigrants. Since 1976, Brennan had taken the lead in listing gay-rights pleas for discussion. He successfully pushed the court to at least talk about Eugene Enslin, the Mississippi Gay Alliance and John Gish. Brennan got John Singer's case listed, and the Civil Service dropped its gay ban. In 1977, Brennan and Marshall dissented from denial of *cert* in the cases of two gay teachers. After reading about how Mad River School District had treated Marjorie Rowland, Brennan decided the time had come to push much harder on gay civil rights.

On Friday, January 4, 1985, at their first conference after the court's Christmas break, the justices rejected Rowland's petition. Afterward, the collegial Brennan strolled out, as usual, with an arm flung up over the shoulders of a taller justice. Back in his own chambers, he briefed his clerks: Once again, he and Marshall had cast the only votes in favor of hearing a gay petition.

Brennan announced to his clerks that this time he wanted to publicly spell out his reasons for dissenting from denial of *cert*. "It was just an article of faith with him that everybody deserves equal rights," Curtis recalls, adding that the message from Brennan was that "we haven't focused on gay people, and this is the time to push it."

Because Brennan's four clerks were swamped, the task of drafting the *Rowland* dissent fell to Rory Little, a go-getter who technically was clerking for retired Justice Stewart. With Stewart's blessing, Little hustled up assignments in various chambers before proving himself so valuable to Brennan that he became an honorary fifth clerk. Little had had gay friends at Yale Law School and suspected (correctly) that the court had gay clerks that term. "It was really sort of an early time in the coming-out movement among professionals. I never really thought much about gay-rights issues until I got [*Rowland*] to look at," he recalls. Little quickly blossomed into a passionate advocate of Rowland's constitutional rights, which he believed had been trampled by "crazy prejudice." But before putting pen to paper, Little brought the case up over coffee.

In Brennan's chambers, sharing morning coffee was elevated to an almost sacred ritual. Tea drinkers quietly converted or hid their preference. While clerks for every other justice were tirelessly cranking out memos on *cert* petitions, memos on cases set for oral argument and even memos on other clerks' memos, Brennan's clerks—coffee mugs in hand—piled into their justice's private office every morning to talk. From 9 A.M. until nearly lunch, Brennan's clerks would methodically hash over pending cases, opinions-in-progress and current events. With Brennan making occasional remarks and whipping out reference books to point out pertinent prior rulings, the clerks were expected to play devil's advocate, to try to poke holes in one another's arguments in order to try to reach the soundest possible legal conclusions.

Brennan's unique morning bull sessions no doubt kept him far more up-to-date than most justices on evolving attitudes toward homosexuality because the discussions kept him in close touch with the thinking of well-educated young people, whom survey research consistently shows are the driving force behind growing public acceptance of gay rights. Clerks' personal attitudes on issues like the place of gay Americans in society were far more likely to surface in the vigorous give-and-take Brennan encouraged than in the written exchanges and brief face-to-face encounters preferred by most justices.

In bringing up *Rowland* over coffee, Little said, "It looks to me, factually, like it's a pure case of dismissal based on status. It's a speech issue." He proceeded to make shorthand references to helpful precedents. ("The whole point is to make it look like prior cases lead exactly to where you want to be, that you're not making much of a new step," he explains.) Brennan asked, "Well, what's your theory?" Taking a legal leap, his borrowed clerk replied, "Well, my theory is that this ought to be a strict scrutiny category," meaning that the court should make discrimination based on sexual orientation as difficult for a governmental body to justify as racism. No judicial standard of review is tougher than "strict scrutiny."

Brennan's other clerks pounced, demanding that Little back up his conclusion. He didn't find that difficult: "To me, it's not a large leap at all to say prejudice against blacks and prejudice against gays should be evaluated the same way. Because to me, they're both the same. They're both irrational; they're both non-individual." Brennan apparently liked what he heard. Little says, "He was consistently concerned with discrimination against the gay community. He would have called it the 'homosexual community,' I think."

During the *Rowland* discussions, Little recalls, Brennan said "general things like, 'Surely there have been wonderfully successful and talented gay people in our culture and our society. Where would the world of arts be without the influence of gay authors?' And he would say, . . . 'I've certainly known people that are gay that are as upstanding citizens as anybody I've ever met.'" Little adds, "I don't think it should be surprising to anyone in the universe that Brennan and Marshall shared the view that any minority deserves strict protection."

Marshall's widow, Cecelia, explains Marshall's attitudes toward gay people by saying, "He always felt that everybody should be treated equally, regardless of who they are and what their beliefs are. And that was his whole premise in life."

Brennan viewed dissents from denial of *cert* as an important means of laying the foundation for the legal breakthroughs. With admiration, former clerk Charles Curtis, now a Wisconsin attorney, describes how Brennan "shamelessly" tried to craft such dissents as legal building blocks—ones that could be cited first by like-minded attorneys, scholars and lower court judges, then cited in a Supreme Court concurrence and finally, perhaps decades later, become the basis for a landmark Supreme Court ruling. Brennan's attitude was, "We don't have a prayer now. Let's lay it all out and build a record for 50 to 100 years from now," Curtis explains. Little agrees, "Brennan was a big believer that dissents can become majorities. He used to say, 'You know, maybe nobody here will pay attention, but somebody out there will.'"

Brennan issued far more dissents from denial of *cert* than usual during 1984–85 because his clerks that term believed in their importance. In other years, clerks sometimes felt too overworked to tackle such dissents and Brennan didn't force the issue. Thus, the timing of Brennan's major statement on the rights of gay Americans may be due at least in part to the fact that *Rowland* popped up when Brennan had clerks willing to take on the extra work.

When Little sat down to pound out the first draft of Brennan's *Rowland* dissent, he took his assignment extremely seriously. "This was a big deal for me. I knew that I was writing a important piece of law . . . something that was going to push the envelope. . . . I knew that it was a potentially earth-shattering piece of writing, but I also didn't really expect that we were ever going to get five votes." He adds, "I viewed my job as being a scribe for Brennan's thoughts."

After completing the draft, Little ran it by Brennan's clerks and incorporated helpful suggestions. Then, Little presented it to Brennan at a second coffee. "More so than any other chambers," Little recalls, "Brennan had a system that was designed to make sure his published opinions reflected his views."

Reflecting "Deep-Seated Prejudice Rather Than Rationality"

Brennan's published dissent in *Rowland v. Mad River* is a stirring and historic plea for the U.S. Supreme Court to begin treating gay Americans and their constitutional rights respectfully. Brennan knew his words would carry extra weight coming, as they did, from the master strategist behind many of the high court's breakthrough decisions against race and sex discrimination. And although he was powerless to restore Marjorie Rowland to her counseling job, Brennan used his secular pulpit to powerfully signal homosexual and bisexual Americans not to give up their fight for equal treatment. Brennan strongly suggested that government discrimination based on "sexual preference" or "sexual orientation" ought to be judged on the "strict scrutiny" standard used in race discrimination cases or by the somewhat looser standard used in sex discrimination cases.

In the court's first public recognition that homosexuals are subjected to irrational prejudice, Brennan clearly attempted to craft his *Rowland* dissent so that it might be looked back upon as a turning point, the place where the court began moving away from the attitude that virtually any anti-homosexual law, policy or interpretation was constitutionally justifiable. Rather than treating homosexuals as immoral, unindicted felons, Brennan depicted them simply as members of yet another minority group whose rights were being unfairly violated.

"This case starkly presents issues of individual constitutional rights that have, as the dissent below noted, 'swirled nationwide for many years,'" Brennan declared. He said that the appeals court's legal reasoning was so clearly wrongheaded that it seemed designed to evade the real question in the case: "May a state dismiss a public employee based on her bisexual status alone?" Rowland was fired, Brennan said, for a non-disruptive and "entirely harmless mention of a fact about [herself] that apparently triggered certain prejudices held by her supervisors." Brennan said that the case record "plainly demonstrates that [Rowland] did not proselytize"—a favorite Brennan word—"regarding her bisexuality, but rather that it became known simply in the course of her normal workday conversations." To Brennan, Rowland's revelation that she was in love with a woman was "no more than a natural consequence of her sexual orientation, in the same way that co-workers generally know whom their fellow employees are dating or to whom they are married."

Scoffing at the notion that Rowland's comments did not involve matters of public concern, Brennan pointed out that the high court had already held that some subjects, including race discrimination, were inherently issues of public concern. "I think it is impossible not to note that a similar public debate is currently ongoing regarding the rights of homosexuals. . . . Speech that 'touches upon' this explosive issue is no less deserving of constitutional attention than speech relating to more widely condemned forms of discrimination."

Brennan's dissent would have been of lasting importance if it had confined itself to a free-speech argument. But its significance was tremendously magnified by Brennan's insistence on going much farther and spelling out why the court ought to pay special attention to protecting the rights of homosexuals. "He was basically inviting the next *cert* petition," points out Brennan Center director Rosenkranz.

Brennan declared,

The Equal Protection Clause protects against arbitrary and irrational classifications, and against invidious discrimination stemming from prejudice and hostility. Under this rubric, discrimination against homosexuals or bisexuals based solely on their sexual preference raises significant constitutional questions under both prongs of our settled equal protection analysis.

First, homosexuals constitute a significant and insular minority of this country's population. Because of the immediate and severe opprobrium often manifested against homosexuals once so publicly identified, members of this group are particularly powerless to pursue their rights openly in the public arena. Moreover, homosexuals have historically been the object of pernicious and sustained hostility, and it is fair to say that discrimination against homosexuals is "likely . . . to reflect deep-seated prejudice rather than rationality." State action taken against members of such groups based simply on their status as members of the group traditionally has been subjected to strict, or at least heightened, scrutiny by this court.

Second, discrimination based on sexual preference has been found by many courts to infringe various fundamental rights, such as the rights to privacy or freedom of expression. . . . Whether constitutional rights are infringed in sexual preference cases, and whether some compelling state interest can be advanced to permit their infringement, are important questions that this court has never addressed, and which have left the lower courts in some disarray.

Even though Brennan couched some conclusions as mere questions, his *Rowland* dissent remains one of the strongest homosexual-rights statements ever issued by any justice.

Little proudly "shopped this [*Rowland*] dissent around the court," pitching it to clerks in Stevens's and Powell's chambers. Marshall, an ardent advocate of equal protection, had already agreed to second the dissent. No other justice was interested. The dissent was announced along with the court's denial of *cert* on February 25, 1985, more than a decade after Marjorie Rowland lost her job at Stebbins High. Rowland, by then an Arizona attorney, took consolation in Brennan's unprecedented dissent. She told herself, "The time isn't right yet. . . . But maybe this dissent will be relied on when the time is better and another case comes along."

As Brennan clearly hoped, his dissent has begun to be noticed and used. In July 1997, a federal judge cited it in a ruling (later reversed) that held the military's gay ban unconstitutional. After Brennan's death at 91 later that month, the first nationally syndicated gay-issues newspaper columnist hailed the *Rowland* dissent in a tribute to the civil rights giant: "Brennan saw our Constitution's purpose as protecting the 'human dignity' of everyone. 'The Constitution's genius,' he declared, 'rests not in any static meaning it may have had in a world that is dead and gone, but in the adaptability of its great principles to cope with current problems and present needs.' Brennan's brilliance lay in finding ways to help our Constitution keep its equal protection promise. He truly was a justice for all."

Little says, "I am flattered that people are starting to notice this [*Rowland*] dissent. And, believe me, I poured my heart and soul into it. And a lot of the writing, of course, is mine and the analysis is mine. But it's clearly Brennan's position that it should be strict scrutiny, and the analysis to get there is Brennan's analysis that it's pernicious and irrational discrimination. . . . I've been telling people about this dissent since the day I left his chambers. I'm very proud of it. And I'm very passionate about the force of the argume   has always seemed to me that the court avoids this issue almost   rather than out of rationality."

In April 1997, when retir   Brennan was no longer capable of granting interviews, his s   iam J. Brennan III, helped put his father's progressive approach to the rights of gay Americans into perspective. The justice's son, an attorney in private practice in New Jersey, had spent many mornings over the years taking walks with Justice Brennan and talking about the work of the court. "I can't recall any discussion with him that focused upon the discrimination which gays faced or any of the issues that are so current today. It would all be in the broader sense of the rights of an individual, the dignity of an individual and the need for the court to uphold those rights and safeguard that dignity," Brennan's son said. ". . . I'm sure that no reason . . . ever suggested itself to him of why gays should be subject to restrictions to which others were not.

". . . And absent any reason to discriminate against gays, Dad would see no reason why they should suffer discrimination. Again, the emphasis would be upon their status as individuals with the right to dignity and, again, the rights would just inhere in them as human beings to be treated decently. And their orientation would be no reason as far as he is concerned—and I can state this with absolute confidence—to oust them from that status or from those rights. And he would tell you directly the same thing," William J. Brennan III added.

In many ways, Justice Brennan's civil rights successes over the decades made the gay-rights battle one that could be waged—if not immediately won—because they established that the Equal Protection Clause applies to women and minorities. (In the mid-1970s, Brennan fell just one vote short of essentially writing the Equal Rights Amendment into the Constitution for women by judicial fiat.) The national gay civil rights debate is "now a very respectable discussion. And the context in which that discussion is taking place is one that my father helped to form," his son proudly noted.

Justice Brennan's widow, Mary, was the justice's secretary from 1957 until she married him in 1983 after the death of his first wife. She said that, as far as she knew, her husband had not been aware of knowing anyone gay. "They weren't coming out then like they are now," she said in November 1997. "I don't remember him ever talking to me about gays. I'm sure he wanted them to get the same courtesies that everybody else did, which I think is what should be. But they still don't. But at least they're coming out of the closet. Of course, the AIDS thing pulled a lot of them out." Mary Brennan's assessment of Justice Brennan's attitude toward gay Americans was much like that offered by her stepson—minus the legal phrasing: "He believed," she said, "that everybody had rights, that they were as good as he and why shouldn't they have the same services, the same jobs and the same everything a regular person had."

Brennan Center director Rosenkranz believes that Brennan's greatest gift as a jurist was his almost superhuman empathy. Brennan himself attributed his reverence for human dignity to the suffering he saw all around him growing up in Newark, New Jersey. Rosenkranz says,

> This was a man who had an enormous ability to put himself in the shoes of others and understand what it felt like to be them. . . . He was born in 1906. I don't think he could really fathom what went on in the bedroom between two men. Yet he understood love and understood human nature and understood how important it was to protect those types of human interactions and those types of bonds. Somehow he was able to transcend his own experience. . . . He believed very firmly that what he was interpreting in the Constitution was actually there. What he saw in the Constitution was the protection of what he called 'common human dignity' in everything. Once you accept that proposition, everything flows from that, so long as you see what's happening to an individual as a violation of that dignity.

"Don't Even Look at Me in a Grocery Store"

By the time Brennan and Marshall publicly scolded their colleagues in early 1985 for failing to take the pleas of gay and bisexual Americans sufficiently seriously, the court was wrestling with a major gay-rights case. Perhaps predictably, the case that had won the conservative court's full attention was not the sort that Brennan and Marshall had in mind: An Oklahoma school board wanted the justices to reinstate a state law allowing teachers to be fired for off-duty advocacy of gay rights. If Brennan and Marshall had had their way, the Supreme Court would have simply affirmed the Tenth Circuit's finding that the law was unconstitutional—a conclusion that the liberal duo considered so obvious that they saw no need to have the case fully briefed and argued.

Board of Education of Oklahoma City v. National Gay Task Force sprang directly out of born-again singer Anita Bryant's viciously homophobic "Save Our Children" crusade. Bryant's 1977 campaign to repeal a Florida gay-rights ordinance had sounded an alarm nationwide about the supposed threat that homosexuals posed to impressionable youngsters.

In January 1978, Oklahoma State Senator Mary Helm, an Oklahoma City Republican, introduced a bill to allow public schools to fire or refuse to hire anyone who engaged in "public homosexual activity" or "public homosexual conduct." The former was defined as publicly breaking the state's "crime against nature" law with a person of the same sex, though that law also prohibited heterosexual sodomy. "Public homosexual conduct," meanwhile, meant "advocating, soliciting, imposing, encouraging or promoting public or private homosexual activity in a manner that creates a substantial risk that such conduct will come to the attention of schoolchildren or school employees." Even heterosexual teachers would be putting their jobs in peril if they uttered anything that could be construed as advocacy of homosexual sodomy.

Shortly after Helm's bill was introduced, the *Oklahoma City Times* reported that more than 100 teenage boys had joined Ku Klux Klan chapters at local high schools for a "declared war on homosexuals." The teenagers claimed responsibility for a baseball bat attack at a gay bar that left several patrons injured and for vandalizing cars at a gay cruising spot. "We are not just against blacks like the old Klan. We are against gays . . . because this activity is morally and socially wrong," one student Klansman declared. Acknowledging that the Klan was indeed organizing in high schools, KKK Grand Wizard David Duke said, "We believe it is a mistake for homosexuals to teach children or for them to be allowed to flaunt their ways in society. . . ."

Oklahoma City public school teachers and administrators condemned the anti-gay violence—public remarks that, under the Helm bill, might well cost them their jobs.

Lawmakers, meanwhile, were focused on ridding their state not of anti-gay violence but of gay and gay-friendly teachers. Without debate, the House passed Helm's bill, 88 to 2 on February 7, 1978. Its House sponsor, Muskogee Democrat John Monks, bragged that the bill targeted "both queers and lesbians" and would empower school boards to "fire those who are afflicted with this degenerate problem—people who are mentally deranged this way."

Anita Bryant, a former Miss Oklahoma, then lobbied the state Senate, telling lawmakers that the bill would curb "the flaunting of homosexuality" and protect schoolchildren from educators who "profess homosexuality," the *Oklahoma City Times* reported February 21, 1978, the day that Justice Rehnquist, tapping into Bryant's poisonous rhetoric, publicly compared homosexuality to a contagious disease requiring a quarantine. The Oklahoma Senate unanimously passed the Helm bill, which became law in April 1978.

The fears that Anita Bryant fanned were widespread. A 1978 poll by the city Human Rights Commission in Norman, Oklahoma, found that only 11 percent of adults favored allowing homosexuals to teach.

Terrified by the Helm law, Oklahoma's gay teachers crawled deeper into their closets. Lesbian Kathleen "Kathy" McKean remembers trying to get gay teachers to come to a meeting. "And they were like, 'Don't even look at me in a grocery store.' They didn't want political activists anywhere near them. They could be fired," she says.

Prosperous oil and gas attorney William B. "Bill" Rogers, a partner in Oklahoma City's oldest law firm, decided that the law had to be challenged and he was the one to do it. "I didn't feel comfortable asking someone else to do what I thought was my own job," he recalls. Rogers, who assumed his law partners knew he was gay, had become the founding chair of the gay Oklahomans for Human Rights because of the influence of his friend Bruce Voeller.

In October 1980, the National Gay Task Force (NGTF) and Stan Easter, a gay man licensed to teach in Oklahoma, sued the Oklahoma City Board of Education in federal court to test the law's constitutionality. (Rogers had failed to find a heterosexual teacher interested in joining the challenge.) Easter soon got frightened and withdrew. Kathy McKean, 24, agreed to take his place as the sole named plaintiff. Fresh out of graduate school, she was a school psychologist for learning-disabled students in the small Oklahoma town of Cushing. "I really expected to be fired," McKean says, recounting how she and her partner braced for hard times.

As it turned out, however, the couple suffered no hardship because Judge Luther Eubanks saw no reason for McKean to join the lawsuit. He ruled that NGTF had sufficient standing to sue alone, based on a sworn affidavit from co-executive director Lucia Valeska that the group's gay members included current and prospective Oklahoma City teachers whose advocacy of gay civil rights was being stifled by their fear of being fired.

Rogers's lawsuit challenged the Helm law's constitutionality: It violated freedom of speech, freedom of association, freedom of religion, the right to privacy and the Equal Protection Clause. Plus, it was too vague, too broad.

Judge Eubanks disagreed on June 29, 1982. The Supreme Court has not extended the right of privacy to same-sex activity, Eubanks said, citing its 1976 *Doe* decision upholding Virginia's sodomy law and Justice Harlan's 1961 *Poe* dissent. Eubanks considered fears about the law overblown. A teacher could not be fired for gay-rights advocacy, the judge contended, unless that advocacy rendered him or her unfit by harming job performance.

Appealing to the Tenth Circuit was risky because of the possibility of reaping far more damaging results, especially if the case reached a Supreme Court increasingly hostile to civil rights pleas of any sort. Lambda Legal Defense and Education Fund, the nation's oldest gay legal group, warned against an appeal. But Rogers, then backed by the ACLU of Oklahoma, and Leonard Graff of the San Francisco–based Gay Rights Advocates fought on. They won the next round. On March 14, 1984, a Tenth Circuit panel ruled 2 to 1 largely in their favor. Firing a teacher for publicly breaking the sodomy law is not unconstitutional, the panel ruled, but the rest of the Helm law unconstitutionally restricts free speech. The panel noted that the Supreme Court had long held that the First Amendment protected even advocacy of illegal activity—including violent revolution—unless it was likely to incite immediate lawlessness. That meant, according to the appeals court, public school teachers had to be free to advocate homosexual activity.

Writing for the majority, Judge James Logan depicted fears about the Helm law's reach as quite justified: Virtually any supportive remark about homosexuals could be used to brand a teacher unfit. "A teacher who went before the Oklahoma legislature or appeared on television to urge the repeal of the Oklahoma anti-sodomy statute would be 'advocating,' 'promoting,' and 'encouraging' homosexual sodomy and creating a substantial risk that his or her speech would come to the attention of school children or school employees if he or she said, 'I think it is psychologically damaging for people with homosexual desires to suppress those desires. They should act on those desires and should be legally free to do so.' Such statements, which are aimed at legal and social change, are at the core of First Amendment protections," Logan wrote.

In a fiery dissent, Judge James Barrett intoned, "Sodomy is *malum in se,* i.e., immoral and corruptible in its nature without regard to the fact of its being noticed or punished by the law of the state. It is not . . . wrong *only* because it is forbidden by law. . . ." Barrett went so far as to say advocacy of the *"unnatural and detestable act of sodomy"* by a teacher was less deserving of constitutional protection than "advocacy of violence, sabotage and terrorism"—a sentiment with which Oklahoma's high school Klansmen would no doubt have agreed.

Because the Tenth Circuit's decision struck down much of a state law, the Oklahoma gag rule case reached the Supreme Court in July 1984 as an appeal. Because the National Gay Task Force—which later added "Lesbian" to its name—chose not to challenge the gay sex portion of the appellate ruling, the case centered entirely on the free speech rights of public school teachers.

Chief Justice Burger listed the case for discussion. On September 24, 1984, six justices—Burger, White, Blackmun, Powell, Rehnquist and O'Connor—agreed with the school board's request to schedule the case for a full hearing. Only the court's two beleaguered civil rights giants—Brennan and Marshall—voted to affirm the Tenth Circuit's protection of the free speech rights of gay-rights advocates. Stevens did not vote.

In urging the justices to find the Helm law constitutional, the Oklahoma City school board's brief argued that the law allowed teachers to be punished only if the prohibited conduct harmed public education. However, elsewhere in the brief, Oklahoma City attorney Larry Lewis made clear that the school board viewed "teacher advocacy of criminal homosexual sodomy" as inherently disruptive. "When it comes to the attention of students . . . it is likely to engender disrespect for law as an institution, the social responsibilities of citizenship. . . . When it comes to the attention of other teachers . . . it is likely to produce sufficient controversy, suspicion and mistrust as to threaten employee discipline, co-worker harmony, . . . " he argued.

The Helm law, Lewis said, targets a "substantive evil" that lawmakers "had a right—and probably a duty—to prevent." That evil, he explained, consisted of the danger that children would commit homosexual sodomy, their education would be disrupted, their "normal" socialization would be harmed and they would see lawlessness as acceptable. Advocacy of gay sex "is not a matter of legitimate public concern" and, therefore, ought to enjoy "little—if any—First Amendment protection, even if uttered by a member of the citizenry as a whole," he argued.

Meanwhile, by the time the National Gay Task Force filed its reply, renowned Harvard law professor Laurence Tribe had taken over as the lead attorney handling the challenge to the Helm law. Tribe, a constitutional law scholar, homed in on the chilling effect of a law whose purpose he described as "the suppression of ideas."

Oklahoma had other laws on the books that provided for dismissal of unfit or immoral teachers, so the Helm law was not needed to achieve those goals, Tribe noted. Instead, Tribe said, the Helm law was an unconstitutional threat: "If you value your job as a teacher, or want ever to hold such a position here, then make no statement in public, or within another's hearing, that might one day brand you as sympathetic to homosexuals or their rights, and take part in no group or activity that might be seen as so inclined."

Tribe pointed out that the Democratic Party's 1984 platform had opposed discrimination based on sexual orientation. Would party membership constitute advocating, promoting or encouraging homosexual activity? Would Ronald Reagan's outspoken opposition to a 1978 California initiative that would have banned teachers from gay-rights "advocacy" rendered him ineligible to teach in Oklahoma? (When Tribe filed his brief, former California governor Reagan was the nation's best-known conservative and had just been elected to a second term as president.)

No Oklahoma teacher had dared find out just where speech crossed the line into forbidden territory, Tribe pointed out. (Oklahoma's attorney general had said the law was needed to rid public schools of "gay-rights activists" and others with "controversial" views.) The First Amendment, Tribe stressed, was intended to protect support for now-outlawed behavior. "The advocacy of activities one generation calls criminal may well be a vehicle for profound political and social change in the next," he argued, pointing to the toppling of laws against interracial marriage, female suffrage and abortion. Homosexual sodomy, he noted, had already been decriminalized in most states.

Attorneys for both sides made their arguments directly to eight justices on January 14, 1985. (Justice Powell, seriously ill with prostate cancer, was absent.) At 1:23 P.M., Chief Justice Burger asked Dennis Arrow, a law professor at Oklahoma City University, to begin. Arrow had barely started sketching the board of education's argument before Rehnquist, long the court's most outspoken foe of gay rights, jumped in to suggest that since no one had been punished under the six-year-old law the time was not yet ripe to decide its constitutionality. The case ought to have been dismissed by the Tenth Circuit, Rehnquist implied.

Sounding equally hostile to the Tenth Circuit's decision, Burger suggested that the Helm law ought to be interpreted by Oklahoma's Supreme Court. Arrow readily agreed.

O'Connor then received Arrow's assurance that the law required a teacher's advocacy to have an adverse effect on students or colleagues before the teacher could be fired. Comparing teacher advocacy of homosexual sodomy to advocacy of heroin use, Arrow argued that the Helm law protected "student morality" and "proper traditional cultural values."

Stevens pressed Arrow hard until the attorney acknowledged that the statute failed to define "private homosexual activity."

Brennan posed a hypothetical question: "Suppose a teacher sat down at lunch with a number of other teachers and said, 'I wish they'd leave these homosexuals alone, they are not hurting anyone except themselves,' and that was heard by everybody in the room, students and everybody else. . . . Would that violate the statute?" Arrow replied that it would not. Then Brennan, who by 1985 rarely spoke in oral argument unless he had especially strong feelings, got Arrow to say that if the law did indeed reach that situation, it would be too broad to be constitutional.

When Tribe, an experienced Supreme Court litigator handling his first gay-rights case, stepped to the lectern to argue on behalf of the National Gay Task Force, he encountered what for him was an "unprecedented" level of hostility, notes legal scholar Arthur Leonard. The original lead attorney, Bill Rogers, found the justices' tone and facial expressions quite disturbing. "I had a distinct feeling that those nine judges had never seen a 'queer' before and were offended at having us in the courtroom," he recalls.

With his opening remarks, Tribe became the first Supreme Court litigator to explicitly frame a case during oral argument as a gay civil
rights issue. "Mr. Chief Justice, and may it please the court," he began,
using the court's traditional phrasing, "writing for the California
Supreme Court a decade ago, the late Justice [Matthew O.] Tobriner
recognized that the modern struggle for homosexual rights in this country is truly a struggle for civil rights. And he said, like other such struggles, it incites heated political debate. The issue in this case is how
open that debate will be. . . ."

Burger jumped in, demanding to know whether teachers should be
allowed to advocate drug use or murder. Tribe calmly replied that First
Amendment protections don't depend on how "silly or disagreeable" a
view is. What about theft, rape? Burger asked. Tribe didn't waver.

Rehnquist then tried to get Tribe to agree that "no one is being
threatened" by the Helm law. Tribe: "It is threatening every day. . . ."

Marshall crankily suggested that Oklahoma's top court should be the
one defining the law's reach, then—when Tribe mentioned anti-gay violence in Oklahoma—grumbled inaccurately that there was no mention
of violence in the court record. Tribe, sounding frustrated, said, "The
court may just have to take notice of some realities."

Burger demanded, aren't lawmakers entitled to take into account the
reality that teachers are role models? Certainly, Tribe replied, but "as a
matter of common sense, there is no reason to believe that homosexuality is something like a contagious disease." Teachers, he added, "have
First Amendment rights every bit as broad as private citizens when they
talk on matters of public interest."

Despite nonstop interruptions, Tribe succeeded in making a coherent, forceful argument against the "vague and opaque and sweeping
and broad" Helm law. ". . . This law in effect tells teachers, 'You had
better shut up about this subject, or if you talk about it, you had better
be totally hostile to homosexuals,'" Tribe told the court. He added that
an important way for teachers to serve as role models is by showing the
"value of free speech." Challenging the notion that morality is a justification for silencing gay-rights advocates, Tribe declared, "One moral
certitude after another has led men to hound others from their midst.
Their ideas seemed too alien. They were too different. But as Justice
Brandeis reminded us long ago, men feared witches and burnt women."

Reverently invoking a nearly sacred pillar of American democracy, Tribe told the justices peering down at him, "in the name of the First Amendment . . . there is only one correct outcome in this case."

When eight justices cast their votes a few days later, they were evenly divided. (Powell was still out sick.) Earlier that month only Brennan and Marshall had stood up for a high school counselor's right to say she was bisexual. Now, with the rights of gay-friendly heterosexual teachers as imperiled as those of their gay colleagues, four justices had come to the defense of free speech. For two months, the outcome of the Oklahoma case was up in the air.

Finally, Powell returned. In missed cases where his vote would be decisive, he could listen to a tape of the oral argument before voting, have the case reargued or simply abstain. On March 22, 1985, Chief Justice Burger circulated an internal memo announcing that three cases would be reargued for Powell. Another five, including the Oklahoma gay-rights advocacy case, would not be. Since a Supreme Court tie vote meant the Tenth Circuit's ruling stood, Powell's decision not to participate meant victory for Oklahoma's gay and gay-friendly teachers.

Given Powell's deep aversion to discussing homosexuality, his choice is not surprising even though it seems quite likely that the case's outcome would have been different if he had voted. School board attorney Arrow thought he would have won if Powell had participated. To Powell, avoiding a homosexual case probably was more desirable than having it go his way.

On March 26, 1985, the court announced simply that the Tenth Circuit's decision was "affirmed by an equally divided court." In keeping with tradition in such cases, none of the justices offered a single public word of explanation or dissent. The court did not disclose how any justice had voted. Stevens and Blackmun most likely joined Brennan and Marshall in finding the law unconstitutional—a line-up strongly suggested by prior and later gay cases. Rehnquist and Burger—both overtly hostile to gay rights—probably were joined by White and O'Connor in voting that Oklahoma had the right to fire any teacher who advocated gay rights.

Triumphant, attorney Bill Rogers felt the fight had been worthwhile even though, he says, it cost him his $100,000-a-year law partnership. The Oklahoma case's outcome "was the first substantive victory for the gay-rights movement in the Supreme Court in almost a quarter century," legal scholar Arthur Leonard notes. Since the early 1960s, gay litigants had won only when the court turned away an anti-gay petition, as in the case of the University of Missouri's gay group, or when the other side folded, as when the Civil Service stopped fighting John Singer.

Although the National Gay Task Force's 1985 Supreme Court victory counted as a decision "on the merits," as lawyers phrase it, that success was an almost accidental result with deeply ominous undertones for gay Americans. There was no huge celebration in Oklahoma's gay communities. "We knew that the Supreme Court hadn't affirmed our rights to be. It was a fluke. We didn't feel that it was any grand victory. Actually, we had a much bigger celebration when we threw Mary Helm out of office," recalls Kathleen McKean, who in 1998 was still a Oklahoma school psychologist and still involved with the same supportive partner. She adds, "Straight people's mouths were shut. That's the only reason we won."

An Invisible Family Smashed to Bits

By the mid-1980s, the Supreme Court had been told for a quarter century about the special vulnerability of homosexual Americans: Homosexual men continued to be approached by handsome undercover vice cops seeking "solicitation" or "lewd" conduct arrests. Police officers who ignored heterosexual lovers' lanes hunted for homosexual men to charge with public sodomy. Courts, cops, prosecutors and government agencies interpreted a host of laws—that on their face had nothing to do with homosexuality—to the disadvantage of homosexuals. Homosexuals in most jobs and in most jurisdictions had no defense against being fired for being gay, regardless of whether they'd ever broken a sex law. The foreign-born partners of American homosexuals perpetually risked deportation. All in all, those justices who were paying attention knew that gay men and lesbians put themselves in jeopardy if they said or did countless ordinary things that their heterosexual counterparts in a "free society" took for granted. But *Kowalski v. Kowalski*, which reached the court in early 1986, had the potential to drive home, with greater emotional force than any case that preceded it, the supreme vulnerability of gay Americans—both as individuals and as couples.

Sharon Kowalski's horrifying situation became American lesbians' worst nightmare: For years, the young woman lay powerless and speechless, warehoused in a nursing home bed—her wishes ignored, her request to see her dearest loved one denied by a father who refused to acknowledge her lesbianism. The severely disabled Kowalski silently taught countless lesbian couples, many of whom had long derided marriage licenses as "just a piece of paper," the value of having a legally recognized relationship and, short of winning the right to marry, the importance of legal documents that offer some measure of protection. Kowalski and her valiant partner, Karen Thompson, who fought tirelessly for their rights, could have taught the Supreme Court a great deal about family, home and commitment, about the ways that homosexuals are the nation's most powerless minority and about homosexuals' special need for the protection of a just court. Yet, as it turned out, the case apparently taught the high court nothing.

Sharon Kowalski was an independent, outdoorsy, motorcycle-riding 23-year-old when she and Karen Thompson, 31, fell in love. The Minnesota women privately exchanged rings and vows to seal a commitment that they considered a marriage. They bought $50,000 life insurance policies that named each other as beneficiary so the mortgage on their St. Cloud home could be paid off if one of them died prematurely. Yet they never gave any thought, Thompson says, to the fact that in the eyes of the law their relationship didn't exist: They were unrelated, single women who happened to live together. It never occurred to them that they would need legal documents to protect the central role that each played in the other's life. They were concerned not with safeguarding their relationship but with keeping it secret.

The high-spirited, life-of-the-party Kowalski, who coached high school basketball and track, confided to a few friends that she and Thompson were lovers. The reserved Thompson, a physical education professor at St. Cloud University, told no one, she says.

The couple's intimate little world was smashed to bits on the afternoon of November 13, 1983, when a drunk driver plowed his pickup truck into Kowalski's car. While in a coma, Kowalski was declared legally incapacitated. Had Kowalski been legally married or if she'd signed a contingency form known as a durable power of attorney, her partner could have made medical decisions for her. Instead, those decisions fell to Kowalski's legal next of kin, her parents.

The head-on accident, which caused severe brain damage, left Kowalski in a near-vegetative state even after she regained consciousness. Almost totally paralyzed, she could not talk or eat. She was barely able to respond at all—sometimes managing to move a finger to signal "yes" or "no." Doctors held out no hope of significant recovery.

Yet Thompson was determined not to give up on the woman she'd loved for four years. Hour after hour, day after day, Thompson worked with Kowalski, struggling to help her regain some control over her battered body, stretching her hands and fingers, reteaching her rudimentary motions needed to comb her hair or brush her teeth. Ever so patiently, Thompson taught Kowalski to very, very slowly type with one finger.

Kowalski's parents were puzzled by the time Thompson was spending at the hospital, bothered by the way she acted as if she had a right to be involved in medical decisions. To them, it didn't seem natural that the woman they'd been told was a "friend" was so intensely concerned about their invalid daughter. Donald Kowalski, a retired miner, ordered Thompson to cut back on her visits. On the advice of a psychologist, Thompson responded by writing Sharon's parents to explain her relationship to Sharon. Donald Kowalski and his wife, Della, were sickened that Thompson was—as they viewed it—accusing their defenseless daughter of being a lesbian. An eight-year legal battle over Sharon Kowalski's guardianship ensued.

Still believing that the nature of her relationship was really nobody's business, Thompson petitioned for guardianship as a concerned, well-qualified friend. Finding Karen Thompson and Donald Kowalski equally capable of guardianship, probate Judge Bruce Douglas chose the father on April 25, 1984. However, he granted Thompson equal visitation rights and equal authority to consult with Sharon Kowalski's doctors. Donald Kowalski soon transferred his daughter to a Duluth nursing home.

Thompson ardently believed that her partner belonged in a state-of-the-art rehabilitation center experienced in treating young adults with serious head injuries. Thompson's constant fear was that Sharon Kowalski's long-term recovery prospects were diminished by every day spent in a nursing home whose primary mission was keeping frail or senile senior citizens comfortable. Thompson was determined to bring Sharon Kowalski home. Donald Kowalski, meanwhile, saw his daughter as a "helpless victim" almost certain to require lifelong institutionalization.

Judge Douglas had urged the warring parties to make peace. When the battle escalated, the judge, acting on the advice of doctors who claimed Thompson's visits depressed Sharon Kowalski, terminated Thompson's rights and granted Donald Kowalski absolute guardianship. That same day, July 22, 1985, Donald Kowalski forbade Thompson to have any contact with his daughter. He ordered the nursing home not to let his daughter have visitors without his approval.

Before Thompson was banished, Sharon Kowalski, whose communication skills were improving a bit, made clear she still loved her, still wanted to live with her. Legal documents (never shared with the Supreme Court) show that in 1985 Sharon Kowalski was asked by a rehabilitation service official, "Are you gay?" She typed, "yes." She was then asked, "Do you have a lover? If 'yes,' what is the person's name?" With maximum effort, Sharon Kowalski slowly typed, "karen t."

At Thompson's request, Janlori Goldman of the Minnesota Civil Liberties Union visited Sharon Kowalski and explained her organization. According to Goldman's sworn affidavit, Sharon Kowalski said her wishes were not being made known to the court by her court-appointed attorney and asked the MCLU to represent her. She repeated the request June 12 to Goldman and Amy Bromberg, the private attorney prepared to handle the case for the MCLU.

The last time Karen Thompson was allowed to visit Duluth's Park Point Manor Nursing Home, she says, Sharon Kowalski typed, "HELP ME! GET ME OUT OF HERE." Utterly powerless at that moment, Thompson had to say "that I couldn't, that my visitation time was up, that I would keep doing everything possible to get her out of there. And she typed, 'PLEASE TAKE ME HOME WITH YOU.'"

A few days later attorney Amy Bromberg discovered that Sharon Kowalski had been moved to what Thompson derisively calls "an old folks' home" in Hibbing, Minnesota, 140 miles from St. Cloud. Officials at the Hibbing facility told Bromberg that if she wanted to see her client she'd need to call Donald Kowalski. His number was unlisted.

The MCLU attorneys who contended that they'd been appointed by Sharon Kowalski appealed the probate judge's order. Two weeks later they filed a second appeal, joined by the disabled woman's court-appointed attorney, Thomas D. Hayes. Judge Douglas had ruled that "the ward [Sharon Kowalski] lacks sufficient understanding or capacity to make or communicate responsible decisions concerning her person." The appeals challenged his conclusion that Sharon Kowalski was completely incapacitated, the appointment of her father as guardian and the decision to deprive Sharon Kowalski of seeing visitors of her own choosing. Hayes also asked that the MCLU's status as Sharon Kowalski's chosen legal team be honored.

In a 2-to-1 decision, the Minnesota Court of Appeals dismissed the MCLU's first appeal on September 9, 1985, because "the trial court has determined the ward is incapable of independently retaining counsel." The court delayed a ruling on the second appeal. After the Minnesota Supreme Court refused to get involved in whether Sharon Kowalski had the capacity to choose her legal counsel, the case advanced to the U.S. Supreme Court.

The only question presented when MCLU lead attorney Brian O'Neill petitioned the justices on February 1, 1986, was whether Sharon Kowalski's constitutional right to the counsel of her choice had been violated. Because that question was, of necessity, so narrow, documents filed with the Supreme Court made it difficult if not impossible for the justices and their clerks to grasp the full sweep of the issues swirling in the background: Ought a committed, long-term gay relationship enjoy some legal protections? Is someone with vociferously anti-gay sentiments an appropriate legal guardian for a lesbian? Does the constitutional right of freedom of association extend to the disabled? And, as Karen Thompson—who technically was not a party to the Supreme Court petition—demanded in speeches to know, "Why can't Sharon Kowalski come home?"

The MCLU, which referred to Thompson as Sharon Kowalski's "friend and housemate," argued that its attorneys and the disabled woman's court-appointed counsel believed that the MCLU had been retained by her. The Minnesota appeals court ruling essentially meant, according to the MCLU, that "a person adjudged incapacitated is prohibited from retaining her own counsel to argue the fact of capacity." That decision, attorney O'Neill argued, denied Sharon Kowalski's right to due process: "What fairness can there be in a proceeding where a handicapped individual is not allowed to have her positions argued by the champion she has selected and hired?" The petition made no mention of Sharon Kowalski's lesbianism or how homophobia might be coloring the decisions of her father, her doctors and the probate judge.

It would have been virtually impossible for the Supreme Court to rule in favor of Sharon Kowalski without contradicting the probate judge's finding that she was incapable of choosing attorneys. One of the high court's basic tenets is that it does not disturb "facts" established by a judge or jury. But if there were any chance the justices would grant *cert,* it surely vanished when Donald Kowalski's response hit the court. Attorney Jack Fena of Hibbing, Minnesota, made certain that the court knew that the case was a hornet's nest pitting Sharon Kowalski's father against the woman "who claims to be Sharon's lesbian lover." Fena depicted Karen Thompson as a dangerously twisted deviant who "disregarded Sharon's wellbeing for her own personal gain." The MCLU was preying on a helpless victim to advance its political agenda, Fena insisted: "How can an incapacitated ward with mental abilities of a six or seven year old, who gives inconsistent answers hire an attorney? The answer is simple; she cannot."

Fena supported his argument with powerful, disturbing letters and reports from Sharon Kowalski's doctors. Dr. S. K. Goff had concluded in October 1984 that the injured woman's mental age was below six or seven and that she was incompetent to make judgments. Psychiatrist George M. Cowan found her answers "inconsistent." On May 7, 1985, attending physician J. C. Moeller, who saw Sharon Kowalski once a month, wrote Fena that nurses "tell me that after Miss Karen Thompson's visits with the patient she seems more depressed and curls up in a fetal position. The nurses consider Miss Thompson's visits as abusive to a vulnerable adult. . . . [T]he visits of Miss Karen Thompson are disruptive and harmful." In a May 8, 1985, letter to Fena, Dr. Goff said that he and Dr. Cowan agreed that Thompson's visits upset Sharon Kowalski and should be stopped. (If a married woman kept in a nursing home against her will became depressed after seeing the husband who longed to take her home, it's difficult to imagine that doctors' solution would be to ban the husband's visits.)

On August 20, 1985, William L. Wilson, attending physician at the nursing home where Sharon Kowalski had then been sent by her father, injected a sick element into the visitation struggle: "Karen Thompson has been involved in bathing Sharon Kowalski behind a closed door for a prolonged period of time. It has also come to my attention that Ms. Thompson has alleged a sexual relationship with Sharon Kowalski that existed prior to the accident. . . . I feel that visits by Karen Thompson at this time would expose Sharon Kowalski to a high risk of sexual abuse."

Finally, in an August 27, 1985, letter to Fena, Dr. Cowan said Thompson had had no right to disclose Sharon Kowalski's sexual orientation. He added, "[T]otal control of Sharon's life should remain in the hands of her parents. I have found through the years that parental love is unconditional and lasting, whereas other associations, many times, disintegrate."

Nothing in the papers filed in *Kowalski v. Kowalski* told the Supreme Court that Sharon Kowalski had never been thoroughly evaluated by independent experts skilled at testing severely brain-injured adults. Minnesota law required guardians to ask adult wards annually whether they wanted their legal capacity tested. But, as Fena later admitted, Donald Kowalski had never asked his daughter. Her competency needed to be tested. Was she getting proper care? Her paid caregivers were hardly the best professionals to ask. Was Sharon Kowalski competent to retain attorneys? The attorneys who thought she'd retained them were not in the best position to judge.

Rather than arguing that Sharon Kowalski's lesbianism made it all the more essential that she have the attorneys of her choice, the MCLU ignored the gay facet of her case and failed to rebut Fena's horrifying portrayal of her devoted partner. Based solely on documents filed with the court, it would be easy to view *Kowalski v. Kowalski* as a battle between a loving father and a possible sexual predator—with the latter's allies begging the court to referee. (And the right-to-counsel dispute seemed to be still knocking around in Minnesota courts. In fact, the MCLU and Sharon Kowalski's court-appointed attorney lost on that issue days before the Supreme Court acted.)

Even without the gay aspect of the case, it's almost impossible to imagine the Supreme Court wading into such a morass. And, in fact, it didn't. Without discussion, the court unanimously denied *cert* on March 24, 1986. By then, Sharon Kowalski had not been allowed to see her partner for eight months.

The Supreme Court skirmish ended up being a small part of the fight only because the high court failed to rule that Sharon Kowalski had a right to the legal counsel of her choice, Thompson believes. A favorable decision would have cut years off Sharon Kowalski's confinement, Thompson contends.

Fighting for her partner's rights turned the once demure Karen Thompson into a lioness. She gradually realized that she was locked in a battle that could not be waged inside a closet. She would have to win in the court of public opinion before she and Sharon Kowalski could win in a court of law. Sharon Kowalski's plight exploded into a cause célèbre within both the lesbian and disability-rights communities as it became clear that a lesbian's disability was being used as an excuse to keep her from having any contact with the woman she loved.

In 1988, major articles in *The Washington Post* and *The New York Times*—the newspapers most likely to be read by Supreme Court justices—depicted Sharon Kowalski as a lesbian whom the courts had allowed to be placed under the total control of a father who was virulently homophobic, an adjective in wide use by then. On the *Post*'s front page on August 5, 1988, Donald Kowalski—whose wife said he spoke for her as well—railed, "On the farm and in the Army, we called them queers and fruits, not gays and lesbians." He insisted he would never believe his daughter was lesbian unless she told him. "What the hell difference does it make if she's gay or lesbian or straight or anything because she's laying there in diapers? . . . Let the poor kid rest in peace," he said, as if his adult daughter were a dead child. He harbored no real hope that she would ever be able to live outside an institution.

Donald Kowalski, who came across to his *Post* interviewer as a fundamentally decent but uneducated man, reserved his harshest language for Thompson. "I think she's an animal," he hissed, attacking her for publicly calling his daughter lesbian. ". . . As far as I am concerned, they should have locked her up a long time ago."

Thompson's concern wasn't Donald Kowalski's opinion of her but the fact he was essentially keeping his daughter locked up: "I cannot condemn a 32-year-old woman to live the rest of her life in a nursing home. She's being held a virtual prisoner in an institution and not being allowed to see people she'd like to see." Thompson, who had not seen her partner for three years, told the *Post*, "I still want to bring

Sharon home. . . . I made a commitment to Sharon for a lifetime. And I mean to keep it."

Committees to "Free Sharon Kowalski" were springing up all around the country. And Sunday, August 7, 1988, the day before Sharon Kowalski turned 32, was marked as "National Free Sharon Kowalski Day" at rallies in several cities. Speaking to any group that would listen, Karen Thompson kept demanding to know, "Why can't Sharon Kowalski come home?"

Very gradually, with public pressure for proper testing and a change of guardianship mounting, Thompson saw progress. In mid-1988, Gary Pagliacetti, then Sharon Kowalski's court-appointed attorney, persuaded Judge Robert Campbell to have the disabled woman thoroughly tested by outside experts. When tests indicated that Sharon Kowalski wanted to see her partner and would benefit from being in a better-equipped facility, Campbell ordered her transferred from the nursing home near her parents to a St. Cloud rehab center near Thompson. On February 2, 1989, after a three-and-a-half-year separation, Sharon Kowalski and Karen Thompson were reunited.

Donald Kowalski no longer wanted to be his daughter's guardian. Thompson did. However, Judge Campbell handed down a decision that stunned Thompson and her advocates: On April 23, 1991, he instead appointed a Kowalski family friend who said she had no intention of trying to bring Sharon Kowalski home.

That decision proved unacceptable to the Minnesota Court of Appeals, which unanimously ordered that Thompson be appointed guardian. Judge Jack Davies declared that Thompson's tireless struggle to maintain a connection to her injured partner and get her the best care showed that she was Sharon Kowalski's best advocate and guardian. "We believe," Davies wrote, "Sharon Kowalski . . . has consistently indicated a desire to return home. And by that, she means to St. Cloud in live with Karen Thompson again. Whether this is possible is still uncertain as her care will be difficult and burdensome. We think she deserves the opportunity to try." Thompson's guardianship became official in early 1992. And eight years after her life was nearly destroyed by a drunken driver, Sharon Kowalski went home.

Of course, things could never be as they had been. Both women had become, in fundamental ways, different people. They live in a fully accessible house with a teacher whom Thompson started loving when she feared she might never see Kowalski again. Thompson, 51, is still showing extraordinary devotion to the 43-year-old Kowalski, who spends her days at an adult day care center. Kowalski is still using a keyboard to communicate and being fed through a tube. Every other evening Thompson and her new partner, Patty, spend four hours giving Kowalski an enema, bathing her and lifting her into a standing-position frame to stretch her organs. Kowalski follows fairly complicated conversations and laughs at appropriate spots. Sometimes she gets out to a basketball or hockey game. Her parents visit her at the day care center twice a month, Thompson says.

Through speaking fees and fundraisers, Thompson, now a full professor at St. Cloud University, has paid off $300,000 in legal bills. She and Kowalski have been honored by a host of professional organizations, including the American Medical Association. (Thompson was invited to President George Bush's signing of the 1990 Americans with Disabilities Act.) She says it's hard to know how much Kowalski grasps of the eight-year legal struggle that had her at its heart. Kowalski laughs when she's told that many people consider her a hero, Thompson adds.

After years of dealing with doctors and judges who couldn't grasp her commitment and treated it as sick, Thompson finds that "people get it. People understand. They don't question that it's love. . . . We go in and out of Coburns, our grocery store in town, and we're just like other people. And they see our family, and they acknowledge that we're a family."

Thompson makes no secret of her new life's frustrations. "Sometimes I think [Sharon] has totally lost her short-term memory. . . . She doesn't know who the president is. When we talk about different issues, she's interested but she won't remember. I would probably go out of my mind without Patty," Thompson admits.

She believes that if she'd been granted immediate guardianship, Kowalski might have recovered the ability to walk. Instead, Thompson thinks, Kowalski spent years curled in a fetal position, the muscles in her legs and an arm becoming rigid. As a result, tendons had to be cut, rendering walking and use of her left arm an impossibility. What would Kowalski's life be like if Thompson had given up? "Well, Patty thinks she'd be dead. . . . I don't know how Sharon survived," Thompson says. "She's an incredibly strong woman."

Thompson shoulders her burdens with a glad heart. "People wonder how we can be happy, but we are. I just never dreamed we could be this happy again. And that's all three of us. . . . When Sharon laughs, it makes anyone smile. That's what the fight was about—Sharon's right to live." Twenty years after committing herself to Sharon Kowalski, Karen Thompson offered a simple description of their incredibly durable bond: "We're a family."

The Supreme Court was never told that Sharon Kowalski and Karen Thompson were a family. But the court had given a cold shoulder to the male couples who had tried to show the justices that homosexuality wasn't simply about sex. By the time it turned *Kowalski v. Kowalski* away, the high court was immersed in a landmark gay case that would demonstrate that most justices saw no possible connection between homosexuality and family.

11

ADRIFT IN A SEA OF GAY CLERKS

BY EARLY 1986, 78-year-old Justice Lewis F. Powell Jr. was weary and set in his old-fashioned ways. He had not yet fully recovered from prostate cancer surgery the year before. Very much an aristocratic Southern gentleman, Powell was unfailingly gracious, polite, proper. The atmosphere in his chambers was warm but a bit formal, much like that in the prominent Richmond, Virginia, law firm where he'd been a founding partner.

On a court with five justices in their late 70s, Powell was the one affectionately described by clerks as grandfatherly. He certainly wasn't ribald like Marshall, pompous like Burger or casual like Brennan, who would sit on a desk and joke with clerks. And, unlike Blackmun, Powell didn't start every weekday by breakfasting with his clerks and catching up on their lives.

Powell's dealings with his clerks were professional, respectful and distant. He treated his clerks humanely, even kindly, but tried to remain oblivious to their private lives, unless one needed his help. Otherwise, he neither offered nor welcomed personal revelations. Soft-spoken to the point of being almost inaudible, Powell communicated with his young assistants mostly through memos, even though their offices were only a few feet from his own.

Powell's notions of propriety meant that rumors ricocheting off the walls inside the closed world of the Supreme Court were unlikely to reach his ears. During the 1984–85 term, for example, gossip swirled that a former gay Powell clerk, David Charny, had had an affair during his clerkship with a conservative Reagan administration attorney. The attorney, who later died of AIDS according to Charny, was in line for a judgeship. Court liberals were hissing that his supposed affair, which Charny insists never happened, had been a scandalous conflict of interest. It was not the kind of talk that clerks or colleagues felt free to share with Powell.

Powell almost invariably devoted Saturdays to catching up on intraoffice memos. He'd spend hours talking into a Dictaphone. At midday, he'd break for lunch and, if the day was warm, go outside to an enclosed courtyard. There, he'd indulge in his weekend treat, drinking half a beer out of a paper bag and eating peanut butter crackers. Then, on Monday, Sally Smith, the faithful assistant he'd brought from Richmond, would transcribe Powell's thoughts and instructions. His clerks would respond by memo. If a case was sufficiently important or difficult, the flurry of memos would be interrupted at least once by an actual face-to-face discussion.

In February or March of 1986—the exact date is lost to history—Powell walked into the office of one of his four clerks, Carter Cabell Chinnis Jr., and struck up a conversation about a Georgia sodomy case, *Bowers v. Hardwick*. Chinnis was startled because *Hardwick* (as it is most often called) wasn't among his cases. "It was very unusual. . . . It was, in fact, to my knowledge the only time he approached an unassigned clerk about a case," Chinnis stresses.

When Powell's clerks had divvied up the term's first wave of cases, *Hardwick* had gone to someone else. Every court insider knew *Hardwick* was one of the term's big cases. Chinnis was no exception. By February he also knew *cert* had been granted, briefs had been filed, and oral argument had been set for March 31.

Powell kicked off the unusual conversation with a few legal questions about *Hardwick,* a case rooted in the arrest of a gay Atlanta bartender for having oral sex in his own bedroom. "The conversation fairly quickly turned to the non-legal aspects of the case. Essentially, he asked me questions about homosexuality," recalls Chinnis, who goes by his middle name, which is pronounced "CAB-all."

Cabell Chinnis was the latest in what he knew was a long line of gay Powell clerks. Chinnis was more open about his sexual orientation than his predecessors, according to office manager Sally Smith. At the time Powell turned to him for information about homosexuality, Chinnis was a 27-year-old graduate of Yale law school, where he'd been managing editor of the *Yale Law Journal*. A strikingly handsome young man with crystal blue eyes and strawberry blond hair, the 6-foot-4 Chinnis, who grew up in Alexandria, Virginia, was a tall and lean southern gentleman like the aged justice for whom he worked.

In his 14 years as a justice, Powell had repeatedly tried to keep homosexuality—a topic he found upsetting and distasteful—off the court's agenda. Yet, suddenly, he wanted to discuss its prevalence. "He said that one of the [friend-of-the-court] briefs had indicated that it was as high as 10 percent or more. And I said that struck me as correct. And he said, 'I don't believe I've ever met a homosexual.' And I was surprised by that remark. I said that that just couldn't be right," Chinnis recalled a dozen years later at his newly renovated townhouse just north of Dupont Circle, the gayest neighborhood in Washington, D.C. Powell's remark about never having met a homosexual "just struck me as the kind of thing a grandmother would say. You'd say, 'Oh, yes, you have.' And she'd say, 'Oh, I guess you're right,'" Chinnis adds.

Powell followed up his declaration of obliviousness by describing his experience as an Army air corps officer. "He said that he had been in North Africa in World War II and that the Allied forces that he was with had been in the desert, hundreds of miles away from women, for an extended period. And there had not been one episode of homosexuality that he knew of," says Chinnis. "I said, 'One could work next to a homosexual for years and a gay person would choose never to disclose that aspect of his private life.'. . . " (Regardless of whether he was aware of it, Powell had rubbed shoulders with homosexuals long before reaching the court. His role in disseminating British code-breakers' intelligence to U.S. forces had introduced him to Alan Turing, the homosexual mathematical genius who cracked the Germans' most daunting encryption machine.)

A few hours after his first questions, Powell returned to Chinnis's office sounding as if he was struggling to understand a phenomenon totally alien to him. Clearly, the cases of Marjorie Rowland, the bisexual guidance counselor, and Sharon Kowalski, the severely disabled lesbian, had made no lasting impression on Powell, who still thought of homosexuality as male. "Justice Powell asked questions about why homosexuals didn't date and marry women," Chinnis recalls.

Chinnis had never told Powell that he was gay but, by that point in the discussions, had jumped to the conclusion that Powell knew. When Chinnis's lover had visited the court, Chinnis had introduced him as a friend he'd lived with in New Orleans. Yet Chinnis, operating in the world of winks, nods and unspoken assumptions inhabited by semi-closeted gay people, thought that the justice might have sensed that he and his partner were a couple. The tenor of Powell's questions, plus the strangeness of his talking to an unassigned clerk, reinforced Chinnis's belief that Powell had singled him out because he thought a gay man could best answer his questions.

Years later, puzzling over what Powell knew, Chinnis wondered, "Would you ask these questions of a straight man?" Chinnis's view in 1986 was that "when a 70- or 80-year-old man walks into my office, having met my boyfriend, to talk about gay people, he wants a pretty clear answer. . . . He said, 'Well, why don't homosexuals have sex with women?' I very bluntly said, 'Justice Powell, a gay man cannot have an erection to perform intercourse with a woman.'"

Powell followed up Chinnis's erection explanation by saying, according to Chinnis, "that he thought that sodomy required an erection. I told him that gay men did, in fact, have erections with men but that was different, they were sexually aroused."

Sitting in the next room, Ann Coughlin, Powell's most liberal clerk that term, overheard the exchange and was shocked that Powell was having such a sexually explicit conversation. "I was as astonished as anyone in the world could be. You know what I mean—your mouth falls open at how strange this whole thing is," Coughlin recalls.

Looking back, Chinnis says, "The thing that struck me most was not, did he know homosexuals? Because I thought he did. I thought we'd worked through that. What struck me . . . is that the concept of homosexuality had no content for him. He had no frame of reference." Telling Powell someone was homosexual would have had as little real meaning to him as saying the person was a Nepalese Muslim—the justice would fail to grasp the cultural, political and emotional implications, Chinnis adds.

Trying to give substance to the concept of homosexuality was no easy task for Chinnis: "It's difficult when you have not talked to someone even about prostate cancer to then talk about sodomy, erections, intercourse and oral sex. And then you hit on the issues—that it's a mark of trust to disclose to someone in your professional environment that you're gay, that because of the bigotry of society it could be used to hurt you. That's the best you can do starting out."

Ann Coughlin knew Chinnis was gay but doubts Powell did. She believes Powell talked to Chinnis because he saw the clerk as a soul mate. "The deep irony here is, I think, he chose Cabell because there was this deep bond between them in Powell's mind, both coming from Virginia, both having that sort of legacy," she says.

The Powell clerk actually handling *Hardwick* never talked with the justice about the nature of homosexuality. "He wouldn't have viewed me as someone who could give him a lot of help on that. I was fresh out of BYU [Brigham Young University law school], married with three children," recalls Michael Mosman, who wasn't sure until late in the term that Chinnis was gay.

Consciously or not, the genteel Powell had an affinity for gay people—male and female—that apparently led him to choose them as clerks more often than did other justices. Powell's gay ex-clerks, like clerks in other chambers, are keenly aware of the phenomenon. Some attribute it to Powell's being drawn to the "preppy, boyish southern jock" style popular for a time among Ivy League gay men. Others say that while many justices gravitated toward hard-charging, argumentative young men, Powell tapped quieter, more academic men and women. One gay Powell clerk recalls he didn't feel any "rapport" when interviewed by macho Justice White. Powell's clerks played more of a role than in many chambers in helping pick their successors. Some members of Powell's unbroken string of gay clerks in the 1980s had been school friends.

Powell also may have been more at ease than some of the less oblivious justices with men and women who fit certain gay stereotypes. Sally Smith, Powell's closest professional companion for 37 years, has never married and fits the description of a comfortable-shoe lesbian so closely that many Powell clerks assume—wrongly, she says with a chuckle— that she must be gay. That's not an idea Powell would have allowed himself to entertain.

Even during the preliminary *Hardwick* discussions, court insiders were well aware that the case had the earmarks of a landmark. The court hadn't handed down a full-length, signed opinion on a case involving homosexuality since 1967, when in *Boutilier* it allowed all homosexual immigrants to be branded "psychopathic" and, thus, deportable.

Only twice since *Boutilier* had the court heard arguments in a homosexual case. Both times it avoided reaching a precedent-setting judgment: In 1984, it dismissed a legally confusing sodomy case, *New York v. Uplinger*. The next year it issued no decision in a case involving gay-rights advocacy by Oklahoma teachers because Powell chose not to break a tie vote.

The place of homosexuals in the United States had changed enormously in the nearly 19 years since the court had treated homosexuality as a mental illness. Homosexuality was no longer unspeakable or invisible. The American Psychiatric Association no longer classified homosexuality as a sickness. The turnabout of national mental health organizations was so great that by the 1980s they were in the forefront of the push for legal recognition of basic gay civil rights. In 1967, the court's three most liberal justices had viewed homosexuals as pitiable. By 1986, millions of openly gay Americans viewed that notion as laughable, insulting. A self-respecting gay-rights movement had not only been born but also matured as a political and social force pushing for recognition that homosexuality was a natural human variation, much like left-handedness, and that it was immoral and un-American to discriminate against people simply for being gay. The AIDS crisis, which first hit in the early 1980s, claimed the lives of tens of thousands of gay men yet helped politicize an entire gay generation—drawing record numbers of gay men and lesbians out of the closet to put a human face on homosexuality for relatives, friends and colleagues. As a result, the news media had finally begun to take gay-rights questions seriously. In 1986, court insiders could be certain that *The New York Times* would not bury *Hardwick*'s outcome on page 33, as it did when it disposed of *Boutilier* in a single sentence.

As gay Americans made tremendous strides toward true first-class citizenship, the Supreme Court—known as a crucial engine of the movement for racial equality—was largely assumed to be absent from the struggle. The court's all-important 1958 freedom of the press decision in *ONE*, which refused to treat material as obscene just for being homosexual, had made possible the eventual blossoming of the gay press. Because of that ruling, gay newspapers and magazines were able to play a vital community-building role by helping fearful homosexuals forge a gay identity and break out of their isolation. Yet the court's largely inadvertent role in helping the gay-rights movement get off the ground was virtually forgotten by the 1980s because neither the news media nor gay history books had focused on the court's gay-rights record. Likewise, few Americans were aware that the Supreme Court had become a drag on the gay movement by, for example, upholding Virginia's sodomy law and by refusing to even listen to the pleas of gay teachers, couples, soldiers and prisoners. But by the time *Hardwick* was accepted for a full hearing, the justices and their clerks knew that the court's final decision would not slip below the general public's radar screen. This time, the nation would be watching.

"The Perfect Case"

Michael Hardwick, the gay young man who risked a 20-year prison sentence to fight Georgia's sodomy law, certainly was no student of the Supreme Court. He was a 28-year-old Atlanta bartender whose gay-rights activism had been limited—until he was arrested in his own bedroom for having oral sex—to marching in a pride parade.

The youngest of four children, Hardwick was born in Miami into a Catholic family in 1954. His childhood was unremarkable, his adolescence rocky. His parents divorced when he was 12; he was never close to his firefighter father. In high school, he dated girls and did gymnastics. He also did drugs—developing a heroin addiction that landed him in a rehabilitation program. By the time he enrolled in Florida State University, Hardwick was intent on becoming a landscape architect. He was also seriously contemplating going through life as a Buddhist monk.

The appeal of monasticism evaporated at 21, when he had sex with another man. The man turned out to already have a lover. Hardwick was crushed but realized homosexuality felt natural to him. He immediately came out to his mother and began living as an openly gay man.

After college, he launched a landscaping company, Growth Concept Environmental Design, in Miami, then sold it to concentrate more on personal growth. His next venture—a health food store—failed. In 1979, Hardwick settled in Atlanta and drifted into tending bar.

Tall with rugged, sculptured features and wavy blond hair, Michael Hardwick looked like a surfer or a GQ model. He was a charmer who "had carefully perfected the skill of looking at you, making you feel special and listening to you," recalls gay-rights attorney Evan Wolfson. By July 1982, Hardwick had been tending bar for a year at the Cove, a gay Atlanta night spot. On the morning of July 5—having spent all night installing insulation in the discotheque that the Cove was about to open—Hardwick grabbed a beer as he headed out the door. Outside, he tossed the beer in the trash, just as Patrolman Keith Torrick spotted him. The 23-year-old policeman slapped Hardwick with a ticket for drinking in public and warned that he'd be arrested if he missed his court date. Hardwick went to court and assumed that paying a $50 fine had ended the matter.

A few weeks later, on August 3, 1982, Hardwick was entertaining a guest, a married North Carolina schoolteacher in town for a job interview. Mistakenly thinking Hardwick was a scofflaw, Torrick showed up at Hardwick's house with an arrest warrant. Accounts differ as to whether a buddy who was sleeping off a hangover on Hardwick's sofa let Torrick in or the front door had simply been left open. Hardwick's hungover pal told Torrick that he didn't know whether Hardwick was home.

Patrolman Torrick began searching the house, stopping outside a back bedroom whose door was open just a crack. He pushed the door and walked—uninvited and unannounced—into the candle-lit bedroom. There, he was "shocked" and "grossed . . . out," as he put it, to discover that Hardwick and his guest were engaging in mutual fellatio. The police officer announced that Hardwick was under arrest. Hardwick shot back, "What are you doing in my bedroom?"

Having destroyed the two men's privacy, Patrolman Torrick further humiliated them by refusing to turn his back as they dressed, according to Hardwick. Torrick handcuffed the men together and drove them to jail, where he "made sure everyone . . . knew I was there for 'cocksucking' and that I should be able to get what I was looking for," Hardwick later recalled. Hardwick and his guest were charged with violating Georgia's sodomy law, which made oral or anal sex a felony punishable by a 1-to-20-year prison sentence. Hardwick posted bail within an hour but wasn't released for 12 hours. He was forced to spend much of that time near convicted criminals who'd been told why he was there. "It was not a pleasant experience," Hardwick said.

A few days later, an ACLU attorney eager to challenge Georgia's sodomy law contacted Michael Hardwick. With his mother in tow, Hardwick went to meet with the ACLU's Atlanta legal team. The attorneys warned that if he agreed to fight the law's constitutionality, instead of quietly pleading guilty to a reduced charge as his sex partner had done, "the judge could make an example out of me and give me 20 years in jail. My mom was saying, 'Do you realize I'll be dead before I see you again?' So they said, 'Just think about it for two or three days.'"

Hardwick had never fought for gay civil rights. But as he thought through how sodomy laws were used to hurt gay people too frightened, embarrassed or vulnerable to fight back, he decided to enlist in the battle. He picked up the phone and volunteered. As he later recalled:

> I realized that if there was anything I could do, even if it was just laying the foundation to change this horrendous law, that I would feel pretty bad about myself if I just walked away from it. . . . [T]hey'd been trying for five years to get a perfect case. Most of the arrests that are made for sodomy in Atlanta are of people who are having sex outside in public; or an adult and a minor; or two consenting adults, but their families don't know they are gay; or . . . they'd be jeopardizing their teaching position. There's a lot of different reasons why people would not want to go on with it. I was fortunate enough to have a supportive family who knew I was gay. I'm a bartender, so I can always work in a gay bar. And I was arrested in my own house. So I was the perfect case.

Hardwick's attorneys first had to clear up a minor imperfection: Hardwick paid a $50 fine for marijuana found in his bedroom. Then, as Hardwick's legal team prepared to tackle the sodomy law, Lewis Slaton, Atlanta's politically savvy district attorney, refused to prosecute.

Unable to pursue their challenge in state court, ACLU attorneys Kathleen Wilde and John Sweet sued in federal court on behalf of Hardwick and "John and Mary Doe," who were—as a Supreme Court clerk later phrased it—"a married couple interested in variety." The Does stated that Hardwick's sodomy arrest had a chilling effect on their sex life. Wilde and

Sweet charged that Georgia's sodomy law was unconstitutional because it trampled the right to privacy, bore "no rational relationship" to any legitimate government purpose, was too broad and violated First Amendment guarantees of freedom of expression and association.

When Judge Robert H. Hall ruled April 15, 1983, he tossed the Does out of the case, declaring that they weren't really threatened—even though the law applied to every couple regardless of sexual orientation or marital status. Hall found Hardwick did have standing to sue. Yet, the judge dismissed the case because the Supreme Court's 1976 *Doe v. Commonwealth's Attorney* ruling had affirmed a decision upholding Virginia's very similar sodomy law.

On May 21, 1985, a three-judge panel of the 11th Circuit Court of Appeals disagreed. Writing for a two-man majority, Judge Frank J. Johnson Jr. handed gay Americans a major, preliminary victory: "The Georgia sodomy statute infringes upon the fundamental constitutional rights of Michael Hardwick. On remand [back to the district court], the state must demonstrate a compelling interest in restricting this right and must show that the sodomy law is a properly restrained method of safeguarding its interests." By requiring Georgia to meet the extraordinarily difficult compelling-state-interest standard in order to keep its sodomy law, Johnson was handing a lower court judge an engraved invitation to strike down the law as unconstitutional.

To Johnson, since the gay Virginians in *Doe* "plainly lacked standing to sue," the Supreme Court might have been essentially dismissing their suit rather than ruling on its merits. Besides, he added, subsequent rulings undermined "whatever controlling weight [*Doe*] once may have had." Pointing to phrases carefully planted in the 1977 *Carey* and 1984 *Uplinger* decisions by the crafty Brennan, Johnson found that the Supreme Court had not definitively ruled on the constitutionality of sodomy laws. (Dissenter Phyllis A. Kravitch wanted to join Johnson's ruling but said she could not because she viewed *Doe* as meaning sodomy laws were constitutional.)

"Write It Strong"

As a federal judge, Frank Johnson had never ducked controversy. He was one of the judicial lions who greatly advanced the movement for racial equality. The KKK branded Johnson "the most hated man in Alabama." The Rev. Martin Luther King Jr. hailed him as giving "true meaning to the word 'justice.'" In 1956, after Rosa Parks refused to sit in the back of a bus, Johnson helped strike down regulations that racially segregated seating on city buses in Montgomery, Alabama. In 1965, Johnson—an Eisenhower appointee later elevated to the appeals court by President Carter—permitted the famous Selma civil rights march. Had Carter—who says his first Supreme Court appointment would have been female—gotten to choose two justices, the second likely would have been Johnson, who believed a judge's job was to "remove injustice."

Much like the dissents from the Supreme Court's "psychopathic" 1967 *Boutilier* decision, Johnson's *Hardwick* decision illustrates that a jurist need not be comfortable with homosexuality or up to date on scientific understanding of it to think that the Constitution protects it. "Personally, I think it's disgusting," he told his law clerks. "But until we find a cure, society ought to tolerate conduct of this kind between consenting adults in the privacy of their home." Johnson, then 64, instructed his clerks to "write it strong" when they drafted his opinion.

Reading the result, Johnson chuckled, "Oh, they're going to call me the sodomy judge." His ruling declares, "The Constitution prevents the states from unduly interfering in certain individual decisions critical to personal autonomy because those decisions are essentially private and beyond the legitimate reach of a civilized society. . . . The intimate association protected against state interference does not exist in the marriage relationship alone. . . . For some, the sexual activity in question here serves the same purpose as the intimacy of marriage."

Attempting to avoid having to justify Georgia's sodomy law to a lower court, Georgia Attorney General Michael J. Bowers asked the Supreme Court to intervene. In a petition filed July 25, 1985, Bowers argued that the justices should take *Bowers v. Hardwick* because Judge Johnson's 11th Circuit ruling "conflicts directly" with a decision by the Court of Appeals for the District of Columbia. The latter, *Dronenburg v. Zech*, upheld discharging a sailor for gay sex. In *Dronenburg,* Judge Robert Bork found the Supreme Court's judgment in *Doe* controlling. Bork, a vociferous foe of recognizing individual rights not listed in the Constitution, further declared that the right of privacy stopped short of protecting homosexuals. "The [Supreme] Court has listed as illustrative of the right of privacy such matters as activities relating to marriage, procreation, contraception, family relationships, and child rearing and education. It need hardly be said that none of these covers a right to homosexual conduct," Bork wrote with a smugness that, combined with his hard-right views, would doom his eventual Supreme Court nomination.

Attorney General Bowers approvingly quoted Bork as well as a New York judge who'd declared in 1980 that ancient scholars "considered even consensual sodomy to be as heinous as the crime of rape." Although Georgia's sodomy law applied to every couple, Bowers attacked Johnson's ruling as if it were only about homosexual sodomy. Bowers direly warned that laws against suicide, prostitution, polygamy, adultery, fornication and drug use would be more difficult to enforce if Johnson's ruling were allowed to stand.

In rebuttal, Hardwick attorney Kathleen Wilde argued that Judge Johnson had been correct in finding that the constitutionality of sodomy laws was still an open question. What's more, Wilde pointed out, the ruling simply spelled out the test that Georgia's sodomy law must meet and did not actually pass judgment on its constitutionality. Thus, she said, Supreme Court consideration of *Bowers v. Hardwick* would be "premature." There was no conflict to be settled: *Dronenburg* was a military case that did not hinge on the legitimacy of civil sodomy laws or the meaning of the *Doe* decision, Wilde contended. And since Johnson had not ruled on constitutionality, his ruling couldn't conflict with a Fifth Circuit decision upholding Texas's sodomy law. Wilde concluded by noting that 24 states had decriminalized sodomy yet had not been "paralyzed in their ability to deal with legitimate areas of state regulation."

Blackmun clerk Helane Morrison wrote the *Bowers v. Hardwick* pool memo and recommended granting *cert*. She saw both a conflict between circuits and sexual privacy issues important enough for the court's attention. She saw pros and cons to waiting for a heterosexual case: ". . . Although it would be a smaller step to find a right of sexual privacy among heterosexuals, it might be difficult to preclude homosexuals from its coverage. And perhaps homosexuals need the protection more. If the court finds no right to sexual privacy, it might be more desirable to render such a decision in [a] case involving homosexuals."

Powell's instinct, as usual with homosexual cases, was to duck: "We can again avoid this highly controversial issue by holding that [the 11th Circuit] misread *Doe*. . . . Or we simply could deny despite conflict," he wrote. Only Brennan, Marshall and Stevens had objected when the *Doe* court upheld Virginia's sodomy law without even having briefs filed. Powell had been part of the six-man majority handing down that decision. To Powell, *Doe* meant that sodomy laws were constitutional: "Kravitch correctly argued that [the 11th Circuit] misread *Doe*."

Since the court was being asked to overturn a gay victory, Chief Justice Burger was predictably interested in *Hardwick*, listing it for discussion. At the court's conference on Friday, October 11, 1985, Justice Byron White cast the first vote in favor of granting *cert* to Georgia's attorney general. Throughout most of his 23 years on the court, the Kennedy appointee had been openly skeptical of reading new rights into the 14th Amendment's Due Process Clause, which says that no state "shall . . . deprive any person of life, liberty, or property, without due process of law." White had once warned that the court "comes nearest to illegitimacy" when it uses that clause to recognize rights that can't easily be traced back to the Constitution's wording. By 1985, a long line of privacy rights, including the right to abortion, rested largely on the Due Process Clause's undefined guarantee of "liberty." Judge Johnson's decision in favor of Michael Hardwick was an attempt to add consensual sodomy to the list. White was ready to fight.

So was Justice William Rehnquist, who with White had dissented from the court's 7-to-2 recognition of abortion rights in 1973. Rehnquist had always insisted *Doe* had established that sodomy is not constitutionally protected. He and White were alone in wanting to take *Hardwick*.

White refused to drop the matter. The following Thursday he circulated a four-page, dispassionate dissent from denial of *cert* that described the legal action that followed Hardwick's arrest for "the crime of sodomy." Saying the lower courts were in conflict, White argued *cert* should have been granted. As soon as he received White's dissent, Rehnquist signed onto it. Oddly, Justice Brennan also added his name—perhaps to appear consistent with his *Rowland* plea just seven months earlier for the court to take gay cases seriously. Or, perhaps upon reflection Brennan had calculated that five votes in favor of Hardwick were within reach.

The justices took a rare second vote October 18. A very unlikely four-some—Brennan, White, Marshall and Rehnquist—provided the necessary votes to grant *cert*. (According to White biographer Dennis J. Hutchinson, Brennan immediately "was besieged by Blackmun, who feared that if the court granted *certiorari*, a majority would not only refuse to protect homosexual conduct but would also undermine *Roe v. Wade* in the process.") Five days after the second vote, Brennan changed his mind again, switching to "Deny." Former Blackmun clerk Pam Karlan says, "No one could understand why Brennan voted to take the case in the first place." Though Marshall often followed Brennan's lead on gay cases, switching once was enough for him. Burger then switched to "grant," ensuring that the case would indeed be heard.

Marshall "never felt under any obligation to explain" himself, recalls Daniel Richman, who worked on *Hardwick* for him. Yet Marshall reassured his clerks that it wasn't bad that the court had taken the case because the issues it raised were going to have to be faced.

"Trying to Move a Conservative Court Beyond Its Instincts"

Once the court accepted the case, Georgia Attorney General Michael Bowers had until mid-December to file a written brief arguing that Judge Johnson's decision ought to be overturned. Michael Hardwick's attorneys would then have 30 days in which to reply. Plotting a strategy to maximize Hardwick's chances of winning was the top item on the agenda when two dozen of the gay-rights movement's best legal minds gathered in New York City in mid-November. They had come together for a two-day meeting of a task force that was attempting to coordinate efforts to rid the nation of sodomy laws.

Would Michael Hardwick's odds be enhanced by rushing a Texas sodomy case to the high court, so that the justices might weigh their merits at virtually the same time? In the Texas case, the Fifth Circuit had ruled against gay activist Don Baker's challenge to the state law that criminalized oral and anal sex only when it involved people of the same gender. By treating same-sex couples differently from male-female couples, the Texas law raised the question of whether it violated the Constitution's guarantee of equal protection.

The task force was split over whether having the justices almost simultaneously think about Hardwick's privacy arguments and Baker's equal protection arguments would be desirable. The matter was quickly settled by Harvard professor Laurence Tribe when he joined the deliberations. Tribe had been recruited to take over as head of Hardwick's legal team.

Stressing the court's increasing conservatism, Tribe told the gay-rights lawyers that it's "no secret that the Supreme Court is not the ideal forum for vindication of threatened rights, but it's not likely to get better in the near future. In particular, Powell is likely to be more open-minded than someone like Bork or [Utah Republican Senator Orrin] Hatch." Tribe said that he saw privacy, not equal protection, as the most promising route in challenging the constitutionality of sodomy laws. "In short," he told the task force, "I've had a change of heart. . . . now I think *Hardwick* would be easier to win without *Baker v. Wade*."

Although Tribe doesn't recall handicapping the odds of winning each justice's vote in *Hardwick*, the task force minutes record him as having said "Burger and Rehnquist are 100 percent impossible, White is about 90 percent impossible, O'Connor about 75 percent impossible, Blackmun and Stevens we have a good chance of winning, Brennan and Marshall we can count on. The biggest question mark is Powell, and so we must aim for him." Underscoring the difficulty of the task ahead, Tribe added, "We're trying to move a conservative court beyond its instincts. . . ."

Tribe's calculation that convincing Powell was the key to winning *Hardwick* did not rest on the fact that Powell had been the missing vote when the court had deadlocked 4-to-4 earlier in 1985 over gay-rights advocacy by Oklahoma teachers. Rather, everything Tribe knew about the justices' records and attitudes pointed toward Powell being the pivotal vote in *Hardwick*.

"It seemed plain to me," Tribe recalls, "that Chief Justice Burger and Justices White and Rehnquist were certain to vote against Hardwick's claim, however that claim might be couched. Their voting histories and philosophies made that clear beyond doubt. My strong sense was that Justice O'Connor would vote the same way, although I thought it possible that she would join Justice Powell if he could be persuaded to vote that the Constitution requires the state to offer a more compelling and precise justification for outlawing a private, non-violent, non-commercial act of sexual intimacy involving two consenting adults than that the state is morally opposed to that act." Overall, Tribe recalls, "my best guess was that, if I could convince Powell, I would have five votes and possibly six but that, if I could not, I would lose 5-4."

Tribe, whose curly hair, boyish face and preppy clothing then gave him a suitably professorial demeanor, knew he'd accepted a Herculean task. "The case was very sharply uphill but not a sure loser," he says. Fellow Harvard professor David Charny, who as a clerk had seen Powell's visceral hostility toward homosexuality, warned him not to count on Powell. Yet, Tribe says, "David Charny's advice didn't affect how I approached the case. I knew the odds of persuading Powell were low. I also knew that I had to try because, without him, we were lost."

Georgia Attorney General Bowers's brief hit the Supreme Court on December 17, 1985. Bowers said he wasn't questioning that the Constitution protects privacy. "However, the lower court has taken an activity which for hundreds of years, if not thousands, has been uniformly condemned as immoral and labeled that activity as a fundamental liberty protected by the Constitution in the same manner as are the intimacies of marriage. . . . Obviously, there is no textual support in the Constitution . . . for the proposition that sodomy is a protected activity," he declared, ignoring that the Constitution doesn't mention marriage, privacy or the mainstays of privacy jurisprudence—contraception and abortion.

Pointing to the roots of sodomy laws, Bowers cited various Bible verses, then quoted 18th-century legal scholar Sir William Blackstone as classifying sodomy as worse than rape, as "an act so heinous 'the very mention of which is a disgrace to human nature,' 'a crime not to be named.'" The attorney general noted that sodomy had been illegal in Georgia since 1816, when it carried a life sentence.

Glossing over the fact that Georgia outlawed both heterosexual and homosexual sodomy, Bowers attempted to rivet the justices' attention on homosexuality. Homosexual sodomy, he argued, "is purely an unnatural means of satisfying an unnatural lust, which has been declared by Georgia to be morally wrong." Bowers depicted homosexual sodomy as not only beyond the bounds of the Constitution's protection but also as a threat to marriage, the family and "our way of life." Edging close to saying sodomy laws are grounded in prejudice, Bowers contended that the Georgia legislature should be left free to pass laws based on its view of morality and its own assumptions—"whereas the judiciary may be inclined to make determinations based upon more empirical evidence, to which this area is not particularly amenable." He claimed the legislature should be able to "find as legislative fact that homosexual sodomy leads to other deviate practices such as sado-masochism, group orgies, or transvestism. . . ." The legislature, he added, also ought to be free to conclude that "homosexual sodomy is the anathema of the basic units of our society—marriage and the family. To decriminalize or artificially withdraw the public's expression of its disdain for this conduct does not uplift sodomy, but rather demotes these sacred institutions to merely other alternative lifestyles."

(Attorney General Bowers failed to tell the justices what he knew firsthand about the degradation of marriage and extramarital heterosexual sodomy. He was then in the midst of a 15-year extramarital affair. In 1997, while running for governor, Bowers admitted the illicit liaison. His former mistress, Anne Davis, then told the world: "As far as sodomy is concerned, Mike Bowers is a hypocrite." Bowers lost the election.)

Attorney General Bowers's brief focused a spotlight on the penis in Michael Hardwick's mouth. In his response, Professor Tribe attempted to shift the spotlight to the cop in Hardwick's bedroom: What right did Georgia law have to invade Hardwick's sexual privacy, regardless of the body parts involved, regardless of his partner's gender? Tribe thought "at least five justices would be instinctively hostile to the very thought of gay sex," he later explained. ". . . I had no illusions that the court could be induced to forget that the primary application of the anti-sodomy statute was to homosexual couples, or indeed that . . . Michael Hardwick was himself gay and been 'caught' in an act of sodomy with another man. My best hope . . . was to persuade the court that these facts were diversions and that the real issue wasn't what Michael Hardwick was doing in his bedroom or with whom but what the state of Georgia was doing in anybody's bedroom!"

One of Tribe's co-counsels, Kathleen Sullivan, once described their *Hardwick* brief as "a love song to Lewis Powell sung in the key of Justice Harlan." Tribe did rely on the right-to-privacy precedents, dating back 25 years to Harlan's *Poe v. Ullman* dissent, that treated both the home and intimate associations as meriting special court protection. (The special court protection granted to the home flows from the constitutional guarantee that "The right of the people to be secure in their . . . houses . . . shall not be violated.") However, Tribe later said, "I never take the risk of 'pitching' a brief and oral argument toward a single justice." In *Hardwick,* he adds, he wasn't so sure of Blackmun and Stevens that he could ignore their particular concerns. Tribe's brief didn't dwell on the sexual details of the case but, he said, that wasn't out of deference to Powell's delicate sensibilities. Rather, "that would have been my choice almost without regard to who sat on the court, if only because it is no more the business of the Supreme Court of the U.S. than it is the business of the state of Georgia who puts which body part into or onto what other body part if the consenting adults whose bodies are involved are acting in a private setting and not imposing their proclivities on any unwilling viewer or unwitting participant," he explains.

Tribe's brief told the justices, "The state of Georgia would extend its criminal law into the very bedrooms of its citizens, to break up even wholly consensual, noncommercial sexual relations between willing adults." All Judge Johnson's ruling required, Tribe stressed, was that Georgia come up with a good reason for its sodomy law—or that law could not stand. Widely respected for his encyclopedic knowledge of court precedents, Tribe delicately attempted to walk the justices through prior cases to show how they would lead, without much of a leap, to a decision in Hardwick's favor. The court's sexual privacy decisions had not—as Bowers argued—been restricted to matters involving marriage, the family and procreation, Tribe argued. ". . . The right to control one's family size cannot by itself explain the protection this court gave to the activities involved in the contraception cases. After all, *that* right can be vindicated, without any recourse to contraceptives, by simply refraining from sexual intercourse. . . . These holdings mandated heightened scrutiny not of state restrictions on procreative sex, but rather restrictions on non-procreative sex . . . whether between married partners or between unmarried individuals." Thus, the court could require a good reason for a total state ban on one particular form of sex for pleasure—sodomy—without going far beyond its birth control decisions.

Noting that the court had already ruled in favor of private possession of pornography in the home, Tribe said it would be "ironic indeed if [the] government were constitutionally barred . . . from entering a man's home to stop him from obtaining sexual gratification by viewing an obscene film—but were free . . . to enter the same dwelling to interrupt his sexual acts with a willing adult partner. The home surely protects more than our fantasies alone."

Tribe argued that decriminalizing private sodomy would not jeopardize laws against public or commercial sex, laws regulating marriage contracts (such as those banning adultery and polygamy) or laws against "self-inflicted harm" (such as those banning "dangerous drugs"). He assured the justices that striking down sodomy laws would not jeopardize heterosexual privilege: States could still structure benefits "to encourage traditional heterosexual unions."

Attorney General Bowers had rested his argument on a one-legged stool—morality—that Professor Tribe tried to kick out from under him. Saying "there is no moral consensus" against sodomy, Tribe pointed out that it had already been decriminalized in 26 states. "Moreover, the nation's major scientific and professional associations, as well as a host of religious organizations, have officially declared their opposition to state regulation of private adult sexual conduct by force of criminal sanction." His all-star list of sodomy law foes included the American Psychological Association, the American Medical Association, the American Bar Association, the American Public Health Association and the National Association of Social Workers as well as prominent Jewish, Catholic, Episcopal, Lutheran, Methodist, Presbyterian, Church of Christ, American Baptist and Quaker organizations. Tribe concluded: "That government must submit to [careful] scrutiny when it would reach deeply into our homes and private lives is simply a feature of our system of ordered liberty."

Meanwhile, in a friend-of-the-court brief filed on Hardwick's behalf, the American Psychological Association and American Public Health Association attempted to bring the justices up to date. "Today," the court was told, "it is safe to conclude that a vast majority of all adult Americans—men and women, married and unmarried, heterosexual and homosexual—have engaged in the intimate conduct made felonious by Georgia." The associations cited studies indicating that up to 90 percent of heterosexual couples had had oral sex—both fellatio and cunnilingus—and that at least one-quarter of married couples under age 35 had engaged in anal sex. Oral and anal sex are more common among younger couples, the associations said, adding that "reliance on vaginal intercourse alone is not [psychologically] healthy."

The idea that sodomy is "unnatural" is a holdover from the Middle Ages, when St. Thomas Aquinas believed that all non-procreative sex was sinful because it supposedly made "extraordinary demands on the body and led to disease," the associations pointed out. However, three-quarters of Americans now consider oral sex a "part of normal sex," the elderly court was told. Oral and anal sex "substantially benefit" many relationships, the associations added. For example, "Married men who engage in oral sex with their wives are happier with their sex lives and more satisfied with their relationships. . . ."

Mental health professionals' understanding of homosexuality had advanced light-years since the mid-1960s, when psychiatrists had depicted Canadian Clive Boutilier as a pitiable creature who might one day be cured: If the court's rulings since *Boutilier* were any measure, the thinking of most justices simply had not kept up. The associations gently tried to disabuse the court of any notion that homosexuals are rare, deviant freaks whose lives and sexual practices bear no similarity to those of heterosexuals. The nation's homosexual population was pegged at 5 million to 25 million people—the estimate that may have triggered Powell's first burst of questions to Cabell Chinnis.

"Homosexuality is not a disorder," the health professionals' stressed. The brief noted that some male couples "form family units just as stable, dependable and contributing to the commonwealth as any traditional nuclear family." Since homosexuality is "not a matter of simple choice," sodomy laws don't keep people from being homosexual, the brief stated. However, it added, sodomy laws are psychologically damaging because their mere existence causes homosexuals to be stigmatized as criminally deviant, fuels heterosexual prejudice and can produce self-destructive self-hatred among homosexuals. Such laws also harm the fight against AIDS "by driving the disease underground," the associations emphasized.

"I Am Sorry You Had to Be Burdened with This Case"

Once all the competing *Bowers v. Hardwick* briefs were distributed around the court, clerks began pounding out "bench" memos, the case summaries that every justice, except Brennan, relied on in preparing for oral argument. An unusual amount of personality shines through in the breezy, five-page memo that Daniel Richman kicked out for Justice Marshall. Richman brushed aside the controversy over the meaning of the court's *Doe* decision, noting that—having accepted *Hardwick*—"the court is now free to do whatever it wants." The only real question, he said, is whether the Constitution protects Michael Hardwick's right to "purely recreational sex with no procreative potential."

But, Richman stressed, "the statute's application to both heterosexuals and homosexuals must be considered. To repeat the point, which I'm sure many members of the court will forget or ignore: THIS IS NOT A CASE ABOUT ONLY HOMOSEXUALS. ALL SORTS OF PEOPLE DO THIS KIND OF THING." Echoing Tribe, Richman said the step that Michael Hardwick was asking the court to take "is a small one. By giving constitutional protection to the right of a heterosexual couple to have access to contraceptives and abortion, this court (though it would never phrase it this way) has essentially established a right to engage in recreational sex. And it is difficult to see why this right should be confined to certain sex acts between consenting adults but not to other acts, which—if the surveys . . . are to be believed—are incredibly popular among a substantial chunk of the population." Richman thought the court should affirm Hardwick's lower court victory. Justice Marshall heartily agreed.

"What was notable about this case was how much of a no-brainer [Justice Marshall] thought this was," says Richman, a law professor at Fordham University. Marshall thought it was obvious that Hardwick's privacy rights had been unconstitutionally trampled. Three factors converged to produce that view, Richman believes, based on conversations with the justice.

First, Marshall strongly believed that if a law targeted any powerless or stigmatized group for discrimination, the government "better have a damned good reason."

Second, Marshall, who wasn't one to pepper his conversations with case citations or legal doctrine, surprised Richman by flatly stating, "This is controlled by *Stanley.*" *Stanley v. Georgia* was Marshall's 1969 majority opinion recognizing that the right to privacy is broad enough to protect using pornography at home. In that, Marshall had quoted a 1928 dissent by Justice Louis D. Brandeis that said the Constitution's framers "sought to protect Americans in their beliefs, their thoughts, their emotions and their sensations. They conferred . . . the right to be let alone—the most comprehensive of rights and the right most valued by civilized men."

The third factor was "just a level of comfort [Marshall] had with gay people," Richman says. "He started reminiscing about Bayard Rustin," the gay man who, as the Reverend Martin Luther King Jr.'s top lieutenant, had orchestrated the 1963 March on Washington.

Meanwhile, in Brennan's chambers, where discussions not memos were the favored currency, there was little talk about *Hardwick* in preparation for oral argument "because it was pretty clear how [Brennan] was going to come out," recalls gay ex-clerk Jay Fujitani, who never disclosed his sexual orientation to Brennan. (Based on a law professor's recommendation, Brennan chose Fujitani for a clerkship before even meeting him.)

Every justice's chambers had a distinct flavor. O'Connor's was predictably southwestern since she'd been raised on an Arizona ranch. On the Saturday before a set of oral arguments, O'Connor would go over the bench memos with her clerks. Often, she'd treat everyone to something southwestern that she'd cooked up at home. The clerk handling *Hardwick* "pitched it heavily as a case that did not have to be understood as a gay case—because . . . that would be much more likely to bring her around," according to an O'Connor clerk.

On the Saturday before the *Hardwick* oral argument, Justice Powell received a strong push in the form of 12-page bench memo from clerk Michael Mosman. If most justices seem guided more by personal instincts and aversions than by any overarching legal doctrine in dealing with homosexuality, the same wasn't true of Mosman. His feelings about gay people were secondary to him, he recalls. "The battle was really about . . . what direction the court was taking on due process," Mosman says. As a personally conservative Mormon from Idaho, he certainly fit many gay Americans' stereotype of a homophobe. In fact, he opposed sodomy laws, though he considered them constitutional, and had to struggle with himself not to be swayed by his empathy for gay friends and relatives. He remembers "trying not to contemplate" what he considered an unprofessional concern—that people dear to him would be disappointed, even hurt, by a ruling against Hardwick.

Mosman insists that labeling him "anti-gay" is unfair. But whatever damage a hostile court ruling might do to gay Americans was of far less concern to him than trying to halt what he considered the illegitimate expansion of privacy rights growing out of the Due Process Clause. "The [sodomy] issue could have come to the court as an equal protection case and would have had a better hearing. I would have been more receptive to it," he says.

With his March 29, 1986, bench memo, Mosman began relentlessly pressuring Powell to vote against Michael Hardwick. The fact that decriminalization of sodomy might be "fairer or more tolerant" was irrelevant, Mosman insisted, because such decisions should be left to lawmakers. Labeling the power to recognize privacy rights "dangerous," he counseled using it with utmost caution. ". . . The right to privacy is not intended to be the vanguard of changes in societal values," he contended. "Personal sexual freedom," he warned, "is a newcomer among our national values, and may well be . . . a temporary national mood that fades." Reading privacy precedents in the narrowest possible light—to him *Stanley* merely involved "freedom of thought"—Mosman insisted that none pointed even remotely toward victory for Hardwick.

Mosman's memo didn't mention that he was deeply upset by the court's *Roe v. Wade* abortion-rights decision, which Powell supported. Mosman definitely did not want a *Hardwick* decision to reinforce *Roe v. Wade* by building upon it. Mosman argued that if the court ruled in favor of Michael Hardwick, it might be opening the floodgates to unchecked sexual freedom, including prostitution, because "no limiting principle comes readily to mind."

Reading Mosman's memo, Powell wrote "no limiting principle." The phrase would nag at him.

"Memo to Mike," Powell said aloud, Dictaphone in hand, as he began a remarkable stream-of-consciousness reply dated March 31, 1986—the day of oral argument in *Bowers v. Hardwick*—but very likely dictated on Saturday, March 29. More than any other document yet unearthed, Powell's response offers telling glimpses of what went through a justice's mind while thinking about homosexuality. Most striking is how offensive Powell found even the blandest parallel between gay lives and his own. To Justice Powell's way of thinking, homosexuals might have houses or apartments but don't have real homes. "Home" is where Mrs. Powell is:

> This case, that we should not have taken, [Powell began] involves the validity of the Georgia statute that makes sodomy a misdemeanor. The facts are straight forward (if one can use that term in this case!). . . . (Possibly the crime is a felony of some level.)
>
> . . . Professor Tribe, with his usual overblown rhetoric, does focus his claim in the narrowest possible language: "Whether the state of Georgia may send its police into private bedrooms to arrest adults for engaging in consensual, non-commercial sexual acts, with no justification beyond the assertion that those acts are immoral". . . .
>
> In view of my age, general background and convictions as to what is best for society, I think a good deal can be said for the validity of statutes that criminalize sodomy. If it becomes sufficiently widespread, civilization itself will be severely weakened as the perpetuation of the human race depends on normal sexual relations just as is true in the animal world.
>
> Despite the foregoing, if I were in the state legislature I would vote to decriminalize sodomy. It is widely prevalent in some places (e.g., San Francisco), and is a criminal statute that is almost never enforced. Moreover, police have more important responsibilities than snooping around trying to catch people in the act of sodomy. . . .
>
> As the briefs all recognize, there is nothing explicit in the Constitution on this subject. Yet, this court has frequently recognized that there are human rights that can be derived from the concept of liberty in the Fourteenth Amendment. The most dramatic example is *Roe v. Wade*. . . . One of the best discussions of this subject that I am familiar with is Justice Harlan's dissent in *Poe v. Ullman*. . . . [He] explicitly refers to homosexuality as not within the right of privacy that he found to exist with respect to the use of contraceptives. . . .
>
> It is clear that, as in *Roe v. Wade*, the issue here is whether there is a substantive due process right—within the meaning of liberty and privacy—to engage in private, consensual sodomy. At present, I think substantial arguments can be made on both sides of this question. The weight of modern thinking at least supports decriminalization. . . .

It is tempting to accept the very narrow argument made by Professor Tribe. Apart from other considerations, it is impossible in any realistic sense to detect and later convict adult citizens who engage consensually in homosexual conduct in a truly private setting—e.g., what fairly may be called home. I must say that when Professor Tribe refers to the 'sanctity of the home,' I find his argument repellant. Also it is insensitive advocacy. 'Home' is one of the most beautiful words in the English language. It usually connotes family, husband and wife, and children—although, of course, single persons, widows and widowers, and others also have genuine homes.

A problem would be to identify some limiting principle if we are inclined to agree with the court of appeals and Professor Tribe. A number of examples come to mind: would the term 'home' embrace a hotel room, a mobile trailer (yes, I think), a private room made available in a house of prostitution or even in a public bar, the "sanctity" of a toilet in a public restroom?

And if sodomy is to be decriminalized on constitutional grounds, what about incest, bigamy and adultery. Incidentally, is there a Supreme Court decision holding that bigamy is unconstitutional? It is not easy for me to see why a husband in the privacy of two homes should not lawfully have two wives if liberty and privacy derived from the Fourteenth Amendment require invalidation of anti-sodomy laws.

As you can see, Mike, I am not talking very much like a lawyer. . . . Both parties rely on my decision in *Moore v. City of East Cleveland* [striking down a zoning ordinance that barred a woman from living with two grandsons because they were not brothers]. If that case is relevant to any extent, it would support reversal.

In sum, Mike, I am sorry you had to be burdened with this case. . . .
LFP, JR.

Bigamy, Incest, Prostitution, Adultery?

Probably about the time that Mike Mosman was reading Powell's apologetic six-page memo, Professor Tribe's Hardwick legal team was having breakfast in the court's ground-floor cafeteria on Monday,

March 31, 1986. Evan Wolfson, then the junior attorney who'd drafted the gay Lambda Legal Defense and Education Fund's friend-of-the-court brief, noticed Blackmun eating with his clerks and then saw a handsome stranger walk into the room. "I thought, 'Oh, my God, who is that gorgeous guy?'" Wolfson says, recalling his first glimpse of Michael Hardwick.

After breakfast, everyone who'd come to Washington for the Hardwick oral argument headed up to the courtroom, which was rapidly filling with spectators and reporters. "We definitely were psyched and really excited and thinking we could win," Wolfson recalls. Smitten, he maneuvered to sit next to the 32-year-old Hardwick, who wasn't spotted by the press since he had never granted interviews. Hardwick had expected the 82-by-91 foot courtroom to be larger. He was surprised that he could clearly see the justices' facial expressions as they filed in from behind their velvet curtain and sat down in high-back leather chairs.

At 10:02 A.M. Chief Justice Burger, whose deep, booming voice and snow white hair made him sound and look the part of the nation's top judicial officer, announced, "The court will hear arguments first this morning in Bowers against Hardwick. Mr. Hobbs, you may proceed. . . ." Michael E. Hobbs, senior assistant attorney general of Georgia, stepped to the lectern in front of the justices and asserted, "This case presents the question of whether or not there is a fundamental right under the Constitution of the United States to engage in consensual private homosexual sodomy."

Hobbs was soon peppered with questions. Why wasn't Hardwick prosecuted? Is the statute really enforced? In response to a question from Justice O'Connor, who'd been advised not to see the case as gay, Hobbs admitted that the law would indeed permit prosecution of married couples. He inaccurately gave the justices the impression that no one in Georgia had gone to prison for private consensual sodomy in a very long time.

Hobbs repeatedly declared that there is no constitutional "right to engage in homosexual sodomy or any other type of extramarital sexual relationship." He tried to de-sex the court's privacy decisions, ignoring that without sexual contact there is no need for contraceptives or abortion. Justice Stevens then began undermining Hobbs by open-

Mysterious Justice Frank Murphy publicly played the role of a debonair ladies' man in the 1940s, but privately forged a deep, lifelong emotional bond with his right-hand man.

Supreme Court Historical Society

To the chagrin of postal censors, the Supreme Court in 1958 told tiny ONE magazine that it could indeed print homosexual articles, even a lesbian love story with a gay ending.

ONE Institute Press

By slamming its door in his face, the Supreme Court inadvertently did homosexuals a tremendous favor by turning shy government astronomer Frank Kameny into a gay-rights dynamo.

Frank Kameny

Beefcake was on the Supreme Court's menu in 1961 when the justices debated whether targeting a homosexual audience made three supposed bodybuilding magazines obscene.

Rare and Manuscript Collections, Cornell University

MAY 1960
Number 17
50c

TRIM

Young America's
Favorite Physique Publication

Ruling that photos of
scantily clad young
men in come-hither
poses could legally be
sent through the mail,
the Supreme Court
rejected psychiatric
testimony that
the pictures could
turn curious boys
into homosexuals.

*Rare and Manuscript
Collections,
Cornell University*

Playing sugar daddy to
young Marines made
Hawaii a sexual paradise
for top-ranking federal
civil servant
Richard Schlegel.

Richard Schlegel

Convinced his government had declared war on him, Frank Kameny—here interviewed outside the White House—fought back by orchestrating gay-rights protests by conservatively dressed gay men and lesbians.

Frank Kameny

Justice William O. Douglas, a rugged, rumpled individualist, counted a lesbian couple among his closest friends.

Supreme Court Historical Society

When President
Nixon chose
Lewis F. Powell Jr.,
an old-fashioned
southern gentleman,
for the Supreme
Court, neither man
would have guessed
that Powell would
unwittingly tap a
long line of
gay clerks.

*Supreme Court
Historical Society*

An ultraconservative
who favored sideburns
and Hushpuppies when
he first joined the court in
1972, William Rehnquist
compared homosexuality
to a contagious illness
like measles before
being elevated
to chief justice.

*Supreme Court
Historical Society*

As "John Doe," Bill Bland–longtime lover of the founder of the National Gay Task Force–failed to get the Supreme Court to strike down Virginia's "crime against nature" law in 1976.

Rare and Manuscript Collections, Cornell University

Atlanta bartender Michael Hardwick, left, spent a sweetly romantic day in Washington, D.C., with young gay-rights attorney Evan Wolfson, when the Supreme Court heard Georgia officials try to justify having arrested Hardwick for having oral sex in his own bedroom.

Evan Wolfson

A former pro ballplayer, Byron White slammed an elbow into the midsections of gay Americans in 1986 when his majority ruling derided gay civil rights arguments as "facetious."

Supreme Court Historical Society

If the court's isolated justices wanted to see the face of gay America, they
needed only to look out their windows in October 1987, when hundreds
of demonstrators were arrested protesting the court's refusal to strike
down sodomy laws.

Supreme Court Historical Society

Attorney Mary Dunlap,
moments after
becoming the first
lesbian to argue a
gay-rights case at the
court, joined dying
athlete Thomas
Waddell in explaining
their passionate fight
for a gay group's right
to use the word
"Olympic."

Mary Dunlap

Justice David Souter, left
has not let unsubstantiated
rumors about his sexuality
keep him from following
in the footsteps
of his predecessor,
William Brennan Jr.,
by becoming a friend of
gay America.

*Supreme Court
Historical Society*

Posing for the official portrait commemorating the 1994 appointment of Justice Stephen Breyer were the nine justices who served together into the 21ˢᵗ century: From left, front row: Antonin Scalia, John Paul Stevens, William Rehnquist, Sandra Day O'Connor, Anthony Kennedy. From left, back row: Ruth Bader Ginsburg, David Souter, Clarence Thomas, Stephen Breyer. Who will be the first to retire? The pace of gay progress will hang in the balance when a new justice is appointed to the deeply divided court. *Supreme Court Historical Society*

Eagle Scout James Dale, who from age 5 had tried to live by the Boy Scouts' rules, was shocked when the organization kicked him out for bravely telling the truth.

Lambda Legal Defense and Education Fund

ing the door to an equal protection argument by getting him to say that prosecuting a married couple for sodomy would be unconstitutional.

As Hobbs steered the subject back to homosexual sodomy, a justice whose voice isn't identifiable on the official audiotape underscored how unfamiliar justices sometimes are with the most basic elements of their cases, asking: "Is the record clear as to whether the conduct was with a male or a female?" Hobbs replied, "Mr. Hardwick was arrested for engaging in [a] sodomitic act with another man." Justice Rehnquist, long the court's most outspoken foe of gay rights, then began assisting Hobbs in clarifying his argument.

Soon, Stevens was back in the debate, pounding Hobbs about why Georgia didn't actually prosecute Hardwick if it was so fired up about keeping its sodomy law: "Does the state really have an interest in stopping this kind of conduct?. . . [W]hy wouldn't they enforce the statute?" Hobbs feebly replied that enforcement was "very difficult." Stevens shot back, "It would have been very easy in this case. . . ." Hobbs murmured "perhaps so" as the image of Michael Hardwick being caught in the act in his own bedroom flashed through a hundred minds and the courtroom rippled with laughter. Landing a final punch, Stevens said, "Presented on a silver platter and they declined to go forward. It seems to me there is some tension between the obvious ability to convict this gentleman and the supposed interest in general enforcement." Momentarily defeated, Hobbs answered, "I would agree, your honor."

In closing, Hobbs made a plea for the status quo much like that once made by defenders of racial segregation: "The Constitution must remain a charter of tolerance for individual liberty. We have no quarrel with that. But, it must not become an instrument for a change in the social order." Hobbs warned the justices that by siding with Hardwick they would be opening a "Pandora's box" and would soon find themselves "confronted with questions concerning the legitimacy of statutes which prohibit polygamy, homosexual same-sex marriage, consensual incest, prostitution, fornication, adultery and possibly even personal possession in private of illegal drugs. Moral and social issues . . . should be decided by the people. . . ."

While watching Hobbs's shaky performance, Justice Powell took notes, rating Hobbs a "good lawyer." Powell's summary of Hobbs's argument ended, "No limiting principle."

Powell's court papers contain an undated note that appears to be Powell's handwritten crib sheet of questions he wanted answered at oral argument:

"limiting principle
"Fundamental right? ?
"Bigamy?
"Incest?
"Prostitution?
"Adultery?
"In a hotel room
"(privacy of home)
"In an automobile
"In a toilet"

Powell put a bracket around the four listed sex crimes and drew an arrow from them to the question that was uppermost in his mind, "limiting principle." What's notable isn't just that Powell was struggling to find a way to rule narrowly against Georgia's sodomy law, it's that Powell's fear evidently wasn't that the court might throw open the doors to gay civil rights. Despite his extreme discomfort with the mere discussion of homosexuality, Powell did not list "Homosexual marriage? Homosexual teachers? Homosexual soldiers? Adoption by homosexuals?" Rather, he wanted to be sure not to undermine laws that attempted to hold libertines in check. Two of the four sex crimes that Powell was concerned about—bigamy and adultery—were breaches of an exclusively heterosexual relationship, civil marriage.

In a 1978 concurring opinion on a non-gay case, Powell had lumped together incest, bigamy and homosexuality in discussing prohibited forms of marriage. With *Hardwick*, he was struggled to find a "limiting principle" that would allow him break that trio apart.

After Hobbs sat down, Professor Tribe stepped up to the lectern and began,

... This case is about the limits of governmental power. The power that the state of Georgia invoked to arrest Michael Hardwick in the bedroom of his own home is not a power to preserve public decorum. It is not a power to protect children in public or private. It is not a power to control commerce or to outlaw the infliction of physical harm or to forbid a breach in a state-sanctioned relationship, such as marriage or, indeed, to regulate the terms of a state-sanctioned relationship through laws against polygamy or bigamy or incest. The power invoked here ... is the power to dictate in the most intimate and, indeed, I must say, embarrassing detail how every adult, married or unmarried, in every bedroom in Georgia will behave in the closest and most intimate personal association with another adult.

Tribe's articulate opening failed to impress Powell, the very justice that Tribe considered key to winning the case. Atop his notes on the Harvard professor's argument, Powell wrote, "Tribe ... (torrent of words!)." Powell interrupted to ask, "Professor Tribe, is there a limiting principle to your argument? You [raised the issue of] how do you draw the line between bigamy involving private homes or incest or prostitution and you move on to place." Continuing, Powell said, "You emphasize the home, and so would I if I were arguing this case" [an odd admission, considering how viscerally Powell had reacted to Tribe's use of the word "home"], "but what about—take an easier one, a motel room or the back of an automobile or a toilet or whatever. What are the limiting principles?"

Unlike the justices who seemed to be using oral argument to try to score points for one side or the other, Powell was genuinely seeking answers. And the tenor of his questions signaled that he was, at the very least, open to the possibility of being persuaded by Tribe's responses.

Tribe said that a mobile home might not legally constitute a "home" but that, however the court chose to define the word, the home did offer limited privacy protection.

"What about incest in the private home?" Powell asked.

Tribe said the home doesn't shield all behavior and that adultery, for example, could be punished regardless of where it occurred.

The back and forth between Powell and Tribe—an exchange that held the outcome of the case in the balance—continued with the rest of the court keeping uncharacteristically silent. Powell asked, "So, the limiting principle is limited to sodomy? Is that a principle?"

"No, no quite," Tribe replied. "I think it is somewhat broader, to be candid, Justice Powell. I think it includes all physical, sexual intimacies of a kind that are not demonstrably physically harmful that are consensual and noncommercial in the privacy of the home. . . . [W]hen the state asserts the power to dictate the details of intimacies in what they call 'irresponsible liaison' even in the privacy of the home, . . . it has a burden to justify its law through some form of heightened scrutiny. . . ."

As Tribe spoke, Hardwick and Lambda attorney Evan Wolfson were hanging on every word. "And whenever Tribe would make a really good point, our knees would touch and there'd be this sort of 'Yeah!'" Wolfson recalls.

Burger, then Rehnquist and O'Connor, jumped in to press Tribe about how, exactly, he'd maintain the illegality of incest and polygamy. Tribe responded that such laws would be "very, very easy" for states to justify. Powell, apparently still not satisfied, pulled the discussion back to homes. Yes, Tribe assured him, a "home" is different from the back of a car, different from a public toilet, somewhat different from a hotel room. Tribe sprinkled his argument with references to Powell-authored rulings that could be read as helping Tribe's case.

At one point Tribe had mentioned former Justice Harlan's classic *Poe v. Ullman* dissent, which laid the foundation for recognition of privacy rights. Powell asked, "but didn't Justice Harlan . . . exclude sodomy. . . ?" (Harlan had said that he wasn't suggesting that "adultery, homosexuality, fornication and incest are immune from criminal inquiry however privately practiced.") Rather than explaining that Harlan's apparent intent was to establish a right of privacy—not permanently define its outer limits—Tribe said simply, "We are not arguing for absolute immunity. We are arguing for heightened scrutiny."

Stevens joined in, making remarks that sounded designed to help Tribe put to rest concerns other justices might not have voiced. "One could argue that the reason for discouraging [sodomy] is to encourage marriage," Steven said, throwing Tribe a verbal softball. Tribe said the state could, indeed, make that argument but probably wouldn't win.

The nation's understanding of what's constitutionally protected has evolved, Tribe continued. Rehnquist pummeled him with hostile questions: Why shouldn't the court let the supposed evolution be expressed by legislative "majority rule"? And, if sodomy wasn't protected when Harlan wrote *Poe*, why should it be now. "What has happened in 25 years?"

Not wanting to focus on homosexuality, Tribe did not respond that understanding of homosexuality had advanced tremendously. He didn't say that the psychiatric profession had come to consider being gay a psychologically normal variant of human behavior. He didn't say that as vast numbers of homosexuals had come out of the closet, public acceptance had grown to an extent that Harlan—personally quite tolerant—probably could not have envisioned. Instead, Tribe expressed doubt that Harlan "would have decided to draw the line based on which body parts come into contact." Rehnquist triggered laughter by firing back: "Then he just wrote that part of his dissent in a fit of absent-mindedness?" No, Tribe calmly replied, but "even the best justices are at their best when they have a genuine case or controversy before them."

Tribe tried to show that the protection he was seeking for Hardwick lay at the intersection of freedom of association and the right to privacy. ". . . If liberty means anything, it means that the power of government is limited in a way that requires an articulated rationale for an intrusion of freedom as personal as this. It is not a characteristic of governments devoted to liberty that they proclaim the unquestioned authority of Big Brother to dictate every detail of intimate life in the home," he declared. Georgia must do more to justify its invasion of privacy than just claim that sodomy is immoral, he added. "It doesn't denigrate the special place of family and parenthood and marriage in our society to recognize the principle of limited government," Tribe argued.

Ignoring the sweep of the law, O'Connor suggested that perhaps Georgia might argue that the sodomy law was a way "to assert its desire to promote traditional families instead of homosexual relationships." Or, she continued, the law might be said to reflect the state's desire to deter disease. Tribe doubted the state could show sodomy laws promoted marriage and said they are "counterproductive" in fighting communicable illnesses. Then his time was up.

As Tribe sat down, "There was a real buzz among the clerks and a buzz, I think, even among the justices. It was like, 'Wow! What happened here?'" recalls Andrew Schultz, the White clerk who handled *Hardwick*. "Tribe blew his oral argument," Schultz says, adding that Tribe was "flailing . . . from the very beginning. I think there was a certain sense that the court smelled blood in the water. . . . The guy is good. But he could not recover." Tribe had won an impressive number of Supreme Court victories. "I thought," Schultz recalls, "there was a sense that, 'Wow! We finally got him!'"

Within at least part of O'Connor's chambers there was an especially disappointed sense that Tribe's pitch had been too much of a gay-rights argument to persuade the staid O'Connor. Although only 55, O'Connor gave her clerks the feeling that she was just as uncomfortable with homosexuality as the court's most conservative old men.

The clerks, of course, had not been around the year before when Tribe had been slammed much harder by the justices while arguing against Oklahoma's anti-gay gag rule on teachers. The 44-year-old Tribe was a seasoned pro at reading the nuances in the tone of questions fired at him from the Supreme Court's bench. "I felt very good during the oral argument in *Bowers v. Hardwick*," he recalls, "mostly because I expected the court to be even more hostile and didn't expect Justice Powell to seem so close to being open-minded even if not persuaded." He adds, "The tone change from the Oklahoma case seemed vaguely hopeful."

Although unaware of Powell's horrified reaction to his use of "home" in his written brief, Tribe says he had "no illusions that [Powell] would easily translate the positive image of 'home' into what he, and most men of his generation, were likely to think of as the sordid picture of gay male sex. Still, I had to try, and I had the sense . . . that I had made some headway. . . . Being exposed to a credentialed and respected straight man carefully and proudly articulating the rights of men and women alike, gay or lesbian as well as straight, in terms as traditional as those I chose might . . . have tentatively . . . moved someone like Powell just a bit."

Immediately after Tribe's oral argument, Hobbs offered a few final words. Georgia wasn't "acting as Big Brother," he insisted. Rather, it was defending "conventional morality" and trying to maintain a "decent society." He concluded, "the liberty that exists under our Constitution is not unrestrained. It is ordered liberty; it is not licentiousness."

Unlike lower courts, where cases are sometime fought in open court for weeks or months, the Supreme Court allots each side a maximum of 30 minutes. After 54 minutes, oral argument in *Bowers v. Hardwick* was complete. The session had failed to put to rest Powell's most nagging question. On his notes about Tribe's presentation, Powell wrote, "(never identified a limiting principle)." If there was a magic phrase that could make the Virginia gentleman feel at ease about holding Georgia's sodomy law to a tough constitutional standard, he had yet to hear it.

Prepared to Plead on Bended Knee

Because it was an oral argument day, tradition dictated that the justices would eat together in their private dining room. Tradition also dictated that retired justices were welcome. The food was unremarkable—cafeteria fare or a brown bag from home. (Powell used paper sacks stenciled "The Justice's Lunch.") The service was extraordinary, though. Each justice was served by his or her office steward. Marshall felt estranged from his colleagues yet often entertained them at lunch with rambling tales of his days as a civil rights gladiator. The court's unwritten code strictly forbids any talk of pending cases. No one breathed a word about *Hardwick*.

A few blocks away at the American Café on Capitol Hill, however, Michael Hardwick's Tribe-led legal team was excitedly doing an instant-replay analysis. "Everyone was very much pre-victory. They were sure I would win," Hardwick said later. He dismissed Georgia's attorney as "an idiot" but had been awed by Tribe. "He was incredible. I've never seen any person more in control of his senses than he was," Hardwick remarked. Evan Wolfson felt exuberant, he recalls, adding, "Tribe was definitely the most cautious of those of us at the table. Some of us were thinking we could have gotten possibly as high as seven votes."

Tribe recalls, "During and after the argument, my hopes were somewhat lifted. In general, I thought that getting a powerful four-justice dissent would make a significant contribution to the legal evolution of these issues in the long run even if, as seemed likely, we were to lose a majority."

Outdoors, instead of Washington's normal March chill, it felt like early June as sunshine warmed the day to a near-record 83. Indoors, Wolfson was sitting across the table from Hardwick. "There was just this moment when we both looked in each other's eyes, and we knew we were going to get out of there. We got up and left. And I remember Tribe had this look on his face of kind of bemused surprise. And there was general snickering amongst the gay people," according to Wolfson. "We had this unbelievably romantic day. It was a lovely spring day. It was gorgeous. . . . We just strolled around the cherry blossoms, strolled around the Tidal Basin. We actually kissed in front of the White House. We were just feeling so high. We just felt like we were going to win, that this was a major day and major case," says Wolfson, who recalls tousling Hardwick's hair in the back of a cab before they parted. Just for the record, he added with a laugh, "We kissed and cuddled. But no sex, no sodomy."

Between the time Justice Powell returned to his chambers on March 31 and the court's conference vote two days later, there was a storm of memos as Powell sought an acceptable means of getting rid of Georgia's sodomy law. "He wanted to strike the [sodomy] law, but he didn't want to use due process to do it," explains ex-clerk Michael Mosman. After a lifetime of refusing to think about homosexuality, Powell was struggling not only to understand it but also to be fair in a case he found "troublesome."

Interestingly, the umbrage that Powell, the oh-so-traditional family man, took at certain homosexual behavior was, perhaps, not as much a reaction to the fact that the people involved were the same sex as it was to their apparent promiscuity. A startling Mosman memo dated April 1, 1986, reveals: The justice who had railed about using the sweet and cozy word "home" in connection with a swinging gay blade like Hardwick apparently could, nevertheless, empathize with gay couples whose private lives seemed somewhat akin to his 50-year marriage. Mosman wrote, "You raised the possibility that the Constitution might protect homosexual relationships that resemble marriage—stable, monogamous relationships involving members of the same sex."

Forever tugging Powell to the right, Mosman warned,

I think this is not a good approach. . . . [T]he kind of marriage that our society has traditionally protected is heterosexual, not homosexual. It would be bootstrapping to say that marriage is protected because of our history and tradition, and then add that homosexual relationships are protected because they "resemble" marriage. Second, once you conclude that homosexual and heterosexual "marriages" are of equal Constitutional status, you would necessarily suggest that homosexuals have a right to adopt and raise children. Further, states would have great difficulty justifying other restrictions on homosexuality—such as no avowed homosexual public school teachers—since the Constitution would place homosexual and heterosexual relationships on a par with each other.

Powell could have pointed out that although tradition protected only intraracial marriages, the court had ruled that the Constitution protected interracial unions as well. Instead, he wrote, "I think Mike is right. I'll forget this possible rationale."

Powell found "considerable logic" in instead using the Eighth Amendment's ban on "cruel and unusual punishment" to gut sodomy laws. The idea behind that approach, as Mosman described it, was that if Hardwick was powerless to change his sexual orientation, it was wrong to punish him for acting on it. Powell could rely on the court's 1962 *Robinson v. California* and 1968 *Powell v. Texas* decisions, Mosman said. The former held that the status of being a drug addict could not be criminalized. The latter held that private drunkenness could not be criminally punished if the person was an alcoholic. An unsigned clerk memo pointed out that, regardless of whether Powell voted to affirm or reverse Hardwick's lower court victory, he could use the Eighth Amendment to declare any punishment for homosexual sodomy unconstitutional.

Cabell Chinnis wasn't involved in the search for a rationale for rendering sodomy laws toothless. But after Powell said he planned to support Hardwick, he and Chinnis talked again. "I initiated the third conversation," Chinnis recalls. "There was a case that we had been talking about that concerned voting rights. And I said, 'It's more important to me to have the right to make love to the person that I love than to vote for a judge in a local election.' And he said, 'The question is not what you would like, but what the Constitution allows.' I had no appreciation about how uncertain he was. That remark doesn't betray any uncertainty at all. It more or less indicates, 'I'm voting in favor of this,' which I knew already, 'and my view is based on what the Constitution allows.' Actually, I found that reassuring. . . .

"I was prepared," Chinns recalls, "to take the most aggressive measures that I could have taken, including, to put it colloquially, pleading on bended knee on the floor. I was prepared to say, 'You're hurting me personally. You're hurting people I care about. You need to understand there's a human face to all of this.' I doubt that would have had any effect. He was just not swayed in his job by emotional appeals. But I don't care. Because if I had known that he was on the fence—

"I talked with [my lover] Chris about it. We actually had an articulated plan of action, but it didn't come to that because we just didn't need to. The boat was headed in the right direction. I wasn't going to rock it," Chinnis adds.

Chinnis's co-clerk Ann Coughlin recalls that "Mike [Mosman] lobbied [Powell] very, very heavily to 'reverse.'" On the day of the conference vote, Mosman told Powell by memo that three of his four clerks, including the liberal Coughlin, supported reversal: "As to the *Robinson/Powell* argument, the three of us who worked on the theory last night—Ann, Bill [Stuntz] and I—continue to recommend that you use that theory to vote to reverse and write separately to introduce the argument, since it was not presented here. [Hardwick] has not yet suffered, nor does it appear likely that he will suffer, any imprisonment. If he or someone else is convicted or sentenced, this argument will be available. We believe it would be a mistake to create a fundamental right to protect this conduct."

Stuntz says that, to him, how Powell voted then seemed less important than that the justice write separately to say that criminal punishment for sodomy is unconstitutional. If the rest of the court split 4-to-4 and Powell took that middle course, then regardless of whether Hardwick won or lost, the court would be saying that sodomy convictions would not stand, Stuntz explains.

Coughlin is adamant that she never advocated reversal; Mosman says that Coughlin's memory of her position is probably better than his. Yet as far as Powell knew, his instinct to affirm Hardwick's lower court victory put him at odds with a least three of his clerks.

When the justices gathered alone in their conference room on Wednesday, April 2, 1986, Chief Justice Burger neutrally summarized *Hardwick,* then strongly pushed for reversal. There is no fundamental right to engage in sodomy, an activity that has been criminalized "for centuries," Burger declared. A privacy decision in favor of Hardwick would undermine laws against incest and prostitution, he warned. The chief justice quoted Harlan's *Poe* dissent and, in an obvious attempt to sway Powell, quoted Powell's language in *Moore v. City of Cleveland,* saying that home and family are constitutionally protected because of tradition.

Brennan spoke next and predictably sided with Hardwick. Having argued the year before in *Rowland* that anti-gay discrimination ought to be subjected to "strict scrutiny," the court's leading liberal had no trouble concluding that Georgia's sodomy law should, at least, be subjected to the lesser "heightened scrutiny." Brennan said his vote to affirm the lower court decision in Hardwick's favor flowed directly out of the privacy rights recognized in contraception cases as well as from the *Stanley* pornography-in-the-home decision.

White said he agreed with Burger and wanted to reverse. Then in a needless crack that surely offended the sensitive Powell, White said Powell had gone too far in *Moore v. East Cleveland.*

Telling his colleagues what he'd earlier told his clerk, Marshall said: *Stanley* controls. He agreed with Brennan's thinking and voted to affirm.

Silently trying to count to five, the 79-year-old Brennan must have felt his pulse quicken as soon as Blackmun started to speak. Blackmun had been nearly crucified by anti-abortion groups for his landmark 1973 *Roe v. Wade* decision, liberalizing the right to privacy to cover most abortions. But on gay rights, Blackmun had never lined up publicly with the court's liberal wing, though he probably had cast one of the four votes against Oklahoma's gag rule on teachers' gay-rights advocacy. Blackmun praised Judge Johnson's ruling in favor of Hardwick, stressing that it was restricted to behavior inside the home. Blackmun compared the sodomy case to England's earlier struggle to decriminalize prostitution. Yes, *Stanley* is relevant, he said, and so is the 1967 *Loving* decision striking down laws against interracial marriage.

Having found a way to sidestep his nagging "limiting principle" worries, Powell voted to affirm. Explaining his novel reasoning, Powell said it would be cruel and unusual punishment to imprison someone like Hardwick "for private conduct based on a natural sexual urge and with a consenting partner." Powell remarked to his colleagues that he'd never known a homosexual. Blackmun, illustrating the sexual predator stereotype that Tribe was up against, responded, "But surely, Lewis, you were approached as a boy?" Later, Blackmun reportedly told his clerks that he had considered saying, "Of course, you have. You've even had gay clerks."

Having spent a decade insisting that the court had already upheld the constitutionality of sodomy laws, Rehnquist, of course, voted against Hardwick.

Stevens cast the crucial fifth vote for affirming, but his support sounded weaker than during oral argument. He signaled that he might agree with Powell's "cruel and usual punishment" approach. Stevens noted that Georgia's law drew no distinction between homosexual and heterosexual sodomy and, according to Powell's notes, said both are considered loathsome. Community moral standards alone do not justify criminalizing conduct, but history would favor reversal, he said. The right to privacy certainly protects marital sodomy, he added. (In *Liberty and Sexuality*, a history of *Roe v. Wade*, Pulitzer Prize winner David J. Garrow quotes Stevens as declaring, "I hate homos." Neither Powell's nor Marshall's conference notes indicate Stevens made any such remark. Since the alleged comment is quite out of keeping with Stevens's approach to gay cases as far back as 1976, this book's authors wrote the justice to express doubt that he'd made the hostile remark and ask him to clear up the confusion. On June 1, 2000, Stevens responded, "Your doubt is fully justified. Even a Pulitzer Prize award winner can put his foot in his mouth when he quotes anonymous sources.")

Voting last, O'Connor stated the right to privacy is not unlimited and Georgia's law was not unconstitutional.

When the justices talked among themselves about Georgia's sodomy law, they weren't focused on how such laws stigmatize millions of gay Americans. Nevertheless, Michael Hardwick had won the secret conference vote, 5-to-4.

As senior justice in the majority, Brennan assigned the enthusiastic Blackmun to write the decision affirming that Georgia had infringed on Michael Hardwick's fundamental rights. When word of the preliminary vote reached Cabell Chinnis, he "declared victory," he says.

The U.S. Supreme Court stood on the brink of the most significant breakthrough in the history of the gay civil rights movement: By siding with Michael Hardwick, it would be declaring that there is no gay exception to the Constitution's privacy protections. The nation would be told that the Constitution is flexible and expansive enough to shield gay citizens. The American public and many lower court judges would, no doubt, interpret the ruling as a decree that anti-gay discrimination is wrong, un-American. It would be hard to overestimate the positive impact that such a declaration would have on gay Americans' lives.

Honor-bound not to let anyone outside the court know the cause for his celebration, Cabell Chinnis "had a nice dinner, drank, partied. It was a big deal. I just said, 'I had a great week at work!' Oh, I was thrilled!"

12

BRANDED SECOND-CLASS CITIZENS

NORMALLY, ONCE A CASE has been voted on in conference, it gets shoved onto a back burner, except in the chambers of a justice writing the majority opinion or a major dissent. Yet Powell was forced to keep thinking about *Hardwick* because he was under extreme pressure to switch his vote. Clerk Mike Mosman kept advocating reversal. And the day after the conference vote, Chief Justice Burger personally delivered a letter practically begging Powell to provide the crucial fifth vote for reversal. It was almost as if Burger were soliciting Powell's vote as a retirement gift even though the chief didn't publicly announce his departure for another month.

Burger's April 3 letter, a rare departure from the justices' tradition of not overtly lobbying one another, offers an invaluable window into the 78-year-old chief justice's hostility toward homosexuals:

Dear Lewis:

I have some further thoughts on your suggestion at conference that Hardwick cannot be punished because of his "status" as a homosexual. . . .

You will remember my "degree" in psychiatry, which led me to be very skeptical about that breed of M.D.'s. [Burger, whose "degree" was earned writing an opinion on psychiatric testimony, was leery of having "the shifting tides of scientific opinion" influence courts.] I have never heard of any responsible member . . . of the A.P.A. [American Psychiatric Association] who recognized homosexuality as an "addiction" in the sense of drug addiction. It is simply without any basis in medicine, science or common sense. In fact these homosexuals themselves proclaim this is a matter of sexual "preference." Moreover, even if homosexuality is somehow conditioned, the decision to commit an act of sodomy is a choice, pure and simple—maybe not so pure!

. . . The Fourteenth Amendment argument goes too far because there is no limiting principle that would allow the states to criminalize incest, prostitution or any other "consensual" sexual activity. Moreover, it would forbid the states from adopting any sort of policy that would exclude homosexuals from classrooms or state-sponsored boys' clubs and Boy Scout adult leadership.

The Eighth Amendment argument . . . creates a potentially greater mischief. . . . [S]urely homosexuals are not "sex crazed" automatons who are "compelled" by their "status" to gratify their sexual appetites only by committing sodomy. Heterosexuals, after all, manage to live in a society where sexual activities are often proscribed except within the bonds of marriage.

The record simply does not remotely support a conclusion that sodomy is compulsive. . . . It is extremely unlikely that what Western Civilization has for centuries viewed as a volitional, reprehensible act is, in reality, merely a conditioned response to which moral blame may not attach. Are those with an "orientation" towards rape to be let off merely because they allege that the act of rape is "irresistible" to them? Are we to excuse every "Jack the Ripper?"

Hardwick merely wishes to seek his own form of sexual gratification. Undoubtedly there are also those in society who wish to seek gratification through incest, drug use, gambling, exhibitionism, prostitution, rape and what not. . . . As Justice [Oliver Wendell] Holmes put it, "pretty much all law consists in forbidding men to something that they want to do." . . .

April 13, an unlucky day, will mark my 30th year on the bench. This case presents for me the most far reaching issue of those 30 years. I hope you will excuse the energy with which I have stated my views, and I hope you will give them earnest consideration.

Powell's former clerks—even the conservative Mosman—don't want to believe that the chief justice influenced their justice to change his vote. Burger was, after all, viciously ridiculed in the chambers of his moderate and liberal colleagues as pompous, shallow, dim, over the hill, a joke. Mary Becker, who clerked for Powell in 1980–81 and later became aware of her lesbianism, recalls that that even the genteel Powell made fun of Burger behind his back. "Honest to God, Powell used to call him the 'the Great White Doughnut'," she says with a giggle, "because he had white hair and a bald spot in the middle, and it signified nothing inside."

Cabell Chinnis recalls that after Burger dropped off the memo Powell disrespectfully rolled his eyes. Mosman insists Burger's letter had "zero influential impact." Even Powell's biographer, former clerk John Jeffries Jr., minimizes the impact of Burger's letter.

Powell wrote "Incredible statement!" by the chief's assessment that *Hardwick* raised the "most far reaching issue" of his career. After the case was settled, Powell wrote atop Burger's missive: "There is both sense and nonsense in this letter—mostly the latter." But Powell's notes to himself immediately after reading Burger's letter are more telling, showing that Burger had caused Powell to renew his struggle:

> I sought a "middle ground" to avoid a court holding that would be w/o [without] a limiting principle. I would not agree that every person has a fundamental right to engage in sodomy any time, any place. There are men who can gratify their sexual desire only with another man. [In the margin, Powell wrote, "Mike—Any medical or other support for this."] Given this fact, I find it difficult to lawfully imprison such a person who confines his abnormality to a private setting with a consenting homo. No one is adversely affected by such conduct.
>
> Incest is different because of genetic consequences. Rape obviously is different.
>
> Possibly I could remand [send the case back to a lower court] to determine whether Hardwick suffers from this abnormality.

The idea that a homosexual orientation could be a normal human variation, much like perfect pitch, apparently didn't occur to Powell.

The conflicting attitudes swirling inside Powell—typified by the fact that he was struggling to justify having sided with Michael Hardwick yet thought of him as a "consenting homo"—robbed him of his equilibrium. In a dramatic gesture perhaps best understood as an exhausted man's attempt to stop his head from spinning, Powell fired off a memo to colleagues announcing that he was switching his vote to "reverse." He noted that in voting to affirm, "I did not agree that there is a substantive due process right to engage in conduct that for centuries has been recognized as deviant, and not in the best interest of preserving humanity." He still thought that imprisonment for homosexual sodomy would be cruel and unusual punishment. However, he said that, since the question argued focused on due process privacy rights—not his Eighth Amendment scheme—"further study" had led him to "conclude that my 'bottom line' should be to reverse."

In a less subtle institution, Powell's "memorandum to the conference" would not have been bizarre. But at the Supreme Court, where justices considering a switch normally keep their own counsel until after reading a proposed majority opinion, Powell's announcement was strange indeed. He was, in effect, sticking his fingers in his ears, running away from the discussion, taking himself out of the game, throwing away his awesome, swing-vote influence. Since he couldn't possibly switch again on such a critical decision without losing enormous amounts of face within the court, he was effectively locking in his vote. The justice writing the majority opinion for reversal would have no reason to temper its language to accommodate Powell's more moderate views because Powell's vote was now a sure thing.

Gay clerk Cabell Chinnis was heartsick. Eyes reddening at the memory of Powell's vote-switching memo, he recalled, "It was the most disappointing moment in my career and one of the most disappointing moments in my life."

Stevens teased Powell that perhaps the nine-member court should just say that it was "equally divided." Powell took the ribbing in good humor, writing "$4^1/_2$ to $4^1/_2$!" in the margin.

"An Intellectual Hit-and-Run Incident"

Suddenly in the majority, Chief Justice Burger assigned Byron White, the justice who had persuaded his colleagues to take the case, to write the court's *Hardwick* opinion. White had written the court's unsigned 1973 *Wainwright v. Stone* decision that Florida's "crime against nature" law forbidding sex *"per os"* or *"per anum"* was clear enough to be constitutional.

The gruff, 71-year-old White displayed no emotion over Powell's vote switch in *Hardwick*. He simply walked two doors down to clerk Andrew Schultz's office and told him, "We are now writing the majority."

Known for his elbows-out roughness in pick-up basketball games on the court's gym, White was both coach and quarterback within his chambers. Abrasively competitive even when playing putt-putt in his office with clerks, White didn't look to his clerks for guidance, reinforcement or friendship. His clerks learned to do their chores without expecting to sway his thinking. "I guess I always had the view that one of the reasons I got hired was because I didn't agree with him," Schultz says. White did 90 percent of his own preparation for oral argument, asking for a short memo or none at all. He read every brief and made notes, which clerks weren't privy to. After making up his mind, he'd talk with clerks just to warm up for oral argument, where he'd deploy hostile body language to rattle attorneys. "'Warm' and 'fuzzy' are not the two words that immediately come to mind when you think Byron White," Schultz admits.

White came to *Hardwick* with a deep respect for privacy—at least his own. His closest friend, Ira C. Rothgerber Jr., called him "a shy man with an aggressive, and encompassing, view of his own privacy." During his years as a pro football star, when he was the highest-paid player of the day, White had learned to hate media attention as much as he despised the nickname "Whizzer" that stuck with him long after he stopped setting records for rushing. When he launched his legal career, one of his goals was to "keep my name out of the goddamn newspapers."

One outgrowth of White's obsessive love of his privacy is that his *Hardwick* files no longer exist. "There are no White papers. And there never will be. White destroyed everything," explains Schultz, who was sickened by having to help destroy box after box of priceless documents. "It just killed me [shredding] some of the stuff—the notes from his original dissent in *Miranda*," the decision requiring police officers to read suspects their rights.

Schultz declined to discuss his own role in the drafting of White's *Hardwick* majority opinion. According to White biographer Dennis J. Hutchinson, White wanted *Hardwick* handled in his office's usual fashion—meaning Schultz was to produce a 12-page draft within 12 days. The clerk met the deadline. White rudely responded that he'd written the opinion himself the night before. The next day, April 21, White circulated his draft, which brusquely rejected Hardwick's privacy claims. Hutchinson has observed, "The terse opinion betrays the impatience with which the author met and ultimately discharged his own assignment. What could have been the culminating expression of longstanding convictions and obviously profound concerns . . . impressed many as an intellectual hit-and-run incident."

In White's hands, the court's *Hardwick* decision became a blunt instrument to use against any gay American seeking any court's protection. White did not say that the constitutional right to privacy is too narrow to cover sodomy. Rather, he said it does not cover homosexual sodomy—with the emphasis on "homosexual." While Georgia's law applied to particular practices, not particular people, White produced the anti-homosexual opinion that Georgia's attorney general had sought. White's ruling claimed to "express no opinion" on heterosexual sodomy. But by treating *Hardwick* as a homosexual sodomy case, rather than just a sodomy case, White was treating homosexual sodomy as different, less acceptable. Homosexuals were being told that when they engaged in certain nearly universal sexual practices the Constitution would not keep cops out of their bedrooms. Intentionally or not, White inserted steel reinforcements into the notion that homosexuals are unconvicted felons whose private lives don't merit the protection accorded the nation's upstanding heterosexual citizens.

"The issue presented is whether the federal Constitution confers upon homosexuals a fundamental right to engage in sodomy and hence invalidates the laws of the many states that still make such conduct illegal and have done so for a very long time," he said. Listing privacy precedents, White stated, "none of the rights announced in those cases bears any resemblance to the claimed constitutional right of homosexuals to engage in acts of sodomy. . . . No connection between family, marriage, or procreation on the one hand and homosexual activity on the other has been demonstrated, either by the court of appeals or by [Hardwick]."

The court had refused to hear gay couples who wanted to marry or be recognized as spouses—as family, in other words—for immigration purposes. And it had failed to educate itself out of the stereotype that homosexuality is shallow, promiscuous and anti-family. So, White glibly asserted that homosexual intimacy had nothing to do with family.

White's hard-edged opinion noted that the court's prior rulings described rights deserving heightened protection as ones "'implicit in the concept of ordered liberty" and "deeply rooted in this nation's history and tradition." Attempting to demonstrate that those descriptions could not fit homosexual sodomy, White pointed to the "ancient roots" of sodomy laws. He noted that all 13 original states forbade sodomy when they ratified the Bill of Rights (the Constitution's first ten amendments) in 1791, that 32 of 37 states prohibited sodomy in 1868 when the 14th Amendment was ratified, that all 50 banned it in 1961 and that in 1986 it was still criminal in 24 states and the District of Columbia. White flatly stated: "Against this backdrop, to claim that a right to engage in such conduct is 'deeply rooted in this nation's history and tradition' or 'implicit in the concept of ordered liberty' is, at best, facetious."

"Facetious." The word slammed an elbow into the midsections of gay Americans. It's not hard to imagine the hyper-competitive White choosing that harsh, insensitive word merely as a way to score a point against court liberals in some game of legal theory one-upmanship. Andrew Schultz thinks that White was trying to ridicule colleagues' theories, not denigrate gay Americans' lives and aspirations. Yet, beyond the court's too-insulated marble walls, "facetious" sounded very much like, "Constitutional rights for homos? You must be joking!"

"Facetious" was pure White, as was all the rest of the language. "Unlike so many modern Supreme Court opinions, the words are absolutely authentic to this author," notes biographer Hutchinson. Using *Hardwick* to get a court majority to endorse one of his favorite themes, White wrote, "The court is most vulnerable and comes nearest to illegitimacy when it deals with judge-made law having little or no cognizable roots in the language or design of the Constitution."

White's court office was so covered with memorabilia from his days working under President John F. Kennedy and Attorney General Robert Kennedy that it seemed stuck in the early 1960s. His *Hardwick* opinion read as if it, too, came from an earlier era. If White was aware that the court would weaken its legitimacy in the eyes of much of the American public by so callously dismissing a gay man's plea for privacy, he gave no indication of it.

Rather, White declared that if the court were to read protections for Michael Hardwick's private sex life into the Constitution, there would be no obvious stopping point—in other words, no limiting principle. "[I]t would be difficult, except by fiat, to limit the claimed right to homosexual conduct while leaving exposed to prosecution adultery, incest and other sexual crimes even though they even though they are committed in the home. We are unwilling to start down that road." White brushed aside Marshall's *Stanley* pornography-in-the-home precedent as an irrelevant First Amendment case that involved reading materials, not sexual privacy.

White added that the "presumed belief of a majority of the electorate in Georgia that homosexual sodomy is immoral and unacceptable" is an adequate justification for outlawing it.

White's harsh, impersonal decision holding sodomy laws constitutional was originally tempered a bit: "Rather than resorting to the courts, those claiming rights involved in this case should take their case to the states, where they have often been successful. As presently advised, however, this court is of the view that it has insufficient constitutional authority to declare laws against homosexual sodomy unconstitutional." White stripped out those sentences, leaving only his brusquely snide denial that a homosexual's plea for privacy could have any legitimacy.

(White apparently did not approach *Hardwick* with a prudish desire to keep the Constitution from protecting sexual, non-marital behavior. A few years later, he would declare that nude barroom dancing was expressive behavior protected by the First Amendment. The erotic message just wouldn't be same if conveyed by a partially clothed dancer, White argued.)

When White circulated his first draft on April 21, 1986, Blackmun responded, "In due course, I shall try my hand at a dissent in this case." The next day, Powell became the first to side with White, saying, "I will join the judgment but will probably write separately." Marshall signaled he'd be joining the dissent. Rehnquist signed on to White's opinion on April 23. The remaining four justices didn't take a final stand for another two months.

As the swing vote, Powell was in the position to essentially speak for the court, if he chose. A strong, separate opinion could have gutted sodomy laws by forbidding imprisonment for private, consensual oral or anal sex. Powell clerk William Stuntz recalls rooting for that outcome. "I think it would be a wonderful thing for the Supreme Court on this particular cultural controversy—rather than to have declared an unequivocal winner (as it did with abortion, which, I think, did not promote social peace in the long run)—to have said, 'You know, it is wrong to fight these cultural battles by trying to throw your opponents in prison.' . . . [T]he middle route in [*Hardwick*] would have been a great arms-control decision."

But clerk Mike Mosman again steered Powell to the right—this time away from writing a concurrence strong enough to halt enforcement of sodomy laws. Mosman successfully pushed Powell to join White's opinion, not merely the result. Powell ended up issuing a toothless concurrence that said, "In my view, a prison sentence for such conduct—certainly a sentence of long duration—would create a serious Eighth Amendment issue. . . . In this case, however, [Hardwick] has not been tried, much less convicted and sentenced."

In a footnote, Powell said sodomy laws were so rarely enforced that they were "moribund." He should have known better: Florida's prisons chief had personally informed Powell in 1972 that at least 85 people were serving sentences of up to 20 years for so-called crimes against nature. On Powell's watch, the court had turned away men sentenced to up to 15 years in prison for oral sex. Yet, in *Hardwick*, Powell naïvely acted as if he would have voted the other way if sodomy convictions actually led to long prison sentences. His concurrence listed existing sodomy laws but deceptively masked their harshness by, for example, failing to note that consensual sodomy in Idaho could lead to a life sentence.

Compared with Powell's quiet concurrence, Chief Justice Warren Burger's was a shrill scream. Burger was in the habit of whipping out short, angry, moralistic dissents and concurrences that he dubbed "little snappers." After wildly venting his spleen, he'd usually let clerks tone down his diatribes. Burger's *Hardwick* snapper is bitingly homophobic and certainly doesn't read as if any clerk dared to touch it. Never before had a justice publicly branded gay Americans immoral or noted with apparent approval that homosexuals were once put to death:

Decisions of individuals relating to homosexual conduct have been subject to state intervention throughout the history of Western civilization. Condemnation of those practices is firmly rooted in Judeao-Christian [*sic*] moral and ethical standards. Homosexual sodomy was a capital crime under Roman law. . . . [Eighteenth-century English legal scholar Sir William] Blackstone described the "infamous crime against nature" as an offense of "deeper malignity" than rape, a heinous act "the very mention of which is a disgrace to human nature," and "a crime not fit to be named.". . . To hold that the act of homosexual sodomy is somehow protected as a fundamental right would be to cast aside millennia of moral teaching.

Burger wasn't very careful with the facts in his venomous sermonette. To depict ancient universal prohibitions on sodomy as specifically targeted at homosexual conduct was a gross distortion—much as if one were to say that Texas forbade black women to have abortions when, in fact, its law made no racial distinctions. Also, as legal scholar Arthur Leonard has pointed out, Blackstone had railed against anal sex whereas Hardwick's supposed crime was oral sex.

Burger's trusted biographer, former clerk Tim Flanagan, is the only researcher with access to the former chief justice's *Hardwick* notes. Flanagan insists that the chief justice's *Hardwick* little snapper was not propelled by "animus," that legalistic blend of animosity, hatred and general ill will. "What we would identify as gay bashing today was not part of his makeup. One thing about Warren Burger that is not widely appreciated is that he rarely said anything negative or unkind about anyone," Flanagan says.

Flanagan, who was Burger's senior clerk the year of *Hardwick*, contends it is important to remember that "people of that generation had limited experience with homosexuality. . . . I don't know of any interaction that he had with respect to homosexuals." The cartoonish depictions of Burger as a puffed-up, empty-headed, untrustworthy, law-and-order fanatic that pepper Supreme Court histories are "absolutely" unfair, according to Flanagan. "I think he's been made into a character of very limited dimension—not only the complexity of his jurisprudence but the dime-store psychoanalysis of Warren Burger that has gone on in terms of why he hated this group or that group. I think it has been unworthy of the academy," Flanagan says.

An Eloquent Plea for "Tolerance of Nonconformity"

On June 23, 1986, the day after Burger unleashed his slapdash "little snapper," Harry Blackmun, the court's most painstakingly meticulous justice, finally circulated an eloquent dissent from White's opinion. Burger and Blackmun had been kindergarten playmates in a working-class neighborhood of St. Paul, Minnesota. Blackmun, best man at Burger's wedding, had been elevated to the Supreme Court in 1970 by Nixon at Burger's suggestion. But, as their responses to Michael Hardwick's plea vividly illustrate, by 1986 their worldviews had diverged dramatically—so much so that Blackmun was unwilling to even put up a pretense of still being friends. Burger's response painted homosexuals as evil; Blackmun depicted them as victims of prejudice and as nonconformists deserving privacy, respect and fairness.

In many ways, the 77-year-old Blackmun was a Minnesota version of Powell, who was a few months his senior. Blackmun was very buttoned down and proper. "I doubt he ever kissed a woman other than his wife," says a clerk, an unabashed admirer. Like Powell, Blackmun agonized over decisions that more ideological justices found easy. He was disciplined, undemonstrative, a stalwart Methodist. He didn't swear. Dubbed "the shy person's justice" by Minnesota radio storyteller Garrison Keillor, Blackmun got a kick out of driving his humble blue Volkswagen to White House dinners packed with limos. Even on conference days, he ate lunch at his desk, preferring the sports page to the company of fellow justices.

Blackmun was appointed as a "strict constructionist" who would not read new individual rights into the Constitution's vague guarantees. And his early Supreme Court votes so mirrored Burger's law-and-order conservatism that he was derided as a "Minnesota Twin" and as "Hip Pocket Harry." Blackmun came to the court a man of limited experience. He'd happily spent the 1950s as legal counsel for the Mayo Clinic, nurturing his love of medicine. He'd devoted much of the rest of his career—first as an attorney, then as a federal appeals court judge—to tax law.

Ironically, cloistered inside the Supreme Court, Blackmun saw more of the world. "He was changed by the cases that came before him. He started getting cases at the Supreme Court that truly challenged him to think about people who were different from himself. He moved from what had been a relatively conservative bent to a real commitment to individual liberty and individual freedom," says ex-clerk Chai Feldblum, now a Georgetown University law professor.

No case changed Blackmun more than the one that made him "the most vilified Supreme Court member in history," as the Associated Press ranked him. Writing for the court in *Roe v. Wade,* Blackmun recognized a constitutional right to abortion during early pregnancy. Though seven justices, including Burger, voted for that 1973 ruling, Blackmun bore the brunt of the wrath of Americans who viewed abortion as murder. Reviled as the "butcher of Dachau," he was constantly picketed at public appearances. Gunfire burst through the front window of his apartment. Death threats were taken so seriously that he reluctantly accepted a bodyguard. He received 60,000 pieces of hate mail, much of it unspeakably vicious, and read every letter.

Blackmun's abortion decision, researched at the Mayo Clinic, was primarily concerned with doctors' rights, even though he had three daughters. As he grew to appreciate his ruling's significance to the push for women's equality, Blackmun became a feminist—focusing later abortion decisions on women's rights and hiring more female clerks than his colleagues.

With *Roe v. Wade,* Blackmun had begun to see the Constitution as a living document whose broad guarantees must be read expansively to meet society's evolving needs. Initially, though, his liberalism rarely extended beyond abortion. In 1976, he had not objected when the court upheld Virginia's sodomy law without even hearing arguments. And in 1978 he had signed onto a Rehnquist outburst that compared homosexuality to a contagious disease. (The clerk who drafted Blackmun's *Hardwick* dissent was not familiar with that 1978 case, *Ratchford v. Gay Lib*—a strong indication that Blackmun didn't view it as having any bearing on his *Hardwick* vote.) Blackmun had never pushed the court to hear gay pleas, though he probably voted in 1985 to strike down Oklahoma's gag rule on gay-friendly remarks by teachers.

Chicago law professor Norval Morris watched Blackmun's attitudes shift on gay rights as they taught two-week seminars on "Justice and Society" every summer at Colorado's Aspen Institute. Asked about Blackmun's gay-rights evolution, Morris gruffly barked, "It was pretty obvious." He added, "I wasn't at all surprised by his position on *Bowers v. Hardwick.*"

Yet Blackmun's dissent was "very, very surprising" to gay-law expert Arthur Leonard. "It seems to me that Blackmun became sort of an inadvertent champion of gay civil rights as part of his larger program of preserving the right of privacy, which is absolutely necessary in order to preserve the right, as he saw it, to an abortion," Leonard says.

Justices without blinders knew there were gay officials in the court's public information and administrative offices, according to Powell aide Sally Smith. Blackmun didn't wear blinders. "We talked about lots of gay people in the court. You forget that there were gay clerks," Morris says. Blackmun had heard rumors about gay Powell clerk David Charny's supposed affair and knew Powell had a gay clerk when he was blithely announcing he'd never known a homosexual, Morris adds. According to Morris and the clerk who drafted Blackmun's *Hardwick* dissent, Blackmun also knew that his own former clerk Al Lauber was gay.

When Lauber clerked for Blackmun in 1978–79, he was married to a woman. But he'd been out of the closet for two years when *Hardwick* hit the court. That's about the time, Lauber believes, that Blackmun heard through the clerks' grapevine about Lauber's sexual orientation. The Reagan White House had wanted the justices to use a Pennsylvania abortion case to overturn *Roe v. Wade.* The task of writing that brief fell to Deputy Solicitor General Lauber. He refused to put his name on the brief because he disagreed with it and found it awkward for a former Blackmun clerk to be arguing against the privacy rights recognized by *Roe v. Wade.* "Everyone was wondering who the hell had worked on this brief," Lauber recalls. "They found that I had done it. And I think at that point there was a lot of 'Well, what a hypocrite. He's gay.'"

To Blackmun, learning about Lauber meant discovering there was someone gay in his family—because the justice treated his clerks as beloved daughters and sons. He called ex-clerks' children "the office grandchildren." Gay ex-clerk J. Paul Oetken, a White House attorney during the Clinton administration, recalls, "Being a law clerk to him meant something very special. And I think it's because when he hired us it was immediately clear that he was accepting us into his chamber's family." Blackmun and his wife, Dottie, entertained the clerks in their home. At Christmas, "there would be little presents—an autographed

copy of the Constitution, the formal photograph of all the justices and
their signatures. He was very fatherly that way," Lauber says. "I think
probably on gay rights he originally thought of it as a sort of kinky, weird
thing. But I think once it became clear to him that there was sort of
family there, too, [in relationships,] then it became much easier for him
to understand and accept," Lauber adds.

Also, unlike his ex-friend Burger, Blackmun didn't sneer at psychiatry. He had voted against allowing death-penalty juries to rely on pre-
dictions of the convicted criminal's future dangerousness because the
American Psychiatric Association had deemed such forecasts unreli-
able. Like Justices Douglas and Fortas before him, Blackmun cared
what mainstream psychiatry had to say about homosexuality. When the
court upheld Virginia's sodomy law in 1976, Blackmun very likely had
not read the court document that mentioned that the APA no longer
considered homosexuality sick. But by *Hardwick,* he had gotten the
message that, in the judgment of leading mental health professionals,
there was nothing wrong with being gay.

When Blackmun discussed the case in his chambers, he gave no indication that supporting Michael Hardwick's privacy rights represented
any sort of switch for him. He saw that position as flowing out of his
abortion-rights decisions. And he depicted it as consistent with what
he'd been saying for years at the Aspen Institute when he conducted
discussions on the debates that led up to Britain's decriminalization of
sodomy. Blackmun's *Hardwick* dissent drew heavily on British legal
scholar H. L. A. Hart's position, articulated during those debates, that
private sexual behavior ought not be outlawed simply because it is
widely considered immoral unless it harms others. Or, as Hart put it,
quoting a 1957 British report that recommended legalizing homosexual
practices between consenting adults: "There must remain a realm of
private morality and immorality which is, in brief and crude terms, not
the law's business."

Former clerk Pam Karlan, a Stanford University law professor, modestly declines to confirm that she drafted Blackmun's *Hardwick* dissent.
Other clerks readily credit her not just with crafting it but with eloquently elevating it to a quotable national landmark on the road to full
equality for gay Americans. "Blackmun's clerks write all his opinions.
He sort of places a comma and changes your adverbs and stuff. So, I'm

not sure that he would have personally written the opinion quite as rhetorically powerful as it was. Pam Karlan wrote it," Lauber says.

Just days before Blackmun circulated his dissent, Burger and O'Connor joined White, giving him the necessary five-member majority.

Blackmun's dissent depicted the court's majority as so blinded by prejudice that it could not see beyond Michael Hardwick's homosexuality to the "fundamental" freedoms that sodomy laws trample. Blackmun's use of the word "fundamental" was critical, a code word signaling that Georgia's law ought to be subjected to "strict scrutiny." To meet that tough standard, the state would need to prove that the law was both justified by a "compelling state interest" and "narrowly tailored" to advancing that interest. His dissent made clear that Blackmun saw no way that Georgia could prove its law valid.

Sodomy laws infringe on the rights to privacy and to freedom of association, Blackmun declared. And homosexuals—the dissent did not use the word "gay"—are civilized people with just as much right as anyone else "to be let alone." Rhetorically wrapping homosexuals in the Constitution's embrace, his ringing dissent began, "This case is no more about 'a fundamental right to engage in homosexual sodomy' . . . than *Stanley v. Georgia* was about a fundamental right to watch obscene movies, or *Katz v. United States* was about a fundamental right to place interstate bets from a telephone booth. Rather, this case is about 'the most comprehensive of rights and the right most valued by civilized men,' namely, 'the right to be let alone'."

Quoting an 1897 *Harvard Law Review* article by Oliver Wendell Holmes, Blackmun declared, "[I]t is revolting to have no better reason for a rule of law than that . . . it was laid down in the time of Henry IV. It is still more revolting if the grounds upon which it was laid down have vanished long since, and the rule simply persists from blind imitation of the past." The right to privacy, Blackmun argued, demands that "before Georgia can prosecute its citizens for making choices about the most intimate aspects of their lives, it must do more than assert that the choice they have made is an 'abominable crime not fit to be named among Christians.'"

Blackmun derided the majority's "obsessive focus on homosexual activity." Georgia's sodomy law applied to everyone, he noted: "Unlike the court, the Georgia legislature has not proceeded on the assumption that homosexuals are so different from other citizens that their lives may be controlled in a way that would not be tolerated if it limited the choices of those other citizens." Hardwick's claim "does not depend in any way on his sexual orientation," he added.

With nods toward Powell's "cruel and unusual punishment" argument and Brennan's historic dissent on behalf of counselor Marjorie Rowland, Blackmun said Michael Hardwick might indeed have valid claims under the Eighth Amendment and, if Georgia's enforcement targeted homosexuals, the 14th Amendment's Equal Protection Clause. However, in his view, Hardwick's privacy and freedom of association claims were so strong that the other protections did not need to come into play.

Just as Justices Douglas, Fortas and Brennan had attempted to be up to date in discussing immigrant Clive Boutilier in 1967, Blackmun tried to wrest homosexuality away from the ancient prejudices that were the bedrock of White's ruling. He declared, "Despite historical views of homosexuality it is no longer viewed by mental health professionals as a 'disease' or disorder. . . . [N]either is it simply a matter of deliberate personal election. Homosexual orientation may well form part of the very fiber of an individual's personality. . . . An individual's ability to make constitutionally protected 'decisions concerning sexual relations' is rendered empty indeed if he or she is given no real choice but a life without any physical intimacy."

Virtually shaking a disapproving finger at the majority, Blackmun declared,

> Only the most willful blindness could obscure the fact that sexual intimacy is "a sensitive, key relationship of human existence, central to family life, community welfare, and the development of the human personality." The fact that individuals define themselves in a significant way through their intimate sexual relationships with others suggests, in a nation as diverse as ours, that there may be many "right" ways of conducting those relationships, and that much of the richness of a relationship comes from the freedom an individual has to *choose* the form and nature of these intensely personal bonds. . . . [W]hat the court has really refused to recognize is the fundamental interest all individuals have in controlling the nature of their intimate associations with others.

Scolding the majority for its "failure to comprehend the magnitude of the liberty interests at stake in this case," Blackmun poked holes in Georgia's justifications for its sodomy law. He seemed to take special pleasure in deriding the argument that ancient, biblical prohibitions against sodomy made Georgia's law valid in 1986. "I cannot agree that either the length of time a majority has held its convictions or the passions with which it defends them can withdraw legislation from this court's scrutiny," Blackmun said, citing rulings that powerfully struck down strong, traditional bans: His 1973 abortion decision, the 1967 *Loving v. Virginia* interracial marriage ruling and the 1954 *Brown v. Board* desegregation decision. "The parallel between *Loving* and this case is almost uncanny," Blackmun noted. He pointed out that the states had been just as opposed to interracial marriage as they were to sodomy when the Bill of Rights and 14th Amendment were enacted. And he quoted the Virginia judge who, in upholding an interracial marriage ban, had stated, "Almighty God created the races white, black, yellow, malay and red, and he placed them on separate continents. . . . The fact that he separated the races shows that he did not intend for the races to mix."

Blackmun argued, "A state can no more punish private behavior because of religious intolerance than it can punish such behavior because of racial animus. 'The Constitution cannot control such prejudices, but neither can it tolerate them'. . . . No matter how uncomfortable a certain group may make the majority of this court, we have held that 'mere public intolerance or animosity cannot constitutionally justify the deprivation of a person's physical liberty.'"

While White's majority opinion smirkily ridiculed gay claims, Blackmun cast *Hardwick* as a vitally important minority-rights case: "It is precisely because the issue raised by this case touches the heart of what makes individuals what they are that we should be especially sensitive to the rights of those whose choices upset the majority." Quoting British legal scholar H. L. A. Hart, Blackmun added, "Reasonable people may differ about whether particular sexual acts are moral or immoral, but 'we have ample evidence for believing that people will not abandon morality, will not think any better of murder, cruelty and dishonesty, merely because some private sexual practice which they abominate is not punished by law.'"

The final, stirring words of Blackmun's dissent provided solace to every gay American. Blackmun told the nation: "I can only hope that . . . the court soon will reconsider its analysis and conclude that depriving individuals of their intimate relationships poses a far greater threat to the values most deeply rooted in our nation's history than tolerance of nonconformity could ever do. Because I think the court today betrays those values, I dissent."

Powell was incensed that Blackmun's dissent dared mention the *Moore v. East Cleveland* decision, Powell's 1977 ruling striking down a strange zoning ordinance that had barred a grandmother from sharing her "single-family" house with two grandchildren if they were cousins, not siblings. "I find it more than a little curious to . . . analogize *Moore's* focus on the importance of the 'family' to the conduct of sodomy in private. The fundamental reason for the condemnation of sodomy has been its *antithesis* to family. The preservation of civilization depends upon family and the bearing of children," Powell seethed in a new footnote. After cooling off, he decided against keeping it. (Of course, contraception and abortion—both of which Powell viewed as constitutionally protected— interfered more directly with procreation.)

Stevens, Brennan and Marshall immediately joined Blackmun's history-making dissent. Stevens also wrote a separate dissent, which Brennan and Marshall joined. Because he wrote his own first drafts, Stevens needed only two clerks, not the usual four. (Rehnquist, whose priority was having a foursome for tennis, had three.) Stevens's *Hardwick* dissent analytically demolished White's claim that Georgia's law was clearly constitutional. Stevens began by echoing Blackmun's effort to set the record straight: Laws down through the ages had been "equally damning" of heterosexual and homosexual sodomy, condemning both as sinfully unnatural. There was no marital exception. Georgia's law fit into that tradition, so White twisted the facts when he "presumed" that Georgians viewed homosexual sodomy as immoral. Rather, Stevens said, Georgia's law "presumably reflects the belief all sodomy is immoral and unacceptable."

To Stevens, *Hardwick* presented two questions: May a state universally outlaw sodomy? If not, may a state preserve its sodomy law by enforcing it only against homosexuals?

Privacy rulings proved, he said, that a law isn't legitimate simply because it is based on a majority view of morality and that marital intimacy—"even when not intended to produce offspring"—is constitutionally protected: "The essential 'liberty' that animated the development of the law in cases like *Griswold, Eisenstadt* and *Carey* surely embraces the right to engage in non-reproductive, sexual conduct that others may consider offensive or immoral. Paradoxical as it may seem, our prior cases thus establish that a state may not prohibit sodomy within 'the sacred precincts of marital bedrooms,' or indeed, between unmarried heterosexual adults."

Stevens read privacy precedents as meaning Georgia's law could not be constitutionally applied to heterosexuals. And unless there was a better reason for discriminatory enforcement than had been offered, he viewed the Equal Protection Clause as barring the targeting of homosexuals. "Either the persons to whom Georgia seeks to apply its statute do not have the same interest in 'liberty' that others have," Stevens said, "or there must be a reason why the state may be permitted to apply a generally applicable law to certain people that it does not apply to others." Stevens continued:

> The first possibility is plainly unacceptable. . . . [T]he principle that 'all men are created equal' . . . must surely mean that every free citizen has the same interest in "liberty." . . . [T]he homosexual and the heterosexual have the same interest in deciding how he will live his own life, and, more narrowly, how he will conduct himself in his personal and voluntary associations with his companions. . . . The second possibility is equally unacceptable. A policy of selective application must be supported by a neutral and legitimate interest—something more substantial than a habitual dislike for, or ignorance about, the disfavored group. Neither the state nor the court has identified any such interest in this case.

With their *Hardwick* dissents, four justices were publicly stating that anti-gay prejudice is not a legitimate foundation for a law. It would be another decade before a Supreme Court majority decision would embrace that view.

On Monday, June 30, 1986, the justices filed into their ornate court-room and dramatically announced their 5-to-4 decision against respecting the sexual privacy of gay Americans. White chose to read large portions of his opinion aloud. So did Blackmun, his voice brimming with barely contained anger at what he saw as the majority's willful blindness. It was the only time Blackmun read aloud from the bench that term, former clerk Pam Karlan recalls.

The Supreme Court's *Hardwick* ruling was gay Americans' most devastating legal setback of the 20th century. For decades, the court had done little and said even less about cases involving homosexuality. The court had ignored the blossoming of the civil rights movement demanding full equality for tens of millions of gay and bisexual Americans. Yet the court's passive hostility, punctuated by active hostility, had had a limited impact because it drew little public attention. Now, with *Hardwick,* the very court whose most lasting glory was its role in ending legalized race discrimination was twisting Georgia's universal sodomy law into a weapon to bash a much-maligned minority group. The court that had spent decades detailing heterosexual privacy rights had suddenly, loudly declared that homosexuals were different. Upholding the sodomy laws that provided the legal underpinnings for anti-gay discrimination put the court squarely on the side of the far-right zealots working to keep gay Americans second class. Everyday gay Americans suddenly realized that the nation's highest court was enemy territory.

"Shame! Shame! Shame!"

Shortly before the Supreme Court ruled, Michael Hardwick moved to Miami. He'd been nervous living in Atlanta, fearful that the Ku Klux Klan would somehow track down the gay man challenging the sodomy law. He'd even taken the precaution of switching his electric bill to someone else's name before deciding it was safest just to leave the state.

On the morning on June 30, 1986, Hardwick was slicing and dicing finger food for the free lunchtime buffet at the Miami gay bar where he worked when a friend showed up in tears and broke the news that he'd lost. "I was totally stunned," he recalled. "I just cried . . . because to me it was frightening to think that in the year 1986 our Supreme Court, next to God, could make a decision that was more suitable to the mentality of the Spanish Inquisition."

Hardwick, 32, was terrified that a TV news crew was able to locate him that night. But a few days later he agreed to go on the *Phil Donahue Show*. Though fearful he'd be shot, he started throwing himself into interviews, talk shows and rallies. He flew to New York City to join civil rights activist Bayard Rustin, who was gay, in speaking at protest rally. Hardwick, then a sculptor as well as a bartender, toyed with the idea of entering law school. "Once you get involved in the legal system, you realize the implications," he explained. "People have no idea about these nine justices who sit up here and make decisions that affect their daily lives in millions of ways. . . . Gays are just a step up from drug addicts in the way society treats us. We're second-class citizens."

The day the high court announced its fateful decision, Hardwick called attorney Laurence Tribe and was surprised to find him "more devastated than I was." Kathleen Sullivan, Tribe's co-counsel, once remarked that losing *Hardwick* "burned a hole in Larry." Tribe agrees: "When I learned we had lost, I felt as though someone had kicked me really hard right in the gut. The wind was knocked right out of me. It's not that I had expected to win. Even after an oral argument that felt unexpectedly good, I realized as an objective matter that the odds were against our winning. But . . . I could still hope. . . . The reason the defeat affected me so strongly, I suppose, was that the basic human right the court denied—the right of sexual intimacy with one's chosen consenting adult partner—seems undeniable in any but a totalitarian vision of the legal order. . . ."

Hindsight hasn't altered Tribe's assessment of the most promising way to approach the case. ". . . I can think even now of no way of briefing and arguing the *Hardwick* case that would have given us any better chance of winning," he says. He believes an equal protection argument accusing Georgia of discriminatory enforcement would have been "a fool's errand." Georgia had prosecuted heterosexuals for private consensual sodomy. Also, Tribe thinks, "a majority of the court would have thought that using the law only for homosexuals liaisons was reasonable."

As news of what both *The New York Times* and *The Washington Post* called the court's "bitterly divided" opinion splashed across front pages, reaction was vociferous and far more negative than the detached justices had probably expected. "What now? Can we expect an army of police to be assigned peeping patrol, instructed to barge into bedrooms and arrest anyone who deviates from the most conventional sexual practice?" the *Post* sarcastically inquired. The *Times* blasted White's opinion as "a gratuitous and petty ruling, an offense to American society's maturing standards of individual dignity." Legal scholars' critiques were similarly scathing.

Meanwhile, the Reverend Jerry Falwell, whose fundamentalist Moral Majority regularly used inflammatory anti-gay rhetoric in fundraising pitches, hailed the ruling against "perverted" behavior. U.S. Attorney General Ed Meese proclaimed the *Hardwick* decision to be the Reagan administration's biggest Supreme Court victory of the term.

The public disapproved of policing bedrooms. A Gallup poll conducted July 1–2, 1986 found by 57 percent to 34 percent American adults thought states should not "have the right to prohibit particular sexual practices conducted in private between consenting adult homosexuals." Adults aware of the *Hardwick* decision disapproved of it, 47 percent to 41 percent. That's the equivalent of a 4-$\frac{4}{5}$-to-4-$\frac{1}{5}$ Supreme Court vote or, forced into whole numbers, a 5-to-4 victory for gay rights. Public sentiment would have pushed the fence-sitting Powell onto Hardwick's side.

Upon hearing the court's decision, Thomas Stoddard, executive director of the Lambda Legal Defense and Education Fund, captured the magnitude of the defeat when he lamented, "For the gay-rights movement, this is our *Dred Scott* case." Stoddard was referring to the court's notorious 1857 decision upholding slavery and ruling that blacks were "beings of an inferior order, so far inferior that they had no rights which the white man was bound to respect."

The years since *Hardwick* haven't tempered gay-rights litigators' assessments. "It was so vicious, so mean—probably the single most vile and unpleasant opinion the Supreme Court decided in the second half of the 20th century. And certainly the most contemptuous of any single group of Americans," says Matt Coles, head of the ACLU's gay-rights division. Lambda director Kevin Cathcart calls *Hardwick* "a clear reminder of the incredible ignorance that many people, including Supreme Court justices, have about gay people and gay life and the role of sodomy laws. We were demonized." Yet he says, Blackmun's dissent was "so beautifully written. I would describe it as really understanding sexuality and its role in life and the importance to gay people of being free of sodomy laws. . . . [Blackmun] gave us hope that it wasn't hopeless."

That dissent showed "Justice Blackmun to be the hero of his own life" and demonstrated "his fierce commitment to enabling others to become the heroes of their own lives as well," according to his clerk Pam Karlan. Another Blackmun clerk, lesbian Chai Feldblum, says, Blackmun's dissent "did start us down the road to having people see us as full human beings. . . . It was a dissent so it didn't have the legal force of law, but it still had the force of rhetoric. And that made a huge difference. . . . It will be cited when, ultimately, *Hardwick* is overturned."

Much like Anita Bryant's homophobic "Save Our Children" campaign nearly a decade earlier, the *Hardwick* decision generated a new wave of gay-rights activists. The monumental defeat felt like a "kick 'em while they're down" decision, coming as it did when the gay community was struggling to cope with the early devastation of AIDS.

Angry but determined to fight for basic civil rights, 500,000 gay men and lesbians marched through the nation's capital on October 11, 1987, setting a record for a gay-rights rally. Two days later, in a carefully choreographed six-hour display of civil disobedience, Michael Hardwick and 571 other demonstrators were arrested in front of the Supreme Court, despite the First Amendment right "of the people peaceably to assemble and to petition the government for a redress of grievances." Never before had so many people been arrested at the court.

Any justice who wanted to see the face of gay America could have looked out the court's front windows as protestors shouted "Shame! Shame! Shame!" and as wave after wave of them were dragged to police cars. "Every day we commit an act of civil disobedience by loving each other," lesbian Pat Norman, an organizer of Sunday's march, shouted. Protesters, most wearing the "Silence = Death" T-shirts of the AIDS activism group ACT-UP, injected characteristically gay humor into the deadly serious protest. "Your gloves don't match your shoes, your gloves don't match your shoes," they shouted at police officers, ridiculing the white plastic gloves donned as supposed protection from the AIDS virus. "Equal justice under the law, that's what it says on the wall," the protesters shouted, pointing at the promise carved into stone. Once arrested, many demonstrators gave powerfully symbolic pseudonyms like

"Harvey Milk," San Francisco's slain gay supervisor, or "Sharon Kowal-ski," the disabled lesbian whom the court had turned away.

By the time of the arrests, the extent of the legal devastation wrought by *Hardwick* was becoming evident. Judges were citing the ruling as proof not just that gay Americans didn't have sexual privacy rights but that virtually any law singling out gay people for second-class treatment was constitutional. "If the [Supreme] Court was unwilling to object to state laws that criminalize the behavior that defines the class, it is hardly open to a lower court to conclude that state-sponsored discrimi-nation against the class is invidious," Judge Laurence Silberman of the D.C. Circuit Court of Appeals wrote in 1987, ruling against a lesbian trying to become an FBI agent.

In the age-old equations perpetuated by Silberman and embraced by many other judges, sodomy = homosexuality and homosexuality = crim-inality. They saw anti-gay laws and policies as restricting criminals. The fact that oral and/or anal sex was featured in the sexual repertoire of many heterosexuals, like some but not all homosexuals, might matter to researchers but apparently didn't to many judges: Homosexuals were "sodomites."

"The *Hardwick* decision has had enormous impact . . . far broader than it ought to have," Lambda director Kevin Cathcart says. "Courts have used it as sort of a blanket reference they throw in whenever they want to just deny any kind of rights to lesbians and gay men."

The Search for a Scapegoat

The court's *Hardwick* decision had hit with explosive force on June 30, 1986—rocking gay Americans back on their heels, instantly radicalizing many who'd never been politically active. Though they lived every day without rights like marriage and military service that heterosexuals took for granted, gay Americans were shocked at being branded second class by the very court that had freed black Americans from racial segrega-tion. It was one thing for gay Americans to believe that the nation's top court had simply not yet gotten around to recognizing the existence of their constitutional rights. It was far more devastating to wake up and read in the morning newspaper that the court had essentially declared a gay exception to the Constitution's guarantees.

The Supreme Court wasn't merely refusing to be an instrument of gay Americans' liberation. Its snidely dismissive majority decision was providing reinforcing sodomy laws—primarily used to hold back gay progress by stigmatizing gay people as deviant, immoral outlaws. Gay anger and bitterness over *Hardwick* were heightened when *The Washington Post* revealed two weeks later that the decision had originally gone the other way: Justice Powell had switched. People who strongly believed *Hardwick's* outcome should have been different now knew it easily could have been. That knowledge was underscored when, after retiring, Powell publicly called his vote to uphold sodomy laws a mistake.

Because the Supreme Court, as an institution, is impossible for voters to hold accountable, there is a natural tendency among Americans deeply upset by a decision to latch on to one individual to blame. Segregationists wanted to "Impeach Earl Warren," even though the court's landmark 1954 *Brown v. Board* desegregation ruling was unanimous. Abortion foes hated Blackmun because he wrote the 7-to-2 *Roe v. Wade* decision. After *Hardwick* was handed down, what little was publicly known about the court's inner workings fueled an unconscious quest for a villain. White and Burger were obvious candidates, as was Georgia's attorney general. But, as the swing vote, Powell made a psychologically more satisfying target because his indecisiveness was a painful reminder that the outcome could have been different. Plus, Powell publicly minimized the case's importance—a dismissive attitude that cut gay Americans to the quick.

Within gay circles, word spread that Powell had had a gay clerk who had not come out. This unnamed gay clerk was forced to shoulder much of the blame for the *Hardwick* decision. Unbeknownst to him for years, Cabell Chinnis became the unidentified subject of gay urban myths. He was labeled a self-hating homosexual, a latter-day J. Edgar Hoover, the devil's handmaiden. Persistent rumors depicted the unknown clerk as too cowardly or selfish to say the three magical words that supposedly would have secured Powell's vote and a gay victory—"I am gay." A recent history of the gay movement quotes a gay-rights attorney, now deceased, as claiming, "Some of the gay lawyers involved in the case knew one of the Powell clerks was homosexual, and they pleaded with him to come out to the justice in hopes that might influence Powell, but the clerk declined. . . ." That scenario is a total fabrication, Chinnis says emphatically: "I never had any communication with anyone outside the Supreme Court about a pending case. I'm absolutely adamant about that." Any such contact, he points out, would have been unethical.

In *The Epistemology of the Closet*, "queer theorist" Eve Kosofsky Sedgwick ruminated about "a hypothetical closeted gay clerk" who worked for the justice who cast *Hardwick*'s decisive vote. She wrote of speculating with friends "what it could have felt like to be a closeted gay court assistant, or clerk, or justice, who might have had some degree, even a very high one, of instrumentality in conceiving or formulating or 'refining' or logistically facilitating this ruling, these ignominious majority opinions, the assaultive sentences in which they were framed."

As recently as 1999 a top gay-rights litigator self-righteously fumed, "You know, there was a gay clerk in Powell's chambers who didn't come out. He ought to be hanged."

From the perspective of Chinnis's co-clerk Ann Coughlin, "The criticisms of Cabell have seemed incredibly unfair because going into conference we were certain that Powell was going to vote [in Hardwick's favor], so why would Cabell have to out himself?" Powell had had "many, many gay clerks," she added. "I guess any one of them could have outed themself. Nobody did."

Chinnis says, quite believably, that he was prepared to beg Powell as an openly gay man but that such an emotional plea seemed both unnecessary and unwise: He had been assured that Powell would vote against the sodomy law. Later, when Powell switched, Chinnis didn't know until it was too late. Chinnis is plagued by the sense that life might now be far better for gay Americans if he'd just done something differently. His gnawing, guilty feeling of somehow not having done the right thing—but still not knowing what it was—is shared by two heterosexual Powell clerks—Ann Coughlin and William Stuntz. Other gay Powell clerks admit that they, too, wonder if they could have made a difference by coming out.

The image of Powell that emerges from the many dizzying *Hardwick* memos in his court papers is of a justice whose head was spinning. Here was an essentially decent, dedicated but intellectually exhausted old man who was flailing about as he tried to understand homosexuality while clinging to the blinders that blocked out the gay parts of his world. If Powell deserves to be blamed by gay Americans, it's perhaps as much for his unprofessional failure to rid himself of his squeamishness about dealing with homosexual cases as for his *Hardwick* vote. If he had bothered to use earlier homosexual cases to educate himself about homosexuality during his first 14 years on the court, his handling of *Hardwick* might have been more level-headed. Powell's more progressive colleagues also can be blamed for not attempting to tear away his blinders. When Powell claimed that he'd never met a homosexual, none of the other justices replied, "Wake up, Lewis. You've probably had more gay clerks than any of the rest of us. In fact, you had two in one year not long ago."

Yes, Powell's *Hardwick* vote might well have been different—if he had gotten different advice, more information, stayed in the struggle longer. But, so might have O'Connor's, according to her ex-clerks. The "what if" scenarios are endless: What if, for example, Abe Fortas, who kept himself up to date on psychiatric thinking, had been confirmed as chief justice? What if Arthur Goldberg, who became vocally gay-friendly in his later years, had never resigned? What if President Carter had gotten the chance to appoint progressive civil rights advocates to the Supreme Court? Carter-appointed lower court judges have been responsible for many of the gay civil rights movement's legal victories.

The fact that four justices sided with gay Americans in *Hardwick* is what's remarkable, given the court's long-time antipathy toward homosexuals. All nine justices had been appointed by presidents whose administrations were hostile to gay civil rights. All nine had been confirmed by an anti-gay Senate. The court's decades-long refusal to take the claims of gay Americans seriously had never sparked an outcry from the press or public. Everyone seeking someone to blame for *Hardwick*'s outcome needs to ask: Why did the basic constitutional rights of millions of Americans hinge on the secret ballot of one worn-out justice?

A Long, Secret Struggle over a "Frivolous" Case

The decent, fundamentally good-hearted man who cast the decisive vote in *Hardwick* agonized over that ruling long after it was handed down. Publicly, Justice Powell played down the case's importance. Privately, he sought to make peace with his anti-gay vote by concocting new justifications for it. His post-ruling mental tug-of-war with himself began in August 1986 as he told the American Bar Association, "The case may not be as significant as press reports suggest." Sodomy laws are "moribund and rarely enforced," he claimed.

Three years after his 1987 retirement, Powell publicly confessed that he'd "probably made a mistake" in *Hardwick*. After Powell branded his vote a mistake, he told a *Washington Post* reporter, "So far as I'm concerned it's just part of my past and not very important. I don't supposed I've devoted half an hour" to thinking about it since the ruling.

An inch-thick legal-sized file that stayed in the retired justice's Supreme Court office after most of his court papers had been shipped to the Washington and Lee University law library puts the lie to Powell's claims. Powell's extensive, handwritten notes and post-retirement memos reveal that he kept rearguing the case with himself, kept fighting with Blackmun's dissent and counted the ruling among the court's most important privacy decisions.

Hardwick was among the cases the retired Powell reviewed most thoroughly in 1988 and 1989 before lecturing at the University of Virginia and Washington and Lee. Girding himself for a March 1988 seminar on due process, Powell wrote two memos, totaling 11 pages, analyzing the case. "I will be grilled as to how *Hardwick* can be reconciled with *Roe v. Wade,* and to a lesser extent with the *City of East Cleveland* [Powell's extended-family zoning decision]," Powell's first memo said. Powell reminded himself to ask law students: "What does 'sodomy' contribute to family life?"

Powell also had clerk Bob Werner produce a due process memo focused on *Hardwick*. Werner found some merit in White's majority decision but ultimately sided with the dissent—spurring Powell to respond "No." To Werner's repeated assertion that homosexual sodomy was victimless, Powell three times wrote "AIDS" in the margin—though the disease had not been among his reasons for siding with White. Powell wrote that the "sanctity of the home," family and history didn't support a sodomy-rights decision. When Werner declared "sexual intimacy . . . is important to the development of the human personality," Powell, aghast, wrote "sodomy!?!!"

Powell's second memo concluded by citing the language in Harlan's classic *Poe v. Ullman* dissent that listed "homosexuality" among activities "the state forbids altogether."

Powell counted the times that Blackmun's dissent had irked him by mentioning "family" and "home." Beside its mention of "family life," Powell hostilely asked, "what family?" Powell saw "no limiting principle" in Blackmun's "right to be let alone." Next to Blackmun's eloquent statement about the threat posed by intolerance, Powell wrote "error" and "history is contrary."

In a handwritten outline of key points for his seminar, Powell showed a male and biblical bias by characterizing the court's contraceptive decisions as establishing a "right to beget." In reference to sodomy he wrote, "AIDS (blood transfusions). There are victims—innocent ones."

Yet in reviewing Chief Justice Burger's contention that knocking down sodomy laws would "cast aside millennia of moral teaching," Powell circled "moral" and put a question mark beside it. Powell wrote, "Not a question of morality w/ [with] me."

Nowhere in his class preparation notes does Powell conclude his *Hardwick* vote was an error. The closest he came was in a margin note on a copy of White's ruling. Powell said, "DC [district court] found no standing. I should have done this." That district court assessment, of course, had applied only to the married couple who had tried to join the case.

When Powell discussed *Hardwick* during his 1988–89 seminars, he didn't call his vote a mistake. However, on October 18, 1990—four years after *Hardwick* branded gay Americans second class—he told students at New York University's law school, "I think I probably made a mistake in that one." That almost unprecedented admission of error by a former justice was triggered, he said, by a question about "any decision I made I had doubts about in retrospect." The 83-year-old Powell was in Manhattan to deliver the school's annual James Madison lecture. Among the guests—invited because of her Powell connection—was a lesbian former clerk. With a pained laugh, she recalls feeling, "Too bad you didn't think of this years ago."

A few days after calling his vote a mistake, Powell inadvertently rubbed salt in gay Americans' wounds by saying, "That case was not a major case, and one of the reasons I voted the way I did was the case was a frivolous case" filed "just to see what the court would do."

Powell somewhat disingenuously explained his change of heart to *The National Law Journal* by saying, "When I had the opportunity to reread the opinions a few months later, I thought the dissent had the better of the arguments." Powell's explanation was misleading because his high-profile switch had effectively cast his vote in concrete months before Blackmun's dissent was even drafted. Blackmun never had had a real chance to win Powell's support by making "the better of the arguments."

Later, in a letter to Tribe, Powell said, "I did think the case was frivolous as the Georgia statute had not been enforced since 1935. The court should not have granted *certiorari*." The damage done by *Hardwick*, of course, could not be undone by a flip-flopping retired justice's change of heart. "There are numerous people in America who wouldn't have gone to jail if Justice Powell had come to his enlightenment earlier," William B. Rubenstein pointed out while director of the ACLU's gay-rights project.

The Powell clerks most upset by Powell's *Hardwick* vote got little satisfaction from his saying that he'd been wrong. Rather, they say, it deepened their feelings of inadequacy because it meant that Powell must have been reachable, that his anti-gay vote had never been chiseled in stone. Three of Powell's four 1985–86 clerks—Cabell Chinnis, Ann Coughlin and William Stuntz—readily admit to nagging guilt feelings.

Gay-friendly liberal Ann Coughlin regrets having taken herself out of the running for handling *Hardwick,* which ended up in the hands of ideological conservative Michael Mosman. She says, "I didn't know why Bill or Cabell didn't end up being the clerk in charge of *Bowers v. Hardwick,* but I know why I didn't. It's because I thought there's no way I could talk about sex with [Powell]. . . . I felt it would potentially backfire if I, as a woman, were to come forward and try to educate him. . . . When we think about these failures in our lives . . . for me, the failure was to think, 'Well, I can't have an explicit conversation with him about sex.'"

William Stuntz, who had wanted Powell to find a way to disarm sodomy laws without proclaiming a new fundamental right, sees the *Hardwick* ruling as a "very sad result." He says,

> In one sense, Tribe blew it. The clerks blew it. . . . Had we given [Powell] the right argument the case would have come out differently. I don't think Tribe can be fairly blamed for that. I don't think we can be

fairly blamed for that. We were 27-year-olds. . . . I feel guilty about it on some level, but I don't think we can fairly be blamed for fumbling around in the dark and not seizing on the right argument. Of course, Powell bears responsibility. It's his vote. But it's a job in which these decisions are made much more quickly than one might assume from reading the files. . . . He is juggling lots of things. He's a very old man. He's very tired. And I don't think he can be fairly blamed for what amounts to failure of judgment on his part.

The passage of time hasn't caused Mosman to feel guilty, he says. The uneasiness evident in his voice when he discusses the decision is, he explains, a result of the clumsy way the court grappled with sodomy. "Everybody—Blackmun, White and Burger's letter—they're all throwing around social science statistics and perceived wisdoms they're picking up who knows where. It's a crummy way to decide an issue. I think we were all just in there using bad tools to decide an important question," he contends.

In describing the struggle over *Hardwick,* Powell biographer John Jeffries Jr. wrote, "Never before had Powell faced an issue for which he was by instinct and experience so uniquely unprepared." Yet if Powell had never before faced sodomy and homosexuality, he had largely himself to blame. More than two dozen homosexual cases—some involving long prison terms for sodomy—had come before the court since he had taken his oath of office in early 1972. Actually reading the court documents filed in those cases would give anyone a fairly thorough understanding of how sodomy laws are used to stigmatize and legally discriminate against a whole class of Americans, including undeniably outstanding teachers and sailors. Powell left that reading to his clerks. Powell usually had as little as possible to do with those cases.

Though Powell had done his best to duck homosexual issues, he was, as his clerks were well aware, a compassionate man capable of understanding the human toll exacted by rigid attempts to control sexuality. Powell's steadfast support for abortion rights was partially grounded in a panicked phone call he'd received from his 19-year-old office boy while working in his Richmond law firm. The distraught teenager's pregnant lover had died as he tried to help her illegally abort her fetus.

Not only was a woman dead because abortion was outlawed, Powell's young assistant could have been sent to prison.

Especially after Powell declared that he'd made a mistake in *Hardwick,* his long line of gay clerks was plagued by questions about whether one or more of them should have come out to him before his 1986 vote. Could they have made him better prepared to wrestle with *Hardwick?* Could they have helped him see that the human toll of sodomy laws?

Not surprisingly, Cabell Chinnis is the ex-clerk most bedeviled by unanswerable questions. "I wish I knew why he changed his vote because then maybe I would be able to say to myself, 'Cabell, anything else you could have done wouldn't have made a difference.'. . . It's the not knowing that really kills you," Chinnis said before war-gaming a series of "what if" scenarios over lunch in 1998.

What if he or Coughlin had handled the case? What if he had invited Powell to lunch and come out to him? What if he had hosted a dinner in which, one by one, gay Powell clerks had risen and said, "Justice Powell, I am a homosexual. This is my partner. We've been together four years." Or, "Justice Powell, I'm a lesbian. I want to be judged on my work and my character not my sexual orientation. I don't want to have to live in fear."

What if Chinnis had done something overt and it had backfired? "I never thought of that," he gasped in horror. "I really think I would have wanted to slit my wrists."

Other ex-clerks also wonder what would have happened if they'd told the grandfatherly Powell they were gay. A clerk from the mid-1980s said, "It's hard to imagine having a conversation like that with your grandfather. . . . He's a great grandfather, but he was still a grandparent." A gay Powell clerk from the 1982–83 term said, "I wondered what I would have done if I had been clerking at the time [of *Hardwick*]. And in my best moments, I'd like to think I would have gone into the justice and said, 'Hey, justice—' . . . [Y]ou don't lobby judges. You know, you don't say, 'Hey, my mother owns a lot of Shell Oil Company.' . . . On the other hand, if in fact having some experience with being gay . . . would help the judge, maybe you would tell him."

A lesbian whose Powell clerkship preceded *Hardwick* remembers thinking at the time the case came up "that Ann Coughlin and Bill

Stuntz were such good people and such decent people that the appeal on behalf of humanity was going to get made." She thought it wouldn't be necessary for gay clerks to out themselves. Powell's anti-gay vote shifted her perspective. She says, "Maybe it would have made a difference if all the gay clerks came out to him because I think some of us were his favorites. But on the other hand, that would have been such an inappropriate thing to do. You just can't do that—try to direct somebody's decision in a pending case with information that is totally outside of the record and really should be irrelevant."

None of Powell's gay clerks ever came out to him, according to his administrative assistant Sally Smith, who kept tabs on virtually every interaction Powell had from 1962 until his death in 1999. A couple of years after *Hardwick*, Smith tried to talk to Powell about the fact that Cabell Chinnis was gay. "I saw it was not going anywhere. He was polite. He didn't tell me to shut up. It was just something he wouldn't deal with," she recalls.

Well into his retirement years, Powell told his lone clerk for that year that he didn't know that he'd ever had a gay clerk. The clerk, who happened to be gay, responded, "Considering the numbers, surely you have." Powell just chuckled. John Jeffries's 1994 Powell biography mentions that the justice had a gay clerk during *Hardwick*'s term. Powell claimed never to have read the book, though his wife read portions aloud to him and Smith caught him peeking at it.

In 1995, Ronald Carr, a gay man who'd clerked for Powell in 1974–75, died of AIDS at 49. He was the first Powell clerk to die. Powell knew the cause of death but ignored it. "He just didn't want to face certain issues, and he didn't," Smith observes. Powell's court papers are archived at the Washington and Lee University law library in Lexington, Virginia. The library bulletin board includes announcements from the law school's gay student group. No one could attend law school at Powell's alma mater today and remain oblivious to gay people.

Though Powell labeled *Hardwick* "frivolous" because he'd been told sodomy laws weren't enforced, prosecutions continued. For example, a Georgia man was sentenced in 1988 to five years in prison for sodomy. James Moseley had successfully defended himself against a charge of raping his estranged wife by persuading the jury they had had consensual oral sex. He later said he hadn't realized he was admitting to criminal behavior. He had thought sodomy laws applied only to homosexuals. He served 18 months, and the conviction was used to deny him visitation rights to see his children.

Many gay-rights attorneys did their best to avoid the hostile Supreme Court after *Hardwick*. Focusing on state courts, state constitutions and state legislatures, they slowly chipped away at sodomy laws. In overturning Kentucky's same-sex sodomy law, that state's top court declared, "We need not sympathize, agree with or even understand the sexual preference of homosexuals in order to recognize their right to equal treatment before the bar of justice."

When *Hardwick* was handed down, 24 states, the District of Columbia and the military had sodomy laws. In 2000, they still existed in 18 states and the military. Gay-rights attorneys' most gratifying breakthrough came in 1998, when the Georgia Supreme Court struck down that state's notorious law. "We cannot think of any other activity that reasonable persons would rank as more private and more deserving of protection from governmental interference than consensual, private, adult sexual activity. . . . [S]uch activity is at the heart of the Georgia Constitution's protection of the right to privacy," Chief Justice Robert Benham declared, overturning the conviction of a man serving a five-year sentence for heterosexual sodomy in his own home.

Michael Hardwick didn't live to see his challenge to the Georgia law vindicated. He died of AIDS at his sister's home in Gainesville, Florida, on June 13, 1991. He was 37.

The Georgia court's ruling was announced just as former Georgia Attorney General Michael Bowers's ex-mistress was revealing his sodomous exploits.

Despite the Georgia breakthrough, the *Hardwick* decision remains a badge of second-class citizenship painfully stitched into the psyches of gay Americans.

Meanwhile, Blackmun grew in his understanding of gay people. Just as reaction to his abortion-rights decision had turned him into a feminist, he was moved by letters of appreciation for his *Hardwick* dissent. He discovered that he knew more gay people than he had realized.

After his clerkship, Cabell Chinnis stayed in Washington, D.C., and specialized in international law. Only gradually did he realize he was being widely demonized because of his association with Powell's swing vote in *Hardwick*. Chinnis recalls being shocked when a stranger at a gay gym refused to lend him a hand with a barbell. "I know who you are," the stranger growled. "You're that guy who drafted anti-gay legislation at the Supreme Court."

In a long interview, Chinnis played another "what if" game: What if the Supreme Court's ruling had gone differently? What if Blackmun's dissent had been the voice of the majority? What if sodomy laws no longer existed?

Lambda executive director Cathcart observes that a favorable *Hardwick* decision "would have changed the world. It absolutely would have changed the world in which we operate."

With a sigh, Chinnis says, "Imagine what it would be like to have people think that that [better] world could have existed and to then hear stories that because of [you] that world didn't come to pass."

Making Criminals out of 700,000 Texans

Though just days away from the end of its term, the court wasn't finished slapping gay Americans when it handed down *Hardwick* on June 30, 1986. On July 7, the court refused to hear one of the strongest, best-documented gay cases ever to reach the high court: Don Baker's equal protection challenge to the Texas sodomy law that criminalized only same-sex behavior.

Despite the legal-theory gloss that Justice White had put on the court's ruling against Michael Hardwick, the court's treatment of Baker indicates that its *Hardwick* decision had far more to do with justices' hostility toward homosexual sodomy than with constitutional limits on privacy rights. When Baker's case had arrived, the court decided to put it aside until *Hardwick* was settled. In *Hardwick*, the court essentially closed off one route—the right to privacy—to a decision in favor of gay challenges to sodomy laws' constitutionality. Baker proposed a different route, equal protection. By refusing to explore Baker's alternate route after blocking the right-to-privacy approach, the court showed itself closed to the idea of the Constitution protecting the sex lives of homosexuals.

Fair-minded people might think that a particular constitutional argument doesn't fit a given case but be open to hearing other arguments. A justice might think, for example, that privacy precedents weren't broad enough to use in knocking down laws against interracial marriage yet find the Equal Protection Clause up to the task. But having upheld laws against homosexual sodomy in *Hardwick,* the court considered the entire subject closed.

Baker's case was tossed aside, with only Marshall publicly listed as dissenting from denial of *cert.* Yet the court could have ruled in Baker's favor without even grappling with homosexuality. Texas's law could have been struck down as unconstitutional sex discrimination. Or, as 26 state governments argued, the court could have overturned the Fifth Circuit Court of Appeals' bizarre decision against Baker because it trampled states' rights. The Fifth Circuit had ridden so roughshod over normal procedures that the attorney generals of 26 states, including 10 with sodomy laws, found themselves asking that Baker's plea be heard. Yet the Supreme Court seems to have felt that it had already handed down a definitive judgment on homosexual sodomy. Any lingering doubts about the court's antipathy toward homosexuality were put to rest when it signaled that *Hardwick's* outcome meant there was no reason to hear *Baker v. Wade.*

To Don Baker's chagrin, his carefully orchestrated assault on Texas's sodomy law now lies permanently in the shadow of *Hardwick.* The court's refusal to take his case reduced it to a little-known echo of gay Americans' most stunning defeat. Yet Baker's case, which began three years before Hardwick's arrest, once held great promise.

After Texas lawmakers revised their state penal code in 1974 some traditional sex "crimes," including fornication and adultery, were no longer illegal. Bestiality was forbidden only in public. Sodomy was downgraded to a $200 misdemeanor and applied only to same-sex couples. So, by the end of 1974, Don Baker could legally have had private oral or anal sex with a woman or even a dog but not with another man.

Abolishing the new sodomy law, toothless except for its power to stigmatize gay people, became the No. 1 priority of Texas's gay-rights groups. "If we can be defined as people habitually involved in criminal activity, then we can be denied housing, child custody, basic job security, everything. So, it was the center of the bull's-eye for us. We had to go for it," recalls Baker.

With repeal attempts getting nowhere, gay lawyers formed the Texas Human Rights Foundation to fight the sodomy law in court. They envisioned a perfectly constructed challenge that could knock down sodomy laws nationwide. Foundation strategists believed that one flaw in *Doe v. Commonwealth's Attorney*, which ended in 1976 with the Supreme Court affirming a decision upholding Virginia's sodomy law, was that the gay challenge had been anonymous.

A 1979 talent search for the ideal plaintiff settled on Don Baker, a bright and articulate former schoolteacher, Navy veteran and devout Christian who'd survived a hellacious, seven-year coming-out struggle. Baker, then a 32-year-old graduate student and vice president of the Dallas Gay Political Caucus, felt honored. Most sodomy challenges in that pre-*Hardwick* era involved public sex, somebody "caught doing some naughty," as Baker phrases it. He had no criminal record and was prepared to bear witness to the harm sodomy laws inflict on homosexuals regardless of whether they're ever arrested.

When Baker sued in federal court on November 19, 1979, he named Dallas County District Attorney Henry Wade (the "Wade" in *Roe v. Wade*) and Dallas City Attorney Lee Holt as defendants. Texas Attorney General Mark White joined to defend the sodomy law on behalf of the state. Other district attorneys declined Holt's invitation to help fight for the law. During preliminary maneuvering, Baker's lead attorney James Barber hit the jackpot: Baker's case was assigned to a 46-year-old liberal Carter appointee, District Judge Jerry Buchmeyer.

A two-day trial in June 1981 turned into yet another psychiatric duel over homosexuality. Psychiatrist James Grigson declared that homosexuality is a "disease" and sodomy laws are beneficial because they prod homosexuals to seek treatment. American Psychiatric Association president Judd Marmor countered that sodomy laws are unjustified and harmful.

Baker witness Victor Furnish, a theologian from Southern Methodist University, testified that the homosexual conduct condemned in the Bible was not consensual.

When Don Baker took the stand, he proved that he was indeed the ideal plaintiff. Baker's lawsuit impersonally described him as "a practicing homosexual . . . constantly in fear of criminal prosecution." But as Baker compellingly told his life story, describing in painful detail how his struggle against his homosexual orientation took him to the brink of suicide, Judge Buchmeyer saw Texas's sodomy law as helping to perpetuate a stigma that causes untold misery. Impressed by the "conservatively" dressed gay man whom he found "very sincere, very credible . . . very articulate," Buchmeyer recounted Baker's story in his ruling, which reached the Supreme Court. Baker himself now tells the story in even richer detail.

Born into a strict, fundamentalist Dallas family in 1947, "Donnie" Baker grew up singing in the choir at the Assembly of God church where his grandfather preached. At school he was ridiculed as a sissy, the boy picked last for ball teams. He didn't consider his strong feelings for other boys homosexual because "queers were bad"—and he was a good boy. Extramarital sex was also "bad," so he felt self-righteous when high school pals fantasized about sex with girls. "I thought I had a special connection with God because I never had those feelings," Baker recalls.

By college Baker was disturbed by his homoerotic feelings because he thought they were "sinful" and "criminal." One Sunday afternoon during his junior year at the University of Texas at Austin, Baker stopped by the student union to watch a Dallas Cowboys game on TV while on break from his job at the bookstore. He became aware that a blond young man was staring at him with a look that was unmistakably sexual. Desire surged through Baker: "It was like a volcano eruption. I just exploded with the emotion of 'Oh my gosh, I want to be with this guy.' But I didn't know what that meant because I had never had any experience. So I just stood up like I was on autopilot. This guy just kind of led me down a hallway into a restroom." The stranger exposed himself. Baker froze. Physically, nothing happened between them. But a war raged inside Baker—pitting everything horrible he'd internalized about homosexuality against "the most wonderful feeling" he'd ever had. He returned to work and started sobbing uncontrollably.

That night, Baker approached his minister for guidance but found himself wailing like a wounded animal, unable to utter a word. "I felt something awful had happened. I went back to my dorm and for two weeks I shut myself off. I thought I had a disease and I didn't want anybody to catch it," Baker says. Convinced his family, society and God hated him, Baker, 20, considered suicide. Instead, he dropped out and joined the Navy. "I wanted to leave Don Baker the homosexual behind," he explains. After four years, Don Baker the celibate homosexual was honorably discharged. Still running away, he enrolled in a New York college. "I was dying inside. . . . How could a good little Christian boy be such a criminal?" he recalls thinking.

Seriously suicidal, Baker overheard co-workers talking about a gay student group at nearby Cornell University. On the night of a meeting, Baker slipped into a Cornell balcony above the floor where the gay students were gathering and peered down at them. Judge Buchmeyer would later note, "It was the first time Donald Baker had ever seen other human beings that he knew were homosexual, too, but who were not ashamed of that fact."

As the 27-year-old Baker went downstairs to get acquainted, he took his first step out of the closet. That first meeting was also a dance: "I can remember for the first time touching a man and holding him and just—I don't know how corny this sounds—feeling rushes of great happiness and joy," Baker recalls. His first sexual experience was that same night. "It was heaven," he says. He soon reconciled his Christianity with being gay, graduated with honors and, having made peace with himself, "packed up my little Pinto and went back to Texas."

With the zeal that he once put into handing out fundamentalist tracts to strangers, Baker began spreading the word that accepting his homosexuality was wonderful. He recalls scolding his parents: "Don't you dare cry for me! I'm the happiest person in the world." (They were in court to show their support when he testified.) Back in Dallas, he was an "excellent" elementary school teacher, according to his evaluations, and devoted his spare time to gay-rights activism.

Baker delivered his powerful testimony in person. District Attorney Wade and City Attorney Holt testified by deposition. They flailed about, proving unable to offer even the flimsiest support for their claim that the sodomy law furthers the state's interest in protecting "morality, decency, health, welfare, safety and procreation." They were stumped when asked how those interests are advanced by a law that allows heterosexual sodomy.

On August 17, 1982, some 14 months after the trial and by coincidence two weeks after Michael Hardwick's arrest, Judge Buchmeyer forcefully struck down the sodomy law that "makes criminals out of more than 700,000 individuals in Texas who are homosexuals, although they did not choose to be." He declared that the law violated the right to sexual privacy that all adults share and violated equal protection by discriminating against homosexuals.

Demonstrating the profound impact that the psychiatric profession's change of heart toward homosexuality was having on the judiciary, Buchmeyer found: "Homosexuals are not ill or mentally diseased. They are not criminals. . . . Homosexuality is not a matter of choice. It is fixed at an early age. . . . Homosexuality is not communicable. . . . There is simply no rational connection between the acts proscribed by [the sodomy law] and the claimed interests of morality, decency, health, welfare, safety and procreation."

The threat posed by the sodomy law is far more than a $200 fine, Buchmeyer stressed, pointing out that it is used to deny homosexuals employment, probation, child custody and citizenship and as an excuse for alleged police harassment. Anticipating criticism, the judge pointed out that his ruling would have "little effect upon the general public."

After his first-round knockout victory, Don Baker recalls being deliriously happy at a news conference: "I was in my typical emotional state—crying and carrying on and yelling and screaming." District Attorney Wade and City Attorney Holt threw in the towel, choosing not to appeal. But on November 1, 1982—shortly before Election Day—Texas Attorney General White, a Democrat then running for governor, did appeal. Jim Maddox, a Democrat who'd tried to repeal the sodomy law while in the state legislature, was elected to succeed White as attorney general. Shortly after taking office, Attorney General Maddox withdrew the state's appeal.

Since the Texas Constitution gave only the state attorney general the power to represent the state in civil legislation, that would have been the end of the case—and the end of Texas's sodomy law—if events had not taken bizarre, even deviant, turns. Danny Hill, newly elected district attorney of Potter and Armstrong counties, asked the Texas Supreme Court to force Maddox to appeal. It refused. Hill and a tiny group called Dallas Doctors Against AIDS petitioned to be allowed to appeal even though they'd never been involved in the case. Both Hill and the doctors were represented by William Charles Bundren, a Dallas attorney.

"I was so mad I could spit nails! It was like, 'Who *are* these people?'" recalls Baker, who couldn't believe that his six-month-old victory was in jeopardy.

Bundren papered the district court and Fifth Circuit with motions citing AIDS as a reason to revive the repeal. Slamming that argument, Judge Buchmeyer asked sarcastically, "if AIDS can be wiped out by statutes such as [this], should the state consider passing criminal laws against other diseases?" A three-judge Fifth Circuit panel also ruled against reopening the case. But the full Fifth Circuit then decided to rehear Hill's argument.

Then in a startling departure from normal procedures and the Texas Constitution's requirements, the full Fifth Circuit voted, 9 to 7, to allow Hill—one of 1,085 Texas district, county and city attorneys—to represent the state of Texas over Attorney General Maddox's objections. The Fifth Circuit's ruling, handed down August 26, 1985, showed how far some judges will go to reach an anti-gay result. As Judge Alvin Rubin wrote in dissent, "Determined to uphold the constitutionality of a Texas statute whatever obstacles bar the way, the majority opinion tramples every procedural rule it considers. No party to the suit has pursued this appeal."

Having created "a special life-support contrivance" for the sodomy law—as the dissenters put it, the Fifth Circuit's majority then upheld it. In a short opinion by Judge Thomas Reavley, the majority first declared that the Supreme Court's 1976 *Doe* decision meant sodomy laws didn't violate the right to privacy. Second, the majority found that there was no violation of equal protection because centuries of antipathy toward homosexuality meant that the law might be rationally related to "implementing morality, a permissible state goal." (The law's legislative history actually indicated that keeping homosexual sodomy illegal was a purely political calculation, not an effort to protect morality.)

Two months later, the Fifth Circuit denied Baker's request for a rehearing. "It is not the role or authority of this federal court to decide the morality of sexual conduct for the people of the state of Texas," Reavley wrote for the court. "The statute affects only those who choose to act in the manner proscribed. . . . Moral issues should be resolved by the people," he claimed.

Acting as if the Fifth Circuit were doing gay Americans a favor by upholding Texas's sodomy law, Reavley contended that if a federal court were to decide a moral question, "The feelings of the losers, perhaps still in the majority, could be elevated by the nature of the [judicial] fiat, and their frustrations might be vented upon the winners to a degree that increased the burdens of the latter beyond the consequences endured under the invalidated statute."

Two weeks after the Fifth Circuit's final ruling against Baker, the Supreme Court agreed to hear *Hardwick*. Baker's case had moved more slowly than Michael Hardwick's because it had actually gone to trial. A Supreme Court victory for Hardwick would have forced Georgia to defend its sodomy law in a district court trial. With the Supreme Court holding Baker's last hope of striking down Texas law, Dallas attorney James Barber reluctantly handed *Baker v. Wade* off to constitutional law scholar Laurence Tribe.

In a *cert* petition filed January 18, 1986, Tribe urged the court to vacate the Fifth Circuit decision on two grounds. First, neither Texas nor any other legitimate party to the case had appealed the original decision striking down the sodomy law. Second, the Fifth Circuit had abdicated its responsibility by failing to apply any real scrutiny to the contested law. Courts could never find a law unconstitutional if the only standard to be met was whether lawmakers had deemed the outlawed behavior objectionable, Tribe pointed out. The Fifth Circuit had not used "any standard of review trenchant enough to flush out unconstitutional legislative animus [toward homosexuals]. Worse than that, it declared that popular antipathy itself tied the court's hands," Tribe argued. The Fifth Circuit's superficial scrutiny was especially inadequate since the same-sex sodomy law discriminates on the basis on gender: Baker could be prosecuted for oral or anal sex with a man. "But if a woman were to commit those identical acts with the very same partner . . . she would be entitled to acquittal on the ground that she is female," Tribe noted.

Dallas attorney Bundren responded that Baker didn't have standing to challenge the sodomy law since he had not been arrested, the law didn't discriminate based on sex and AIDS proved that outlawing "homosexual sodomitic acts" was necessary to protect public health and safety. "Homosexuals are a reservoir of serious transmissible diseases," he said.

Meanwhile, half the nation's attorney generals told the justices, "[A] federal court must respect the decision by a state attorney general to withdraw an appeal of a judgment declaring a state criminal statute unconstitutional."

Obsessed with his crusade, Don Baker "ate, drank and slept gay activism." He lived off credit cards, part-time jobs and garage sales as he crisscrossed the country to enlist contributions to help the Texas Human Rights Foundation with its legal bills. "I don't want this to sound whiny, but I set my career back about seven years," he admits. He flew to Washington to hear the oral argument in *Hardwick*. When Michael Hardwick lost, Baker was "heartsick."

The record in *Baker v. Wade* practically begged the justices to see that the damage inflicted by sodomy laws had almost no relationship to how many homosexuals were or were not prosecuted. But there's no reason to think any justice, except Brennan, ever read anything more than some clerk's very short summary of Judge Buchmeyer's account of the trial testimony.

When the court then refused to hear *Baker v. Wade*, Baker plunged into a depression. "It's just unbelievable that we all would work so hard, and we could not be heard. . . . I can appreciate the fact now that many people will read Judge Buchmeyer's decision and they'll say, 'Oh, wow! It's such an inspiration.' But at the time, [being turned away] was very painful."

News that the Supreme Court had slammed its door in Baker's face was virtually lost on a gay community that was reeling over *Hardwick*. "Part of the pain," Baker recalls, "was that I felt America never knew this happened. *Hardwick* was the critical case, but no one knows there was another case going on and how it was designed and what it was supposed to do."

Baker wishes he could have talked to the eight justices who refused to grant him a hearing: "All we want is to be treated equally. We aren't looking for some kind of exceptional rights. We are just talking about average folks like me, people that are schoolteachers, people who are nurses, people that are contributing. Whenever you don't hear us, you are saying to us we don't matter. . . . We're all brought up in a system where we think we all have voices. And to be shut out like this is just unimaginably devastating."

After his case died on the justices' doorstep, Baker, feeling drained, curbed his activism. He fell in love and left Texas. In 1996, Don Baker, 49, was happily settled in Boston with his "wonderful husband" of nine years and was director of training for a 1,500-employee firm that assists the mentally disabled. He was pushing his company to extend benefits to gay workers' partners. And he was actively involved in the Episcopal Church.

Baker still believes that within his lifetime Supreme Court justices will fling open the door to full legal equality for gay Americans: "I never, ever have just given up on them. . . . You've got to keep knocking."

More than two decades after Don Baker sued, Texas still has a sodomy law—one of five in the nation that targets only same-sex behavior. As governor, George W. Bush opposed repeal.

When the Supreme Court's 1985–86 term came to a close, the *Hardwick* ruling branding gay Americans second class was the one that was seared into countless minds. An institution that to casual observers had seemed—like the tired old man who cast the decisive *Hardwick* vote—grandfatherly, formal, distant but kind, now appeared dangerously out of touch, not just with gay lives but with a modern-day America that took sexual freedom for granted. If five justices had no problem with a cop in Michael Hardwick's bedroom, was anyone's sexual privacy assured?

The court had been absent from the national debate over gay civil rights for so long—punting, ducking and muttering one-word rulings that never caught the public's eye—that its harsh *Hardwick* decision was treated as its definitive statement on gay rights: There's nothing immoral, un-American or unconstitutional about discrimination if homosexuals are the target.

The court's liberal, activist days had faded away before gay Americans had a chance to be recognized as a legitimate, wrongly oppressed minority. As the court swung far to the right and shunned civil rights activism, observers often remarked that it didn't want to get too far out in front of the country. Yet the court wasn't just refusing to lead a gay civil rights parade. By the summer of 1986, the court was undeniably an active drag on gay Americans' progress. To this day, *Bowers v. Hardwick* is a millstone around the neck of every gay American.

13

CONFIRMING HOSTILITY

"DOES YOUR ORGANIZATION ADVOCATE any kind of treatment for gays and lesbians to see if they can change them and make them normal like other people?" asked 83-year-old Senate Judiciary Committee Chairman Strom Thurmond, his thin voice crackling like a gramophone.

Jeffrey Levi, executive director of the 10,000-member National Gay and Lesbian Task Force, had waited 13 hours to testify before the Senate Judiciary Committee. Only moments before Thurmond's curveball, Levi had become the first person ever to speak on behalf of gay Americans at the confirmation hearing of a Supreme Court justice, forcefully opposing William Rehnquist's elevation to chief justice of the United States.

Momentarily speechless, Levi responded, "Well, senator, we consider ourselves to be quite normal, thank you." Levi heard a pair of liberal straight women giggling sympathetically behind him. "We just happen to be different from other people," continued Levi, conservatively dressed in a dark suit and burgundy tie. "And the beauty of the American society is that ultimately we do accept all differences of behavior and viewpoint. To answer the question more seriously, the predominant scientific viewpoint is that homosexuality is probably innate; if not innate, then formed very early in life. The responsible medical community no longer considers homosexuality an illness but rather something that is just a variation of standard behavior."

The hour was very late, nearly midnight, on July 31, 1986. The brightly lit, high-ceilinged Senate Judiciary Committee hearing room had earlier overflowed with spectators and camera crews. Now it seemed eerily cavernous. In the front of the room, nameplates marked the places of the committee's 18 senators, all of whom but Thurmond had vanished. Behind the green-cloth-covered witness table, row after row of leather chairs was largely vacant.

"You don't think gays and lesbians are subject to change?" Thurmond shot back.

"No more so, senator, than heterosexuals," Levi replied.

Thurmond, a South Carolina Republican first elected to the Senate as a Democrat in 1954, owed his political longevity to his adaptability. A hard-core segregationist who had fought the Voting Rights Act tooth and nail, he found it advantageous to see the light on racial equality once barriers to black voting were outlawed and his reelection, thus, depended on gaining some black support. As Levi was quickly discovering, Thurmond had not felt the need to similarly modernize his attitudes toward homosexuality. Oddly, Thurmond's terminology was up to date, probably an indication he was drawing on staff-written questions.

"You don't think they could be converted so they'd be like other people in some way?" Thurmond doggedly asked.

"Well, we think we are like other people with one small exception, . . . " Levi answered.

"That 'small exception,' though, that is a pretty big exception, isn't it?" a grinning Thurmond said, looking mighty pleased with himself.

"Unfortunately, society makes it a big exception. We wish it wouldn't, and that is why our organization exists," Levi said.

The Supreme Court had derided gay-rights claims as "facetious" in *Hardwick* just a month earlier. President Reagan, whose attorney general had hailed *Hardwick's* outcome, had shown his contempt for minority rights by nominating Rehnquist for chief justice. Yet even in that hostile atmosphere, Levi was stunned by what he calls Thurmond's "bizarre" questions.

"It was just so unreal that you had to suspend reality for a while in order to be able to engage in that conversation," Levi says. The irony was that coverage of Thurmond's queries—*The New York Times* ran a brief article—helped publicize Levi's late-night testimony.

Levi had used his allotted three minutes to read a forceful statement attacking Rehnquist's track record as an associate justice. It was, Levi pointed out, one of relentless disdain for gay Americans' civil rights: "Mr. Chairman, my organization represents the 10 percent of the

American population—and the 10 percent of your constituents—who are lesbian and gay. As citizens of this country, we ask for no special favors, merely the same fundamental constitutional rights that all Americans should have. Justice Rehnquist . . . would judge us and deny us our basic constitutional rights of free speech, free association, and privacy simply because of who we are."

Two Democratic senators had asked Levi questions pertinent to Rehnquist's confirmation before departing, leaving Thurmond alone at the committee table. The ancient South Carolinian had hurled himself into quizzing Levi by proclaiming himself "shocked" by the 10 percent figure.

Thurmond's view of homosexuality as a problem to be fixed was "symbolic of what we would continue to be up against," Levi says. The fact that Thurmond, the member of Congress most responsible for assessing the fitness of judicial nominees, voiced psychiatric attitudes from 30 years earlier when he was a freshman senator—attitudes disavowed by the American Psychiatric Association in 1973—was a potent reminder that the Supreme Court was unlikely to embrace gay Americans as long as Congress and the White House remained hostile.

However, Rehnquist's 1986 confirmation hearings demonstrated not only how far the gay movement had to go but also how far it had come. A gay-rights spokesman had a place at the witness table. Also, the broader civil rights community showed that it was beginning to embrace gay Americans. Rehnquist's extraordinarily narrow interpretation of the Constitution's guarantees of liberty and equal protection made him the justice most hostile to safeguarding human rights, whether those of gay people, women, racial minorities or children born out of wedlock. Rehnquist contends that the 14th Amendment's prohibition on denying "any person . . . the equal protection of the laws" only bans the racial discrimination that triggered its enactment in 1868. For example, he blasted *Roe v. Wade* for recognizing "a right that was apparently completely unknown to the drafters of the [14th] Amendment." As an associate justice, Rehnquist almost invariably found justifications for voting even against victims of racial discrimination.

Civil rights groups that had warned the Senate in 1972 that Rehnquist, a Nixon nominee, was too hostile to minority rights to serve on the Supreme Court were back in 1986, saying, "We told you so." In 1972, Rehnquist had sported long sideburns, Hushpuppies and an unfashionably far-right philosophy that opposed most judicial efforts to make society fairer or more humane.

During 14 years on the nation's top court, Rehnquist had updated his appearance but not his outlook. Instead, his "antipathy toward civil liberties and minority groups has found dangerous new outlets," testified Congressman Ted Weiss (D–New York), speaking as president of the liberal Americans for Democratic Action (ADA). Weiss declared, "We believe his positions will further divide this country between the privileged and the poor, between black and Hispanic and white, between men and women, between homosexual and heterosexual, between the majority and minority." The 1986 testimony of the ADA and the Leadership Conference on Civil Rights, an umbrella group of civil rights organizations, cited Rehnquist's outspoken opposition to gay civil rights as evidence of his consistent, unacceptable extremism. The clear implication of Rehnquist's 1978 dissent from denial of *cert* in *Ratchford v. Gay Lib* was that he viewed enacting a sodomy law as giving a state carte blanche to discriminate against homosexuals.

Rehnquist gave senators fair warning that if they wanted an advocate of minority rights, they'd best look elsewhere. Illinois Democratic Senator Paul Simon said that in reviewing Rehnquist's record "I do not see someone who is a champion of justice for all citizens, for the minority, for women, for people who need a champion and who may not have one. Am I misreading the record?" Rehnquist replied, "I would say partly but not entirely," explaining that he generally voted against groups seeking a broad interpretation of the Equal Protection Clause.

The Supreme Court's composition and, to a large extent, its rulings reflect the choices of presidents and senators. If Reagan or a majority of the Senate had wanted the court to grant gay Americans equal protection, Rehnquist would not have become chief justice. Instead, he was confirmed, 65 to 33. The Republican-controlled Senate thus endorsed a narrow vision of justice that left out gay Americans. During Rehnquist's confirmation hearing, not one senator asked Rehnquist about gay Americans' rights, even though he twice mentioned *Hardwick*.

The picture painted of Rehnquist, an amateur artist, during the 1986 hearings was of an amiable, learned man, who got along well with colleagues but who was astoundingly insensitive to minorities. That portrait has stood the test of time. As chief, Rehnquist is fair to colleagues, never engaging in the Burger trickery of assigning a majority opinion despite having voted on the losing side. Rehnquist revels in leading sing-a-longs using a baton given by a clerk. He insists on a Christmas caroling party, despite the discomfort it causes Jews and the strangeness of holding a Christian celebration at a court that enforces the separation of church and state. And Rehnquist has upset black judges by insisting on the singing of "Dixie," a Confederate marching song, at a federal judicial conference. His voting record has remained deeply hostile to minority rights.

While the Senate was wrangling over whether to make the 61-year-old Rehnquist chief, the Judiciary Committee held confirmation hearings on the younger, feistier ideological clone nominated to succeed him as an associate justice. Antonin "Nino" Scalia, 50, was a pugnacious law school professor who had been tapped by Reagan four years earlier for an appeals court judgeship. Enthralled with the idea of naming the first Italian-American justice, Reagan chose Scalia for the Supreme Court. In his academic writing, Scalia delighted in shouting "gotcha" at liberals whose minority-rights arguments he felt he had demolished. He exhibited no empathy for the discrimination victims who were the real losers of what he treated like an intellectual game.

As an appeals court judge, Scalia had joined Robert Bork's 1984 *Dronenberg v. Zech* ruling that the military's prohibition against sodomy was constitutional. Scalia explicitly rejects the idea that the Constitution is a dynamic, flexible document whose vaguely worded guarantees evolve as society matures and notions of equality expand. "I would never use the phrase 'living Constitution,'" Scalia bluntly informed the Judiciary Committee.

Scalia advocates a two-prong test of constitutionality: Does a law violate the Constitution's "original meaning"? Does it violate the "national consensus," as "reflected in the legislation that [lawmakers] have adopted?" The test is rigged against groups—like gay people—who weren't recognized as victims of discrimination in the 18th and 19th centuries but who are now the target of discriminatory laws. Under Scalia's approach, the Constitution's promises become dead letters, as he virtually admitted in a 1985 article: "[T]o some degree, a constitutional guarantee is like a commercial loan; you can only get it if, at the time, you don't really need it."

For nearly a half century, the Supreme Court had attempted—in fits and starts—to protect minority rights and to limit government intrusion into purely personal decisions. Scalia's philosophy, like Rehnquist's, would virtually close off that avenue of appeal. As AFL-CIO general counsel Lawrence Gold testified, "I do not understand how he thinks we could have fought racial discrimination if we had to wait for a consensus. I do not understand how we are ever going to fight successfully any form of discrimination if we have to wait for consensus."

Gay Americans suffered in countless ways from government-sponsored discrimination in 1986. Yet no gay group was invited to testify at Scalia's hearing. No senator asked Scalia about gay rights. Delaware Senator Joseph Biden, the Judiciary Committee's ranking Democrat, inquired whether Scalia recognized a right to privacy but stressed he wasn't asking whether it covered "the right to engage in homosexual activities in your home." Scalia declined to answer.

Scalia left no doubt that he would be at least as ferocious as Rehnquist in trying to force the court to drastically reduce its guardianship of minority rights. No senator found that a sufficient reason to vote against a popular president's choice. He was confirmed, 98–0, on September 17, 1986.

And so the Rehnquist era, which would last into the 21st century, began. The court started its 1986–87 term with a new chief and a new associate. The court's lineup had last changed in 1981, when O'Connor was confirmed after saying "the state of the law concerning homosexuality is . . . unsettled." *Hardwick,* plus the advancement of Rehnquist and Scalia, seemed to settle the issue for the time being: Gay people would be wise to look elsewhere for protection. Yet with the number of gay Americans willing to fight openly for their rights skyrocketing, some gay cases nevertheless wound up before the Supreme Court.

Clashing with Dignity

New York City Police Commissioner Benjamin Ward and Mayor Ed Koch petitioned for *cert* in December 1986. The dispute stemmed from police attempts to stop a gay Catholic group, Dignity–New York, from standing in front of St. Patrick's Cathedral during gay pride parades.

New York City's first pride parade, in June 1970, marked the first anniversary of the Stonewall rebellion. Unable to get a parade permit, gay New Yorkers marched on the sidewalk. Soon, the annual parade was permitted to use Sixth Avenue, then Fifth Avenue, the normal path for big parades. The Fifth Avenue route passed in front of St. Patrick's Cathedral, headquarters of the Roman Catholic Archdiocese of New York. From 1976 to 1982, when marchers representing Dignity-New York reached St. Patrick's, they would leave the parade to stand in front of the cathedral. As the rest of the gay pride parade passed by, Dignity members prayed and sang.

Especially for members of a faith steeped in symbolism, Dignity's joyful presence in front of the cathedral conveyed—far more than the words of its hymns and banners—its message. Dignity members were affirming their dual identity as gay Catholics, despite their church's hostility to homosexuality. "Dignity's presence there was never a protest," recalls spokesman Matthew Foreman. "Nobody held up any signs critical of the church's position. . . . Dignity's presence was meant to communicate, 'We're Catholics. You don't have to hate the Catholic Church in order to be gay. You don't have to give up your Catholic beliefs in order to be gay.'"

During the 1981 pride parade, two anti-gay Catholics tried to rip down Dignity's hand-held banner and were arrested. Dignity was back on the cathedral steps in 1982; there was no violence. Yet, the next year police declared that because Catholics who said they considered Dignity's presence a "symbolic desecration" of the cathedral were threatening violence, no one could stand in front of the cathedral during the gay parade. Police again declared the front of St. Patrick's off-limits in 1984. Dignity filed a legal challenge, but it was too late, a federal judge ruled.

Long before the June 1985 parade, Dignity was back in federal court. Chief Judge Constance Baker Motley, a former NAACP attorney, ruled that the police were wrong to bar Dignity "from its preferred public forum because of fear of disruption by its foes." She declared, "It is precisely when speech in the public forum is provocative, challenging and hotly contested that . . . the state's duty to protect the speaker's right to speak is most pointedly called into play." She ordered that Dignity be allowed to resume its traditional place in front of the cathedral.

Two days before the 1985 parade, the Second Circuit overturned Judge Motley. The 2-to-1 decision, bowing to police "expertise," held that she had erred in seeing little threat of violence.

In early 1986, Motley found that the police had questionably cozy relationships with church officials. The police, for example, had suggested that scheduling a church service during the gay parade would provide an excuse for closing the sidewalk. Motley ordered that 100 Dignity members be allowed in front of St. Patrick's.

Again, she was overruled. The Second Circuit ruled that Motley had been insensitive to anti-gay groups. It ordered that first 25 Dignity members, then 25 anti-gay protestors, be allowed inside a police barricade in front of St. Patrick's for 30 minutes during the two-hour parade.

In petitioning the Supreme Court, New York's police commissioner and mayor argued that closing the sidewalk in front of St. Patrick's was a fair police decision—"a result of caution, perhaps an excess of caution." Federal courts, they contended, should not meddle with "reasonable" police restrictions. Dignity, led by president Michael J. Olivieri, countered that the restrictions were "neither 'reasonable' nor 'good faith.'" In a separate petition, Dignity asked that Motley's order opening the St. Patrick's sidewalk to Dignity be reinstated. Anti-gay Catholics, Dignity argued, had never wanted to be in front of the cathedral—they just wanted to keep Dignity away.

Justice O'Connor added the competing petitions to the court's "discuss" list. A Marshall clerk commented, "This is one of those disputes between people so stubborn that they'd rather fight than win." During the court's March 6, 1987 conference, Rehnquist said he'd be willing to provide a fourth vote for accepting the police commissioner's case, *Ward v. Olivieri*. No one else wanted to take it. The court didn't vote on Dignity's petition.

Matthew Foreman, who was Dignity's spokesman, recalls being "incredibly naïve" in thinking *Hardwick* was an "aberration" and that the Supreme Court would want to stand up for Dignity in a "classic First Amendment case." He says, "I have come to realize that there is very little justice and enormous prejudice in the legal system around anything that is gay or lesbian."

Dignity's original joyful message no longer reaches its intended audience. Whatever symbolism is left is mainly a statement about silencing gay people. During pride parades, Dignity exercises its option to spend 30 minutes inside a police barricade. "No one [else] actually realizes they are there because they're hidden by this solid blue line of police officers," says Foreman, who left the group. "So it's very hollow."

An "Olympic" Tug-of-War

Two weeks after voting to stay out of the St. Patrick's dispute, the justices heard arguments in the case of another gay-rights group being thwarted from delivering a powerful, symbolic message. San Francisco Arts & Athletics Inc., a non-profit group, had been prohibited from calling its international sports competition the "Gay Olympic Games." According to the Ninth Circuit Court of Appeals, a 1978 federal law rendered the word "Olympic" the property of the United States Olympic Committee (USOC), the federally chartered organization responsible for fielding U.S. Olympic teams. The Ninth Circuit ruled that, since the USOC objected, the gay group could not use "Olympic." Such a ban did not violate the First Amendment, the appeals court declared, even though the linking of "gay" and "Olympic" sent a strong political message that challenged the stereotypes that homosexuality is unhealthy and gay men are unathletic.

Beating tremendous odds, San Francisco Arts & Athletics and its founder, Dr. Thomas F. Waddell, had successfully petitioned the justices to referee the "Olympic" tug-of-war: Could a commonplace word with roots reaching back to ancient Greece really be private property?

Tom Waddell was a tall, graceful gay man who had once dreamed of a dancing career. He was also a physician, former paratrooper and lifelong athlete. At the advanced age of 30, he had competed in the 1968 Olympics in Mexico City, coming in a respectable sixth in the decathlon.

Born Thomas Joseph Michael Flubacher in 1937, he grew up poor in an industrial part of New Jersey. He changed his surname to Waddell out of respect for the couple who gave him encouragement he'd never found at home. Tom joined his high school track and football teams. His "adopted" parents, who'd been in vaudeville, taught him acrobatics and ballet. "I really wanted to be a dancer," Tom Waddell recalled, "but who were the dancers in the '50s? They were 'faggots.'. . . I didn't want to be 'a homosexual.' I wanted to be a person."

Waddell knew very early that he was attracted to other males. He built a tiny altar at home and prayed to be changed. Much later, after graduating from college, he began his first serious gay relationship, with a man three times his age, but kept fighting homosexuality.

Despite his trouble accepting an unapproved sexual orientation, he had no difficulty bucking political orthodoxy. In medical school, he was derided as "Tommie the Commie" for opposing the Vietnam war and volunteering at a Black Panther health clinic. In 1966, a year after earning his M.D., Waddell was drafted. Ordered to serve in Vietnam, he threatened to become a "conscientious objector." The Army blinked—transferring him to its track team rather than risking a public relations nightmare by court-martialing an anti-war doctor. At the '68 Olympics, Waddell irked Olympic officials by speaking up for the U.S. athletes who gave Black Power salutes during the national anthem. At the 1976 Olympics, he was team physician for the Saudis. By then, he had settled down in San Francisco with landscape architect Charles Deaton.

The idea of a Gay Olympic Games came to Waddell when he spotted a gay bowling tournament while channel surfing. He dreamed up a new quadrennial international sports festival, one open to all without regard to sexual orientation, sex, age or even skill level. He wanted to challenge homophobia, sexism, ageism and the idea that winning mattered more than the sheer joy of participation. Waddell and two friends formed the United States Gay Olympic Committee in June 1980. They tried to incorporate as the "Golden State Olympic Association" but were told corporate names couldn't include "Olympic." Thus, San Francisco Arts & Athletics Inc. was born.

Having heard he needed permission to call his festivities the "Gay Olympic Games," Waddell wrote the U.S. Olympic Committee in December 1981. His letter crossed in the mail with a USOC demand that his group immediately stop using "Olympic." That demand, according to USOC executive director F. Don Miller, had "nothing to do with the issue of homosexuality."

Waddell agreed to drop "Olympic." But after American Civil Liberties Union attorneys advised him that the USOC was on shaky legal ground, he resumed using "Gay Olympic Games" for the 17-sport competition. San Francisco Mayor Dianne Feinstein proclaimed August 28 to September 5, 1982 "Gay Olympics Games Week." But before the games could begin, the USOC sued, winning an order August 9 blocking Waddell's use of "Olympic."

Sports Illustrated ridiculed USOC's action, pointing out that "the ancient Olympics, an all-male event in which participants competed in the nude, was staged by a society in which homosexuality flourished." Los Angeles alone had 140 "Olympic" businesses—everything from Olympic Donuts to Olympic Memorial Funeral Home. Plus, it seemed that everyone and his brother was holding some sort of "Olympics" without drawing the USOC's fire. There were, for example, Special Olympics, Firemen's Olympics, Crab Cooking Olympics, Xerox Olympics, Alcoholic Olympics, Armenian Olympics, Explorer Olympics, Wrist-Wrestling Olympics, Senior Olympics and Rat Olympics. "The bottom line is that if I'm a rat, a crab, a copying machine or an Armenian, I can have my own Olympics. If I'm gay, I can't," Waddell complained.

Under a court order to stop using the disputed word, Waddell and his fellow volunteers spent the days leading up to their 1982 gathering furiously striking through "Olympic" on tickets, T-shirts, posters, brochures and medals. The "Gay Olympic Games" became simply the "Gay Games." Waddell was upset by the change. "I say 'Gay Games' to a gay person and you know what reaction I get? Just imagine! Drag races? Pocketbook races? Spoon-and-egg races?"

At opening ceremonies in the stadium that had been the home of the San Francisco '49ers, Congressman Phillip Burton and San Francisco Supervisor Doris Ward defied the court by announcing the "Gay Olympic Games." Some 1,300 athletes from 12 counties competed in such traditional Olympic sports as swimming and boxing as well as in such popular pastimes as softball, rugby and billiards. Waddell, a handsome 44-year-old with a strawberry blond beard, took home a gold medal for the discus. Gay Games I was a modest box office success, ending $15,000 in the black. It had drawn an amazing 250 reporters. "It really attracted our attention when the USOC asked them to drop the 'Olympics' from their name," explained a German journalist. Waddell and three other Olympians—Susan McGreivey (1956, swimming), George Frenn (hammer throw, 1968, 1972) and Bill Paul (judo, 1964)—scolded the USOC for having "debased the honorable world 'Olympic.'"

Six months later, a Ninth Circuit panel ruled that "there is no First Amendment right to use the word 'Olympic' . . . so long as there are other adequate means" to communicate a message. The dispute then bounced back to district court, where Judge J. P. Vukasin Jr. ordered Waddell and his group to pay $96,600 in attorneys' fees for not heeding the USOC's original request. The judge slapped a lien on Waddell's Victorian house.

The USOC's claims rested on the Amateur Sports Act of 1978, which decreed that the USOC's consent was required for anyone to use "for the purpose of trade, to induce the sale of goods or services, or to pro-mote any theatrical exhibition, athletic performance, or competition" the five-ring Olympic symbol or "the words 'Olympic,' 'Olympiad,' *Citius Altius Fortius*' [the Olympic motto: "faster, higher, stronger"], or any combination or simulation thereof tending to cause confusion . . . or to falsely suggest a connection" to what was sometimes called the real Olympic Games. The act appeared to make lawbreakers out of the thou-sands of businesses named "Olympic." However, under trademark law, non-confusing uses are legal. A builder could advertise "Olympic" swim-ming pools because, in that context, the word is recognized as a size.

Nevertheless, in January 1986, a different Ninth Circuit panel ruled that the USOC had been granted more than a trademark. ". . . The word 'Olympic' and its associated symbols and slogans are essentially property. Such property rights can be protected without violating the First Amendment," the panel ruled. The Ninth Circuit punted on the "difficult issue" of whether the USOC was engaging in anti-gay dis-crimination. The question was irrelevant, it ruled, because the USOC was a private organization.

Three months later, when the Ninth Circuit refused to have the Olympics case heard by its entire membership, three judges forcefully dissented. Judge Alex Kozinski, joined by Harry Pregerson and William A. Norris, sounded an alarm, arguing that if the Amateur Sports Act re-ally did turn "Olympic" into the USOC's private property, then it "raises serious First Amendment concerns." Kozinski declared that "'Olympic' has a meaning unique in our language. . . . I have great difficulty with the idea that Congress can deny all of us that word, and the ideas it em-bodies, in connection with all public endeavors."

Quoting a 1971 Supreme Court decision establishing the right to wear a jacket with "Fuck the Draft" emblazoned on it, Kozinski wrote,

"we cannot indulge in the facile assumption that one can forbid particular words without also running a substantial risk of suppressing ideas
in the process." Then, in his own words, he added, ". . . To say that
SFAA could have named its event 'The Best and Most Accomplished
Amateur Gay Athletes Competition' no more answers the First Amendment concerns here than to suggest that Paul Robert Cohen could have
worn a jacket saying 'I Strongly Resent the Draft.'"

Accepting allegations of discrimination as true—a requirement in a
federal court of appeals when the court below has rendered a judgment
without first holding a trial to establish the facts—Kozinski found that
"the USOC is using its control over the term 'Olympic' to promote the
very image of homosexuals that the SFAA seeks to combat: [The] handicapped, juniors, police, Explorers, even dogs are allowed to carry the
Olympic torch, but homosexuals are not."

In August 1986, San Francisco attorney Mary C. Dunlap petitioned
the justices to take *San Francisco Arts & Athletics, Inc. and Thomas F.
Waddell, M.D., v. United States Olympic Committee and International
Olympic Committee*. She broke a thumb that month playing goalie in a
soccer semi-final at Gay Games II, which drew 3,500 athletes and
cleared $25,000.

Waddell was in financial trouble, worried the USOC was going to
seize his house. He was dying of AIDS and wanted to leave his house to
the daughter born three years earlier to him and a lesbian friend. He'd
checked himself out of a hospital to speak at Gay Games II. On behalf
of the "400 million gay people in this world," Waddell declared, "we
hereby serve notice that we are . . . worthy of the respect and esteem of
all the other citizens of this world." Though his body was being ravaged,
he won a gold medal in the javelin.

Up against the USOC's clout, San Francisco Arts & Athletics had
lost every step of the way. "We had little to lose and much to gain by
confronting the [Supreme] Court with the discrimination involved,"
Dunlap recalls. Even though SFAA could not afford an attorney, she
waged its battle because she considered the struggle important. "Some
donors bought me an electric typewriter so that I could type the briefs,"
she says. Dunlap saw *Hardwick* as all the more reason to take gay cases
to the Supreme Court: "We'd lost a lot, and we needed to gain it back.
And we needed to gain it back as soon as we could."

Petitioning the justices six weeks after the *Hardwick* decision, Dunlap presented her case as one in which the Ninth Circuit had ignored the will of Congress by interpreting the Amateur Sports Act too broadly. The law, she contended, granted the USOC just a trademark. Turning a word with a rich history predating the USOC by more than 2,000 years into private property "cuts a menacing . . . hole in the heart of the Constitution," Dunlap argued. Her petition accused the Ninth Circuit of having too hastily brushed aside questions of discrimination. Her brief said that "gay" and "lesbian" "connote persons of homosexual orientation having the common cause of overcoming homophobia and discrimination."

In reply, USOC's team argued that the case merely involved the breaking of a perfectly constitutional law by a group seeking "a free ride on the goodwill created by [the USOC]."

In the Supreme Court's pool memo, White clerk Samuel Dimon thought the case had been "wrongly decided." Under the Ninth Circuit's interpretation of the disputed law, "an ad for Olympic Avenue Pizza would appear to be subject to injunction, a result which I doubt Congress intended," Dimon said. Justice Powell demonstrated the power of the name Gay Olympic Games to shape how gay people are perceived: "[Petitioners] want to have international games between 'Gays,'" he wrote. Just months earlier, Powell had referred to a "consenting homo."

Rehnquist saw no reason to discuss the case; Brennan added it to the "discuss" list. On October 10, 1986, Brennan, Marshall and Stevens voted to take the case and, in her first sign of any receptiveness to a gay plea, O'Connor cast the crucial fourth vote for *cert* by voting "Join 3." Blackmun passed but later echoed O'Connor's "Join 3."

In winning the right to be heard, SFAA attorney Mary Dunlap cleared a monumental hurdle. The last time the court had heard oral argument in a case brought on behalf of a homosexual cause was on March 14, 1967, when immigrant Clive Boutilier was trying to stay in this country. Only Brennan and White remained from that pre-Stonewall era.

Dunlap's written brief reiterated that the United States Olympic Committee did not have unlimited authority to police the use of "Olympic." A law granting the USOC that much power would violate freedom of speech, she argued. Contending that the USOC was being "intentionally discriminatory," she noted that USOC gave its blessing to the Special Olympics for the mentally disabled and to the Junior Olympics and Explorer Olympics for youth. The USOC had never sued the International Police Olympics, whose five-ring symbol included a pair of handcuffs. In fact, the USOC had sued only one other non-profit group, the March of Dimes, over unauthorized athletic use of "Olympic." That lawsuit, Dunlap stressed, was filed after she'd leveled her discrimination charge. She argued that the USOC was so closely tied to the government that its behavior amounted to "state action" and, thus, unconstitutional discrimination.

In reply, attorney Edward Bennett Williams said that the USOC was fairly policing commercial infringement on its rights. San Francisco Arts & Athletics had "no more First Amendment right to market the 'Gay Olympics' than they would 'Gay Coca-Cola,'" Williams argued. "Petitioners as a group," he contended, don't enjoy the same constitutional protection as racial minorities. "Bluntly, blackness and homosexuality are not the same phenomenon," he said.

Dunlap shot back that the name "Gay Olympics Games" was inherently political. She argued that it was wrong to depict SFAA, which one judge noted was in "dire financial straits," as "just another . . . profit-crazed commercial imitator of the Olympics." Branding USOC actions "homophobic," Dunlap quoted a USOC attorney as saying that for "Olympic" to be used by a homosexual group "makes the harm to us even greater" because "'Gay Olympics' suggests very strongly that they have to do it because the Olympics themselves are not available to gay people."

Clerk Margaret Raymond advised Justice Marshall that the gay group's rights were being violated by denying it access to "an essentially generic term" that "represents a historic idea with a modern counterpart, a Greek tradition, an ideal of competition, the whole shebang."

Meanwhile, Powell clerk Leslie Gielow, a University of Michigan law school graduate, who was unaware of Justice Powell's struggles over *Hardwick*, told Powell, "Alternate methods for SFAA to convey its message seem almost as good." Powell, whose failure to grasp the significance that Michael Hardwick's sodomy challenge had had for gay Americans had proven him a poor judge of the gay community's needs, responded, "True."

Powell's immediate instinct was to side with the USOC. He apparently would have viewed the case much differently if he had seen it in terms of a minority group whose rights he wanted to protect. Gielow's bench memo asked rhetorically, "could the USOC without violating the Constitution issue a policy statement that no black groups would be allowed to use the word 'Olympic' whereas white groups would be allowed to do so?" Powell penned, "Of course not." Later Powell wrote to himself, "Couldn't allow use by whites—not Blacks." (Former clerk Gielow says, "It's not surprising to me that a race discrimination issue would resound more with Justice Powell," given his experiences as a white Southerner.)

Powell summarized his responses: "Congress intended to grant USOC something broader than [trademark]. . . . I could hold that [SFAA's] First Amendment interest is insubstantial. . . . Its purposes probably are to gain stature and favorable recognition by creating the belief that Gays participate in approved Olympic events. This in itself would 'tend to cause confusion. . . .'"

Mary Dunlap and her lover flew to Washington, D.C., at their own expense for oral argument in what Dunlap says "no one will ever be able to prevent me from calling the Gay Olympics case." On Tuesday, March 24, 1987, the atmosphere in the nation's most prestigious courtroom was charged. She says, "A large number of people were saying to the court, 'Here we are. We're gay. We're lesbian. We're queer. We're visible. We're vocal. You can see us. We're not hiding in your woodwork.'"

Yet entering the courtroom, Dunlap felt that she was walking into the lion's den. "The *Hardwick* case represented a rejection of gay and lesbian people. I went into the oral argument with a very keen awareness that the Supreme Court was against us. Going in, I certainly couldn't count five votes." (She had no way of knowing that five justices had voted to hear her plea.)

At 59 minutes after noon, Chief Justice Rehnquist announced the case and Dunlap rose to address the court. The justices saw a tall, trim, short-haired, 38-year-old brunette wearing a $275 navy blue Pendleton skirted suit, off-white pleated collarless shirt, heels, pantyhose, a gold necklace and no makeup. (The heels later fetched $225 at a gay fundraiser.) "You have to make really conscious choices when you are about to become a symbol," Dunlap says of her "flight attendant" outfit. She hoped that her use of the word "we" would signal the justices that she was the first lesbian to argue a gay-rights case at the Supreme

Court. "I had fantasies before I went into the court about being even more explicit than I was," she remembers. She knew she would be the first attorney in a gay-rights case to say "gay" to the justices.

Dunlap felt very strongly that past gay-rights oral arguments had been too defensive. "It seemed to me terribly important," she says, "that we put a positive, affirmative, proud, strong, unapologetic face before the Supreme Court on a case involving gay and lesbian rights."

Since the court generally likes to rule as narrowly as possible, Dunlap dove first into the specifics of why she believed the Ninth Circuit's interpretation of the law giving the USOC control of "Olympic" was wrong. Contending that the only unlawful uses of "Olympic" were those likely to cause confusion, Dunlap read from a Waddell letter: "Our outreach and emphasis differ widely from the traditional Olympic Games in that we openly gay people around the world are struggling to produce an image that more closely resembles the facts, rather than some libidinous stereotype generated over decades of misunderstanding and intolerance."

Dunlap's plan was to move quickly into broader constitutional questions. But the court's newest member, Scalia, pounced on what he saw as a fatal flaw in her legal interpretation. Scalia loves jumping into the fray and arguing cases himself. He debated Dunlap about the law's punctuation. Refusing to lapse into the obsequiousness common during oral argument, Dunlap moved ahead to say that Gay Olympic Games was chosen as a name because "Olympic" dates from ancient Greece, where "homosexuality was more widely tolerated than in this culture." Scalia fired back, "They could have also said the Hellenic Games."

Justice Stevens asked for a clarification of a couple of legal points. Rehnquist joined the discussion and became irked when Dunlap answered before he had finished piling on questions.

Scalia steered Dunlap into a long exchange about whether one could trademark "Bird Soap," "Soap Soap" or a shoe polish called "Soap." Frustrated, Dunlap told him, "What I'm trying to do . . . is move the court to the consideration of the constitutional implications of having, not of 'Soap Soap' but of a 'Gay Olympic Games.'" Scalia, sounding pleased that he was running out the clock on the side he clearly opposed, continued the soap discussion. Dunlap barely had time to sketch out her free speech and equal protection claims.

Dunlap found Scalia "playfully hostile—as opposed to Rehnquist who was just hostile. Rehnquist I really felt . . . just loathed that I was even there." White, who asked a few questions, "spent much of the oral argument depriving himself of oxygen by keeping his arms so tightly across his chest I really honestly thought he'd pass out. The environment was pretty unapologetically hostile," she says. She remains frustrated that "Scalia started frothing about soap" and kept her from making key points. "To this day, I wish I had said to him, 'This is not about soap. It's about soapboxes.' Because it was really a case about the First Amendment," Dunlap says.

Attorney John G. Kester of a prominent Washington, D.C., law firm represented the USOC. He said that when people hear "Olympic" they think of the modern games, not "something that happened in a valley under Mount Olympus as a religious festival in honor of Olympian Zeus." O'Connor asked about "fair use" defenses. Then Rehnquist asked—and Stevens pursued—Kester's opinion on whether Congress could give control of the word "baseball" to one organization. Kester eventually said probably not. Trying to rescue him, Scalia argued "Olympic" was different because it referred to something "created by" the USOC. That answer clearly wasn't good enough for Stevens, who kept pressing Kester's argument to its logical conclusions. Kester reluctantly admitted that he believed the law gave the USOC the right to stop a laundry in a town named Olympic from calling itself the "Olympic Laundry."

O'Connor asked if the USOC was a "state actor." Kester claimed the issue was irrelevant, that the bias charge was a "bum rap." His time ran out as Stevens and O'Connor quizzed him about what cereal boxes could legally say about the breakfast habits of Olympic champions.

Tom Waddell felt he'd already won "in the court of public opinion" but confided to his diary, "I did not get a good feeling about the hearing. . . . Mary Dunlap was brilliant. . . ."

When the justices met privately, Rehnquist didn't buy Dunlap's interpretation of the law, thought giving monopoly control over words did not violate the Constitution and said the USOC was not a state actor so there could be no valid discrimination claim. Brennan disagreed, finding the law too broad and seeing the USOC as essentially an arm of the government.

White, who had written the *Hardwick* ruling, echoed Rehnquist in siding with the USOC. Marshall seconded Brennan. Blackmun, who had so eloquently dissented in *Hardwick,* passed. Powell saw no merit in the gay group's positions.

Having pressed the USOC attorney quite hard, Stevens was convinced the law was "overbroad." Yet he found that fact irrelevant in what he viewed as a "commercial" case because the Gay Games "raise [a] great deal of money." Stevens added, "Probably not state action; there is no showing of discriminatory enforcement."

O'Connor, taking the gay side for the first time since joining the court in 1981, voted to send the case back down for a trial on whether there was state action. "There are serious First Amendment issues. 'State action' is close and difficult, and if there is state action, there may be discrimination," she told her brethren.

Scalia, predictably, sided with the USOC. Blackmun, having been persuaded by Stevens's thinking, made it a 6-to-3 victory for the USOC.

Perhaps hoping to avoid another Powell flip-flop in a gay case, Rehnquist asked Powell to write the majority opinion, a task that fell largely to clerk Leslie Gielow. After what Powell aptly called "light editing," the opinion was circulated on April 20. Powell held that federal law granted the USOC more than a trademark and that giving USOC control over "Olympic" did not violate the First Amendment. Powell said the USOC's behavior did not constitute government action and that, in any event, there was no sign of discrimination. He treated the non-profit Gay Olympic Games as if its name raised no greater constitutional questions than a purely commercial venture called, say, "K-mart Olympics." Just as he later minimized his *Hardwick* "mistake," Powell played down the impact of his decision to rule against a gay group, saying, "neither Congress nor the USOC has prohibited the SFAA from conveying its message."

Powell attracted the votes of Rehnquist, White and Scalia—one shy of a majority. Six weeks passed. Stevens was waiting to read Brennan's dissent. "I am inclined to think that even if there is state action, that there is no constitutional violation," Stevens explained.

After checking with clerks in other chambers, Gielow told Powell, "The Brennan clerks are still trying to figure out a convincing state action theory. . . . Justice O'Connor has no theory of her own. She was intrigued by Justice Brennan's state action argument at conference and wants to read his dissent before she makes up her mind. Justice Stevens is in somewhat the same position. . . . [Blackmun] is letting Justice Stevens take the lead." Powell suggested making cosmetic changes to have an excuse to recirculate his opinion. Brennan finally unveiled his dissent June 17. Two days later, Stevens's vote in hand, Powell exclaimed, "Cheers! A court"—meaning a majority. It was the first Supreme Court majority opinion to use "gay"—though only as a part of a formal name or in a quote. Otherwise, gay people remained "homosexuals."

Powell ended up with seven votes—everyone but Brennan and Marshall—for his ruling that the law governing "Olympic" was constitutional and provided much more than a trademark. But the court split 5-to-4 in favor of USOC on equal protection. In a one-paragraph part-concurrence/part-dissent, O'Connor, joined by Blackmun, found that the government and the USOC were "joint participants in the challenged activity and as such are subject to the equal protection" requirements. O'Connor and Blackmun wanted a lower court to determine whether there had, in fact, been discrimination. So, Dunlap fell just one vote short of getting to take her Olympics case to trial.

No justice thought that the USOC had been granted a mere trademark. But Brennan and Marshall agreed with Dunlap on every other major point: Yes, there was government action. Yes, there was unconstitutional discrimination. And, yes, a law that gave the USOC sweeping censorship power was too broad. "By preventing the use of the word 'Olympic,' the statute violates the First Amendment by prohibiting dissemination of a message for which there is no adequate translation. . . . Here, the SFAA intended, by use of the word 'Olympic,' to promote a realistic image of homosexual men and women that would help them move into the mainstream of their communities," Brennan sympathetically declared.

Brennan's dissent detailed the cozy, symbiotic relationship between the federal government and the USOC. In a section joined by O'Connor and Blackmun as well as Marshall, Brennan compared the USOC's actions to those of a restaurant on government property refusing to serve a black customer. Brennan cited the court's 1961 ruling in *Burton v. Wilmington Parking Authority,* which held the restaurant's bigotry equaled governmental discrimination because the restaurant was located in a public parking garage. Thus, four justices were drawing a notable parallel between alleged anti-gay discrimination and race discrimination.

When the decision writing an "Olympic" exception into the First Amendment was announced on June 25, 1987, Dunlap called Tom Waddell. "It was one of the harder things I've had to do as any attorney," she says. Waddell died less than two weeks later at 49. "The Supreme Court's terrible decision probably did not hasten Tom's death. It just made it all the more bitter," Dunlap recalls. Only after Waddell's death did the USOC lift the lien on his house.

Gay Games continued growing. Gay Games IV in New York City in 1994 set a record as the largest athletic competition in world history. Sydney, Australia, will host Gay Games VI in 2002.

A federal judge's rush to judgment had left key facts in dispute: Was there "state action"? Was there discriminatory enforcement? Fair-minded legal scholars disagree over the answers. Yet, the case's 5-to-4 outcome is a reflection of the Supreme Court's continuing refusal to treat anti-gay discrimination as an injustice. At least one majority justice—Powell—would have switched sides if the USOC had targeted a black group while leaving white groups alone.

Mary Dunlap recalls being "shocked" that Powell's majority opinion gave such short shrift to constitutional issues she had tried to raise. The justices in the majority "lost themselves by choice in the trademark issues . . . because I think they weren't ready to deal with gay and lesbian rights." Calling the court's handling of gay cases "irrational," Dunlap says, "I don't see their decisions as following some kind of principled path from one case to the next. They are instead a group of nine individuals who are very much swayed by personal experience—whether people are out to them, whether members of their family are gay or lesbian, bisexual or transgendered, and whether any of them is a gay or lesbian person. I think all those things ultimately and unfortunately matter more" than the constitutional issues at stake in a gay case.

"Bork Without the Bite?"

The day after his gay Olympics decision was announced, 79-year-old Justice Powell retired. The departure of the man in the middle meant the court's future direction on abortion, gay rights and a host of other subjects was hanging in the balance when the Senate began weighing whether to confirm President Reagan's nominee. Reagan had chosen appeals court Judge Robert Bork, a bellicose critic of all things liberal, including tolerance of homosexuality. When, as solicitor general, he had asked the Supreme Court in 1976 to vacate an appeals court ruling against fired federal worker John Singer, Bork apparently was merely carrying out the wishes of the Civil Service Commission, which had ended its ban on homosexuals.

While teaching at Yale, Bork had angrily denounced the idea of barring military recruiters from campus to protest the military's gay ban. "Societies can have very small or very great amounts of homosexual behavior, depending on the degrees of moral disapproval or tolerance shown," Bork lectured his colleagues. Elevated to the federal bench by Reagan, Bork scoffed at the idea that homosexuals are protected by the Constitution.

Bork's rabid homophobia, no doubt, would not have been enough to derail his nomination, even though hundreds of thousands of gay-rights demonstrators had marched—by coincidence—through the nation's capital just two weeks before the Senate's final Bork vote. In his Senate testimony, Bork made no secret of his view that the right to privacy is an illegitimate branch of constitutional law, a figment of liberal imaginations. He clearly relished the idea of wielding the pruning shears, lopping off even married couples' right to use contraceptives in the privacy of their bedrooms. Abortion rights would bite the dust, if he had his way, and that would just be the beginning of his efforts to rewrite landmark civil rights decisions.

Whereas Powell had fretted and struggled and reluctantly made choices, often ending up aligned with liberals on non-gay cases, Bork aggressively pursued an extremist agenda. For the nation's leading civil rights groups, Bork's nomination was a five-alarm fire: Generations of hard-won gains were in danger of going up in smoke. Bork was so far out of step with the nation on civil rights that he even disagreed with the unanimous 1948 Supreme Court decision holding that house deeds with language barring sales to blacks, say, or Jews were unconstitutional.

The belligerent Bork proved to be his own worst enemy, gruffly refusing to play the standard confirmation game of being politely evasive about his views. He dug in his heels—and lost on a 58-to-42 Senate vote on October 23, 1987.

Reagan's second pick, federal appeals court Judge Douglas Ginsburg, lasted just days: The "Just Say No" Reagan administration was embarrassed by the revelation that Ginsburg had smoked marijuana as a Harvard law professor. Amid jokes about Reagan's "high court" nominee, Ginsburg quickly withdrew his name from contention.

The president then turned to a straitlaced Californian. Anthony Kennedy, born and raised in Sacramento, had been a Boy Scout, a Roman Catholic altar boy, a good boy. He was so very good that his hard-drinking, freewheeling father, a liquor industry lobbyist, futilely offered him $100 if he'd just do something, anything, bad enough to get in trouble with the police, according to an oft-repeated anecdote. After Anthony Kennedy took over his father's law practice, he drafted a tax-cut ballot initiative for then-Governor Reagan. As a favor to Reagan, President Ford appointed Kennedy, 38, to the Ninth Circuit in 1975, making him youngest federal appellate judge at the time. Kennedy got the most satisfaction from teaching a Monday night class in constitutional law. Showing a flair for the theatrical, he sometimes delivered a lecture while dressed as James Madison, whose Bill of Rights amended the Constitution to begin protecting personal freedoms.

Kennedy didn't don a powdered wig for his Senate confirmation hearings in December 1987, but when he testified, the third-graders there from his wife's class got an early lesson in constitutional law. Stressing that the Constitution protects rights—including privacy—not explicitly listed in it, Kennedy said that "there is a zone of liberty, a zone of protection, a line that is drawn where the individual can tell the government: Beyond this line, you may not go." The eloquent Kennedy, 51, didn't sound like a Bork or, for that matter, a Rehnquist or Scalia. He was difficult to pigeonhole. Civil rights advocates worried that he was "Bork without the bite." His views on gay rights were murky enough to worry both their advocates and opponents.

Kennedy had ruled in five gay-rights cases. All five times he had ruled against the gay side. Yet because he clearly took gay issues seriously and once raised the possibility that some anti-gay discrimination might be unconstitutional, North Carolina Republican Senator Jesse Helms's knee-jerk reaction to Kennedy's nomination was "No way, Jose!"

Kennedy had written the *Beller v. Middendorf* decision upholding Navy regulations banning homosexuals. In *Sullivan v. INS,* he ruled that deportation was not a "special hardship" for Australian Anthony Sullivan, even if it separated him from his American partner. Kennedy had joined decisions finding that John Singer had no right to regain his federal job because he had "flaunted" his homosexuality, that the gay Olympics case did not merit the attention of the entire Ninth Circuit and that gay people who'd lost federal jobs were not entitled to class-action relief despite a lower court decision finding the government guilty of unconstitutional discrimination. In a sixth case, Kennedy ruled that it was not sex discrimination to treat the forcible sodomizing of a man as a more serious crime than the rape of a woman. "It is rational to determine that the harm, both physical and mental, suffered by victims of these two crimes are of a different quality. . . . [L]aws may properly take account of such differences. . . ," he said.

In opposing Kennedy's confirmation, the National Organization for Women, Americans for Democratic Action and the Center for Constitutional Rights pointed to his gay record as well as to his pattern of ruling against women and blacks. National Gay and Lesbian Task Force executive director Jeffrey Levi testified, "Judge Kennedy's views may be expressed without the vitriolic rhetoric associated with Judge Bork, but his conclusions are the same. . . . Judge Kennedy's notion of justice is too narrow. . . ." The Democrats had retaken the Senate, so Strom Thurmond no longer chaired the Judiciary Committee. This time, the only senators who quizzed Levi—Chairman Joe Biden and Arlen Specter, a moderate Pennsylvania Republican—sounded supportive of gay Americans. The committee reprinted an article by legal scholar Arthur Leonard that concluded Kennedy's record made his appointment "no cause for joy among gay people."

Yet Kennedy's 1980 *Beller* decision, despite its outcome, set him very much apart from jurists who gave no indication of being acquainted with learned arguments in favor of protecting the basic civil rights of gay Americans. In a remarkable bow to liberal legal scholars, Kennedy wrote, "We recognize, as we must, that there is substantial comment which argues that the choice to engage in homosexual action is a personal decision entitled, at least in some instances, to recognition as a fundamental right and to full protection as an aspect of the individual's right of privacy." He proceeded to cite the work of liberal constitutional law scholar Laurence Tribe and a host of law review articles favoring gay civil rights. Kennedy's *Beller* decision marked the first time that a federal appeals court had suggested that government-sponsored anti-gay discrimination (outside the military) might have to pass a test of "heightened scrutiny" to be constitutional.

Kennedy's effort to educate himself about homosexuality made some conservatives so nervous that they had persuaded the Reagan White House to pass over him when Bork's nomination failed. After Kennedy became Reagan's third pick, ultraconservative New Hampshire Republican Senator Gordon Humphrey worried aloud about Kennedy's nod in *Beller* toward liberal academic thought. Kennedy responded, "This was the first case involving a challenge to the discharge of homosexuals from the military, and I spent a great deal of time on it, and I thought it important for the reader and for the litigants to know that I had considered their point of view."

From a gay-rights perspective, Kennedy's most promising characteristic was the fact that he was not repelled by discussion of homosexuality. He clearly found gay cases intellectually stimulating. For a 1986 address to Canadian judges attending a Stanford University legal forum, Kennedy chose to talk about *Bowers v. Hardwick,* contrasting it with a European court decision striking down a sodomy law. Carefully avoiding passing judgment on the Supreme Court's *Hardwick* decision, Kennedy dealt very respectfully with gay rights but stressed that judges must stay within the confines of their particular government's legal framework: "One can conclude that certain or fundamental rights should exist in any just society. It does not follow that each of those rights is one that we, as judges, can enforce under the written Constitution. The Due Process Clause is not a guarantee of every right that should inhere in an ideal society. Many argue that a just society grants a right to engage in homosexual conduct. If that view is accepted, the *Bowers* decision says the state of Georgia has the right to make a wrong decision—wrong in the sense that it violates some people's view of rights in a just society."

Levi told the Judiciary Committee that Kennedy's *Hardwick* remarks weren't reassuring.

Yet to have a prospective justice—and a conservative one, at that—entertain the idea that gay rights might be fundamental in an ideal society was remarkable indeed. This was a Supreme Court, after all, that had just ruled that the right to sexual privacy did not include homosexuals, that had never disavowed the view that all homosexuals are mentally ill, whose chief had compared homosexuality to a contagious disease and whose previous chief apparently considered homosexual sodomy worse than rape. Tribe, the attorney who had lost *Hardwick,* urged Kennedy's confirmation, saying that Kennedy's writings indicated that he is "deeply committed to an evolving understanding of the Constitution."

Kennedy won confirmation 97-to-0 on February 3, 1988.

Terminated with Extreme Prejudice?

When Kennedy took his place on the Supreme Court, Chief Justice Rehnquist was in the midst of drafting a ruling in a gay "John Doe" case. The openly gay man, who would have preferred the pseudonym "Jim Doe," concealed his identity not because he was embarrassed or secretive about his sexual orientation but to protect his employer, the Central Intelligence Agency. (Apparently out of lingering loyalty to the CIA, he asked to remain anonymous in this account.)

Doe was a 17-year-old West Virginia boy when he landed a clerk-typist job with the CIA in 1973. "The company," as the agency is often called, tracked him into its upward mobility program. He was trained as an electronics engineer rather than a demolition expert because, he says, he "didn't want anything to do with bombs and possibly killing or maiming somebody."

For five exciting years, Doe worked undercover on state-of-the-art James Bond–style circuitry. "Everything was miniature," he recalls, avoiding classified details. As instructed, he told friends that he worked at the Defense Department. A gung-ho company man whose work was excellent, Doe had extremely high security clearances and dealt with CIA Director William Colby and his successor, George Bush. "I have autographed pictures from Colby and Bush," Doe brags.

The CIA had asked Doe only once—when he was 18—about his sex life. He replied that he didn't have one. Two years later he became a sexually active gay man and soon revealed his sexual orientation to his family and friends, including a few co-workers. Despite its vaunted intelligence-gathering capabilities, the CIA was virtually alone in being unaware that Doe was gay. "All I wanted to do was cross that off the list," he recalls. He didn't want to wake up at 45 and discover himself unemployed because his bosses had finally figured out his sexual orientation. Confident that a valued employee wouldn't be fired for being gay, Doe voluntarily told a security officer that he was homosexual in January 1982. He was 26 at the time.

Doe was wrong, even though lie detector tests confirmed that he had never had sex with a foreigner or leaked secrets. Two security agents told him that his homosexual activities violated agency regulations. A top CIA official said each homosexual case was evaluated individually. Finally, Doe was informed that the "circumstances of his homosexuality" rendered him a security risk. After Doe refused to resign, CIA Director William Casey fired him in May 1982—snuffing out a distinguished eight-year career. The CIA informed Doe that if he applied for a classified job, his prospective employer would be told that he'd been branded a security threat because of his homosexuality. That essentially rendered him unemployable in the field in which he had been trained.

CIA officials refused to say why, in their view, Doe's sexual orientation made him a security risk. "They told me that if I cooperated . . . and I was fired, that they would give me an explanation of the reasons. But they never did. They just terminated me. And so I felt like they had lied. I hadn't lied, but they had," Doe says. Angry and disappointed, he began an 11-year campaign to force one of the world's most secretive institutions to rehire him or explain his firing: Had his employment been terminated with extreme prejudice?

Doe had consulted Frank Kameny, who was eking out a living by advising homosexuals who had government-related job trouble. Doe recalls, "He was like, 'Don't give them your badge!' I thought he was a little bit too militant." Doe turned to ACLU attorney Mark Lynch, who pursued the case free of charge even after going into private practice. Doe sued the CIA, charging that its refusal to explain his firing violated agency regulations, federal law and due process.

CIA regulations allowed the agency to bypass its fair-employment safeguards when immediate dismissal was required. However, U.S. District Judge Barrington Parker noted that there apparently was nothing urgent about Doe's dismissal since the CIA waited three months to do it. Parker ruled in 1985 that the CIA had run roughshod over its own procedures and ordered the agency to put Doe on paid administrative leave until he was dealt with properly.

The CIA appealed, claiming that federal law barred the courts from interfering after someone was fired by its director. In a 2-to-1 decision, the U.S. Court of Appeals for the D.C. Circuit reversed Doe's victory, saying Judge Parker had not shown enough deference to the CIA director's judgment, and sent the case back down for a fact-finding inquiry. Judge Harry T. Edwards, joined by future justice Ruth Bader Ginsburg, ruled on August 1, 1986, that the director of central intelligence had broad but not absolute discretion over ousting CIA employees. "Without doubt, for example the director could not terminate black employees simply because they are black, female employees simply because they are female, or even blonde employees simply because they are blonde," the appeals court declared.

Directing a district court to clear up "confusion" over Doe's firing, the D.C. Circuit ruled that there would be nothing wrong with having fired Doe for no reason or because his particular sexual behavior posed a security risk. However, Doe would have an "arguable" constitutional claim if the CIA banned homosexuals, the court said. Broadly reading the month-old *Hardwick* decision as holding that "homosexual conduct is not constitutionally protected," the appeals court noted that the Supreme Court "did not reach the difficult issue of whether an agency of the federal government can discriminate against individuals merely because of sexual *orientation*."

Reagan administration Solicitor General Charles Fried petitioned the justices to take a case of "exceptional public importance," warning that the appeals court's Doe ruling imperiled the CIA by letting courts snoop into the reasons for dismissals. Federal law gives the CIA director "absolute discretion" over dismissals, even unconstitutional ones, Fried insisted.

Doe's attorney Mark Lynch replied that Fried was crying wolf because courts already second-guessed CIA employment decisions if they allegedly involved race or sex discrimination. The appeals court had ruled that the CIA director would not have to explain Doe's firing unless there was evidence his reason was unconstitutional. But in a separate petition, Lynch asked that the director be required to give an explanation, if he could do so without compromising security.

Solicitor General Fried countered that Doe had been told quite enough—that the CIA was bothered by "the duration and frequency of Mr. Doe's sexual activity, his failure to reveal his homosexuality to the agency for six years, and his unwillingness to identify his homosexual partners." (Doe says he told the CIA that he would identify his partners if he were allowed to give them the courtesy of being told that the CIA wanted their names. Permission was denied.)

To the CIA's contention that the director's firing decisions were not reviewable, Marshall clerk Eben Moglen said, "Phooey." Yet the court voted May 14, 1987, to turn the case away.

Warning that "secrecy in national security matters" might be in jeopardy, White circulated a dissent from denial of *cert*. He wrote that the district court had been ordered to find out whether the CIA had a policy of firing "all persons with homosexual orientation"—stilted phrasing that nevertheless shows how the court gradually updates its language. Rehnquist joined the dissent, as did the indecisive Powell, who had voted in conference to "grant," then switched to "deny." White's dissent was never published because the court reconsidered and granted *cert* on June 8, 1987, with Scalia providing the fourth vote. (The court turned away Doe's separate petition.)

By the time Fried filed the government's brief in August 1987, Powell had retired. Fried attempted to persuade the justices that Doe couldn't possibly have a valid constitutional claim, approvingly quoting a lower court decision against a lesbian would-be FBI agent: "It is not irrational . . . to conclude that the criminalization of homosexual conduct coupled with the general public opprobrium toward homosexuality exposes many homosexuals, even 'open' homosexuals, to risks of possible blackmail to protect their partners, if not themselves."

As a clerk to Justice Harlan two decades earlier, Fried had injected homosexuality into his draft of the justice's *Poe* dissent, gratuitously declaring that the constitutionally of outlawing homosexual liaisons wasn't being questioned. As solicitor general, Fried tried to place gay CIA employees beyond the reach of the Constitution's protection, implying that Doe's homosexual "conduct"—which may not have broken any law—meant his discrimination claim was illegitimate.

Doe's attorney Lynch replied that dismissing Doe wasn't rational and that Doe had been punished more severely than heterosexuals having sex outside of marriage. Lynch argued Doe was entitled to know whether the CIA director's decision to fire him was "tainted by an impermissible antipathy toward homosexuals."

On the morning of Tuesday, January 12, 1988, Fried and Lynch squared off in the Supreme Court's ornate courtroom. Since Fried represented the side that had persuaded the court to hear the case, he spoke first, objecting to allowing courts to go "rummaging around" in the CIA's business. Unbeknownst to the justices, Doe was in the courtroom, a few rows behind his attorney.

Fried deflected an O'Connor question about whether Congress intended to shield the CIA director even if there were "a policy not to hire a black or a woman or something of that kind." Fried's answer that dismissals are different from other employment decisions didn't satisfy Scalia. With the undisguised glee of a butterfly collector pinning down his latest specimen, Scalia pointed out that, under federal civil rights laws, the CIA sometimes must defend itself in court against promotion lawsuits.

Scalia continued, "And I say I do not see why that doesn't open up the CIA to the same kind of probing that you're objecting to here." Fried replied, "Well, it does, but that is Congress' decision. We are saying that Congress made quite a different decision as to the termination of employment. And I think that is a rational line to draw." Scalia: "It seems to me irrational. . . ."

Trying to recover, Fried declared, "It is also worth noting that Title VII [Civil Rights Act] lawsuits involve particularly serious and, traditionally, particularly important constitutional rights," implicitly contrasting discrimination based on age, sex or race with anti-gay discrimination.

Then, Stevens asked whether the law protecting the CIA's director's power would prevent judicial review of a policy of firing "everybody who wasn't a born-again Christian." Fried replied that the law would indeed shield even that decision. He conceded, however, that the Supreme Court might well find the law unconstitutional as applied to that particular situation. "But I do not think that that extreme but perhaps useful ability to keep the door unlocked, though closed, applies in this case with these claims," Fried said. Translation: This isn't a traditional civil rights case.

Fried's concessions to Scalia and Stevens, combined with the anti-gay attitudes that seemed to lurk just under the surface of his entire oral argument, raised a very real question of what the solicitor general was trying to achieve in the CIA case. Obviously, the goal wasn't blocking all constitutional challenges to CIA dismissals. And the courts were already rummaging around in the agency's business. What's more, the CIA already knew it could defeat Doe in district court simply by saying it didn't have a gay ban, since Doe would have no way of proving such a ban existed. And government attorneys originally had not tried to say that Doe's firing was immune from court review even if it was for an unconstitutional reason. That claim had surfaced only when Fried took over. The more Fried focused on why the court should rule in the CIA's favor in Doe's case, regardless of how it might react to hypothetical other cases, the more Fried stressed homosexuality. It almost seemed that Fried's unspoken goal was to get the Supreme Court to give such a sweeping interpretation to its *Hardwick* ruling that anti-gay discrimination would be placed well beyond the Constitution's reach.

When Lynch spoke, he stressed that before Fried no government attorney had suggested that the CIA director's dismissals were immune to constitutional challenges. Stevens told Lynch, "I don't understand this case. I would have thought the government would have been happy with its [D.C. Circuit] victory, would have . . . filed an affidavit saying we do not have any such policy [banning homosexuals] and that would have been the end of the lawsuit. . . ." Lynch replied, "I would have thought that the court would have declined *certiorari* on that ground as well."

Three days after oral argument, Rehnquist kicked off discussion of the CIA case by siding with a gay plaintiff for the first time. Federal courts do have the authority to review allegations that a CIA employee was fired unconstitutionally, he declared. Thus, Doe's case should go back down to the district court for an inquiry into whether the CIA bans homosexuals. Brennan, White, Marshall, Blackmun and Stevens agreed. Only O'Connor and Scalia did not. The court voted unanimously that the 1947 law that had created the CIA barred judges from second-guessing dismissal complaints involving anything less than questions of unconstitutionality.

Rehnquist assigned the majority opinion to himself and quickly circulated a draft that, with only slight changes, cemented Doe's 6 to 2 victory. "Dear Chief: I am pleased to join your opinion," wrote Brennan, who had knocked heads with Rehnquist on gay cases for 15 years.

The ruling announced June 15, 1988, in *[William] Webster, director of central intelligence v. Doe* represented a significant but little-noticed milestone for the gay civil rights movement. Though written by a justice who'd been aggressively hostile to gay litigants, *Webster v. Doe* was neither disrespectful nor dismissive of Doe. It did not equate Doe's "sexual orientation" with criminality, immorality or susceptibility to blackmail. In fact, it did not draw any conclusions about homosexuals. Rehnquist's opinion was so judicious in its few references to homosexuality that it might well have been discussing something as uncontroversial as left-handedness.

"It is difficult, if not impossible, to ascertain from the amended complaint whether [Doe] contends that his termination, based on his homosexuality, is constitutionally impermissible, or whether he asserts that a more pervasive discrimination policy exists in the CIA's employment practices regarding all homosexuals. This ambiguity . . . is no doubt attributable in part to the inconsistent explanations [Doe] received from the agency itself. . . ," Rehnquist wrote.

By treating *Webster v. Doe* as raising legitimate, unresolved questions, a six-member majority implicitly reached a conclusion that Anthony Kennedy had articulated eight years earlier in *Beller:* Government discrimination against homosexuals might be unconstitutional in certain circumstances.

The court refused to accept Solicitor Fried's invitation to treat gay CIA employees' constitutional claims as inherently illegitimate. Fried argued *Hardwick* was proof that banning homosexuals would not violate the Constitution. Rehnquist's ruling replied, "This question was not presented in the petition for *certiorari,* and we decline to consider it at this stage of the litigation." Thus, the court signaled that *Hardwick* did not dictate the outcome of every gay case.

In dissenting from the decision to let Doe's lawsuit continue, O'Connor did not mention homosexuality.

Scalia's dissent ridiculed the logic of the majority opinion, arguing that CIA dismissals cannot be both reviewable and unreviewable and warning of the harm of litigating dismissal of "our spies." However, in a roundabout way, Scalia joined the majority in indicating that certain anti-gay discrimination might be unconstitutional. He said, "Even if the basis for the director's assessment was [Doe's] homosexuality, and if the connection between that and the interests of the United States is an irrational and hence an unconstitutional one, if that assessment is really 'the director's alone' there is nothing more to litigate about."

Doe's case bounced down to Judge Aubrey Robinson Jr., who required the CIA to show him an internal memo written before Doe was fired. Robinson then ruled in 1991 that there was a rational and, thus, constitutional basis for firing Doe. "Homosexuals engaging in homosexual conduct pose a greater security risk than heterosexuals," Robinson declared. A three-judge panel of the D.C. Circuit then ruled entirely in the CIA's favor.

In June 1993, Doe was back at the Supreme Court, asking that his firing be declared unconstitutional yet still not knowing the reason for his dismissal. Doe had no way to know whether he had been treated differently from heterosexual CIA employees. Clinton administration Solicitor General Drew Days III told the justices that the CIA does not ban homosexuals and directed their attention to lower court decisions that had held homosexuals might be security risks. The justices turned away *Doe v. Woolsey* on October 12, 1993.

The CIA had kept Doe on paid leave for eight years. Unable to find a new job in electronics, he switched to telecommunications and returned to West Virginia. He lived in limbo, not knowing whether the agency was going to demand its money back. After his final defeat, the CIA threatened to sue him for a quarter million dollars and backed down only after he threatened to go public, he says. Bitter that his anonymity prevented the gay community from rallying to his side, Doe ended up feeling that he'd accomplished nothing. "Had I known what the toll was originally, I wouldn't even have pursued it," Doe says. "Emotionally, I'm not the person that I was. I don't trust anybody or anything." Doe says he's met other gay men fired by the CIA and still believes the agency targets homosexuals. He just can't prove it.

In 1995 President Clinton issued an executive order barring federal agencies from denying security clearances "solely on the basis of . . . sexual orientation." In June 2000, Congressman Barney Frank addressed a gay-pride celebration at CIA headquarters that drew 100 gay intelligence workers. Former CIA director R. James Woolsey welcomed the changes: "If the blackmail threat is removed, which has been done socially and culturally over the years and was ratified by the Clinton order . . . it seems to me gays and lesbians ought to be able to be CIA officers."

By happenstance, the first gay-rights petitions to reach the Supreme Court after Justice Kennedy's confirmation involved the one area in which he'd made clear that he considered anti-gay discrimination clearly constitutional: the military. James Woodward and Miriam Ben-Shalom had run afoul of military regulations in the mid-1970s simply for acknowledging being gay. After long bouncing around in lower courts, their separate, exhausting fights to regain their military careers ended up on the Supreme Court's private conference table on the same day in early 1990.

If any justice was under the illusion that *Hardwick*'s impact was limited to sodomy prosecutions, the Woodward and Ben-Shalom cases put the lie to that notion. In the appeals court rulings against Woodward and Ben-Shalom, gay speech (admitting a homosexual orientation) was equated with action, action with criminal sodomy.

The formal question before the Supreme Court in the Woodward and Ben-Shalom cases was whether gay Americans can be barred from military service because of their sexual orientation. The informal question was: Did the court care that *Hardwick* was being used to deny a host of constitutional protections to gay Americans never charged with any crime?

14

CRAWLING TOWARD EMPATHY

JIM WOODWARD DIDN'T FLINCH in 1972 when his low draft lottery number meant that Uncle Sam wanted him in the military. A college Republican who backed the Vietnam War, "I felt that stopping communism in Southeast Asia was the right thing to do," he says. After graduation, the handsome 20-year-old signed up to become a Navy flight communications officer.

Woodward, who as a college senior had fallen in love with a male classmate, told the truth on his enlistment questionnaire: "Are you attracted sexually or do you desire any sexual activity with persons of the same sex as yourself?" "Yes." "Have you ever engaged in sexual activity with another person who is the same sex as yourself?" "No." Despite its policy of barring homosexuals, the Navy commissioned Ensign Woodward and, after flight school, assigned him to a squadron in the Philippines.

In September 1974, trying to bolster the self-esteem of a suicidal "19-year-old kid" being discharged for being gay, Woodward took an enlisted man to the Subic Bay Officers' Club. In explaining why he'd broken the club's rules, Woodward said he was gay himself, naïvely thinking honesty would be appreciated. His commander promptly recommended his discharge. The Navy transferred him to its unpaid, inactive reserve.

Woodward, 24, fought for reinstatement. The Navy said he would have been ousted even if he had not been homosexual. That claim was weakened by the fact that Woodward's above-average performance ratings had been downgraded based on his sexual orientation.

Woodward's case bounced around in federal district and appeals courts for more than a decade. On Woodward's third trip to the D.C. Circuit, a three-judge panel finally addressed the major issues in the case and sided with the Navy. In March 1989, Judge Glen L. Archer Jr., writing for the court, said Woodward's admissions of homosexuality were not protected speech. Interpreting *Hardwick* as meaning "homosexual conduct" is not constitutionally protected, Archer tossed aside Woodward's privacy plea because "there is no claim . . . that he is celibate." Rejecting Woodward's equal protection claim, Archer asserted, "After *Hardwick* it cannot logically be asserted that discrimination against homosexuals is constitutionally infirm."

In August 1989, Woodward's attorney petitioned the Supreme Court, arguing that the appeals court erred in "equating Ensign Woodward with persons guilty of criminal acts." Bush administration Solicitor General Kenneth Starr, now best known as the independent counsel who investigated President Clinton, replied that the D.C. Circuit's ruling was absolutely correct.

Marshall clerk Jonathan Schwartz recommended voting to deny "for defensive reasons," arguing that "this case does not present a promising vehicle for carving out some protection for homosexuals in the military." He thought Woodward's chances of victory were hurt by his "non-sexual associations with other homosexuals" and the job-performance dispute.

Rehnquist put Woodward's case on the "discuss" list for January 5, 1990, making it the first gay military case considered in conference. Rehnquist, Brennan, Blackmun and Kennedy got a final decision postponed until Miriam Ben-Shalom's case could be reviewed.

"If I Had Lied, I Wouldn't Be in This Position"

The Navy had succeeded in muddying Woodward's challenge, but Ben-Shalom's was undeniably pure: She was a superb Army drill sergeant booted out for admitting being lesbian.

Born in 1948, Ben-Shalom was a Tom Sawyerish tomboy who grew up in a very strict family in rural Wisconsin. "There were no excuses for doing less than your best," she recalls. She learned to swim before she could walk and has vivid memories of hunting raccoons with her father and floating down the Fox River on homemade rafts. She married at 19 and divorced a year later, having borne a daughter. At 23, Ben-Shalom discovered she was gay when she kissed her best friend after a night on the town: "When my lips touched her cheek, it was as if the shutters came undone, the blinds were open, the lights turned on. And I knew."

Five years later in 1974, while completing her college degree, she enlisted in the Army Reserve. She explains, "My father was a Marine in the Pacific theater in World War II. . . . I really didn't have any idea that gays weren't allowed." She began as a chaplain's assistant, then became a drill instructor when new opportunities opened to women. In 1975, she was furious to read that Bronze Star winner Leonard Matlovich was being discharged for being gay.

Her anger aroused suspicion. She was summoned by her commander: "He said, 'Sgt. Ben-Shalom, are you a homosexual?' It's true what they say—your whole world does flash in front of your eyes. But my father had not raised me to be a liar. And I said, 'Yes, I am.'" In 1976, she was discharged because of her sexual orientation.

On May 20, 1980, federal Judge Terence Evans ruled that the Army had violated Ben-Shalom's freedom of speech, freedom of association and privacy. "[I]t cannot be assumed that all who have personalities oriented toward homosexuality necessarily engage in homosexual conduct," Evans lectured the Army. Ben-Shalom's record demonstrated that "her sexual preferences had as much relevance to her military skills as did her gender or the color of her skin," he declared. Evans ordered Ben-Shalom reinstated.

The Army failed to appeal. It also failed to obey. The court then ordered Ben-Shalom to be paid for the 11 months left on her tour of duty. Wanting to serve, not financial gain, Ben-Shalom got the Seventh Circuit to order reinstatement. She reentered the Army Reserve in 1987, eleven years after being ousted, then tried to reenlist. The Army refused to let her.

Judge Myron Gordon ordered the military to consider the "exemplary" sergeant's reenlistment application without regard to sexual orientation. When the Army found her qualified but refused to take her back, Gordon held it in contempt and levied a $500-a-day fine until Ben-Shalom was returned to uniform. Ten days later, the Army let her reenlist.

The Army continued fighting Ben-Shalom. Gordon again sided with her. He pointed out that the Army discriminated against homosexuals: It actually banned homosexual people, not homosexual conduct, because heterosexuals who committed homosexual sodomy could avoid discharge by claiming they had been drunk, immature or simply curious. To the Army's demand that he make the "common sense" connection between homosexuality and sodomy, Gordon said in that usage, "common sense" amounted to "little more than a euphemism for prejudice."

Quoting Justice Brennan, Gordon said anti-gay discrimination often reflects "deep-seated prejudice rather than rationality." He added, "Such hostility is evident in the very pleadings in this case wherein homosexuals are analogized to kleptomaniacs and arsonists."

On August 7, 1989, the Seventh Circuit ruled against the "avowed homosexual." Writing for a three-judge panel, Judge Harlington Wood Jr. declared that "the Army should not be required by this court to assume the risk . . . that accepting admitted homosexuals into the armed force might imperil morale, discipline, and the effectiveness of our fighting forces." Twisting speech into action, Wood ruled, "Ben-Shalom is free under the regulation to say anything she pleases about homosexuality and about the Army's policy toward homosexuality. . . . What Ben-Shalom cannot do, and remain in the Army, is to declare herself to be a homosexual. . . . [I]t is the identity that makes her ineligible for military service, not the speaking of it aloud."

Wood said it was reasonable to assume Ben-Shalom "has in the past and is likely to again" commit sodomy. (She insists she never violated the military's code while she was subject to it.) Because "homosexual conduct may constitutionally be criminalized," discrimination is not unconstitutional if it is rational, Wood ruled. The Army's gay ban is rational, he concluded.

In December 1989, Milwaukee attorney Patrick Berigan asked the Supreme Court to intervene, arguing that the Army's treatment of Ben-Shalom was irrational and unconstitutional. He noted that the Pentagon had "suppressed studies which show that homosexuals are no less suitable for military service than other minority groups." He pointed out, "Those of homosexual orientation are the last minority group to which the federal government sanctions outright discrimination without any evidence of individual misconduct." Berigan added, "This court should rule conclusively as to the effect of *Bowers v. Hardwick* on equal protection claims."

Solicitor General Starr told the justices there was no reason to bother with Ben-Shalom's case. According to Starr, "since the Army's concern is with the potentially disruptive effect of homosexual conduct, it is obviously rational to exclude homosexuals while allowing heterosexuals to serve." He pointed to a military case in which the justices had denied *cert, Hatheway v. Secretary of the Army,* and allowed selective prosecution of homosexual sodomy. Starr compared the military's exclusion of Ben-Shalom to its ban on minors and felons.

Marshall clerk Jonathan Schwartz thought Ben-Shalom's case was stronger than Woodward's because everyone agreed she was a superior sergeant discharged for acknowledging her lesbianism. "Whether or not [her] claim prevails, it is worth forcing the military to defend its outrageous policy in a public forum," Schwartz said.

The Supreme Court voted in its Friday, February 23, 1990, conference to deny *cert* in both *Woodward v. United States* and *Ben-Shalom v. Stone, secretary of the Army et al.* The United States was still at war with homosexuals. Through inaction, the justices had stripped Sergeant Ben-Shalom, who'd been promoted to teaching other drill sergeants, of her uniform for the last time.

A half-dozen years later, Ben-Shalom, 48, still owed $13,000 on a $55,000 legal bill. "I will tell you the cost of fighting the military," she says. "I lost the house I had. I lost custody of my daughter. I didn't see her for three years. It is very hard to fight all by yourself for 13 years." Driven by "a need for justice," she'd been undeterred by failing to get free legal help. "Nobody wanted to deal with a military issue because of the old animosity left over from the Vietnam war," she says, adding that lesbians often asked, "Why would you want to be a baby killer?"

Every time a court ruled in her case, she'd had to cope with the negative side effects of publicity, including being denied an apartment, being fired from a civilian job and receiving anonymous death threats. She regrets the years spent in dead-end jobs—driving a bus, working in a factory, tending bar—while fighting to serve. She doesn't regret standing up for herself.

She wishes that she could have told the justices, "I am in this position because I was asked a question by my commanding officer and I refused to lie. If I had lied, I wouldn't be in this position. So, what do you expect of your [non-commissioned officers]?" She says, "There just comes a point in your life where you just can't lie, when you realize there's something more than just words that are in the balance. I believe I would have lost my soul if I had lied."

Ben-Shalom, a Milwaukee substitute teacher, would now be eligible for a military pension had her career not been derailed. "It was my pride and great joy to serve my country," she says. "I know I changed the minds of the soldiers that I worked with because they told me so. I know that I've touched thousands of people's lives," she says. The Army told her that she was an outstanding soldier but unfit to serve. The Supreme Court didn't disagree. Yet, in the end, she says, her integrity was victorious: "I kept my heart and my soul intact."

Meanwhile, Woodward, 46, was chipping away—$100 a month—on bills from his 15-year struggle. A top official in San Diego's health department, he'd helped Ben-Shalom found the Gay, Lesbian and Bisexual Veterans Association. But after President Clinton couldn't keep his promise to lift the military's gay ban, Woodward was too filled with rage to stay involved.

Fighting for rights that heterosexual Americans can take for granted, Woodward lost his patriotism: "That whole thing changed my life radically. It changed me from being an American to being a gay man. I no longer felt a loyalty to the United States of America that caused me to join the Navy at a period when probably the majority of my peers would have gone to Canada instead. . . . And until homosexuals are considered whole human beings and citizens of this country, I will not support this country as a full citizen is obligated and responsible to do."

The Exceptional Simone

The Supreme Court had been rejecting gays-in-the-military cases for nine years when, for the first time, the government petitioned the justices to hear one. In May 1990, Solicitor General Starr asked the court to end one of the most remarkable military careers in U.S. history.

Army Staff Sergeant Perry Watkins had served 16 years as an openly gay man before being discharged in 1984 for being gay. The full Ninth Circuit ordered Watkins's reinstatement, ruling in 1989 that the Army could not repeatedly allow Watkins to reenlist, promote him and praise his performance, then turn around and oust him for a characteristic that it had been fully aware of all along. Yet the Bush administration didn't want Watkins treated as an exception.

But almost from his birth in racially segregated Joplin, Missouri, in 1948, Perry James Henry Watkins was exceptional. His strong-willed mother, the first black woman admitted to the local nursing school, taught him, "Don't give a hoot what anybody thinks about you. You can do anything and be anybody you want. . . . Never lie." As a boy, Watkins knew he enjoyed changing dolls' hairstyles, watching the June Taylor Dancers on TV and playing jump rope. So, that's what he did. At 13, he added sex with boys to his favorite pastimes. When a classmate demanded to know "Are you queer?" Watkins fearlessly answered yes. His inquisitor slunk off, reinforcing in Watkins's mind the value of honesty: He would never make any secret of his homosexuality.

After high school, he followed his stepfather, a military man, to Germany because he had heard it was an ideal place to study ballet. He didn't try to get a draft deferment; he knew the military had rules against accepting homosexuals. Yet at 19, he was drafted. On his induction questionnaire, Watkins readily acknowledged "homosexual tendencies." An Army psychiatrist grilled him about his sex life and, after being told Watkins enjoyed oral and anal sex with men, rated him "qualified" to serve. Watkins told his mother that the military must have changed its rules.

The Army's treatment of Watkins was schizophrenic right from the start. When he found out that a white draftee had been dismissed for admitting being gay, Watkins asked to be discharged. No, you can't prove you're homosexual, the Army replied. When he then applied to become a chaplain's assistant, the Army replied, no, you're homosexual.

Watkins was transferred to Ft. Belvoir, Virginia, to be trained as a company clerk. There, on a Sunday afternoon in 1968, five soldiers tried to rape 20-year-old Private Watkins in his barracks. He escaped, then told his commander, "I want out of this motherfucker Army, and I want out today. You put me in here knowing I'm gay, and it's your job to protect me." The Army launched an investigation—of Watkins. He named civilians he'd had sex with. Deciding there was no proof of sodomy, the Army kept him. At the end of his two-year tour, he was honorably discharged.

Watkins quickly realized that he wasn't going to get far in civilian life without more education. He reenlisted to get a college degree. Posted to a Pershing missile unit in West Germany, Watkins, who'd discovered his inner drag queen, was soon performing in Army clubs all over Europe as "Simone." When the *Stars and Stripes* gushed that "[Simone] Makes the 56th Artillery Guys Flip," Watkins laughed that the Army had no idea how many guys he'd flipped. Simone even won an Army beauty pageant, defeating 11 biological women.

In 1972, Watkins was denied a security clearance because of his homosexuality. The Army nevertheless allowed him to reenlist again in 1974. The next year, while Specialist Watkins was serving as a company clerk at a post in South Korea, an Army discharge board sat in judgment on whether he should be expelled for acknowledging being gay. His commander, Captain Albert J. Bast III, testified that Watkins was "the best clerk I have known." First Sergeant Owen Johnson told the board, "Everyone in the company knows that Watkins is a homosexual. There have been no complaints or trouble." The board unanimously agreed to keep Watkins.

In 1977, Watkins received a "secret" clearance. He was, however, barred from a NATO nuclear weapons program because of being gay until his new commander fought for "one of our most respected and trusted soldiers." The Army accepted him for reenlistment a third time.

Promoted to staff sergeant, Watkins was intent on rising to sergeant first class. But in 1980 the Army revoked his security clearance, citing his sexual orientation and his officially applauded drag performances. Watkins sued. Once again, in October 1981, he was summoned before a discharge board because of his stated homosexuality. This time, he lost.

Just 48 hours later, federal Judge Barbara Rothstein blocked Watkins's ouster, ruling that he couldn't be tried twice for the same thing. When the Army responded by waiting for Watkins's enlistment to expire and blocking his return, Rothstein ordered the Army to readmit him, which it did. Watkins again received superb performance ratings and was unanimously recommended for promotion.

But a Ninth Circuit panel ruled that Rothstein could not tell the Army to disobey regulations unless they were invalid. Reluctantly agreeing, Judge William Norris said the Army's "regressive policy demonstrates a callous disregard for the progress . . . made toward acknowledging that an individual's choice of life style is not the concern of government." The Army booted out openly gay Sergeant Watkins, 35, in May 1984. He was four years shy of retirement.

Watkins's ACLU attorney, James Lobsenz of Seattle, refused to surrender. After Rothstein ruled that the Army's gay ban didn't violate federal law or the Constitution, a divided Ninth Circuit panel disagreed and handed down a groundbreaking decision in 1988. "We hold that the Army's regulations violate the constitutional guarantee of equal protection of the laws because they discriminate against persons of homosexual orientation, a suspect class, and because the regulations are not necessary to promote a legitimate compelling government interest," wrote Judge Norris, joined by Judge William Canby. As Norris explained, the Supreme Court had ruled in 1982 that government "discriminations that burden some despised or politically powerless groups are so likely to reflect antipathy against those groups that the classifications are inherently suspect and must be strictly scrutinized."

Norris said, "We agree with Justice Brennan that 'discrimination against homosexuals is likely . . . to reflect deep-seated prejudice rather than . . . rationality.'" The Army, he added, "argues that homosexuals, like burglars, cannot form a suspect class because they are criminals." Norris shot down that argument by noting that the Army bans homosexuals, regardless of their sexual conduct. He added that most gay sexual behavior is not illegal.

Norris rejected most of the Army's justifications as illegitimately catering to prejudice, saying the military cannot bow to anti-gay bias any more than it could to racism.

Dissenting Judge Stephen Reinhardt thought that *Hardwick,* a ruling he despised, left him no choice but to rule against Watkins. "The anti-homosexual thrust of *Hardwick,* and the [Supreme] Court's willingness to condone anti-homosexual animus in the actions of the government, are clear," he declared, adding that he was confident *Hardwick* "will be overruled by a wiser and more enlightened court."

The full Ninth Circuit soon intervened. In a 10-to-1 ruling on May 3, 1989, Judge Harry Pregerson shoved aside broad constitutional questions to rule very narrowly in Watkins's favor: It simply wasn't right for the Army to tell Watkins for 16 years that he was fit to serve despite being gay and then discharge him on the basis of homosexuality. "Equity cries out and demands" that Watkins be allowed to serve, Pregerson said, reviving the order requiring reenlistment.

Solicitor General Starr petitioned the Supreme Court a year later. In reply, Watkins's attorney stressed that Watkins's situation was unique and asked the justices to let his victory stand. Starr then urged that the case be sent back down for reconsideration in light of a new non-gay ruling that he saw as restricting judges' authority to require the government to play fair.

By the time *U.S. Army et al. v. Watkins* was discussed in conference, gay Americans had lost the 84-year-old Brennan—their most vocal ally—to retirement. A stroke had ended the civil rights giant's 34-year career. Justice Marshall's notes show the court had trouble sorting out how it wanted to deal with Watkins. After an inconclusive vote, Blackmun persuaded colleagues to wait for Brennan's successor. David Souter joined the court in early October 1990. Five justices voted to erase Watkins's victory and send his case back down—Rehnquist, Blackmun, O'Connor, Kennedy and Souter. Instead of making Watkins's setback final, the court voted a third time.

A very odd five-member majority, including the newest justice, turned the case away, sealing Watkins's victory. On November 5, 1990, the court announced that *cert* was denied. What it didn't say was that Marshall, Stevens, O'Connor, Scalia and Souter had made Perry Watkins the first openly gay member of the armed forces to walk away from the Supreme Court victorious.

For six years, Perry Watkins, whose military potential had been rated "unlimited," had been reduced to being a telephone operator at the Social Security Administration office in Tacoma, Washington. He was at work there when he got word of his triumph. He immediately called the woman who'd taught him the value of candor—his mother. Watkins had spent 14 years proving that an openly gay soldier could win the respect of his comrades in arms. At 42, he chose not to return to uniform. Instead, he settled for $135,000 in back pay, full pension benefits and promotion to sergeant first class. Watkins's court victory—like his life—was truly exceptional. The military's gay ban remained firmly in place. Watkins died of AIDS in 1996.

The "Stealth" Justice

Three days after Brennan announced his retirement in April 1990, President George Bush nominated his replacement—a 50-year-old bachelor. David Hackett Souter's never-married status immediately sparked unsubstantiated rumors that he might be gay. Press reports that quickly raised questions about his sexual orientation then just as quickly shot them down only fueled the speculation.

Bachelors are rare in public life. When Souter was nominated, the nation had not had an unmarried justice since Frank Murphy's death in 1949. The press had reveled in depicting Murphy, who very well may have been homosexual, as a ladies' man. Whispers of homosexuality weren't deemed fit to print. But in the half century since Murphy's 1940 nomination to the court, the news media and the American public had changed tremendously.

Though confirmation that Souter was gay undoubtedly would have doomed his nomination, by 1990 being gay was no longer generally considered so unspeakably horrible that it was either unimaginable or unprintable. "Well, is he gay?" was a typical Washington, D.C., reaction to hearing that Souter was a life-long bachelor.

The increasingly confrontational news media, which in Murphy's era had jealously guarded the private lives of public men, thought nothing of injecting the gay talk into articles introducing Souter to the nation. The ethics that once would have kept leading publications from spreading gossip under the guise of debunking it no longer controlled journalism.

Souter was a stranger to virtually all of official Washington. Latching onto meaningless little details like the fact that Souter's New Hampshire farmhouse needed painting and that he enjoyed hiking alone, press profiles cast the stranger as strange. The gay rumor served to make him seem even more odd.

Time dubbed Souter the "Stealth candidate," invisible to radar. Describing him as looking like comedian Pat Paulsen with a Nixonian 5 o'clock shadow, the magazine presumptuously declared Souter was "the man nobody knows." To *Newsweek*, the nominee was "a man without tracks" and "a man without a shadow." Everyone who'd never heard of Souter before Bush passed over better-known conservatives, including

Kenneth Starr, for him had ample reason to feel uneasy. The abortion-rights crowd, for example, was alarmed because White House chief of staff John Sununu, who was strongly anti-abortion, was vouching for his fellow New Hampshirite. (Less well known was that Souter's best friend was New Hampshire Republican Senator Warren Rudman, who was pro-choice.) Abortion foes, meanwhile, were worried (with good reason, it turned out) because Souter had been board president at a hospital that performed abortions. The last time a Republican president had appointed a "conservative" interested in medicine—Harry Blackmun—the court had gotten its most ardent advocate of abortion rights.

In reality, Souter had methodically chiseled a fine reputation for himself in the Granite State. He was intelligent, frugal and kind, a man devoted to old friends and good books. He had not written enough on constitutional law, though, for his legal philosophy to be easy to label.

The unkempt Souter farmhouse that suddenly had reporters tramping across its yard and passing judgment on its appearance was in Weare, New Hampshire, and had once belonged to Souter's parents and, before them, to his grandparents. Souter, an only child, grew up in that small town but his academic excellence propelled him to Harvard. After college he won a Rhodes scholarship to Oxford, then returned to Harvard for law school. Souter briefly practiced law with a private New Hampshire firm before becoming an assistant state attorney general at 29.

Two years later, Souter got the break of a lifetime: He was taken under the wing of his state's ambitious and politically savvy attorney general, Warren Rudman. Soon Souter found himself elevated to deputy attorney general by Rudman, who envisioned great things for Souter and devoted much of the next two decades to making that vision a reality. As Rudman's political career advanced, he pulled strings to get Souter named his successor as attorney general in 1976, then appointed to a state judgeship and promoted to the state Supreme Court. Rudman talked Bush into naming him to the First Circuit in April 1990. Less than two months after Souter was sworn in as a federal judge, Rudman secured a U.S. Supreme Court nomination for him. "I can guarantee you that he has no skeletons in his closet," Rudman had assured the president.

Very soon, however, the press started making its veiled insinuations that what was in Souter's closet was his sexual orientation. With Souter on its August 6, 1990, cover, *Time* reported, "Some [unidentified 'activists'] wondered if the 50-year-old lifelong bachelor might be gay. (Friends assured them he is not.)" In a companion story, *Time* continued, "Souter had barely left the podium in the press room of the White House before Republican Party officials were raising 'the 50-year-old bachelor thing,' which was widely interpreted as a way of introducing speculation that Souter is homosexual. In fact the question has been dealt with twice," in 1978 and again in 1983 when he was nominated to state courts. By claiming the gay rumor had been circulating for a dozen years, *Time* fueled it even as it went on to name women Souter had dated.

Newsweek, meanwhile, boosted the rumor in its Souter profile: "No, he assured White House aides, he had never used drugs. And no, the 50-year-old bachelor said, he was not a homosexual." *Newsweek* continued, ". . . White House aides moved quickly to manage 'the lifestyle issue.' His friend Rudman assured a GOP Senate caucus meeting that the nominee was 'a very normal guy,' who had been disappointed in two heterosexual relationships. Journalists found two women he had dated in the '60s and '70s, who rated him 'very warm, friendly' and 'a real gentleman.' Perhaps more telling, a gay New Hampshire lawyer who spoke on condition of anonymity says there is 'not a particle of evidence' to suggest Souter is homosexual."

Implying that dating women necessarily meant a man was heterosexual was absurd, of course. Even more ludicrous was the idea that if Souter were gay, every gay lawyer in New Hampshire would know it.

Rudman was livid: ". . . Why raise such an issue gratuitously and then knock it down? Why raise it at all? If someone is homosexual that's his or her business, but if someone is not, he shouldn't be accused of homosexuality simply to titillate newspaper and magazine readers. . . . To print sheer gossip . . . without a shred of evidence strikes me as the height of irresponsibility." According to Rudman, who offered Senate Judiciary Committee Chairman Biden names of women who supposedly could attest to Souter's heterosexuality, "The gay issue arose simply because David was 50 years old and had never married. There was absolutely nothing to support such speculation." In Rudman's view, "The law was his mistress."

Souter, who was bunking at Rudman's Washington apartment while making get-acquainted calls on Capitol Hill, was upset by the endless rumors and innuendoes. "Warren," he told Rudman, "if I had known how vicious this process is, I wouldn't have let you propose my nomination." Rudman, who in 19 years had rocketed Souter from assistant attorney general of a tiny state to U.S. Supreme Court nominee, feared Souter was going to withdraw his name.

The intensely private Souter was primarily upset that women he'd known were being embarrassed, says longtime friend Tom Rath, who succeeded Souter as state attorney general. Labeling the gay gossip "ridiculous," he adds, "Those of us who knew him were certainly surprised at the rumors."

The Bush administration had asked lobbyist Kenneth Duberstein, who as Reagan's congressional liaison spearheaded Anthony Kennedy's confirmation fight, to orchestrate Souter's confirmation drive. "Some of the opposition was trying to make [Souter] out as Anthony Perkins in *Psycho*, that he lived at the end of the long, dark dirt road, sometimes with his mother, and that he was a bit 'odd,'" recalls Duberstein. He denies a published report that he had slipped reporters the name of one of Souter's ex-girlfriends. That wasn't necessary, he says, because the woman, Eleanor Stengel Fink, was talking to the press before he knew she existed. "The irony is that a reporter from *The Washington Post* gave her my phone number," Duberstein adds.

Over the years, Eleanor Fink had lost touch with the man she'd known as Hackett Souter. They met on a blind date when she was a college freshman and he was a law student. "We really dated seriously two or three years," she recalls. Souter had been a down-to-earth young man with a wry sense of humor. When Souter's nomination was announced, Fink was a homemaker. "I had my hands in the kitchen sink doing my dishes. I had the radio on. . . . I said, 'Oh, my God, they got Hackett! . . . This is incredible. I dated a Supreme Court justice,'" she recalls. When the press started fanning rumors about her old flame, she contacted *Washington Post* columnist Judy Mann. "It was my attempt to throw a little sanity into the equation," Fink explains. "The idea of his being gay strikes me as pretty funny. I thought it was a laugh and a half."

By the time of Souter's Senate confirmation hearings in September 1990, gay-rights groups had come out against him. Their public testimony focused on Souter's public record.

While on the New Hampshire Supreme Court, Souter had joined an unsigned 4-to-1 advisory opinion in 1987 telling the New Hampshire legislature that a blanket prohibition on gay adoptive and foster parents would not violate either the U.S. Constitution or the state constitution, even though sodomy was no longer illegal in the state. Declaring homosexuals unfit to be adoptive or foster parents would be "rationally related" to the state's goal of offering children "a healthy environment and role models," the opinion declared. It found lawmakers could conclude that homosexuals aren't fit role models because they might affect a child's "developing sexual identity."

Dissenting Judge William F. Batchelder said, "The state is never less humanitarian than when it denies public benefits to a group of its citizens because of ancient prejudices against that group." He pointed out that "the overwhelming weight of professional study on the subject concludes that no difference in psychological and psychosexual development can be discerned between children raised by heterosexual parents and children raised by homosexual parents." (The New Hampshire legislature, which had sought guidance from the state's top court, proceeded to prohibit gay men and lesbians from becoming adoptive or foster parents. That ban was repealed in 1999.)

Because of the anti-gay advisory opinion, Paula Ettelbrick, legal director of the Lambda Legal Defense and Education Fund, and Urvashi Vaid, executive director of the National Gay and Lesbian Task Force, testified against Souter's confirmation. The Senate's leading liberal, Massachusetts Democrat Edward Kennedy, termed the advisory opinion "troubling."

Asked about the advisory opinion by Alabama Democrat Howell Heflin, Souter cited the "role model function served by adoptive parents." Sounding almost apologetic, he added that one problem with advisory opinions is they're often based on skimpier evidence than other rulings.

Souter was confirmed, 90-to-9, on October 2, 1990.

Rumors and assumptions that Souter is a closeted gay man persist in gay circles. Yet a gay man who clerked for Blackmun during Souter's tenure says, "I don't think he's gay. I was kind of hopeful we would have a gay justice in him, but I know tons of his clerks, and I've asked them, 'Confidentially, do you think he might be?' And everyone says, 'No, I really don't think he is.'" Plus, the clerk adds, "To the extent there is anything to 'gaydar,'" Souter's manner of speaking, walking and dressing gives no hint that he might be gay. Gay-friendly Souter clerks consistently said in off-the-record interviews that they firmly believe he is heterosexual.

The "Slur" That Helped Clarence Thomas

Less than a year after Souter's confirmation, President Bush got a second chance to give the Supreme Court a hard shove to the far right. Justice Marshall—exhausted and disgusted at the increasing lack of respect a majority of his colleagues were showing for what he saw as basic constitutional protections—threw in the towel in June 1991. The Bush administration had already promised far-right conservatives, disgruntled that Souter was an enigma, that a second Bush pick would have unquestionably hard-core conservative credentials.

Bush kept that promise by selecting 43-year-old Clarence Thomas, a black man whose open disdain for such traditional civil rights remedies as affirmative action had fueled his meteoric rise through the Reagan and Bush years. Thomas caricatured black civil rights groups, reducing their liberal activism to what sounded like a particularly unfortunate name for a law firm: "bitch, bitch, bitch, moan and whine." From a purely political perspective, picking Thomas was ingenious. Many senators who might have balked at replacing a lion of the civil rights movement with a white nominee who ridiculed that movement would have great difficulty voting against any black nominee to an otherwise all-white Supreme Court.

Directly out of Yale law school, which had admitted him as part of a racial quota, Thomas worked for Missouri Attorney General John Danforth. In 1979, two years after the Republican Danforth won a Senate seat, Thomas followed him to Washington. Soon after winning the White House, Reagan appointed Thomas to the Education Department as assistant secretary of civil rights. Ten months later, Reagan named Thomas director of the Equal Employment Opportunity Commission. Civil rights activists accused Thomas of rendering the EEOC toothless—criticism that further endeared him to fellow conservatives. In March 1990, Thomas advanced to a federal court of appeals, thanks to President Bush. Just 14 months later, Bush nominated him for the Supreme Court.

Appearing before the Senate Judiciary Committee, Thomas played up his poverty-stricken childhood while playing down his Bork-like extremism. He depicted himself as a firm believer in self-reliance but no ideologue. Thomas seemed well on his way to a sure, if unenthusiastic, confirmation by the Democratic-controlled Senate when a thunderbolt struck him: A University of Oklahoma law school professor named Anita Hill was accusing him of having harassed her while she worked for him at the EEOC. The charge of sexual harassment—a problem that until then had been largely treated as a predictable, boys-will-be-boys characteristic of the working world—glued Americans to their TVs as Hill testified in lurid detail. Thomas denied everything. It was a classic, ugly "he said, she said" battle, with no easy way of telling who was lying and with Thomas certain to win if it ended in a draw.

Suddenly, a second former EEOC employee, newspaper editor Angela Wright, was ready to testify that Thomas had made repeated, unwanted suggestive remarks to her. Two women, who had not met, hurling similar charges would do far more than boost the credibility of the first. It would suggest that Thomas habitually accosted women and that he was very likely lying under oath. Desperate to discredit Wright, Thomas's allies made sure that articles reporting her claims included a countercharge—that she'd been fired by Thomas for calling a co-worker a "faggot." As a Thomas friend described the counteroffensive, "We got across that she was a gay-bashing sewer mouth. If [her] story had had a day to sit there, it could have killed Clarence Thomas."

On national TV, Senator Alan Simpson (R-Wyoming), a Thomas defender, asked why Wright had been fired. "I summarily dismissed her," Thomas said, because of "a report to me . . . that she referred to another male member of my staff as a 'faggot.'" Sounding horrified, Simpson repeated, "As a 'faggot'?" Forging ahead, Thomas added, "And that is inappropriate, and that is a slur, and I was not going to have it."

It was a truly strange moment in American politics. Thomas was trying to win confirmation from one anti-gay institution, the Senate, to another anti-gay institution, the Supreme Court, by discrediting the witness who might well have derailed his nomination by accusing her of having made an anti-gay remark. The image of Thomas casting himself as a zealous protector of homosexuals was especially bizarre because national support for his confirmation was being orchestrated by anti-gay activists Gary Bauer of the Family Research Council and Lou Sheldon of the Traditional Values Coalition. Thomas's politics left no doubt that as a justice he would be unreceptive to discrimination claims from anyone, including gay people.

The "faggot" accusation proved important. The Judiciary Committee refused to let Wright testify and a pattern of sexual harassment was not established on national television. On October 15, 1992, Thomas, who had charged that he was the victim of "a high-tech lynching," was confirmed, 52 to 48. No other 20th-century justice won confirmation so narrowly. Later, *Strange Justice: The Selling of Clarence Thomas,* a triumph of investigative journalism honored as a National Book Award finalist, cast grave doubt on Thomas's honesty. Three senators—enough to have cost Thomas confirmation—said that they never would have voted for him if they'd known what was later revealed. By then, of course, Thomas was a life-tenured Supreme Court justice, one who'd vowed to serve the second 43 years of his life on the court just to spite his detractors.

As for the alleged "faggot" remark, its reported target, Thomas supporter John Seale, later said he couldn't recall Wright saying anything of the sort. Thomas backer Ricky Silberman, a former EEOC boss, said Wright was fired because of her work. In *Strange Justice,* Wright insisted, "The faggot line was made up out of thin air. I'd never say that—I'd put my hand on a stack of Bibles! I believe they sat down and cooked it up because it says all the negative things you can say—that a person is homophobic and insensitive."

On the Supreme Court, Thomas, who sits in stony silence during oral arguments, initially seemed little more than Scalia's echo. He soon proved to be the most right-wing justice.

Painting the First Sympathetic Portrait

Before 1992, a Supreme Court majority opinion never expressed the slightest empathy for any homosexual, except perhaps in 1963 when immigrant George Fleuti was described as having taken an "innocent" day trip to Mexico. The saga of "respondent Hardwick" was stripped of every humanizing detail, even Michael Hardwick's first name.

The court's first empathetic homosexual majority opinion was handed down not in the wholesome cases involving Americans whose only "crime" was admitting being gay—gifted teachers, first-rate soldiers. Rather, the case involved a convicted recipient of child pornography. Even more oddly, the opinion in that 1992 case, *Jacobson v. United States,* was written by Bryon White, the justice who had treated gay-rights arguments with flippant disdain in *Hardwick.*

White's willingness to put himself in Keith Jacobson's shoes six years after refusing to symbolically put himself in Michael Hardwick's bedroom is, almost certainly, not evidence of a change of heart—or a heart implant. White and a majority of his colleagues seem to lack any overarching philosophical framework into which they could fit gay demands for equal justice. Most justices over the past 50 years seem to have approached every homosexual plea on a case-by-case basis, willfully ignoring the impact of anti-gay laws, regulations and rulings on millions of everyday gay Americans. Justices like White don't seem motivated by conscious anti-gay hostility. One can almost hear them explain, "It's nothing personal." *Jacobson* illustrates only that even justices who feel zero responsibility for protecting the rights of homosexuals as a group are not necessarily immune from being touched by a particular homosexual's legal woes.

Despite the nature of his conviction, Keith Jacobson is a remarkably sympathetic character. Born in Newman Grove, Nebraska, in 1930, Jacobson grew up on his family's 80-acre farm. At 20, he enlisted in the Navy and fought in Korea. He then joined the Army and won a Bronze Star in Vietnam. In 1972, Jacobson received a "compassionate reassignment" to a post near his hometown after his father suffered a stroke. Honorably discharged in 1974, he returned home to raise livestock and, eventually, drive a school bus.

Jacobson says he had a few homosexual encounters while in the military but never gave his orientation much thought during those years. Back home in tiny Newman Grove, he broke out of his isolation by ordering gay books and magazines through the mail—the only way he had access to anything gay. In an interview, Jacobson seemed hungry for human contact: It was easy to see how government agents were able to lure him into a trap by striking up a correspondence with him. He insists, "I'm not someone who thinks it's okay to buy kiddie porn."

In February 1984, Jacobson, 53, spotted an ad in a national gay magazine, the *Advocate,* by a San Diego adult bookstore, Electric Moon. He ordered two magazines, *Bare Boys I* and *Bare Boys II*. When they arrived, Jacobson was startled, he later testified, that some of the naked "boys" were clearly minors. They weren't depicted having sex, though. The magazines broke no law. Three months later, Congress outlawed receiving child pornography, defined as the "visual depiction . . . of a minor engaging in sexually explicit conduct," and postal inspectors found Jacobson's name on a mailing list when they raided Electric Moon.

Though Jacobson had no criminal record, except for a 1958 drunken driving conviction, he became the target of five undercover operations designed to entice him into breaking the new child pornography law. Using fictitious groups as a cover, postal inspectors and customs agents wrote Jacobson a dozen times. He was pressured into filling out sex surveys and corresponding with a bogus pen pal claiming to share similar sexual interests. Jacobson expressed an interest in homosexual material dealing with "pre-teen sex" but said he opposed pedophilia. He said that he liked "good looking young guys (in their late teens and early 20s) doing their thing together."

Government agents used Jacobson's responses to refine their pitches, luring him ever closer to illegality. After two years, Jacobson's curiosity got the best of him. He ordered *Boys Who Love Boys*. Its ad said, "11 year old and 14 year old boys get it on in every way possible. Oral, anal sex and heavy masturbation. If you love boys, you will be delighted with this."

On June 16, 1987, Jacobson picked up the illegal magazine at the Newman Grove Post Office, took it home, looked at it and shoved it in a drawer before heading back to town for a cup of coffee. On his return home, he was greeted by the sheriff and four armed federal agents with a search warrant. Their hour-long search of his house turned up the new magazine plus the lawful 1984 *Bare Boys* magazines but nothing else depicting minors.

Jacobson wasn't arrested. "I couldn't understand what was going on," he recalls. "I was terrified." Three months later, the local school superintendent called Jacobson to say that the 10 P.M. news said he'd indicted on a child pornography charge. That was the end of his 10-year job as a school bus driver. A federal jury then found Jacobson guilty of receiving child pornography, even though he had testified that he had not known he was ordering illegal material.

Shocked and embarrassed, Jacobson became reclusive, even though Newman Grove was rallying to his side. He faced up to 10 years in prison. On June 30, 1988, Jacobson, 57, was given a three-year suspended sentence and ordered to perform 250 hours of community service: He spent the rest of the summer painting his parson's garage and volunteering at a library.

On appeal, an Eighth Circuit panel reversed Jacobson's conviction, ruling 2-to-1 that he'd been entrapped. The government has no business targeting someone because of lawful conduct, "no matter how distasteful," the majority declared.

The full Eighth Circuit then reinstated Jacobson's conviction in October 1990. Judge George C. Fagg's ruling held that "the Constitution does not require reasonable suspicion of wrongdoing before the government can begin an investigation."

In dissent, Chief Judge Donald P. Lay called the government's behavior "reprehensible." Judge Gerald W. Heaney denounced the government's "deliberate manufacture of a crime." Heaney argued, "Had the Postal Service left Jacobson alone, he would have, on the basis of his past life, continued to be a law-abiding man, caring for his parents, farming his land and minding his own business. Now he stands disgraced in his home and his community with no visible gain to the Postal Service in the important fight against the sexual exploitation of children."

Pursuing vindication to the Supreme Court meant Jacobson would have to foot a $25,000 bill for printing and other expenses, he recalls. To raise the money, Jacobson sold his half of the family farm to his sister.

Jacobson's *cert* petition claimed he'd been impermissibly entrapped. Federal rules didn't allow someone to be targeted without good reason to suspect that a crime had been committed or would be committed without enticement. The petition said, "Just showing that [Jacobson] had an interest in preteen sex is not proof that he would commit a crime to satisfy it any more than showing that someone . . . watches 'Columbo,' for instance, is proof that they will commit murder," it argued.

Solicitor General Starr argued there was nothing improper about Jacobson's conviction.

Clerk Scott Brewer told Justice Marshall, "There is some chance that the center-conservatives might get upset by this kind of government targeting of admittedly completely innocent citizens, in part because [Jacobson] is a very very sympathetic [defendant]."

Brewer's assessment of the justices who passed for moderates on a court tilted far to the right was correct. White's "preliminary view of the record," according to his biographer, "was that Jacobson had been harassed by federal agents run amok." Justice Stevens added the case to the court's March 27, 1991 "discuss" list after Rehnquist, never sympathetic toward convicted criminals, left it off. Jacobson initially failed to win the necessary support. White pushed the court to vote again, and White, Blackmun, Marshall and Stevens produced the necessary foursome to take the case. Rehnquist, Scalia, Kennedy and Souter wanted to turn Jacobson away. O'Connor didn't vote. Then, before oral argument, Marshall retired.

On Monday, November 4, 1991, Keith Jacobson, 61, boarded a Greyhound bus in Omaha. The nation's top court was set to hear his case, and the prospect of a 22-hour bus ride wasn't nearly enough to keep him away. When he reached Washington, D.C., Jacobson walked proudly into the ultimate tribunal. "Here's a man," he later said, speaking of himself, "who's a single individual who got his case to the Supreme Court—me and my lawyer did. Sometimes you think of organizations being there, or big companies or whatever. But I wasn't that."

Just before 1 P.M. on November 6, Jacobson attorney George Moyer rose to face the justices and present his client's entrapment argument. The jury verdict was "fatally flawed," Moyer said, "because the government was permitted to offer to the jury evidence Mr. Jacobson suffered from a weakness, that he had a sexual desire to look at pictures, sexually explicit pictures of boys, and that he was a homosexual." Moyer contended that the only relevant factor was that government agents had had no evidence Jacobson was predisposed to commit his alleged crime.

Several justices grilled Moyer. O'Connor seemed worried that Moyer's predisposition requirement would rule out pawnshop stings, a common way to catch thieves who fence stolen goods. Kennedy wasn't buying the idea that doing something when or where it was legal didn't necessary predispose someone to the same behavior in an illegal setting. He told Moyer, "So under your position if someone used marijuana, say in the Netherlands where it's legal, that's irrelevant as to whether he is predisposed to use it here? I find that very difficult to accept."

Taking Moyer's place at the lectern, Assistant Solicitor General Paul Larkin Jr. said the "short answer" to Moyer's arguments was that the *Bare Boys* magazines were graphic enough to prove Jacobson was predisposed to buying child porn. White, who in the past had devoted his energy to throwing homosexuals' attorneys off-stride, disputed Larkin's sexually charged description and said most *Bare Boys* photos "are boys standing up all by themselves." Larkin then argued committing a crime proves predisposition. White hammered Larkin, questioning the active "targeting . . . and pursuing" of someone in contrast to "passive" pawn-shop stings.

When the justices voted a few days later, only White and Stevens sided with Jacobson. Rehnquist assigned O'Connor to write the 7-to-2 decision. Back in Newman Grove, unaware the conference vote had gone against him, Jacobson was entertaining the press, enjoying what he calls his "15 minutes of fame" for much of the winter. "I put the town on the map," Jacobson recalls with a chuckle. "How many little towns can say that they were visited by Mike Wallace?"

On the morning of April 6, 1992, Jacobson got a call at the farm co-op where he worked part-time. His attorney's assistant had news: "The Supreme Court decided your case, and you won. You won." Jacobson, ecstatic even in the retelling, adds, "And the majority decision was written by Byron 'Whizzer' White." Four years after being convicted, Jacobson was vindicated. It was a sweet moment for him, even though it had cost his entire 40-acre stake in Nebraska.

How did Jacobson win? Whizzer White, the retired gridiron great, had pulled off a come-from-behind miracle. The gruff justice wasn't one for sweet-talking or arm twisting. "Talk is cheap," he was known to grumble. "All the persuasion around here is done on paper." While Jacobson was being profiled on *60 Minutes,* White was painting a sympathetic portrait in what began as a dissent. White described Jacobson as a "56-year-old veteran-turned-farmer who supported his elderly father in Nebraska," an "innocent" person who had ordered the illegal magazine solely because the government "succeeded in piquing his curiosity."

White argued Jacobson's conviction should be reversed because there was no evidence he'd been predisposed to break the law. The legal *Bare*

Boys purchase "may indicate a predisposition to view sexually oriented photographs that are responsive to his sexual tastes; but evidence that merely indicates a generic inclination to act within a broad range, not all of which is criminal, is of little . . . value in establishing a predisposition," White said. "A person's inclinations and fantasies . . . [are] beyond the reach of government," he added. "When the government's quest for convictions leads to the apprehension of an otherwise law-abiding citizen who, if left to his own devices, likely would have never run afoul of the law, the courts should intervene," White concluded.

Stevens had agreed with White about Jacobson from the start. The force of White's very human argument swiftly swept Blackmun and Thomas to Jacobson's side. The decisive fifth vote has been incorrectly attributed to Thomas. Actually, two months after White circulated his draft, Souter provided the fifth vote. Souter did not consider it a gay case, according to the gay clerk who handled it for him. Thomas's vote constitutes his only known support for a homosexual litigant. Thomas reportedly sympathized with being the victim of overzealous investigators.

Having lost her majority, O'Connor dissented, saying Jacobson was no "innocent dupe." Joined by Rehnquist, Kennedy and Scalia, she added, "The government contends that from the enthusiasm with which Mr. Jacobson responded to the chance to commit a crime, a reasonable jury could permissibly infer . . . that he was predisposed to commit the crime. I agree."

After his victory, Jacobson's life settled back down. Several people who wrote him during his legal ordeal became pen pals. In 1994, he rode to New York City with an Omaha gay-rights group to celebrate the 25th anniversary of the Stonewall rebellion and to march down Fifth Avenue. Four years later, he was 65, retired and still reading gay magazines.

The Long Khaki Line

With *Jacobson*, the Supreme Court showed it was capable of empathizing with a veteran who happened to be gay. The court still wasn't prepared to show the same level of concern for gay people still serving in the military. Yet, by letting Sergeant Watkins's Ninth Circuit victory stand, the court had signaled the Pentagon in 1990 that it could not rely on the court's active help in ridding the military of known homosexuals. The justices repeated that signal in late 1992 by refusing to disturb Army Reserve Captain Carolyn "Dusty" Pruitt's preliminary victory.

Pruitt was yet another member of the long khaki line of outstanding gay soldiers with perfect evaluation scores and "unlimited potential." After five years as an Army recruiter, she shifted to the Army Reserve in 1976 in order to enter the ministry. She was slated for promotion. But after the brass read about her lesbianism in the *Los Angeles Times,* they ousted her. In a January 27, 1983 interview, Pruitt, a Metropolitan Community Church pastor, had described wrestling to reconcile her Baptist upbringing and military career with being gay.

Pruitt argued that her freedom of speech had been violated. A district judge and a Ninth Circuit panel disagreed. Though ruling against her on free speech, Ninth Circuit Judge William Canby said she might have valid equal protection claim. Ordering the Army to offer a district court a "rational basis" for its gay ban, Canby strongly implied that the military would have to do more than cite the prejudice of heterosexuals. He pointed to recent civil rights decisions.

In 1984 in *Palmore v. Sidoti,* the Supreme Court had ruled that racial prejudice was not a valid reason to take custody away from a mother in an interracial marriage: "The Constitution cannot control such prejudices but neither can it tolerate them. Private biases may be outside the reach of the law, but the law cannot, directly or indirectly, give them effect." In 1985 in *City of Cleburne v. Cleburne Living Center Inc.* the court said "mere negative attitudes or fear" did not provide a rational basis for requiring a group home for the retarded to clear extra zoning hurdles.

In petitioning the Supreme Court not to require the Army to justify its gay ban, Solicitor General Starr said the Ninth Circuit had erred in ruling that the ban "could not be justified on the basis of social disapproval of homosexuality." The relevant precedent, he said, was *Hardwick.*

Most justices jump at any excuse not to take a homosexual case. Pruitt's legal team handed the court a perfect one: "President-elect Bill Clinton has stated that, upon taking office, he will immediately rescind the military's ban on service by lesbians and gay men." On December 7, 1992, the court denied *cert* in *[Richard] Cheney, Secretary of Defense, et al. v. Pruitt.* To avoid returning to lower court, the Army settled with

Captain Pruitt, retiring her with a promotion to major and with a guarantee of full pension benefits. She kept serving in the ministry.

Even as many lower courts continued using *Hardwick* as a excuse to deny gay Americans all sorts of basic civil rights, the Supreme Court had begun to tone down its hostility. And Clinton's election signaled that if the court, always sensitive to how it is perceived, didn't want to look out of step with society, it might well have to change a great deal more.

15

Turning a Major Corner

"Come on, Chai. You know he really likes you. You know it makes a difference when people know someone who's gay. You should *do* it."

Georgetown University law professor Chai Feldblum was giving herself a coming-out pep talk, summoning the courage to share an important aspect of her identity with her beloved mentor, Justice Blackmun. She'd remained close to him after clerking for him in 1986–87, the term after his ringing *Hardwick* dissent. Blackmun knew all about Feldblum's career, including her part in pushing the Americans with Disabilities Act of 1990 through Congress. She wanted to be equally forthcoming about her personal life. But, she recalls, "I knew it was not going to be easy for him."

Blackmun was on record advocating "tolerance of nonconformity" in his *Hardwick* dissent. By then, he knew, via the grapevine, that ex-clerk Al Lauber was gay. But, as Feldblum was keenly aware, the chasm between uneasy tolerance and true acceptance can be difficult to cross. She'd watched Blackmun, who'd nearly drowned in hate mail after his 1973 *Roe v. Wade* abortion ruling, react with surprise at the number of gay people, including the son of dear friends, who wrote to express gratitude for his *Hardwick* dissent. "So," Blackmun told clerks, "I guess there are a lot of homosexuals in this country." Feldblum recalls, "He was shocked."

Chai (pronounced "Hi") Feldblum finally talked herself into coming out to Blackmun in late 1992. Over breakfast, a meal she had shared with him countless times in the justices' private section of the court cafeteria, she broke the news. "Well," Blackmun responded, "you know we love you *anyway*," speaking not only for himself but also his wife and assistants. The 84-year-old justice instantly caught himself, apparently having realized that he'd made it sound as if there were something wrong with being gay. "And then he stopped," Feldblum remembers, her voice brimming with emotion as she relived the moment. "And he said, 'No. No. We *love* you.'"

Serving on a court where justices choose every word with great care, weigh every nuance, Blackmun was reassuring his former clerk not just that his deep affection for her remained unchanged but also that he didn't see being gay as a flaw.

Feldblum was one of a number of current and former gay clerks who by the early 1990s were coming out to justices. Michael Conley never sat Blackmun down and declared "I'm gay" during his 1990–91 clerkship but says he talked so openly about his life with his partner that Blackmun knew. "One of my co-clerks would say, 'Well, my husband, Sean, and I are going here or there. And I would say, 'Yeah, Mark and I have been there.'" Conley adds, "Seeing us as real people, not just clerks, but human beings about whom he cared greatly and then knowing that some of us existed in gay relationships that were happy" helped Blackmun keep evolving.

Similarly, J. Paul Oetken brought his lover of four years to the court several times for breakfast with Blackmun during his 1993–94 clerkship. Oetken's introductions left no room for doubt. "Sometimes I would say 'boyfriend.' Sometimes I would just say, 'This is Tom.' Sometimes I would say, 'partner'," recalls Oetken, who says Blackmun was "warm and cordial."

Blackmun retired at the end of Oetken's clerkship but continued keeping close tabs on his "office family," as he called it. If the elderly justice forgot the name of an ex-clerk's spouse or partner, he could consult his office roster. By 1998, Blackmun's list included the same-sex partners of Chai Feldblum, Al Lauber, Michael Conley and J. Paul Oetken. The list was a testament to how comfortable Blackmun had become with openly gay people.

Unlike Blackmun, Souter was near the start of his Supreme Court career when the first clerk came out to him. Before landing a 1991–92 Souter clerkship, Bill Araiza interviewed with several justices, including ones who'd voted in the majority on *Hardwick*. He resolved to come out to any justice who hired him; he didn't want his justice to "walk away thinking he's never met a gay person." Araiza decided to first develop a good working relationship with Souter. He fretted that by coming out he might lose the justice's confidence. Also, Araiza, who considers Souter an old-time bachelor, admits that "one of the concerns I had about coming out to him was I didn't want him to think that I was reaching out to what I thought was a kindred spirit."

One spring weekend when they were working alone, Araiza told Souter he wanted to talk:

> I basically spilt it very bluntly. I didn't want to do a lot of hemming and hawing. You know, he took it very well. He's not a real gushy kind of person. There wasn't a hug.
>
> I think he was slightly uncomfortable with the idea of me telling him, not because he was uncomfortable with someone being gay in his chambers, but because, I think, his conception of what's appropriately private . . . would entail that this kind of conversation not happen. . . . I tried to explain to him why I thought it was appropriate that I tell him—that it is important for people in authority to realize that people who work for them and who are their trusted confidants are gay. And then I used the analogy that this is maybe what it would have been like to have been a Jewish clerk in the '20s—easy to hide . . . it wouldn't come out, but I just want you to know.
>
> He thought about it for a second and said, "Well, that's a good analogy." He asked if I had any problems at the court. I really appreciated that concern for my comfort level. After assuring him that I had not had . . . that was really the end of the conversation. . . . He certainly was not in the mood to continue the conversation.

Araiza chose not to bring up the court's gay-rights record during the 10-minute encounter. He and Souter never again discussed anything gay.

While growing numbers of clerks have come out, court traditions have limited the impact of their revelations. Justices are often retired or dead before their gay ex-clerks come to terms with their orientation and are ready to risk coming out in legal circles. Reunions bring one justice together with his or her clerks; sitting justices don't mingle socially with the ex-clerks of former justices. Of the 18 living openly gay Supreme

Court clerks located, only three worked for a justice still serving in 2000. Another two gay people clerked at circuit courts for current justices.

Justices' isolated work environment makes it very difficult, if not impossible, for them to know how much of their court's work has been done by gay people. Most of today's justices are unlikely to be aware, for example, of Powell's long string of gay clerks. There is no Gay and Lesbian Former Supreme Court Clerks Association filing briefs or inviting justices to dinner.

The Supreme Court changes far more slowly than the outside world, but it does change. As the stories of Paul Oetken and Bill Araiza illustrate, the current generation of gay clerks is more likely to be aware of their sexual orientation by the time they reach the court and more likely to be out. A growing number were openly gay in law school, as their résumés show. The résumé of William Hohengarten, who landed a Souter clerkship in 1996–97, prominently listed a gay-rights article from *Yale Law Journal*, "Same-Sex Marriage and the Right of Privacy."

Clerks weren't the only court employees letting justices—at least those without blinders—know they were gay. The sexual orientation of a top member of the court's small professional staff had long been an open secret. "I never advertised, and I never denied," he says. Hired early in the Burger era, he works closely with justices. He and his partner of more than 20 years "would run into Justice and Mrs. White at the ballet or at the symphony. We would be at a cocktail party where the Powells would be."

Shortly after Thanksgiving 1987, the man's partner suddenly died of leukemia. The first condolence letter to arrive at the couple's Georgetown townhouse was a handwritten note from Chief Justice Rehnquist. The grieving court employee received a "several-page handwritten letter" in Justice O'Connor's large script, he recalls, adding that both letters left no doubt that the justices knew the exact nature of his loss. Most other justices called to offer sympathy. Marshall kindly scolded him— "Get out of here!"—for dropping by the court before the funeral.

In 1993, the court professional threw himself a birthday party. "The O'Connors, the Scalias and the Whites came," he recalls, adding. "I would find them to be very narrow if they refused to come to my house because I'm gay. And they're not like that." He's never discussed gay issues with the justices. He thinks most justices (except Powell) have known his orientation. He's not ready to tell the rest of world: "I've cracked the door of the closet, but I'm not out."

"No Jews or Dogs"

Justice Ruth Bader Ginsburg arrived at the Supreme Court in August 1993 fully aware that she'd had a lesbian clerk midway through her 13 years as a federal appeals court judge. Ginsburg also knew that she owed the former clerk, Barbara Flagg, a profound debt of gratitude. Flagg had masterminded a behind-the-scenes lobbying campaign that helped defuse the feminist criticism that had threatened to destroy Ginsburg's chances of advancing to the Supreme Court.

Ginsburg ought to have been the feminist movement's darling. As an ACLU attorney, she had carefully orchestrated sex discrimination cases that gradually inched the all-male Supreme Court toward recognition of equal rights for women. While pursuing her intentionally cautious strategy, Ginsburg was fond of quoting Justice Benjamin Nathan Cardozo: "Justice is not to be taken by storm. She is to be wooed by slow advances."

Born to Brooklyn Jews in 1930, Ruth Bader felt the sting of bigotry early. Riding through Pennsylvania as a girl, she saw "No Jews or Dogs" posted outside a resort. After marrying Martin Ginsburg and becoming a Social Security claims adjuster, she was passed over for promotion because she was pregnant. Ruth Bader Ginsburg graduated from Columbia University law school tied for first place in 1959 but couldn't interest any New York City law firm in hiring her or any justice in interviewing her for a clerkship. "To be a woman, a Jew and a mother to boot—that combination was a bit too much," she recalls. By 1963 she was a law professor and pregnant again. She borrowed her mother-in-law's clothes to hide her condition because she feared it would cost her job. Reading Simone de Beauvoir's *The Second Sex* jolted Ginsburg into realizing that obstacles unfairly placed in her path because of her sex were part of a societal problem—one reinforced by discriminatory laws.

For more than a century after the 1868 ratification of the 14th Amendment, the right that it guaranteed to all citizens—"equal protection of the laws"—remained out of reach for women. The Supreme Court, for example, upheld laws that kept women out of the legal profession (1873), barred women from voting (1875) and excluded women from jury duty (1961). Pushing the courts in the 1960s to say that the Constitution required laws to have a better justification than that they fit stereotypical notions about "proper" gender roles, Ginsburg found jurists needed considerable education. "Race discrimination was immediately perceived as evil, odious and intolerable. But the response I got when I talked about sex-based discrimination was, 'What are you talking about? Women are treated ever so much better than men.' [They thought] I was somehow critical about the way they treated their wives . . . [and] daughters," she recalls.

With Melvin Wulf, Ginsburg wrote the ACLU brief that in 1971 led the Supreme Court to strike down a law as unconstitutional sex discrimination for the first time. Building on that breakthrough, she argued six sex discrimination cases—often having targeted laws that worked a hardship on men—at the high court between 1973 and 1978. She won five. By the time President Carter appointed her to the D.C. Circuit, the Supreme Court had ruled that sex-based laws must be subjected to heightened scrutiny. In Ginsburg's view, the huge number of women entering the workforce had transformed public attitudes and led to landmark rulings. There was "no chance" the Supreme Court "was going to move until there were pervasive changes in society," she says.

As a judge, Ginsburg maintained her reserved, cautious approach. As the Thurgood Marshall of the women's rights movement and as a seasoned judge moderate enough to win easy confirmation, she was a natural Supreme Court contender when 75-year-old Justice White announced his retirement on March 19, 1993. Her name quickly surfaced. Just as quickly, top feminists and other liberals questioned her suitability. They focused on a speech, delivered ten days before White's announcement, in which Ginsburg argued that an abortion-rights ruling less sweeping than Roe v. Wade might have been more productive and less divisive in the long run. Ginsburg's liberal critics were also bothered by her 1984 vote not to have her entire circuit rehear Dronenburg v. Zech, the case in which Bork upheld the military's prohibition on sodomy.

As controversy swirled around Ginsburg's possible nomination, Dayna Deck, the partner of Ginsburg's lesbian ex-clerk Barbara Flagg, attended a board meeting of the National Abortion Rights Action

League (NARAL). Deck was outraged to learn NARAL was pushing a male Justice Department official as White's replacement. She argued that NARAL should be backing a woman and that Ginsburg was the best pro-choice woman for the job.

Three years earlier, Deck had attended a dinner marking the tenth anniversary of Judge Ginsburg's appointment to the bench. Flagg, who'd been unattached while clerking, introduced Deck to Ginsburg as "my partner" and made their relationship clear. Later, Ginsburg responded to an invitation to the couple's commitment ceremony by sending a crystal vase.

Back home in St. Louis after the 1993 NARAL meeting, Deck shared her frustration with Flagg, who swung into action on behalf of her mentor. Flagg launched a reputation-mending campaign, an effort that decorum dictated Ginsburg could not undertake on her own behalf.

In a May 21, 1993, letter on Washington University law school stationery, Flagg, a professor of constitutional law, told influential feminist Harriet Woods:

> I'm writing to urge the National Women's Political Caucus to consider supporting Judge Ruth Bader Ginsburg as President Clinton's nominee to fill retiring Justice White's position on the Supreme Court. I've heard expressed some concerns about her views on the constitutionally protected right of privacy, especially as it applies to homosexuals and to abortion. I'm a law professor, a lesbian, and a former law clerk to Judge Ginsburg. . . . I want to assure you that I'm completely comfortable with, and confident of, her views on both issues. . . . I believe that if she were [a justice], our rights would be more secure than they are today.

Flagg's four-page letter, which Ginsburg deemed factually accurate before it was mailed, explained the judge's abortion speech and sodomy vote. The speech, Flagg said, emphasized "the value of a measured, step-by-step approach to doctrinal change." Ginsburg's goal, Flagg stressed, was to make abortion rights more secure. As for sodomy, Flagg said—as Ginsburg had in a concurrence—that Ginsburg felt that the Supreme Court's 1976 action upholding Virginia's sodomy law made it impossible for a lower court to topple the military's sodomy ban. Flagg concluded, "Her substantive style is generally moderate, but her commitment to equality is not."

Enhancing the reach of Flagg's heart-felt endorsement, Deck wrote a cover letter identifying herself as Flagg's partner and sent it on to NARAL president Kate Michelman and key friends at the gay Human Rights Campaign and the Women's Legal Defense Fund.

Just when it seemed that the Supreme Court nomination would go to Stephen Breyer, Ginsburg was summoned to the White House. Clinton chose her on June 14, 1993. At the Rose Garden announcement, Ginsburg looked sternly judicial—her dark hair pulled back in a severe ponytail, her dark eyes obscured by coaster-sized glasses, her lips pursed. If confirmed, she would be the second female justice in history, the first new Democratic justice since Marshall's appointment in 1967 and the first Jewish justice since Fortas's resignation in 1969.

Her confirmation was never in doubt. Senators of both parties competed in bestowing accolades on her, grateful her nomination would not cause a Clarence Thomas–style bloodbath. Harriet Woods, president of the National Women's Political Caucus and prime recipient of Flagg's letter, was among those hailing Ginsburg. NARAL, the Human Rights Campaign and Lambda Legal Defense and Education Fund expressed worry but not outright opposition.

Senate confirmation hearings for Supreme Court nominees are cat-and-mouse games with senators pouncing with substantive questions they know won't be answered and nominees darting for the cover of ambiguity. Judiciary Committee members use the encounters to telegraph which legal controversies senators actually care about. No Supreme Court nominee could possibly miss, for example, that key senators are obsessed with and deeply divided over abortion rights. Volleying questions at Ginsburg, the committee for the first time showed real interest in finding out where a Supreme Court nominee stood on gay rights. Ginsburg skillfully dodged direct answers yet gave gay Americans real reason to be hopeful.

Seven years after quizzing a gay-rights advocate about changing homosexuals into "normal people," 90-year-old Senator Strom Thurmond asked whether adoption could constitutionally be limited to heterosexuals. Ginsburg declined to answer.

Two days later, Senator Edward Kennedy, the Senate's leading gay-rights advocate, asked Ginsburg whether she stood by her 1979 assertion that "rank discrimination based on sexual orientation should be deplored." Sidestepping a direct answer, Ginsburg forcefully declared, "I think rank discrimination against anyone is against the tradition of the United States and is to be deplored. . . . This country is great because of its accommodation of diversity."

Pressing for clarification, Senator William Cohen, a moderate Maine Republican, asked what exactly "rank" discrimination based on sexual orientation meant. With intentional vagueness, Ginsburg replied, "I think base discrimination is deplorable and against the spirit of this country. Discrimination, arbitrary discrimination without reason." Cohen said his understanding of the Constitution was that discrimination with "a rational basis" was allowable.

Ginsburg responded, "If I discriminate against a person for reasons that are irrelevant to that person's talent or ability, that is what I meant when I said rank discrimination. Arbitrary discrimination, unrelated to a person's ability or worth, unrelated to a person's talent, discrimination simply because of who that person is and not what that person can do. . . . A person's birth status should not enter into the way that person is treated. A person who is born into a certain home with a certain religion or is born of a certain race, those are characteristics irrelevant to what that person can do or contribute to society."

"What about sexual orientation?" Cohen asked.

Ginsburg attempted to duck, saying, "Senator, you know that is a burning question virtually certain to come before the court. I cannot address that question without violating what I said had to be my rule about no hints, no forecasts, no previews."

When Cohen contended that her reply to Kennedy had already broken that rule of silence, Ginsburg summed up: "I think rank discrimination for any reason—hair color, eye color, you name it, rank discrimination is un-American. There must be a reason . . . for any classification."

Later in the day, Senator Hank Brown, a conservative Colorado Republican, reopened the topic, saying it was open to debate whether homosexuality involved "a class of people or forms of behavior. But in the event we are dealing with forms of behavior, would homosexuals be protected under the provisions of the Equal Protection Clause?" Ginsburg replied that she couldn't address a question that "ultimately" the Supreme Court must decide.

Pennsylvania Senator Arlen Specter, a moderate Republican, asked what standard the court should use in gauging the constitutionality of "discrimination against gays." Ginsburg wouldn't say. Utah Senator Orrin Hatch, the committee's ranking Republican, then closed out the history-making focus on gay rights by praising Ginsburg's *Dronenburg* vote.

The next day, a front-page *Washington Post* headline, no doubt read by more senators than had watched the televised hearings, flatly declared: "Ginsburg Deplores Bias Against Gays." That was exactly the sort of unhedged gay-rights statement that she'd spent much of the day avoiding. Yet she'd come closer than any prior nominee to deploring anti-gay bias. She had stopped just short of saying that discrimination based on sexual orientation is as irrational as discrimination based on eye color and just as difficult to justify under the Constitution.

The Senate confirmed the 60-year-old Ginsburg on August 3, 1993 by a vote of 96 to 3. In voting against her, North Carolina Republican Jesse Helms cited her support of what he called the "homosexual agenda."

On Tuesday, August 10, in a brief ceremony at the Supreme Court, Chief Justice Rehnquist swore in Ruth Bader Ginsburg to succeed the justice who had authored the 1986 ruling that handed gay Americans their greatest legal setback. Seated in the third row was a lesbian couple, Barbara Flagg and Dayna Deck. They were there at Ginsburg's invitation. From a gay-rights perspective, Ginsburg had brought incremental progress to the court on her first day in office.

Just as Ginsburg's statements told justices that the outside world was changing—blatant anti-gay discrimination was less and less socially acceptable—two cases that arrived during Ginsburg's first term showed that state and local governments were no longer uniformly hostile to gay rights. In both, governments took what amounted to the gay side—a first for the court.

In one, an anti-gay Florida organization called The Take Back Tampa Political Committee and its leader, Richard M. Clewis III, claimed that their constitutional right to petition the government had been denied. A Tampa ordinance outlawing discrimination based on sexual orientation in employment, housing and public accommodations had been signed into law in May 1991. Take Back Tampa spearheaded a petition drive to put a repeal initiative on the ballot. Take Back fell 180 short of the required 12,310 signatures after 462 signatures were thrown out because they belonged to people recently purged from the active voter rolls. A state court ordered the purged names restored. After a state appeals court also sided with Take Back, the city put repeal on the 1992 ballot. Repeal won with nearly 60 percent of the vote. The Florida Supreme Court then ruled that the 462 disputed signatures were invalid.

Documents filed with the U.S. Supreme Court left the justices in the dark about whether the final Florida ruling had revived the gay-rights law. Those papers just showed that Take Back Tampa considered the voter-roll purge unconstitutional while the county attorney and county elections supervisor Robin Krivanek thought the purge had been required by law. The U.S. Supreme Court turned away *Richard M. Clewis III and The Take Back Tampa Political Committee v. Robin C. Krivanek* on April 18, 1994. Through their inaction, the justices kept gay Tampa residents protected: Fifteen days after the Florida Supreme Court ruled, city attorneys infuriated Take Back by declaring that the decision meant the gay-rights ordinance was once again law.

Similarly, gay rights won when the justices refused on June 13, 1994, to hear a challenge to a New York state agency's inclusive definition of "family." The state legislature had clamped rent controls on New York City apartments in response to a serious housing shortage after World War II. Landlords then became eager for apartments to turn over because new tenants could be charged more. If a leaseholder died or moved out, the landlord could evict the apartment's other tenants—unless they were related by blood or marriage to the original tenant.

In 1989 New York's top court redefined "family" to bar the eviction of a gay man from the apartment he'd shared with his partner of 10 years. The state housing authority then reworked its regulations to protect tenants with a committed, interdependent relationship to the leaseholder—regardless of whether it fit the traditional definition of "family."

The landlords of more than 1 million apartments argued in *The Rent Stabilization Association of New York City et al. v. Richard L. Higgins et al.* that the new rules representing an unconstitutional "taking" of private property. Among those joining housing Commissioner Higgins in urging the justices to turn the landlords' case away was a giant of off-Broadway theater, Everett Quinton. He'd had to fight eviction after AIDS claimed his lover, comic genius Charles Ludlam. By letting New York's expanded definition of "family" stand, the justices allowed the state to put a surviving gay partner on equal footing with a widow or widower when it came to being protected from eviction.

A Plain Vanilla Nominee

Nine months after Ginsburg's confirmation, Blackmun's retirement enabled Clinton to nominate a second justice. By the time he stepped down at 85, Blackmun had gone from being a law-and-order conservative to being the most liberal justice—a shift showing not only Blackmun's evolution but also how the court's changing composition had pulled it to the right after his 1973 *Roe v. Wade* decision. Brennan had been the court's leading liberal when he retired in 1990. Marshall then filled that role until retirement. With Blackmun's departure, the moderate, unpredictable Stevens was as close as any justice got to being liberal. But rather than expend political capital trying to rebuild the court's left wing, Clinton selected a plain vanilla nominee with no clear views on any major social issue, including gay civil rights, even after 14 years as an appeals court judge. Clinton's choice, First Circuit Chief Judge Stephen Breyer, 55, had been the runner-up when the president chose Ginsburg.

Born into a Jewish middle-class San Francisco family, Breyer's academic prowess took him to Stanford, Oxford and Harvard law school. As a clerk to Justice Arthur Goldberg, he drafted Goldberg's concurrence in the 1965 *Griswold* birth control case—a right-to-privacy landmark that has been twisted to justify anti-gay rulings. Breyer then worked at the Justice Department, married a wealthy British aristocrat, taught at Harvard, served as an assistant Watergate prosecutor and became chief counsel to the Senate Judiciary Committee while Senator Edward Kennedy was chairman. President Carter tapped Breyer for the court of appeals in 1980. Senate Republicans were so fond of Breyer that they allowed him to be confirmed even though Carter had already lost to Ronald Reagan.

A political odd couple—Kennedy and conservative Republican Orrin Hatch—successfully pushed the Clinton White House to elevate Breyer to the Supreme Court. The Senate's four-day confirmation hearing focused on regulatory reform and antitrust law, Breyer's dry specialties. Defined by friends as a pragmatist, Breyer spoke in vague, moderate-sounding platitudes, saying the Constitution guarantees rights that enable people to "lead lives of dignity." Which people, what rights? He didn't say, other than to deem the right to abortion "settled law."

Two senators' questions touched on sexual orientation; Breyer's bland replies didn't. Breyer's one gay case, *Matthews v. Marsh,* wasn't mentioned. In it, Breyer had dissented from a decision vacating a trial judge's gay-rights ruling. The judge had held that discharging Diane Matthews for telling her Army Reserve commander that she was gay violated the First Amendment. The First Circuit instructed the trial judge to reconsider the case and to take into account Matthews's later admission of homosexual conduct. "We don't know why [Breyer] dissented," noted gay law expert Arthur Leonard, who felt that gay Americans should be "cautiously optimistic" about him.

As a First Circuit judge, Breyer had at least two gay clerks, those clerks confirm. However, he neither talked about his private life nor inquired into his clerks'. To him, as with Justices Douglas and White, law clerks aren't adopted children, protégés or pals. They're just assistants. Breyers' clerks don't even hold reunions, according to a gay ex-clerk who says Breyer would have never thought about a clerk's sexual orientation. Breyer gets so focused on work that he's been known to forget to change shirts. He didn't notice when a caged mouse moved into his office.

Breyer's Supreme Court appointment was confirmed on July 29, 1994.

In the eight years after *Hardwick,* six justices retired. Scalia, Kennedy, Souter, Thomas, Ginsburg and Breyer took their places. Only Rehnquist, Stevens and O'Connor were holdovers. When Breyer took his seat in August 1994, the nation's top tribunal stopped playing Musical Chairs. Breyer and the justices who greeted him would serve together into the 21st century.

Less than a year after Breyer's arrival, the Supreme Court turned a major corner with a unanimous decision that treated the gay-rights movement with unprecedented respect. That 1995 case was *Hurley et al. v. Irish-American Gay, Lesbian and Bisexual Group of Boston*.

The Court Learns to Say "Gay"

The St. Patrick's Day Parade is Boston's biggest party. "We just wanted to be part of it," Cathleen Finn wistfully recalls.

In early 1992 Finn, the bisexual daughter of Irish immigrants, spotted a flier on her church bulletin board for the new Irish-American Gay, Lesbian and Bisexual Group of Boston (GLIB). Three Irish-American women—Barbra Kay, Cindy Toombs and Ellie Rudolph—had created the group after deciding that Boston's parade should have an openly gay contingent. Finn jumped at the chance to join. "The Irish culture is very heterosexually oriented," Finn says. "So if you are not heterosexual, you can somewhat lose your sense of your Irishness. I saw [GLIB] as a way of reconnecting, of not having to check either being bisexual or being Irish at the door."

Boston's St. Patrick's Day Parade, which draws a million spectators, honors not only the patron saint of Ireland but "Evacuation Day." On March 17, 1776, British troops evacuated their posts in South Boston as George Washington scored his first victory of the Revolutionary War. Boston's government long sponsored the St. Patrick's/Evacuation Day Parade. After World War II, the city continued to help finance the celebration but turned responsibility for it over to the South Boston Allied War Veterans Council. Year after year, as many as 20,000 marchers paraded through working-class South Boston. The Veterans Council generally welcomed any group that applied to march. McGruff the Crime Dog paraded alongside Miss Ice-O-Rama, the Boston Bruins, the AFL-CIO, the South Boston Baptist Bible Trolley and politicians of every ethnic stripe. Over the decades, the Veterans Council had turned away only the Ku Klux Klan and, at the height of South Boston's furor over court-ordered busing, an anti-busing group. Yet the Veterans Council, led by John J. "Wacko" Hurley, voted to bar GLIB for "safety reasons."

GLIB soon won a state court order allowing 25 members to march, provided they carried only one banner and handed out nothing to the crowd—restrictions catering to the Veterans Council's expressed fear that GLIB members were disruptive ACT-UP and Queer Nation radicals.

Two decades after forced busing sparked a violent reaction, the idea of court-ordered anything hit a raw nerve in South Boston. In the days leading up the 1992 parade, death threats rained down on GLIB members whose names surfaced in the news media. Several would-be GLIB marchers wrote out their wills, Finn recalls. She chose to march because "I knew that if something happened to me I really wouldn't be the first Irish bisexual to be killed for that."

Wearing warm clothes and nervous smiles, she and 24 other GLIB members marched behind a banner bearing their group's name and decorated with gay-pride pink triangles inside Irish shamrocks. Hostility intensified as the march progressed. Above the sirens of GLIB's motorcycle cop escort, menacing shouts rang out, sometimes as chants from knots of young men: "Hope you guys die of AIDS! Fucking homos!" "No fags! No fags! No fags!" "Queers—every one of you!" Almost anywhere the GLIB marchers looked, they saw obscene gestures. A middle-aged man holding a "Choose Life" sign dropped his trousers and mooned them.

Pelted with generally harmless objects, including a smoke bomb, GLIB's marchers kept smiling, kept waving and shouted "Thank you" and "We love you, Boston" back to the occasional supportive spectator. "We didn't throw condoms. We didn't swear. We were not disrespectful in any way in the face of a lot of hostility," Finn recalls. No one was injured.

The next year, 1993, the Veterans Council turned down GLIB's application, this time saying that "sexual themes" were inconsistent with the parade's "traditional religious and social values." GLIB again won a court order allowing it to join the parade.

Then in December 1993, Massachusetts Judge J. Harrold Flannery held that the Veterans Council was breaking the state's anti-bias law. The council's shifting explanations for barring GLIB were attempts to camouflage its real, illegal reason, he ruled. "The evidence establishes that GLIB was excluded . . . on account of its members' sexual orientation," he found. However, Flannery said the discrimination was not unconstitutional because the 1993 parade wasn't government-sponsored—the city had refused to underwrite it because organizers barred GLIB.

Flannery also ruled that the Veterans Council did not have a First Amendment right to exclude GLIB because the parade was such a crazy quilt that it had no discernible overall message. Also, in Flannery's view, "a proper celebration of St. Patrick's and Evacuation Day requires diversity and inclusiveness." He concluded, "History does not record that St. Patrick limited his ministry to heterosexuals or that General Washington's soldiers were all straight."

The Veterans Council responded by canceling the 1994 parade. Everyone who loved the parade was upset. GLIB came under intense pressure, including from many gay people, to back down. The cancellation put a national media spotlight on GLIB's fight for inclusion. One GLIB member appeared on *Larry King Live*. Finn went on *The Today Show*. "I was able to do well with [media appearances]," she says, "but it takes a toll, it really does. You are totally out. You are no longer able to be in the closet. That's great. But it's also terrifying. I remember right after the ABC-TV thing . . . I had a death threat on my answering machine."

In July 1994, Massachusetts's top court seconded Flannery's finding of illegal discrimination. The Veterans Council had unsuccessfully argued that because groups had to apply to march, the parade was not a "public accommodation" and excluding GLIB, thus, did not violate the anti-bias provisions of the state's public accommodations law. "Under the defendants' reasoning," the court ruled in its 4-to-1 decision, "a restaurant which admits only diners who have made reservations . . . would be exempt from the public accommodations laws."

The court's lone dissenter lamented, "Today will be regarded as a sad and frustrating day in the history of the First Amendment. . . . [T]he Veterans Council does not need a narrow or distinct theme or message in its parade to be protected under the First Amendment."

The Veterans Council petitioned the U.S. Supreme Court in October 1994. Since a state's top court is the final arbiter of what a state law means, the fact that the Boston St. Patrick's Day parade was a public accommodation and the fact that parade organizers had broken the state's anti-bias law were no longer open to debate. The only question before the justices was whether Massachusetts's anti-bias law violated the Veterans Council's First Amendment rights.

Boston attorney Chester Darling argued that any parade amounted to constitutionally protected speech. He told the justices that the Veterans Council had canceled its 1994 parade "rather than showcasing a message they deemed offensive." He contended that GLIB was banned because of its message, not its members' sexual orientation. The Veterans Council had never barred any marcher for being homosexual or bisexual and would allow GLIB members to march if they carried no identifying banner, he said. Raising the specter of requiring a "Salute to Israel Parade" to accept a Nazi contingent, Darling concluded, "It is beyond dispute that the First Amendment rights of everyone require that there be no forced mixing of [parade] messages."

GLIB's reply minimized its Massachusetts victory, calling it a mere "state-law decision" not warranting the justices' attention.

The Supreme Court accepted the parade case on January 6, 1995. GLIB immediately tried to get the case dismissed as moot, arguing that the controversy had vanished because the Veterans Council had adopted explicit themes for the upcoming 1995 parade: It was to "honor St. Patrick," "celebrate . . . traditional families" and protest judicial intervention into the parade. Attorney Darling countered that the dispute was very much alive because "the veterans emphatically wish to return to the way they have run the parade for the last 47 years."

In his written brief, Darling repeated his argument: The St. Patrick's Day celebration was a "private parade" and that all such parades are entitled to First Amendment protection from government interference with their messages. Saying the veterans found GLIB's message "morally objectionable," Darling stated, "The veterans cannot be forced to include someone else's message in their parade and they have a First Amendment Right to remain silent on the subject of homosexuality." GLIB's presence in the 1992 and 1993 parades turned "a source of pride and accomplishment" into "a source of anger and embarrassment" for the Veterans Council, he contended. "If [GLIB members] wish to proclaim their homosexuality and Irish heritage as a group, they can hold their own parade," he added.

GLIB attorney John Ward of Boston replied that the Massachusetts courts didn't force the Veterans Council to express any particular message: The courts simply required the veterans to stop discriminating. The veterans have no more right to discriminate against a gay group than a restaurant owner has to refuse to serve blacks or an employer has to refuse to hire Jews, Ward said. He argued that anti-bias laws would be toothless if event organizers or business owners could get exempted by saying they didn't want to be compelled to send a message of tolerance.

What's more, GLIB's parade banner expressed no "message" beyond the fact that Irish-American gay and bisexual people exist, Ward argued. "The very purpose of public accommodations statutes is to protect the right . . . to participate in public life without having to hide identity or remain silent about it," he said.

It was as if the Veterans Council had said it didn't bar Jews and claimed that a group carrying an "Irish-American Jews" banner was barred not because of its religion but because of the "message" implied by their name. The Veterans Council's position amounted to a civilian version of "Don't Ask, Don't Tell." If you don't identify yourself, we won't discriminate against you. What good are non-discrimination guarantees to an invisible group if visibility is deemed a legitimate excuse for exclusion?

The Supreme Court had never shown any understanding of sexual orientation. It had always treated homosexuality as a form of misbehavior, not an innate characteristic. In 1987, the court had refused to treat the name "Gay Olympic Games" as protected political speech. How would the 1995 court view "Gay, Lesbian and Bisexual Group of Boston"? Would "gay" now be considered a message-laden word, a protected expression of identity or both?

A New, Respectful Tone

Five GLIB members traveled down to Washington, D.C., to see John Ward square off against the Veterans Council's Chester Darling before the Supreme Court on the morning of April 25, 1995. GLIB had already put a human face on homosexuality for any justice who saw the *Boston Globe* photo reproduced in court documents. It showed four ordinary-looking people smiling, waving and holding GLIB's banner.

The *Hurley* oral argument quickly proved quite telling. Gone was the overt anti-homosexual animosity that had marked several past oral arguments. But the justices' respectful tone did not seem to indicate receptivity to GLIB's argument. Darling had barely begun presenting the Veterans Council's argument when justice after justice, including moderates whom GLIB couldn't win without, started trying to guide him to victory.

Souter wanted Darling to say that any parade is constitutionally protected even if it expresses nothing. When Darling missed his cue, Souter helped him, saying, ". . . It seems to me that your answer would be that even if your parade is non-expressive in its history and its tradition, that you have the right to keep it that way."

Running with Souter's argument, Scalia said that if the St. Patrick's Day has no expressive purpose, "It seems to me that you still have an argument. . . . [Y]ou have the right to say that it cannot be used for some other person's message."

Next Ginsburg summarized Darling's argument for him, saying, "It's your parade to make it do whatever you want it to do." When Darling agreed, Scalia corrected him. Using respectful terminology, Scalia said, "I thought you conceded that you could not exclude gays, lesbians and bisexuals from marching in the parade . . . so long as they are not trying to convey a message which you do not want conveyed."

Taking that cue, Darling responded that "my clients do not have a litmus test so far as sexual orientation is concerned. . . . [M]y clients have excluded messages, not the people."

When Darling stumbled in describing the Veterans Council's message, Souter again lent a hand: "The message is, it's great to be Irish." Darling: "That's one of them, Justice Souter." Souter: "That's enough, isn't it?"

Rehnquist took his turn steering Darling toward a winning argument by helping him articulate messages. "Well," Rehnquist said, "what you're saying I gather, Mr. Darling, is, it isn't just a message 'it's great to be Irish,' but that 'it's great to be Roman Catholic,' too."

Of the eight justices who participated in the oral argument—Thomas kept his usual stony silence—only Stevens showed no interest in assisting Darling. "Why do they let the Baptists join the parade if it's a Catholic parade?" Stevens inquired. When Darling quipped in reply, "They're ecumenical in their Irish—," Stevens cut him off, saying, "Up to a point."

GLIB attorney Ward went into the oral argument assuming that the justices knew he was gay because he'd told a gay court official. (That official did not pass along the information.) When Ward's turn came, he stressed, "This is a case about discrimination," noting that the trial judge had found GLIB's members had been excluded "for who they were, not what they said."

Kennedy wasn't buying that explanation. "I assume," Kennedy said, "you concede that your clients wanted to be in the parade because they wanted to proclaim a message."

Struggling to make what was clearly a losing argument, Ward responded, "Well, I think the term 'message' as it's been used in this case really is more confusing than illuminating, Justice Kennedy. My clients wanted to be included in the parade," pointing out that every other group was allowed to identify itself.

But Kennedy insisted that "if messages are the grounds for the exclusion from the parade, it would seem to me that that is the end of it"—meaning, GLIB loses.

Scalia said GLIB's mere existence had expressive purposes, including expressing "its members' pride in their dual identities."

Rehnquist pushed Ward to agree that "forcing" a parade to accept signs "inconsistent" with its desired message would violate the First Amendment. Ward insisted, "that didn't happen."

O'Connor then spoke up, asking what would happen if an animal-rights group wanted to join a circus parade and carry signs protesting the use of animals in circuses—a question implying that gay rights are inherently at odds with an eclectic St. Patrick's Day parade.

Ward continually failed to get the justices to focus on discrimination, to focus on the rationales that discriminators use to mask illegal behavior.

Sounding uncharacteristically moderate, Scalia said that the Veterans Council "does not believe, whether you agree with it or not, that being homosexual is something to be proud of, and therefore do[es] not want that idea to be expressed in their parade." Ward stressed that GLIB's sign said only the group's name. "That is enough to show that you are proud," Scalia responded.

Stevens noted that *Hurley* was remarkable because of the two sides' common ground: Both agreed that excluding GLIB based on its members' identity would be unlawful but that a message-based exclusion would be lawful.

Kennedy slammed Judge Flannery's ruling, saying that for a court "to tell a private speaker how to celebrate St. Patrick's Day is antithetical to the First Amendment."

When Ward's half hour was exhausted, Darling returned for his left-over four minutes. Stevens quizzed him about whether the GLIB's sign was mere "self-identification" or an actual message. "I'm wrestling with this, to be honest with you," Stevens said, wondering aloud about what if Jews were permitted in the parade only if they didn't wear yarmulkes—an identifying sign. When oral argument ended at 11:08 A.M., GLIB seemed likely to win, at most, one vote.

The Supreme Court ruled unanimously against the Irish-American Gay, Lesbian and Bisexual Group of Boston in a decision written by Souter and announced June 19, 1995.

In his first four years on the court, Souter had blossomed into a justice beloved by clerks. He stands alone in having the clerks of other justices speak of him almost universally in heroic, almost reverential terms: He treats the court like a family, memorizes the names of clerks and elevator operators, takes the time to write personal notes, forms friendships across ideological lines and is described as kind, generous, accommodating.

Much of Souter's admirable behavior seems modeled after that of the justice he replaced, William Brennan. Souter and Brennan forged a warm, loving friendship after the much younger man's arrival in Washington. Though far from Brennan's ideological clone, Souter became a great admirer of Brennan, who had worked tirelessly to make the Constitution keep its promise of equal rights. Brennan, an Irish-American charmer who believed in the "dignity of every human being," lavished praise on Souter's early handiwork as a justice and, perhaps, in the process nurtured Souter's most humane traits. It doesn't take much of an intellectual leap to read Brennan's influence into the totally respectful tone of Souter's *Hurley* decision.

That tone made the outcome a gay-rights landmark even as the entire court ruled against forcing the organizers of Boston's St. Patrick's Day parade to accept an openly gay group. Souter consciously wanted to be respectful and did not want his opinion to be interpreted as anti-gay, recalls clerk Kent Greenfield. In using the gay community's preferred terminology, in talking about being gay as an identity, in praising the Massachusetts law that attempted to protect gay people from discrimination and in explicitly refusing to endorse the Veterans Council's anti-gay views, Souter's opinion marked a major turning point for the court.

The Supreme Court ruled that forcing the St. Patrick's Day parade to include "a parade contingent expressing a message not of the private organizers own choosing" violated the First Amendment. A parade, by its very nature, constitutes protected speech, even if its organizers' choices produce a jumble of messages, the court decided.

Souter said GLIB members had wanted to join the parade "as a way to express pride in their Irish heritage as openly gay, lesbian, and bisexual individuals, to demonstrate that there are such [Irish American] men and women." A Supreme Court majority ruling had never before used "gay," except in a formal name or a quote. *Hurley* put the court on record as acknowledging that gay, lesbian and bisexual Americans are a victimized minority "group" that governments may lawfully try to protect from discrimination. In contrast, *Hardwick* had treated homosexuals as essentially a class defined by criminal behavior, like burglars, not by a sense of "identity."

Souter praised the "venerable history" of Massachusetts's public accommodations law, whose protections had gradually expanded to outlaw discrimination based on "sexual orientation." Souter wrote, "Provisions like these are well within the state's usual power to enact when a legislature has reason to believe that a given group is the target of discrimination."

The point of the First Amendment's free speech provision, Souter said, is "to shield . . . choices of content that in someone's eyes are misguided, or even hurtful." Government may not force a private parade to include an unwanted message, and GLIB definitely was trying to send a message, the court found. ". . . A contingent marching behind the organization's banner would . . . bear witness to the fact that some Irish are gay, lesbian, or bisexual, and the presence of the organized marchers would suggest their view that people of their sexual orientations have as much claim to unqualified social acceptance as heterosexuals. . . . The parade's organizers may not believe these facts. . . ," Souter wrote. His strong, supportive word choice—"facts" instead of the neutral "claims"—implied that he agreed that gay people ought to be accepted.

Souter went on to say that, arguably, Massachusetts's anti-bias law might have "a broader objective" than just ensuring equal access: "the ultimate point of forbidding acts of discrimination toward certain classes is to produce a society free of the corresponding biases." (A Supreme Court majority had never before, even obliquely, talked of anti-homosexual attitudes as "biases.") However, Souter ruled, "While the law is free to promote all sorts of conduct in place of harmful behavior, it is not free to interfere with speech for no better reason than promoting an approved message or discouraging a disfavored one, however enlightened either purpose may strike the government."

Though disappointed by the outcome, GLIB spokeswoman Cathleen Finn was delighted with the court's language. "Now they are using our language to describe us," she noted.

The defeat pretty much destroyed GLIB, which cleaned out its bank account to pay a financial settlement partially covering the Veterans Council's court costs, Finn says.

Yet the parade struggle wasn't for nothing, she believes, explaining that it made "the somewhat abstract notion of gay rights into something very concrete and very topical." The subject stopped being taboo to the Boston news media, and local politicians were forced to show where they stood on gay rights. "I felt much stronger as a person having gone through it," Finn says. "For Boston, it really made homophobia visible. . . . Parts of Massachusetts are very liberal, and so people can be lulled into a sense of complacency. But when they saw on TV what happened . . . people bursting with anger and hatred and lots of venom—it was like a wakeup call, to say that we really haven't won this yet."

GLIB attorney John Ward calls *Hurley* "one of those cases that we were doomed to lose." However, he vehemently disagrees with those gay-rights attorneys who consider the ruling constitutionally correct. "If this had been Jews, it would have gone the other way," Ward insists, saying the outcome was an example of the notorious "gay exception"—the loser would have won, except for being gay. He had tried in vain to get the justices to focus on what the Veterans Council was doing to GLIB, not on what the state was doing to the Veterans Council.

The Supreme Court largely guides itself by looking backward at its own prior decisions. Perhaps the most lasting national impact of *Hurley*

is that its tone tells the court that in 1995 it wasn't hostile to gay people. Regardless of whether that message is true, it serves as a subtle,
progressive influence. Because *Hurley* marked such a major turning
point, the court seems unlikely to turn to hostile, dismissive language
that it knows would make it look erratic.

Three months before handing down *Hurley,* the justices agreed to
settle a Colorado controversy whose outcome would almost certainly
have a huge impact on gay Americans' rights. The case, *Romer v.
Evans,* would decide the constitutionality of a 1992 state constitutional amendment that forbade the protection of gay civil rights. The
Colorado case, accepted on February 21, 1995 and scheduled to be argued early in the court's term 1995–96 term, seemed likely to produce
the court's most significant gay-rights decision since its 1986 *Hardwick* ruling.

Other gay cases that, coincidentally, landed at the court while the
Colorado case was pending had virtually no chance of being heard. A
court with a long history of being loath to take gay cases wasn't likely to
give its full attention to more than one at a time. At most, the justices
might be willing to hold on to another gay case, decide the Colorado
dispute, then send the other case back to a lower court for reconsideration "in light of" the Colorado case's outcome.

Hurley's respectful handling of the concept of gay identity represented an important departure from the attitude that homosexuals are
criminals. But even as the court was moving away from that view, a new
kind of conflict offered a poignant reminder that gay Americans remain
outlaws in the original meaning of that concept—that is, outside the
law's protection.

As far back as 1972, gay couples had turned to the Supreme Court
with problems arising out of their outlaw status. Richard John Baker
and James Michael McConnell wanted the court to force Minnesota to
recognize them as legally married. Then, in 1982, Richard Adams
wanted the court to stop his longtime partner, Australian Tony Sullivan,
from being deported—an action triggered by the federal government's
refusal to recognize their legal marriage license. In 1986, the court was
asked to help Sharon Kowalski, a severely disabled lesbian denied the
right to be with the woman she loved, Karen Thompson, because their
inability to marry allowed Kowalski's anti-gay father to become her

guardian after she became incapacitated. Despite the Supreme Court's unwillingness to help, all three relationships survived.

In September 1995, Baker was still with McConnell, Adams was still with Sullivan and Kowalski was back home with Thompson—demonstrating the remarkable durability of many gay relationships even in the absence of government recognition and support. That month the Supreme Court received a new brand of gay outlaw case, one demonstrating that problem breakups are not unique to heterosexual couples and, more importantly, that when gay couples are treated as outlaws their children are left unforgivably vulnerable.

For the first time, gay people were on opposite sides of a Supreme Court case. *Elsbeth Knott v. Sandra Lynn Holtzman* pitted a biological mother against her former lover in a fight over visitation rights. The biological mother, Knott, was petitioning the justices to overturn a Wisconsin Supreme Court decision that opened the door to Holtzman's gaining the right to spend time with the 4-year-old boy who considered her his second mother.

Harrison Has Two Mommies

Sandra Holtzman and Elsbeth Knott first met in Boston in 1983 and quickly became a couple. Within months, they bought a house together. They privately exchanged rings and vows on September 15, 1984, and for the next eight years celebrated the anniversary of that date. The women wanted to have a child together and opted for insemination by an unknown donor so that they'd be the only parents their child would know.

After Knott became pregnant, Holtzman went with her to every childbirth class. Harrison Samuel Holtzman-Knott was born on December 15, 1988. For the next four years, the couple and their son "led their lives as a normal family," as a Wisconsin county judge, George A. W. Northrup, later put it. Holtzman was the primary breadwinner and shared parental duties with her partner. The women assured their son "that he had two parents who loved him very much," Northrup said. Holtzman taught her non-biological son, Harrison, how to ride a tricycle, throw a ball, ice skate, shoot baskets, fish and ski. She read to him and took him to the zoo, to an art museum and to swimming lessons.

Harrison called Sandra Holtzman—whose childhood nickname was "San"—"My San" because he couldn't say "Momma San." The family moved to Wisconsin so that Holtzman could attend law school.

In late 1992, Knott began having serious emotional problems and was placed on a suicide watch, court papers show. On January 1, 1993, she announced that she no longer wanted to be involved with her partner of eight years. In May, Knott took Harrison and moved out. Three months later, Knott informed Holtzman that she could no longer see him. As the boy's sole legal parent, Knott sought a court order to back up that decision. Holtzman petitioned for custody.

Using gay couples' outlaw status as a weapon, the biological mother claimed that since Holtzman had no legally recognized relationship to their son, Holtzman had no right to seek custody or visitation. Holtzman recalls feeling "a tremendous sense of betrayal. . . . The world suddenly didn't seem like a very safe place. If something like that, something so unimaginable, so unjust could occur, then it was like all bets were off—anything could happen."

Judge Northrup ruled in October 1993 that Wisconsin law gave him no choice but to say that Harrison's non-biological mother had no legal right to seek custody or visitation. Handing down a decision that he clearly saw as a miscarriage of justice, Northrup said, "Bad law makes hard cases. This court sees this as a case where a family member ought to have the right to visit and keep an eye on the welfare of a minor child with whom she has developed a parent-like relationship. Unfortunately, because the law does not recognize the alternative type of relationship which existed in this case, this court cannot offer the relief Holtzman seeks."

Saying his decision was dictated by a 1991 Wisconsin Supreme Court ruling in a similar lesbian custody dispute, Northrup declared, "Under current Wisconsin law the best interests and general welfare of children of a dissolving nontraditional relationship are ignored. . . . This court urges the appellate courts and the legislature to reexamine the law in light of the realities of modern society and the interests of its children."

Though Judge Northrup believed he had to ignore Harrison Holtzman-Knott's interests, the little boy's wishes were clear: He said he missed Holtzman and wanted to be able to visit Holtzman and call her, even though he knew that would upset his biological mother. According to his court-appointed attorney, Linda Balisle, "He knows that his mother, Elsbeth Knott, does not consider Sandra his parent, but he disagrees with her." Four-year-old Harrison offered Holtzman's address and phone number without being asked. He said he wanted to grow up to be a doctor like his Aunt Sherry, Holtzman's sister.

The boy's attorney persuaded the Wisconsin Supreme Court to intervene. On June 13, 1995, Wisconsin's top court ruled that while Holtzman had no right to seek custody so long as her ex-partner was a fit parent, she did have standing to seek visitation under the guidelines its ruling created. The court said it was sending the case back to the lower court to give Sandra Holtzman the opportunity to prove the existence of a "parent-like relationship." Holtzman would need to show that the legal parent had consented to formation of a parent-like relationship, that she'd lived with the child, that she had assumed major parental responsibilities and that she had bonded with the child.

Refusing to treat Harrison Holtzman-Knott as an outlaw, the Wisconsin Supreme Court declared that the ultimate decision on visitation would hinge on his best interests. "When a non-traditional adult relationship is dissolving, the child is as likely to become a victim of turmoil and adult hostility as is a child subject to the dissolution of a marriage. Such a child needs and deserves the protection of the courts as much as a child of a dissolving traditional relationship."

The biological mother turned to the U.S. Supreme Court, claiming "the Wisconsin Supreme Court has granted an unrelated biological stranger the right to interfere with an intact family unit." Suddenly, the woman who had been the family's primary provider for the first four years of Harrison's life was cast as a "stranger." Knott's petition charged that Wisconsin was unconstitutionally interfering with the rights of a fit parent. A footnote gave the justices a clue about the real nature of the disputed relationships: Harrison was "a nonmarital child because Knott and Holtzman cannot marry."

Sandra Holtzman asked the justices not to disturb the Wisconsin visitation guidelines drawn for her son's protection: "What matters to the child is the continuation of important relationships." Harrison's attorney, joining in asking the justices to turn the case away, declared that "ending this bonded relationship would plainly harm this child."

Although the U.S. Supreme Court wasn't informed, a Wisconsin judge ruled in October 1995 that Harrison's best interests required that Sandra Holtzman, his non-biological mother, be granted full guardianship. On November 13, 1995, a month before Harrison turned 7, he and Holtzman were visiting Disney World. Holtzman called the Supreme Court and was "delighted" to learn that *cert* had been denied. The justices refused to disturb a legal breakthrough for gay families.

A fifth-grader in the spring of 2000, Harrison is a very funny boy with a stable home. He loves to Rollerblade and snowboard and dreams of growing up to be a comedian or cartoonist. He lives with Holtzman, a family law attorney, and visits his biological mother on Friday afternoons, Holtzman said one night after putting her son to bed. Her legal battle cost $300,000, money she would have rather spent on her son's education. She fought, she says, because "I had no choice. I had nothing to lose. . . . When you take away a parent you are damaging that kid. He would never have been okay." She credits the outcome to "a series of miracles."

"People Knew It Wasn't Right"

Unlike *Knott v. Holtzman*, Daniel Miller's case didn't ask the justices to explore completely new territory. As far back as 1948, eight years before Miller's birth, the Supreme Court had ruled that it was unconstitutional for judges to enforce certain bigoted private contracts. That ruling sounded the death knell for the "restrictive covenants" on house deeds that had kept certain neighborhoods closed to blacks or Jews. When Miller pleaded with the justices for help in December 1995, he was under a Pennsylvania court order to pay more than $110,000 to his ex-boss for supposedly violating an anti-gay contract. In desperate financial straits, Miller wanted the justices to declare that there is no gay exception to the principle that government must not assist private discrimination.

Miller was a 29-year-old certified public accountant, just back home in Pennsylvania and on the verge of accepting his homosexuality, in 1985 when he joined Donald DeMuth's financial management firm in Camp Hill, across the Susquehanna River from Harrisburg. A few weeks later a *Newsweek* article about a male couple "hit me like a ton of bricks," Miller recalls. "They just seemed so normal. I came out then. That week." He shyly called Harrisburg's gay switchboard, which gave him a "very non-threatening" way to make friends—gay volleyball.

Six weeks after being hired by DeMuth, Miller, who'd been out to himself less than a week, was asked to sign a contract. If Miller quit or was fired "for cause" there would be serious financial consequences if he took clients with him, said the contract, which listed "homosexuality" as cause for dismissal. Miller thought he couldn't legally be fired for being gay. "I was naïve," he explains. "People say, 'Well, why did you sign that?' If I didn't sign it, well, then I didn't have my job. So I thought, 'Well, I'll sign it and deal with this later.'" Miller assumed that his boss's anti-gay hostility would fade as he got "to know me."

Four years passed. Miller played gay volleyball and rose to being president of the gay switchboard. Clients—mostly doctors and dentists—liked the way he did their books. His pay climbed to $50,000 a year as his boss put him on a partnership track. He had kept signing annual contracts with the "insulting" anti-gay provision but eventually resolved not to sign another.

Miller's contract had expired when he came out, by accident, on the local news. His group had been trying to meet with the Harrisburg City Council about recent gay bashings. Miller confronted a councilman at city hall. TV news teams rushed over to film the encounter. Miller was terrified because "we were on every single news channel that night." He went to work; nothing happened. Three weeks later, Miller finished a major project and DeMuth fired him.

Being fired for being gay wasn't illegal under local, state or federal law, Miller discovered. Furious and advised by an attorney that the old contracts would never stand up in court, Miller set up a competing firm. "When I took a third of his clients," Miller says, "I'm sure that just crushed him. How could any client choose a gay man over him?" DeMuth warned deserting clients that they'd be wise to find out Miller's HIV status if they hoped to do business with him for long. DeMuth also sued his former employee. Miller recalls, "When he sued me, there was no way that I could imagine that I was going to lose. But, again, I was being naïve. I didn't know the law."

During a three-day trial, DeMuth freely admitted he fired Miller for being gay. A jury decided that the expired contract was still binding on

Miller. He was ordered to pay his former boss $123,648.43 for becoming a competitor in violation of the contract restriction on what he could do after being fired "for cause." Miller asked the judge to overturn the verdict, arguing that state enforcement of a bias-based contract violated his constitutional rights.

Judge Kevin Hess responded in November 1993 by noting that the 1948 Supreme Court decision barring enforcement of restrictive covenants in effect endorsed the view that "our Constitution is color-blind." According to Hess, "At the heart of this case is the question of whether or not the Constitution is equally blind to sexual orientation." Hess, who cited "broad disagreement . . . on whether a disdain for a lifestyle equates to bigotry," said the trial record wasn't adequate to settle constitutional questions. He left the verdict in place, reducing Miller's penalty to $110,000—the expired contract's top limit.

In 1995, the Pennsylvania Superior Court upheld that penalty, ruling 2-to-1 that Miller was being penalized for going into competition, not for his "sexual predilections" or "sexual preference." The dissenter argued that enforcing an anti-gay contract violated equal protection. Citing Brennan's 1985 *Rowland* language, the dissent suggested anti-gay discrimination might be subject to strict scrutiny. It added, "nothing in *Hardwick* . . . suggests that a state may discriminate against or penalize an individual because of the status of sexual orientation alone."

The Pennsylvania Supreme Court turned down Miller's appeal. Meanwhile, the Lambda Legal Defense and Education Fund had taken over Miller's case; he'd run up a $35,000 bill with a private attorney.

In petitioning the U.S. Supreme Court on Miller's behalf, Lambda attorney Beatrice Dohrn depicted DeMuth as using the Pennsylvania court system "as a sword—in the service of his private efforts to carry out invidious discrimination." She told the justices, "This case calls upon the court to make plain that discriminatory state action based solely on antipathy toward gay people lacks any rational basis and is unconstitutional."

In reply, DeMuth's attorney, Samuel Andes, said the contract was legal and its enforcement by Pennsylvania judges was constitutional.

Miller recalls, "I really thought that the Supreme Court was going to take this case and they were going to rule for me." On February 20, 1996, his case was turned away without comment.

The "invidious discrimination" argument so echoed Ginsburg's remarks about sexual orientation during her confirmation hearing that her silence was especially notable. Did she not see Miller as a victim of "invidious discrimination"? Did his case not fit in with her master plan for securing full equality for gay Americans? Or, did she have no master plan? During her confirmation hearings Ginsburg had stressed she was giving no "hints" about her intentions. She was continuing that practice as a justice. In earlier times, Douglas, Brennan and Marshall had publicly signaled that they had wanted the court to hear gay pleas. Is Ginsburg's public silence when gay cases are turned away just a bow to collegiality, which she prizes, or is it evidence she's unwilling to take a leading role in fighting anti-gay discrimination? She's not telling.

The court's refusal to hear his case was "demoralizing," Miller, 40, says. "You lose some faith in America. . . . People knew it wasn't right yet allowed it to happened."

The Supreme Court's inaction meant Daniel Miller had to pay $148,000—the original $110,000 plus interest—because he was homosexual. Pennsylvania had no other "cause" for enforcing the contract. "I feel I was a slave to this man [DeMuth] for three or four years," says Miller, whose penalty exceeded what he had earned in his final three years as a DeMuth accountant.

"After I lost the case and I had this big bill looming, I was just petrified of where I was going to get that money," Miller recalls. Selling all his investments raised only $20,000. "I borrowed from my parents, my grandmother, my sister and friends. I borrowed close to $130,000." Miller also faced monstrous legal bills. "My first bill was for over $10,000. Well, I don't come from a wealthy family. I was stunned," he recalls.

Miller says, "I'm glad I stood up to [DeMuth]. . . . They wanted to settle the day before the trial for $60,000. And I sometimes think about that. But, what good would that have done? I was much better off fighting." Yet the inaction of the Supreme Court, which he had trusted to provide "the right justice," still gnaws at him. "It's hard to understand why they didn't take my case. I feel like the government and DeMuth just reached into my wallet and took $200,000 out."

The Continuing Adventures of the Sex Police

Just days before the justices passively allowed Pennsylvania to help an anti-gay boss financially crush a former employee, they received the petition of a gay man who was the victim of a far more pervasive brand of government-sponsored discrimination—the targeting and intentional humiliation of gay men for the kind of sexual remark that never leads to the arrest of any heterosexual, except suspected prostitutes. Brian Sawatzky was a reluctant soldier in the ACLU's war on laws primarily used as justifications for arresting gay men.

On a blistering July day in 1994, Sawatzky decided to check out Hobie Point, a gay cruising spot that juts into Oklahoma City's Lake Hefner. Sawatzky, 25 and openly gay, worked as a lens grinder in an optical lab and was, he says, "as comfortable as could be expected" with his orientation, given that the police routinely hassled gay people outside bars and at parks.

Sawatzky was strolling down a deserted Hobie Point road when he met a stranger leaning against a car and smoking a cigarette. The stranger started spinning a tale intended to create the impression that he was a gay man looking for sex. The stranger, undercover officer Raymond Ledford, claimed, for example, to be a Kansas City construction worker staying at a hotel in a gay neighborhood. He pretended to be nervous that Sawatzky might be an undercover cop.

"Pretty soon he started saying, 'What do you like to *do?*' I took him literally, and I was ticking off my hobbies. I said, 'I play guitar. . . .' And he would look at me like, 'Hey, what do you like to *do?*' Finally, I got him. He asked the question probably six to 10 times. I finally started becoming annoyed because, obviously, I wasn't interested. I expressed in a very sarcastic tone what I like to do. . . . I like to suck dick," Sawatzky recalls, saying he was trying to brush the stranger off. (According to the police report, Sawatzky announced, "I want to suck a dick.")

Hearing the answer he'd worked to get, Officer Ledford told Sawatzky he had "a dick" for him and whipped out his badge. "I didn't believe it was real. I didn't think I was being arrested. . . . Then I felt like I went pale. All of a sudden I was like, 'Oh, my God!'. . . I knew it was going to look terrible to everyone just because I had been arrested," Sawatzky says.

Moments later, Sawatzky found himself steaming inside a closed police car between two other gay men. One started complaining, "You know, it's really hot back here! Let's get this over with." A policewoman answered, "Well, as soon as we get a couple more." Disgust shot though Sawatzky as he realized that the police were luring as many homosexuals as possible into making allegedly illegal remarks.

From jail, Sawatzky called his mother, who was furious at him. She and his sister bailed him out. He was charged with "offering to engage in an act of lewdness," a catchall misdemeanor that included asking anyone other than one's spouse to have oral sex. His family was mortified when the police department's gay roundup hit the newspapers. Brian Sawatzky, who goes by his middle name, was listed as "Kenneth Sawatzky," the name his father uses.

The ACLU persuaded Brian Sawatzky to challenge the lewdness ordinance and, through it, the state sodomy law. He was outraged at the double standard used in prosecuting him for sexual banter: "My lawyer found that there had never been any straight people arrested. . . . How many times do you think a guy walks up to a girl in a bar and does what I was accused of?"

Recounting the "suck dick" portion of his story, Sawatzky turned shy. "That was probably the hardest thing about it, the embarrassment part, in the courtroom. I'm not ashamed . . . of my proclivities, but it's just like a bashful thing. It's private," he explained. His discomfort at having to repeat what was meant to be a private sexual remark spotlights the fact that even though gay men are often depicted as flaunting their sexuality, shoving it upon uninterested strangers, the reality is usually quite different.

Sawatzky's attorneys tried to get the lewdness charge dismissed, arguing that Sawatzky couldn't be punished for proposing anything lawful. Since Oklahoma's courts had struck down the state sodomy law as it applied to heterosexuals, the attorneys said it would violate equal protection to prosecute same-sex fellatio. Convicted on November 4, 1994, Sawatzky was fined $250.

Sawatzky then lost in a state appeals court, which ruled that the lewdness statute was valid regardless of whether gay fellatio was lawful.

"[T]he solicitation of some sexual acts . . . is simply not appropriate in public places. To suggest that government cannot prohibit such solicitation is unfathomable," the court ruled. A marital exception was permissible, it ruled, because a married person is presumed to have consented to being solicited by his or her spouse.

The lone dissenter argued that outlawing all unmarried advances was too restrictive. He noted that the undercover cop's testimony made clear that Sawatzky "was purposely led to believe that a sexual solicitation would be welcome."

ACLU attorney Steven Shapiro's petition on Sawatzky's behalf reached the Supreme Court on February 15, 1996. He argued that the appeals court had ignored the well-established First Amendment principle that non-obscene speech cannot be suppressed just because it might upset someone. He said the lewdness law was too broad, equally banning a polite, welcome, private solicitation and "a loud and vulgar offer shouted to a repulsed stranger." He asked the justices to say that freedom of speech protects lawful gay sexual propositions—a stand that would have forced Oklahoma's top court to rule on the constitutionality of its same-sex sodomy ban.

Richard C. Smith, representing Oklahoma City, responded by saying that before Sawatzky's arrest the police had received complaints about "moral violations" at Hobie Point. Smith argued that soliciting a "criminal act" was not protected by the First Amendment. He cited *Hardwick* as proof that laws can properly be grounded in morality. Stressing the government's interest in policing "morality" in a park used by "children, sail boaters and nature lovers," Smith claimed Sawatzky's "offer was made in a public park to an obviously unwilling participant."

Just as the court ultimately chose not to decide the constitutionality of Uplinger's sexual remarks in 1984, the court wanted nothing to do with Sawatzky's case. Brian Sawatzky had practically handed the court an engraved invitation to say that gay Americans are just as protected by the First Amendment as heterosexuals. By overturning his conviction, the court could have begun setting constitutional limits on police harassment of homosexuals. Instead, cert was denied in *Kenneth B. Sawatzky v. City of Oklahoma City* on April 22, 1996.

Though his legal battle lasted less than two years, Sawatsky felt as if "it dragged out forever. . . . At one point I almost backed out because it was on my mind 24 hours a day." In the end, Brian Sawatzky's main satisfaction was that his father finally said that he was proud of him for fighting for his rights and that his mother became an ACLU volunteer.

By the mid-1990s, the Supreme Court's overt hostility had been replaced the respectful language of the *Hurley* parade decision. Yet the legal place of gay Americans was still largely defined by the court's anti-gay *Hardwick* decision. "What does the U.S. Supreme Court say about homosexuality?" *The Denver Post* asked. The newspaper answered, "The highest federal courts do not recognize homosexuals as a group that deserves protection from discrimination."

On November 3, 1992, Colorado voters went to the polls to decide whether to officially relegate gay men, lesbians and bisexuals to second-class citizenship. The outcome of that vote eventually led the Supreme Court to squarely confront the question of whether there is a gay exception to the Constitution's guarantee of Equal Protection.

The 1986 *Hardwick* decision had been decried as the equivalent of the racist *Dred Scott* decision. But issues raised by *Romer v. Evans,* the monumental case growing out of Colorado's referendum, more closely paralleled those in the notorious 19th-century *Dred Scott* ruling that declared blacks weren't citizens and had "no rights which the white man was bound to respect."

Did gay Americans have no rights that heterosexuals were bound to respect? In early 1995, the U.S. Supreme Court decided to decide.

16

"THE CONSTITUTION 'NEITHER KNOWS NOR TOLERATES CLASSES AMONG CITIZENS'"

A HANDSOME, GLEAMING CITY tucked just in front of the Rocky Mountains, Colorado Springs, Colorado, has long taken a distinctly conservative bent from its best-known institutions, the Air Force Academy and the Army's Fort Carson. While Denver embraced the liberalism of aging antiwar baby boomers, Boulder threw its heart into environmentalism and Aspen thrived as a trendy ski resort, Colorado Springs tilted farther to the right.

In the late 1980s, the city's economic development teams actively recruited far-right religious organizations. James Dobson's Focus on the Family pulled up stakes in California and resettled in Colorado Springs. Soon, so many conservative Christian groups had moved their national headquarters to Colorado Springs that the city was being called the "Vatican of evangelical Christianity" and "Ground Zero in the culture wars." The influx of ultraconservative activists into Colorado Springs coincided with anti-gay politics becoming a cash cow for far-right groups desperate to fill the void created by Communism's collapse as a reliable bogeyman.

Colorado's gay citizens generally were oblivious to the threat that the growing ranks of hardcore conservatives posed to them. "Nobody really understood what was going on. We didn't see the danger," recalls lesbian Linda Fowler, who chaired the gay-rights advisory committee of Denver's liberal mayor. Although Colorado wasn't among those few states that outlawed discrimination based on sexual orientation, it had re-pealed its sodomy law. Denver, Boulder and Aspen banned discrimination based on sexual orientation in employment, housing and public accommodations. What's more, Democratic Governor Roy Romer had signed an executive order protecting state government workers from dis-crimination based on sexual orientation.

In 1991, new protections were proposed for gay Coloradans: a state law targeting hate crimes and a Colorado Springs anti-bias ordinance. Both failed. But in response to them, Tony Marco, who made his living ghostwriting fundraising letters for fundamentalist groups, and Kevin Tebebo, whose mother was a state lobbyist for far-right causes, formed Colorado for Family Values (CFV). Its ambitious goals: Roll back exist-ing protections against anti-gay discrimination and write a ban on fu-ture gay-rights laws into Colorado's state constitution.

A Colorado Springs Chrysler dealer, Will Perkins, was recruited to chair the board of the anti-gay campaign and bankroll its early efforts. Perkins, in turn, enlisted former U.S. senator Bill Armstrong and the University of Colorado's popular football coach as outspoken proponents of the view that gay people are a menace, a threat to decent society. Tel-evangelist Pat Robertson's legal team advised CFV on the wording of its proposed amendment to the state constitution. And hundreds of listeners to the Focus on the Family radio broadcasts volunteered to circulate pe-titions to put the amendment on the November 1992 ballot.

On March 20, 1992, CFV chairman Perkins pulled up in front of the state capitol in an armored car loaded with 17 boxes of petitions bear-ing 85,500 signatures. Reporters laughed at Perkins's theatrics as he declared, "We consider these to be among the most important pieces of paper in the entire United States." The secretary of state determined Perkins had well over the required 49,000 names and put the anti-gay referendum on the ballot as "Amendment 2."

Even as Colorado's leading gay activists shifted into combat mode—mapping a strategy, filling a war chest, setting up phone banks—most weren't terribly worried. They assumed that a venomously anti-gay ini-tiative would win in Oregon, long under siege from anti-gay zealots, while Colorado would defeat its mildly worded amendment. "We thought Colorado was a liberal state," explains lesbian Linda Fowler.

Nevertheless, six months before Election Day, 1992, Fowler and six other gay-rights leaders secretly gathered in a dingy Denver conference room to prepare for the unthinkable: passage of Amendment 2. How would they fight back? Though all seven felt sure Amendment 2 would lose, they began laying the groundwork for filing the strongest possible challenge to its legitimacy under the U.S. Constitution immediately after the ballots were counted—just in case.

Quietly working behind the scenes, they asked a respected civil rights attorney, Jean Dubofsky of Boulder, to head their legal team. Dubofsky, 50, was chosen for her trustworthiness and experience. Her heterosexuality wasn't a factor, Fowler says. A former state Supreme Court justice, Dubofsky readily accepted, though she, too, expected Amendment 2 to fail. Tennis star Martina Navratilova, an Aspen resident and then the nation's best-known lesbian, agreed to be a plaintiff if a lawsuit proved necessary. Fowler also signed on, as did a lesbian police officer, a gay professor, a heterosexual with AIDS and Richard Evans, a gay aide to Denver's mayor.

The Reverend Priscilla Inkpen, a United Church of Christ campus minister at the University of Colorado in Boulder, was floored when she was approached about joining the potential lawsuit. Someone who'd seen her lead an Amendment 2 discussion had correctly assumed she was gay. Inkpen, 45, thought of the biblical patriarchs who had shouldered unwanted burdens. "It felt like a calling to me—like, 'Here it is. Nothing you expected. But the moment is at hand. You are the person to step in. So do it,'" she recalls. Yet she held back. Finally, she says, "It came down to, 'Well, how do I want to live my life? Do I want to live out of fear or out of what I believe?' I decided I should come out 100 percent, regardless of what happened. I began seeing drawbacks of being even somewhat in the closet. . . . A lot of people came out because of Amendment 2—before and after [Election Day]. It was a feeling that this is the time to stand up and say who we are. 'We are not freaks. We are your next door neighbors. We don't want to be put down.'"

Colorado for Family Values was busily painting gay men, lesbians and bisexuals as sinful, sex-crazed, child-molesting freaks, who wanted more than their fair share of rights. Chairman Perkins claimed homosexuals have "a radically deviant obsession with sex."

After CFV charged that homosexuals are responsible for one third to one half of all child molestation, a husband and wife team of Denver physicians put the lie to that claim. Their review of recent Denver abuse cases found that children are 100 times more likely to be molested by heterosexual male relatives—pedophiles who take sexual advantage of children without regard to their gender—than by someone gay. Instead of passing an anti-gay initiative, "It would make more sense to outlaw being a father or stepfather," one of the researchers remarked.

Yet CFV persisted, charging in a brochure distributed to 800,000 households on the day before the election that "sexual molestation of children is a large part of many homosexuals' lifestyle—part of the very lifestyle 'gay-rights' activists want government to give special class, ethnic status!" CFV hired anti-gay psychologist Paul Cameron, whose research had been repudiated by the American Psychological Association. He told Coloradans that homosexuals should be quarantined.

At churches, CFV leaders called homosexuality an abomination, a violation of God's will. In more public forums, they downplayed their religious message. CFV's TV commercials showed vulgar snippets from San Francisco gay pride parades and warned that Colorado could be next. But CFV's concerted effort to depict being gay as a deviant "lifestyle" wasn't nearly as damaging as the seemingly all-American message it hammered home: "No special rights."

Sue Anderson headed the Denver gay community center and served on the board of Equal Protection, the group formed to defeat Amendment 2. She recalls what Equal Protection was up against: "In a microsecond they can say 'special rights' and send a message out. 'Gays don't deserve special rights.' And from our side it takes 10 or 15 minutes to undo that message when we sit down with people and say, 'Okay, here is the reality. We don't have civil rights. We can be fired from our jobs.'. . . So when you had 'special rights' versus something that takes 10 minutes to explain, who is going to win? We tried 'Equal rights, not special rights,' 'Basic civil rights.' Early on, it was 'Hate is not a family value.' That was not a good message—people don't want to be called haters. It just makes people mad."

Linda Fowler says, "We didn't find a way to make an argument in a sound bite that there are no 'special rights' here. We never effectively countered that."

Nothing in Amendment 2's wording alerted voters that, far from merely blocking "special rights," it would deprive Colorado gay men, lesbians and bisexuals of ordinary rights that American citizens take for granted. Amendment 2 read: "Neither the state of Colorado, through any of its branches or departments, nor any of its agencies, political subdivisions, municipalities or school districts, shall enact, adopt or enforce any statute, regulation, ordinance or policy whereby homosexual, lesbian or bisexual orientation, conduct, practices or relationships shall constitute or otherwise be the basis of, or entitle any person or class of persons to have or claim any minority status, quota preferences, protected status or claim of discrimination."

Right up to November 3, Election Day, polls showed Amendment 2 losing. It did lose in Denver, Boulder and Aspen, the three cities with gay-rights laws. But as votes rolled in from Colorado Springs, suburbs and rural counties, Amendment 2 passed, winning 53.4 percent of the vote statewide. Ironically, Colorado simultaneously helped elect Bill Clinton, who promised to be the first gay-supportive president. Oregon's anti-gay measure lost.

On election night, gay Coloradans who had gathered at a Denver hotel for what they'd expected to be a victory celebration were stunned, frightened. Some wept. Sensing rising panic in the room, Fowler woke Denver Mayor Wellington Webb. He and Governor Romer, outspoken foes of Amendment 2, commiserated with the crowd and helped restore a semblance of calm.

Sue Anderson turned in early, sensing that she wouldn't have another good night's sleep for a very long time. She was back at the gay community center by 6:15 A.M., and the phone was already ringing off the hook with distraught gay people pleading for answers: "How could this happen?" "What can we do?" Knowing that 813,966 of their fellow Coloradans had voted for Amendment 2, gay people were afraid for their safety, afraid for their jobs.

There was a widespread sense that Colorado had declared open season on gay people. Amendment 2's passage felt like "a declaration that you can do anything to gays because they aren't going to be protected," recalls Inkpen, whose daughter came from Boulder High School in tears after classmates declared that "gays ought to be shot." One sign at a gay-rights rally read: "I wish I was a black bear"—a reference to hunting restrictions approved November 3.

A 26-year-old gay man from Colorado Springs committed suicide a week after the referendum. "I refuse to live in a state where a few people can, at will, make my life a living hell," he wrote in a note blaming his death on Amendment 2.

Therapists reported that their gay patients felt betrayed, angry, grief-stricken. Some openly gay people tried to return to the closet; other fled the state. But Amendment 2 propelled record numbers of people out of the closet as they stood up for themselves. At least 150 new gay groups sprang up almost overnight. Many were led by rural gay people like Linda Dunn, who'd been "in the closet so deep you would have had to have a bulldozer to dig me out."

Meanwhile, reports of anti-gay harassment and attacks skyrocketed nine times higher in November 1992 than the previous November. "People felt they had permission to say really hateful, hurtful things. Yet at the same time, [heterosexual] folks who had never voiced any support [for us] before were standing up and saying, 'This is wrong,'" Anderson recalls.

Outside the state, outrage at Amendment 2's passage translated into a boycott that cost Colorado $40 million in convention business and tourism. Scores of national associations branded the state's anti-gay stand repugnant.

Fenced Out but Still Fighting

Just nine days after Amendment 2 passed, attorney Jean Dubofsky filed the carefully planned challenge to its constitutionality. Denver, Boulder and Aspen joined seven individuals as plaintiffs in the lawsuit that named Governor Romer and Attorney General Gale Norton, a conservative Republican, as defendants. Soon two more people and Boulder Valley School District joined as plaintiffs. The immediate goal was preventing Amendment 2 from taking effect as scheduled January 15, 1993.

In the first victory for Amendment 2's foes, state District Court Judge Jeffrey Bayless issued a temporary order January 15 barring Amendment 2 from becoming part of Colorado's constitution. Bayless, a 47-year-old ex-prosecutor, based his ruling on his findings that Amendment 2 might be unconstitutional and its implementation would cause immediate, irreparable harm. Scheduling a trial, Bayless said that for the state to win it would need to show that a compelling government interest justified violating what he deemed a fundamental right, "the right not to have the state endorse and give effect to private biases."

Bayless vowed that the trial would take into account what Chief Justice Earl Warren had called "the evolving standards of decency that mark the progress of a maturing society."

Hoping to avoid a trial, the state's attorneys appealed to the Colorado Supreme Court, which upheld Bayless's preliminary injunction, though on different grounds. In a 6-to-1 ruling on July 19, 1993, Chief Justice Luis Rovira said, "We conclude that the Equal Protection Clause of the United States Constitution protects the fundamental right to participate equally in the political process, and that any legislation or state constitutional amendment which infringes on this right by 'fencing out' an independently identifiable class of persons must be subject to strict judicial scrutiny." The state's top court found that Amendment 2 fenced out gay and bisexual voters by rendering government officials powerless to respond to their pleas—and only their pleas—for protection from discrimination. Rovira said the referendum's results told gay men, lesbians and bisexuals that "you can appeal to government . . . but you will, by virtue of Amendment 2, lose—irrespective of your ability to summon the support of others or carry a majority in an election." He concluded, "Strict scrutiny is thus required because the normal political processes no longer operate to protect these persons. Rather, they, and they alone, must amend the state constitution in order to seek legislation which is beneficial to them."

The Colorado Supreme Court based its preliminary decision to slap down Amendment 2 largely on the U.S. Supreme Court's 1969 *Hunter v. Erickson* ruling. In that case, a real estate agent in Akron, Ohio, had drawn up a list of houses to show prospective buyer Nellie Hunter. But the moment the agent laid eyes on Hunter, all the houses became unavailable. The agent explained that the property owners "did not wish their houses shown to Negroes," Hunter stated in a 1965 complaint. Akron's mayor and city council were powerless to help her because Akron voters had repealed a fair-housing ordinance and amended the city charter to forbid any future ordinance from outlawing housing dis-crimination based on "race, color, religion, national origin or ancestry." Thus, victims of housing discrimination were effectively fenced out of Akron's normal political process—until the U.S. Supreme Court inter-vened. Striking down the city charter amendment, the court said that Akron "may no more disadvantage any particular group by making it more difficult to enact legislation in its behalf than it may dilute any person's vote or give any group a smaller representation than another of comparable size."

After the Colorado Supreme Court ruled, the Amendment 2 case bounced back to the Denver courtroom of Judge Bayless. During an eight-day trial that began October 12, 1993, the burden was on the state to prove that the amendment met the "strict scrutiny" require-ments of advancing a "compelling" state interest and being "narrowly tailored" to do so. Colorado contended that Amendment 2 advanced six compelling interests. First, it deterred "factionalism," meaning political disagreement. Second, it protected the state's political functions by fending off what Perkins called "militant gay aggression." Third, it safe-guarded the state's ability to pay for enforcement of more traditional civil rights protections. Fourth, it prevented government interference in individual, family and religious privacy. Fifth, it blocked government subsidization of a special interest group. Finally, it promoted children's well-being.

(Before Bayless could rule, the U.S. Supreme Court announced on November 1, 1993 that it had denied a Colorado petition for *cert;* the case clearly wasn't yet ripe for its review.)

Scoffing at most of the rationales concocted by the state's attorneys after Amendment 2's passage, Bayless found that only religious freedom and family privacy were compelling interests and that Amendment 2 wasn't narrowly drawn to advance either one. On December 14, 1993, the judge declared Amendment 2 unconstitutional.

Colorado appealed again to its state Supreme Court. That court re-examined the asserted state interests that Bayless had found wanting. And it looked at one that Colorado's attorneys claimed he'd neglected—

"allowing the people themselves to establish public social and moral norms." Amendment 2 advanced that interest, Colorado claimed, by preserving heterosexual marriage and branding gay men, lesbians and bisexuals immoral.

Finding no compelling interest advanced by Amendment 2, Colorado's top court ruled on October 11, 1994, that the anti-gay measure unconstitutionally violated the 14th Amendment's guarantee of equal protection. The court ridiculed the notion that married heterosexuals "will 'choose' to 'become homosexual' if discrimination against homosexuals is prohibited."

Agreeing with that unsigned ruling, Justice Gregory Scott argued that Amendment 2 also violated the right "peaceably to assemble and petition the government for redress of grievances." He said, "Like the right to vote which assumed the right to have one's vote counted, the right peaceably to assemble and petition is meaningless if by law government is powerless to act."

In dissent, Justice William Erickson moaned that the Colorado Supreme Court had done "exactly what the voters . . . sought to prevent" by creating "heightened protection for homosexuals, lesbians and bisexuals."

The landmark Colorado ruling, *The New York Times* noted, "marked the first time that the highest court of any state had found it unconstitutional to deny certain rights to homosexuals."

"Worse Off Than Hotdog Vendors"

With its top state court branding Amendment 2 unconstitutional, Colorado had one last place to seek permission to erect that measure's enormous barrier to basic gay civil rights. Colorado Attorney General Norton again petitioned the U.S. Supreme Court on December 12, 1994.

Adopting CFV's "no special rights" theme, Norton characterized laws and policies against discrimination based on sexual orientation as "special" protections for homosexuals and bisexuals. She leaned heavily on *Hardwick* even though her state did not outlaw sodomy. "If homosexual activity may be criminalized outright, it is assuredly nonsensical to say that restricting special legal protections to those professing a desire to engage in such activity requires a compelling [state] interest," she argued. Norton also charged that the Colorado Supreme Court's ruling struck "at the heart of voter sovereignty."

A former Reagan administration solicitor general, Rex Lee, had helped Colorado's attorneys prepare their *cert* petition. And rejected Supreme Court nominee Robert Bork kept his ultraconservative credentials up to date by filing a friend-of-the-court brief warning the justices that the Colorado ruling was already being used to attack anti-gay initiatives in other states.

Before Jean Dubofsky could file a rebuttal, she had to fend off national legal groups that thought they should handle a gay-rights case once it hit the big time. Dubofsky believed it was important for a Coloradan to be the one the justices heard arguing against the state constitutional amendment—if the case reached that point. The Amendment 2 challengers stuck with her.

Since Amendment 2 would be dead if *cert* were denied, Dubofsky argued that there was no reason for the justices to hear *Romer v. Evans,* as the Amendment 2 case was called. Stressing that Amendment 2 had an "undisputed discriminatory purpose," she said that the Colorado Supreme Court decision to overturn it was consistent with prior U.S. Supreme Court rulings.

On February 21, 1995, the U.S. Supreme Court sent a shiver down the spines of every gay-rights attorney in America: The court had agreed to decide the constitutionality of Colorado's Amendment 2. The court's decision to take a case is bad news for the side that won in the lower court. Often, it's a signal that at least four justices think they have the votes to overturn the lower court's decision. However, according to a clerk familiar with the deliberations, most justices viewed Amendment 2 as weighty enough to merit a hearing because a state wanted a last chance to defend the constitutionality of a voter-passed addition to its constitution.

Colorado Attorney General Norton's brief depicted Amendment 2 as a benign attempt to "withdraw a deeply divisive social and political issue from elected representatives and place its resolution in the hands of the people." Colorado's gay men, lesbians and bisexuals "continue to have the same rights as anyone else who has lost an election," she said. She warned, however, that if the Colorado Supreme Court decision were correct, "then laws restricting marriage, certain tax benefits and military service to heterosexuals are also constitutionally suspect."

Norton argued that Amendment 2 was rationally related to three government interests, including giving priority to spending anti-discrimination monies on groups "particularly deserving of special protection," deferring to the "legitimate preferences" of citizens who want to discriminate against gay people and promoting statewide uniformity.

Since the Supreme Court likes to depict its rulings as the predictable outgrowth of prior decisions, Norton downplayed the relevance of its 1969 ruling in favor of prospective homebuyer Nellie Hunter. That decision, she argued, merely meant that racial minorities could not be fenced out of the political process. To support that claim, she cited *James v. Valtierra,* a 1971 ruling in which the Supreme Court had refused to strike down a California requirement that state officials get local voter approval before building public housing. The requirement disadvantaged Californians who supported public housing, yet the court ruled that "a lawmaking procedure that 'disadvantages' a particular group does not always deny equal protection."

The Colorado Supreme Court had ruled that it didn't need to calculate the sweep of Amendment 2 because it was already declaring it unconstitutional for fencing gay people out of the normal political process by banning gay-rights laws. Yet in challenging Amendment 2, attorney Dubofsky directed the U.S. Supreme Court's attention to the way Amendment 2 swept away a vast array of legal protections that citizens can ordinarily take for granted. Amendment 2 rendered public officials powerless to respond to "any . . . claim of discrimination" by gay men, lesbians or bisexuals. She argued that even the Colorado law intended to shield all workers from being fired for lawful, off-duty behavior could no longer be used to protect gay workers.

"Under Amendment 2," Dubofsky contended, "all efforts by the government to protect gay people from discrimination are swept away. . . . From the police officer who refuses to patrol gay neighborhoods or provide backup assistance to lesbian police officers like [Amendment 2 challenger] Angela Romero, to the judge who decides cases based on animus toward lesbians and gay men, even state actors who irrationally and maliciously discriminate based on sexual orientation are immune from state legislative, executive, administrative or judicial remedy." She noted that Amendment 2 would strangely distort laws banning discrimination based on sexual orientation—removing protections from gay men, lesbians and bisexuals while leaving them in place for heterosexuals. Dubofsky argued that Amendment 2 has "no rational relationship to any legitimate state purpose." Asserting that Amendment 2's "true purpose" is "to harm a politically unpopular group," she stressed, "If bare antipathy toward a group could justify discrimination against that group . . . the Equal Protection Clause would be meaningless."

In its separate brief, the City of Aspen said "it can hardly be argued rationally that any legitimate public purpose is served . . . by the christening of a new class of 'untouchables.'" Aspen and Dubofsky both argued Amendment 2 amounted to a open-ended invitation to discriminate.

The word "discrimination," state Attorney General Norton replied, "once divested of its emotional connotation, simply means to distinguish or to draw a line." She scoffed at the idea that voters who backed Amendment 2 were motivated by hostility: "The record demonstrates that Coloradans are largely tolerant of homosexuality, yet unwilling to support governmental action which confers benefits on a relatively privileged group at the expense of the less-privileged."

Dubofsky, understandably, devoted much of her brief to echoing the Colorado Supreme Court's finding that Amendment 2 must be subjected to extraordinary scrutiny. However, as the U.S. Supreme Court shifted to the right, it had grown extremely reluctant to expand "strict" and "heightened" scrutiny—the ill-defined levels above ordinary "rational basis" scrutiny.

While countless legal tomes have debated the appropriate scrutiny levels for various equal protection cases, the U.S. Supreme Court did not need to wade into that morass to find Amendment 2 unconstitutional, Laurence Tribe insisted. His argument, which four other eminent constitutional law scholars joined, was a model of simplicity, clarity and persuasiveness: "Never since the enactment of the Fourteenth Amendment has this court confronted a measure quite like Amendment 2—a measure that, by its express terms, flatly excludes some of a state's people from eligibility for legal protection from a category of wrongs."

The very language of Amendment 2 obviously violates the 14th Amendment's guarantee that "no state shall . . . deny to any person within its jurisdiction the equal protection of the laws," Tribe wrote in his friend-of-the-court brief. "Amendment 2 on its face thus makes homosexuals worse off than heterosexuals—and worse off than hot dog vendors, optometrists, left-handed people, and every other group that remains free to claim discrimination, and even to seek preferential treatment, under state law," he declared.

`    ` the attorney who'd lost *Hardwick,* Tribe was painfully aware that `      ` . Supreme Court could hardly be counted as friendly territory `          ` Americans. Striking down Amendment 2, he told the justices, ᴉᴄզᴜᴉᴄ̣s no benign or even neutral view" of homosexuality.

Tribe's brief gently escorted the justices one step back from the quicksand that courts often sink into when asked to resolve disputes involving anti-gay discrimination. "Had Colorado explicitly declared some people within its jurisdiction completely ineligible for the protection of its laws from some other form of mistreatment—from robbery, for example, or blackmail . . . no one would doubt that such discriminatory state action would 'deny (such persons) the equal protection of the laws,' regardless of the rationale the state might offer to defend it," Tribe argued. The denial of protection to one class of people is "just as unconstitutional," he insisted, when the mistreatment "takes the form of discrimination," instead of robbery or blackmail.

As a veteran of civil rights battles of all sorts, Dubofsky was gratified by the national outpouring of mainstream support for the gay challenge to Amendment 2. Among those filing friend-of-the-court briefs against Amendment 2 were the American Bar Association, American Psychological Association, NAACP Legal Defense and Education Fund, Women's Legal Defense Fund, National Education Association, American Association of University Professors, Japanese American Citizens League, Mexican American Legal Defense and Education Fund, American Federation of State County and Municipal Employees, Puerto Rican Legal Defense and Education Fund, the states of Oregon, Iowa, Maryland, Massachusetts, Minnesota, Nevada and Washington and the District of Columbia. Missing was the Clinton administration, which—depending on whose explanation is believed—didn't see a federal issue at stake or was afraid of looking too liberal (meaning, pro-gay). Walter Dellinger, a top Justice Department official at that time, later confessed, "Nothing makes me unhappier than the fact that we didn't file in *Romer.*"

Amendment 2 was scheduled for oral argument at the start of the high court's 1995–96 term. Unless the justices ducked a real ruling, they finally would have to draw a line. That line would either bring gay and bisexual Americans into the Constitution's protections or put them—and them alone—outside. Never in history had the U.S. Supreme Court struck down any explicitly anti-gay law or regulation as unconstitutional. Brennan and Marshall, who in 1985 had declared that anti-gay discrimination was largely based on "irrational prejudice," were gone by 1996. In the decade after its hostile *Hardwick* decision, the court had passively allowed lower courts to twist that sodomy decision into an all-purpose anti-gay weapon. The tone of its 1995 St. Patrick's Day parade ruling had sounded respectful toward gay people and toward Massachusetts for extending anti-bias protections to them. But, as that decision illustrated, a respectful tone didn't necessarily translate into a gay victory. Would the justices shackle gay and bisexual Coloradans to Amendment 2, even though their state's top court had ruled it intolerably unfair?

One of Amendment 2's original challengers died and two others dropped out before their case reached the U.S. Supreme Court. The remaining six flew to Washington for oral argument.

The night before their case was heard they attended a rally outside the court. As the Reverend Priscilla Inkpen approached the court, she was moved by the democratic promise carved above the entranceway: Equal Justice Under Law. "It just struck me," she says, "that this is exactly what we were coming here for—equal justice. And I thought about all of the other people who had come there, all the other minorities. And I thought, 'Well, some have gotten justice and some have not.'" When she addressed the banner-waving crowd, Inkpen declared, "I don't know what is going to happen tomorrow, but I do believe in the end we will have justice."

"I've Never Seen a Case Like This"

As Supreme Court clerks filed into their reserved seats on the warm, sunny morning of October 10, 1995, several thought they did know what was going to happen: Scalia was going to win—meaning that U.S.

Supreme Court would ultimately declare anti-gay Amendment 2 constitutional. Clerks trying to handicap the outcome of one of their term's
most exciting cases had found they could not "count to five"—as Brennan had phrased it—when listing justices prepared to strike down
Amendment 2: Scalia, Rehnquist and Thomas definitely would side
with Amendment 2. Assuming the right-leaning Kennedy joined them,
O'Connor would be the swing vote. She had not tipped her hand to her
clerks as they'd strenuously debated Amendment 2. But she certainly
couldn't be counted on to provide the crucial fifth vote for a landmark
gay-rights decision, especially since she'd upheld the constitutionality
of sodomy laws in *Hardwick*.

The clerks' calculations were quite similar to those of Arthur
Leonard, author of *Sexuality and the Law* and the gay-rights attorney
with his fingers closest to the Supreme Court's pulse. Without insider
information, Leonard assumed that Stevens, Ginsburg and Breyer were
likely to oppose Amendment 2 and that Souter might join them.
Leonard was skeptical but not without hope that Kennedy or O'Connor
would provide a fifth vote against Amendment 2.

For the Amendment 2 oral argument, the court's majestic but surprisingly intimate courtroom was so crammed with spectators that
their elbows were jammed into one another's sides. Attorney Dubofsky,
seated at a table immediately in front of the justices' bench, felt calm,
despite the enormity of the stakes and the grandeur of the occasion.
Behind her were Amendment 2's challengers—the human face of the
minority group that Colorado wanted to brand second-class. Challenger Linda Fowler was wearing the lucky bracelet her daughter had
given her.

Shortly before 10 A.M. the audience was commanded to rise. Black-
robed justices materialized from behind the huge velvet curtains. And a
marshal loudly recited the ceremonial words that intensify the court's
aura of timeless dignity: "The honorable, the chief justice and the associate justices of the Supreme Court of the United States. Oyez, oyez,
oyez. All persons having business before the honorable, the Supreme
Court of the United States, are admonished to draw near and give their
attention, for the court is now sitting. God save the United States and
this honorable court."

"When they said 'oyez, oyez,' and the justices came into the room, I started to sob," recalled Richard Evans, lead challenger because his name happened to be listed first on the lawsuit. "A lady sitting next to me gave me her lace handkerchief," Evans added. As Evans wiped away tears, Chief Justice Rehnquist announced that the court would hear argument in *Roy Romer v. Richard G. Evans.*

Taking his cue to step to the lectern in front of Rehnquist, Colorado's thin, young solicitor general, Timothy Tymkovich, launched into a dry defense. ". . . Colorado's Amendment 2 reserves to the state the decision of whether to extend special protections under state law on the basis of homosexual or bisexual conduct or orientation. The sole question here is whether . . . that statewide reservation of authority should be nullified under this court's prior holdings in *James v. Valtierra* and *Hunter v. Erickson.* . . . [T]he logic and holding of *James* is indistinguishable and controls here."

Less than a minute into Tymkovich's presentation, just as the minds of non-lawyers teetered on the brink of wandering, Justice Kennedy energetically pounced. ". . . Usually when we have an equal protection question, we measure the objective of the legislation against the class that is adopted, against the statutory classification. Here, the classification seems to be adopted for its own sake. I've never seen a case like this," Kennedy said, sounding almost as if he were quoting Tribe's brief. Kennedy demanded to know, "Is there any precedent that you can cite to the court where we've upheld a law such as this?"

As Tymkovich, fumbling, pointed again to *James,* Kennedy calmly bagged his quarry: "But the whole point in *James* was that we knew that it [involved] low-income housing, and we could measure the need, the importance, the objectives of the legislation to control low-cost housing against the classification that was adopted. Here, the classification is just adopted for its own sake, with reference to all purposes of the law, so *James* doesn't work." After giving Tymkovich a few seconds to speak, Kennedy hammered what to astute listeners sounded like a final nail being driven into Amendment 2's coffin: ". . . Here, the classification is adopted to fence out . . . the class for all purposes, and I've never seen a statute like that."

For more than 40 years, gay Americans had been courting justice. As Kennedy kicked away the one-legged stool that was Colorado's main defense and signaled that Amendment 2 appalled him, the hearts of gay and gay-friendly spectators leapt. "I felt we were fine then," Dufobsky recalls. In examining Amendment 2 closely enough to see it as discrimination for discrimination's sake, Kennedy fulfilled the promise implicit in his 1980 ruling upholding the Navy's gay ban: He would treat gay constitutional claims with the utmost seriousness.

By signaling his disdain for Amendment 2, Kennedy tremendously lightened O'Connor's intellectual burden. One O'Connor clerk recalls, "That was *the* moment in the case. That was the first point where I thought, 'Yeah, the left's going to win this.'" Inside her chambers, O'Connor made no secret of the fact she'd always been bothered by *Hardwick.* And the announcement that her old ally, Lewis Powell, thought he'd made a mistake in upholding Georgia's sodomy law had given her all the more reason to fret. "Assume you're Sandra Day O'Connor," says a clerk familiar with her thinking. "Assume you're very troubled by this [Amendment 2] case. Assume you think it's very difficult. Assume that you go into oral argument thinking, 'There's probably four [votes] on the left. There's obviously three on the right that would never consider going that way. Tony [Kennedy] usually votes with those guys. Geez, I don't know.' Tony suddenly comes out with the guys on the left quite strongly. It's much easier to join five than to join four."

With Colorado's attorney reeling from Kennedy's blows, O'Connor politely chimed in, asking whether Amendment 2 stripped ordinary legal protections away from homosexuals. Tymkovich said no. Sounding almost apologetic, like someone reluctantly pointing out that the emperor has no clothes, O'Connor said, "How do we know that? I mean, the literal language would indicate that, for example, a public library could refuse to allow books to be borrowed by homosexuals and there would be no relief from that, apparently." Tymkovich struggled with assurances that Amendment 2's sweep was narrow, but O'Connor again asked, "Well, how do we know that?"

Linda Fowler began getting ecstatic as it "became obvious that we were getting the support that we needed."

One by one, all the justices, except Thomas-the-silent, made a re-markable display of showing their hands during Tymkovich's half-hour. By the time Ginsburg followed up O'Connor's questions, court ob-servers believed they saw a 6-to-3 defeat for Amendment 2 in the cards. Underscoring Amendment 2's unprecedented breadth, Ginsburg noted that *James* dealt only with low-income housing "but here, it's every-thing—'Thou shalt not have access to the ordinary legislative process for anything that will improve the condition of this particular group.' And I would like to know whether in all of U.S. history there as been any legislation like this. . . ."

Seeing Amendment 2 getting mauled, Scalia tried to rescue it by feeding answers to Tymkovich. ". . . [I]f all 'orientation' means is some-one who engages in homosexual, lesbian or bisexual acts, then you have plenty of precedent . . . namely, state laws that absolutely criminalize such activity—bigamy, homosexuality." Tymkovich: "That's right, the—" In her most withering voice, Ginsburg cut in: "Colorado has no law that prohibits consensual homosexual conduct." Reduced to carrying am-munition for his opponents, Tymkovich noted that Colorado's sodomy law had been repealed in 1972.

Souter, the author of the first Supreme Court ruling to deal respect-fully with gay identity, got Tymkovich to concede that "orientation means something more than conduct," thus effectively moving the Amendment 2 challenge out of *Hardwick*'s shadow. Souter noted that the current case was an equal protection challenge because it involved discrimination. ". . . [N]o invidious discrimination," Tymkovich said, trying to hide behind a legalism. Sounding professorial, Souter in-quired, "What does 'invidious' mean?" The ground crumbling beneath him, Tymkovich lamely answered, "I think it means an arbitrary and ir-rational classification. . . . I think we've shown that there are reasons for the classification."

Then Ginsburg, the court's resident civil rights scholar, fit the gay-rights movement into the nation's long, slow march toward equal rights. "Mr. Tymkovich," she said, "I was trying to think of something compa-rable to this, and what occurred to me is that this political means of go-ing at the local level first is familiar in American politics. In fact, it was the way that the suffragists worked." She wanted to know whether an Amendment 2–style ban on local ordinances letting women vote would have been constitutional. Before Tymkovich could finish saying "no" because the court treats discrimination against women as "suspect," Ginsburg made him look ridiculous. "Well," she instructed, "cast your mind back to the days before the Nineteenth Amendment," which granted women the right to vote. The audience gently chuckled.

Scalia saw an opening and tried to pull O'Connor over to his side, saying that the answer to her earlier library question was, "No homosexual can be treated differently from other people. He simply cannot be given special protection by reason of that status." Tymkovich interjected, "That's right."

The task of further mapping Amendment 2's vast sweep then was shouldered by Stevens, who, after beating back contradictory answers, got Tymkovich to say gay and bisexual people could be refused service in a restaurant, turned away from an inn or turned down for a job because of their sexual orientation. "Having the right not to be refused a job . . . on that ground is a 'special right'? It's not being just like everybody else?" Stevens asked, sounding incredulous. Stevens wanted to hear the "rational basis" for Amendment 2, especially the "rational basis" for its telling the people of Aspen that they can't protect homosexuals.

Tymkovich said Amendment 2 "was a response to political activism by a political group that wanted to seek special affirmative protections under the law." He added that it was a "political response to what the [voters] might have perceived as laws going too far or being too intrusive." Rehnquist tried to help, suggesting that the rational basis could be that voters preferred to make rules at the state, not local, level.

Souter then flung a question that, in effect, said that rationale wouldn't explain why "protections for homosexuals cannot be dealt with at a certain level, whereas affirmative protections for the aged, for the handicapped, and so on, can be." When Tymkovich said Amendment 2 simply reflected a "quintessential political judgment," Souter said that to survive an equal protection challenge it must have a justification "independent merely of majority will."

Seeing Amendment 2 going down for the count, Scalia intervened more aggressively than before. "Mr. Tymkovich, if this is an ordinary equal protection challenge and there's no heightened scrutiny, isn't it an adequate answer to Justice Souter's question to say this is the only area in which we've had a problem? If localities started passing special laws giving favored treatment to people with blue eyes, we might have a statewide referendum on that as well. . . ." Tymkovich: "That's exactly what happened here. . . ."

Souter inquired, "What is the problem that you supposedly have been having?" Tymkovich offered a vague reply about "sensitive liberty concerns." Clearly deeming that inadequate, Scalia said localities were "giving preferences which the majority of the people in the state did not think desirable for social reasons." Tymkovich: "That's right." Silently drawing a slippery-slope analogy—that protecting gay people would open the door to protecting bigamists—Scalia declared Colorado would act again if local governments gave "special preferences to bigamist [sic] couples."

Stevens quietly inquired, "What is the 'special preference' that a homosexual gets?" Although Aspen, Boulder and Denver law banned discrimination based on sexual orientation, thus protecting everyone, Tymkovich answered that the anti-bias laws created "a cause of action on the basis of the characteristic that's not available to the general population at large."

In the final minutes of what must have felt like the longest half hour of his life, Tymkovich wrestled with Ginsburg, Kennedy and Breyer. Ginsburg asked what if a hospital with a dialysis machine said, "We're not going to have any gay, any lesbian person." (Ginsburg knew that the audience included a lesbian couple to whom she'd given admission tickets, former clerk Barbara Flagg and her partner, Dayna Deck.) Firing blanks, Tymkovich told Ginsburg that perhaps federal law could stop the hospital from discriminating or maybe the state could "enact a policy."

Breyer then homed in on the part of Amendment 2 barring any government "policy" against anti-gay discrimination. He asked, "if the police department says, 'There's been a lot of gay-bashing. . . . Stop it.' If the head librarian says, 'You're making gays sit—you're being mean to them and not letting them in. Stop it.' If the health department says the same thing, if the insurance commissioner says the same thing, doesn't the word 'policy' cover that?" Sounding angry as he pressed the point and ignored Scalia's attempts to answer for Tymkovich, Breyer asked, "Does it prevent the police department, the librarian, the dozens of state agencies from putting up a piece of paper that says, 'Policy: It is our policy in this department not to discriminate against gays.' You're saying it doesn't prohibit that. Then what does it prohibit?"

Tymkovich said Amendment 2 prohibits "special protection." Kennedy slammed him, saying his answer was "inconsistent" with what the Colorado Supreme Court had determined. With Breyer still dogging him with "policy" questions and one minute left on the clock, Tymkovich asked permission to return to his seat.

It had been an historic half hour. Never before had U.S. Supreme Court justices talked publicly about gay people as ordinary folks who check out library books, eat in restaurants, hold jobs and might need police protection or kidney dialysis. Never before had a majority of justices hammered away at a blatant attempt to discriminate against gay people. Never before had a majority sounded so ready to wrap gay and bisexual Americans in the Constitution's protection.

Dubofsky's allotted half hour was lively but anticlimactic. Peppered with nonstop questions, Dubofsky repeatedly found herself responding, "That's correct," as Breyer, Kennedy, Ginsburg, Souter and Stevens phrased derogatory remarks about Amendment 2 in the form of questions. Those five justices continued their earlier efforts to emphasize Amendment 2's potentially gigantic sweep, then stressed that—even if narrowly construed—it would leave gay and bisexual people completely vulnerable to the irrational and arbitrary discrimination that Colorado law otherwise protects against. The five seemed obsessed with what Amendment 2 would do to gay and bisexual Coloradans if allowed to take effect. They had no interest in debating levels of scrutiny or majority rights.

The five didn't constitute a rescue squad; Dubofsky didn't need one. She was neither intimated nor flustered by Scalia's efforts to cast the anti-bias laws blocked by Amendment 2 as "special provisions giving special protection" and prohibiting discrimination based on "homosexual orientation." Dubofsky placidly reminded him that they banned discrimination based on "sexual orientation" and, thus, protected everyone.

Still working to score a "special rights" point, Scalia, the court's first Italian American, said, ". . . if I go and ask a homeowner to take me in [at a] bed and breakfast and the homeowner says, 'I don't like Italians,' that's my tough luck unless there's a law against it." (As Scalia was surely aware, a federal civil rights law prohibits any public accommodation from discriminating based on national origin.) Breyer responded to Scalia by pointing to regulations covering everyone's sexual orientation. Scalia then insisted that homosexuals were given protections not available "to people at large. You can refuse to hire someone because you don't like the way he combs his hair." Dubofsky said Colorado law actually would prohibit firing someone for such an "improper reason."

Rehnquist compared Amendment 2 to a hypothetical amendment stating that polygamy will always be a felony but dropped the line of questioning when Dubofsky wasn't shaken by it.

With oral argument nearly over, Scalia hurled the question Dubofsky had been expecting: "Are you asking us to overrule *Bowers v. Hardwick?*" Dubofsky: "No, I am not." Scalia then proceeded to make the classic anything-goes-because-of-*Hardwick* argument. "Well," he said, "there [in *Hardwick*] we said that you could make homosexual conduct criminal. Why can a state not take a step short of that and say, 'We're not going to make it criminal, but on the other hand, we certainly don't want to encourage it. And, therefore, we will neither have a state law giving it special protection, nor will we allow any municipalities to give it special protection. It seems to me the legitimacy of the one follows from the legitimacy of the other."

Scalia knew that three days later, in the justices' private conference, he wouldn't get a chance to talk about Amendment 2 before the more senior O'Connor voted. (Rehnquist, Stevens and O'Connor had been on the *Hardwick* court. Rehnquist and O'Connor voted with the anti-gay majority.) Scalia's "legitimacy" argument served to put O'Connor on notice that he was prepared to blast her as intellectually inconsistent if she voted against Amendment 2. O'Connor was the only justice whose second-half remarks made her vote seem less certain. Before Scalia threw down the *Hardwick* gauntlet, she'd twice said she wasn't sure how to interpret Amendment 2.

Dufobsky thanked the court, sat down and watched as Souter slammed Tymkovich one last time in his remaining minute.

A *Denver Post* reporter gasped that both attorneys had been "treated like dirt." That wasn't quite accurate. Tymkovich had been handed his head. But Dubofsky emerged not only unbowed but unbloodied. Though things could change radically before the court handed down its written ruling, Dubofsky walked out of the courtroom and into the fall sunshine looking as if she'd very likely win 6 to 3, or 5 to 4 if she lost O'Connor.

After talking to reporters, Dubofsky, the six challengers and the rest of their lawyers headed to a Capitol Hill restaurant for lunch. Dubofsky was amused to see retired Justice Powell, whose flipflop had handed gay Americans their *Hardwick* defeat, at the next table. "We didn't need to tell him what we were there for," Dubofsky says. "We felt high. We felt like we would be all right." As she began the long wait for the court's ruling, she was buoyed by remembering that the justices had seemed at ease saying "gay" and "lesbian"—words that no one uttered during *Hardwick's* oral argument. "I think the U.S. Supreme Court is much more knowledgeable about both discrimination and sexual orientation than it was when [*Hardwick*] was decided—and a lot of it is because there has been so much in the news media about it," Dubofsky said then.

The day after oral argument Barbara Flagg and Dayna Deck dropped by Ginsburg's office, which is off-limits to the public. Deck introduced Ginsburg to her daughter and son, then asked the justice to sponsor her admission to the Supreme Court bar. Ginsburg agreed. Flagg and Deck didn't mention Amendment 2; that would have breached protocol. Yet they felt confident that the woman whose nomination they had so vigorously pushed would be a strong advocate for gay Americans' basic civil rights when the court voted.

"This Colorado Cannot Do"

On Friday, the 13th of October 1995, gay Americans finally got lucky at the Supreme Court. The justices voted 6-to-3 to strike down Amendment 2 as unconstitutional, lining up just as they had in the oral argument's first half. Stevens, O'Connor, Kennedy, Souter, Ginsburg and Breyer versus Rehnquist, Scalia and Thomas. Based on interviews with eight of that term's 35 clerks, it is possible to piece together a coherent picture of what happened behind the velvet curtain. The clerks all spoke very guardedly and only on condition of anonymity. Each attempted not to provide significant clues to the court's secret deliberations. Yet a pattern—which probably cannot be checked against justices' records for many years—emerged from their overlapping remarks.

Most justices had a "visceral reaction," as one clerk phrased it, to the sweeping discrimination that Amendment 2 would have licensed. Stevens, as senior justice in the majority, had the honor and responsibility of choosing the author of the court's first landmark gay-rights decision. He chose Kennedy, apparently out of a desire to keep him and O'Connor from straying.

"Kennedy definitely wanted the case. . . . His big shtick was this was an exceptional case, this was an outrage. He wanted to sock it to the people of Colorado. The emphasis on motive, bad guys is very much Kennedy," recalls a clerk for a majority justice. Clerks coyly said that a certain friend-of-the-court brief that they felt honor-bound not to identify played an unusually influential role in shaping the court's ruling. The brief was Tribe's, the reasoning of Kennedy's opinion suggests. Amendment 2 apparently hit a nerve with Kennedy, who strongly believes the Constitution bars government from classifying people based on characteristics such as race.

O'Connor, who'd signaled in the 1987 Olympic dispute that she was open to a gay equal protection argument, wasn't particularly interested in motive. Though she would have written the opinion differently from Kennedy, O'Connor was pleased that the task had not fallen to her because she wasn't eager to spotlight that she was the only justice to vote for the anti-gay *Hardwick* decision but against anti-gay Amendment 2. As in gerrymandering cases, she was concerned about the message that government action was sending to the public and about that message's real-world social and psychological effects.

Knowing that they could expect the take-no-prisoners Scalia to try to undermine their decision's legitimacy, the majority wanted a strong, undiluted ruling. "There was definitely a lot of eagerness to make it 6-3 rather than 5-4. That was considered a big deal by everyone," one clerk confided. Ginsburg was especially intent on the court handing down a 6-to-3 decision unmuddied by concurrences. The majority discussed whether to mention *Hardwick* but doing so probably would have meant the loss of O'Connor's vote. "O'Connor voted in the majority on [*Hardwick*]. She obviously couldn't go back on that," one of her clerks said.

Nancy Combs was the chief clerk handling Amendment 2 for Kennedy, whose usual practice is to breathe life into a clerk's draft. Kennedy circulated a draft fairly quickly. And though most justices in the majority made editorial suggestions, there were no major revisions. "The opinion in every sense of the word was Justice Kennedy's. It is definitely an opinion for the ages," a Kennedy clerk proudly declared. Scalia fired the expected broadside but failed to trigger a significant response. O'Connor's vote against Amendment 2 held firm.

During his 1987 confirmation hearings, Kennedy had demonstrated his gift for eloquence as he assured the Senate of his respect for individual rights, including the right to privacy. Kennedy stressed, "It is central to the idea of the rule of law that there is a zone of liberty, a zone of protection, a line that is drawn where the individual can tell the government: Beyond this line, you may not go." Confirmed in the era when clerk-written drafts usually lead to judicial opinions that resemble sausage more than literature, Kennedy's ear for the English language deftly elevated the court's landmark Amendment 2 ruling with eminently quotable touches of grandeur and solemnity. That Kennedy was the author of *Romer v. Evans* injected not just poetic language but poetic justice into the forceful ruling: He's the successor of Lewis Powell, who had indecisively cast the decisive vote against gay civil rights in *Hardwick* and lived to regret it.

As the court's 1995–96 term wound toward its close, gay Americans aware of the tremendous stakes in the Amendment 2 case grew increasingly nervous. Week after week, every Monday morning—decision day—gay-rights activists around the country held their breath and waited. Civil disobedience plans had been laid, just in case. Colorado's gay leaders were prepared to respond—win or lose.

The obsessively secretive court never provides even a moment's notice that a particular decision is about to be handed down. So only those reporters and tourists who happened to be in its courtroom on the morning of May 20, 1996, heard the announcement of the biggest legal victory in the history of the gay civil rights movement. The chief justice called on Kennedy, who quietly summarized *Romer v. Evans,* then said that the Colorado Supreme Court's decision against Amendment 2 was "affirmed" but on different grounds.

The majestic opening of Kennedy's ruling was missing from his spoken summation but leapt off the printed page: "One century ago, the first Justice Harlan admonished the court that the Constitution 'neither knows nor tolerates classes among citizens.' Unheeded then, those words are now understood to state a commitment to the law's neutral-ity where the rights of persons are at stake. The Equal Protection Clause enforces this principle and today requires us to hold invalid a provision of Colorado's constitution." Kennedy was drawing a strong, unmistakable parallel between the fight for gay rights and the fight for racial equality. He was quoting the heroic dissent by Justice John Mar-shall Harlan's grandfather from the court's infamous "separate but equal" *Plessy v. Ferguson* decision upholding racial segregation in 1896.

Speaking for the six-member majority, Kennedy, 59, found it unnec-essary to get bogged down in questions about levels of scrutiny. Instead, the court broke with its own anti-gay past to declare that hatred is not a legitimate reason to treat gay Americans as second-class citizens. Measuring Amendment 2 against the minimal requirement that it bear a rational relationship to a legitimate government purpose, Kennedy found that it simply did not make sense—except as an expression of "animus," or animosity.

"If the constitutional conception of 'equal protection of the laws' means anything, it must at the very least mean that a bare . . . desire to harm a politically unpopular group cannot constitute a legitimate gov-ernment interest," Kennedy declared, quoting the 1973 *Department of Agriculture v. Moreno* decision that knocked down a federal attempt to deny food stamps to hippies. Never before had a U.S. Supreme Court ruling even inquired into whether anti-gay hostility was a legitimate jus-tification for a government policy disadvantaging "gays and lesbians," as Kennedy referred to them.

Kennedy described Amendment 2 as probably sweeping away a vast number of ordinary legal protections but said that blocking anti-bias laws intended to protect gay people was enough to render it unconsti-tutional. He wrote:

> [W]e cannot accept the view that Amendment 2's prohibition on spe-cific legal protections does no more than deprive homosexuals of spe-cial rights. To the contrary, the amendment imposes a special disability upon those persons alone. Homosexuals are forbidden the safeguards that others enjoy or may seek without constraint. They can obtain spe-cific protection against discrimination only by enlisting the citizenry of Colorado to amend the constitution or perhaps, on the state's view, by trying to pass helpful laws of general applicability. This is so no matter

how local or discrete the harm, no matter how public and widespread the injury. We find nothing special in the protections Amendment 2 withholds. These are protections taken for granted by most people either because they already have them or do not need them; these are protections against exclusion from an almost limitless number of transactions and endeavors that constitute ordinary civic life in a free society.

Noting that virtually every law disadvantages some group of people, Kennedy pointed out that judges routinely evaluate whether there's a legitimate end that justifies the means. "By requiring that the classification bear a rational relationship to an independent and legitimate end, we ensure that classifications are not drawn for the purpose of disadvantaging the group burdened by the law. . . . [Amendment 2] is at once too narrow and too broad. It identifies persons by a single trait and then denies them protections across the board. The resulting disqualification of a class of persons from the right to seek specific protection from the law is unprecedented in our jurisdiction," Kennedy lectured Colorado.

Then in grand cadences worthy of his hero James Madison, Kennedy marched to his finale: "We must conclude that Amendment 2 classifies homosexuals not to further a proper legislative end but to make them unequal to everyone else. This Colorado cannot do. A State cannot so deem a class of persons a stranger to its laws. Amendment 2 violates the Equal Protection Clause, and the judgment of the Supreme Court of Colorado is affirmed."

On May 20, 1996, six justices of the U.S. Supreme Court gave gay Americans their promise that laws serving no purpose other than to advance prejudice will not survive their scrutiny. To gay Americans, that sounded like a promise to ultimately be freed from every form of government-sponsored discrimination since every overtly anti-gay law or regulation is rooted in animosity.

The Supreme Court majority opinion striking down Amendment 2 for unconstitutionally attempting to reduce gay men, lesbians and bisexuals to outlaws was a fitting climax to an odd minuet that Anthony Kennedy and Laurence Tribe had been dancing at arm's length for 16 years. In 1980, the moderately conservative jurist had, as an appeals court judge, cited the work of the progressive constitutional law scholar in saying that homosexual activity outside the military "might be constitutionally protected." That aside, especially since it cited the liberal Tribe, caused the Reagan White House to initially pass over Kennedy for a Supreme Court nomination. After Reagan nominee Douglas Ginsburg withdrew and Kennedy replaced him, Tribe—whose damning testimony against Bork had ruined his own chances of serving on the court—testified in Kennedy's favor. Tribe drew the ire of liberal colleagues for that endorsement. Kennedy's Tribe-influenced Amendment 2 decision not only eased Tribe's lingering pain over his *Hardwick* defeat but also showed Kennedy to be the kind of moderate that Tribe had predicted.

Just as Supreme Court's landmark 1954 school desegregation decision did not discuss laws against, say, interracial marriage, Kennedy's opinion did not address gay-rights issues not directly raised by Amendment 2. The ruling did not mention the military's ban on openly gay soldiers, school districts that fire bisexual guidance counselors, state bans on gay adoption or the court's own *Hardwick* decision. The majority's omission of *Hardwick* was hypocritical and intellectually dishonest, Scalia charged in a ferocious dissent joined by Rehnquist and Thomas.

"The court has mistaken a *Kulturkampf* for a fit of spite," seethed Scalia, whose use of the German word for the term "culture war" popularized by right-wingers like Pat Buchanan intensified his image as dangerously far-right. He continued, "The constitutional amendment before us here is not the manifestation of a 'bare . . . desire to harm' homosexuals, but is rather a modest attempt by seemingly tolerant Coloradans to preserve traditional sexual mores against the efforts of a politically powerful minority to revise those mores through use of the laws."

Then Scalia, whom clerks say was in a lather over having lost a series of 1996 cases he'd expected to win, transformed the majority opinion into a far stronger gay-rights statement than it was on its face: "In holding that homosexuality cannot be singled out for disfavorable treatment, the court contradicts a decision, unchallenged here, pronounced only 10 years ago, see *Bowers v. Hardwick,* and places the prestige of this institution behind the proposition that opposition to homosexuality is as reprehensible as racial or religious bias." Scalia's view of homosexuality was that "Since the Constitution of the United States says nothing about this subject, it is left to be resolved by normal democratic means"—meaning, the court has no business stopping any sort of anti-gay discrimination.

Holding the *Hardwick* ruling "unassailable" and Amendment 2 "eminently reasonable," Scalia, who read much of his opinion aloud, said, "If it is constitutionally permissible for a state to make homosexual conduct criminal, surely it is constitutionally permissible for a state to enact other laws merely disfavoring homosexual conduct." Once again, as in Burger's venomous *Hardwick* concurrence, homosexuality equaled sodomy equaled criminality.

After blowing a dart at Kennedy by quoting from his 1980 opinion upholding the Navy's gay ban, Scalia railed, "I had thought that one could consider certain conduct reprehensible—murder, for example, polygamy, or cruelty to animals—and could exhibit even 'animus' toward such conduct. Surely that is the only sort of 'animus' at issue here: moral disapproval of homosexual conduct. . . ." Then having compared homosexuals to murderers, polygamists and animal torturers, Scalia claimed, "It is nothing short of preposterous to call [them] 'politically unpopular'. . . ." He then assailed the majority justices as elitists imposing the values of "the lawyer class" on a defenseless nation.

Though not mentioned by name, O'Connor bore the brunt of Scalia's vicious attack. She alone had voted to uphold Georgia's sodomy law and strike down Colorado's Amendment 2. Had she had a change of heart? Had her understanding of gay people evolved? Or, did she consider the constitutional issues raised so different that she could have cast both votes simultaneously? O'Connor clerks from 1986 and 1996 always considered her potentially persuadable that sodomy laws violate equal protection by being used primarily to smear gay people as criminals. Of course, *Hardwick* did not reach the Supreme Court as an equal protection challenge, though Stevens ruled against Georgia's sodomy law largely on those grounds.

A 1986 O'Connor clerk, Stephen Gilles, says, "I could see her going either way [on *Romer*], depending on whether she saw it in equal protection terms or not. In other words, whether it looked to her like a case where the court would be intruding in a novel, large-scale fashion into the [political] process or just protecting a minority from a new kind of overreaching by a [state] that's out of control. You can characterize *Romer* either way. You can characterize [*Hardwick*] either way. And how does she know where you put one and not the other? I don't know that she would have a great answer to that."

Powell biographer John Jeffries believes that Powell, in many ways O'Connor's intellectual soul mate, would have seen *Romer* as quite different from *Hardwick*. Jeffries said, "If you look at *[Hardwick]* from his point of view, it looks like an offensive claim, not a defensive one. It would have been defensive if there were actual criminal prosecutions. . . . What's distinctive about *Romer* is it looks defensive. It looks like the government is beating up on gay people. And I feel very certain Powell would have been in the majority on *Romer*."

On *Romer*, Kennedy led and O'Connor followed. Had the Senate not rejected Bork's nomination to succeed Powell, the relentlessly anti-gay Bork, not Kennedy, would have been on the *Romer* court. O'Connor very likely would have been unwilling to be a fifth vote against Amendment 2—especially under assault by two ideologues so aggressive that they make Rehnquist's hard-edged conservatism seem almost mild. With Bork on its bench, the Supreme Court likely would have ruled 5-to-4 that Amendment 2 was perfectly constitutional.

But the word that sped to Colorado in a heartbeat was very different indeed: The U.S. Supreme Court had tossed anti-gay Amendment 2 into the dustbin of history. It would never be allowed to take effect.

"When we won, I was giddy and light-headed. I felt like I was rising off the ground," Amendment 2 challenger Priscilla Inkpen recalls. A jubilant celebration at the state capitol in Denver drew 2,000 people. The gay-rights governor whose name ironically came to stand for the case's anti-gay side, Romer called the court's ruling "reasoned."

In Washington, D.C., Elizabeth Birch, executive director of the Human Rights Campaign, the nation's largest gay-rights organization, ecstatically welcomed the court's decision. "We are jubilant, and this is an outstanding moral victory. All the way to the Supreme Court the tone of this country has changed with regard to gays and lesbians: Gay people are full citizens of this country and have to be treated as such."

Colorado for Family Values Chairman Will Perkins impotently vowed to impeach the majority justices and warned that the court had opened the door to gay marriage. Colorado Attorney General Norton called the ruling "disappointing in its failure to provide useful guidance." (She went on to lose the 1996 Republican Senate nomination to anti-gay

Congressman Wayne Allard, whose campaign blamed her for losing Amendment 2. In November 1996, Colorado elected Allard to the Senate. Then in 2001 Norton became secretary of the interior under President George W. Bush.)

The court's gay-rights breakthrough was the lead story in *The New York Times*, *The Washington Post* and, of course, *The Denver Post*.

For the first time since Amendment 2 passed in 1992, a Colorado poll taken the day after the Supreme Court's ruling found the amendment trailing—46 percent to 43 percent.

Legally, the *Romer* ruling preserved the status quo for Colorado's gay community. Emotionally and organizationally, the successful fight to defeat Amendment 2 had transformed their state. Four years later, Equality Colorado had a paid staff of eight, headed by Sue Anderson, and list of 12,000 supporters, making it one of the nation's strongest statewide gay groups.

Amendment 2 challenger Linda Fowler says, "I often have thought that Colorado for Family Values and the religious right did some wonderful things for us in terms of pushing [gay rights] forward and pushing it into the limelight. It created enormous dialogue among all kinds of people who had never thought of this issue. People could actually say the words. You would be sitting in a restaurant and hear people discussing it. It was terrific! It was so incredibly beneficial. [CFV] had no idea what a gift they were giving us. We wouldn't be where we are today without Amendment 2."

A Monumental Puzzle

In striking down Amendment 2, the court seemed to ring the death knell for similar rights-blocking initiatives. (It did nothing to stop mere repeal of gay-rights laws.) Yet for all of Kennedy's eloquence, it was difficult to discern exactly how much "equal protection" gay Americans had won. The six majority justices had drawn a line and scolded Colorado for having crossed it, yet they gave no reliable hint of what else— if anything—they'd view as over the line.

Dubofsky says *Romer* signals that gay claims ought not to be brushed aside: "'We won't listen to you'—that had been the tenor of most of the opinions in the country before. *[Romer]* basically says, 'In this country you don't treat a group of people the way Amendment 2 would.' The main impact comes from the change in the tenor. And that is felt all the way through the country."

Tribe thinks *Romer* is reason for "cautious optimism in bringing before the court claims of unjust discrimination whenever a state or local civilian agency refuses to hire someone or promote someone (preferably not an elementary school teacher or a daycare worker, given likely judicial prejudices among the nine) just because he or she is openly gay."

Gay-law scholar Arthur Leonard says *Romer* might mean the nation has a Supreme Court majority "comfortable with the idea of gay people as citizens, as people who exist beyond sexual acts. . . . And if we do, then we've made a real breakthrough. Because it means when we come back with other equal protection challenges, we don't have to start from square one trying to persuade them there's a difference between sodomy and homosexuals. And that's crucial for military cases, absolutely crucial." He cautioned, however, "We certainly shouldn't build castles in the sky on the basis of suddenly proclaiming Anthony Kennedy as a great hero of gay rights."

A *Romer* clerk says, "*Romer* doesn't necessarily tell you that much about what they'd do in the next case. It gives you [something] that does counterbalance *[Hardwick]*. And now Justice Scalia's argument in dissent is that *[Hardwick]* held that gay people aren't people and therefore don't have any rights. And *Romer* says, 'No, gay people are people; gay people have rights.' I think it just kind of levels the playing field. You'd have to make normal constitutional arguments now. There's no huge thumb on the scale against gay people—I hope that's what it means."

The U.S. Supreme Court had ruled that gay Americans were not "strangers to the law." Time would tell which justices really meant it.

17

COUNTING TO ~~FIVE~~ FOUR

ON JUNE 17, 1996, just four weeks after sternly intoning, "This Colorado cannot do," the same six-justice majority that had struck down Colorado's anti-gay Amendment 2 seemed to add, "And neither can Cincinnati."

The Supreme Court erased a Sixth Circuit decision upholding Cincinnati's very similar anti-gay amendment to its city charter, then sent the case back down "for further consideration in light of *Romer v. Evans*"—code meaning, "Our earlier ruling dictates the outcome of your case."

Those actions seemed to suggest that six justices were committed to using *Romer* on behalf of gay Americans. Perhaps more than anything else, *Romer* gave gay people a promise of fairness. Reading between the lines of *Romer's* soaring prose, it's easy to see Justices Kennedy, Stevens, O'Connor, Souter, Ginsburg and Breyer pledging not to let prejudice rule them.

Romer lectured Colorado that there is no gay exception to the Constitution's guarantee of equal protection, that government must not put its stamp of approval on anti-gay animosity. Yet for all its grandeur, that ruling generated more questions than answers: Was the court being honest in signaling gay Americans that it was no longer hostile territory? When push came to shove—as it inevitably would—how many real friends would gay Americans have? Could they count on the *Romer* six—or, at least, five of the six?

For four years, gay Americans waited impatiently to learn whether a majority of the court was really willing to use its first real gay-rights ruling as a cornerstone for decisions moving gay Americans toward full legal equality. When, in June 2000, the Supreme Court finally addressed gay rights again, gay Americans received an unwanted math lesson: On a court where five votes can do anything, gay Americans have four strong allies.

Between *Romer* and that 2000 lesson, the court dealt directly with gay rights only in the Cincinnati case. And in the end, the court chose not to tell Cincinnati what it can or cannot do.

The saga of Cincinnati's anti-gay amendment was almost identical to that of Colorado's Amendment 2 in fencing gay people out of the normal political process by making it more difficult for them than anyone else to seek government help. In 1991, the Cincinnati City Council banned discrimination based on sexual orientation in city employment. The next year the council outlawed such discrimination in private employment, housing and public accommodations.

As a direct result, Take Back Cincinnati—later called Equal Rights Not Special Rights—got an anti-gay amendment to the city's charter onto the ballot. That amendment, known as Issue 3, passed on November 2, 1992, with 62 percent of the vote. Issue 3 declared that city officials "may not enact, adopt, enforce or administer any ordinance, regulation, rule or policy which provides that homosexual, lesbian or bisexual orientation, status, conduct or relationship constitutes, entitles or otherwise provides a person with the basis to have any claim of minority or protected status, quota preference or other preferential treatment."

Equality Foundation of Greater Cincinnati, which had led the fight against Issue 3, joined a housing group, a lesbian mother and four gay men in suing. (One man, Chad Bush, had had a discrimination complaint pending until the city said it could no longer enforce its anti-bias law.)

Federal Judge S. Arthur Spiegel blocked Issue 3 from taking effect, then struck it down as too vague and as a violation of a host of constitutional rights. He denounced "grossly inaccurate" Issue 3 campaign materials that depicted homosexuals as pedophiles and as people whose sexual practices "involve . . . rodents." Building on Brennan's *Rowland* dissent Spiegel ruled that gay people have "suffered a history of invidious discrimination." Issue 3's purpose, he declared, was to give "effect to private prejudice. This, the Constitution will not tolerate."

As Issue 3 headed to the Sixth Circuit, the anti-gay side recruited Robert Bork and former attorney general Edwin Meese. When the Clinton administration refused a gay request to get involved, *The New York Times* accused it of "cowardice." Meanwhile, Cincinnati voters deleted sexual orientation protections from the city's anti-bias law.

On May 12, 1995, a Sixth Circuit panel leaned on *Hardwick* in finding nothing unconstitutional about Issue 3. It ruled the measure might advance "a litany of valid community interests," such as expressing majority "moral views" and enhancing "liberty" for people who want to be free to "dissociate themselves from homosexuals"—that is, free to discriminate.

In August 1995, the Equality Foundation petitioned the Supreme Court, which sat on the request while grappling with *Romer*'s Amendment 2. When the court's June 1996 one-sentence Cincinnati ruling cited *Romer,* that action was "widely regarded as the fatal blow for Issue 3 because the two laws were considered nearly identical," the *Cincinnati Enquirer* noted.

Yet a short dissent by the Scalia-led trio of *Romer* protesters that included Rehnquist and Thomas almost begged the Sixth Circuit to stick to its anti-gay guns. The dissenters pointed to an obvious difference from Amendment 2: Issue 3 was a local, not a state, measure. (Yet the landmark *Hunter v. Erickson* ruling had overturned a discriminatory addition to a city charter.)

On October 23, 1997, the same Sixth Circuit panel—Robert Krupansky, Cornelia Kennedy and Alan Norris—shocked observers by again upholding Issue 3. Trying to justify what certainly seemed like a slap at the Supreme Court, the panel claimed *Romer* was not relevant. In contrast to "conscience-shocking" Amendment 2, Issue 3 involved a local measure and "merely prevented homosexuals . . . from obtaining special privileges and preferences" rather than blocking all protection for discrimination, it ruled. Of course, *Romer* had explicitly ruled that Amendment 2 was unconstitutional regardless of whether it canceled all discrimination protections.

When Issue 3 bounced back, the Supreme Court ducked, denying *cert* in *Equality Foundation of Greater Cincinnati et al. v. City of Cincinnati* on October 13, 1998. No justice publicly dissented. Yet Stevens, joined by Souter and Ginsburg, issued an extraordinary explanation that, while not citing *Romer,* served to caution against reading the court's inaction as undercutting *Romer.* Denial of *cert,* Stevens stressed, "is not a ruling on the merits. Sometimes such an order reflects nothing more than a conclusion that a particular case may not constitute an appropriate forum in which to decide a significant issue." He added that "confusion" over Issue 3's reach "counsels against" taking the case.

Except for the Sixth Circuit, lower courts had struck down or blocked Amendment 2–style anti-gay initiatives in the wake of *Romer.* The Supreme Court's passivity allowed Cincinnati's Issue 3 to be the only such measure to survive.

Court watcher Arthur Leonard saw Stevens's usual statement as a defensive, strategic move. "It means that those on the court that we like to think of as supportive of gay and lesbian rights didn't have the votes. . . . I've got to believe the problem is with O'Connor and Kennedy," he said, pointing ominously to the most conservative justices in *Romer*'s six-member majority.

Between its Cincinnati responses, the court repeatedly batted away challenges to the military's gay ban.

Don't Listen, Don't Rule

If the Supreme Court wanted to break its 15 years of silence on the military's ouster of homosexuals, Paul Thomasson offered it an ideal opportunity. He had been cruising at top speed toward an admiralty until his sense of integrity and his determination to combat anti-gay stereotypes forced him to come out to the Navy's top brass. A week later, the Navy formally began torpedoing his outstanding career solely because he acknowledged being gay. After serving openly for 15 months, Thomasson was honorably discharged in July 1995.

On the steamy morning of July 1, 1996, Thomasson briskly walked two blocks from the Capitol Hill restaurant he'd recently bought to the Supreme Court. Demonstrating the take-charge attitude that had made admirals swoon, he personally filed the required 40 copies of his *cert* petition, the first challenging the "Don't Ask, Don't Tell" rules signed into law in late 1993.

Just days after Bill Clinton took office in January 1993, a firestorm enveloped his young presidency because of Pentagon and congressional opposition to his campaign pledge to lift the ban on gays in the military. Bowing to political realities, Clinton agreed to a compromise that pleased almost no one: Simply being gay would no longer be declared incompatible with military service. However, any "homosexual act" (physical contact, no matter how casual, that an onlooker might interpret as gay), coming-out statement or same-sex marriage would be grounds for discharge. In other words, gay Americans could serve if they remained closeted and celibate.

Pentagon "Don't Ask, Don't Tell" regulations specifically said that statements such as "I am gay" would be presumed to mean someone had engaged in or would engage in homosexual acts. Unless successfully rebutted, that presumption would lead directly to discharge.

On March 2, 1994—the day after the Navy issued its "Don't Ask, Don't Tell" rules—31-year-old Lieutenant Paul Thomasson wrote to four admirals whom he'd served with distinction: "I can remain silent no longer. I am gay."

During Thomasson's 10 years on active duty, his superiors pinned an endless string of star-studded compliments on him: "magnificent," "spectacularly good," "a true superstar," "destined for great things." When Thomasson worked for the Joint Chiefs of Staff, Chairman Colin Powell awarded him medals for his excellent briefings of Powell and Defense Secretary Richard Cheney. After working with Thomasson, Rear Admirable Lee Gunn gushed, "If you are in your right mind, you want Paul Thomasson working for you. . . . Lt. Thomasson has genuine flag [admiral] potential." A year after Thomasson came out, Rear Admiral Albert Konetzni said Thomasson "commands the respect of his subordinates and seniors alike." On Thomasson's last day in uniform, Konetzni, whose duties ironically included enforcing the revised gay ban, recommended him for promotion to lieutenant commander.

By then, Thomasson, who claimed that his rights of free speech, equal protection and due process had been violated, had lost his first round in court. A federal judge had said courts aren't competent to "second guess" Congress's military decisions. On April 5, 1996, the full Fourth Circuit agreed, 9 to 4, and declined to "upset . . . a carefully crafted national political compromise."

The dissenters, led by Judge Kenneth Hall, found it wrong to assume Thomasson would break conduct rules, comparing that to assuming someone who said "I am an Orthodox Jew" would violate regulations by wearing a yarmulke while in uniform. Seeing evidence that the ban was "motivated by a desire to accommodate prejudice," Hall noted that retired Admiral Thomas Moorer, who helped revise the ban, had claimed homosexuals are "inherently promiscuous."

When Thomasson petitioned the Supreme Court, six weeks after *Romer* declared that expressing anti-gay animosity was not a legitimate government purpose, his case seemed like a textbook test case. Would the court be willing to examine whether "Don't Ask, Don't Tell" violated the equal protection principles spelled out in *Romer?* Thomasson's petition informed the justices that the military's ban had ruined the careers of 772 Americans in fiscal 1995 alone.

Responding for the Clinton administration, Acting Solicitor General Walter Dellinger said "Don't Ask, Don't Tell" is not "unconstitutionally grounded in prejudice." Rather, he argued, it is "narrowly tailored" to meet the military's unique needs and to advance the "legitimate objectives of prohibiting homosexual acts in the military, promoting unit cohesion, protecting privacy interests and reducing sexual tension." Comparing the military's gay ban to its ban on "ex-felons," Dellinger pointed to Colin Powell's contention that "open homosexuality in units is not just the acceptance of benign characteristics such as color or gender or background."

In paying his Supreme Court filing fee, Thomasson wrote a $300 check. On the line used to record the transaction's purpose, he wrote, "Equal justice." The court delivered its curt reply in *Paul G. Thomasson v. William J. Perry, secretary of defense, and John H. Dalton, secretary of the Navy* on October 21, 1996: *Cert* denied. Despite *Romer,* the court's response to "Don't Ask, Don't Tell" was just what it had been to earlier versions of the gay ban: Don't get involved.

"God Hates Fags"

Though there's not yet any way to peek behind the velvet curtain to see how the court privately dealt with cases it turned away between 1996 and 2000, those cases provided the justices windows into the contradictory ways the outside world was responding to gay demands for full equality. The justices were offered glimpses of the most virulent strand of homophobia produced in the 1990s, competing churches' tug-of-war over homosexuality, the increasing efforts of many state and local governments to protect their gay citizens and the continued use of the *Hardwick* sodomy decision as an all-purpose anti-gay weapon.

In October 1996, a petition challenging minor restrictions on anti-gay picketing by Westboro Baptist Church introduced the justices to the shockingly extremist views of that Topeka, Kansas, church. In the words of its own attorney, Margie Phelps, "Beginning in early 1991 Westboro began a ministry of public religious pickets with a central message of 'God Hates Fags.'" She explained, "Westboro uses this term ["fags"] not to be gratuitously pejorative. . . . The word means, loosely, fuel for fire, and is appropriate given Westboro's message."

Led by Pastor Fred Phelps, Westboro had paraded its burn-in-hell message all over the country. Church members picketed more than 10,000 times with such signs as "Hate is a Bible Value," "Fags = AIDS = Death" and "Fag God = Rectum." In 1992, a Topeka church critical of Westboro's hateful message—St. David's Episcopal—became a prime target of its picketing. St. David's sued, alleging that anti-gay picketing interfered with its members' "worship experience."

A county judge restricted how closely Westboro could picket to St. David's property before or after services. A state appeals court upheld the limits.

Westboro argued that its freedom of religion was being violated because its sidewalk picketing constituted a "worship service." The Supreme Court turned *Westboro Baptist Church Inc. v. St. David's Episcopal Church* away unheard on January 21, 1997.

Ten months later, the justices refused to give the time of day to a fundamentalist preacher ousted from San Francisco's anti-discrimination board for "implicitly endorsing"—as the Ninth Circuit phrased it—the Old Testament punishment of death by stoning for homosexuals. The Reverend Eugene Lumpkin Jr. of Ebenezer Baptist Church had been appointed in 1992 to the Human Rights Commission, which is charged with investigating discrimination complaints and ridding the city of bigotry, including anti-gay prejudice.

Lumpkin sparked a controversy in June 1993 when a *San Francisco Chronicle* article on black homophobia quoted him: "It's sad that people have AIDS . . . but it says right there in the *Scripture* that the homosexual lifestyle is an abomination against God." The furor might have burned itself out if Lumpkin had not appeared on a local TV show. When he declared, "I believe everything the Bible sayeth," his interviewer responded, "*Leviticus* also says that a man who sleeps with a man should be put to death. Do you believe that?" Lumpkin answered, "That's what it sayeth." Interviewer: "Do you believe that?" Lumpkin: "That's what God sayeth."

Mayor Frank Jordan fired Lumpkin, who claimed his freedom of religion and freedom of speech had been violated. A federal judge sided with the mayor. The Ninth Circuit agreed, saying "the First Amendment does not assure [Lumpkin] job security when he preaches homophobia while serving as a city official charged with . . . 'eliminat(ing) prejudice and discrimination.'"

By the time Lumpkin petitioned the Supreme Court, the city had a new mayor. Lumpkin told the justices that he'd never actually advocated violence against homosexuals. On November 3, 1997, *cert* was denied in *Eugene Lumpkin Jr. v. Willie L. Brown, mayor of San Francisco et al.*

Just as the federal crackdown on homosexuals that began in the 1950s caused homosexuals to look to the high court for help, the spread of state and local laws protecting gay people inevitably produced *cert* petitions from heterosexuals claiming a right to discriminate.

Ann Hacklander-Ready wanted the justices to say she had a First Amendment right to refuse to rent to a lesbian after advertising for female housemates. In 1989, Hacklander (then unmarried) had been leasing a four-bedroom house in Madison, Wisconsin. When two women moved out, she and housemate Maureen Rowe sought replacements. Rowe decided living with a lesbian would be too much like "living with a man." So, a day after accepting a deposit from Caryl Sprague, Hacklander and Rowe told her that she could not move in because she was gay.

A county judge ruled that the city's fair housing ordinance, which outlawed discrimination based on sexual orientation, applied to anyone who rented housing for profit. The judge awarded Sprague $3,300 in damages, an amount reduced to $300 on appeal.

In petitioning the Supreme Court, Hacklander's attorney said, "From time immemorial, one's reputation has been determined in part by the company he keeps." Denying *cert* on May 12, 1997, the justices chose not to keep company with *Ann Hacklander-Ready v. Wisconsin.*

"If It's Homosexual, It Would Have to Be Sodomy"

If the Supreme Court had been eager to expand on what four dissenting 11th Circuit judges hailed as the "teaching" of its *Romer* gay-rights decision, it might have viewed a Georgia case that landed on its doorstep at the start of its 1997 term as an extraordinary opportunity. Georgia Attorney General Michael Bowers, winner of the 1986 *Bowers v. Hardwick* sodomy decision, was again defending his actions against a gay Georgian. This time, Bowers had revoked a job offer from a promising young lawyer because she planned to wed another woman.

In siding with Bowers, the 11th Circuit demonstrated how *Hardwick* could still be used to trump virtually any gay-rights claim. The 11th Circuit apparently had not learned from *Romer* that the existence of sodomy laws was no reason to treat homosexuals as second-class citizens. Petitioning on behalf of the rejected lesbian lawyer, Lambda Legal Defense and Education Fund, the nation's leading gay legal aid society, asked the Supreme Court to repeat the lesson.

Robin Joy Brown's story is yet another of the wholesome sagas that practically beg the justices to see gay Americans as upstanding citizens deserving judicial protection. Raised in a traditional Jewish family, she attended Hebrew school until 16. While in college in 1986, Brown met Francine Greenfield, who'd grown up in a strictly observant, kosher family. The women dated, fell in love and settled down, eventually buying a house in Atlanta together.

In the summer of 1990, Brown, an Emory University law student, was a law clerk in the Georgia state Department of Law. By then, she and Greenfield were making wedding plans. And they began premarital counseling with a rabbi. Unaware of Brown's upcoming commitment ceremony, Georgia Attorney General Bowers offered her a permanent job. She accepted, agreeing to start in September 1991.

After graduation, Brown told Deputy Attorney General Robert Coleman that she wanted to start work in late September because she was going to Greece on her honeymoon. When Coleman mentioned Brown's plans around the office, he and Bowers discovered that she was marrying a woman. Bowers decided to have Coleman give Brown a dismissal letter.

On July 9, 1991, Coleman handed Brown the letter and, following a bizarre script, said, "Thanks again for coming in and have a nice day." Bowers's letter told Brown, "This action has become necessary in light of information which has only recently come to my attention relating to a purported marriage between you and another woman. . . . [I]naction on my part would constitute tacit approval of this purported marriage and jeopardize the proper functioning of this office." Floored, Brown asked to see the attorney general but was instead shown the door.

Brown and her partner went ahead with what invitations described as a "Jewish, lesbian-feminist, out-door wedding." On Sunday, July 28, 1991, about 100 guests watched as the couple stood under a traditional Jewish wedding canopy in a South Carolina park, exchanged rings, signed a marriage contract and smashed a glass. As Rabbi Sharon Kleinbaum later explained, the ceremony—though having no legal significance—represented the women's commitment to each other, their synagogue and their faith. That month, the couple legally adopted the surname Shahar, Hebrew for "seeking God."

Robin Joy Shahar sued Bowers in October 1991, just weeks after she had been scheduled to start handling death penalty appeals for him. She claimed that Bowers had violated her rights to freedom of association, freedom of religion, equal protection and due process. (The Supreme Court has recognized a right to "intimate association" protecting close, personal relationships.)

According to Bowers, Shahar's relationship was not qualified for protection because it "does not involve a heterosexual relationship connected with . . . creating or maintaining a family." Judge Richard C. Freeman disagreed in 1993, ruling that a relationship involving "a lifetime commitment which cannot end unless formally dissolved within her religion" is protected. Yet, he dismissed the lawsuit out of deference to Bowers's need to keep his office "efficient."

An 11th Circuit panel unanimously overturned Freeman's ruling on December 20, 1995. Judge John Godbold and Judge Lewis R. Morgan said Shahar's intimate relationship merited the highest judicial deference and sent the case back down with orders that Bowers's job-offer withdrawal be subjected to "strict scrutiny." Judge Phyllis Kravitch would have preferred to go ahead and rule in Shahar's favor on the basis of protected intimate association.

Kravitch brushed aside Bowers's claim that he was protecting his office's credibility. She quoted him as saying his behavior was based on "the public perception that 'the natural consequence of a marriage is some sort of sexual conduct . . . and if it's homosexual, it would have to be sodomy.'" (In prosecuting a heterosexual sodomy case, Bowers had insisted that his attorneys' sex lives were irrelevant.) Noting there was "no evidence that Shahar violated Georgia's sodomy law," Kravitch declared, "Catering to private prejudice is not a legitimate government interest"—the point that would be at the heart of the *Romer* ruling six months later.

Instead of letting the case return to district court, the full 11th Circuit intervened. In May 1997 it ruled, 8 to 4, against Shahar. Judge J. L. Edmondson's ruling said "reasonable people" might equate a same-sex marriage with violating Georgia's sodomy law and, therefore, having Shahar on Bowers's staff could "undermine confidence" in his commitment to law enforcement. The decision quoted a judge who'd said, "Sodomy is an act basic to homosexuality."

Slapping down Shahar's claim that she was a victim of the kind of anti-gay discrimination prohibited by *Romer,* Edmondson declared, "*Romer* is about people's condition; this case is about a person's conduct." He added, "We also note that in deciding *Romer* the court did not overrule or disapprove (or even mention) *Bowers v. Hardwick.*"

Judge Gerald Tjoflat's concurrence quoted *Hardwick* as saying "no connection between family, marriage or procreation on the one hand and homosexual activity on the other has been demonstrated."

In dissent, Judge Stanley Birch, joined by Judges Godbold, Kravitch, and Rosemary Barkett—forcefully argued that "with *Romer* in the balance, the scales tip decidedly in favor of Shahar." They noted that Bowers assumed a homosexual would break Georgia's sex laws but did not make a similar assumption about heterosexuals. Bowers dismissed evidence "that lesbians prefer . . . non-sodomy sexual practices" by arguing the public was unaware of those findings.

Less than a week after the 11th Circuit ruled in his favor, Bowers, then a Republican gubernatorial candidate, admitted a 15-year adulterous affair with a female employee. (His ex-lover declared, "As far as sodomy is concerned, Mike Bowers is a hypocrite.") Shahar petitioned for a rehearing because of the new light that Bowers's sex life cast on his winning claims.

On August 1, 1997, the 11th Circuit voted, 9 to 3, not to reopen the case.

Robin Shahar, who'd become an attorney for the city of Atlanta, turned to the Supreme Court in October 1997. Petitioning the court on Shahar's behalf, Lambda attorney Ruth Harlow stressed that the case involved a government employee's rights of intimate association and expressive association (people gathering to express shared beliefs or ideas)—not any attempt to win legal recognition of same-sex marriage. Harlow argued that Shahar's interests should prevail because "Bowers' decision rests on irrational prejudice toward gay people."

The very facts that argued most strongly in favor of the Supreme Court putting Shahar's case in the balance with its *Romer* decision made the odds of its doing that infinitesimally low. *Robin Joy Shahar v. Michael J. Bowers et al.* spotlighted the undeniable tension between *Romer* and *Hardwick*. It also drew into sharp focus Bowers's hypocrisy in treating Georgia's universal sodomy law as an anti-gay law when he was among its heterosexual violators.

The six-member majority that had carefully sidestepped *Hardwick* in issuing the court's first major gay-rights ruling in May 1996 was not prepared 20 months later to squarely face the damage that government actions equating homosexuality with sodomy were still inflicting. *Cert* was denied January 12, 1998. (Georgia's top court struck down the state sodomy law later that year.)

"Any Decision That Treats Us As Equal . . . Is a Good Thing"

In grappling with gay-related cases after *Romer,* the justices demonstrated increasing sophistication and increasing comfort in dealing with homosexuality:

• In the 1997 oral argument in *Oncale v. Sundowner Offshore Services Inc.*, the justices talked matter-of-factly about homosexuals without exhibiting squeamishness or a sense of moral superiority. Joseph Oncale had been subjected to vulgar, frightening sexual harassment while working as a roustabout on an offshore oil rig. (He and his alleged attackers were heterosexual.)

On March 4, 1998, the court unanimously ruled harassment claims cannot be dismissed just because the victim and victimizer are the same sex. The justices disagreed with judges who'd held that same-sex harassment is discrimination based on sexual orientation—not sex—and, thus, not outlawed by the Civil Rights Act. ACLU gay-rights project chief Matt Coles cheered: "In effect, the court said we gay people are protected by the same rules and we are bound by the same rules as everybody else. And any decision that treats us as equal and unexceptional members of the workforce is a good thing."

• Three months later, the court ruled 8-to-1 against performance artists who had challenged Congress's 1990 requirement that the National Endowment for the Arts defer to "general standards of decency" in awarding grants. No justice used the homoerotic details of *National Endowment for the Arts et al. v. Karen Finley et al.* as a provocation to launch an anti-gay tirade.

Karen Finley, John Fleck, Holly Hughes and Tim Miller had challenged the "decency" rule as a violation of their First Amendment rights after being denied grants. All four specialize in shocking audiences, breaking taboos. Hughes's razor-edged monologues painfully probe her tortured psyche in ways guaranteed to make even many fellow lesbian feminists squirm. Miller uses vegetables as sexual props while ruminating on his life as a gay man in the age of AIDS.

• Nine months later the Supreme Court accepted a case vital to the continued good health of fledging gay-rights groups at public colleges and universities.

Scott Southworth and a handful of fellow conservative law students at the University of Wisconsin claimed that the school's mandatory student activities fees unconstitutionally forced them to subsidize views that they found offensive. Of 100 student groups funded by those fees, Southworth and his friends objected to 18, four of them gay. The lawsuit was part of a nationwide "effort by right-wing groups to attack student campus activities of a progressive nature—and that included gay and lesbian groups," notes gay law scholar Arthur Leonard.

The University of Wisconsin argued that encouraging a diversity of student groups was a proper educational enterprise at a public university. On March 22, 2000, the Supreme Court agreed in *University of Wisconsin v. Southworth,* and gay-rights attorneys sighed with relief.

• The gay civil rights movement's top attorneys were even more relieved two months later when the Supreme Court carefully tiptoed across a family-law minefield. The case pitted a mother against her daughters' paternal grandparents. After the suicide of their unmarried son, Jenifer and Gary Troxel sought visitation rights to see his daughters more often than their mother permitted. Washington state law allowed "any person . . . at any time" to seek visitation rights.

Gay-rights attorneys worried that a court unused to venturing into domestic disputes would stumble badly—harming gay parents' children: A ruling siding with the grandparents might harm lesbian mothers' attempts to fend off anti-gay relatives. A ruling against the state law might make it more difficult for a gay adult to protect a parental bond with an ex-partner's child.

When the court ruled June 5, 2000, it respectfully signaled its awareness of the growth of nontraditional families. "The demographic changes of the past century make it difficult to speak of an average American family," O'Connor, joined by Breyer, Ginsburg and Rehnquist, pointed out. Though striking down what O'Connor called a "breathtakingly broad" visitation law, the court made clear that such laws can be narrowly crafted to maintain important relationships.

Six justices issued *Troxel* opinions. "A common thread running through the opinions is that our society's once-rigid definition of 'family' is evolving and that our domestic laws need to reflect that," ACLU attorney Michael Adams noted.

By then, the Supreme Court had agreed to hear *Boy Scouts of America v. Dale,* a case that would force the court to talk directly about gay Americans for the first time since 1996.

Standing Up to the "Biggest Bully"

Little five-year-old James Dale wanted to be a Scout like his father and older brother. Scout rules said he had to wait. So, until he turned eight, he settled for being a YMCA Indian Guide. "The second that I could join the Cub Scouts, I got rid of the Indian Guides and joined the

Scouts," recalls Dale, whose first troop met at his family's Lutheran Church in Middletown, New Jersey.

By 11, he was a full-fledged Boy Scout and had earned the first of 27 merit badges, three of them for citizenship. He loved the camping and crafts, but the camaraderie mattered most: "I never found that I was as accepted as I was in the Scouts. The feeling of acceptance and belonging—that's why I joined and why I stuck with it. They made me feel good about myself."

Even though his troops kept folding for lack of adult leadership, Dale excelled. He soared from bugler to Eagle Scout. Scout rules said that at 18 he could no longer be a youth member, so as a Rutgers University freshman he became assistant scoutmaster of his old troop.

Sixteen months later, in mid-August 1990, Dale received the second certified letter of his life. The first had arrived August 5 from the Monmouth, New Jersey, Council of the Boy Scouts. It said his membership was being revoked. Having lived since age five by Scout rules, Dale had written back to ask why. Holding the unopened reply, he braced himself. But, he recalls, when he tore open the envelope the words of council executive James W. Kay "felt like a kidney punch." Kay wrote, "The grounds for this membership revocation are the standards of leadership established by the Boy Scouts of America, which specifically forbid membership to homosexuals."

The Boy Scouts had taught Dale to stand up for himself, have integrity and follow his own moral compass. Suddenly, he was being tested. "If they said they didn't like my politics or they didn't like me being this, that or the other thing, maybe I would have walked away. But being discriminated against because of my sexuality was not something I was going to walk away from. . . . Growing up, people would call me 'fag' and 'queer'. . . . I ran away from kids who would say things like that or threatened to beat me up. . . . [T]his was a fight that I wasn't going to walk away from. This was like maybe the biggest bully that I had ever dealt with," Dale recalls.

Dale had spent much of his adolescence fleeing from his growing awareness of his sexual orientation. "My perceptions of being gay were sex, bathrooms, bars, pornography. I had the middle-class dream of a two-car garage, white picket fence, a dog named Spot, wife and 2.5

kids. . . . It didn't seem like I could be gay and have a life," he recalls. But when a gay friend introduced him to the more wholesome sides of gay culture after his freshman year, Dale accepted himself and "pretty much started telling everybody." He did not tell his Scout troop.

Having gained experience in public speaking as a Scout, Dale agreed to address a Rutgers seminar for high school educators focused on lowering gay teens' suicide rates. *The Newark Star-Ledger* reported July 8, 1990 that "James Dale, 19, co-president of the Rutgers University Lesbian/Gay Alliance said he lived a double life while in high school, pretending to be straight while attending a military academy. He remembers dating girls and even laughing at homophobic jokes." A photo of Dale accompanied the article, which did not mention Scouting.

Dale had always assumed some Scout officials would react negatively if they learned he was gay and others would not. Nothing in the Scout handbook mentioned homosexuality. Neither did the Scout oath, the Scout law or the application for adult membership (A Boy Scouts magazine had once said the group barred homosexuals.) Dale didn't know that the Boy Scouts' National Council had banned gay Scouts at least since 1978—the year he became a Cub Scout. Several Scout leaders mailed the *Star-Ledger* article to Monmouth council executive Kay, who stripped James Dale of his Boy Scout uniform. (Left leaderless, Dale's troop disbanded.)

Dale secured the free assistance of the Lambda Legal Defense and Education Fund. He appealed to a higher Boy Scouts council but was brusquely informed that "avowed homosexuals" were unwelcome. Dale's legal fight appeared to be over before it began: Since neither federal nor New Jersey anti-bias laws prohibited anti-gay discrimination, Dale had no grounds for a lawsuit. But in 1991 the New Jersey legislature amended the state's public accommodations law to prohibit discrimination based on "affectional or sexual orientation." Suddenly, Dale had a very promising legal argument. Shortly after the new amendment took effect in 1992, he sued.

By then, attorneys for the Boy Scouts of America were arguing that homosexuality was forbidden by the Scout Oath's requirement that Scouts be "morally straight" and the Scout Law's demand that they be "clean." The oath, written long before "straight" became slang for "heterosexual," reads: "On my honor I will do my best to do my duty to God and my country and to obey the Scout law; to help other people at all times; to keep myself physically strong, mentally awake and morally straight." Defining "morally straight," the Scout handbook said, "To be a person of strong character, guide your life with honesty, purity and justice. Respect and defend the rights of all people. Your relationships with others should be honest and open. . . . The values you follow as a Scout will help you become virtuous and self-reliant." Defining "clean," it said, "A Scout keeps his body and mind fit and clean. . . . A Scout knows there is no kindness or honor in . . . mean-spirited behavior. . . . He defends those who are the targets of insults."

Dale was the target of insults when New Jersey Superior Court Judge Patrick J. McGann ruled in 1995, branding him an "active sodomist." Pointing to the Bible as proof that sodomy had long been condemned as a "gravely serious moral wrong," McGann declared, "Men who do those criminal and immoral acts cannot be held out as role models." (New Jersey had repealed its sodomy law when Dale was nine.) The judge said the public accommodations law did not apply to the Boy Scouts of America.

When Dale decided at 20 to fight back, he naïvely imagined it would be over very quickly. "I really honestly thought, 'I am right. They are wrong. The court will agree.'" Seven years later, he found a court that did agree. A New Jersey appeals court ruled 2-to-1 in 1998 that the Boy Scouts could not expel him for being gay. (The dissenter thought the organization could ban gay men but not gay boys.)

That court found "absolutely no evidence . . . that a gay scoutmaster . . . does not possess the strength of character necessary to properly care for . . . the young boys in his charge." It pointed to the "patent inconsistency in the notion that a gay Scout leader . . . who adheres to the Scout laws by being honest and courageous enough to declare his homosexuality publicly must be expelled."

"The Human Price of . . . Bigotry"

The Boy Scouts of America appealed. The New Jersey Supreme Court then handed Dale a monumental victory, unanimously ruling on August 4, 1999 that the group must abide by the state's anti-bias law. Chief Justice Deborah T. Poritz's ruling declared, "The human price of . . . bigotry has been enormous. . . . New Jersey has always been in the vanguard in the fight to eradicate the cancer of unlawful discrimination of all types from our society. . . . It is unquestionably a compelling interest of this state to eliminate the destructive consequences of discrimination."

The New Jersey Supreme Court ruled that because the five million–member Boy Scouts of America was huge, closely tied to government and publicly advertised itself as open to "all boys" of certain ages, it was a public accommodation—much like any restaurant, movie theater or swimming pool that sought the public's business. The New Jersey court pointed to a string of U.S. Supreme Court decisions limiting the right of expressive association. Beginning with a 1984 decision allowing Minnesota to force the Jaycees to admit women, the Supreme Court had held that large, generally non-exclusive groups were exempt from anti-bias laws only when accepting a certain sort of member would violate its fundamental purpose. (A group like the KKK whose members join to express white supremacist views could not be forced to admit black members.)

Noting that the Boy Scouts teach tolerance and that its troop sponsors have sharply conflicting views of homosexuality, New Jersey's top court found, "Nothing before us . . . suggests that one of Boy Scouts' purposes is to promote the view that homosexuality is immoral."

Concurring, Judge Alan Handler denounced the Scouts' ban as rooted in "anachronistic stereotypes about homosexuality." Handler declared, "One particular stereotype that we renounce today is that homosexuals are inherently immoral. . . . [Also], the myth that a homosexual male is more likely than a heterosexual male to molest children has been demolished."

James Dale's New Jersey Supreme Court triumph was announced two days after he turned 29. He'd matured into a strikingly handsome young man who gave the challenge to the Boy Scouts' gay ban a terrific poster boy. Dale exclaimed, "this is best birthday gift I could have asked for. The decision vindicates everything I have learned through Scouting—to be true to yourself, to be helpful to others and to believe that justice and goodness will prevail."

The Boy Scouts of America turned to the U.S. Supreme Court. (The group had been turned away in 1984 after losing a preliminary California decision in its successful attempt to exclude gay Eagle Scout Tim

Curran.) The question of whether New Jersey's anti-bias law applied to the Boy Scouts was no longer open to debate. The sole remaining question, according to the petition filed October 25, 1999, was: "Whether a state law requiring a Boy Scout troop to appoint an avowed homosexual and gay-rights activist as an assistant scoutmaster responsible for communicating Boy Scouting's moral values to youth members abridges First Amendment rights of freedom of speech and freedom of association." Attorney George Davidson argued that the *Hurley* ruling—saying organizers of the Boston St. Patrick's Day parade had a right to exclude a banner-carrying gay group—meant the Boy Scouts could exclude homosexuals. "We recognize that the issue [of] whether homosexual conduct is moral or immoral is controversial, and that many people of good will believe that Boy Scouting's position is misguided," Davidson said, arguing that the group ought not be forced to conform to a court's "idea of egalitarian values."

Lambda attorney Evan Wolfson countered that no particular message about sexual orientation is fundamental to Scouting. He noted that scoutmasters are instructed to avoid sex education and that *The Boy Scout Handbook* says "most boys join Boy Scouting for one reason—to have fun in the outdoors." Pointing out that heterosexual gay-rights advocates are not banned from Scouting, Wolfson stressed that Dale was expelled merely for being gay—not for anything he'd said or done. He urged the justices not to disturb New Jersey's landmark gay-rights decision.

Many gay-rights attorneys had long pointed to a Boy Scouts case as the sort of dispute they wanted to keep away from the Supreme Court. Cases involving a gay adult serving as a role model—whether as a troop leader, teacher or parent—were considered the least likely to get a fair hearing because of the lingering image of gay people as immoral and as sexual predators. The gay legal community would have preferred to try to build on its *Romer* success with a less emotionally charged case involving, say, a lesbian fired from a state highway department. But at least four justices wanted *Boy Scouts of America et al. v. James Dale* to be their court's first post-*Romer* statement on the rights of gay Americans. *Cert* was granted January 14, 2000.

The Boy Scouts of America's full-length brief then depicted James Dale as a human billboard: "Whether he intends it or not, Dale's pres-

ence as an openly gay scoutmaster would convey the message that homosexuality is consistent with Scouting's ideals and values."

In rebuttal, Wolfson accused the group of falsely claiming to have an
anti-gay message in order to evade New Jersey's civil rights law. "Dale's
identity is not a message," he added. ". . . Learning someone is gay tells
you nothing about his or her political party, religious beliefs, lifestyle or
moral code." He warned against creating an "escape hatch for discriminators" that would let them, say, bar women by claiming they didn't
want to send a "women's lib" message.

The flood of friend-of-the-court briefs supporting Dale showed how
much American society had changed from the days when gay people
were continually at odds with government. New Jersey, New York, California, Hawaii, Maryland, Massachusetts, New Hampshire, Oklahoma, Oregon, Vermont, Washington and several cities backed Dale.
Mental health, gay-rights, racial equality, religious and educational organizations also chimed in on his behalf.

"You Have to Make Room for Luck"

The day after gay Americans lost *Hardwick* on June 30, 1986, Evan
Wolfson bought pink-triangle lapel pins for himself and Michael Hardwick. "I said to myself, 'The reason this happened is because not
enough gay people are visible.' And I swore I would not stop wearing
that pin until we had overturned that hideous decision," he recalls. He
wanted to wear it during his argument on behalf of Eagle Scout James
Dale but knew court rules forbade insignia.

"So," he recalls, "here I was going from having sat in the [*Hardwick*]
audience as a junior, junior gay attorney . . . sitting with Michael on
what was an intense, romantic, exciting day, and losing, and taking this
vow to wear this pin" to knowing that he couldn't wear the pin while arguing before the very court that had foisted the *Hardwick* decision
upon gay Americans. "So what I wanted was to find a tie that would
have a very, very, very subtle pink-triangle motif," he says. He settled on
a dignified green tie with a pattern composed of teensy pink triangles.

One of Wolfson's gifts is his ability to simultaneously focus on small
but emotionally significant details and the big sweep of history that is
carrying gay Americans forward. He's convinced that the gay civil rights

movement will advance most quickly if gay Americans reach for the gold rings of first-class citizenship—legal marriage, for example. As a result, he leads battles that some gay-rights attorneys view as premature but that he sees as no-lose engagements because they educate the rest of the nation about gay Americans' wants and needs.

"We are winning so much culturally because of the political and legal battles—some of which we win. . . . We could be further along if luck had broken our way. But you have to make room for luck. If you don't make room for it, you will never get it," Wolfson explains.

Ranked by *National Law Journal* as one of the nation's 100 most influential lawyers, Wolfson is best known for making countless Americans share his faith that the marriage fight will be won. As the Boy Scouts' oral argument neared, he put his faith in substance and symbolism—prepping himself to be an undeniably strong advocate for gay Americans and to look the part. With oral argument scheduled for Wednesday, April 26, 2000, Wolfson sat in on the court's Monday and Tuesday arguments just to absorb the tone and rhythm of the courtroom he'd visited many times.

Wolfson found himself remembering the day, 14 springs before, that *Hardwick* had been argued. "Walking through the halls of the court, walking past where I met Michael [Hardwick], walking past where Larry Tribe and the rest of us had breakfast before going up to argue, it kept flooding back. And now being the openly gay lawyer who would argue the case for gay inclusion, building on what the non-gay lawyer [Tribe] had done in arguing just for us to be left alone. I kept trying to remind people, 'To win this case we need to get our fifth vote from a Reagan appointee [Kennedy or O'Connor]. This is an uphill fight.' That we dared to dream—with good reason—that we might actually get it is a testament to how far we have come," he says.

For luck, Wolfson had dinner the night before his oral argument with his parents, brother, sister and new sister-in-law, his Lambda colleagues and James Dale. On the morning of the argument, he put on the expensive black suit that, despite his frugal nature, he'd bought for his brother's wedding. Wolfson, a sturdily-built 43-year-old, accidentally over-trimmed his goatee and ended up shaving it off. The Vermont legislature's decision to create civil unions for gay couples was front-page news that morning, vividly reminding him and the justices just how rapidly progress was being made in one gay battle that long seemed impossible.

When Wolfson arrived at the court, it was packed with a Who's Who of the gay legal world and veterans of civil rights legal wars. He recalls being shocked but pleased to see New Jersey Supreme Court Chief Justice Poritz there. Seated near Wolfson was James Dale, who felt that his lucky charm was having his parents—Doris and Jerry Dick (Dale's surname until age 18)—with him. They had been uneasy with his sexual orientation, then with his lawsuit. The turning point, Dale says, was when their pastor congratulated them on his New Jersey Supreme Court victory and said, "This is what being a Christian is all about."

"Do You Ask If They're Ax Murderers?"

Chief Justice Rehnquist quickly dispensed with preliminary court business then announced the final oral argument of the 1999–2000 term—the case of the gay Boy Scout. At 10:10 A.M., the Boy Scouts of America's attorney, George Davidson, began: "This case is about the freedom of a voluntary association to choose its own leaders." He immediately found himself fielding questions from all six justices in *Romer's* gay-rights majority. They wanted him to explain what, precisely, the Boys Scouts were targeting with their gay ban.

Kennedy, whose *Romer* opinion eloquently cloaked gay Americans in the Constitution's protection, led off, asking whether James Dale was expelled for advocacy or for being gay? Davidson replied that the Boy Scouts are "not concerned about status. Souter pressed him, ". . . If he simply says, 'I am a homosexual,' would he be excluded from a leadership position for that?"

As Davidson hemmed and hawed, Ginsburg cut in: "Are you saying the policy is 'Don't Ask, Don't Tell,' or is the policy, 'If you are gay, you are not welcome in the Boy Scouts'? Which is it?" Davidson said, "The policy is not to inquire. The policy is to exclude those who are open."

Then O'Connor, adopting the puzzled professor persona that had signaled her opposition to Amendment 2, said, "Well, where do we look, though, to determine what the policy is, because it is a little confusing. . . . What about the heterosexual Scout leader who openly espouses the view that homosexuality is consistent with Scout law and oath and that it's not immoral?"

As Davidson fumbled for an adequate reply, Rehnquist helped him: "Well, I take it from what you're saying . . . that perhaps the Scouts have not adopted a comprehensive policy covering every single conceivable situation that might come up." Davidson agreed, "the Scouts have general moral principles in the morally straight and clean requirement of the oath and law."

Ginsburg inquired whether the Scouts expelled celibate homosexuals or cohabiting heterosexual couples. When Davidson's response generated more confusion, Souter got him to say that the Scouts expel anyone "openly homosexual" who comes to their attention. Davidson said "being openly homosexual . . . communicates the concept that this is okay, this is an alright lifestyle to pursue." Souter then got him to admit that the Scouts' gay ban isn't spelled out in its handbook. Souter also elicited an acknowledgment that expelling Dale had nothing to do with a fear that he might molest boys.

Breyer established that in Dale's situation being "open" simply meant that he had come out in the Newark newspaper. Breyer wasn't able to get Davidson to say whether a heterosexual who "had said every word exactly the same" as Dale would have his membership revoked.

Kennedy jumped in to point out that as far back as 1978 a top Scout executive had issued a memo calling homosexuality incompatible with being a scoutmaster. Sounding as if were musing aloud, he suggested that a Supreme Court victory for the Boy Scouts would likely mean that New Jersey would force its public schools and fire departments to stop sponsoring troops.

Having waited until his more talkative younger colleagues had had their say, Stevens pointedly asked, "If homosexual conduct violates the Scout code . . . why is it relevant whether the man is open or not?" Davidson admitted that the Scouts would oust even the most secretive gay man if his orientation were discovered.

Breyer wondered whether the organization was concerned about homosexuality or about how the public might react to openly gay Scout leaders. He calmly said, if the real concern is that homosexuality is "very, very bad conduct, it's surprising you don't look into it. . . ." Scalia tried to lessen the damage Breyer had inflicted on the anti-gay side. "Do you ask, Mr. Davidson, if Scouts or proposed Scout leaders are adulterers? . . . Do you ask if they're ax murderers?"

James Dale had to suppress an urge to raise his hand and ask, "May I say something?" He wanted to point out that his leadership application had asked whether he'd ever been convicted of a crime and that most ax murderers would be weeded out by that question.

Souter dealt the Boy Scouts another major blow, saying it was significant that the organization had been fighting gay Scouts in court for decades but still didn't mention its gay ban in its handbook. What's more, Souter, the author of the *Hurley* decision allowing parade organizers to bar a sign-carrying gay group, stated that the two cases were not parallel: "Mr. Dale has not . . . asked to carry a banner. He's saying, 'I'm not going to carry a banner. . . .'"

"Justice Souter," Davidson responded, "he put a banner around his neck when he . . . got himself into the newspaper."

Although the Boy Scouts' attorney had not been hammered as the Colorado attorney defending Amendment 2 had been in 1996, a crackle of excitement shot through the courtroom as Davidson sat down. Gay people sensed that five votes—perhaps even a sixth—were almost within reach. Souter, Stevens, Breyer and Ginsburg seemed like good bets for Dale. O'Connor and, perhaps, Kennedy were also possible. Most justices seemed dubious about granting constitutional protection to a discriminatory policy that the Boy Scouts' attorney could not clearly articulate and that the organization obviously did not want spelled out in its materials.

Rehnquist signaled Wolfson to begin. With his pink-triangle lapel pin hidden in his pocket, Wolfson started describing New Jersey's civil rights law. O'Connor immediately wanted to know whether it meant the Boys Scouts would have to admit girls. Wolfson said, no, there was a single-sex loophole. Rather than letting Wolfson proceed, Souter and Ginsburg kept asking about girls. Ginsburg, the court's resident women's right expert, witheringly asked Wolfson if his response was "the best that you can come up with." At that instant, all bets were off. The Boy Scouts could count on Scalia, Rehnquist and the mum Thomas supporting the right not to associate with homosexuals. But not one justice was indisputably in Dale's corner.

O'Connor voiced skepticism about applying a public accommodations law to a non-commercial organization. Then Rehnquist tried unsuccessfully to get Wolfson to say that government has a stronger interest in protecting people with such "immutable characteristics" as race and national origin from discrimination. ". . . Presumably homosexuals are not quite the same," Rehnquist said.

Breyer wondered if religious groups could be forced to accept people of other faiths.

Wolfson kept trying to focus the court's attention on the "expressive purpose that brings [Scouts] together" and to his view that an anti-gay message was not central to Scouting. But Scalia went on the attack: ". . . Is there any doubt that one of the purposes of the Boy Scouts . . . is moral formation. . . . And they say—and I don't know why we have the power to question it if the leadership of the organization says so—that one of the elements of that moral formation is that they think homosexuality is immoral." How, Scalia demanded, can letting "someone who embodies a contradiction of [the Scouts'] message" be a scoutmaster "not dilute the message?"

Wolfson replied that "a human being, such as Mr. Dale, is not speech." He warned the justices not to create a "free-floating freedom of disassociation" that would let discriminators evade civil rights laws virtually at will.

After Souter indicated that the Boy Scouts might have a stronger argument if they made their anti-gay ban more explicit, Scalia lectured Wolfson that if Dale won "what you will have succeeded in doing is inducing the Boy Scouts of America to be more openly and avowedly opposed to homosexual conduct in all of its publications." Wolfson disagreed. The Boy Scouts of America, he said, "are afraid of losing the non-gay people who . . . do not agree with this policy."

Wolfson's time expired. By then the gay audience's hopes had been dampened as thoroughly as a campfire doused by nine buckets of water.

Dale wishes he could have told the justices, "I am standing up against this policy because of what the Scouts taught me. How can an organization that made me feel so good about myself for so long suddenly not want me because they found out one small thing about who I am? . . . I am somebody the Scouts thought was great for so long."

Wolfson left the courtroom feeling more hopeful about O'Connor's vote and less hopeful about Kennedy's than when he'd arrived. As Wolfson and Dale walked outside to talk with the press, the sun broke through the clouds. Dale took that as good sign. A gay-rights victory was still possible to imagine but so was a 9-to-0 defeat. Dale seemed very unlikely to win.

Two days later, the justices gathered in their private conference room, which has honey-colored paneling, a black marble fireplace and a large desk, left over from the Burger era, tucked in one corner. Seated around their 12-foot conference table, the justices voted on whether New Jersey could force the Boy Scouts to take Dale back. The chief justice spoke first, of course.

James Dale began waiting for announcement of the ruling that, one way or another, would close a ten-year chapter of his life. He was sick of trying to live up to an idealized media image of "the gay Boy Scout" by being careful not to even cross against a light. And he was tired of having his privacy exposed in articles that snidely remarked on his upscale taste for medium-rare tuna steak or described his physical endowment. At 29, he was advertising director for *POZ*, a magazine for HIV-positive people. He had a Brooklyn apartment with no space for camping equipment. He was in a new relationship and still dreaming of someday becoming a parent.

Dale knew the passage of time had boosted his chances: "Gay marriage was an oxymoron ten years ago; today it is almost a reality. Gays in the military. *Ellen*. The Big Three auto makers just last week announced they are providing domestic partner benefits. . . . It would be easy for me to say, 'Oh, isn't this great what I've done?' But I am not that foolish or egocentric."

Five Votes Against an "Avowed Homosexual"

Seven weeks after Wolfson argued Dale's case, the court alerted him that—as part of an experiment—it was going to notify him of its *Boy Scouts* decision by e-mail rather than by telephone. Taking that as a strong hint that the ruling would be handed down on the next decision day—Wednesday, June 28, 2000—Wolfson and his Lambda colleagues had their attention riveted to his computer screen that morning. Lambda attorney Suzanne Goldberg heard a news flash on the radio and burst into Wolfson's office: James Dale had lost.

The six-member *Romer* majority had shattered, with Kennedy and O'Connor moving to the right to join Rehnquist, Scalia and Thomas in a 5-to-4 decision against Dale. The Supreme Court ruled that forcing the Boy Scouts of America to readmit "an avowed homosexual and gay-rights activist" would violate the organization's First Amendment right of expressive association.

The ruling forcefully demonstrated both how very far gay Americans had come in their quest for full equality and how far they still had to go. Rehnquist, who chose to write the majority opinion, was careful to use generally respectful language toward gay Americans, to call Dale an "exemplary Scout" and not to endorse the Boy Scouts' view that homosexuality is immoral. Yet his decision is a classic example of the "gay exception." Normal judicial procedures and constitutional safeguards were abandoned to produce an anti-gay result.

Boy Scouts v. Dale, nevertheless, is something of a gay-rights milestone because it revealed that four justices are vocal foes of anti-gay discrimination and strongly support the continued integration of openly gay people into American society. Writing for the dissenters, Stevens spoke out against anti-gay bias more powerfully than any prior justice.

In the past, the Supreme Court had looked skeptically at organizations' First Amendment excuses for discriminating and had tried to gauge whether being forced to abide by civil rights laws would actually interfere with the group's true expressive purpose. Rehnquist's decision instead accepted the Boy Scouts' contentions at face value: "The Boy Scouts asserts that it 'teach(es) that homosexual conduct is not morally straight' and that it does 'not want to promote homosexual conduct as a legitimate form of behavior.' We accept the Boy Scouts' assertion. We need not inquire further to determine the nature of the Boy Scouts' expression with respect to homosexuality. . . . As we give deference to an association's assertions regarding the nature of its expression, we must also give deference to an association's view of what would impair its expression." Rehnquist's ruling upheld what he termed the "freedom not to associate."

According to Rehnquist, "Dale's presence in the Boy Scouts would send a message . . . that the Boy Scouts accepts homosexual conduct as a legitimate form of behavior." The decision clearly allowed Dale to be barred not for his presumed views but for his sexual orientation. Dale's presence, the ruling declared, "sends a distinctly different message" than the presence of a heterosexual assistant scoutmaster who opposes the Scouts' gay ban.

Rehnquist acknowledged that "the terms 'morally straight' and 'clean' are by no means self-defining"—that is, their meanings are debatable. Yet by accepting the claim that those words are essentially Boy Scout code for "no homosexuals allowed," the court treated gay Americans in a way that is difficult to imagine it now treating any other minority group.

Thirty-three years earlier, the *Boutilier* justices who allowed "psychopathic" to be used as a blanket ban on homosexual immigrants had—consciously or not—seen a link between homosexuality and mental illness that they presumably would not have seen between, say, "shiftlessness" and left-handedness. Likewise, the five-justice *Boy Scouts* majority—despite claiming "not [to] be guided by our views of whether the Boy Scouts' teachings with respect to homosexuality are right or wrong"—was willing to read homosexuality into a ban on immorality in a way it almost certainly would not have been willing to read in, say, being Jewish or black, though both traits were long considered immoral in certain strands of American society. It is almost inconceivable that the court would have accepted any group's claim in 2000 that "morally straight" was just another way of saying "no Jews allowed" or "no blacks allowed."

In declaring homosexual sodomy unprotected by the Constitution, the *Hardwick* court had deferred in 1986 to the supposed judgment of the people of Georgia that homosexuality is immoral. Rehnquist's *Boy Scouts* ruling acknowledged that "homosexuality has gained greater societal acceptance." With public opposition to homosexuality no longer strong enough to be used as a reason for an anti-gay ruling, public acceptance of homosexuality became the justification. ". . . The fact that an idea may be embraced and advocated by increasing numbers of people is all the more reason to protect the First Amendment rights of those who wish to voice a different view," the court ruled.

In 1988, the court's Rehnquist-written preliminary decision in favor of a fired CIA technician had said nothing derogatory about being gay. Yet the moderate tone of Rehnquist's *Boy Scouts* ruling, especially its refusal to endorse the view that homosexuality is immoral, perhaps reflected not a change of heart by the justice who once compared homosexuality to a contagious disease but an effort to hold the essential votes of Kennedy and O'Connor. Stridently anti-gay language might have driven one or both into Dale's camp.

On gay issues, as O'Connor goes, so goes the Supreme Court. She voted in the majority in *Hardwick*, *Romer* and *Boy Scouts*. (By 2000, O'Connor was a barometer of court sentiment on most issues; she voted in the majority in 70 of 74 cases given a full hearing.) Her vote largely depends on whether on she sees a gay litigant as victimized or as trying to score a political gain, her clerks say. If she pigeonholed Dale as an "activist" trying to send a message by regaining his Scout uniform, that probably was reason enough for her to vote against him.

A "Symbol of Inferiority"

Justice John Paul Stevens, appointed in 1975 by President Ford, turned 80 two months before he handed down his impassioned *Boy Scouts* dissent. Best known for jaunty bow ties and his refusal to march to any particular ideological tune, Stevens first bucked an anti-gay majority in 1976, saying Virginia's sodomy law ought not to have been upheld without even hearing oral arguments. His *Hardwick* dissent a decade later raised serious equal-protection concerns.

As his more liberal elders retired and the progressives among his junior colleagues remained largely untested, Stevens emerged as gay Americans' most reliable ally. In 1996, he assigned Kennedy to write the ruling striking down Colorado's Amendment 2. That choice may have been critical to holding the *Romer* majority together. In *Boy Scouts*, with Kennedy and O'Connor lined up with the anti-gay majority, Stevens chose to write himself—in dissent.

In an unprecedented attack, Stevens—joined by Souter, Ginsburg and Breyer—flatly accused the justices in the majority of creating a gay exception to the Constitution's protections: "The only apparent explanation for the majority's holding . . . is that homosexuals are simply so different from the rest of society that their presence alone—unlike any other individual's—should be singled out for special First Amendment treatment. Under the majority's reasoning, an openly gay male is irreversibly affixed with the label 'homosexual.' That label, even though unseen, communicates a message that permits his exclusion wherever he goes. His openness is the sole and sufficient justification for his ostracism. Though unintended, reliance on such a justification is tantamount to a constitutionally prescribed symbol of inferiority."

Slamming the majority's reasoning as "astounding," "astonishing," "mind-boggling" and "far-fetched," Stevens argued that the court was supposed to figure out whether forcing the Boy Scouts to readmit Dale would seriously impede its attempt to achieve its basic, shared goals. The simple answer, Stevens said, was that it would not because the Boy Scouts had never expressed a "clear and unequivocal view" of homosexuality. At most, he argued, the Boy Scouts of America had a "secret" anti-gay policy at odds with its "public posture . . . of tolerance." Blasting the majority for failing to scrutinize the Boy Scouts' claims, he said, "It is plain as the light of day that neither one of these principles—'morally straight' and 'clean'—says the slightest thing about homosexuality."

Gasping in horror at the total deference the majority gave to the unexamined claims of the Boy Scouts of America's attorneys, Stevens declared, "I am unaware of any previous instance in which our analysis of the scope of a constitutional right was determined by looking at what a litigant asserts in his or her legal brief and inquiring no further."

In order to side with the Boy Scouts, the majority had to ignore every prior Supreme Court ruling in similar freedom of expressive association cases, Stevens stressed. "In fact," he pointed out, "until today, we have never once found a claimed right to associate in the selection of members to prevail in the face of a state's anti-discrimination law."

The Boy Scouts case, Stevens added, is "nothing like" the Boston St. Patrick's Parade case because "Dale did not carry a banner or sign . . . he expressed no intent to send any message."

Woven into Stevens's dissent was recognition of the role-model positions filled by gay Americans—as Olympic gold medalists, Wimbledon tennis champs, teachers, police officers, librarians, coaches and, more generally, as people viewed as moral by an increasing number of "major religious institutions."

Fifteen years earlier, Justices Brennan and Marshall had recommended strict scrutiny of anti-gay discrimination because it might well reflect "irrational prejudice." With Stevens's dissent, four justices were branding anti-gay prejudice a product of ignorance.

Stevens pointed out that even Supreme Court justices can evolve out of anti-gay stands once they get to know openly gay people: "Unfavorable opinions about homosexuals 'have ancient roots.' [A phrase from] *Bowers v. Hardwick*. Like equally atavistic opinions about certain racial groups, those roots have been nourished by sectarian doctrine. [He cited the religious roots of now-forbidden state bans on interracial marriage.] . . . Over the years, however, interaction with real people, rather than mere adherence to traditional ways of thinking about members of unfamiliar classes, [has] modified those views."

As evidence of that more enlightened thinking, Stevens cited the fact that homosexuality is no longer officially classified as an illness, Blackmun's *Hardwick* dissent, the Georgia ruling eliminating the very sodomy law upheld in *Hardwick* and the New Jersey civil rights law itself.

In an amazing footnote, Stevens violated the court's unwritten rule against saying anything truly personal about a colleague's intellectual development. He pointed out that the "significance of [Blackmun's *Hardwick* dissent] is magnified by comparing it with Justice Blackmun's vote 10 years earlier" upholding Virginia's sodomy law. Stevens also contrasted Blackmun's *Hardwick* dissent with Blackmun's 1978 decision to join Rehnquist's dissent from denial of *cert* in *Ratchford v. Gay Lib*. As Stevens noted, in discussing a gay student group's bid for university recognition, the Rehnquist dissent had said perhaps that "the question is more akin to whether those suffering from measles have a constitutional right, in violation of quarantine regulations, to associate together and with others who do not presently have measles. . . ." Stevens had managed not just to spotlight how Blackmun had changed but also how the author of the *Boy Scouts* ruling had viewed a gay freedom of association claim.

Having indirectly pointed out that Rehnquist had stood still while society evolved, Stevens continued, "Indeed, the past month alone has witnessed some remarkable changes in attitudes about homosexuals." He cited *New York Times* reports that General Motors, Ford and Daimler-Chrysler were offering domestic partner benefits to gay autoworkers, the CIA had celebrated gay pride day and a prep school had welcomed gay couples as dorm parents.

Stevens continued, "That such prejudices are still prevalent and that they have caused serious and tangible harm to countless members of the class New Jersey seeks to protect [by outlawing anti-gay discrimination] are established matters of fact. . . . That harm can only be aggravated by the creation of a constitutional shield for a policy that is itself the product of a habitual way of thinking about strangers. As Justice [Louis] Brandeis so wisely advised, 'We must be ever on our guard, lest we erect our prejudices into legal principles.'

"If we would guide by the light of reason, we must let our minds be bold," Stevens grandly concluded.

In a short separate dissent, Souter, joined by Ginsburg and Breyer, explained that their awareness of the "laudable decline in stereotypical thinking on homosexuality" had not dictated their votes. Rather, Souter said, they sided with Dale because the Boy Scouts of America's materials failed to convey any clear message about homosexuality. In other words, in their view, if the Boys Scouts of America were an overtly, actively homophobic group, it would have a constitutional right to exclude gay people because they would interfere with its core message.

"Dinosaurs Became Extinct"

James Dale sounded anything but defeated after hearing how the court had ruled: "Dinosaurs became extinct because they didn't evolve. I think the Boy Scouts are making themselves extinct, and that is a very sad thing."

The question of which side had actually lost most surfaced immediately. Lambda attorney Ruth Harlow contended, "The Boy Scouts have won a hollow victory. Their leaders and lawyers have convinced five [justices] that they are an anti-gay institution. And now they will have to live with that narrow discriminatory vision."

The Boy Scouts of America, meanwhile, hailed the ruling: "We believe an avowed homosexual is not a role model for the values espoused in the Scout Oath and Law."

Gay-law scholar Arthur Leonard said the ruling showed that "normal rules of constitutional interpretation fall by the wayside when gay people are involved." The ACLU's Matt Coles agreed: "I don't think that the court would allow this kind of purely identity-based discrimination against any other group." They were especially disappointed in Justice Kennedy.

Around the nation, calls for churches and government institutions, including schools, to sever ties to the Boy Scouts intensified. The United Methodist Church, which sponsored 15 percent of troops, urged its churches to cut links to the group. A California Democratic congresswoman proposed revoking the Scouts' federal charter. She and 10 other congressional Democrats futilely demanded that President Clinton resign as honorary president of the Scouts. Clinton said he hoped that the *Boy Scouts* ruling was "just one step along the way of a movement toward greater inclusion." United Way chapters started joining the dozen that already refused to accept contributions for the Boy Scouts because of its anti-gay stance.

On many editorial pages, the Boy Scouts and, to a lesser extent, the Supreme Court took it on the chin. *Philadelphia Daily News:* "No Scout's honor in court ruling." *Kalamazoo* [Michigan] *Gazette:* "We disagree with the idea that moral straightness or cleanliness are attributes only of heterosexuals. . . . [T]he Girl Scouts of America has no such ban." *Seattle Times:* The court's majority opinion was "tinged with homophobia." *Des Moines Register:* "Now [the Boy Scouts] must live with an image of intolerance."

Nationally syndicated cartoonist Mike Peters ridiculed the Boys Scouts of America's discriminatory policy: A little Boy Scout was pictured asking the old woman whom he was preparing to walk across the street, "You're not *gay* are you?"

A *Los Angeles Times* poll shortly before the *Boy Scouts* ruling found the public split into four camps: 26 percent said excluding gay Scouts is wrong because it's discrimination; 20 percent said excluding gay Scouts is wrong, but there should be a "Don't Ask, Don't Tell" policy for them; 22 percent said the Scouts have a right as a private group to exclude gays; 25 percent said the group's moral code gives it a right to exclude gays. A Gallup poll the day after the ruling found that 64 percent of adults were opposed to requiring the Scouts to accept gay leaders.

Reflecting on *Boy Scouts*, Wolfson says, "The dissent is so strong, so powerful, so better reasoned that it will stand the test of time in a way that this very superficial majority [ruling] will not." Noting that Souter, Ginsburg and Breyer had not been very tested, he adds, "They came through with flying colors." All four dissenters "showed a very powerful and clear understanding of gay identity. So, I think we have solidified those four. We now need a fifth."

A dedicated gay civil rights commando, Wolfson refuses to measure the progress of the gay movement strictly in terms of wins and losses: "By fighting, by engaging, you force discussion. Discussion is what we need to move forward. You can lose but still lose *forward* if you fight and you fight well. The only way to really lose is to give up."

CONCLUSION

SEEKING THE SHORTEST PATH
TO EQUAL JUSTICE

CHIEF JUSTICE ANTONIN SCALIA riveted his gaze on the young female attorney preparing to argue that the U.S. Supreme Court ought to declare a state law against same-sex marriage unconstitutional. The emotionally charged case, the first of its kind ever heard by the nation's top court, was brought by a lesbian couple who had been together for 17 years.

Willamina Wallace and Murron McGregor had met at a gay pride parade in Frossel City when Wallace was a medical resident and McGregor was an architecture student. Drawn together by a love of art, the women's passion for Picasso quickly blossomed into a passion for one another. After McGregor landed a job with a respected local architectural firm, she and Wallace began living together. Wallace completed her residency, secured a permanent job at St. Laughlin Memorial Hospital and proceeded to establish a reputation as an outstanding pediatrician.

After 14 years as couple, the women decided they wanted their relationship to enjoy the legal protections of marriage. However, they were turned down for a marriage license by a clerk who showed them a copy of the state law that decreed, "A marriage is valid only if it is . . . between an unmarried male and an unmarried female. . . ." The next year McGregor, by then an employee of the state housing department, was diagnosed with a fatal form of lymphoma. Knowing McGregor faced a death sentence, the couple challenged the state marriage law in federal court: McGregor wanted Dr. Wallace to be the beneficiary of her state-provided life insurance policy. To be eligible, Wallace would have to be McGregor's lawful spouse.

Federal courts dealt with the couple's lawsuit unusually swiftly. The women won a landmark district court ruling, then lost at the appeals court level. The Supreme Court, decades after dismissing a gay marriage case for supposedly raising "no substantial federal question," quite shockingly granted *cert*. On September 12—an unheard-of day for oral argument—the lesbian couple's attorney, Gina Okum, met Chief Justice Scalia's steely gaze and began.

Real as the Supreme Court oral argument seemed, it actually was a 1996 student competition at New York Law School with professors and judges serving as "justices" to test students' skills. Scalia, elevated to "chief" for the occasion, was the only real justice and seemed to immensely enjoy playing himself—the court's most outspoken foe of basic gay civil rights.

Student "attorney" Okum said her clients were challenging their state's marriage law as an unconstitutional violation of equal protection. Because the law discriminated on the basis of sex, the court must subject it to heightened scrutiny, she argued. "If either one of petitioners was a male, [the state] would grant them a marriage license," Okum pointed out. (The sex-discrimination approach had produced the initial, phenomenal 1993 Hawaii Supreme Court breakthrough in the still unsuccessful effort to legalize same-sex marriage.)

Okum said her clients weren't claiming to be victims of sexual orientation discrimination because that would mean the law would only have to be subjected to the lowest level of scrutiny, the "rational basis" test that almost invariably results in the law being ruled constitutional.

Unwilling to let a gay marriage case be cast in anything but the starkest homosexual terms, Chief Justice Scalia began hurling the rapid-fire, loaded questions that are his trademark: "Is it not the law in [the state] that one of the perquisites of marriage is intercourse? . . . And is it not a ground for annulment of a marriage in any state—and certainly for divorce in any state—that the partner refuses to engage in intercourse? . . . If it is so, then it's not just a matter of sex, it's a matter of homosexuality whether they proclaim themselves to be homosexual or not. They are claiming a right to enter into a relationship one of the obligations of which is intercourse."

Pausing momentarily here and there to let Okum utter a few words in reply, the heavyset Scalia barreled forward: "When you are working with the Equal Protection Clause, you are essentially saying that a social judgment is valid or invalid. For example, I suppose on your theory you would say that having separate toilets for men and women discriminates on the basis of sex. It certainly does. Now whether that's valid or invalid—should we sit as a court to decide whether the 50 states of the union can have separate toilets for men and women. . . ?"

Justice Karen Burstein, who in real life unsuccessfully ran as an openly gay candidate for New York state attorney general, cut Scalia off. Barely containing her disdain for his line of reasoning, she asked him, "Do you really think toilets are the same thing as marriage?"

Scalia shot back: ". . . In so far as the fact that 50 states have separate toilets and 50 states do not permit homosexual marriages . . . they are exactly the same. And what I am asking is: What makes you think that this court has a capacity to make the judgment for the society that not even a single state has made in that direction?"

Uncowed by Scalia's infamous aggressiveness, Okum calmly answered, "Because this court has the final say . . . of what is constitutional." She went on to argue that the state's claimed justifications for its marriage law—promotion of procreation and prevention of sexually transmitted diseases—failed even the lowly rational basis test.

SCALIA: "What about just moral objection to it? What do you think justifies single-sex toilets? What do you think justifies the law against bigamy? . . . Can a society justify a law just because it has a moral objection to it? Like a law against torturing animals?"

OKUM: "Your honor, this is not a moral issue, though."

SCALIA: "But many people think it is. Don't you think these laws were originally just morality-based laws, just as bigamy laws? Are such laws unconstitutional?"

The court's other woman, "Justice" Nadine Strossen, president of the American Civil Liberties Union, pounced: "In *Loving* it was!" The Supreme Court's 1967 *Loving v. Virginia* decision struck down state bans on interracial marriage, saying they were unconstitutional race discrimination because the legality of a marriage depended on the race of one's partner.

Ignoring the liberal zinger, Scalia kept pounding Okum. "Do you deny," he asked, "that simply the moral offensiveness of a practice justifies a law against it?" Battling back, Okum told him, "Morality is something in this country that everyone has a different view of."

Scalia exploded, "Fifty states have the same view of this one! . . . I mean, it's been in the common law forever."

Having thoroughly dominated the first half of the oral argument by challenging the attorney representing the gay side, Scalia spent much of the second half trying to rescue the young attorney arguing against same-sex marriage. Known for throwing lifelines when his side is sinking, Scalia tried several tactics: ". . . Aren't you thinking of the fact that [banning interracial marriage] was not a uniform tradition in all the 50 states going back into the mists of common law? You're not going to raise that? Are you going to accept equating that some states prohibited miscegenous marriages with the fact that no state has ever permitted homosexual marriages?"

Scalia continued, "How would the state go about assuring that no one who can't procreate will marry? It would be very intrusive, wouldn't it? The American Civil Liberties Union wouldn't like it at all. So, it seems like a rational thing for the state to say, 'Anyone who wants to get married—so long as there is on the face of it a chance of procreation— go ahead and get married.' Maybe the state wants the stability in a family unit that has both a man and a woman in it. . . . Are there statistics to show that children that don't have a male influence in the house don't turn out as well?"

Scalia challenged the state's attorney only when the argument against same-sex marriage was being actually undermined by the claim that preventing it deters disease. Sounding annoyed, Scalia said, "I really don't understand this argument of yours at all, counselor. . . . [P]romoting stable, monogamous homosexual relationships will surely reduce the sexually transmitted diseases that are from promiscuity. I mean, it's the same

thing as stable married couples are not great hotbeds of sexually transmitted diseases but promiscuous heterosexuals are. . . ."

In the end, Chief Justice Scalia had left no doubt where he stood.
(The mock court did not rule on the constitutionality of limiting marriage to male-female couples. Instead, the student lawyers were judged
on their skills.) Karen Burstein says it was obvious "Scalia thinks there
is no equal protection argument that can prevail here." She adds, "I
wouldn't want to put my fate in his hands," knowing full well that to
some extent the fate of every gay American is in his hands.

Most justices are extraordinarily meticulous about not doing or saying
anything in public that might be taken as an indicator of how they would
vote in a future case. Yet Scalia makes no attempt to hide his opposition
to same-sex marriage. Scalia and civil libertarian Nadine Strossen are
friends, despite being ideological opposites. Shortly after Scalia handed
down his vitriolic dissent from gay Americans' *Romer* victory, he heard
that Strossen was headed to Hawaii to fight for same-sex marriage. Scalia
burst out laughing and said, "Tell her I wish her the worst of luck!"

What If . . .

The September 12, 1996 moot court—as such competitions are called—
offered an extraordinary glimpse of one possible future: Scalia serving as
chief justice and sparring with an openly gay justice while debating the
scrutiny that should be given to a law barring same-sex marriage.

Is such a scenario probable? Is it likely that the Supreme Court will
remain deeply and closely divided over gay civil rights? Is it realistic to
think the court will become willing to referee the high-stakes battle over
the equal protection claim that strikes at the very heart of heterosexual
privilege—gay marriage? Will the court finally decide to resolve the critical issue of what level of scrutiny judges must give to laws that discriminate against gay Americans? Will we have a president willing to
elevate the most vocally anti-gay justice to chief—as Reagan did with
Rehnquist in 1986? Will we have a Senate willing to confirm such a
nominee? Is an openly gay justice a realistic possibility in the foresee-
able future?

The 2000 presidential election offered the American public one of its
clearest opportunities to chart the future course of the closely divided

court, which split 5-to-4 against allowing New Jersey to force the Boy Scouts to accept an openly gay scoutmaster. While successfully campaigning as a "compassionate conservative," Republican George W. Bush pointed to ultraconservatives Antonin Scalia and Clarence Thomas as models for the justices he'd choose. Democrat Al Gore, in contrast, said he'd appoint justices in the mold of William J. Brennan Jr. and Thurgood Marshall, old-style activist liberals with strong gay-rights records. Since every president except Carter who has served at least a full term has gotten at least one Supreme Court pick, President George W. Bush can be expected to put a long-lasting mark on the court. Justice O'Connor, long the court's swing vote in major gay cases, is said to be actively considering retirement. She turned 70 before fellow conservative Republican George W. Bush took office. The record number of justices appointed in any four-year period is seven.

We can perhaps best understand the varied possibilities the Supreme Court's future holds by looking, briefly, again at its past. As far back as 1958, the court has had justices who attempted to set aside their prejudices and apply one standard of justice without regard to sexual orientation. Yet those justices have never been able to sustain a critical mass—one open to learning from advances in scientific understanding of the nature of homosexuality, open to seeing the pernicious impact of sodomy laws on average gay couples, open to treating gay citizens not as a collection of law breakers—like tax dodgers or cat burglars—but as yet another beleaguered minority group victimized by irrational prejudices. There's never been a critical mass of justices to carry homosexuals' groundbreaking *ONE* and *Manual* victories over the Post Office censors forward to, say, the immigration cases or carry the *Romer* gay-rights triumph forward to the *Boy Scouts* case.

Nevertheless, it's easy to imagine how the course of history might have been different. Without ever making any grand gay-rights gestures or pronouncements, the court could have slowly brought gay Americans to the brink of full legal equality by the end of the 20th century.

What if, for example, Justice Goldberg had gotten the Immigration and Naturalization Service off George Fleuti's back in 1963, not by concocting a special loophole for him, but simply by providing the fifth vote to declare that "psychopathic" was too vague a term to constitute a ban on all homosexual immigrants?

Or what if Justice Black had stuck with his original stance and "psychopathic" had been ruled unconstitutionally vague in *Boutilier* in 1967? What if the court had followed that ruling by matter-of-factly declaring that "crime against nature" also was too vague and that any state wanting to outlaw oral and anal sex had to enact a law that explicitly said so?

What if, instead of resigning in 1965, Goldberg had still been on the court when he developed into a gay-rights supporter? What if Fortas, the justice most attuned to changing psychiatric opinion, had chosen not to resign and instead had just let the congressional furor over his finances die out? What if President Johnson had not lost his chance to appoint as Chief Justice Warren's successor someone far more progressive than Nixon-appointed Warren Burger?

What if the court had been willing to acknowledge its contraception rulings as sex-for-pleasure decisions and overturned the lower court decision upholding Virginia's sodomy law in 1976 by simply saying, "Reversed. See *Griswold v. Connecticut, Eizenstadt v. Baird*."

What if the court had said a government worker (librarian Mike McConnell) couldn't be deprived of a job for applying for a marriage license or a government worker (teacher Joe Acanfora) couldn't lose his job for talking to the press about why he'd been thrown out of his classroom?

What if Carter—whose federal judicial appointees have been in the vanguard of recognizing gay civil rights—had gotten to make a Supreme Court appointment? What if Carter had gotten to make several—so many that Ronald Reagan and/or George Bush (who together named five justices) got to make none?

What if gentlemanly Justice Powell, a man with considerable empathy, had realized that many of his most trusted clerks were gay and, thus, decided to provide the crucial fifth vote to strike down Georgia's sodomy law? What if the Senate had heard Angela Wright's testimony and refused to confirm Clarence Thomas?

What if writing *Romer* had transformed Justice Kennedy into an ardent supporter of gay rights, the way writing the *Roe v. Wade* abortion-rights ruling forever changed Blackmun?

What if the Supreme Court had tossed gays-in-the-military cases back to lower courts with instructions that the Pentagon needed to find a better justification than heterosexual animosity for its ban on openly gay soldiers? Or what if the court had struck down that gay ban?

On the other hand, what if the 5-to-4 conference vote in favor of *ONE* magazine had gone the other way—strangling the newborn gay press in its crib in 1958? And what if the third Reagan appointee to win a Supreme Court seat had been stridently anti-gay Robert Bork instead of Anthony Kennedy? With Bork on the court in 1996, gay Americans almost certainly would have lost the *Romer* decision and its history-making promise of equal protection.

Clearly, there were many paths the Supreme Court could have followed. The route it chose was not chiseled in stone. And, certainly, the court's handling of any particular gay case doesn't definitively establish that the justices' thinking was clouded by prejudice. Even gay-rights attorneys disagree on the constitutionally correct outcome in some disputes, the 1987 tug-of-war over a gay athletic group's use of the word "Olympic," for example, and the 1995 bid of a sign-carrying Boston gay group to march in the local St. Patrick's Day parade. Yet the results of each of the court's gay cases must be viewed through a lens that takes into account the court's overall approach to anything gay: Usually, if a case has involved homosexuality, the gay side has lost.

The Supreme Court has fluctuated between passively permitting and actively creating a "gay exception" to the standard approaches to determining a law's meaning and constitutionality. As a result, gay people have been read into criminal laws and civil restrictions that make no mention of homosexuality—the federal law against "psychopathic" immigrants, for example. And gay people have been read out of legal benefits that don't mention homosexuality—marriage laws that don't specify male-female couples, for example.

The reasoning of many justices who probably have not considered themselves homophobic has often seemed colored by assumptions—perhaps unconscious—about what it means to be gay and whether gay people are a legitimate minority group. For example, during the oral argument in the Boston St. Patrick's Day parade case, Justice O'Connor compared carrying a gay banner in that parade to carrying an animal-rights banner in a Barnum & Bailey Circus parade. Her unspoken assumption: Being openly gay is completely at odds with the message of a St. Patrick's Day parade. (Gay groups routinely march in Ireland's St.

Patrick Day parades.) Likewise, Justice Powell had no trouble voting to allow a gay group to be barred from using "Olympic" yet said he would have stood up for a black group if it had been denied the use of "Olympic" while white groups were allowed to use it.

Certainly Justice Souter, the author of the court's unanimous St. Patrick's Day parade decision, has shown that he's not hostile to gay people. Yet the reasoning of justices like O'Connor and Powell creates the nagging suspicion that a group wanting to use the name "Black Olympic Games" or to march in Boston's parade carrying an "Irish-American Jews" banner would have won at the Supreme Court.

A Drag on the Nation

The U.S. Supreme Court of recent decades is often described as not wanting to get too far ahead of the rest of the nation on social issues. But the reality is that the court entered the 21st century as a drag on U.S. progress toward full inclusion of gay citizens in mainstream American life. Much like a ship trying to sail with its anchor still out, the United States is held back by the court's handling of gay cases.

The court's 1986 *Hardwick* sodomy decision continues to be used by judges and lawmakers to justify equating gay people with criminals. Although a six-member majority grandly declared in *Romer* a decade later that gay Americans must not be relegated to second-class status, the court has yet to say what yardstick ought to be used in measuring the constitutionality of anti-gay government actions. Given no guidance, most lower court judges have chosen the weak "rational basis" standard that almost always means discrimination wins.

Prime evidence that the U.S. Supreme Court has indeed impeded this country's progress on gay rights is found both abroad and in state capitals. The 1969 Stonewall Rebellion in New York City's Greenwich Village triggered a gay-pride movement that swept the world. Three decades later, the U.S. military still bans openly gay people, 18 states and the military still outlaw sodomy and only Vermont offers same-sex couples all the state-level rights of marriage. Meanwhile, most other westernized countries—thanks largely to their courts—have erased their sodomy laws and opened their militaries to gay people. And quite a few nations, including Denmark, Norway, Iceland, the Netherlands,

France and Canada, have taken great strides toward offering gay couples the legal protections long available only through marriage.

Closer to home, the fact that the U.S. Supreme Court is not just refusing to lead the fight to end anti-gay discrimination but is an active drag on the nation's evolution to a more just society is illustrated by advances made at the state Supreme Court level—not usually known for being in the forefront of civil rights movements. A few examples:

Hawaii's top court handed down the favorable 1993 ruling that sparked the national debate over same-sex marriage. Vermont's top court first approved second-parent adoption for gay couples, then ordered the state legislature to give gay couples all the legal protections of marriage. The highest courts of Georgia, Kentucky and Tennessee struck down their sodomy laws. The Oregon and Washington top courts acted on partner benefits for gay state workers. The Supreme Courts of Wisconsin and New Jersey protected the rights of gay parents. And the New Jersey Supreme Court, of course, attempted to take one more step toward eradicating the "cancer of discrimination" by protecting gay Boy Scouts. Often, these state courts—whose justices tend not to enjoy the protection of lifetime tenure—have read their state constitutions as more protective of individual rights than the U.S. Constitution, since the U.S. Supreme Court has made it very difficult for them to read significant gay civil rights protections into the Bill of Rights or the 14th Amendment.

A Promise to Keep

The promise of equal protection that the U.S. Supreme Court finally gave gay Americans in its 1996 *Romer* ruling remains unfulfilled. Gay soldiers and gay couples—to name two obvious examples—continue to be a "stranger to the laws" because of government-sponsored discrimination. The court silently watches as openly gay Americans are booted out of the military, just as it mutely allowed lesbian Robin Shahar to lose a government job offer for having a commitment ceremony with her partner. Yet *Romer* remains a powerful weapon, one waiting to be used when the Supreme Court again musters a majority to protect basic gay civil rights.

The gay community may never get its equivalent of the 1954 *Brown v. Board* decision, which had the effect of branding racial segregation un-American. Gay Americans may never have a *Brown*-level blockbuster, a decision that forever marks a turning point away from government-authorized discrimination. And it's unlikely that future generations will be able to look back upon one particular ruling and say, "On that day, gay Americans achieved full legal equality."

Yet the justices already have all the tools they need to tear down any barrier to equal rights for gay Americans. Whether a future case involves equal protection, privacy, freedom of association or freedom of speech, the legal reasoning to support any reasonable gay claim can be found in four prior gay cases plus a variety of other civil rights cases. Listen to their language:

- The Constitution "neither knows nor tolerates classes among citizens." (Harlan dissent, *Plessy v. Ferguson,* 1896)
- "The Constitution cannot control . . . prejudices but neither can it tolerate them. Private biases may be outside the reach of the law, but the law cannot, directly or indirectly, give them effect." (Palmore v. Sidoti, 1984)
- "If the constitutional conception of 'equal protection of the laws' means anything, it must at the very least mean that a bare . . . desire to harm a politically unpopular group cannot constitute a legitimate government interest." (U.S. Department of Agriculture v. Moreno, 1985)
- "Homosexuals have historically been the object of pernicious and sustained hostility, and it is fair to say that discrimination is 'likely to . . . reflect deep-seated prejudice rather than rationality.' State action against members of such groups based simply on their status traditionally has been subjected to strict, or at least heightened, scrutiny by this court." (Brennan dissent from denial of cert, Rowland v. Mad River, 1985)
- "It is precisely because the issue raised by this case touches the heart of what makes individuals what they are that we should be especially sensitive to the rights of those whose choices upset the majority. . . . [D]epriving individuals of their intimate relationships poses a far greater threat to the values most deeply rooted in our nation's history than tolerance of nonconformity could ever do." (Blackmun dissent, Bowers v. Hardwick, 1986)
- "Amendment 2 classified homosexuals not to further a proper legislative end but to make them unequal to everyone else. This

Colorado cannot do. A state cannot so deem a class of persons
a stranger to its laws." (Romer v. Evans, 1996)

- "Unfavorable opinions about homosexuals 'have ancient
roots'. . . . Like equally atavistic opinions about certain racial
groups, those roots have been nourished by sectarian doctrine. . . . Over the years, however, interaction with real people,
rather than mere adherence to traditional ways of thinking
about members of unfamiliar classes, have modified those
views. . . . That such prejudices are still prevalent and that they
have caused serious and tangible harm to countless members of
the class New Jersey seeks to protect are established matters of
fact. . . . That harm can only be aggravated by the creation of a
constitutional shield for a policy that is itself the product of a
habitual way of thinking about strangers. . . . 'We must be ever
on our guard, lest we erect our prejudices into legal principles.'"
(Stevens dissent, Boy Scouts v. Dale, 2000)

There's Going to Be More Evolution

Gay Americans headed into 2001 in the unenviable position of needing
to win five out of six available justices to make any significant headway
at the U.S. Supreme Court. Three justices—Rehnquist, Scalia and
Thomas—were clearly out of reach in any major gay-rights case.

The good news for gay Americans was that the *Boy Scouts* dissent established that four justices are firmly opposed to anti-gay discrimination and to any ruling that treats gay people as inferior simply because
of their sexual orientation. Stevens, Souter, Ginsburg and Breyer probably can be counted on to take the gay side in sodomy, employment
and, possibly, adoption and custody cases. Gay Americans are far less
likely to be able to count on their support if the court accepts gay challenges to the military's "Don't Ask, Don't Tell" policy or marriage laws.

Kennedy and O'Connor would probably be willing to join the gay
side in the least controversial sort of job discrimination case involving,
say, a lesbian fired from a state agriculture department.

The current court, whose membership hasn't changed since 1994, is
likely to continue trying to avoid gay disputes, because neither the most

progressive justices nor those with the most anti-gay records can be certain of their outcome. Since the early 1960s, the Supreme Court has stubbornly abdicated its responsibility to be a unifying national force on issues involving homosexuality. And as states advance on gay rights at tremendously different paces, the need for the court to keep the country from fracturing into a state of 50 nations, as far as gay people are concerned, becomes greater and greater. When the court heard its first homosexual case, every state had a sodomy law and not one state protected gay workers or gay couples in any way. Today, a state like Vermont has no sodomy law, outlaws anti-gay discrimination and provides gay couples all the benefits of marriage. But a gay Vermonter who moves to another state may suddenly find herself—and her family—as vulnerable as if she'd slipped back to the 1950s.

It seems inevitable that the U.S. Supreme Court, which has proclaimed marriage a "fundamental" right, will eventually have to sort out the rights of gay couples. Yet a few years ago it appeared the court would have to rule on the constitutionality of the military's ban. Now it appears that gay Americans may have to wait until Congress decides to repeal that law.

The high court has a history of waiting for some controversies to run out of steam. It never ruled, for example, on the constitutionality of the undeclared war in Vietnam or on states' conflicting divorce laws. The court waited until Congress rewrote immigration laws to remove language that might be construed as barring homosexuals. It waited until President Clinton prohibited discrimination based on sexual orientation within the federal civilian workforce.

The court's composition will change. That much is certain. And the addition of a new generation of judges who have had openly gay friends since college, attended law schools with anti-bias and domestic partnership policies, seen the growing public acceptance of homosexuality and dealt comfortably with gay issues throughout their professional lives may well make the court far more responsive to gay Americans than its past would suggest. And a new generation of senators will include men and women more attuned to their gay constituents' needs in questioning court nominees. The mild tone of Rehnquist's *Boy Scouts* majority decision strongly suggests that even some of the most conservative justices know that they can no longer hold a majority—or the public's respect—if they show overt hostility to gay Americans.

And the Supreme Court might include an openly gay justice early in this century. Thirteen years after *Brown v. Board,* the first black justice was confirmed. Ten years after the court first struck down a law as unconstitutional sex discrimination, the first woman joined the court. If the 1996 *Romer* decision—the moment when the court first explicitly declared that gay Americans are protected by the constitutional guarantee of equal protection—counts as the starting point for gay Americans, an openly gay justice might be confirmed between 2006 and 2009, provided the historical pattern holds.

The phenomenal progress of gay Americans in accepting themselves and gaining the respect of others points directly toward full legal equality. Three-quarters of Americans now think anti-gay job discrimination is wrong. Just like the justices, average American citizens believe in the constitutional ideal of equality and are continually redefining what it means.

As gay Americans continue courting justice, the question is not whether justice will be won, but when. Gay-rights attorney Evan Wolfson is fond of quoting the Reverend Dr. Martin Luther King Jr. as saying, "The arc of the moral universe is long, but it bends toward justice." The Supreme Court still has the opportunity to seize a leading role in making the Constitution's promises come true for gay Americans. Prodding the court to evolve out of the anti-gay prejudices that have so colored its rulings, Justice Stevens declared in June 2000, "If we would guide by the light of reason, we must let our minds be bold."

Openly gay Americans still have the opportunity to influence the court's thinking. As Stevens's *Boy Scouts* dissent illustrated, a gay man or lesbian doesn't have to be a Supreme Court clerk or a justice's nephew or neighbor to have an impact. The justices read *The New York Times.* They read that openly gay workers at General Motors have won partner benefits, and they see that the nation's definition of fairness is evolving. Every American who comes out as gay or gay-supportive has the potential to influence how future Supreme Court decisions interpret the Constitution's timeless guarantees.

We cannot change the past. We can help shape the future.

APPENDIX

The Supreme Court dealt with homosexuality in the following cases, listed chronologically. A case summary is provided only for cases not detailed in the text. Cases not directly involving homosexuality are bracketed.

ONE Inc. v. Olesen, postmaster of Los Angeles. Reversed lower court decision censoring homosexual magazine, Jan. 13, 1958.

Franklin Edward Kameny v. Wilber M. Brucker, secretary of the Army, et al. Cert denied, March 20, 1961.

Womack v. United States. Cert denied, March 27, 1961.

Shields v. Sharp, secretary of the Air Force. Cert denied, May 8, 1961. Joseph Shields, civilian chief of personnel statistics for the Air Force, fired for "immoral conduct off duty," specifically, allegedly having sex with a Navy officer, attending a party with "known homosexuals" and living at a "known hangout" for homosexuals.

[*Poe v. Ullman.* Dismissed, June 19, 1961.]

Manual Enterprise Inc. et al. v. J. Edward Day, postmaster general of the United States. Reversed lower court decision censoring homosexual magazine, June 25, 1962.

Williams v. Zuckert, secretary of the Air Force. Cert dismissed as improvidently granted, Jan. 14, 1963. Dismissal vacated and case returned to lower court, April 22, 1963. Daniel Alton Williams, recreation supervisor at the Air Force Academy, fired after being accused of three homosexual assaults and destruction of property; case focused not on homosexuality but on whether proper procedures were followed in administrative hearing.

Caplan v. Korth, secretary of the Navy. Cert denied, May 13, 1963. Purchasing clerk Eugene S. Caplan fired from Navy Department for "immoral and disgraceful conduct," specifically for allegedly having four homosexual encounters including one in which he was raped.

Rosenberg v. Fleuti. Lower court ruling vacated with instructions that homosexual immigrant George Fleuti was not to be deported unless his afternoon trip abroad was for a nefarious purpose, June 17, 1963.

Poore et al. v. Mayer. Cert denied, Dec. 7, 1964. Four men arrested on sodomy charges after police videotaped activities inside Mansfield, Ohio, restroom.

Dew v. Halaby, administrator, Federal Aviation Agency, et al. Dismissed when settled out of court, Dec. 17, 1964. Federal employee fired in 1957 for homosexual acts and marijuana use in early adulthood; not accused of being a homosexual.

[*Griswold v. Connecticut.* State ban on contraceptives struck down as invasion of marital privacy, June 7, 1965.]

Chamberlain v. Ohio. Cert denied, Oct. 10, 1966.

Robillard et al. v. New York. Cert denied, Nov. 7, 1966.

Clive Michael Boutilier v. Immigration and Naturalization Service. Affirmed lower court decision allowing immigrant Clive Boutilier to be deported under INS policy defining all homosexuals as "psychopathic," May 22, 1967.

Immigration and Naturalization Service v. Lavoie. Reversed lower court ruling blocking deportation of homosexual immigrant, June 5, 1967.

Landau v. Fording. Affirmed, 5 to 4, that *Un Chant d'Amour,* a homosexually explicit sadomasochistic silent film by French literary great Jean Genet could be banned as obscene, June 12, 1967.

Tovar v. Immigration and Naturalization Service. Cert denied, June 12, 1967. Fifty-six-year-old David Belmonte Tovar, a legal resident since age 15 and the sole supporter for his ill, homemaker wife, lost last chance to avoid deportation; lower court ruled his arrests for homosexual activity meant he'd failed to show "good moral character."

Talley v. California. Cert denied, April 22, 1968.

Schlegel v. United States. Cert denied, April 20, 1970.

Adams v. Melvin R. Laird, secretary of defense. Cert denied, April 20, 1970.

Wade v. Buchanan and Buchanan et al v. Wade. Vacated appeals court decision finding Texas's sodomy law too broad, March 29, 1971.

Buchanan v. Texas. Cert denied, Feb. 22, 1972.

McConnell v. Anderson. Cert denied, April 3, 1972.

Baker v. Nelson. "Dismissed for want of a substantial federal question," Oct. 10, 1972.

Wainwright, corrections director, et al. v. Stone. Reversed appeals court ruling finding Florida's "crime against nature" law too vague, Nov. 5, 1973.

Connor v. Arkansas. Dismissed, Nov. 5, 1973.

Canfield v. Oklahoma. Dismissed, Nov. 5, 1973.

Acanfora v. Board of Education of Montgomery County. Cert denied, Oct. 15, 1974.

Doe et al. v. Commonwealth's Attorney for the City of Richmond et al. Affirmed lower court ruling upholding Virginia's sodomy law, March 29, 1976.

Enslin v. North Carolina. Cert denied, March 29, 1976.

Singer v. United States Civil Service Commission. Vacated lower court decision against gay federal employee at request of Civil Service Commission, which had dropped its gay ban, Jan. 10, 1977.

Mississippi Gay Alliance v. Goudelock. Cert denied, April 25, 1977.

[*Carey v. Population Services International.* Court struck down New York ban on distribution of birth control devices to minors under age 16, June 9, 1977.]

Gaylord v. Tacoma School District No. 10 et al. Cert denied, Oct. 3, 1977.

Gish v. Board of Education of the Borough of Paramus. Cert denied, Oct. 3, 1977. Outstanding teacher removed from classroom for refusing to take mental exam for being a high-profile gay-rights advocate.

Ratchford, President, University of Missouri et al. v. Gay Lib et al. Cert denied, Dec. 9, 1977.

New York v. Onofre and New York v. Peoples et al. Cert denied, May 18, 1981.

Beller v. Lehman, secretary of the Navy, et al. Cert denied, June 1, 1981.

Hatheway v. Marsh, secretary of the Army. Cert denied, Oct. 5, 1981.

Gray, treasurer of Harris County, Texas v. Van Ooteghem. Cert denied, Jan. 18, 1982.

Adams et al. v. Howerton, Acting District Director, Immigration and Naturalization Service. Cert denied, June 28, 1982.

Longstaff v. Immigration and Naturalization Service. Cert denied, May 29, 1984.

New York v. Uplinger. Cert dismissed as improvidently granted, May 30, 1984.

Mount Diablo Council of the Boy Scouts of America v. Curran. Dismissed "for want of a final judgment," July 5, 1984. Boy Scouts had lost preliminary judgment in battle with gay Eagle Scout Tim Curran, an assistant scoutmaster expelled after taking boy to his senior prom. Curran finally lost in the California Supreme Court in 1998.

Rowland v. Mad River Local School District, Montgomery County, Ohio. Cert denied, Feb. 25, 1985.

Board of Education of Oklahoma City v. National Gay Task Force. Lower court ruling striking down ban on teachers' gay-rights advocacy "affirmed by an equally divided court," March 26, 1985.

Kowalski v. Kowalski. Cert denied, March 24, 1986.

Bowers, attorney general of Georgia v. Hardwick et al. Upheld constitutionality of Georgia's sodomy law, June 30, 1986.

Baker v. Wade. Texas v. Hill. Hill v. Texas. Hill v. Baker. Cert denied in all four interlocking cases, July 7, 1986.

Arcara v. Cloud Books, Inc. Ruled that closing adult bookstore in the Village of Kenmore, N.Y., because of illicit sex on premises—four men had approached an undercover deputy—did not violate the First Amendment, July 7, 1986.

Ward v. Olivieri and Olivieri v. Ward. Cert denied, March 9, 1987.

San Francisco Arts & Athletics, Inc. and Thomas F. Waddell, M.D., v. United States Olympic Committee and International Olympic Committee. Allowed U.S. Olympic Committee to deny use of word "Olympic" to Gay Olympic Games, June 25, 1987.

Webster, director of central intelligence v. Doe. Ruled federal courts have authority to inquire into whether gay CIA technician was fired unconstitutionally, June 15, 1988. (Returned as *Doe v. Woolsey. Cert* denied, Oct. 12, 1993.)

Woodward v. United States. Cert denied, Feb. 26, 1990.

Ben-Shalom v. Stone, secretary of the Army et al. Cert denied, Feb. 26, 1990.

U.S. Army v. Watkins. Cert denied, Nov. 5, 1990.

Schowengerdt v. United States. Cert denied, March 23, 1992. Richard Neal Schowengerdt lost job as Navy civilian employee after evidence of bisexual extramarital affairs was found in his desk.

Jacobson v. United States. Overturned conviction of gay man lured by federal agents into ordering child pornography, April 6, 1992.

Cheney, Secretary of Defense, et al. v. Pruitt. Cert denied, Dec. 7, 1992.

Jan Krc. v. United States Information Agency. Cert denied, Feb. 22, 1994. Gay man lost job as a USIA Foreign Service officer after being branded security risk for sexual escapades that included encounters with two nationals of a Communist country.

Richard M. Clewis III and The Take Back Tampa Political Committee v. Robin C. Krivanek. Cert denied, April 18, 1994.

The Rent Stabilization Association of New York City et al. v. Richard L. Higgins et al. Cert denied, June 13, 1994.

Jackson v. Brigle. Cert denied, Oct. 3, 1994. Lt. Col. Kenneth L. Jackson failed to win right to sue military investigators who, during unrelated probe, discovered his homosexuality—a finding that led to his discharge.

Hurley et al. v. Irish-American Gay, Lesbian and Bisexual Group of Boston. Organizers of Boston's St. Patrick's Day Parade allowed to bar sign-carrying gay group, June 19, 1995.

Walmer v. Department of Defense et al. Cert denied, Nov. 13, 1995. Army Major Joyce Walmer discharged after female ex-lover accused her of lesbianism and she admitted it.

Elsbeth Knott v. Sandra Lynn Holtzman. Cert denied, Nov. 13, 1995.

Miller v. DeMuth. Cert denied, Feb. 20, 1996.

Kenneth B. Sawatzky v. City of Oklahoma City. Cert denied, April 22, 1996.

Roy Romer v. Richard G. Evans. Colorado's anti-gay Amendment 2 struck down as unconstitutional, May 20, 1996.

Equality Foundation of Greater Cincinnati, Inc. et al. v. City of Cincinnati et al. Returned to lower court for reconsideration "in light of *Romer v. Evans*," June 17, 1996. Cert denied, Oct. 3, 1998.

Paul G. Thomasson v. William J. Perry, Secretary of Defense, and John H. Dalton, secretary of the Navy. Cert denied, Oct. 21, 1996.

Westboro Baptist Church Inc. v. St. David's Episcopal Church. Cert denied, Jan. 21, 1997.

Richard Dirk Selland v. William J. Perry et al. Cert denied, May 12, 1997. Lt. Selland, a supply officer, was kicked off his attack submarine after coming out to commander in order to ask for protection from anti-gay harassment.

Ann Hacklander-Ready v. Wisconsin. Cert denied, May 12, 1997.

Laurie Arbeiter et al. v. New York. Cert denied, May 12, 1997. Eighty-eight people—most of them lesbian—arrested for marching down Fifth Avenue to protest gay group's exclusion from New York City's St. Patrick's Day Parade.

Richard F. Richenberg Jr. v. William J. Perry et al. Cert denied, Oct. 6, 1997. Air Force captain who'd flown 25 combat mission during Desert Storm lost career after coming out to commander.

John Doe v. Massachusetts Department of Social Services. Cert denied, Oct. 6, 1997. Catholic man objects to placing his 14-year-old son in foster home of gay male couple.

Sandra S. Nelson v. McClatchy Newspapers Inc. et al. Cert denied, Oct. 6, 1997. Lower court finds freedom of the press protects newspaper's decision to demote lesbian journalist for high-profile political activism on gay rights and other issues.

Eugene Lumpkin Jr. v. Willie L. Brown, mayor of San Francisco et al. Cert denied, Nov. 3, 1997.

Robin Joy Shahar v. Michael J. Bowers et al. Cert denied, Jan. 12, 1998.

[*Oncale v. Sundowner Offshore Services Inc.* Rules sexual harassment claims cannot be dismissed just because victim and victimizer are the same sex, March 4, 1998.]

[*National Endowment for the Arts et al. v. Karen Finley et al.* NEA decency regulation does not unconstitutionally restrict free speech of grant seekers, June 25, 1998.]

Thorne v. Department of Defense et al. Cert denied, Oct. 19, 1998. Navy "Top Gun" pilot Tracy W. Thorne discharged after coming out on ABC News' *Nightline.*

Andrew Holmes et al. v. California Army National Guard et al. Cert denied, Jan. 11, 1999. Navy Lt. Richard P. Watson and California Army National Guard Lt. Holmes stripped of uniforms after gay statements that lower court equated with "homosexual conduct."

[*Davis v. Monroe County Board of Education.* Schools receiving federal funds liable if their officials react with "deliberate indifference" to student-on-student sexual harassment, May 24, 1999.]

[*University of Wisconsin v. Southworth.* Using mandatory fees to encourage diversity of campus groups does not violate students' First Amendment rights, March 22, 2000.]

[*Troxel v. Granville.* Strikes down Washington state's "breathtakingly broad" child visitation law but signals awareness of family diversity, June 4, 2000.]

Boy Scouts of America and Monmouth Council, petitioners, v. James Dale. New Jersey cannot force the Boy Scouts to readmit gay Eagle Scout James Dale, June 28, 2000.

NOTES ON SOURCES

Each chapter of *Courting Justice* is treated separately, with citations grouped under chapter subtitles. All interviews by the authors were conducted between 1996 and August 2000, in person, by telephone or, in a few cases, by e-mail. Of the hundreds of people interviewed, generally only those quoted by name are cited below. Many, many others provided information that shaped our thinking about the court, its justices and the era covered. In a few instances, individuals asked that their identities not be made public. All quotations are from interviews with the authors unless otherwise noted. Full citations of books and other documents are given when they are first mentioned.

Memos to or from a particular justice are located in that justice's papers unless otherwise noted. Justices' papers are housed at the Library of Congress's Manuscript Reading Room (Warren, Douglas, Marshall, Black, Frankfurter, Burton), Princeton University (Harlan), the University of Texas (Clark), Washington and Lee (Powell), Yale (Fortas), Northwestern University (Goldberg), and the University of Michigan (Murphy). Justices' private conference votes are listed on "docket sheets," usually kept in a separate section of justices' papers from their cases files.

Every case discussed relied, at least in part, on the official documents filed with the U.S. Supreme Court, such as the *cert* petition, a response in opposition and, if *cert* was granted, briefs from both sides. Generally, an appendix containing the lower courts' rulings was also filed with the court. Those documents are not cited individually below. All the court documents are available at the U.S. Supreme Court library, unless it is noted that they are at the National Archives in Washington, D.C. Audiotapes of oral arguments are available at the audio/visual branch of the National Archives in Maryland. Identification of justices in oral arguments was made by the authors by listening to official tapes or from notes taken from press seats at oral arguments in *Hurley, Romer, Oncale v. Sundowner Offshore Services Inc., Troxel v. Granville* and *Boy Scouts v. Dale.*

The portrait of the inner workings of the Supreme Court and justices' personalities and habits reflects more than 100 interviews with former clerks and court officials, tens of thousands of pages of court documents including the justices' working drafts of opinions and numerous books listed in the Bibliography. In particular, the following books were helpful: Laurence H. Tribe, *American Constitutional Law* (Mineola, N.Y.: The Foundation Press, 1988). Michael Les Benedict, *The Blessings of Liberty: A Concise History of the Constitution of the United States* (Lexington, Mass.: D.C. Heath, 1996). Bernard Schwartz, *A History of the Supreme Court* (New York: Oxford University Press, 1993). David G. Savage, *Turning Right: The Making of the Rehnquist Supreme Court* (New York: John Wiley & Sons, 1992). Bob Woodward and Scott Armstrong, *The Brethren: Inside the Supreme Court* (New York: Avon Books, 1979). Clare Cushman, editor, *The Supreme Court Justices: Illustrated Biographies, 1789–1995* (Washington, D.C.: Congressional Quarterly, 1995).

INTRODUCTION: "PAY NO ATTENTION TO THAT MAN BEHIND THE CURTAIN"

Authors' interviews: Frank Kameny, Tony Sullivan, Jim Woodward, Daniel Miller, Miriam Ben-Shalom. Other sources: Jonathan Ned Katz, *Gay/Lesbian Almanac: A New Documentary* (New York: Harper & Row, 1983), p. 130 (early sodomy statutes). Nat Hentoff, "Profiles: The Constitutionalist," *The New Yorker*, March 12, 1999, p. 58 ("It was fascinating"). David G. Savage, *Turning Right: The Making of the Rehnquist Supreme Court* (New York: John Wiley & Sons, 1992), p. 210 (Stevens photo story). Joan Biskupic, "Has the Court Lost Its Appeal?" *The Washington Post*, Oct. 12, 1995, p. A23 (Three stooges/justices poll). UPI, "Washington News," *The Washington Post*, Jan. 31, 1985, p. A21 ("Sandy, baby"). Deb Price, "Lady Justice," *The Detroit News*, Jan. 3, 1997 ("let's kill"). Ruth Bader Ginsburg quoting Justice Benjamin Cardozo at her Senate confirmation hearing, "Nomination of Ruth Bader Ginsburg to Be Associate Justice of the Supreme Court of the United States" (Washington, D.C.: U.S. Government Printing Office, 1994), p. 51, Ginsburg quoting Cardoza ("wooed by slow advances").

Close Encounters of a Gay Kind

Authors' interviews: Rand Hoch, Judge Michael Sonberg of Criminal Court of the City of New York. Court documents: Justice John Paul Stevens letter to the authors, June 1, 2000 (denying "I hate homos" quote). Kennedy, Breyer confirmation hearings (sensitivity to Hispanics, women). *Boutilier v. Immigration and Naturalization Service*, 1967 ("afflicted with homosexuality"). *Boy Scouts of America v. Dale*, Stevens's dissent ("symbol of inferiority"). Other sources: Bernard Schwartz, *Decision: How the Supreme Court Decides Cases* (New York: Oxford University Press, 1996), p. 99 (influence of Warren chauffeur), p. 159 ("trust a dog"). Jennifer M. Lowe, ed., *The Jewish Justices of the Supreme Court Revisited: Brandeis to Fortas* (Washington, D.C.: The Supreme Court Historical Society, 1994), p. 3 (Ginsburg on Jewish justices). Joan Biskupic, "Breyer Presents Moderate Image," *The Washington Post*, July 13, 1994, p. A1 (Breyer on daughters). Michael Les Benedict, *The Blessings of Liberty*, p. 173 (slaveholding justices), p. 211 ("paramount destiny"). David G. Savage, *Turning Right*, p. 59 (on architect). John C. Jeffries Jr., *Justice Lewis F. Powell Jr.: A Biography* (New York: Charles Scribner's Sons, 1994), p. 347 (Powell on abortion). *Hoyt v. Florida*, 1961 jury-duty decision. Clare Cushman, editor, *The Supreme Court Jus-*

tices: Illustrated Biographies, 1789–1995 (Washington, D.C.: Congressional Quarterly, 1995), "James C. McReynolds," pp. 330 (anti-Semitism), 400.

An Imprecise Art

Authors' interviews: W. H. Perry, Mary Brennan, Michael Conley. Other court documents: *Chambers v. Florida* ("havens of refuge"). Other sources: William O. Douglas, *The Court Years 1939–1975: The Autobiography of William O. Douglas* (New York: Random House, 1980), p. 8 ("other 90 percent"), p. 281 (FDR's shock). H. W. Perry, *Deciding to Decide: Agenda Setting in the United States Supreme Court* (Cambridge, Mass.: Harvard University Press, 1991), pp. 257–258 ("gay rights"). Rehnquist dissent from denial of *cert, Ratchford v. Gay Lib* ("storm cellar"). Brennan dissent from denial of *cert, Rowland v. Mad River* ("important questions"). Mary Ann Harrell and Burnett Anderson, *Equal Justice Under Law: The Supreme Court in American Life* (Washington, D.C.: Supreme Court Historical Society, 1988), p. 144 (Latin translation).

A Gay Justice?

Authors' interview: Sidney Fine. Other sources: Sidney Fine, *Frank Murphy: The Washington Years* (Ann Arbor: University of Michigan Press, 1984), pp. 6, 8, 9, 15, 170, 171, 201, 202, 212 479. *Frank Murphy, The Detroit Years* (Ann Arbor: University of Michigan Press, 1975), pp. 28, 33, 38, 255. *Frank Murphy: The New Deal Years* (Chicago: University of Chicago Press, 1993), pp. 2, 23, 284, 285. Frank Murphy obituary, *The Washington Post*, July 20, 1949, p. A1. Abe Garfinkel letter to Frank Murphy, Jan. 10, 1940, Frank Murphy papers, Bentley Library, University of Michigan, pp. 6, 15, 170, 171, 212. FBI files on Frank Murphy. "E. G. Kemp Dead; Aide to Murphy," *The Detroit News*, Nov. 23, 1962, p. B10. "Frank Murphy," *Current Biography*, 1940. FBI files on Frank Murphy and Edward Kemp.

An Archeological Dig

Authors' interviews: Bob Woodward, Jim Graham. Other sources: Joan Biskupic, "Breyer: Pragmatic Lawyer and Judge," *The Washington Post*, June 27, 1994, p. A1 (goldfish).

CHAPTER 1: *ONE* STANDARD OF JUSTICE

Authors' interviews: Jim Kepner, Dale Jennings, Eric Julber. Other sources: Jim Kepner, *Rough News, Daring News: 1950s' Pioneer Gay Press Journalism* (New York: The Harrington Park Press, 1988), p. 3 ("Ain't you one?"), pp. 11, 12 (circulation figures); p. 256 (Judge Clarke's ruling). (Note: The Post Office pegged ONE circulation at 8,978, but Kepner said thousands of copies were returned by newsstands.) Jim Kepner, letter to the authors, March 4, 1997 ("Who would choose to be this way?"). *ONE*, Vol. 1, No. 1, Jan. 1953, contents page ("mystic bond"), p. 6 (Julber read every word); Vol. 1, No. 5, May 1954, p. 5 (British homosexual uproar); Vol. 1, No. 8, August 1953, pp. 10–12 (marriage), pp. 12–15 ("Sappho Remembered"), pp. 18–19 ("Lord Samuel poem"); Vol. 1, No. 10, October 1953, cover ("not grateful"); Vol. 2, No. 8, October 1954, contents page (extra charge), pp. 5–6 (Julber's content rules); March 1958, p. 6 (Judge Clarke's ruling); January 1962, p. 6 (on ONE's skipped issues). Don Slater, letter to the authors, Oct. 31, 1996 ("smoke and sparking conversation"), ("cocksucker!"), (*ONE*'s Mattachine roots), ("unequal enforcement"). Don Slater, letter to authors, Nov. 22, 1996 ("band of radicals"), ("tired of the uncertainty"), ("can happen to me"), ("too delicious"). Minutes, *ONE* staff meeting, Nov. 12, 1954 (Post Office seizure of magazines, *ONE* finances). Federal Bureau of Investigation files on *ONE*, Feb. 10, 1956 memo; March 6, 1956, memo, p. 2 (*ONE* not communist). FBI files on Mattachine Society, file No. 100–403320–21, p. 3 (Julber's filing delay).

"Perverts Called Government Peril"

Other sources: Allan Berube, *Coming Out Under Fire: The History of Gay Men and Women in World War Two* (New York: The Press Press, 1990), p. 262. William S. White, "Never Condoned Disloyalty, Says Acheson of His Stand," *The New York Times*, March 1, 1950, p. 1 ("in the shady category"). William S. White, "Miss Kenyon Cites Patriotic Record to Refute Charges," *The New York Times*, March 1, 1950, p. 3 (Senator McCarthy's activities). Special to *The New York Times*, "Perverts Called Government Peril," *The New York Times*, April 19, 1950, p. 25. Senator Styles Bridges (R-N.H.), Congressional Record, p. 4120, March 27, 1950 ("Who put the 91 homosexuals"). David K. Johnson, "Homosexual Citizens," *Washington History*, Vol. 6, No. 2, fall/winter 1994–95, pp. 47–49, 53, 54 ("Stalin's Atom Bomb," Senator Wherry demands probe, quoting columnist Max Lerner). William S. White, "Inquiry by Senate on Perverts Asked," *The New York Times*, May 20, 1950, p. 8 (Lt. Blick's "quick guess"). John D'Emilio, *Sexual Politics, Sexual Communities: The Making of a Homosexual Minority in the United States, 1940–1970* (Chicago: The University of Chicago Press, 1983), pp. 35, 37 (impact of fear of Kinsey research, fear of communism), p. 44 (loyalty investigations), pp. 46–47 (FBI, vice squads, Post Office crack down), p. 112 (ACLU's 1957 stand on homosexuality). Subcommittee on Investigations, Committee on Expenditures in the Executive Departments, *Employment of Homosexuals and Other Sex Perverts in Government* (Washington, DC: United States Government Printing Office, 1950), Dec. 15, 1950, pp. 1, 4 ("one homosexual can pollute"), pp. 5, 13 ("FBI began furnishing") pp. 19, 21 ("to pussyfoot"). Anthony Summers, *Official and Confidential: The Secret Life of J. Edgar Hoover* (New York: Pocket Star Books, 1993) (alleged evidence of Hoover's homosexuality woven throughout).

Reaching the High Court

Other court documents: Chief Justice Warren's docket sheet (conference votes), clerk memo, *ONE v. Olesen*. Clerk memo to Justice Burton, *ONE v. Olesen*. Justice Douglas docket sheet (conference votes), clerk memo, *ONE v. Olesen*. Other sources: Eric Marcus, *Making History: The Struggle for Gay and Lesbian Equal Rights 1945–1990* (New York: HarperCollins, 1992), p. 52 (Kepner theory on FBI role in *ONE* seizure). FBI files on *ONE*. Jim Kepner, *Rough News, Daring News*. FBI files on Mattachine Society, Senator Wiley's letter to postmaster. *ONE*, March 1958, p. 5 ("a rational view . . . would prevail"). Clare Cushman, editor, *The Supreme Court Justices*, "Harold Burton," pp. 416–420; "Charles E. Whittaker," pp. 453, 455.

"We Made It"

Authors' interviews: Jim Kepner, Dale Jennings. Other sources: Anthony Lewis, "Nudist Magazines Win Mail Rights," *The New York Times*, Jan. 14, 1958, p. 35 (*ONE* ruling). *ONE*, Feb. 1958, p. 17 ("by winning this decision"); March 1958, p. 6 ("rendered UNANIMOUSLY"). Don Slater, letter to the authors, Nov. 27, 1996 ("we had no party").

Homosexual G-Men—"It's True!"

Sources: *ONE*, Nov. 1955, p. 5 ("How much do we know?"). FBI files on *ONE*, FBI memos, Jan. 26, 1956 ("put up or shut up"); Feb. 17, 1956 (on pressing Post Office, Justice Department); Feb. 10, 1956, March 31, 1958 (stop sending *ONE* Hoover). Anthony Summers, *Official and Confidential: The Secret Life of J. Edgar Hoover* (Hoover's relationship with Tolson).

CHAPTER 2: "A BURNING SENSE OF INJUSTICE"

Authors' interview: Frank Kameny. Other sources: U.S. Office of Personnel Management, record of Civil Service pay levels. Deb Price, "Former Astronomer Thanks His Lucky Stars He Turned to a Life of Activism," *The Detroit News*, Oct. 8, 1993 ("declare war on me").

"The Passion of the Aggrieved"

Authors' interview: Frank Kameny, Philip Heymann. Court documents: *Kameny v. Brucker*, cert petition, response in opposition. Clerk Philip Heymann, March 1961 memo to Justice Harlan on *Kameny*, Harlan files. Clerk Bernard Jacob, March 1961 memo to Justice Douglas, Douglas files. Clerk Markham Ball, undated memo to Chief Justice Warren. Warren, Douglas docket sheets on *Kameny*. Other sources: John D'Emilio, *Sexual Politics, Sexual Communities*, p. 147 ("passion of the aggrieved").

The Undefeated

Authors' interviews: Frank Kameny. Other sources: Deb Price, "Former Astronomer Thanks His Lucky Stars He Turned to a Life of Activism," *The Detroit News*, Oct. 8, 1993 ("slit trench by slit trench"), ("one fell swoop"). John D'Emilio, *Sexual Politics, Sexual Communities*, pp. 152, 155–156, 214 (all on ACLU's turnaround), p. 162 (government leans on illness label). Ronald Bayer, *Homosexuality and American Psychiatry* (New York: Basic Books, 1981), p. 81 ("no one was of greater importance").

CHAPTER 3: BEEFCAKE ON THE MENU

Court documents: Douglas docket sheet on *Womack*. Clerk memo on *Womack* for Warren. Clerk memo to Douglas on *Manual*. Clerk Gordon Gooch memo to Warren on *Manual*. Clerk John B. Rhinelander memo to Harlan on *Manual*. Clerk memo to Clark on *Manual*. *Manual* docket sheets of Douglas, Harlan, Warren. Other sources: James Griffin, "Dr. Womack and the Nudie Magazines," *The Washington Daily News*, April 30, 1970 (Womack's appearance, early life). Roger K. Newman, *Hugo Black: A Biography*, p. 553 ("My belief"). Jackie Hatton, "The Pornography Empire of H. Lynn Womack,"

Viewing Culture 7 (Spring 1993), p. 9 ("unsung anti-hero"). *MANual*, April 1960. *Trim*, May 1960, pp. 14–15 ("Robert Kimball"). *Grecian Guild Pictorial*, May 1960.

Aroused Angels and the Empire State Building

Authors' interviews: Gordon Gooch; anonymous Clark clerk. Other sources: Gordon Gooch bench memo to Warren on *Manual*. Official audiotape of *Manual* oral argument, U.S. National Archives. Oral argument transcript created by the authors. *Jacobellis v. Ohio*, Stewart majority opinion ("I know it when I see it").

"No Worse Than Striptease Calendars"

Authors' interviews: Gordon Gooch, Sally Smith (Harlan greeting lamppost), Robert Mnookin, Philip Heymann, James Knox, Ramsey Clark. Court documents: Douglas conference notes on *Manual. Roth v. United States,* Douglas dissent. Douglas, Clark, Warren docket sheets on *Manual.* Black's case assignment sheet on *Manual. Manual v. Day,* Harlan majority opinion, Clark dissent. Harlan first draft of *Manual* ruling, May 3, 1962, pp. 4, 16, Harlan papers. Stewart letter to Harlan, June 5, 1962, Harlan papers ("obnoxiously debasing"). Brennan letter to Harlan, June 9, 1962, p. 1 ("refine the *Roth* test"). Gordon Gooch last-minute memos to Warren on *Manual,* June 1962. James Knox memo to Clark, June 1962. First draft of Clark's *Manual* dissent, June 1, 1962, Harlan papers ("Wow!"). Other sources: Bernard Schwartz, *Super Chief: Earl Warren and His Supreme Court* (New York: New York University Press, 1983), pp. 221–222 ("strangled with my own hands"). Clare Cushman, editor, *The Supreme Court Justices,* "Hugo L. Black," p. 380 ("no law means no law"); "Charles E. Whittaker," p. 455 (Whittaker's breakdown). Roger K. Newman, *Hugo Black*, p. 588 ("if they were all like Harlan"). Bob Woodward and Scott Armstrong, *The Brethren: Inside the Supreme Court* (New York: Avon Books, 1981), p. 47 ("quintessential patrician"). David J. Garrow, *Liberty and Sexuality: The Right to Privacy and the Making of Roe v. Wade* (New York: Lisa Drew Books, 1994), pp. 182, 184 ("colorless," "mustard").

A Second Green Light

Authors' interview: Stanley Dietz. Other sources: Special to *The New York Times*, "Court Lifts Ban on 3 Magazines," *The New York Times*, June 26, 1962. Herman L. Womack, death certificate, Office of Vital Statistics, state of Florida. Jackie Hatton, "The Pornography Empire of H. Lynn Womack," *Viewing Culture* 7 (Spring 1993), p. 22 ("Womack was proud"), p. 24 ("Gaining the right"). James Griffin, "Dr. Womack and the Nudie Magazines," *The Washington Daily News*, April 30, 1970 ("pay taxes and die").

Twisting a Shield into a Weapon

Authors' interviews: Howard Lesnich, Charles Fried, Philip Heymann, Robert Mnookin, Robert Goldberg. Court documents: *Poe v. Ullman,* Frankfurter majority decision, Harlan dissent. *Bowers v. Hardwick. Griswold v. Connecticut* (contraceptives for married couples). *Eisenstadt v. Baird* (contraceptives for unmarried adults). *Carey v. Population Services International* (contraceptives for minors). *Loving v. Virginia* (interracial marriage). *Stanley v. Georgia* (private possession of pornography).

Roe v. Wade (abortion rights). Other sources: Howard Lesnich memo to Harlan on *Poe*, spring 1960 ("farfetched as this may be").

CHAPTER 4: "MORE THAN A HOMOSEXUAL"

Authors' interview: Hiram Kwan. Court documents: *Rosenberg v. Fleuti, cert* petition, response in opposition, "transcript of record" (Fleuti quotes, background, history of immigration law). Other sources: William Booth, "'Slow Growth' on Fast Track in Southern California," *The Washington Post*, Nov. 27, 1998, p. 2.

"He Performs Publicly"

Authors' interviews: Peter R. Taft, Barbara Goldberg. Court documents: *Rosenberg v. Fleuti*, first circulated draft of Goldberg opinion (June 5, 1963), Clark dissent, brief for petitioner, brief in opposition. Clerk *Fleuti* memo to Warren, Aug. 20, 1962. Clerk *Fleuti* memo to Harlan, Aug. 17, 1962, Harlan papers. Warren, Douglas dockets sheets on *Fleuti*. Peter R. Taft bench memo on *Fleuti* for Warren, March 22, 1962. Douglas conference notes on justices' remarks on *Fleuti*. In the Goldberg papers on *Fleuti*: Goldberg "MEMORANDUM TO THE CONFERENCE," June 4, 1963; Goldberg memo to Douglas, June 7, 1963 (on idea for "entry" loophole); Black note to Goldberg, June 6, 1963 ("although I would prefer"); Warren note to Goldberg, June 6, 1963; Brennan note to Goldberg, June 6, 1963 ("splendid job"); Douglas note to Goldberg, June 6, 1963 ("a just, liberal construction"); Harlan note to Goldberg, June 1963 ("ever been to Ensenada"). Clerk Richard Higel note to Harlan on Goldberg draft ("ingenious"). Other sources: David L. Stebenne, *Arthur G. Goldberg: New Deal Liberal* (New York: Oxford University Press, 1996), pp. 4, 6 ("as a Jew"). Associated Press, "Court Seeks Ruling in Alien's Brief Trip," *The New York Times*, June 18, 1963, p. 29.

"The Yellow Person of Today"

Authors' interviews: Hiram Kwan, Peter Edelman, Robert Goldberg, Barbara Goldberg. Other sources: Harry Hay, *Radically Gay: Gay Liberation in the Words of Its Founder* (Boston: Beacon Press, 1996), p. 79 ("solitary confinement"). Dudley Clendinen and Adam Nagourney, *Out for Good: The Struggle to Build a Gay Rights Movement in America* (New York: Simon & Schuster, 1999), p. 79 (Goldberg's gubernatorial campaign, "more important things"). David L. Stebenne, *Arthur G. Goldberg*, p. 373 (Goldberg loses chance of being chief).

CHAPTER 5: "AFFLICTED WITH HOMOSEXUALITY"

Authors' interviews: Ramsey Clark, Mimi Clark Gronlund, Cathy Douglas Stone. Court documents: Clerk *cert* memos on *Boutilier* to Harlan, Clark, Warren. Warren, Douglas, Clark docket sheets on *Boutilier*. Other sources: Bruce Allen Murphy, *Fortas: The Rise and Ruin of a Supreme Court Justice* (New York: Morrow, 1988), pp. 79–80 (Fortas's lavish life), p. 86 ("competency test"); pp. 137–138 (Jenkins scandal), p. 163 ("no wiser man"), p. 216 ("He was not afraid"). Clare Cushman, editor, *The Supreme Court Justices*, "Abe Fortas," pp. 471–475 (Fortas background, "fine-boned").

"A Homo Might or Might Not Be Psychotic"

Authors' interviews: Douglas Kranwinkle, Stuart Ross, Ramsey Clark, Burt Rein. Court documents: *Boutilier v. INS*, brief for petitioner, brief for respondent, drafts of Clark majority decision. Justices, memos reacting to Clark's *Boutilier* draft, Clark files. Douglas Kranwinkle bench memo on *Boutilier* for Warren, Feb. 16, 1967. Douglas, Fortas conference notes on *Boutilier*. Justice Clark's retirement press release, February 28, 1967 ("filled with pride"), Warren papers. Other sources: Ronald Bayer, *Homosexuality and American Psychiatry*, pp. 39–40 (psychiatric diagnoses of the 1950s), p. 88 ("after a protracted debate"). Audiotape of *Boutilier* oral argument, March 14, 1967, National Archives. Roger K. Newman, *Hugo Black*, pp. 256, 258 (furor over KKK membership), pp. 281–282 (quoting Black's *Chambers v. Florida* decision, "havens of refuge"). Clare Cushman, editor, *The Supreme Court Justices*, "Tom C. Clark," pp. 426–430 (Clark background, "biggest mistake").

A Beloved Homosexual Nephew

Authors' interviews: Ramsey Clark, Mimi Clark Gronlund.

A Dissenting Diagnosis

Authors' interview: Cathy Douglas Stone. Court documents: Warren memo to Clark, May 19, 1967, joining *Boutilier* majority decision, Warren papers. *Boutilier v. INS*, Douglas dissent, Douglas dissent drafts (Douglas papers), Brennan dissent. Lewis B. Merrifield memo to Douglas with editing suggestions for *Boutilier* first draft, Douglas papers. Clerk John Griffith note to Fortas on first circulated Douglas draft of *Boutilier* dissent, May 18, 1967. Fortas memo to Douglas on *Boutilier* draft, May 18, 1967, Douglas papers. Fortas's racy limerick to Douglas, "To WOD—a poem—No. 395," April 10, 1967 (Douglas papers, *Loving v. Virginia* file). Fortas letter to Douglas, Aug. 24, 1954 ("continue . . . as a director"), Douglas papers (Fortas file). Douglas letter to Fortas, Oct. 12, 1954 ("happy to serve"), Douglas papers (Fortas file). Other sources: Bruce Allen Murphy, *Fortas*, p. 214 ("Bill just got bored"). John D'Emilio, *Sexual Politics, Sexual Communities*, p. 112 (Hooker research).

The Lesbian Couple Next Door

Authors' interviews: Cathy Douglas Stone, Clive Boutilier. Other sources: William O. Douglas, *Go East, Young Man: The Autobiography of William O. Douglas* (New York: Vintage Books, 1974), pp. 104–105 ("the first homosexual I ever knew"), p. 240 ("Some 30 years ago"). Kay Kershaw letter to Douglas, June 12, 1972 ("Happy Hour"), Douglas papers. Isabelle Lynn letter to Douglas, February 23, 1978 ("lovely valentine"), Douglas papers. "William Frazier" (William O. Douglas), unpublished play, "The Couch," 1970, pp. 57–59. (No byline), "Supreme Court's Actions," *The New York Times*, May 23, 1967, pp. 1, 33.

A "True Homosexual"?

Court documents: *INS v. Lavoie*, rulings, respondent's petition, respondent's petition for a rehearing ("I do not even regard"), Douglas, Warren docket sheets on Lavoie. Report of Daniel Beittel, M.D., to INS investigator William A. Sherrill, October 9 1961 ("Patient categorically states"), National Archives. "Matter of Gerard Joseph Lavoie," brief on Appeal to Board of Immigration Appeals by George R. Anderson, undated, p. 12 ("maladjusted confused person"), National Archives. Douglas docket sheet on *Lavoie* rehearing petition. Other sources: Ronald Bayer, *Homosexuality and American Psychiatry,* p. 193 (1979 actions on immigration ban).

CHAPTER 6: NOWHERE TO HIDE

Authors' interviews: Bill Spognardi, James Chamberlain, Larry I. Inscore. Court documents: James S. Campbell memo on Poore to Douglas, August 13, 1964 ("invasion of privacy"), Douglas papers. Clerk memo on Poore to Douglas, Nov. 11, 1964. Clerk memo to Warren on Poore. Douglas, Warren docket sheets. Daniel P. Levitt memo on Chamberlain to Fortas, Fortas papers. James T. Hale memo on Chamberlain to Warren, May 31, 1966. Lewis B. Merrifield memo on Chamberlain to Douglas, Sept. 26, 1966 ("I just don't see"). Douglas docket sheet on Chamberlain. Other sources: Donn Gaynor, "Hidden Movie Camera Used by Police to Trap Sexual Deviates at Park Hangout," *The Mansfield News-Journal,* Aug. 22, 1962, p. 1. Allan Berube, *Coming Out Under Fire,* pp. 258–259 (history of "sexual psychopath" laws). John D'Emilio, *Sexual Politics, Sexual Communities,* p. 51 (29 Iowa homosexuals put in asylum). Ohio prison records on Chamberlain, Ohio prison officials.

"I Know I Look Like I'm a Queer"

Authors' interview: Herb Selwyn. Court documents: Douglas Kranwinkle memo to Warren on *Robillard,* Oct. 20, 1966. Lewis B. Merrifield memo to Douglas on *Robillard,* Oct. 27, 1966. Douglas, Warren docket sheets on *Robillard.* Other sources: John D'Emilio, *Sexual Politics, Sexual Communities,* p. 183 (gay bars), p. 187 ("resort for sexual perverts"), p. 207 ("instructed officers"), pp. 211–212 (bar licensing). "The Consenting Adult Homosexual and the Law: An Empirical Study of Enforcement and Administration in Los Angeles County," 13 *U.C.L.A. Law Review* 643 (1966).

Nightstick Nightmares

Authors' interviews: Edward Vasquez, Buddy Ball, Jim Kepner, Herb Selwyn. Court documents: *Talley v. California* documents, National Archives. Other sources: Clare Cushman, editor, *The Supreme Court Justices,* "Thurgood Marshall, pp. 476–479," ("Mr. Civil Rights"). Lincoln Caplan, *The Tenth Justice: The Solicitor General and the Rule of Law* (New York: Knopf, 1987) pp. 4–6 (role of solicitor general). Lillian Faderman, *Odd Girls and Twilight Lovers: A History of Lesbian Life in Twentieth-Century America* (New York: Penguin, 1992), p. 165 ("think you're a man"). John D'Emilio, *Sexual Politics, Sexual Communities,* p. 227 ("gay demonstration"). Clark clerk Larry Nichols memo on Talley, April 2, 1967 ("frivolous"), Warren papers. William Reppy memo to Douglas on Talley, April 12, 1967 ("vagueness only"). Peter Zimroth memo to Fortas on Talley. Douglas docket sheet on Talley.

Nixon's "Law and Order" Chief Justice

Court documents: *Bowers v. Hardwick,* Burger concurrence ("deeper malignity"). *Scott v. Macy,* D.C. Circuit Court of Appeals decision, 1965, Burger dissent ("whether it is sound"). Other sources: Bruce Allen Murphy, *Fortas,* p. 270 (on Warren's resignation strategy). Bernard Schwartz, *Super Chief,* p. 86 ("inherent inferiority"). Clare Cushman, editor, *The Supreme Court Justices,* "Earl Warren," p. 440 ("But was it fair?"); "Abe Fortas," p. 475 (Fortas resigns). John D'Emilio, *Sexual Politics, Sexual Communities,* p. 184 ("leading sheep"), pp. 231–232 (Stonewall rebellion, *Village Voice* quote), p. 233 ("within a year"). Deb Price, "One Night at the Bar, Gays Learned to Say: 'No More!'" *The Detroit News,* April 23, 1993 (Stonewall rebellion). "4 Policemen Hurt in 'Village' Raid," *The New York Times,* June 29, 1969.

Trouble in Sexual Paradise

Authors' interview: Richard Schlegel. Court documents: *Schlegel v. United States,* *cert* petition, appendix, brief in opposition. Other sources: Richard Schlegel's treatise on homosexual, sent to Col. Jean P. Sams, July 19, 1961, Schlegel records, Cornell University, Carl A. Kroch Library, Rare and Manuscript Collections ("accept the moral responsibility"). Army "Notice of Proposed Removal," May 26, 1959, Schlegel personal papers, Lewisburg, Pa. ("immoral and indecent"). Robert Mnookin memo on *Schlegel* to Harlan. Thomas C. Armitage memo on *Schlegel* to Douglas. Douglas docket sheet on *Schlegel.*

"A Reckless, Irresponsible or Wanton Nature"

Authors' interview: Charles Fabrikant. Court documents: Charles Fabrikant memo to Harlan on *Adams.* Thomas C. Armitage memo to Douglas on *Adams.* Douglas docket sheet on *Adams.*

"An Outlaw of Society"

Authors' interview: Ray Hill. Court documents: Friend-of-the-court brief by the North American Conference of Homophile Organizations. (All Buchanan documents are at National Archives.) Douglas docket sheet on Buchanan cases. *Younger v. Harris, Samuels v. Mackell* and *Fernandez v. Mackell,* 1971 rulings on "standing." *Eisenstadt v. Baird* ruling, 1972 (contraceptives for unmarried couples). William Alsup memo to Douglas on Buchanan ("three-sided john"). Other sources: Arthur S. Leonard, *Sexuality and the Law,* p. 59 ("not the ideal"), p. 62 (first federal court to strike down sodomy law), p. 137 (Texas law revised).

CHAPTER 7: NOTHING TO HIDE

Authors' interviews: Mike McConnell, Richard L. Jacobson. Court documents: Jacobson memo to Douglas. Douglas docket sheet on *Baker v. Nelson.* Barbara Underwood memo on *Baker* to Marshall, April 30, 1972. Carol Bruch memo on *Baker* to Douglas, Aug. 9, 1971. Other sources: Baker-McConnell fact sheet 1997, Baker-McConnell personal papers. Dudley Clendinen and Adam Nagourney, *Out for Good: The Struggle to Build a Gay Rights Movement in America* (New York: Simon & Schuster, 1999), p. 56 ("media celebrities"), p. 70 (*Look* spread), 71 (student president), p. 229 ("cocksucker"). William M. Hohengarten, "Same-Sex Marriage and the Right of Privacy," 103 *The Yale Law Journal,* No. 6, April 1994, pp. 1506, 1508. American Civil Liberties memo, Dec. 20, 1971, from the ACLU files at Princeton ("Calvinist

Puritan"). Deb Price, "Civil Rites: Arguments Against Same-Sex Marriage Mirror Those That Kept the Races Apart," *The Detroit News,* April 18, 1997 (ducking inter-racial marriage cases).

"The Abominable and Detestable Crime Against Nature"

Authors' interview: William P. Porter. Court documents: Opposition to Application for Stay of Mandate of the United States Court of Appeals for the Fifth Circuit. *Wainwright v. Stone* files in the National Archives. Douglas docket sheets on *Wainwright, Canfield, Connor.* Clare Cushman, editor, *The Supreme Court Justices,* "Byron R. White," pp. 462–464.

"A Duty of Privacy"

Authors' interview: Joe Acanfora. Court documents: Douglas docket sheet. Other sources: *Pennsylvania Mirror,* June 15, 1972, p. 1 (Acanfora comes out). Minutes of University Teacher Certification Council, July 10, 1972, Acanfora's personal papers. "Homosexual Gains Authority to Teach," *The New York Times,* Sept. 24, 1974. "Courage, Honesty, Strength," *The Daily Collegian,* Feb. 28, 1973 ("meaning of courage"). "'Gay' Teacher," *Montgomery County Sentinel,* Oct. 26, 1972. "Homosexuality Flares as School Board Issue," *Washington Star & Daily News,* Oct. 26, 1972. "MCEA, Homosexual Teacher File Suit," *Bethesda Tribune,* Nov. 10, 1972. "Homosexual Teacher Wins in State, Takes Fight to Maryland," *Philadelphia Inquirer,* Nov. 12, 1972. *60 Minutes,* Feb. 25, 1973.

Rubber-stamping a Stigmatizing Law

Authors' interview: Frank Kameny. Other sources: Dudley Clendinen and Adam Nagourney, *Out for Good,* pp. 188, 190–192, 374 (Voeller and NGTF). Arthur S. Leonard, *Sexuality and the Law,* p. 274 (naked bar dancing). Bernard Schwartz, *A History of the Supreme Court,* p. 358 ("freedom to do"). Clare Cushman, editor, *The Supreme Court Justices,* "John Paul Stevens," pp. 503–505. Bob Woodward and Scott Armstrong, *The Brethren,* p. 505 ("Marshall was outraged").

Nobody's Poster Boy

Authors' interview: Eugene Enslin. Court documents: Lambda Legal Defense and Education Fund friend-of-the-court brief. Consolidated Petition for Rehearing. National Gay Task Force friend-of-the-court brief ("specific guidance"). Other sources: E. Carrington Boggan, April 6, 1976, letter to Melvin Wulf ("quite disastrous"). Leigh W. Rutledge, *The Gay Decades* (New York: Plume, 1992), p. 94 (Carswell nomination). "G Harrold Carswell Is Dead at 72; Was Rejected for Supreme Court," *The New York Times,* Aug. 1, 1992, p. 11. "G. Harrold Carswell, 72, Dies; Rejected for Supreme Court," *The Washington Post,* Aug. 1, 1992, p. B6.

CHAPTER 8: A MARBLE STORM CELLAR

Authors' interviews: John Singer, Paul Barrick, Frank Kameny.

"An Off-Campus Cell of Homosexuals"

Authors' interview: Anne DeBary. Court documents: *Mississippi Gay Alliance et al. v. Goudelock et al., cert* petition. Burger's "Memorandum to the Conference," April 19, 1977, listing *Mississippi Gay Alliance* for discussion, Marshall papers. Powell's *Carey v. Population Services* memo, Oct. 29, 1976 ("difficult for me").

"I Had to Tell My Parents"

Authors' interviews: James "Jim" Gaylord, John Gish. Court documents: Gaylord added to "discuss" list by Marshall, Gish by Brennan—Marshall papers.

A Contagion Like Measles?

Court documents: *Ratchford v. Gay Lib,* drafts of Rehnquist dissent from denial of *cert,* Marshall papers. Blackmun memo joining Rehnquist's *Ratchford* dissent, Marshall papers. Other sources: Ronald Bayer, *Homosexuality and American Psychiatry,* pp. 36, 141 (on APA rejection of Socarides, Voth views.) (Note: Socarides's gay son, Richard, served as President Clinton's liaison to the gay community.) Leigh W. Rutledge, *The Gay Decades* (New York: Plume, 1992), pp. 100, 101, 103, 108 (for Anita Bryant material). David Savage, *Turning Right,* pp. 21, 31, 36, 40 (on Rehnquists' rights record, including "choose his customers," "holy deadlock"). Bob Woodward and Scott Armstrong, *The Brethren,* p. 261 (Rehnquist's view of 14th Amendment).

"I Felt So Lonely, So Useless"

Authors' interview: Ronald Onofre. Court documents: Marshall adds *Onofre* to "discuss" for May 11, 1981, Marshall papers.

Stripped of Their Uniforms

Court documents: Judge Anthony Kennedy's Ninth Circuit *Beller* ruling, 632 Federal Reporter, 2nd series, pp. 792, 809, 811. Marshall "discuss" lists for May 1981 show no justice listed *Beller.* Other sources: Arthur Leonard, *Sexuality and the Law,* p. 501 (Kennedy ruling a first).

CHAPTER 9: OMINOUS, "UNSETTLED" TIMES

Authors' interview: Gary Van Ooteghem. Court documents: Justices' private, internal "discuss" lists for the 1981–82 term, Marshall papers. Marshall's "discuss" list, January 12, 1982. Other sources: John C. Jeffries Jr., *Justice Lewis F. Powell Jr.,* p. 504 (honorific changes). Jack Bass, *Taming the Storm: The Life and Times of Judge Frank M. Johnson, Jr. and the South's Fight over Civil Rights* (New York: Doubleday, 1993), p. 358 (Carter would have appointed a woman). Clare Cushman, editor, *The Supreme Court Justices,* "Sandra Day O'Connor," pp. 506–508. O'Connor's comments on homosexual rights come from the official transcription of the Senate Judiciary Committee hearings on the confirmation of Sandra Day O'Connor, Sept. 9–11, 1981, p. 247. Randy Shilts, *Conduct Unbecoming: Lesbians and Gays in the U.S. Military* (New York: St. Martin's Press, 1993), pp. 221–223, 244, 260 (Hatheway's early life, plus

"HOMO," "heard a blow job"), pp. 194, 195, 198 (Matlovich material). Arthur Leonard, *Sexuality and the Law*, p. 237 (final outcome of Van Ooteghem case).

A Couple Without a Country

Authors' interviews: Tony Sullivan, Richard Adams, Clela Rorex. Court documents: Sullivan/Adams Supreme Court documents at National Archives. *Adams v. Howerton*, 673 Federal Reporter 2d Series, pp. 1040, 1041. *Sullivan v. INS*, 772 F. 2d 609, pp. 609, 611, 612; government response (National Archives); Marshall "discuss" lists June 1982. Other sources: Copy of Sullivan/Adams marriage license and INS letters, Nov. 24, 1975 ("two faggots") and Dec. 2, 1975 ("legally insufficient"), and other legal and personal documents from Sullivan/Adams personal files. Sullivan/Adams Internet message on Queer Law bulletin board, posted Aug. 9, 1996.

The Case of the "Soliciting Homo"

Authors' interviews: David Charny, second gay Powell clerk. Court documents: Gary Born, *New York v. Uplinger* pool *cert* memo, June 1, 1983, p. 2 ("What!"), Powell papers. *Uplinger* docket sheet, Marshall papers. Marshall's *Uplinger* bench memo, Jan. 16, 1984. Marshall records. Charny's *Uplinger* bench memo to Powell. *New York v. Uplinger* official transcript of oral argument, Jan. 18, 1984, Official audiotape of oral argument for identification of justices. *New York v. Uplinger*, Powell's conference notes, Jan. 20, 1980. Justices' memos casting final *Uplinger* votes, Powell and Marshall papers.

"These Bastards Will Not Win!"

Authors' interview: Richard Longstaff.

CHAPTER 10: THE CHESS MASTER MAKES HIS MOVE

Authors' interview: Marjorie Rowland.

Wading into the Flood

Authors' interviews: Marjorie Rowland, Charles Curtis, Rory Little, E. Joshua Rosenkranz, Mary Brennan, Cecelia Marshall, William J. Brennan III. Other sources: Stuart Taylor Jr., "Supreme Court. Brennan: 30 Years and the Thrill Is Not Gone," *The New York Times*, Oct. 5, 1986, p. B8 ("no soul but my own"). Joan Biskupic, "Justice Brennan, Voice of the Court's Social Revolution, Dies," *The Washington Post*, July 25, 1997, p. A1. Deb Price, "The High Court's William J. Brennan Jr. Leaves a Legacy of Justice for Gay Rights," *The Detroit News*, Aug. 8, 1997.

"Don't Even Look at Me in a Grocery Store"

Authors' interviews: Kathleen McKean, William B. Rogers, Keith Smith, Laurence Tribe. Court documents: *Board v. NGTF* bench memo, Marshall files; *Board v. NGTF*, official transcript of oral argument, Jan. 14, 1985. Official tape of oral arguments. Marshall's files, March 22, 1984, memo from Chief Justice Burger to the court. Burger memos to the justices, March 15, 1984, March 22, 1984, showing Powell having some cases reargued but not *Board v. NGTF*, Marshall papers. Other sources:

William B. Rogers letter to NGTF co-director Lucia Valeska, Sept. 9, 1981 (affidavit sufficient). Mike Hammer, "Teacher Firings Allowed/Homosexual Reins Voted," *The Daily Oklahoman*, Feb. 8, 1978, p. 1. Associated Press, "High School Ku Klux Klan Terrorizes Gays in Oklahoma City," *Gaysweek*, Feb. 6, 1978, plus other wire stories from National Gay and Lesbian Task Force records, Box 90, Cornell University Library, The Norman Human Rights Commission poll, National Gay Task Force files. Box 90, Cornell University Library. Arthur Leonard, *Sexuality and the Law*, p. 616 ("first substantive victory"). "Court Axes State Anti-Gay Statute," The Oklahoma Publishing Co., March 27, 1985 (Arrow on Powell).

An Invisible Family Smashed to Bits

Authors' interview: Karen Thompson. (Donald Kowalski, Della Kowalski, Jack Fena, Janlori Goldman, all 1988.) Other sources: Joyce Murdoch, "Fighting for Control of a Loved One," *The Washington Post*, Aug. 5, 1988, p. A1. "Why Can't Sharon Come Home?" 1988 Thompson speech, reprinted in *Plain Brown Rapper*, Vol. II, No. 3, p. 13. Karen Thompson and Julie Andzejewski, *Why Can't Sharon Kowalski Come Home?* (San Francisco: Spinters Ink, 1989).

CHAPTER 11: ADRIFT IN A SEA OF GAY CLERKS

Authors' interview: Court documents: David Charny, Cabell Chinnis, Sally Smith, Ann Coughlin, Michael Mosman, Mary Becker and John C. Jeffries Jr. Other sources: John C. Jeffries Jr., *Justice Lewis F. Powell Jr.*, p. 90 (Chinnis interview). Andrew Hodges, *Alan Turing: The Enigma* (New York: Simon and Schuster, 1983), p. 496.

"The Perfect Case"

Authors' interviews: Evan Wolfson. Daniel Richman's bench memo to Marshall, March 1986, p. 2. Other sources: Michael Hardwick, quotes and background are from Peter Irons, *The Courage of Their Convictions: Sixteen Americans Who Fought Their Way to the Supreme Court* (New York: Penguin, 1988), pp. 381–403; and Art Harris, "The Unintended Battle of Michael Hardwick," *The Washington Post*, Aug. 21, 1986, p. C1.

"Write It Strong"

Authors' interviews: Pam Karlan, Daniel Richman. Court documents: *Bowers v. Hardwick* pool *cert* memo, pp. 1, 13, Powell files. Other sources: Jack Bass, *Taming the Storm*, p. 280 ("remove injustice"), p. 424 ("write it strong" and other Johnson exchanges with clerks), p. 427. J. Y. Smith, "Judge Frank M. Johnson Jr. Dies; Rulings Shaped Civil Rights," *The Washington Post*, July 2, 1999, p. C8 ("true meaning," "most hated"). Dennis J. Hutchinson, *The Man Who Once Was Whizzer White: A Portrait of Justice Byron R. White* (New York: Free Press, 1998), p. 452.

"Trying to Move a Conservative Court Beyond Its Instincts"

Authors' interviews: Laurence Tribe, David Charny. Court documents: *Bowers v. Hardwick*, American Psychological Association and American Public Health Association friend-of-the-court brief. Other sources: Official minutes, Ad Hoc Task Force to Challenge Sodomy Laws, Nov. 15 and 16, 1985, from personal records of Don Baker. Krista Reese, "The Lights Went Out in Georgia," *George* magazine, p. 73, May 1998 ("Bowers is a hypocrite"). Jeffrey Toobin, "Supreme Sacrifice," *The New Yorker,* July 8, 1996, p. 47 ("a love song").

"I Am Sorry You Had to Be Burdened with This Case"

Authors' interviews: Daniel Richman, Jay Fujitani. Court documents: Daniel Richman's bench memo to Marshall on *Hardwick,* pp. 3, 4, March 1986. *Olmstead v. United States,* Brandeis dissent ("the right to be let alone"). Michael Mosman bench memo to Powell, March 29, 1986.

Bigamy, Incest, Prostitution, Adultery?

Authors' interviews: Evan Wolfson, Andrew Schultz, Laurence Tribe. Court documents: *Bowers v. Hardwick,* oral argument, March 31, 1986, official transcript. Undated memo in Powell's handwriting, *Bowers v. Hardwick* main file, Powell papers. *Zablocki v. Redtail,* 1978. *Bowers v. Hardwick,* Powell notes on oral argument, March 31, 1986, Powell papers. Other sources: Peter Irons, *The Courage of Their Convictions,* p. 399 (Hardwick sees courtroom).

Prepared to Plead on Bended Knee

Authors' interviews: Evan Wolfson, Laurence Tribe, Cabell Chinnis, Ann Coughlin, William Stuntz. Court documents: Michael Mosman, memo to Justice Powell, April 1, 1986. Mosman memo to Powell, April 2, 1986. Unsigned, undated memo to Powell, 1986, Powell papers. Powell, Marshall conference notes on *Hardwick.* Personal notes Powell used during court's conference on *Hardwick,* Powell papers. *U.S. Department of Agriculture v. Moreno* (hippie food stamps case). Other sources: Peter Irons, *The Courage of Their Convictions,* p. 399 ("pre-victory'). *The Washington Post,* April 1, 1986, p. C1 (Washington weather). John C. Jeffries Jr., *Justice Lewis F. Powell Jr.,* p. 528 ("Of course, you have"). David J. Garrow, *Liberty and Sexuality,* p. 660 ("I hate homos"). Justice John Paul Stevens, letter to the authors, June 1, 2000 (denying "I hate homos" quote).

CHAPTER 12: BRANDED SECOND-CLASS CITIZENS

Authors' interviews: Mary Becker, Cabell Chinnis, Mike Mosman. Court papers: Burger's April 3, 1986 letter to Justice Powell, Powell papers. Powell's notes to himself on Burger letter, Powell papers. Powell's "Memorandum to the Conference," April 8, 1986, Powell papers. Stevens memo to Powell, April 8, 1986, Powell papers. Other sources: John C. Jeffries Jr., *Justice Lewis F. Powell Jr.,* p. 524 (Jeffries minimizes impact).

"An Intellectual Hit-and-Run Incident"

Interviews: Andrew Schultz, William Stuntz, Mike Mosman, Tim Flanagan. Court papers: Burger's memo to White, April 9, 1986 (assigning *Hardwick* majority opinion). *Bowers v. Hardwick,* first draft, Powell papers. Powell papers describe when justices signaled their views. *Bowers v. Hardwick,* Powell concurrence drafts, Powell papers. Michael Mosman memo to Justice Powell, June 12, 1986, Powell papers. *Barnes v. Glen Theatre Inc.,* White dissent on nude barroom dancing. Other sources: Dennis Hutchinson, *The Man Who Once Was Whizzer White,* pp. 2–5 ("shy man," "goddamn newspapers"), 452–453 ("terse opinion," "absolutely authentic"). Arthur Leonard, *Sexuality and the Law,* p. 160 (on Blackstone).

An Eloquent Plea for "Tolerance of Nonconformity"

Authors' interviews: Tim Flanagan, Chai Feldblum, Norval Morris, Arthur Leonard, Sally Smith, Albert Lauber, J. Paul Oetken, Pam Karlan. Draft of rejected footnote to Powell concurrence on *Hardwick,* June 24, 1986, Powell papers (*"antithesis* to family"). Powell's timetable of court actions on Hardwick, Powell papers. Other sources: On Blackmun, Clare Cushman, editor, *The Supreme Court Justices,* pp. 487, 489 (reference to *Barefoot v. Estelle* death penalty juries case), 490; Richard Carelli, "Retired Justice Blackmun, Author of Roe-Wade Abortion Ruling, Dead at 90," *Associated Press,* March 4, 1999; Richard Carelli, "Blackmun Wanted to Be Remembered for More Than Abortion," *Associated Press,* March 4, 1999. H. L. A. Hart, *Law, Liberty and Morality* (Stanford: Stanford University Press, 1963), pp. 4, 5, 13, 14–15 ("There must remain a realm").

"Shame! Shame! Shame!"

Authors' interviews: Evan Wolfson, Laurence Tribe, Matt Coles, Kevin Cathcart, Chai Feldblum. Court documents: *Dred Scott v. Sanford,* opinion of Chief Justice Roger Taney ("no rights which the white man"). Arthur Leonard, *Sexuality and the Law,* p. 450–452 (quoting Laurence Silberman 1987 opinion in *Padula v. Webster).* Other sources: Peter Irons, *The Courage of Their Convictions,* p. 400–403 (Hardwick quotes). Jeffrey Toobin, "Supreme Sacrifice," *The New Yorker,* July 8, 1996, p. 47 ("burned a hole"). Lincoln Caplan, *The Tenth Justice,* p. 253 (Meese reaction). "Barging into Bedrooms," *The Washington Post,* July 1, 1986, p. A14 ("What now?"). "Crime in the Bedroom," *The New York Times,* July 2, 1986, p. A30 ("gratuitous and petty"). Stuart Taylor Jr., "High Court, 5-4, Says States Have the Right to Outlaw Private Homosexual Acts," *The New York Times,* July 1, 1986. Gallup poll results reported in *Newsweek,* July 14, 1986, p. 38. Al Kamen, "Court Upholds State Law Prohibiting Sodomy," *The Washington Post,* July 1, 1986, p. A1. Larry Rohter, "Friend and Foe See Homosexual Defeat," *The New York Times,* p. A19, July 1, 1986 (Falwell, Stoddard reactions). Karlyn Barker and Linda Wheeler, "Gay Activists Arrested at High Court," *The Washington Post,* Oct. 14, 1987, p. A1 (details, quotes from gay-rights demonstration at court). Pamela S. Karlan, "Some Thoughts on Autonomy and Equality in Relation to Justice Blackmun," *Hastings Constitutional Law Quarterly,* Fall 1998, Vol. 26, No. 1, p. 71 ("hero of his own life").

The Search for a Scapegoat

Authors' interviews: Cabell Chinnis, Ann Coughlin and William Stuntz. Other sources: Ruth Marcus, "Powell Regrets Backing Sodomy Law," *The Washington Post,* Oct. 26, 1990, p. A3. Al Kamen, "Powell Changed Vote in Sodomy Case," *The Wash-*

ington Post, July 13, 1986, p. A1. Dudley Clendinen and Adam Nagourney, *Out for Good,* p. 539 ("the clerk declined"). Eve Kosofsky Sedgwick, *The Epistemology of the Closet* (Berkeley: University of California Press, 1990), pp. 74, 75, 77. Gay-rights attorney's remark to author, Human Rights Campaign national dinner, Washington, D.C., 1999 ("ought to be hanged").

A Long, Secret Struggle over a "Frivolous" Case

Authors' interviews: Ann Coughlin, William Stuntz, Mike Mosman, Cabell Chinnis, Mary Becker, Sally Smith, Kevin Cathcart. Court documents: Justice Lewis Powell speech to the American Bar Association litigation section meeting, Aug. 12, 1986, Powell papers, *Hardwick* file. Powell class preparation notes, 1988, 1989, Powell papers. Bob Werner due process memo to Powell, 1988, Powell papers. *Commonwealth v. Wasson* (Kentucky ruling striking down sodomy law). *Powell v. State* (Georgia ruling striking down sodomy law). Other sources: Ruth Marcus, "Powell Regrets Backing Sodomy Law," *The Washington Post,* Oct. 26, 1990, p. A3 ("made a mistake," "frivolous case," "half an hour"). Anand Agneshwar, "Ex-Justice Says He May Have Been Wrong: Powell on Sodomy," *The National Journal,* Nov. 5, 1990, p. 3 ("When I had the opportunity"). John C. Jeffries Jr., *Justice Louis F. Powell Jr.,* pp. 511 ("Never before had"), 347 (office boy and abortion), 530 (Powell letter to Tribe). Joyce Murdoch, "Laws Against Sodomy Survive in 24 States," *The Washington Post,* April 11, 1993, p. A20 (Moseley sodomy conviction). Deb Price, "Protect privacy by repealing sodomy laws," *The Detroit News,* Nov. 30, 1998 (Georgia's law repealed, Scarborough quote). "Michael Hardwick Died Five Years Ago at His Sister's Home," *The Washington Blade,* 29 March, 1996, p. 19 (Hardwick's death). Krista Reese, "The Lights Went Out in Georgia," *George* magazine, p. 73, May 1998 (Bowers's ex-mistress).

Making Criminals Out of 700,000 Texans

Author interviews: Don Baker. Court documents: Marshall's docket sheets on *Baker v. Wade. Buchanan v. Texas,* decided March 29, 1971. Friend of court brief in *Texas v. Hill* for Alabama, Delaware, Florida, Illinois, Iowa, Kansas, Louisiana, Maine, Massachusetts, Michigan, Minnesota, New Hampshire, New Mexico, New York, North Carolina, Ohio, Oregon, Pennsylvania, South Dakota, Tennessee, Utah, Vermont, West Virginia, Wisconsin and Wyoming. Other sources: Norma Adams Wade, "Teacher Files Suit Against Homosexual Conduct Law," *The Dallas Morning News,* Nov. 20, 1979 ("a practicing homosexual").

CHAPTER 13: CONFIRMING HOSTILITY

Authors' interview: Jeffrey Levi. Other sources: Videotape of WETA-TV broadcast of Levi testimony before Senate Judiciary Committee, July 31, 1986, provided by Levi. Senate Judiciary Committee transcript of Rehnquist confirmation hearings, July 29–Aug. 1, 1986. "Required Reading: Thurmond on Homosexuality," *The New York Times,* Aug. 2, 1986, p. 6. Craig Timberg, "Sing-along Strikes a Sour Note; Chief Justice's Selection of 'Dixie' Distasteful, Some Say," *The Washington Post,* July 22, 1999. Scalia's Senate Judiciary Committee hearings, Aug. 5–6, 1986 (quotes from hearings transcript). *Dronenburg v. Zech,* Bork ruling for D.C. Circuit Court of Appeals.

Clashing with Dignity

Authors' interview: Matthew Foreman. Court documents: Memo to Marshall from Eben Moglen, March 4,1987. Marshall docket sheet. Arthur Leonard, *Sexuality and the Law,* p. 238 (history of parade route).

An "Olympic" Tug-of-War

Authors' interviews: Mary Dunlap, Leslie Gielow (Jacobs). Court documents: Samuel Dimon pool memo on *SFAA v. USOC,* Sept. 29, 1986, Powell papers. Robert Long memo to Powell, Oct. 2 1986. Margaret Raymond memo to Marshall, Oct. 3, 1986. Powell and Marshall docket sheets. Margaret Raymond bench memo to Marshall, Feb. 11, 1987. Leslie Gielow (Jacobs) bench memo to Powell, Feb. 11, 1987. Powell handwritten notes to himself on *SFAA v. USOC,* Feb. 23, 1987 and March 21, 1987, Powell papers. Official transcript of oral arguments, March 24, 1987. Powell conference notes on SFAA votes. Leslie Gielow (Jacobs) draft of SFAA opinion with Powell handwritten responses April 11, 1987 ("light editing"), Powell papers. Justices' memos in response to Powell opinion, Powell papers. Leslie Gielow (Jacobs) memo to Powell ("the Brennan clerks"), June 5, 1987. Powell reply memo to Leslie Gielow (Jacobs), on changes to justify recirculation, June 5, 1987. Powell reaction on Stevens memo, June 19, 1987 ("Cheers!"), Powell papers. Other sources: Tom Waddell and Dick Schaap, *Gay Olympian: The Life and Death of Dr. Tom Waddell* (New York: Knopf, 1996) (for Waddell quotes, personal life and view of Gay Olympics Games fight).

"Bork Without the Bite?"

Authors' interview: Laurence Tribe. Other sources: David Savage, *Turning Right,* (on Bork) pp. 134, 136 ("Societies can have"); 142, 145, 146, (on Kennedy); 169, 170, 172, 175 ("no way, Jose"). Deb Price, "Gays find unexpected Supreme Court friend in Anthony Kennedy," *The Detroit News,* June 7, 1996. Linda Greenhouse, "Justice Kennedy's Influence," *The New York Times,* May 27, 1996. Official transcript of the Kennedy hearings, Dec. 14–16, 1987. Kennedy's *Beller v. Middendorf* ruling, 632 Federal Reporter, 2d series, pp. 792, 811. Kennedy ruling in *United States v. Smith* 574 F. 2d 988 (1978), on difference between rape of man, woman. Anthony Kennedy, unpublished address, "Unenumerated Rights and the Dictates of Judicial Restraint," to the Canadian Institute for Advanced Legal Studies, The Stanford Lectures, Stanford University, July 24–Aug. 1, 1986.

Terminated with Extreme Prejudice?

Authors' interviews: "John Doe" (ex-CIA technician), Frank Kameny. Court documents: Marshall docket sheet. Eben Moglen memo to Marshall, May 1, 1987. Powell memo to White, June 2, 1987, Marshall papers. Rehnquist memo to White, May 28, 1987, Marshall papers. White unpublished dissent from denial of *cert* in *Gates v. Doe,* Marshall papers. *Webster v. Doe* oral argument, Jan. 12, 1988, official transcript and audiotape. Marshall conference notes on *Webster v. Doe.* Brennan memo to Rehnquist,

March 9, 1988, Marshall papers. Other sources: Vernon Loeb, "At CIA, Gay Pride Comes in from the Cold," *The Washington Post,* p. A1, June 9, 2000. (Woolsey quote).

CHAPTER 14: CRAWLING TOWARD EMPATHY

Authors' interview: Jim Woodward. Court documents: Jonathan Schwartz memo to Marshall, Dec. 4, 1989. Marshall docket sheet (for which justices voted to delay).

"If I Had Lied, I Wouldn't Be in This Position"

Authors' interviews: Miriam Ben-Shalom, Jim Woodward. Court documents: Jonathan Schwartz memo to Marshall, Dec. 4, 1989. Docket sheet in Marshall papers.

The Exceptional Simone

Authors' interview: Perry Watkins. Court documents: Marshall docket sheet on Watkins. Other sources: Randy Shilts, *Conduct Unbecoming* (for personal details of Watkins's life and legal battle), pp. 60–64, ("give a hoot," "are you queer"); 79, 83 ("motherfucker Army"); 155, 156, 162 ("GUYS FLIP"); 218, 242 ("best clerks," "no complaints"); 309 ("respected and trusted"); 383, 384, 398, 448, 729. Perry Watkins biographical sketch, *Contemporary Black Biography,* 1996, Col. 12, Gale Research Inc. (final settlement, death). David W. Dunlap, "Perry Watkins, 48, Gay Sergeant Won Court Battle with Army," *The New York Times,* March 21, 1996 (final settlement, death), p. B8.

The "Stealth" Justice

Authors' interviews: Tom Rath, Kenneth Duberstein, Eleanor Fink. Other sources: Margaret Carlson, "An 18th Century Man," *Time,* Aug. 6, 1990. Richard Lacayo, "A Blank Slate," *Time,* Aug. 6, 1990. Aric Press, "The Quiet Man," *Newsweek,* Aug. 6, 1990, pp. 14–16. Warren Rudman, *Combat: 12 Years in the U.S. Senate* (New York: Random House, 1996) (for Rudman quotes, perspective and Souter "if I had known" quote), pp. 154, 158, 160, 162, 178, 179, 181, 182. Senate Judiciary Committee's transcript of Souter confirmation hearings, Sept. 13–19, 1990. Clare Cushman, editor, *The Supreme Court Justices,* "David H. Souter," pp. 521–522. Arthur Leonard, *Sexuality and the Law,* pp. 352–354 (on New Hampshire adoption ruling, "never less humanitarian").

The "Slur" That Helped Clarence Thomas

Other sources: Jane Mayer and Jill Abramson, *Strange Justice: The Selling of Clarence Thomas* (New York: Plume, 1995), pp. xv, 11–13, 118, 151, 192, 195, 321, 322, 324, 326 ("out of thin air"), ("sewer mouth"), 360, 338 ("dismissed her," "As a 'faggot'?"). David Savage, *Turning Right,* pp. 423, 424 ("bitch, bitch"), 444 ("high-tech lynching"). Clare Cushman, editor *The Supreme Court Justices,* p. 528. Arthur Leonard, *Sexuality and the Law,* pp. 473 (on Canby ruling).

Painting the First Sympathetic Portrait

Authors' interviews: Keith Jacobson. Bill Araiza. Court documents: Scott Brewer memo to Justice Marshall on *Jacobson,* March 21, 1991. Transcript of Jacobson oral argument, Nov. 6, 1991 and oral argument tape. Dennis J. Hutchinson, *The Man Who Once Was Whizzer White* (White turns court around, conference votes), pp. 420 ("preliminary view"), 421. David Savage, *Turning Right,* p. 464 (attributing fifth vote to Thomas). Jane Mayer and Jill Abramson, *Strange Justice,* p. 358 (on Thomas's reason). Note: During its 1992–93 term, the court also denied *cert* in *Jantz v. Muci.* Kansas teacher Vernon R. Jantz sued after a principal failed to hire him in 1988 because of his alleged "homosexual tendencies."

The Long Khaki Line

Other sources: *Lesbian/Gay Law Notes,* June 1995, Lesbian & Gay Law Association of Greater New York (on final settlement of Pruitt's case).

CHAPTER 15: TURNING A MAJOR CORNER

Authors' interviews: Chai Feldblum, Michael Conley, J. Paul Oetken, Bill Araiza, William Hohengarten.

"No Jews or Dogs"

Authors' interviews: Barbara Flagg, Dayna Deck. Other sources: Biographical information about Ginsburg largely came from her Senate testimony, July 20–23, 1993 and Clare Cushman, editor, *The Supreme Court Justices,* pp. 532–533. Barbara Flagg letter, May 21, 1993 to Harriet Woods. Anthony Lewis, "How Not to Choose," *The New York Times,* May 10, 1993, p. A19 (controversy over Ginsburg). Ruth Marcus, "Judge Ruth Bader Ginsburg Named to High Court; Clinton's Unexpected Choice Is Women's Rights Pioneer," *The Washington Post,* June 15, 1993, p. A1. Lambda Legal Defense and Education Fund press release, June 15, 1993. Joan Biskupic, "Ginsburg Deplores Bias Against Gays," *The Washington Post,* July 23, 1993, p. A1. Joan Biskupic, "Senate, 96–3, Approves Ginsburg as 107th Supreme Court Justice," *The Washington Post,* Aug. 4, 1993, p. A4 ("homosexual agenda"). Richard Danielson, "Tampa Won't Fight Gay Rights Law," *The St. Petersburg Times,* Oct. 29, 1993, p. 3B. Arthur Leonard, *Sexuality and the Law,* pp. 364–365 (background on ruling barring gay man's eviction after partner's death).

A Plain Vanilla Nominee

Authors' interviews: Arthur Leonard, George Fisher. Other sources: Official transcript of Breyer's Senate confirmation hearings July 12–15, 1994. Clare Cushman, editor, *The Supreme Court Justices,* "Stephen G. Breyer," pp. 536–538. Ann Devroy, "Boston Judge Breyer Nominated to High Court," *The Washington Post,* May 14, 1994, p. A1. Joan Biskupic, "Breyer Presents Moderate Image," *The Washington Post,* July 13, 1994, p. A1. Joan Biskupic, "Breyer: Pragmatic Lawyer and Judge," *The Washington Post,* June 27, 1994, p. A1.

The Court Learns to Say "Gay"

Authors' interviews: Cathleen Finn, John Ward. Other sources: "St. Patrick's Day Parade: March 15, 1992," *Primetime* (videotape provided to authors by Finn).

A New, Respectful Tone

Authors' interviews: John Ward, Kent Greenfield, Cathleen Finn. Court documents: Official transcript of *Hurley* oral argument, April 2, 1995. Audiotape of *Hurley* oral argument. Other sources: "In Memoriam: William Brennan Jr," *Harvard Law Review,* November 1997, Vol. 111, No. 1, p. 2 (reprint of Souter's eulogy at Brennan's funeral mass).

Harrison Has Two Mommies

Authors' interviews: Sandra Holtzman; Linda S. Balisle.

"People Knew It Wasn't Right"

Authors' interview: Dan Miller.

The Continuing Adventures of the Sex Police

Authors' interview: Brian Sawatzky. Other sources: "Questions about Amendment 2," *The Denver Post,* Nov. 12, 1992, p. A13.

CHAPTER 16: "THE CONSTITUTION 'NEITHER KNOWS
NOR TOLERATES CLASSES AMONG CITIZENS'"

Authors' interviews: Linda Fowler, Priscilla Inkpen, Sue Anderson, Jean Dubofsky. Other sources: Tom Kenworthy, "Colorado Springs Culture Wars," *The Washington Post,* Nov. 18, 1997, p. A3 (for "Vatican of evangelical Christianity" and details on conservative Christian groups' move to Colorado). *The Denver Post*'s superb coverage of the Amendment 2 battle provided many factual details. We drew on Michael Booth, "From Dramatic Start, Momentum Built," *The Denver Post,* May 21, 1986, p. 6A ("We consider these"). Michael Booth, "Colorado: Gay-Rights Battlefield," *The Denver Post,* Sept. 27, 1992, A1. Michael Booth, "TV Ad Blitz to Promote Amendment 2," *The Denver Post,* 20 Oct. 1992, p. B1. Michael Booth, "Gay-Rights Ban Narrowly Winning," *The Denver Post,* Nov. 4, 1992, p. A14. Carol Kreck, "Gays Not Sex Abusers, Study Says," *The Denver Post,* Sept. 28, 1992, p. 8A ("make more sense"). Virginia Culver, "Amendment 2 Focuses on Child Abuse," Sept. 11, 1992, p. 6B. Will Perkins, "Drive for Homosexual Rights Undermines Family Values," *The Denver Post,* May 23, 1992, p. B7 ("radically deviant"). Kelly Richmond and Stacy Baca, "Anti-Gay Incidents Soaring, Group Says," *The Denver Post,* Dec. 23, 1992, p. B1. Michael Booth, "Therapists Hear Gays Pour out Their Anguish and Anger," *The Denver Post,* Nov. 4, 1992, p. A9. Jeffrey Roberts, "Amendment 2 a Call to Arms for Rural Gays," *The Denver Post,* Sept. 19, 1993, p. D1 ("bulldozer"). Associated Press, "Gay Man's Suicide Note Cites Passage of Amendment 2," *The Denver Post,* Nov. 12, 1992, p. A13 ("refuse to live"). Bruce Finley, "400 Activists Rally At Capitol In First Action By New Coalition," *The Denver Post,* p. 8A ("black bear"). Dirk Johnson, "Colorado Justices Strike Down a Law Against Gay Rights," *The New York Times,* Oct. 12, 1994, p. A1 ($40 million).

Fenced Out but Still Fighting

Other sources: Lisa Keen and Suzanne Goldberg, *Strangers to the Law: Gay People on Trial,* p. 24 (Bayless personal details). Deb Price, "A 1969 Court Ruling Is Still Being Used to Cut Down the Ugly Weeds of Bigotry," *The Detroit News*, Dec. 2, 1994. Dirk Johnson, "Colorado Justices Strike Down a Law Against Gay Rights," *The New York Times*, Oct. 12, 1994, p. A1 ("first time").

"Worse Off Than Hotdog Vendors"

Authors' interviews: Jean Dubofsky, Priscilla Inkpen. Court documents: Robert Bork's *Romer v. Evans* friend-of-the-court brief for attorneys general of Alabama, Idaho and Virginia. Aspen's friend-of-the court brief. Friend-of-the-court brief by Laurence Tribe, John Hart Ely, Gerald Gunther, Philip Kurland and Kathleen Sullivan. Other sources: Jeffrey Toobin, "Clinton's Left-Hand Man," *The New Yorker*, July 28, 1997, p. 30 ("Nothing makes me unhappier").

"I've Never Seen a Case Like This"

Authors' interviews: Jean Dubofsky, Arthur Leonard (1995), Linda Fowler, Barbara Flagg, Dayna Deck. Court documents: Official transcript and audio tape of oral arguments in *Romer v. Evans*. Other sources: Michael Booth and Adriel Bettelheim, "Supreme Court Aura Eerily Undemocratic," *The Denver Post*, Oct. 11, 1995, A1 ("started to sob," "treated like dirt."). Deb Price notes from oral argument.

"This Colorado Cannot Do"

Authors' interviews: Laurence Tribe, Stephen Gilles, John Jeffries, Priscilla Inkpen, Linda Fowler, Sue Anderson. Other sources: Official transcript of Justice Kennedy's Senate confirmation hearings, Dec. 14–16, 1987 ("beyond this line"). "Colorado Reaction," *The Denver Post*, p. 5A ("reasoned"). Jeffrey Roberts, "Court Ruling Is Fodder for Senate campaign," May 21, 1996, p. 9A. "Voters Evenly Split on Issues," *The Denver Post*, May 21, 1996. Gale A. Norton, "Reflections on Amendment 2," *The Denver Post*, June 22, 1996, B7 ("disappointing in its failure"). Dick Foster, "Amendment 2 Leader Starts Bid to Oust Justices," *Rocky Mountain News*, p. 14A. "Supreme Court Backs Gay Rights in Ruling," *The San Francisco Examiner*, May 20, 1996, p. A1 ("jubilant"). Linda Greenhouse, "Justice Kennedy's Influence," *The New York Times*, May 27, 1996, p. 2A (on Kennedy's outlook on government classifying people). Adriel Bettelheim and Michael Booth, "Court Rejects Amend. 2," *The Denver Post*, May 21, 1996, p. 1A. Linda Greenhouse, "Gay Rights Laws Can't Be Banned, High Court Rules," *The New York Times*, May 21, 1996, p. A1. Joan Biskupic, "Court Strikes Down Colorado's Anti-Gay Amendment," *The Washington Post*, May 21, 1996, p. A1.

A Monumental Puzzle

Authors' interviews: Jean Dubofsky, Laurence Tribe, Arthur Leonard.

CHAPTER 17: COUNTING TO ~~FIVE~~ FOUR

Authors' interview: Arthur Leonard. Other sources: "Coalition of Civil Rights Groups Join to Oppose Anti-Gay Measure," Lambda Legal Defense and Education Fund news release, Dec. 8, 1994 (on Bork, Meese). "Cowardice at the Justice Department," *The New York Times*, Dec. 3, 1994, p. A22 ("Cowardice"). Kristen Delguzzi,

"Gay Rights in City Set Back," *The Cincinnati Enquirer,* Oct. 24, 1997 ("nearly identical"). Linda Greenhouse, "Justices Leave Intact Anti-Gay Measure," *The New York Times,* Oct. 14, 1998 (only such measure to survive).

Don't Listen, Don't Rule

Authors' interview: Paul Thomasson. Other sources: Deb Price, "Discharged officer takes heart in recent court decisions as he challenges gay ban," *The Detroit News,* July 5, 1996 (Thomasson details, including "equal justice" check). Deb Price, "Supreme Court Can Throw Lieutenant The Life Preserver His Naval Career Needs," *The Detroit News,* Dec. 29, 1995 (quotes from Thomasson's superiors).

"God Hates Fags"

Court documents: Used ordinary filings.

"If It's Homosexual, It Would Have to Be Sodomy"

Other Sources: Krista Reese, "The Lights Went Out in Georgia," *George,* p. 73, May 1998 ("Bowers is a hypocrite").

"Any Decision That Treats Us As Equal . . . Is a Good Thing"

Authors' interviews: Matt Coles, Jon Davidson, Arthur Leonard, Ruth Harlow, Michael Adams, Holly Hughes, Dixon Osburn, Nancy Polikoff, Pat Logue. Other sources: Deb Price, "Supreme Court Heads in the Right Direction with Harassment Ruling," *The Detroit News,* March 14, 1998 ("any decision"). Deb Price, "Supreme Court Shows Its Progress by Not Treating Gay Issues As Dynamite," *The Detroit News,* Dec. 5, 1997 (on *Oncale* ruling). Deb Price, "Sexual Harassment on the Job Can Be Same-Sex, Too, but the Courts Deal with It Differently," *The Detroit News,* Jan. 10, 1997 (on *Oncole v. Sundowner*). Deb Price, "Ending College Fees Would Hurt Free Speech, Diversity," *The Detroit News,* April 5, 1999. Deb Price, "Court Grasps Changing Nature of Families," *The Detroit News,* 12 June 2000 (on *Troxel v. Granville*). Deb Price, "Court Must Tread Carefully in Custody Case," *The Detroit News,* Nov. 8, 1999 (on *Troxel v. Granville*). Deb Price, "Sexuality, Controversy Should Not Hold Back Artist," *The Detroit News,* April 4, 1998 (on Holly Hughes).

Standing Up to the "Biggest Bully"

Authors' interview: James Dale. Other sources: "James Dale: Former Eagle Scout," Lambda Legal Defense and Education Fund press release, February 2000 (details on Dale's Scouting career). Monmouth Council Executive James W. Kay letters to James Dale, dated July 19, 1990, Aug. 10, 1990. "Boy Scouts Can Discriminate Against Gay Members, High Court Rules," Lambda news release, June 28, 2000 (Dale's troop disbanded).

"The Human Price of . . . Bigotry"

Authors' interviews: Evan Wolfson, Michael Adams, Arthur Leonard. Court documents: *Roberts v. Jaycees.* Other sources: "Unanimous New Jersey Supreme Court Strikes Down Boy Scout Anti-Gay Ban," Lambda Legal Defense and Education Fund press release, Aug. 5, 1999 ("birthday present"). Deb Price, "Will Court Be Brave on Boy Scouts Case?" *The Detroit News,* Jan. 24, 2000 (on hazards of Supreme Court taking a gay Boy Scouts case).

"You Have to Make Room for Luck"

Authors' interviews: Evan Wolfson, James Dale.

"Do You Ask If They're Ax Murderers?"

Authors' interviews: James Dale, Evan Wolfson. Court documents: Transcript of oral argument in *Boy Scouts of America et al. v. James Dale,* April 26, 2000. Deb Price, "Will Justices' Scrutiny Help Gay Scouts," *The Detroit News,* May 1, 2000 (on oral argument).

Five Votes Against an "Avowed Homosexual"

Authors' interviews: Evan Wolfson. Joan Biskupic, "O'Connor, the 'Go-to' Justice," *USA Today,* July 12, 2000, p. 1 (O'Connor pivotal justice). Edward Walsh, "The Supreme Scorecard," *The Washington Post,* July 3, 2000, p. A17 (O'Connor in majority on 70 of 74 cases).

A "Symbol of Inferiority"

Court documents: *Hurley v. GLIB,* Souter majority opinion; *Ratchford v. Gay Lib,* Rehnquist dissent from denial of *cert.*

"Dinosaurs Became Extinct"

Authors' interviews: Matt Coles, Arthur Leonard, Evan Wolfson. Other sources: Deb Price, teleconference interview with James Dale, Ruth Harlow, Evan Wolfson on June 28, 2000 ("extinct," "hollow victory"). Peter Freiberg, "Battle Decided; War Looms," *The Washington Blade,* July 21, 2000, p. 1. Peter Freiberg, "Clinton Asked to Resign Honorary Post," *The Washington Blade,* July 21, 2000, p. 19. Lambda online press kit, "Recent editorials" (www.lambdalegal.org). Mike Peters cartoon, *Dayton Daily News,* June 2000. Los Angeles Times poll, conducted June 8–13, 2000. "CNN Early Edition," June 29, 2000, Gallup poll results.

CONCLUSION: SEEKING THE SHORTEST PATH TO EQUAL JUSTICE

Authors' interviews: Nadine Strossen, Karen Burstein, Gina Okum, Raafat S. Toss. Other sources: New York Law School videotape of "oral argument," Sept. 12, 1996. Mock same-sex marriage case fictitious court documents: *"Willamina Wallace and Murron McGregor v. State of Frossel,"* brief of petitioners.

What If . . .

Other sources: Laurence H. Tribe, *God Save This Honorable Court: How the Choice of Justices Shapes Our History* (New York: Random House, 1985) (record number of appointments: FDR, Aug. 1937 to June 1941: Justices Black, Reed, Frankfurter,

Douglas, Murphy, Byrnes, Jackson). Deb Price, "Next President Likely to Reshape Court," *The Detroit News,* Jan. 19, 2000, p. A1.

A Drag on the Nation

Other sources: Deb Price, *The Detroit News,* nationally syndicated weekly column, May 1992–September 2000 (charting progress of gay-rights movement here and abroad).

A Promise to Keep

Court documents: *Plessy v. Ferguson,* Harlan dissent. *Palmore v. Sidoti. U.S. Department of Agriculture v. Moreno. Rowland v. Mad River,* Brennan dissent from denial of cert. *Bowers v. Hardwick,* Blackmun dissent. *Romer v. Evans. Boy Scouts v. Dale,* Stevens dissent.

There's Going to Be More Evolution

Authors' interviews: Laurence Tribe, Matt Coles, Chai Feldblum, Evan Wolfson, Arthur Leonard.

SELECTED BIBLIOGRAPHY

Bass, Jack. *Taming the Storm: The Life and Times of Judge Frank M. Johnson, Jr. and the South's Fight Over Civil Rights.* New York: Doubleday, 1993.

Bayer, Ronald. *Homosexuality and American Psychiatry.* New York: Basic Books, 1981.

Benedict, Michael Les. *The Blessings of Liberty: A Concise History of the Constitution of the United States.* Lexington, Mass.: D.C. Heath, 1996.

Berube, Allan. *Coming Out Under Fire: The History of Gay Men and Women in World War Two.* New York: The Free Press, 1990.

Blumstein, Philip, Pepper Schwartz. *American Couples: Money Work Sex.* New York: Morrow, 1983.

Caplan, Lincoln. *The Tenth Justice: The Solicitor General and the Rule of Law.* New York: Knopf, 1987.

Clendinen, Dudley, and Adam Nagourney. *Out for Good: The Struggle to Build a Gay Rights Movement in America.* New York: Simon & Schuster, 1999.

Contemporary Black Biography 1996, Col. 12, Gale Research Inc.

Cushman, Clare, ed. *The Supreme Court Justices: Illustrated Biographies, 1789–1995* Washington, D.C.: Congressional Quarterly, 1995.

D'Emilio, John. *Sexual Politics, Sexual Communities: The Making of a Homosexual Minority in the United States, 1940–1970.* Chicago: The University of Chicago Press, 1983.

Douglas, William O. *The Court Years 1939–1975: The Autobiography of William O. Douglas.* New York: Random House, 1980.

_____. *Go East, Young Man: The Autobiography of William O. Douglas.* New York: Vintage Books, 1974.

Faderman, Lillian. *Odd Girls and Twilight Lovers: A History of Lesbian Life in Twentieth-Century America.* New York: Penguin, 1992.

Fine, Sidney. *Frank Murphy: The Detroit Years.* Ann Arbor: University of Michigan Press, 1975.

_____. *Frank Murphy: The New Deal Years.* Ann Arbor: University of Michigan Press, 1984.

_____. *Frank Murphy: The Washington Years.* Chicago: University of Chicago Press, 1993.

Garrow, David J. *Liberty and Sexuality: The Right to Privacy and the Making of Roe v. Wade.* New York: Lisa Drew Books, 1994.

Hart, H. L. A. *Law, Liberty and Morality.* Stanford: Stanford University Press, 1963.

Hay, Harry. *Radically Gay: Gay Liberation in the Words of Its Founder*. Boston: Beacon Press, 1996.

Hodges, Andrew: *Alan Turning: The Enigma*. New York: Simon and Schuster, 1983.

Hutchinson, Dennis J. *The Man Who Once Was Whizzer White: A Portrait of Justice Byron R. White*. New York: The Free Press, 1998.

Irons, Peter. *The Courage of Their Convictions: Sixteen Americans Who Fought Their Way to the Supreme Court*. New York: Penguin, 1988.

Jeffries, John C. Jr. *Justice Lewis F. Powell Jr.: A Biography*. New York: Charles Scribners' Sons, 1994.

Katz, Jonathan Ned. *Gay American History: Lesbians and Gay Men in the U.S.A.* New York: Thomas Y. Crowell Company, 1976.

_____. *Gay/Lesbian Almanac: A New Documentary*. New York: Harper & Row, 1983.

Kepner, Jim. *Rough News, Daring News: 1950s' Pioneer Gay Press Journalism*. New York: The Harrington Park Press, 1988.

Keen, Lisa, and Suzanne Goldberg. *Strangers to the Law: Gay People on Trial*. Ann Arbor: University of Michigan Press, 1998.

Leonard, Arthur S. *Sexuality and the Law: An Encyclopedia of Major Legal Cases*. New York: Garland Publishing, 1993.

Lowe, Jennifer M., ed. *The Jewish Justices of the Supreme Court Revisited: Brandeis to Fortas*. Washington, D.C.: The Supreme Court Historical Society, 1994.

Marcus, Eric. *Making History: The Struggle for Gay and Lesbian Equal Rights 1945–1990*. New York: HarperCollins, 1992.

Mayer, Jane, and Jill Abramson. *Strange Justice: The Selling of Clarence Thomas*. New York: Plume, 1995.

Murphy, Bruce Allen. *Fortas: The Rise and Ruin of a Supreme Court Justice*. United States: Morrow, 1988.

Newman, Roger K. *Hugo Black: A Biography*. New York: Pantheon Books, 1994.

Perry, H. W. *Deciding to Decide: Agenda Setting in the United States Supreme Court*. Cambridge, Mass.: Harvard University Press, 1991.

Rubenstein, William B., ed. *Lesbians, Gay Men, and the Law*. New York: The New Press, 1993.

Rudman, Warren. *Combat: 12 Years in the U.S. Senate*. New York: Random House, 1996.

Rutledge, Leigh W. *Gay Decades: From Stonewall to the Present: The People and Events That Shaped Gay Lives*. New York: Plume, 1992.

Savage, David G. *Turning Right: The Making of the Rehnquist Supreme Court*. New York: John Wiley & Sons, 1992.

Schwartz, Bernard. *A History of the Supreme Court*. New York: Oxford University Press, 1993.

_____. *Decision: How the Supreme Court Decides Cases*. New York: Oxford University Press, 1996.

_____. *Super Chief: Earl Warren and His Supreme Court*. New York: New York University Press, 1983.

Sedgwick, Eve Kosofsky. *The Epistemology of the Closet*. Berkeley: University of California Press, 1990.

Shilts, Randy. *Conduct Unbecoming: Lesbians and Gays in the U.S. Military.* New York: St. Martin's Press, 1993.

Stebenne, David L. *Arthur J. Goldberg: New Deal Liberal.* New York: Oxford University Press, 1996.

Summers, Anthony. *Official and Confidential: The Secret Life of J. Edgar Hoover.* New York: Pocket Star Books, 1993.

Thompson, Karen, and Julie Andzejewski. *Why Can't Sharon Kowalski Come Home?* San Francisco: Spinsters Ink, 1989.

Tribe, Laurence H. *American Constitutional Law.* Mineola, N.Y.: The Foundation Press, 1988.

_____. *God Save This Honorable Court: How the Choice of Justices Shapes Our History.* New York: Random House, 1985.

Waddell, Tom, and Dick Schaap. *Gay Olympian: The Life and Death of Dr. Tom Waddell.* New York: Knopf, 1996.

Woodward, Bob, and Scott Armstrong. *The Brethren: Inside the Supreme Court.* New York: Avon Books, 1979.

INDEX

411, 412; *New York v. Uplinger* and, 228, 229, 230, 231; *Romer v. Evans* and, 465, 467, 469, 472, 473, 474, 475, 479–480; *San Francisco Arts & Athletics v. USOC* and, 368, 372, 373–374; *Troxel v. Granville* and, 496; *U.S. Army et al. v. Watkins* and, 397; voting pattern of, 511; *Ward v. Olivieri* and, 362; *Webster v. Doe* and, 384, 385, 386
Oetken, J. Paul, 323, 416
Ohio, sodomy and sexual psychopath laws, 135, 136–138
Ohio Education Association, 238
Oklahoma, Helm law controversy, 251–260
Oklahoma City, 175; lewdness statute challenge, 446–449
Oklahoma City Times (newspaper), 252, 253
Oklahomans for Human Rights, 253
Okum, Gina, 420, 518, 519
Olesen, Otto K., 29
Olivieri, Michael J., 362
Olivieri v. Ward, 533
Oncale, Joseph, 494–495
Oncale v. Sundowner Offshore Services, Inc., 494–495, 535
O'Neill Brian, 264–265
ONE Inc. v. Olesen, 22, 69, 78, 531; federal court decision, 31–34; granting of *certiorari* in, 41–47; *Roth v. United States* and, 41–42, 43–44, 46; significance of, 50, 82–83, 276–277
ONE (magazine), 27–34, 39–40, 47–50
Onofre, Ronald, 206, 207
Oral argument, 15; time allotted for, 303
Oral sex; cases concerning, 175–176, 185–186, 207; friend-of-the-court brief in *Bowers v. Hardwick* on, 289–290
Oregon, 452, 455, 526
O'Rourke, Eugene, 132

Pagliacetti, Gary, 268
Palmore v. Sidoti, 413, 527
Parker, Barrington, 381–382
Parks, Rosa, 281
Partner adoption, 165
Patterson, Edgar, 9
Paul, Bill, 365
Pearson, Drew, 19
Penn State, 177
Pennsylvania Superior Court, 444
Performance artists, 495
Perkins, Will, 452, 453, 458, 480
Perry, H. W., 16
Perry, Troy, 220
Peters, Mike, 515
Petitioners, 42
Peurifoy, John E., 34–35

Phelps, Fred, 489
Phelps, Margie, 489
Philadelphia Daily News (newspaper), 515
Phil Donahue Show (television show), 331
Planned Parenthood, 85–86
Plessy v. Ferguson, 204, 476, 527
Poe v. Ullman, 83–86, 167, 182, 240, 254, 287–288, 294, 300, 307, 339, 531
Police; anti-homosexual policies, 25–26, 38, 88, 99; Black Cat kissing case and, 143–144, 146–147; enforcement of sodomy and sexual psychopath laws, 135–138, 159; entrapment of homosexuals, 139–141; gay bar raids, 141, 142–143, 149–150; harassment of lesbians, 142–143
Poore et al. v. Mayer, 531
Poritz, Deborah T., 499–500, 504
Pornography; Jacobson entrapment case, 407–412; Earl warren and, 76; *See also* Obscenity
Porter, William P., 175
Post Office, 62; anti-homosexual policies, 37; Jacobson child pornography case, 407–412; obscenity cases and, 65–68; *ONE* magazine and, 29, 31–34, 39–40, 49
Powell, Colin, 487, 488
Powell, Lewis, Jr., 9, 467, 480; abortion rights and, 341–342; appointed to Supreme Court, 161; attitudes toward homosexuality, 225–226, 272–275, 293–295; *Board of Education of Oklahoma City v. National Gay Task Force* and, 255, 257, 259; *Bowers v. Hardwick* and, 174, 272–275, 283, 285–286, 292, 293–295, 298, 299–300, 302, 303, 304–305, 307–308, 311–314, 318–319, 328, 335–343; *Carey v. Population Services International* and, 196; gay clerks of, 23, 272–275, 335–336, 342–343; *New York v. Uplinger* and, 227, 228, 231; personality of, 271; relationship with clerks, 271–272; retirement of, 375; *San Francisco Arts & Athletics v. USOC* and, 368, 369–370, 373, 374, 375, 525; *Singer v. United States* and, 192; *Wainwright v. Stone* and, 174; *Webster v. Doe* and, 383
Powell v. Texas, 305
POZ (magazine), 508
Pregerson, Harry, 223–224, 366, 397–398
Privacy rights, 12, 376. *See also* Sexual privacy
Pruitt, Carolyn, 413–414
Psychiatry, 91, 93–94, 104, 105; *Baker v. Wade* and, 347, 350; Blackmun and, 324; Abe Fortas and, 110; Gaylord discrimination case and, 197; Franklin Kameny's influence on, 62; views of homosexuality, 38, 111–112, 350

ABOUT THE AUTHORS

Joyce Murdoch is managing editor for politics of *The National Journal*. She served as an editor and reporter at *The Washington Post* for more than a decade. Before joining the *Post* in 1982, she founded and operated Murdoch News Service, which covered Congress for Georgia newspapers.

Deb Price of The *Detroit News* writes the first nationally syndicated column in mainstream journalism that is devoted to exploring life from a gay perspective. Price's prize-winning weekly column is distributed to more than 100 newspapers and is available online at detnews.com. Before joining the *News'* Washington bureau in 1989, Price was a *Washington Post* editor.

Murdoch and Price also co-authored *And Say Hi to Joyce: America's First Gay Column Comes Out*. A couple since 1985, they live in Takoma Park, Maryland.